# MEL BAY'S COMPLETE BOOK OF HARMONY, THEORY & VOICING

By Bret Willmott

1 2 3 4 5 6 7 8 9 0

MEL BAY

# Biography

Bret Willmott is a highly acclaimed professor at Berklee College of Music and a noted educator and performer world-wide. He has been a faculty member of the College for more than eighteen years and a performing guitarist for over twenty-five years.

Mr. Willmott's musical history would include studies *and* performances with Pat Metheny, Gary Burton, Mick Goodrick, Mike Stern, Bill Frisell, Wolfgang Muthspiel, Jeff Berlin, and Steve Smith, as well as currently appearing on CDs that include notables Bob Moses and Mike Stern. Bret was also a teacher to several of these aforementioned musicians.

Mr. Willmott is a major author and contributor to the Berklee College curriculum including many personal arrangements and compositions used in the Guitar Department there. He is also the creator and primary teacher of two popular courses offered at the College dealing with harmonic and rhythmic development on the guitar.

# Credits

My thanks to:

Larry Baione, Gary Burton, Larry Monroe, Barrie Nettles, Paul Schmeling, Tony Marvuglio, Dan Bowden, Morris Acevedo, Yasutaka Yoshioka, and the many others who supported and assisted me in various ways.

Special thanks to William Leavitt, whose memory and spirit are "between the lines," and Dorothy Ours, whose many *extra* hours (no pun intended) of work helped make this book possible.

Personal thanks to my wife, Kathy, and my three sons, Mathew, Devin, and Daniel. Their support, patience, and love allowed the continuation and completion of this work.

# Table of Contents

# INTRODUCTION

This text is a combination harmony/theory/voicing text with emphasis placed on "voice-leading." Harmonic motion and understanding are key elements for "comping" in today's jazz and pop idioms. Through knowledge and listening, students will discover and compose new voicings and sounds.

Many guitarists have a unique physical/visual approach to harmony, due to the nature of this complicated instrument and the lack of traditional music training. The material in this book will be *common* musical knowledge that can be shared by all musicians. It will not be another guitaristic approach to harmony for guitar players only. It is hoped that this text will give an approach and begin a process that will continue far beyond its pages.

This text's primary focus will be that of presenting and examining four-note voicings on the middle four strings (2, 3, 4, 5) of the guitar. By eliminating the top and bottom strings (1 and 6), the voicings produced are in a relatively "safe" range for comping, conflicting less with bass lines and melodies (or solos). The initial approach to voicing construction will use what is referred to as *"drop 2"* type voicings, and will include tension additions and enharmonic chordal substitutions. The top note of each drop 2 type voicing will be notated and consequently always appear on the 2nd string, eliminating the need for position markings. Students will become aware of the top note of each chord voicing, whether it be a chord tone or a tension, and the different linear or voice-leading possibilities the 2nd string produces over various chord changes. This indirectly helps in a student's eventual involvement with chord melodies and chord soloing as well. In later sections, the remaining strings will receive the same voice-leading considerations as the top string. Students will learn to recognize each note's relation to the chord (vertical) as well as each note's linear motion to the next chord (horizontal).

Students are encouraged to transpose all applicable information presented on the middle four strings to the top four strings and, to a lesser extent, the bottom four strings. Consider further that each four-note voicing has <u>four</u> three-note voicings within it:

Using a C7 chord:

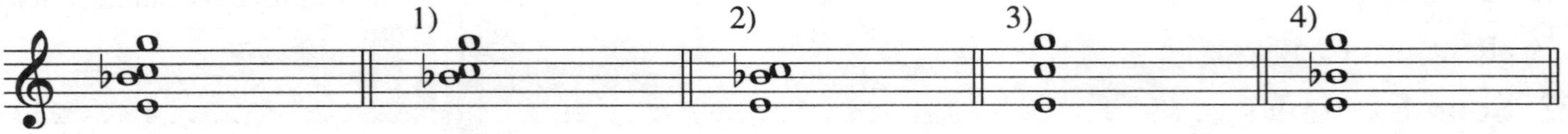


*Note that the last two voicings contain the same "width" (or two outside notes) as the original four-note voicing.*

Most guitar students will find three- and four-note voicings to be the most appropriate in jazz/pop "comping" situations.

The "width" of any voicing is determined by physical or fingering limitations. By assuming five frets as our physical limitation, the following interval widths are made available between the 2nd and 5th strings:

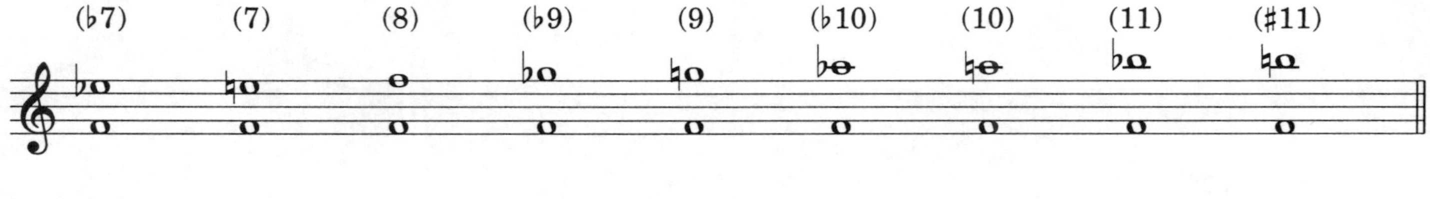

The octave (8) and ♭9th intervals can be temporarily removed since voicings containing these intervals will be initially avoided. They will reappear in later chapters where their unique sound is more appropriate. This leaves somewhat of a leap in width from the 7th intervals to the remaining intervals, producing potential voice-leading problems. For this reason, and again with some isolated exceptions, voicing containing the outside width of a 7th interval will generally be avoided. Conveniently, *drop* 2 type voicings utilize the remaining interval widths; (9), (♭10), (10), (11), (♯11). This text will also explore some substitute chords that are not drop 2 type voicings, but continue to utilize these widths, allowing them to voice-lead smoothly with the traditional drop 2 type voicings. In an attempt to be thorough and include most every conceivable voicing within this established framework, some physically difficult and/or "strange sounding" voicings will occasionally appear. More desirable substitute voicings can be used in these cases and most certainly should if it is felt certain isolated voicings "ruin" an otherwise pleasant sounding exercise or song.

Alterations and tension additions on the basic four-part chords (7th and 6th chords) sometimes produce upper-structure triads or hybrid chords. When this occurs, they will be listed as such. Upper-structure triads and hybrid chords will be more specifically dealt with in the later chapter entitled **Triad over Bass Voicings**.

As tensions are added to the basic four-part chords, the enharmonic chordal substitution possibilities increase dramatically. The enharmonic substitution possibilities of each chord will be listed as they are exposed by tension additions. Students will become proficient at enharmonically realizing a group of notes (a chord voicing) in more ways than one. Example:

C6 = A-7 = Fmaj9 (no root) = D9sus4 (no root) = B♭maj7 (13/♯11/9) (no root) = etc.

The majority of voicing examples presented in this text will contain very little rhythmic variation and it is highly recommended that some of those ideas suggested in the **Rhythm** chapter toward the end of this book be applied toward musical examples contained in each chapter. The **Conclusion** chapter contains additional information on different string combinations and voicing sizes that can also be applied to existing musical examples throughout the book. Coordinating information between these two chapters and the rest of this book will ultimately enhance its content.

# Chapter 1.
## Drop 2 Type Voicings

By dropping the second note from the top of a four-way close voicing down an octave, a larger sounding voicing (referred to as "drop 2") is produced. These drop 2 voicings in turn produce a chord physically more accessible on the guitar than some of the original four-way close voicings.

This book will explore all four inversions of the drop 2 type voicings and their placement on the middle four strings of the guitar (2, 3, 4, 5).

Cmaj7 = C E G B
R 3 5 7

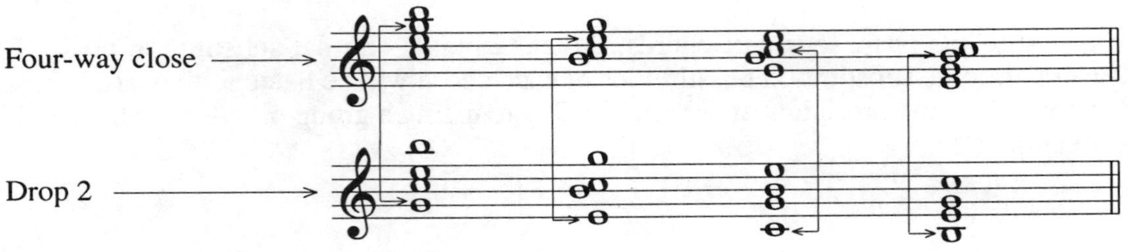


Drop 2 type voicings
arranged by inversions:

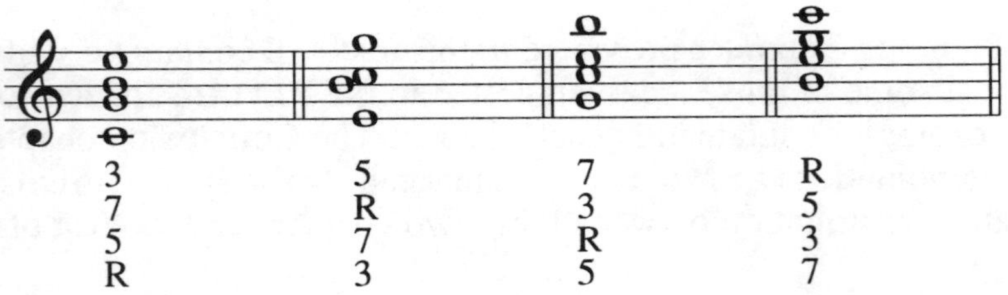


The following maj7th chord forms are produced by the above voicings on the middle four strings of the guitar:
(strings vertical/frets horizontal)

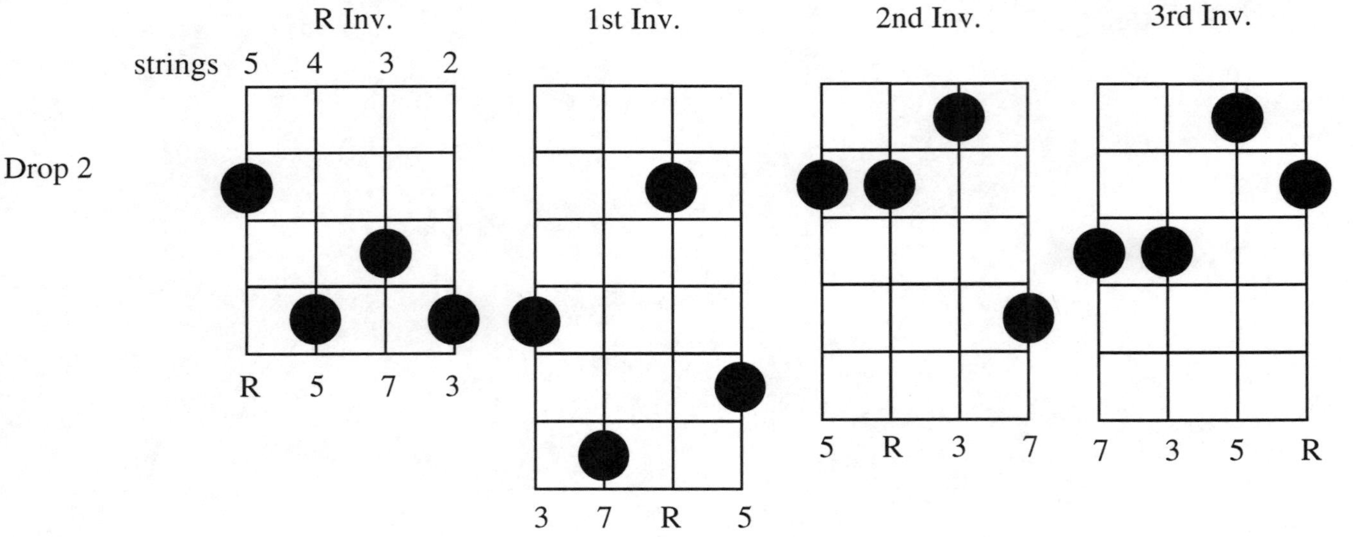


*The above forms can be transposed or moved to different keys.

We now have four inversions of a Cmaj7 chord on the middle four strings of the guitar.

At this point, it should be mentioned that a ♭9th interval is generally considered an avoid interval in traditional "Jazz - Pop" harmony. This book will initially continue that approach, with the dom7(♭9) chord being the only exception. Thus, the ♭9th interval contained in the 3rd inversion of the Cmaj7 chord (between B and C) will negate use of that inversion as a maj7 type chord. Similarly, the 3rd inversions of Cmaj7♭5, Cmaj7♯5, and C-maj7 will be avoided. Voicings containing ♭9th intervals will be presented later, especially in those chapters exploring triad-over-bass structures where the 3rd inversion of Cmaj7 will be available as a C triad over a B bass; C/B.

Assignment: Construct all four inversions for each four-part chord listed. All of these chords can be perceived as "altered" maj7th chords.

| | | | | | |
|---|---|---|---|---|---|
| **Cmaj7** | (1 3 5 7) | **C-6** | (1 ♭3 5 6) | **C7sus4** | (1 4 5 ♭7) |
| **Cmaj7♭5** | (1 3 ♭5 7) | **C6** | (1 3 5 6) | **C°7** | (1 ♭3 ♭5 ♭♭7) |
| **Cmaj7♯5** | (1 3 ♯5 7) | **C7** | (1 3 5 ♭7) | **C°maj7*** | (1 ♭3 ♭5 7) |
| **C-7** | (1 ♭3 5 ♭7) | **C7♯5** | (1 3 ♯5 ♭7) | **C-maj7** | (1 ♭3 5 7) |
| **C-7♭5** | (1 ♭3 ♭5 ♭7) | **C7♭5** | (1 3 ♭5 ♭7) | | |
| **C-7♯5** | (1 ♭3 ♯5 ♭7) | | | | |

Follow these three approaches in preparing the inversions of the four-part chords:

1) Prepare all 15 listed chords on the root inversion only in the key of D. Next, prepare chords on the 1st inversion only in the key of C. Next, prepare chords on the 2nd inversion in the key of B♭. Finally, prepare chords on the 3rd inversion in the key of G. Include inversions containing the ♭9th interval for purposes of this exercise.

2) In the key of F, prepare all four inversions on one chord type, then move to the next chord type. Continue until all 15 types are completed.

3) With an established tempo, prepare the following symmetrical chord progression using one chord type for all four chords and inversions. Continue through the entire list of the 15 chord types, following the given chordal/inversion pattern. Note that this exercise is "voice-led."

| 1st Inv. | 2nd Inv. | 3rd Inv. | R Inv. |
|---|---|---|---|
| Cmaj7 | Amaj7 | G♭maj7 | E♭maj7 |

Mixing different chord types while going through the different inversions and chords might make an interesting additional exercise.

***C°(maj7)** ( 1 ♭3 ♭5 7 ) and its available tensions will be examined more thoroughly in the **Tension Additions on Diminished Chords** chapter.

In contemporary music, upper-structure triads and fourth voicings play a major role. The following chordal inversions contain such voicings and should be noted:

1) Fourths: The <u>root inversion</u> of the maj7♭5 and the <u>2nd inversion</u> of the dom7sus4 are the most common fourth voicings used.

2) Upper-structure triads:

Root Inv. Cmaj7♯5 = E/C
3rd Inv. C-7♯5 = A♭/B♭
Root Inv. C°maj7 = B/C

Additional upper-structure triads will be revealed in later chapters.

The examples using drop 2 type voicings throughout this text will indicate such voicings by notating only the top note or voice on the 2nd string, eliminating the need for position markings. This lead note will directly indicate the inversion of the drop 2 voicing introduced:

**Third** of chord notated (top voice) = **root** inversion

**Fifth** of chord notated = **first** inversion

**Seventh/Sixth** of chord notated = **second** inversion

**Root** of chord notated = **third** inversion

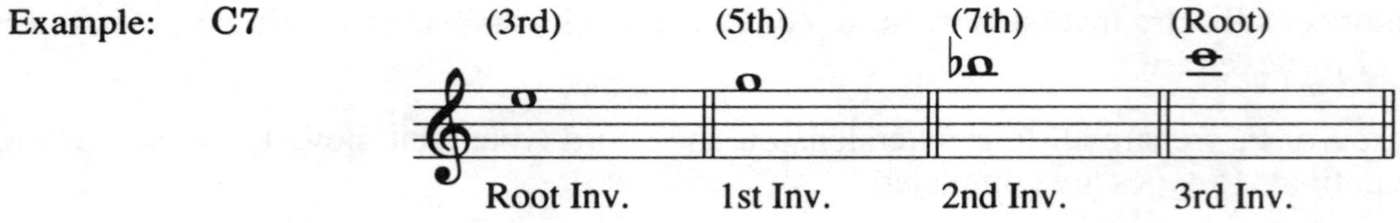


The following chord progression examples consist of only 7th and 6th drop 2 type chords. These drop 2 chord progressions are actually substitutions for more basic chord progressions listed directly below each voicing in parentheses.

After preparing each example, students should record and play back the roots of the basic chord progression in parentheses while again playing the example. This will allow students to "hear" the example in relation to the basic chord progression. Students should also write or realize the tensions produced on the basic chord progression by the original 7th and 6th chords.

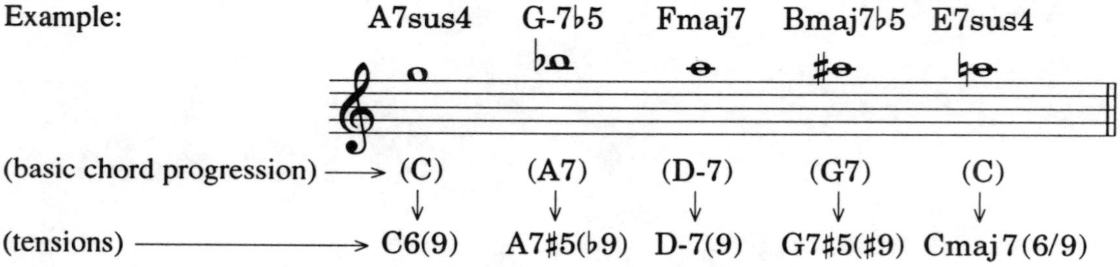

#1) The following example makes use of only four different 7th chords: maj7♭5, maj7♯5, min7♭5, and dom7sus4. These chord types will prove quite useful due to their versatile enharmonic substitution possibilities throughout this text.

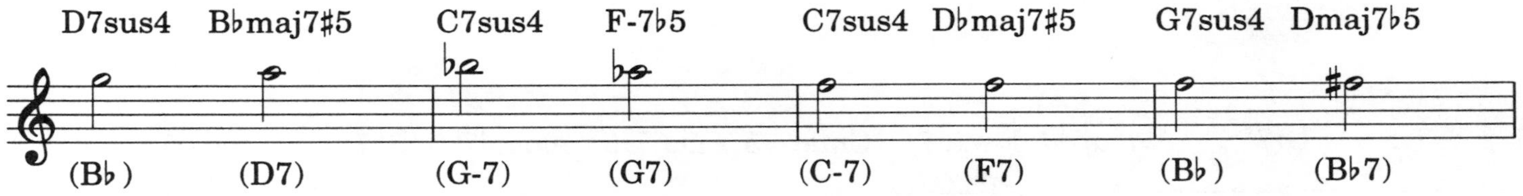


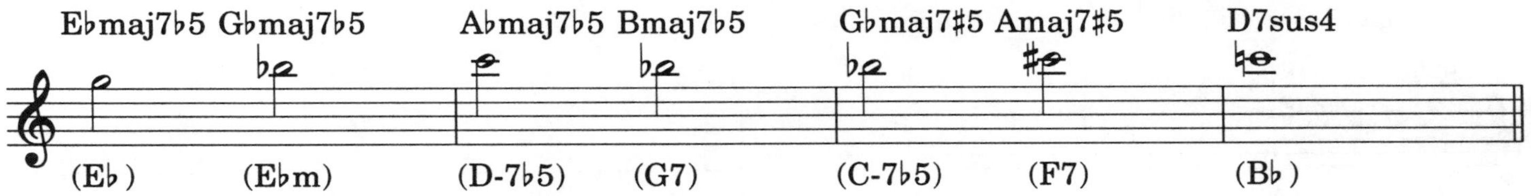


#2) The following two examples are minor chord progressions.

a)

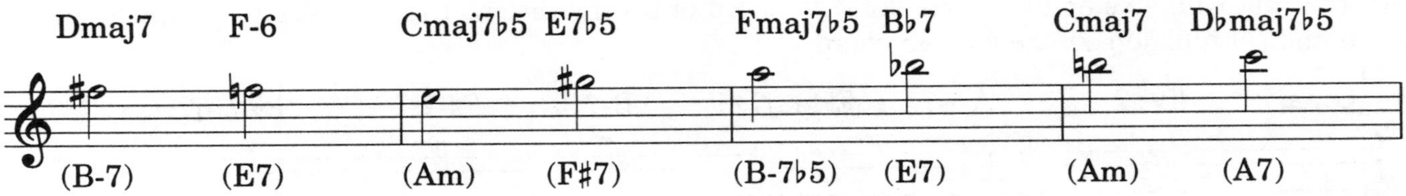


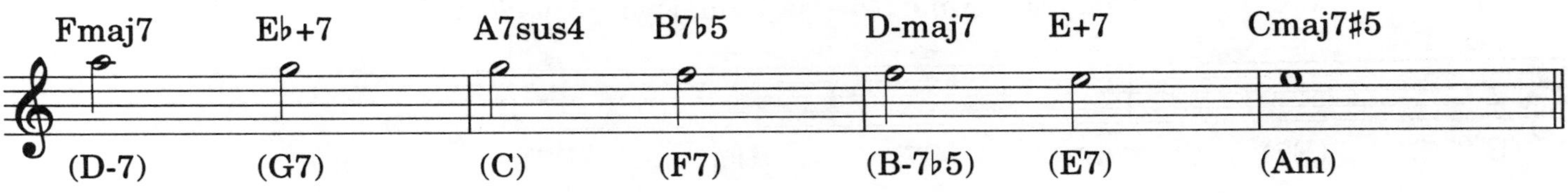

b)

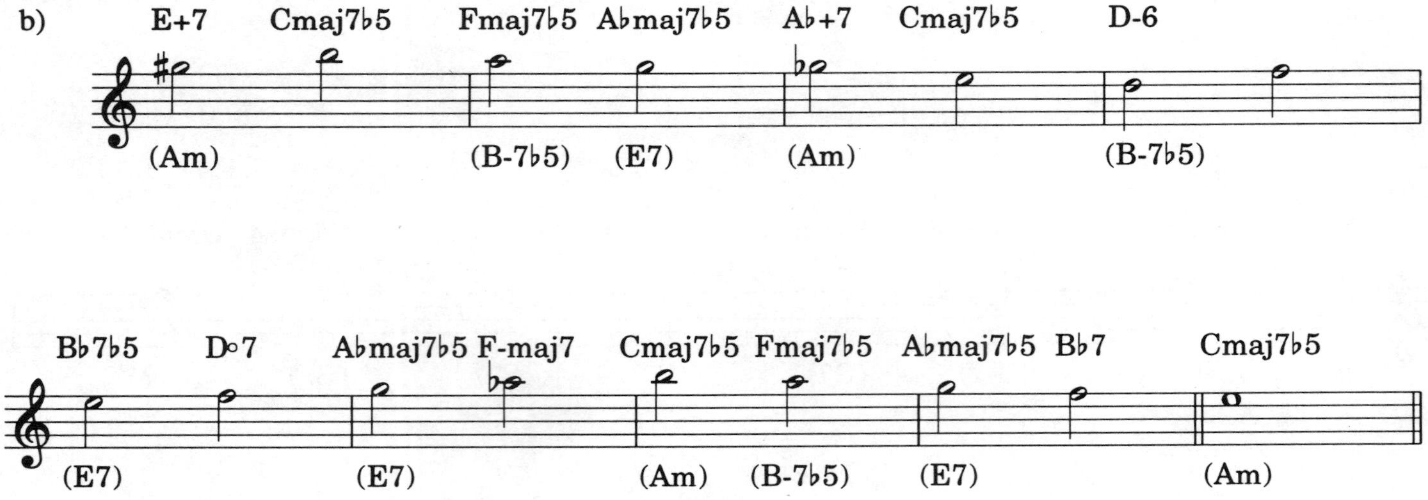


#3) This next example uses the min7(♯5) chord in several different functions and ends with a constant structure example.

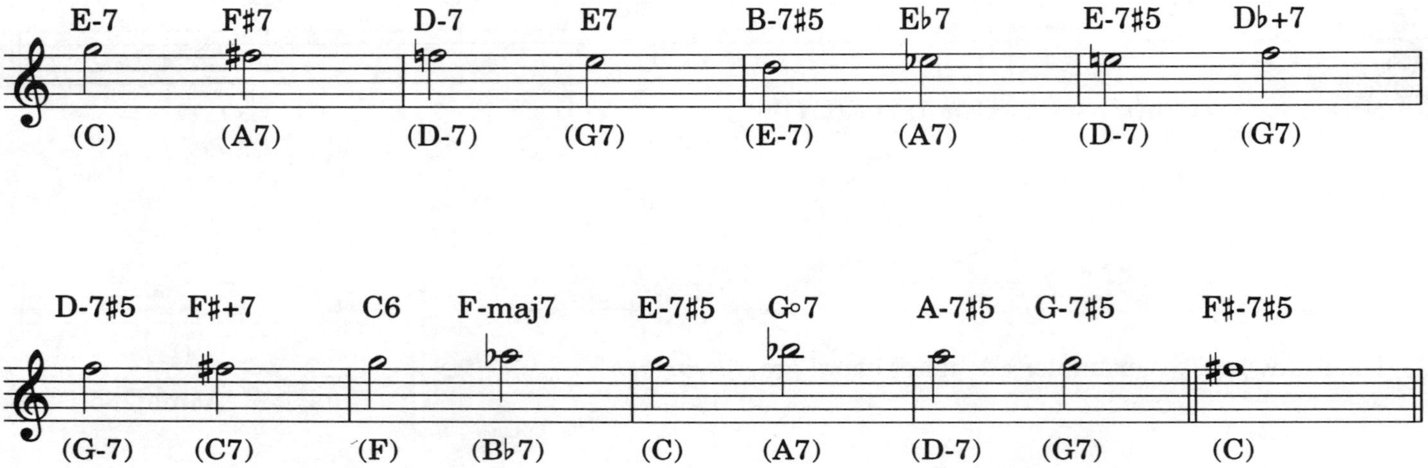


#4) The following example uses the dom7♯5 chord in several different functions. Also, note the two different dominant functions of the maj7♯5 chord.

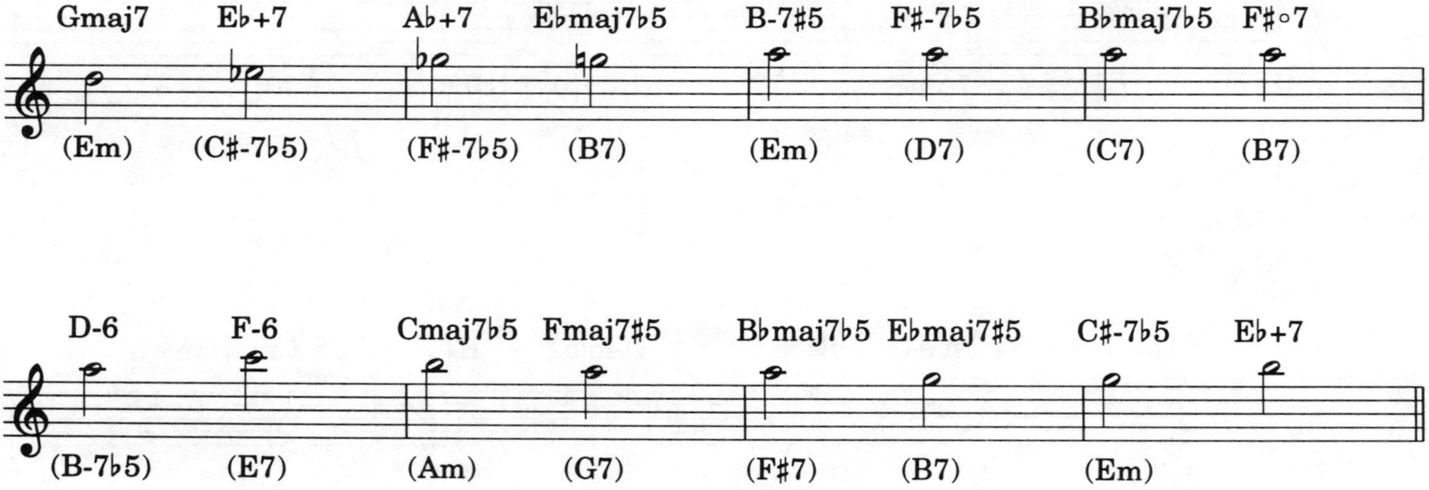

#5) In the following progression, the min7♯5 and dom7sus4 chords again receive multiple functions. The dom7 chords at the end of this example receive four different dominant functions in symmetrical minor thirds.

The following two exercises complete the examination of various 7th and 6th chords and their multiple functions. Most of these chords will reappear under their relative tension chapters. As an example:

Cmaj7♭5 = A-6 (9) = A♭7(♯9/♯5) = D7(13/9) = F♯-7♭5(11)

In each appropriate chapter they will receive a chord progression example utilizing their new functions. A list of all the substitutions for any one 7th or 6th chord can be found in the **Enharmonic Chordal Substitutions** chapter.

#6 a)

b)

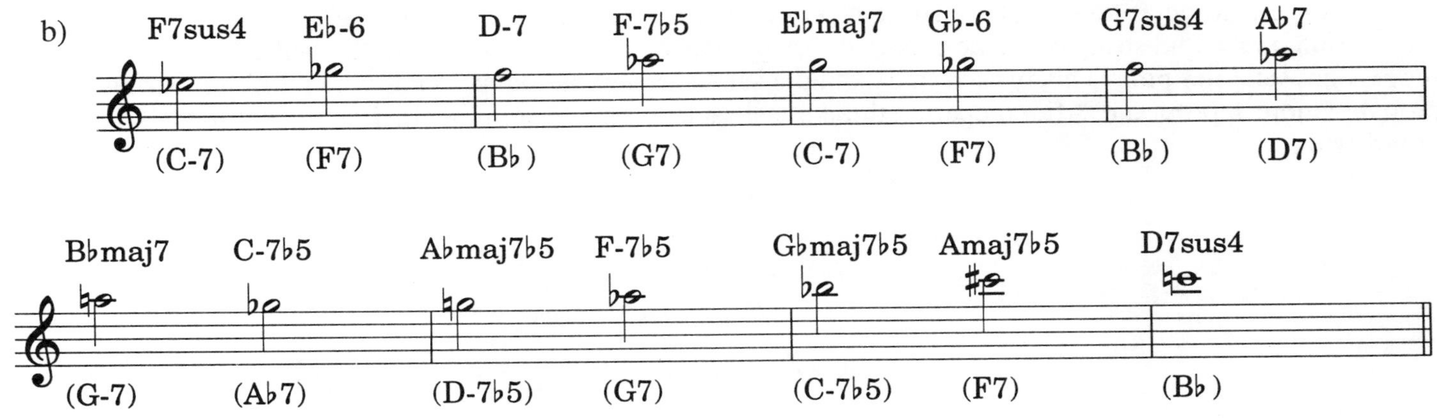

# Chapter 2.
## Voice-Leading

Voice-leading is a simple concept intended to make chords move smoothly from one to another. By allowing the top note (2nd string) of different chords to move step-wise through those chords, a smooth sound is achieved over the entire chord progression.

There are three basic choices when voice-leading from one chord to the next:

1) move up a step
2) move down a step
3) stay on same note

If there is a leap of a third or more, try to resolve the leap by using one of the notes that was skipped over in the following chord:

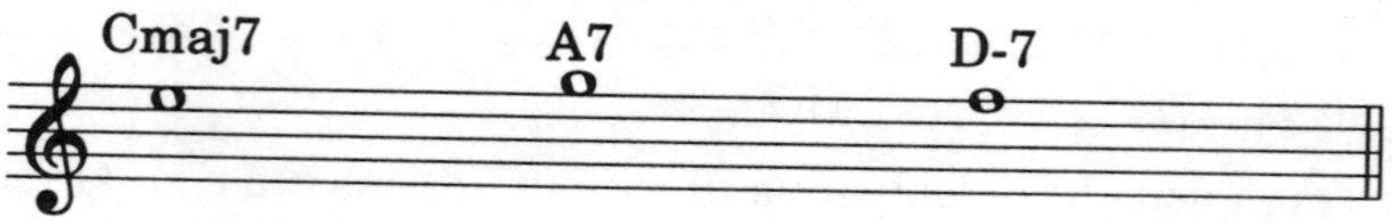


An exception to this rule is when two or more voicings appear on the same chord (often different inversions). In this case, leaping is acceptable and sometimes desirable, since the harmony is stagnant. In contrast, voice-leading is most desirable when chords change.

The above example could also be viewed as indirect voice-leading, (often melodically referred to as "indirect resolution"), since the "E" note does resolve step-wise to the "F" note with the "G" note temporarily delaying that resolution. Indirect voice-leading could be extended by two or more voices, but does begin to compromise smooth voice-leading over chord changes. In the following example, the "E" note still resolves step-wise to the "F" note although delayed by two voices:

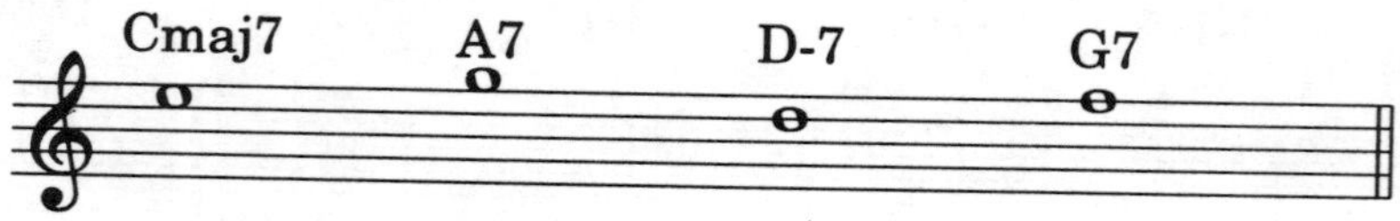


By altering chord tones or adding tensions, many different line patterns can be produced while voice-leading through a single chord progression. The following chord progression receives a variety of voice-leading ideas ranging from more traditional concepts (step-wise, chromatic, and common tones) to several line patterns that actually break basic voice-leading concepts while still offering an acceptable comping idea through "predictable" patterns.

Prepare the following lines using **any** voicing that will accommodate the lead note. In some cases, drop 2 type voicings are not appropriate and a more conventional voicing placing the root in the bass might be more desirable. Be sure to realize what tension the lead note produces on the original chord. While all lines are intended for preparation on the 2nd string only, the example "Leaps" can be prepared on both the 1st and 2nd strings, allowing for less physical jumping. This broken line example serves as a good indication of when different string sets are probably more appropriate. After preparing these lines, students should compose their own lines to the given chord progression.

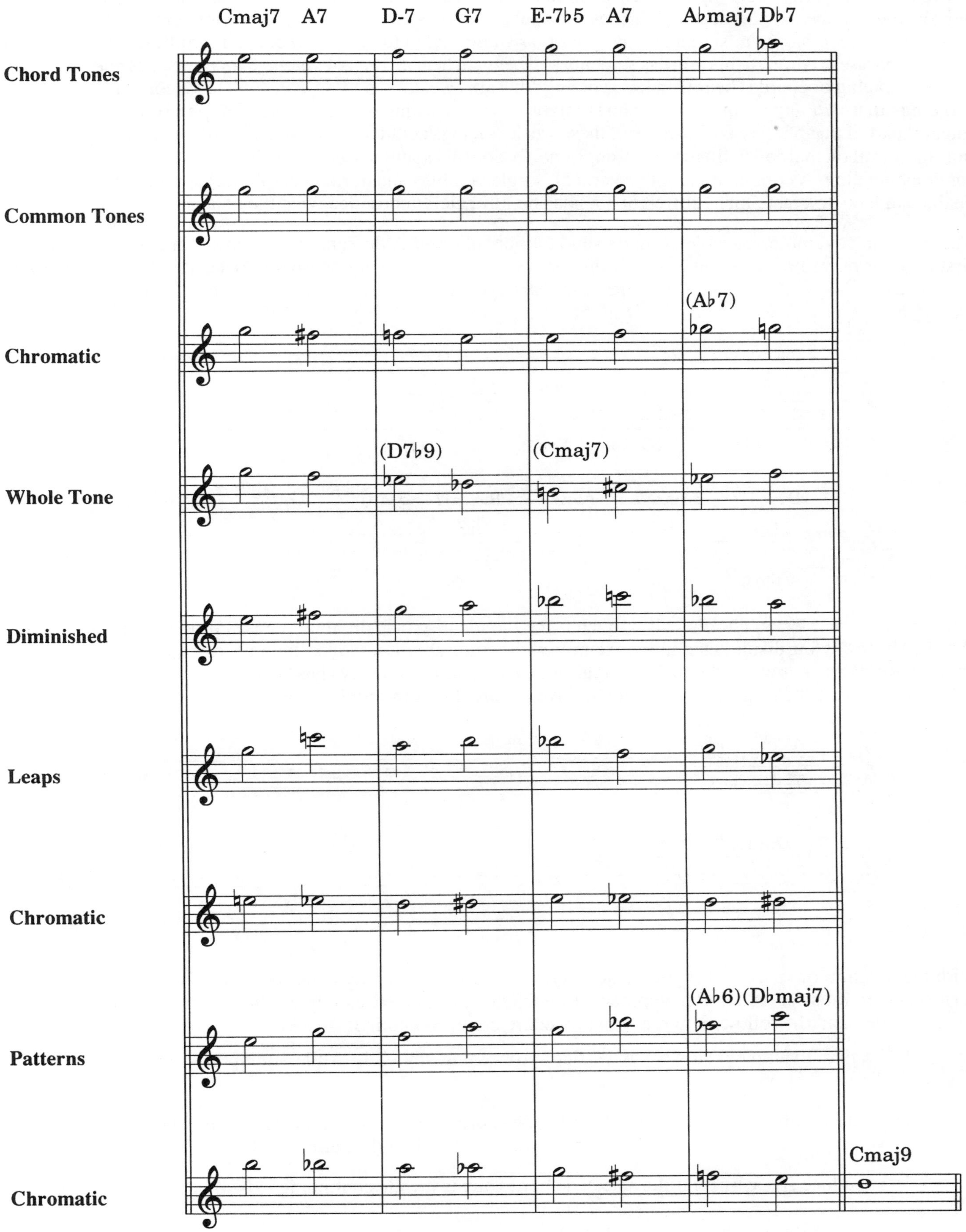
Cmaj7 A7 D-7 G7 E-7♭5 A7 A♭maj7 D♭7
Chord Tones
Common Tones
Chromatic
(A♭7)
Whole Tone
(D7♭9)
(Cmaj7)
Diminished
Leaps
Chromatic
Patterns
(A♭6)(D♭maj7)
Chromatic
Cmaj9

Chromatic lines and sustained notes (common tones) are considered the strongest approaches to voice-leading. Although the majority of examples given in this text will be voice-led throughout the entire example, a more realistic approach would be to voice-lead by phrases (two bars, four bars, or eight bars), sometimes breaking voice-leading at the end of each phrase to start a new phrase or, as suggested in the **Rhythm** chapter, omitting chords or *resting* between phrases. Through this process students will begin to hear a group of voicings (or phrase) as *one* sound, much like one voicing or chord is heard. In fact, voicings that are "weak" sounding, incomplete, or contain "wrong" notes (voicings that *will* appear in later chapters) might be found within a strong voice-led phrase and function as an integral part of that phrase. While many of these weak voicings could only be used in a voice-led passage and would not stand well on their own, there are "strong" and "beautiful" sounding voicings that can be used with little regard for voice-leading. A combination of this vertical (single voicing) and horizontal (phrase) approach to harmony will enable students to create many different sounds and ultimately reproduce what they "hear."

The following example voices-leads in two and four bar phrases. A descending chromatic line is established in the first two-bar phrase while a common leading tone is used in the second two-bar phrase, and the example finishes with an ascending chromatic line in the last four bars. Note the descending triads (top three voices) in the *first* two bars; **F** **E** **E♭** **D** (with 5th string added); **F/G** **E/F** **E♭/F** **D/E♭**

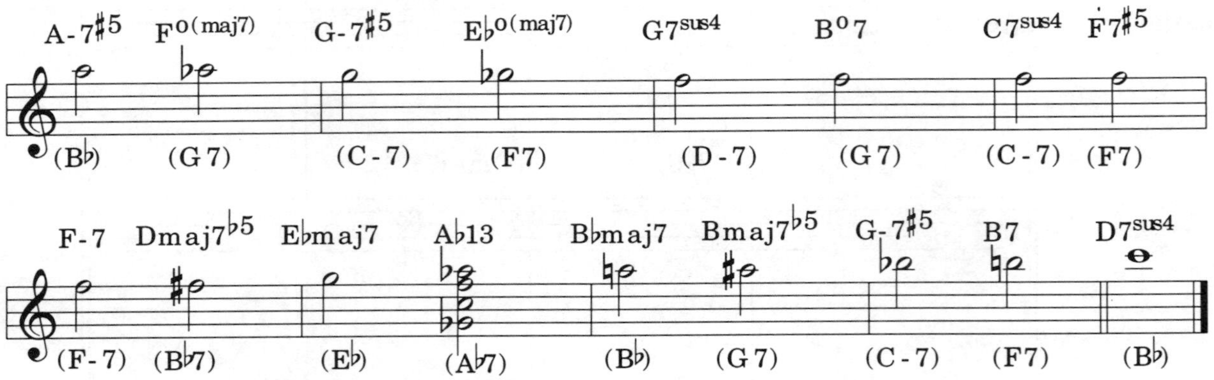


The omission of selected chords will only enhance the identity of individual phrases produced by the remaining chords. The following displays the above example with certain chords removed, helping to better define the remaining phrases. Rhythmic variety in the form of eight-note anticipations or delays has been added to enhance the exercise. A bass line stating the original progression (above in parenthesis) should accompany this exercise as well.

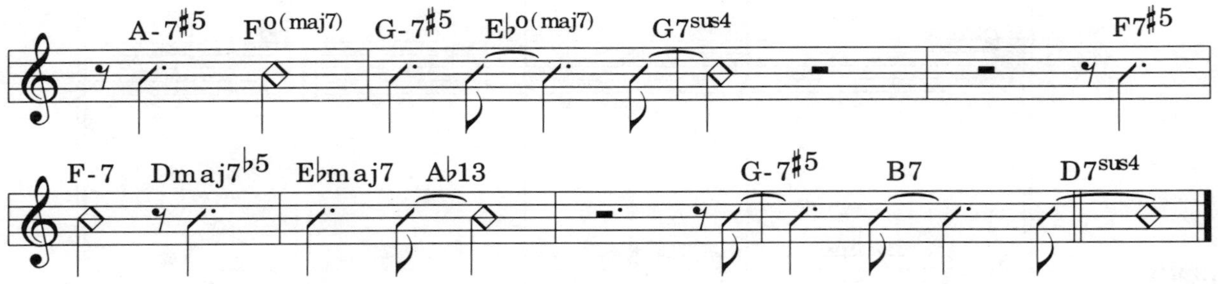


With the addition of space and rhythmic activity, this example probably better represents what occurs in a "real" performance situation. A similar approach to each of the notated examples throughout this text is strongly recommended and the following three-step procedure could be applied:

1) Prepare examples (slowly) as written, proceeding smoothly while attempting to perform in a "legato" fashion.

2) Add rhythmic variety (predominantly eight-note anticipations and delays) while performing all voicings. A mix of long and short rhythmic attacks should be attempted.

3) Introduce space by omitting selected chord voicings while continuing to be rhythmically active.

Students should continue the process established in this chapter and compose a variety of lines over different chord progressions and songs. As we progress further, these *original* lines can be harmonized by the new voicings introduced.

# Chapter 3.
## Voicing Considerations

There are various considerations involved in determining a voicing's strength or weakness in a given situation. Obviously, a "good sound" is a primary consideration, and several factors can be isolated that contribute to this. Substitution possibilities and voice-leading are very important considerations in a voicing's worth and will be discussed further in later chapters.

We have already discussed the avoidance of ♭9th intervals and will continue to avoid use of voicings containing this interval. Whenever a chord contains two notes a half-step from each other, one of the inversions will form a ♭9th interval. There are eight different available half-steps with the potential of producing an inversion containing a ♭9th interval:

| | | |
|---|---|---|
| (R - ♭9) | - | dom7(♭9) |
| (9 - ♭3) | - | min7(9) |
| (♯9 - 3 ) | - | dom7(♯9) |
| (11 - ♭5) | - | min7♭5(11) |
| (♯11 - 5) | - | maj7(♯11) / dom7(♯11) |
| (5 - ♭13) | - | dom7(♭13) |
| (13 - ♭7) | - | dom7(13) |
| (7 - R) | - | maj7 / maj7♭5 /maj7♯5 / min. maj7 / etc. |

There remain two important considerations while constructing different voicings:

1) low interval limits (LIL).

2) physical difficulty in fingerings.

Low interval limits refers to the lowest possible placement of a chord tone or tension in a voicing. Below this limit, the original chord sound begins to deteriorate and lose its primary function. LIL will apply to chord tones and tensions on the 5th string. A "bright" tone and/or a light gauge string will accommodate lower placement of tensions and chord tones, while a "dark" tone and/or heavy gauge string will not accept lower placements quite as well.

The following chart will determine *generally* how low a tension or chord tone can appear on the 5th string.

| | | |
|---|---|---|
| R | - | unlimited |
| ♭9 | - | E♭ |
| 9 | - | F (avoid tension 9 on 5th string) |
| ♯9 | - | AVOID: produces ♭9th interval with major 3rd |
| ♭3 | - | C |
| 3 | - | C |
| 4 [11] | - | D |
| ♭5 [♯11] | - | C |
| 5 | - | unlimited |
| ♯5 [♭13] | - | C |
| 6 [13] | - | D |
| ♭7 | - | C |
| 7 | - | E |

These limits are slightly lower than those determined by the Berklee College of Music Arranging Department. It is the student's responsibility to know what chord tone or tension is in the bass (5th string) on each voicing and how low that voicing can be safely used. In the **Approach Voicings** chapter later in this text, concepts will be introduced that allow violation of Low Interval Limits on the weak harmonic rhythm of a given chord or measure.

The physical difficulties involved in fingering different voicings is perhaps the largest and most diverse consideration in chord choice for most guitarists. There are basically four factors in determining the difficulty of fingering any chord or chords:

1) range
2) fingerings before and after a given chord
3) tempo
4) individual abilities

1) Range: Some voicings that are difficult on the lower, wider frets become easier as they are moved up the fretboard to the higher, thinner frets.

2) Fingerings: Fingerings of chords immediately before and after a given chord will affect the difficulty of fingering that chord. A difficult fingering can lead to a similar fingered chord, requiring little finger change and consequent physical ease of the passage. Some chords have several different ways of fingering them, while others have only one possible fingering. Use the fingering that best prepares the next chord fingering. Example:

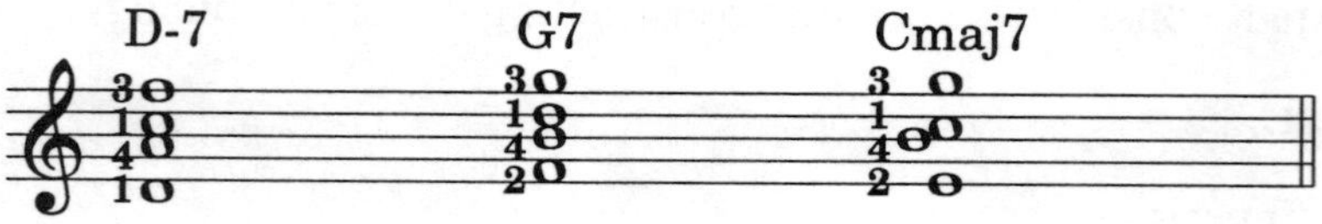


3) Tempo: Tempo is perhaps the single most important consideration in chord choice. A ballad might accommodate the time to prepare difficult fingerings of chords that could not be attempted at a quicker tempo.

4) Individual: Each student's personal technical abilities will determine what is considered a "difficult fingering." Students are reminded that difficult-fingered voicings might become easier when applied to the top four strings (1 2 3 4) or when a non-essential note is removed to produce a 3-note voicing and subsequently easier fingering.

As we move into the tension addition sections, we see some voicings becoming physically easier as tensions are added.

# Chapter 4.
## Chord Symbol Notation

Before examining tension additions to the basic four-part structures, I would like to discuss some of the approaches and difficulties involved in chord symbol notation. I must start by first stating that it is not my intent to re-organize or establish a new system of chord symbol notation. To the contrary, I would rather have avoided the need for this section altogether, but my attempt to complete a comprehensive volume of voicings and substitutions, and feedback I received from many of my colleagues, suggested I should address this topic at some level. Please keep in mind that the primary focus of this text is not that of chord symbol notation but that of discovering various four-note voicings and their enharmonic uses as different chords and substitutions, while examining different *voice-leading* possibilities between those voicings.

The initial approach to the discovery of new voicings in this text is based on the addition of different tension combinations to the basic four-part structures (7th and 6th chords). This is also where I received the most diverse and controversial responses from my colleagues. Opinions ranged from those favoring little or no tension addition to the basic structure (allowing more freedom of interpretation) to those who felt that tensions should dictate specific scales as well as describe their vertical placement in a voicing. The most notable and surprising differences appeared to center around the enharmonic interpretations of tensions ♯11 and ♭13 and their melodic or harmonic implications. A majority of responses supported the assumption that tensions ♭13 and/or ♯11 would include or imply a natural 5th in the same dominant type voicing. Although the natural 5th could accompany one or the other tension, both tensions with a natural 5th would produce consecutive half-steps:

♯11 — 5 — ♭13

1/2 1/2

While this is a melodic possibility, it has limited, if not problematic, harmonic value. When posed with a dom7(♭13/♯11) chord, responses were confusing at best. My reaction and recommendation is to avoid this particular tension combination on a dominant chord. If the same notes are desired with no natural 5th, the following symbols would suffice:

dom7♯5(♯11) / dom7♭5(♭13) / dom7(♯5/♭5) / dom7(alt5)/ dom7♯5(♭5) /dom7♭5(♯5) / etc.

If the natural 5th is desired in the voicing, dom7(♭13/♯11) would suffice for those who responded that ♯11 and ♭13 imply natural 5 (do you guys really want this chord?). For those who would not assume the natural 5th was implied, it would have to be included in the chord symbol: dom7(♭13/♯11) add 5. Yikes! At this point, I personally would prefer that the desired voicing be notated on a staff. Even if I could not read music, I'd probably produce the voicing quicker off the staff than from the above chord symbol.

This segues well to another issue and personal recommendation I have. I think that tension additions are appropriate when used as suggestions to desired "colors" or sounds on basic structures or to describe melodic effects on different voicings. On the other hand, I believe that symbols that are made more complicated or confusing by attempting to communicate vertical placement of tensions or by their dictation of specific scales should be avoided. At this point, the voicing would be served better by notation on a staff.

Although this book will possess many complicated symbols, they are used as descriptions of specific staff notated voicings and are not implying or endorsing their use as "standard" chord symbol notation. To the contrary, most voicings introduced in this text are to be used as various available "colors" or sounds (including available tensions and chord tones) over a more basic chord symbol. A collection of many different voicings will be made available to one basic chord type. Your choice of specific voicings to use is your "interpretation" of that basic chord.

Example:

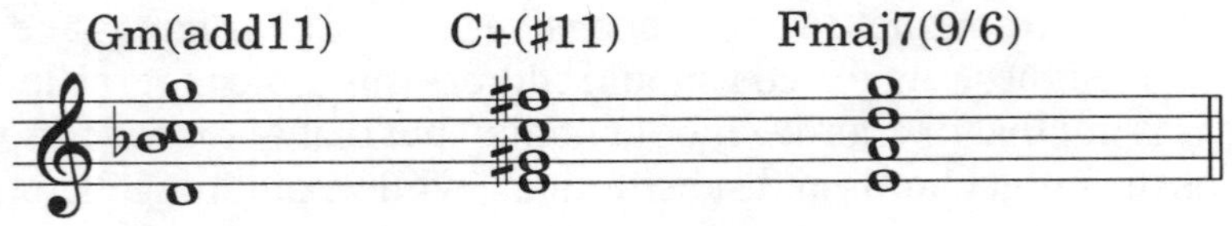


The above voicings could be used to "color" or substitute the basic II-V-I cadence in the key of "F" (G-7, C7, Fmaj7). Gm(add11), C+(♯11), and Fmaj7(9/6) are chord symbol descriptions of the above voicings in the key of "F."

The attempt will be made to use the "least" offensive chord symbols when notating these complicated, and in many cases incomplete, voicings. I have tried to reach a "compromise" in my chord symbol selections that would satisfy most, knowing that some (hopefully not most) will certainly find fault.

At this point, I should summarize some of the basic assumptions that have been presented and will be used in this text. The following suggestions specifically deal with the ♯11/♭13 controversy introduced earlier:

I. Tension ♭13 might imply or include a natural 5th when used in a chord symbol. If the ♭5th is notated in the symbol, natural 5 is not a choice. If ♭13 is desired without natural 5 (or ♭5), enharmonic ♯5 instead of ♭13 can be used. A more complicated symbol choice could be ♭13(no5).

II. Tension ♯11 might imply or include a natural 5th when used in a chord symbol. If the ♯5th is notated in the symbol, natural 5 is not a choice. If ♯11 is desired without natural 5 (or ♯5), enharmonic ♭5 instead of ♯11 can be used. A more complicated symbol choice could be ♯11(no5).

These suggestions make clear the need for caution when using ♭13 or ♯11 in a chord symbol. They contain inherent controversy harmonically and melodically. My personal inclination is to avoid their use as much as possible. I prefer the enharmonic ♭5 and ♯5 spelling of the same notes. ♭5 and ♯5 produce exact harmonic interpretation and retain freedom of interpretation melodically.

C7(♭13/♯11) might imply natural 5 harmonically and "who knows what" melodically.
C7(♭13/♭5) to some implies the "altered" scale.
C7(♯11/♯5) to some implies the "whole tone" scale.

C7(♯5/♭5), C7(alt5), C7♭5(♯5), C+7(♭5): precise harmonic description and freedom of melodic or scale interpretation.

*Note the C7(alt5) symbol could be confused with the C7(alt) symbol which implies any combination of ♭5, ♯5, ♭9, ♯9.

For organizational purposes, the first introduction of these two notes together in the same voicing occurs under the **Tension 11** chapter as a C+7(♯11) chord. They appear again under the **Tensions 9 and 13** chapter as C9♭5(♭13), C7♭5(♭13/♭9), and C7♭5(♭13/♯9) chords. In this chapter, ♭5 and ♯5 will be noted as the preferred symbol choices:

C9(♯5/♭5), C+7(9/♭5), or C7♭5(9/♯5)
C7(♭9/alt5), C+7(♭9/♭5), or C7♭5(♭9/♯5)
C7(♯9/alt5), C+7(♯9/♭5), or C7♭5(♯9/♯5)

# Chapter 5.
## Tensions

As tensions are added to the basic four-part chords (7th and 6th chords), different basic four-part chords often reappear on different roots (i.e., B♭9 = D-7♭5 / F-6), beginning the enharmonic chordal substitution process that will continue throughout this book. These substitute chords might sound clearer or more obvious than the original chord receiving tensions. D-7♭5 or F-6 is more defined or complete than the original B♭9 chord, which is missing its root. For this reason, it is recommended that a bass line containing the original chord roots be recorded and played back while playing chords containing tensions.

In each tension chapter the majority of voicings produced by tension additions will most likely have been introduced enharmonically in earlier chapters, many originating as basic four-part 7th or 6th chord voicings. When this occurs, the original chords introducing those voicings for the first time will be listed. For example:

*Under the **Tension 9** chapter, the min7(9) {♭3 5 ♭7 9} voicings were originally introduced as maj7 (1 3 5 7) voicings, A-7(9) = Cmaj7.

*Under the **Tensions 9 & 13** chapter, the dom7sus4(13/9) {4 ♭7 9 13} voicings were originally introduced as maj7 {1 3 5 7} voicings, D7sus4(13/9) = Cmaj7.

*Under the **Tensions 9 & 11** chapter, the maj7(♯11/9) {5 7 9 ♯11} voicings were originally introduced as maj7 {1 3 5 7} voicings, Fmaj7(♯11/9) = Cmaj7.

A list of all the possible substitutions for any one voicing can be found in the **Enharmonic Chordal Substitutions** and **Additional Chordal Substitutions** chapters following the tension chapters. In these chapters, the previous examples would combine their substitutions in order of their appearance in this text:

Cmaj7 = A-9 = D7sus4(13/9) = Fmaj7(♯11/9)

A minimal understanding of harmony and theory is required to make the appropriate tension selections for different chords. Some basic harmonic assumptions will be presented to allow for a choice of tensions that will sound appropriate in a common pop or jazz idiom. While tensions are usually dictated by chord function and/or key of the moment, a strong voice-led guide-line often can make use of tensions that might appear inappropriate or non-diatonic to the key of the moment. This is especially true of dominant chords, which can accept many different tension combinations (both diatonic and non-diatonic), while other chord types are more demanding of fewer and more specific tensions. Tensions on diminished 7 chords will be examined separately in the **Tension Additions on Diminished Chords** chapter later in this book.

In the following examples, the guide-line in example #2 is not as diatonic as the #1 example (E-9 and G7(♭13) are not diatonic to the key of C), yet example #2 sounds better due to the strong chromatic guide-line produced by these tensions.

#1
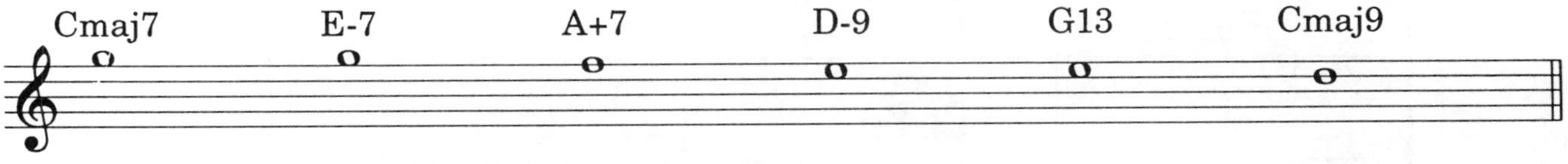


#2
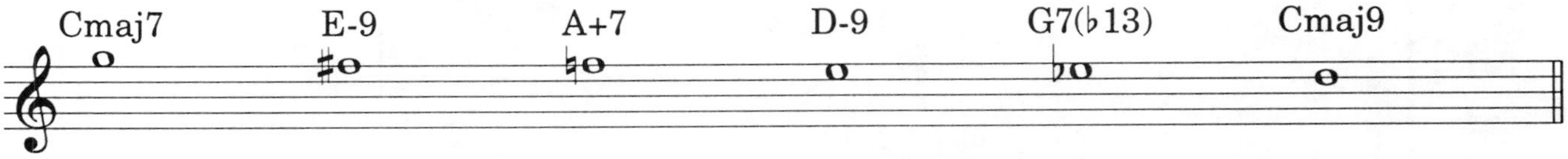


When a "strong" or effective guide-line is not present, a more conservative or diatonic approach to tension additions might be in order.

There are only seven different tensions available in the more common pop or jazz idioms:

| | | |
|---|---|---|
| ♭9 | 9 | ♯9 |
| 11 | ♯11 | |
| ♭13 | 13 | |

Note the enharmonic functions some tensions might possess:

| | | |
|---|---|---|
| 11 | = | sus4 |
| ♯11 | = | ♭5 |
| ♭13 | = | ♯5 |

The following will examine each tension's characteristics in these more common idioms. Of course, different styles and concepts could condition or change these basic assumptions. For example, "modal music" often requires use of tensions that are not desirable in a more diatonic situation.

1) Natural 9 can appear on any chord type and can be accompanied by any other tension except ♭9 or ♯9.

2) ♭9 and ♯9 can accompany each other and any other tension except natural 9. ♭9 and ♯9 can only appear on dom7 type chords.

3) Natural 11 can appear on any chord type except maj7 type chords. Natural 11 can accompany any tension except ♯9 and ♯11. Natural 11 often functions enharmonically as a suspended 4th on dom7 and maj6 chords. The use of natural 11 with the major third is a more contemporary sound which will be examined later.

4) ♯11 can appear only on major type chords (maj7 / maj6 / dom7). ♯11 can accompany any tension except natural 11.

5) Natural 13 can appear on any chord type except min7♭5. Natural 13 can accompany any tension except ♭13.

6) ♭13 can appear on any chord type except minor chords containing a natural 5th. ♭13 can accompany any tension except natural 13.

The following tension chart attempts to clarify and classify available tensions and chord tones on the most common chord types (excluding dim7 chords).

**CHORD TENSION CHART**

| CHORD | FREELY | CAREFUL | WEAK |
|---|---|---|---|
| maj7 | 6, 9 | ♯11, ♯5 | 11 |
| maj6 | 9 | 7, ♭7, ♯11 | 11 |
| min7 | 9, 11 | 13 | ♭13 |
| min6 | 9 | 7, ♭7, 11 | |
| min7(♭5) | 11, ♭13 | 9 | ♭9 |
| min maj7 | 9 | 6, 11 | ♭13 |
| dom7sus4 | 9, 13<br>♭9, 13 | 3, ♭13 | ♯9 |
| dom7 | 9, 13<br>9, ♭13<br>9, ♯11<br>9, ♯11, 13<br>9, ♯11, ♭13<br>♭9, ♯9, 13<br>♭9, ♯9, ♭13<br>♭9, ♯9, ♯11<br>♭9, ♯9, ♯11, 13<br>♭9, ♯9, ♯11, ♭13 | 11 | 7 |

Again, some of the tensions listed under the "weak" or "careful" column might in fact be strong or characteristic notes in a modal setting, or appear in a common diatonic progression were a melody or strong voice-leading could make use of an otherwise "weak" tension.

In the following common chord cadence, the ♭9 tension is not normally available to a min7♭5 chord, but sounds and voice-leads quite well in this particular example. Note the A-7♭5(♭9) chord forms a complete C-7 chord over an "A" bass note; ( C-7/A ).

A-7♭5(♭9) D7(♭9) G-6

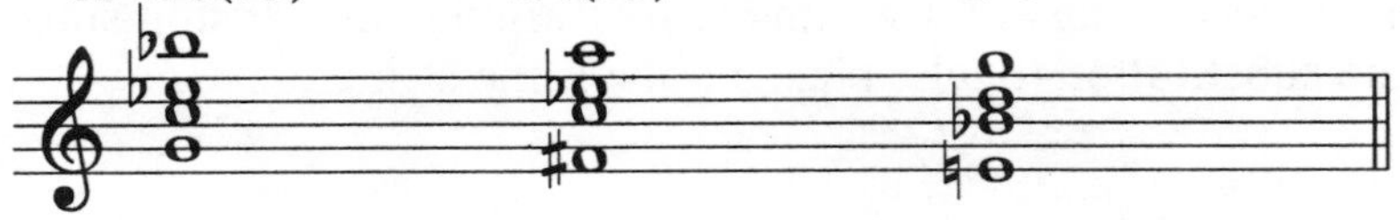

Note that some of the above tension combinations under the dom7 chord dictate specific chord scales:

| | | |
|---|---|---|
| 9, ♯11, 13 | - | Lydian ♭7 |
| 9, ♯11, ♭13 | - | whole tone |
| ♭9, ♯9, ♯11, 13 | - | dominant diminished |
| ♭9, ♯9, ♯11, ♭13 | - | altered |

With the exception of dom7 type chords, the tension chart accurately describes available tensions on these chord types in the majority of harmonic situations in which they would appear. The dom7 type chord needs some harmonic clarification in order to chose the appropriate tensions in relation to its function; keep in mind that the nature of a dom7 chord can accept most any tension combination, regardless of its function. The following describes the tension tendencies of a dom7 chord in a given function.

1) **V7 of major**

Common
1) natural tensions (9, 13)
2) altered tensions (♭9, ♯9, ♭5, ♯5)
3) tension combinations: ♭9/13, 9/♭13, etc.
4) natural to altered (before resolving)

Not Common
1) (9, ♯11, 13) sub V sound
2) altered to natural (before resolving)

2) **V7 of minor**

Common
1) ♭9, ♯9, ♭13 and natural 5 or ♭5
2) tension combinations: ♭9/13, 9/♭13, etc.

Not Common
1) natural
2) natural to altered
3) altered to natural
4) (9, ♯11, 13) sub V sound

3) **Sub V and/or non-diatonic dom 7th,** as well as **IV7** and **II7**:

(Lydian ♭7) 9, ♯11, 13

Upon establishing some basis for tension possibilities on a given chord, it is now important to discuss the placement of tensions in a four-note voicing, commonly referred to as "tension substitution."

When a tension is introduced to a four-note voicing, one of the basic chord tones is removed. The least needed chord tone is usually chosen. The root and fifth (unless altered) are the least needed, while the guide-tones (third and seventh or sixth) are more important to the sound and function of the chord. Due to enharmonics, some tensions are already built into the basic four-part chords:

Cmaj7♭5 = Cmaj7(♯11); C7♭5 = C7(♯11); C7(♯5) = C7(♭13).

These tensions could be considered as substituting for the fifth of the chord.

Tension substitution on drop 2 type voicings follows this basic formula: any tension substitutes a chord tone next to that tension. This allows the substitution to take place on the same string.

9 substitutes the root or third
11 [4] substitutes the third or fifth
13 [6] substitutes the fifth or seventh

Since the guide-tones are needed, we are left with the following tension substitution formula for drop 2 type voicings:

9 substitutes the root {3 5 7 9}
11 [4] substitutes the fifth {1 3 7 11}
13 [6] substitutes the fifth {1 3 7 13}

An exception to this formula which must be addressed is when the fifth is altered (♭5 or ♯5). An altered fifth is an important part of the chord sound that should be included. In this case, 11th and 13th type chords would have to substitute guide-tones instead of the fifth; 11 for 3/13 for 7. If the original chord sound and function are not lost, these substitutions are possible. An example would be a min7♭5(11) chord with tension 11 substituting the 3rd. A min7♭5 chord is the only type of chord that will accommodate a ♭5th and an 11th. By deduction, the minor 3rd of the chord is "heard" even though it is not played. If the chord sound is lost by removing a guide-tone on one of these altered fifth voicings, an alternative voicing to the drop 2 type voicing is required:

| | | |
|---|---|---|
| 11th chord | - | 3 5 7 11 |
| 13th chord | - | 3 5 7 13 |

The fifth and the guide-tones are accommodated in these voicings and will be used when appropriate.

In the following tension sections, with some isolated exceptions, the attempt will be made to retain the guide-tones in every voicing. When this is not possible, the 7th will be retained in favor of the 3rd. This will present some new voicings that are not drop 2 type voicings but share the same width as drop 2, allowing compatible voice leading. More "incomplete" type voicings with various tension additions will be examined in the later **Enharmonic Chordal Substitution** chapters.

The following tension substitution formulas will be used in their appropriate sections:

| | | | |
|---|---|---|---|
| **Tension 9** | 9 for 1 | {3 5 7 9} | (drop 2) |
| | 9 for 5 | {1 3 7 9} | |
| | 9 for 3 | {1 5 7 9} | |
| **Tension 11** | 11 for 3 | {1 5 7 11} | (drop 2) |
| | 11 for 5 | {1 3 7 11} | (drop 2) |
| | 11 for 1 | {3 5 7 11} | |
| ***Tension 13** | 13 for 5 | {1 3 7 13} | (drop 2) |
| | 13 for 1 | {3 5 7 13} | |

(* With the exception of a dom13♭5 chord, {1 5 7 13} proves too ambiguous or limited to examine.)

| | | |
|---|---|---|
| **Tension 9 & 13** | 9 for 1 / 13 for 5 {3 7 9 13}<br>9 for 1 / 13 for 3 {5 7 9 13} | (drop 2) |
| **Tension 9 & 11** | 9 for 1 / 11 for 5 {3 7 9 11}<br>9 for 1 / 11 for 3 {5 7 9 11} | (drop 2)<br>(drop 2) |
| **Tension 11 & 13** | 11 for 5 / 13 for 1 {3 7 11 13}<br>11 for 3 / 13 for 1 {5 7 11 13} | |

As more tensions are added to a four-note voicing, one or both of the guide-tones will eventually be removed, resulting in what is commonly referred to as an "incomplete" voicing. Some of these voicings can sound ambiguous or begin to lose their original chord sound, while others can define their original chord sound by use of unique tensions or a predictable chord progression. These latter chords often sound better and more "colorful" than the original "obvious" chord sound.

Here are some examples of incomplete voicings being defined by their tensions:

1) ♭9 or ♯9 must accommodate a dom7 type chord
2) 11th with ♭5th must accommodate a min7♭5 or dim7 chords
3) 11th with 7th must accommodate min maj7 or dim7 type chords

Here is an example of an incomplete voicing being defined by a predictable chord progression:

(II) G-7 ↓ — (V) C7 ↓ (A♭7♯5) — (I) Fmaj7 ↓

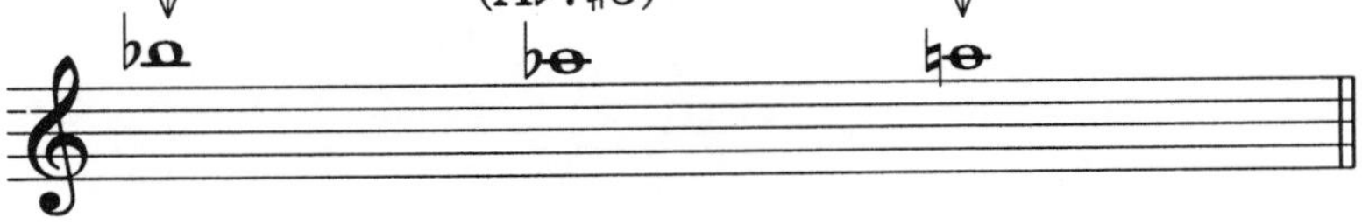

The A♭7♯5 is an incomplete C7(alt5) chord:

| | | | | |
|---|---|---|---|---|
| A♭7♯5 | 1 | 3 | ♯5 | ♭7 |
| | ↓ | ↓ | ↓ | ↓ |
| | A♭ | C | E | G♭ |
| | ↑ | ↑ | ↑ | ↑ |
| C7(alt5) | ♯5 | 1 | 3 | ♭5 |

The A♭7♯5 chord standing alone has no particular C7 sound. When placed in the above chord progression in substitute of the normal C7 (and perhaps accompanied by a C bass note), it no longer sounds like and A♭7♯5 chord.

By examining each tension, we can see which tensions dictate guide-tones and which do not:

1) ♭9 can appear only on dominant type chords, dictating their guide-tones when missing from a voicing.

2) Natural 9 can appear on any type of chord, thus cannot dictate the guide-tones of any particular chord type.

3) ♯9 can appear only on dominant type chords. It can dictate the ♭7th but requires the 3rd to accompany it. Without the 3rd, ♯9 might sound enharmonically like the third of a minor chord, ♯9 = ♭3.

4) Natural 11 can appear on any chord type except the maj7 type chord. With the exception of an 11 with natural 7 dictating a min. maj7 (11) chord, 11 usually dictates a ♭7th guide-tone. Natural 11 cannot dictate a major or minor third, although it often can take the place of the third by enharmonically functioning as a suspended 4th guide-tone.

5) ♯11 can appear only on major chord types, dictating the major 3rd when missing, but not the 7th.

6) ♭13 can appear on any chord type except minor chords containing the natural 5th. It can dictate the ♭7th, with the maj7(♯5) chord being enharmonically an exception. It cannot dictate the 3rd.

7) 13 can appear on any chord type except the min7♭5 chord. It cannot dictate guide-tones.

As more tensions and chordal substitutions are presented, the use of incomplete voicings will become more common.

The maj7♯5 and min7♯5 chords have been omitted from the following tension chapters, due to their unique sound being compromised by tension additions. The min7♯5 chord will reappear in the **Additional Enharmonic Chordal Substitutions** chapter with tension additions. Although tensions will not be added to the maj7♯5 and min7♯5 chords, their four-part structures will reappear as enharmonic substitutions in various tension chapters. As an example, in the **Tension 11** chapter, G-7♯5 will appear as C-7(11) (♭3 5 ♭7 11).

# Chapter 6.
## Dominant Sub V Chords

Every dominant type chord, with the exception of those containing a suspended fourth, can be substituted by another dominant chord a tritone away. This chord is commonly referred to as a "Sub V" chord (D♭7 is the Sub V chord of G7, and vice-versa). Any tensions added to a dominant chord will appear as chord tones or different tensions on the Sub V chord.

The following is a simple tension conversion model for Sub V chords that should be memorized:

| R | ♭9 | 9 | ♯9 |
|---|---|---|---|
| ↕ | ↕ | ↕ | ↕ |
| ♯11 (♭5) | 5 | ♭13 (♯5) | 13 |

The above model in relation to C7 and its Sub V chord:

| | | | | | |
|---|---|---|---|---|---|
| | C7 | R | ♭9 | 9 | ♯9 |
| ↗ | | ↑ | ↑ | ↑ | ↑ |
| (Sub V) | | C | D♭ | D | D♯ |
| ↘ | | ↓ | ↓ | ↓ | ↓ |
| | F♯7 | ♯11 | 5 | ♭13 | 13 |

There are four dominant chords that "mirror" themselves on their Sub V chords:

| | | |
|---|---|---|
| C7♭5 | = | F♯7♭5 |
| C7(♭9) | = | F♯7(♭9) |
| C9(♯5) | = | F♯9(♯5) |
| C13(♯9) | = | F♯13(♯9) |

Remember the tension substitutions [9 for R] and [13 for 5] for the above examples, leaving three of the chords rootless.

All the dominant chords that will be introduced in the forthcoming tension chapters will also examine their Sub V chords. The only exceptions will be dominant chords that contain both a ♭13 and natural 5. These notes produce ♭9 and natural 9 on the Sub V chord, which is not an acceptable tension combination, producing consecutive half-steps (R - ♭2 - 2). These chord types will be omitted from the tension chapters but will reappear for examination in the **Additional Enharmonic Chordal Substitutions** chapter.

Remember to be aware of Low Interval Limits and ♭9th intervals when placing dominant tensions on the 5th string. Tensions ♯9 and 13 will not be allowed on the 5th string. Both tensions are Sub V substitutes for each other and both produce ♭9th intervals (tension ♯9 over the 3rd and tension 13 over the ♭7th). Tensions 9 and ♭13 [♯5] are also Sub V substitutes for each other, but only the 9th (with some exceptions) will be omitted from the 5th string due to low interval limits.

Before beginning the tension chapters, a brief discussion of the "altered" dominants should be given. Altered (or alt) on a dom7 chord refers to the 9th and 5th being flatted and raised (♭9, ♯9) and (♭5, ♯5) or enharmonically (♭9, ♯9, ♯11, ♭13). Any combination of these tensions will satisfy an "altered sound," but tensions ♯9 and ♭13 [♯5] are most characteristic because they are also tensions on the Sub V chord: (♯9 = 13) and (♭13 = 9). Example:

| | | |
|---|---|---|
| C7(♯9/♯5) | = | F♯7(13/9) |
| (altered) | | (natural) |

An additional observation of interest shows the ♯9 and ♯5 of a V7 chord to be the "blue" notes ♭7 and ♭3 of the related I chord;

| | | |
|---|---|---|
| (V7) C7(♯9/♯5).................... | ♯9 | ♯5 |
| | E♭ | A♭ |
| ( I ) F.................................. | ♭7 | ♭3 |

More information on altered dominants is presented in the **Altered Dominant** chapter later in this text.

# Chapter 7.
## Tension 9

By substituting 9 for the root on all of the previous four-part drop 2 inversions, we see many of those original four-part 7th and 6th chords reappearing on different roots. The following list contains all possible tension 9 additions to the original four-part chords and the consequent four-part enharmonic substitute chords produced:

| | | |
|---|---|---|
| Cmaj7(9) | = | E-7 / G6 |
| Cmaj7♭5(9) | = | refer below |
| C-maj7(9) | = | E♭maj7♯5 |
| C-7(9) | = | E♭maj7 |
| C-7♭5(9) | = | E♭-maj7 |
| C6(9) | = | A7sus4 |
| C-6(9) | = | E♭maj7♭5 |

| | | |
|---|---|---|
| C7(9) | = | E-7♭5 / G-6 |
| C7(♭9) | = | C♯°7, E°7, G°7, B♭°7 |
| C7(♯9) | = | refer below |
| C7♭5(9) | = | F♯+7 (Sub V) |
| C7♭5(♭9) | = | F♯7 (Sub V) |
| C7♭5(♯9) | = | refer below |
| C+7(9) | = | E7♭5/B♭7♭5 |
| C+7(♭9) | = | B♭-7♭5/D♭-6 |
| C+7(♯9) | = | Emaj7♭5 |
| C7sus4(9) | = | G-7/B♭6 |
| C7sus4(♭9) | = | G-7♭5/B♭-6 |

Cmaj7♭5(9), C7(♯9), and C7♭5(♯9) do not produce basic four-part 7th or 6th enharmonic substitute chords, but do produce their own interesting substitute chords:

| | | |
|---|---|---|
| C7♭5(♯9) | = | G♭7(13) (Sub V) |
| C7(♯9) | = | G♭7(♭9/13) (Sub V) [1st inv. of C7(♯9) = D♯/E).] |
| Cmaj7♭5(9) | = | D6(9) {1 3 6 9}, which is not a drop 2 voicing. This maj6(9) voicing will be discussed later in this chapter. |

C7sus4(♯9) has been omitted, since it has become a C-7(11) chord. As mentioned earlier, Cmaj7♯5 and C-7♯5 will not be included in the tension chapters, but will appear later in this book with tension additions. C°7 will receive tensions in the **Tension Additions on Dimin 7 Chords** chapter.

Realize the enharmonics involved in the above ninth chords with an altered 5th :

| | | |
|---|---|---|
| Cmaj7♭5(9) | = | Cmaj7(9/♯11) |
| C7♭5(9 /♭9 / ♯9) | = | C7(♯11/9) (♯11/♭9) (♯11/♯9) |
| C7♯5(9/♭9/♯9) | = | C7(♭13/9) (♭13/♭9) (♭13/♯9) |

If not already listed, realize the Sub V chord for each dominant chord:

| | | |
|---|---|---|
| C7(9) | = | F♯7(♯5/♭9) |
| C7(♭9) | = | F♯7(♭9) |
| C7♯5(9) | = | F♯+7(9) |
| C+7(♭9) | = | F♯7(9) |
| C+7(♯9) | = | F♯7(13/9) |

Look at the previous enharmonic substitutions from a common four-part chord root:

| | | |
|---|---|---|
| Cmaj7 | = | A-9 |
| Cmaj7♭5 | = | A-6(9) / A♭7(♯5/♯9) / D7(9/13) |
| Cmaj7♯5 | = | A-maj7(9) |
| C-maj7 | = | A-9♭5 |
| C-6 | = | F9 / D7sus4(♭9) / B7(♯5/♭9) |
| C6 | = | Fmaj9 / D7sus4(9) |
| C-7 | = | A♭maj9 / F7sus4(9) |
| C-7♭5 | = | A♭9 / F7sus4(♭9) / D7(♯5/♭9) |
| C7 | = | G♭7(♭5/♭9) |
| C7♭5 | = | G♭7♭5 / A♭9+/ D9+ |
| C7♯5 | = | G♭9(♭5) |
| C°7 | = | B7(♭9) / D7(♭9) / F7(♭9) / A♭7(♭9) |
| C7sus4 | = | E♭6(9) |

Tensions ♭9 and ♯9 can combine to form available dom7 tensions (i.e. C7(alt9) / C7♭5(alt9) / C+7(alt9)). These chords will be examined later in the **Altered 9 Tensions on Dom7th Chords** chapter.

With the exception of the ♭9 tension on a dom7 chord, this text will avoid using tension 9 on the 5th string. Some isolated exceptions to this rule might appear in later chapters.

The following is a convenient model which will be used to display different chord voicings and inversions:

| | | | | | | |
|---|---|---|---|---|---|---|
| **maj7(9) {3 5 7 9}:** | | 3 | 5 | 7 | 9 | ⟶ 2nd string |
| | ↕ | 7 | 9 | 3 | 5 | ⟶ 3rd string |
| | | 5 | 7 | 9 | 3 | ⟶ 4th string |
| | | 9 | 3 | 5 | 7 | ⟶ 5th string |

Note that the previous seventh chords that avoided their 3rd inversions due to the ♭9th interval they contained (Cmaj7, Cmaj7♭5, and C-maj7) are now available as 9th chords (Cmaj9, Cmaj9♭5, C-maj9), since tension 9 has removed the ♭9th interval that was produced between the 7th and root. Although these inversions are now available, they do run the risk of violating "Low Interval Limits" since the 7th is in the bass. To avoid this problem, non-drop 2 type voicings, which contain the same basic "width" as drop 2 type voicings, can be used to substitute these third inversion drop 2 ninth chords:

By removing the fifth degree from a root-inversion close position ninth chord, a four-note voicing containing tension 9 in the top voice is produced:

Cmaj7(9) no 5 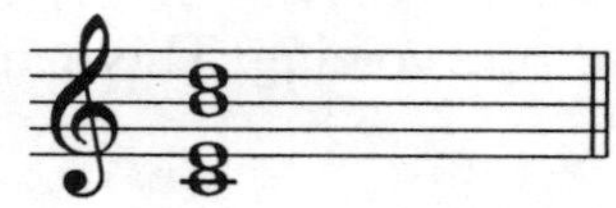

C6(9) no 5 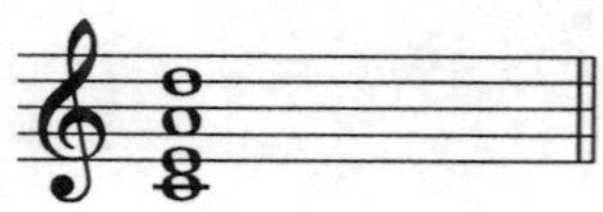

These voicings can effectively substitute the third inversion drop 2 ninth chords while retaining the desired tension 9 in the lead:

| | | |
|---|---|---|
| 9 | can substitute | 9 |
| 7(6) | | 5 |
| 3 | | 3 |
| 1 | | 7(6) |

If the 5th degree is needed in these substitute ninth chords, the *third* can be removed:

| | |
|---|---|
| Cmaj9(no3) | 9 |
| | 7(6) |
| | 5 |
| | 1 |

When LIL is not an issue, voice leading, sound, and fingering will determine which voicing is best. Examine the previous list of 9th chords using the new omitted 5th or omitted 3rd ninth chords discussed:

| | | | | | |
|---|---|---|---|---|---|
| Cmaj7(9) | = | 1 3 7 9 | C7(9) | = | 1 3 ♭7 9 |
| Cmaj7♭5(9) | = | 1 ♭5 7 9 | C7(♭9) | = | 1 3 ♭7 ♭9 |
| C-maj7(9) | = | 1 ♭3 7 9 | C7(♯9) | = | 1 3 ♭7 ♯9 |
| C-7(9) | = | 1 ♭3 ♭7 9 | C7♭5(9) | = | 1 ♭5 ♭7 9 |
| C-7♭5(9) | = | 1 ♭5 ♭7 9 | C7♭5(♭9) | = | 1 ♭5 ♭7 ♭9 * |
| C6(9) | = | 1 3 6 9 | C7♭5(♯9) | = | 1 ♭5 ♭7 ♯9 * |
| C-6(9) | = | 1 ♭3 6 9 | C+7(9) | = | 1 ♯5 ♭7 9 |
| | | | C+7(♭9) | = | 1 ♯5 ♭7 ♭9 * |
| | | | C+7(♯9) | = | 1 ♯5 ♭7 ♯9 * |
| | | | C7sus4(9) | = | 1 4 ♭7 9 |
| | | | C7sus4(♭9) | = | 1 4 ♭7 ♭9 * |

*These voicings will be omitted from this chapter, due to the ♭9th intervals or the ambiguous sounds produced. Most will reappear later in more appropriate chapters.

**Note:** Four of the above voicings have produced previously introduced drop 2 type voicings:

Cmaj7♭5(9)........................{1 ♭5 7 9} = A♭7♭5(♯9) / D13
C-7♭5(9) and C7♭5(9).........{1 ♭5 ♭7 9} = D+7/ A♭9♭5
C9sus4................................{1 4 ♭7 9} = D-7♯5

Since the drop 2 inversions are known, they can be applied to these ninth chords:

| | | | | |
|---|---|---|---|---|
| Cmaj7♭5(9); | 9 | ♭5 | 7 | 1 |
| | 7 | 1 | 9 | ♭5 |
| | ♭5 | 7 | 1 | 9 |
| | 1 | 9 | ♭5 | 7 |
| C-7♭5(9) or C7♭5(9); | 9 | ♭5 | ♭7 | 1 |
| | ♭7 | 1 | 9 | ♭5 |
| | ♭5 | ♭7 | 1 | 9 |
| | 1 | 9 | ♭5 | ♭7 |
| C9sus4; | 9 | 4 | ♭7 | 1 |
| | ♭7 | 1 | 9 | 4 |
| | 4 | ♭7 | 1 | 9 |
| | 1 | 9 | 4 | ♭7 |

*Common notation for the root inversion of C9sus4 is B♭/C.

Two additional ninth (omit 5) chord voicings whose inversions will be examined are maj6(9) and dom7(9):

| | | | | | | | | | |
|---|---|---|---|---|---|---|---|---|---|
| **maj6(9)** | 9 | 3 | 6 | 1 | **dom7(9)** | 9 | 3 | ♭7 | 1 |
| | 6 | 1 | 9 | 3 | | ♭7 | 1 | 9 | 3 |
| | 3 | 6 | 1 | 9 | | 3 | ♭7 | 1 | 9 |
| | 1 | 9 | 3 | 6 | | 1 | 9 | 3 | ♭7 |

*The 1st inversion of the maj9 {1 3 7 9} and 3rd inversion of the dom7♭9 {1 3 ♭9 ♭7} will be examined in later chapters.

Note the C+7(9) no 3 voicing {1 ♯5 ♭7 9} is equivalent to the B♭7(9) no 5 voicing {1 3 ♭7 9}.

| | | | | |
|---|---|---|---|---|
| C+7(9); | 1 | ♯5 | ♭7 | 9 |
| | ↓ | ↓ | ↓ | ↓ |
| | C | G♯ | B♭ | D |
| | ↑ | ↑ | ↑ | ↑ |
| B♭7(9); | 9 | ♭7 | 1 | 3 |

Since the dom7(9) inversions will be used, they can be realized on the dom7♯5(9):

| | | | |
|---|---|---|---|
| 9 | ♯5 | ♭7 | 1 |
| ♭7 | 1 | 9 | ♯5 |
| ♯5 | ♭7 | 1 | 9 |
| 1 | 9 | ♯5 | ♭7 |

At this point, we should summarize the substitution possibilities presented for each chord, including Sub V chords of the non-drop 2 dominant ninth chords with omitted 3rd or 5th:

| | | |
|---|---|---|
| C-7♯5 | = | B♭9sus4 {1 4 ♭7 9} |
| C+7 | = | G♭9♭5 = B♭9♭5 / B♭-9♭5 {1 ♭5 ♭7 9} = E(alt5) {1 3 ♭5 ♯5} [Sub V of B♭9♭5] |
| C7(9) | = | G♭7(♯5/♭9) = E-7♭5 = G-6 = A7sus4(♭9) |
| C7(9) {1 3 ♭7 9} | = | D+7(9) {1 ♯5 ♭7 9} = F♯7(alt5) {3 ♭5 ♯5 ♭7} [Sub V of C9] = A♭9(alt5) {1 ♭5 ♯5 9} [Sub V of D+7(9)] |
| Cmaj7(9) | = | E-7 = G6 = A9sus4 |
| C7♭5 | = | G♭7♭5= A♭+7(9) = D+7(9) |
| Cmaj7♭5 | = | A-6(9) = A♭7(♯5/♯9) = D7(9/13) |
| Cmaj9♭5 | = | D6(9) {1 3 6 9} |
| Cmaj7 | = | A-9 |
| C-maj7 | = | A-7♭5(9) |
| Cmaj7(♯5) | = | A-maj9 |
| C6(9) | = | A7sus4 |
| C7(♭9) | = | (C♯° / E° / G° / B♭°) (C7(♭9)/F♯7(♭9)/A7(♭9)/E♭7(♭9)) |
| C7(♯9) | = | F♯13(♭9) |
| C7 | = | F♯7(♭5/♭9) |
| C7♭5(♯9) | = | G♭7(13) = Emaj9♭5 {1 ♭5 7 9} |
| C7(♯9) {1 3 ♭7 ♯9} | = | F♯13♭5 {3 ♭5 ♭7 13} [Sub V of C7] |

The Sub V chord of the C7(♭9) {1 3 ♭7 ♭9} chord is F♯7(♯11) {3 5 ♭7 ♯11}. This Sub V chord will not be available to the root inversion C7(♭9) chord because of the ♭9th interval between the 5th and ♯11th of the F♯7(♯11) chord. In the next chapter, F♯7(♯11) will reappear on the third inversion of the C7(♭9) chord. These ninth (omit 3rd or 5th) chord voicings, as well as the drop 2 type voicings, will have some very interesting additional substitution possibilities in later chapters.

Each 9th chord and applicable inversions previously examined will be presented in the following II-V-I chord cadence examples. As mentioned earlier, when a single voice is notated on the staff, it will be considered the top note of a drop 2 type voicing. If a non-drop 2 type voicing is used, all four voices will be notated. This approach will be used throughout this text.

**maj7(9)**

drop 2 type voicings:

| | | | | | | |
|---|---|---|---|---|---|---|
| Imaj7(9) | = | III-7 | = | V6 | = | VI9sus4 |
| Cmaj7(9) | = | E-7 | = | G6 | = | A9sus4 |

Avoiding tension 9 on the 5th string leaves three applicable drop 2 inversions with the addition of one ninth (omit 5) voicing:

| | | | |
|---|---|---|---|
| 5 | 7 | 9 | 9 |
| 9 | 3 | 5 | 7 |
| 7 | 9 | 3 | 3 |
| 3 | 5 | 7 | 1 |

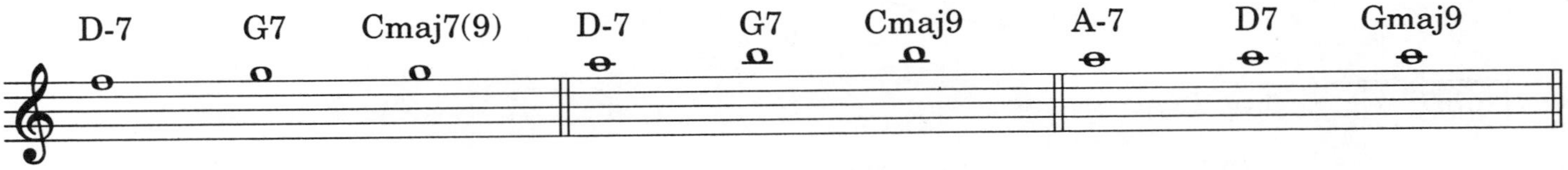


**maj7♭5(9)**

This is a unique chord in that the drop 2 type voicings produce ninth (omit 5) enharmonic substitute voicings and the ninth (omit 3) chord produces a drop 2 type enharmonic substitute chord.

| | | |
|---|---|---|
| Imaj7♭5(9) (drop2) | = | II6(9)no 5 |
| Cmaj7♭5(9) (drop 2) | = | D6(9)no 5 |
| Imaj7♭5(9)no 3 | = | ♭VI7(♭5/♯9) (drop 2) / II13 (drop 2) |
| Cmaj7♭5(9)no 3 | = | A♭7♭5(♯9) (drop 2) / D13 (drop 2) |

Avoiding tension 9 on the 5th string leaves three applicable drop 2 inversions with the addition of one ninth (omit 3) voicing.

| | | | |
|---|---|---|---|
| ♭5 | 7 | 9 | 9 |
| 9 | 3 | ♭5 | 7 |
| 7 | 9 | 3 | ♭5 |
| 3 | ♭5 | 7 | 1 |

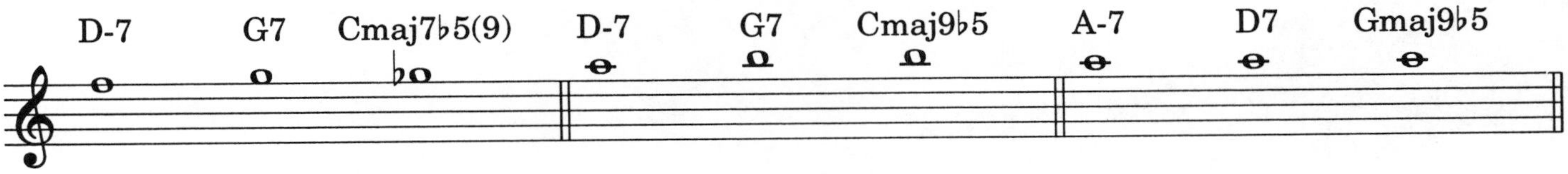

**min. maj7(9)** drop 2 type voicings:

| | | |
|---|---|---|
| I-maj7(9) | = | ♭IIImaj7♯5 |
| C-maj7(9) | = | E♭maj7♯5 |

Three applicable drop 2 inversions with the addition of one ninth (omit 5) chord. Due to the physically awkward fingering produced by the 2nd inversion, its register might be limited.

| | | | |
|---|---|---|---|
| 5 | 7 | 9 | 9 |
| 9 | ♭3 | 5 | 7 |
| 7 | 9 | ♭3 | ♭3 |
| ♭3 | 5 | 7 | 1 |

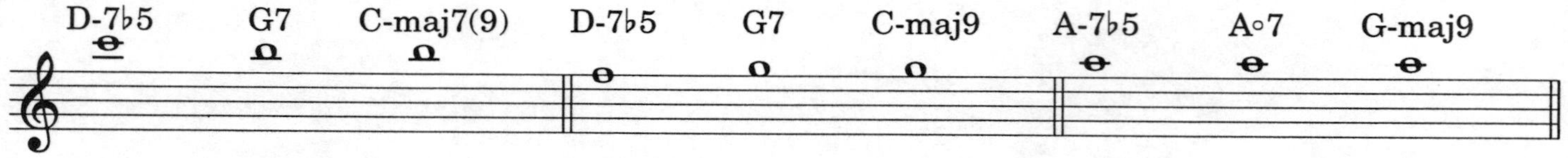


**min7(9)** drop 2 type voicings:

| | | |
|---|---|---|
| I-7(9) | = | ♭IIImaj7 |
| C-7(9) | = | E♭maj7 |

Three applicable drop 2 inversions with the addition of one ninth (omit 5) chord.

| | | | |
|---|---|---|---|
| 5 | ♭7 | 9 | 9 |
| 9 | ♭3 | 5 | ♭7 |
| ♭7 | 9 | ♭3 | ♭3 |
| ♭3 | 5 | ♭7 | 1 |

**min7♭5(9)**

| | | |
|---|---|---|
| I-7♭5(9) (drop 2) | = | ♭III-maj7 (drop 2) |
| C-7♭5(9) (drop 2) | = | E♭-maj7 (drop 2) |
| I-7♭5(9)no 3 | = | II+7 (drop 2) / ♭VI9♭5 (drop 2) |
| C-7♭5(9)no 3 | = | D+7 (drop 2) / A♭9♭5 (drop 2) |

Three applicable drop 2 inversions with the addition of three good ninth (omit 5) chord inversions. Due to the physically awkward fingerings produced by the 2nd and 3rd drop 2 inversions, their registers might be limited.

| drop 2; | | | | ninth (omit 3); | | | |
|---|---|---|---|---|---|---|---|
| | ♭5 | ♭7 | 9 | | 9 | ♭7 | 1 |
| | 9 | ♭3 | ♭5 | | ♭7 | 9 | ♭5 |
| | ♭7 | 9 | ♭3 | | ♭5 | 1 | 9 |
| | ♭3 | ♭5 | ♭7 | | 1 | ♭5 | ♭7 |

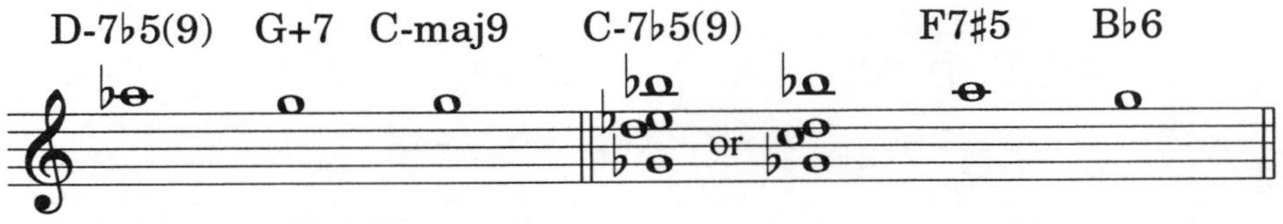


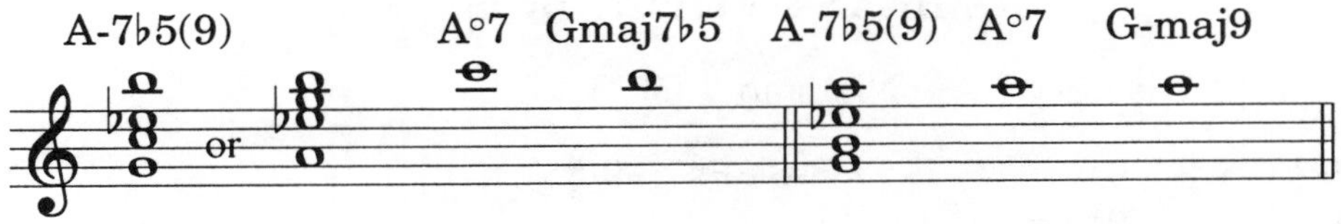


Those min7♭5(9) voicings containing no third will be examined later in this chapter for their dominant quality as well; dom7♭5(9).

**maj6(9)**

| | | |
|---|---|---|
| I6(9) (drop 2) | = | VI7sus4 (drop 2) |
| C6(9) (drop 2) | = | A7sus4 (drop 2) |
| I6(9)no 5 | = | ♭VIImaj9♭5 (drop 2) |
| C6(9)no 5 | = | B♭maj9♭5 (drop 2) |

Three applicable drop 2 inversions and three applicable ninth (no 5) chord inversions:

| drop 2; | | | | ninth (no 5); | | | |
|---|---|---|---|---|---|---|---|
| | 5 | 6 | 9 | | 9 | 6 | 1 |
| | 9 | 3 | 5 | | 6 | 9 | 3 |
| | 6 | 9 | 3 | | 3 | 1 | 9 |
| | 3 | 5 | 6 | | 1 | 3 | 6 |

**Drop 2;**

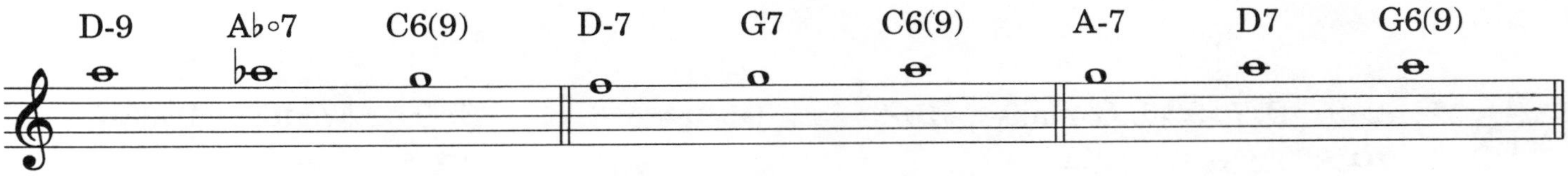


**Ninth (no 5) Chord;**

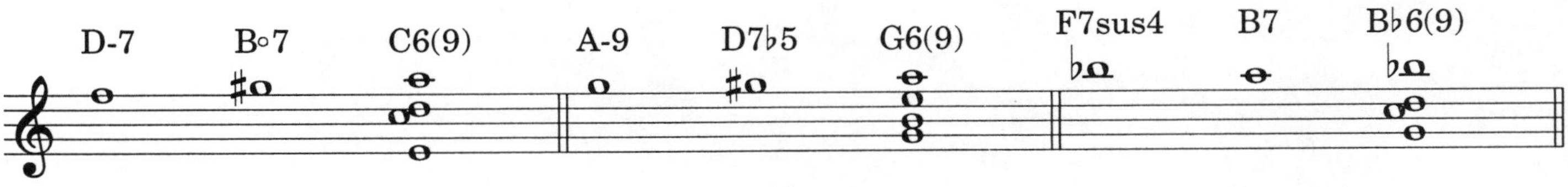

**min6(9)** drop 2 type voicings:

| | | | | |
|---|---|---|---|---|
| I-6(9) | = | ♭IIImaj7♭5 | = | VII7(♯5/♯9) / IV7(9/13) |
| C-6(9) | = | E♭maj7♭5 | = | B7(♯5/♯9) / F7(9/13) |

Three applicable drop 2 inversions with the addition of one ninth (no 5) chord voicing. Due to the physically awkward fingerings produced by the drop 2 (2nd inversion), its register might be limited.

| | | | |
|---|---|---|---|
| 5 | 6 | 9 | 9 |
| 9 | ♭3 | 5 | 6 |
| 6 | 9 | ♭3 | ♭3 |
| ♭3 | 5 | 6 | 1 |

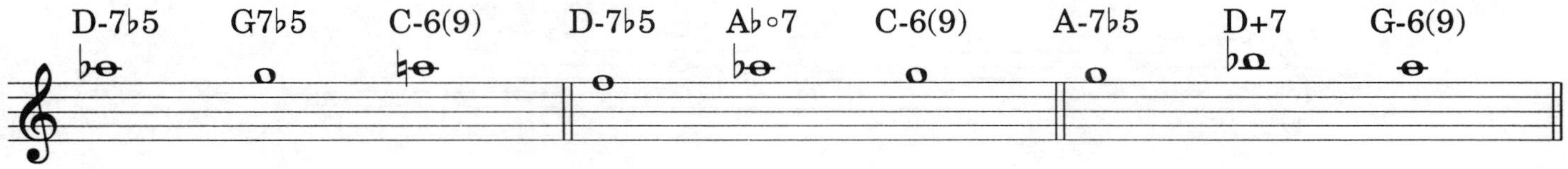


## DOMINANT 9TH CHORDS

**dom7(9)** drop2 {3 5 ♭7 9} - Ninth no 5 {1 3 ♭7 9}

C9 {3 5 ♭7 9} = E-7♭5 / G-6 / F♯7(♭9/♯5)
C9 {1 3 ♭7 9} = F♯7(alt5)

Avoiding tension 9 on the 5th string leaves three applicable drop 2 inversions and three applicable ninth (no 5) chord inversions:

| drop 2; | | | | ninth (no 5); | | |
|---|---|---|---|---|---|---|
| 5 | ♭7 | 9 | | 9 | ♭7 | 1 |
| 9 | 3 | 5 | | ♭7 | 9 | 3 |
| ♭7 | 9 | 3 | | 3 | 1 | 9 |
| 3 | 5 | ♭7 | | 1 | 3 | ♭7 |

**Drop 2;**

SUB V

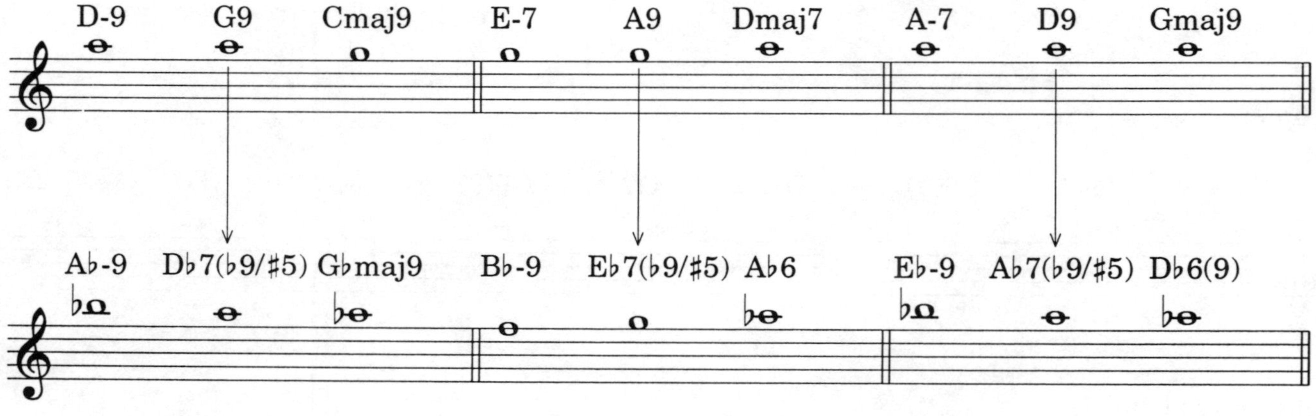

**Ninth (no 5);**

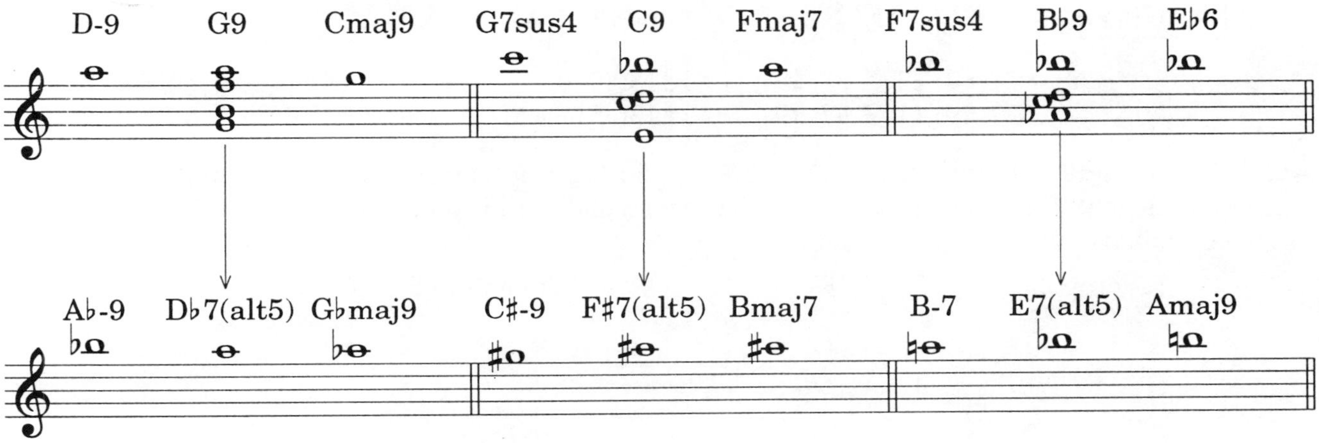


SUB V

| **dom7(♭9)** | drop2 {3 5 ♭7 ♭9} | ninth (no 5) chord {1 3 ♭7 ♭9} |
|---|---|---|
| | C7(♭9) {3 5 ♭7 ♭9} = | D♭, E, G, and/or B♭dim7 (E♭7(♭9), F♯7(♭9), and/or A7(♭9)) |

Four applicable drop 2 inversions plus one additional ninth (no 5) chord inversion. The drop 2 Sub V chords need not be presented, since transposing these exercises by a tritone (and minor thirds) will produce the same examples. The Sub V will be avoided on the ninth (no 5) chord voicing due to the ♭9th interval produced by 5 over ♯11. The ♭9th interval produced by ♭9 over the root is available on dominant chords.

**Drop 2;**

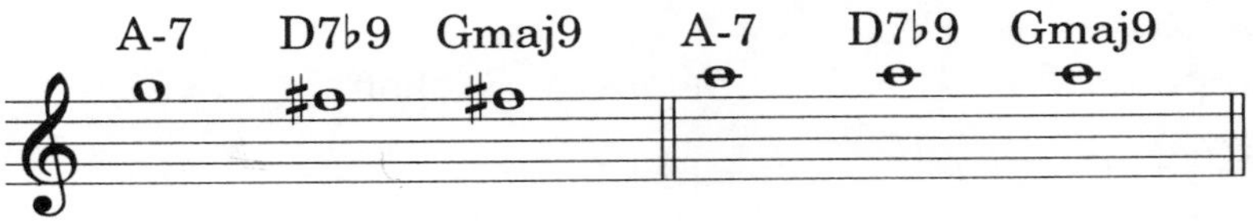


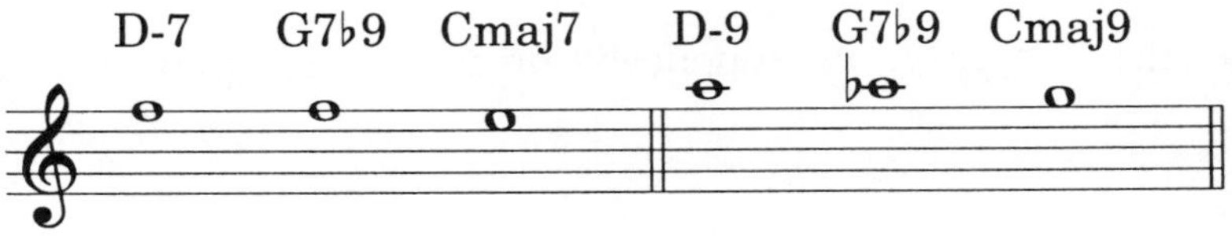


**Ninth (no 5);**

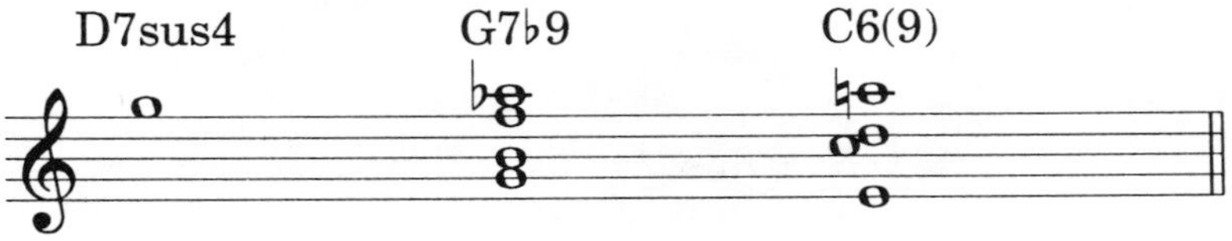

**dom7(♯9)** drop2 {3 5 ♭7 ♯9} ninth (no 5) chord {1 3 ♭7 ♯9}

C7(♯9) {3 5 ♭7 ♯9} = F♯13(♭9)
C7(♯9) {1 3 ♭7 ♯9} = F♯13(♭5)

Avoiding tension ♯9 on the 5th string leaves three applicable drop 2 inversions plus one ninth (no 5) chord inversion. Due to the difficult fingerings produced by the second and third inversions of the drop 2 voicings, their registers might be limited.

| | | | | | |
|---|---|---|---|---|---|
| drop 2; | 5 | ♭7 | ♯9 | ninth (no 5); | ♯9 |
| | ♯9 | 3 | 5 | | ♭7 |
| | ♭7 | ♯9 | 3 | | 3 |
| | 3 | 5 | ♭7 | | 1 |

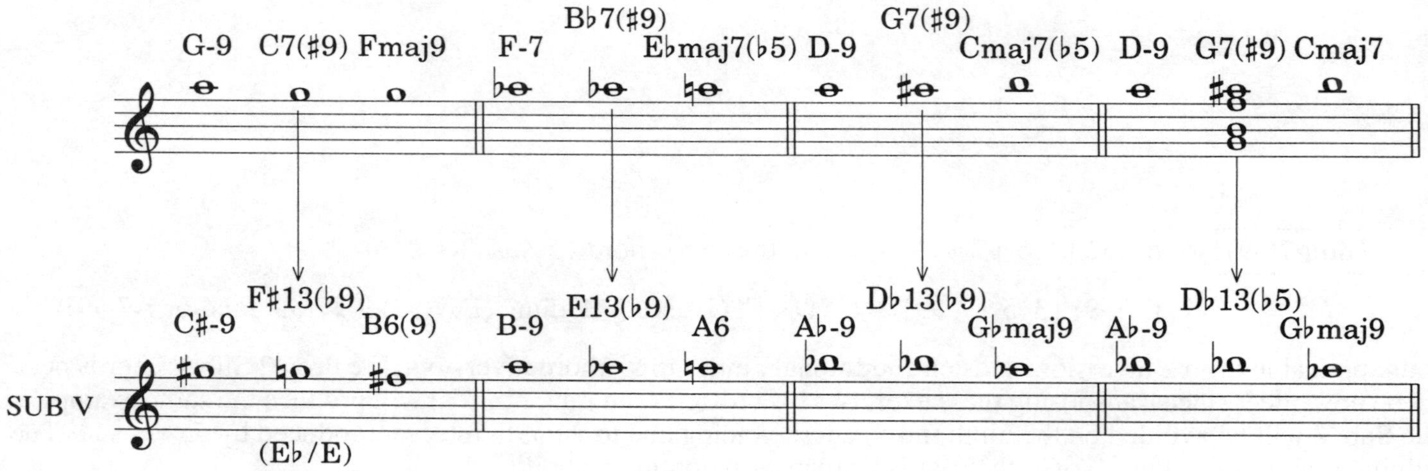


**dom7♭5(9)** drop2 {3 ♭5 ♭7 9} ninth (no 3) chord {1 ♭5 ♭7 9}

C9(♭5) {3 ♭5 ♭7 9} = F♯+7
C9(♭5) {1 ♭5 ♭7 9} = D+7 / A♭9(♭5)

Avoiding tension 9 on the 5th string leaves three applicable drop 2 inversions and three applicable ninth (no 3) chord inversions:

| | | | | | | | |
|---|---|---|---|---|---|---|---|
| drop 2; | ♭5 | ♭7 | 9 | ninth (no 3); | 9 | ♭7 | 1 |
| | 9 | 3 | ♭5 | | ♭7 | 9 | ♭5 |
| | ♭7 | 9 | 3 | | ♭5 | 1 | 9 |
| | 3 | ♭5 | ♭7 | | 1 | ♭5 | ♭7 |

**Drop 2;**

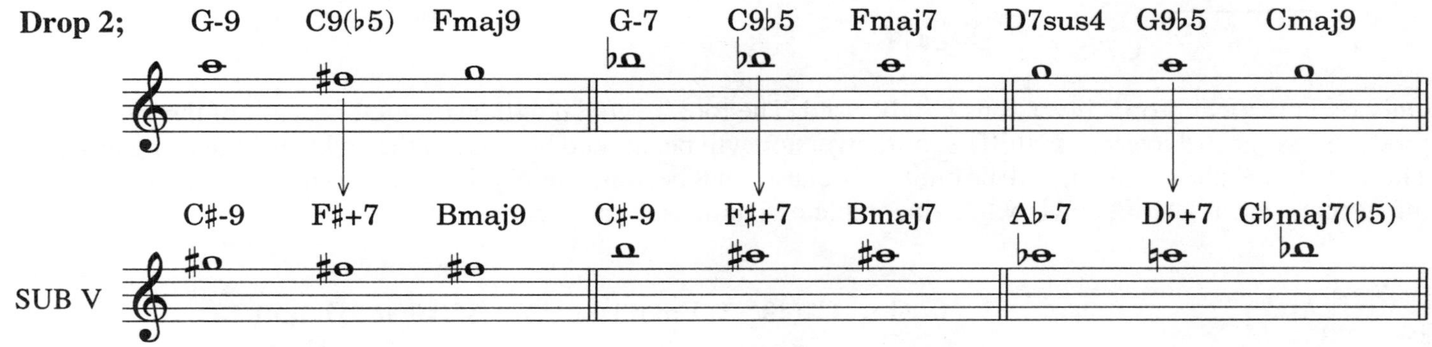


**Ninth (no 3);**

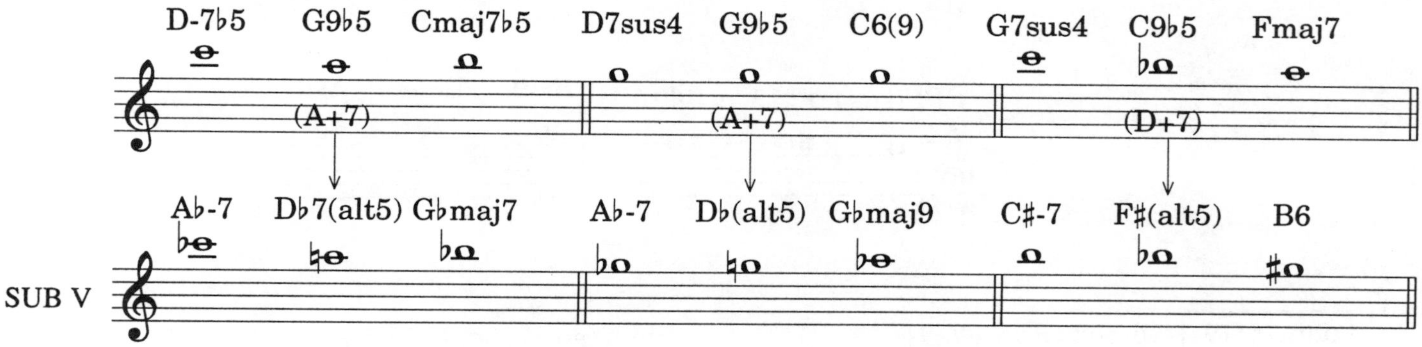


**dom7♭5(♭9)** drop2 {3 ♭5 ♭7 ♭9}

C7♭5(♭9) {3 ♭5 ♭7 ♭9} = F♯7

The ninth (no 3) voicing will be omitted, due to the ♭9th interval produced. This voicing will reappear in a later chapter as a hybrid chord.

Four applicable inversions:

| | | | |
|---|---|---|---|
| 3 | ♭5 | ♭7 | ♭9 |
| ♭7 | ♭9 | 3 | ♭5 |
| ♭5 | ♭7 | ♭9 | 3 |
| ♭9 | 3 | ♭5 | ♭7 |

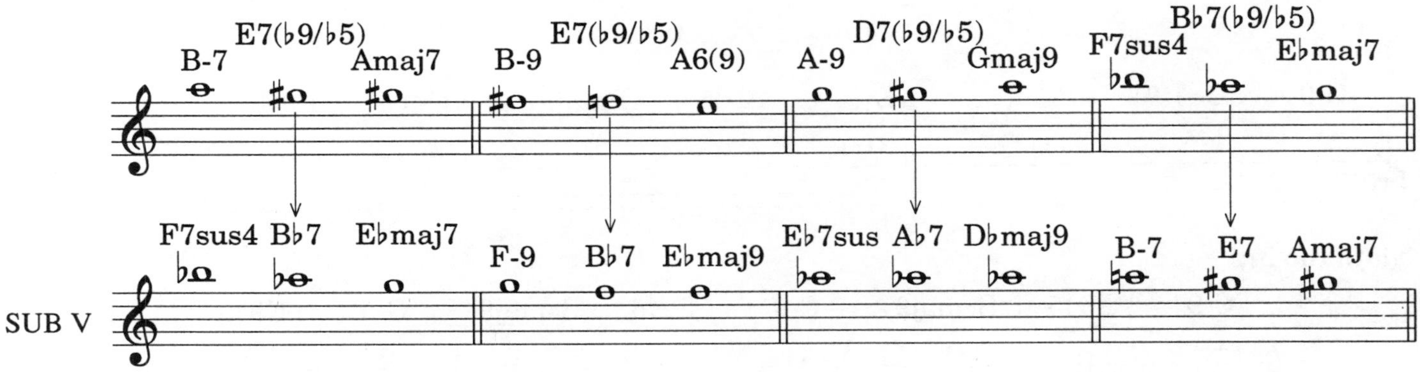

**dom7♭5(♯9)** drop 2 {3 ♭5 ♭7 ♯9}

C7♭5(♯9) = F♯13

Only two practical drop 2 inversions will be used. The root inversion will be omitted because of the ♭9th interval produced by the 3rd over the ♯9th. The third inversion will be omitted because of the awkward fingering produced. The ninth (no 3) chord voicing will be omitted because it has become a min7♭5 chord. This ninth (no 3) chord voicing might reappear in later chapters where incomplete voicings are more appropriate.

| | |
|---|---|
| ♭5 | ♭7 |
| ♯9 | 3 |
| ♭7 | ♯9 |
| 3 | ♭5 |

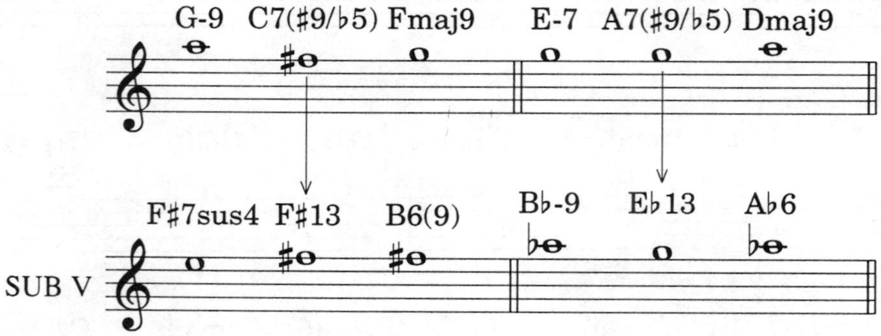


**dom7♯5(9)** drop2 {3 ♯5 ♭7 9} ninth (no 3) chord {1 ♯5 ♭7 9}

C9♯5 {3 ♯5 ♭7 9} = E7♭5 / B♭7♭5 / F♯9♯5
C9♯5(no 3) {1 ♯5 ♭7 9} = F♯9(alt5)/ B♭9(no 5) {1 3 ♭7 9} / E7(alt5)

Avoiding tension 9 on the 5th string leaves three applicable drop 2 inversions and three applicable ninth (no 3) chord inversions. The Sub V chord will not be included in the drop 2 examples because, like its dom7♭5 substitute, it "mirrors" its original dominant chord: C9♯5 = F♯9♯5.

| drop 2; | | | | ninth (no 3); | | | |
|---|---|---|---|---|---|---|---|
| | ♯5 | ♭7 | 9 | | 9 | ♭7 | 1 |
| | 9 | 3 | ♯5 | | ♭7 | 9 | ♯5 |
| | ♭7 | 9 | 3 | | ♯5 | 1 | 9 |
| | 3 | ♯5 | ♭7 | | 1 | ♯5 | ♭7 |

**Drop 2;**

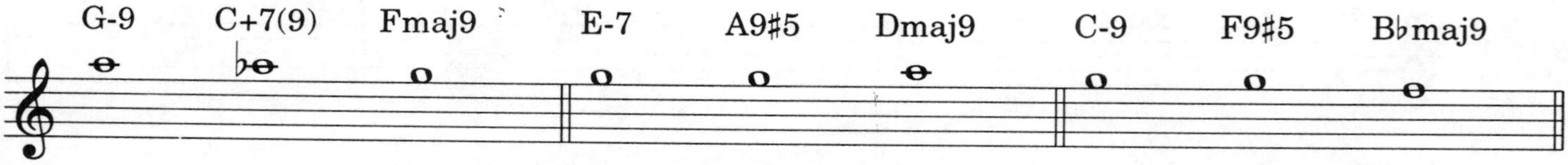


**Ninth (no 3);**

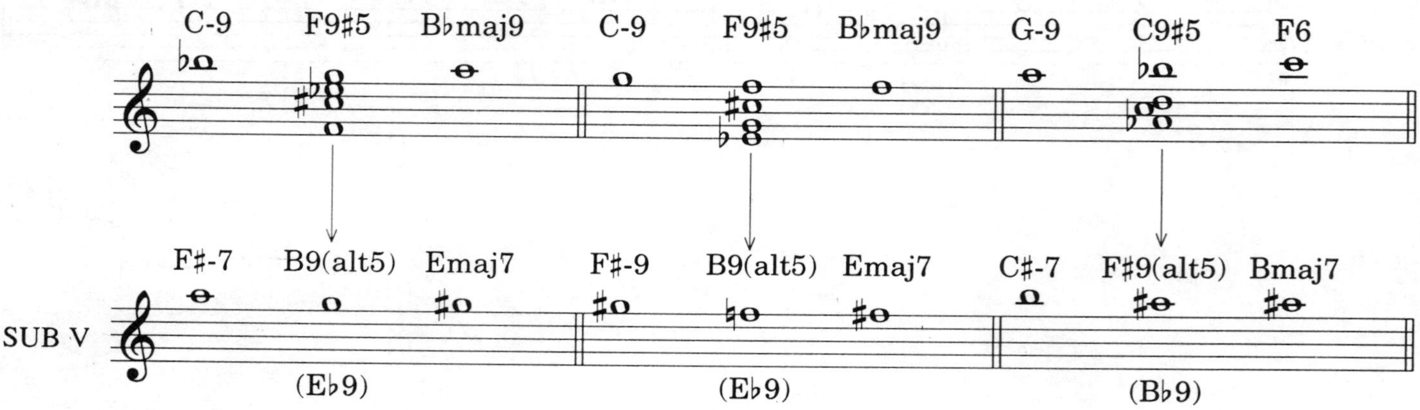

**dom7♯5(♭9)** drop2 {3 ♯5 ♭7 ♭9}

C7(♭9/♯5) = D♭-6 / B♭-7♭5 / F♯9

The ninth (no 3) chord voicing will be omitted, due to the awkward fingering and the ♭9th interval produced. The drop 2 Sub V chord produced is a dom9 chord, and although all four inversions are available to the dom7♯5(♭9) chord, the inversion producing tension 9 on the 5th string on the dom9 Sub V chord will be omitted. There are four applicable inversions:

| | | | |
|---|---|---|---|
| 3 | ♯5 | ♭7 | ♭9 |
| ♭7 | ♭9 | 3 | ♯5 |
| ♯5 | ♭7 | ♭9 | 3 |
| ♭9 | 3 | ♯5 | ♭7 |

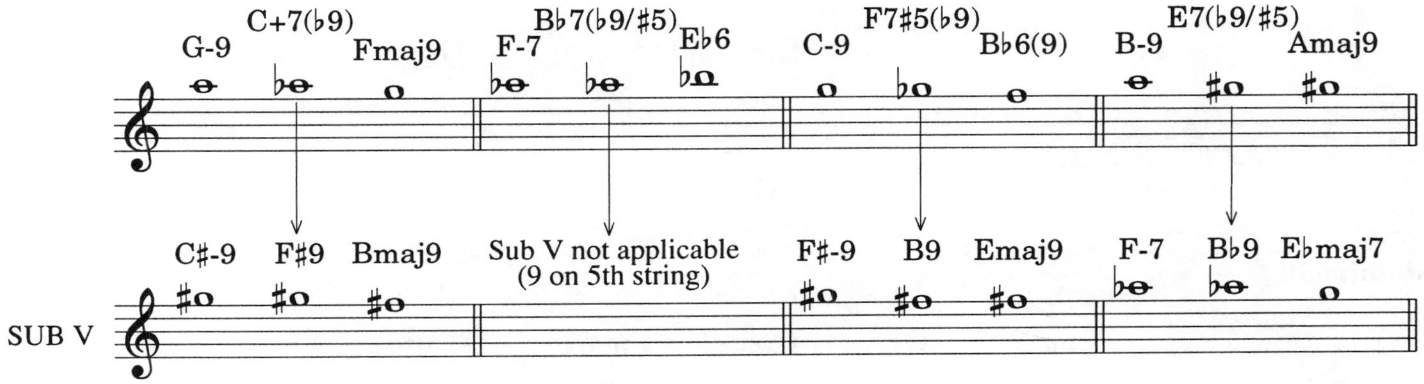


**dom7♯5(♯9)** drop2 {3 ♯5 ♭7 ♯9}

C7(♯9/♯5) = Emaj7♭5

The ninth (no 3) voicing will be omitted, due to its incomplete nature. It forms a complete min7♯5 chord, which will be examined later for its dominant qualities.

Avoiding tension ♯9 on the 5th string leaves three applicable drop 2 voicings:

| | | |
|---|---|---|
| ♯5 | ♭7 | ♯9 |
| ♯9 | 3 | ♯5 |
| ♭7 | ♯9 | 3 |
| 3 | ♯5 | ♭7 |

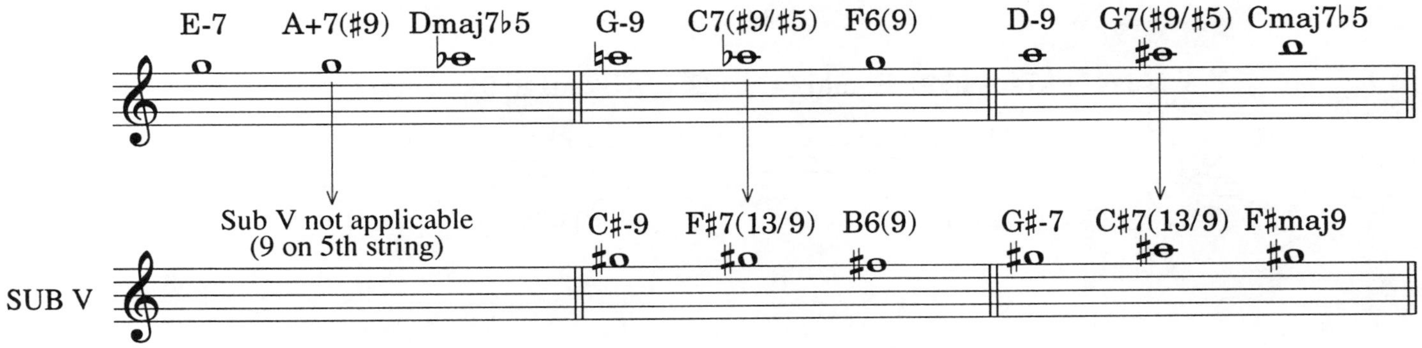

**dom7sus4(9)** drop2 {4 5 ♭7 9} ninth (no 5) {1 4 ♭7 9}

C9sus4 {4 5 ♭7 9} = G-7 / B♭6
C9sus4 {1 4 ♭7 9} = D-7♯5

Avoiding tension 9 on the 5th string leaves three applicable drop 2 inversions and three applicable ninth (no 5) chord inversions:

drop 2;

| | | |
|---|---|---|
| 5 | ♭7 | 9 |
| 9 | 4 | 5 |
| ♭7 | 9 | 4 |
| 4 | 5 | ♭7 |

ninth (no 5);

| | | |
|---|---|---|
| 9 | ♭7 | 1 |
| ♭7 | 9 | 4 |
| 4 | 1 | 9 |
| 1 | 4 | ♭7 |

**Drop 2;**

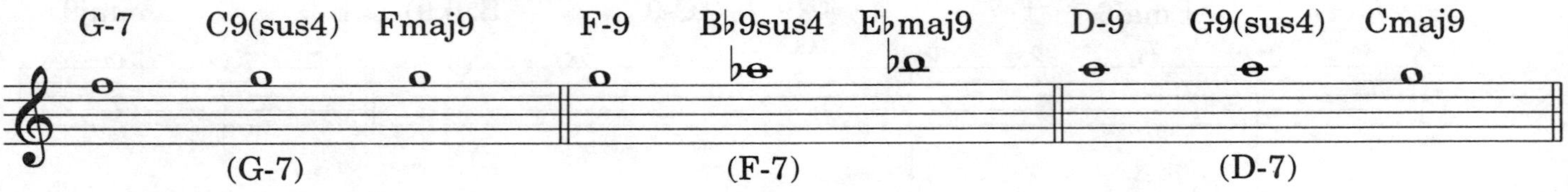


**Ninth(no5);**

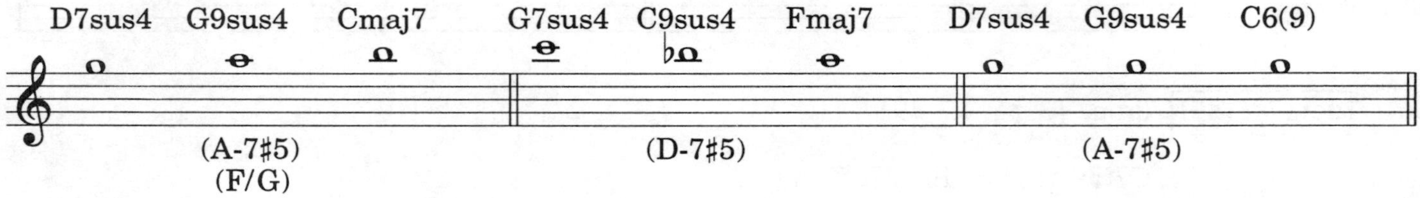


**dom7sus4(♭9)** drop2 {4 5 ♭7 ♭9}

C7sus4(♭9) = G-7♭5 / B♭-6

The ninth (no 5) chord voicing will be omitted due to the ♭9th interval. It will reappear later as a hybrid chord. There are four applicable drop 2 inversions:

| | | | |
|---|---|---|---|
| 4 | 5 | ♭7 | ♭9 |
| ♭7 | ♭9 | 4 | 5 |
| 5 | ♭7 | ♭9 | 4 |
| ♭9 | 4 | 5 | ♭7 |

## TENSION ADDITION BY STRING

In the following chord progression, voice tension 9 on the 2nd string only. Use drop 2 type voicings first, then repeat using the ninth (no 5) chord voicings only. This is a good example of the ninth (no 5) voicings being more appropriate since the drop 2 voicings, having the 7th in the bass, travel below the recommended Low Interval Limits.

G7(9) F♯7(♯9) Fmaj7(9) E7(♭9) D-7(9) D♭7(9) Cmaj7(9)

Now voice tension 9 on the 3rd string only in the *above* chord progression.

Finally, voice tension 9 on the 4th string only in the *below* chord progression.

C7(9) B7(♭9) B♭maj7(9) A7(♭9) G-7(9) G♭7(9) Fmaj7(9)

Tension 9 on the 5th string will be avoided.

In the following chord progression, tension 9 alternates between the 2nd, 3rd, and 4th strings. After preparing this progression, the student should compose his or her own line on the same progression using a 9th tension on each chord.

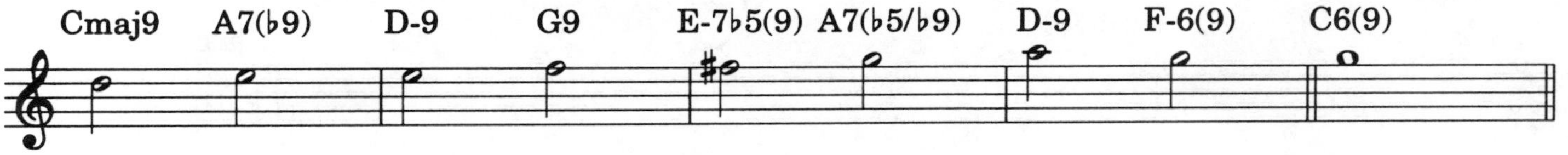


The following examples will use various ninth chords over a typical "Jazz" or "II–V" blues form. Remember to try both drop 2 and ninth with omitted 3rd or 5th voicings when tension 9 is in the lead. Inversions of the ninth (no 3) or ninth (no 5) chord voicings beyond the root inversion with 9 in the lead will be completely notated.

This next example makes use of several different ninth chord inversions with the omitted third or the omitted fifth. Note the chromatic voice-leading in bars two, three, and four into bar five. Also note the voice-led scale pattern in the last three bars before the end. The same "II–V" blues form used above has been transposed to the key of "B♭" for this example.

The following dominant "turnaround" example uses all four of the inversions of the dom9(no 5) chord.

Tension 9 on the 5th string for the above F9 chord has been included for demonstrative purposes. It is above the L.I.L. for tension 9.

# Chapter 8.
## Tension 11

There are three basic substitution approaches to adding tension 11 to basic four-part 7th & 6th chords:

| | |
|---|---|
| 11 for 5 | {1 3 7 11} |
| 11 for 3 | {1 5 7 11} |
| 11 for R | {3 5 7 11} |

11 for 3 or 5 is the traditional drop 2 substitutional approach, while 11 for the root can often produce a new drop 2 or ninth chord with omitted 3rd or 5th. 11 for the root or 5th, subsequently retaining the guide tones, is in most cases preferable. If the 5th is needed, the root would be the preferred note to omit with the 3rd being the last choice.

The addition of tension 11 to some of the basic four-part chords can produce both physical and harmonic difficulties within certain inversions. This in itself might dictate which note the 11th should substitute. As these problems arise they will be addressed and appropriate recommendations will follow. Some of these difficult inversions will become quite useful as additional tensions are added.

By use of enharmonics, the previous four-part 7th & 6th chords and 9th chords produce some of the most useful 11th chord structures:

| | | | |
|---|---|---|---|
| **Cmaj7(♯11)** | [11 for 5] | = | Cmaj7♭5 |
| **C6(♯11)** | [11 for 5] | = | C6♭5 / A-6 / F♯-7♭5 |
| **C-7(11)** | [11 for 5] | = | F7sus4 |
| | [11 for 3] | = | C7sus4 |
| | [11 for R] | = | G-7♯5 |
| **C-7♭5(11)** | [11 for 3] | = | G♭maj7♭5 |
| **C7(♯11)** | [11 for 5] | = | C7♭5 |
| **C+7(♯11) / C7(alt5)/ C7(♭5/♭13)** | | | |
| | [11 for R] | = | G♭9(no 5) |
| | [11 for 3] | = | A♭9(no 5) |

Note the unique substitutions arising from the [11 for 3] C+7(♯11) chord. Since this voicing is the same as A♭9 {1 3 ♭7 9}, the past A♭9 substitutions can be added to C+7(♯11) and its Sub V chord G♭9♭5 {1 3 ♭5 9}. When this is done, a dominant type chord appears on each note of a whole tone scale:

| | **C** | **G♭** | **G♯** | **B♭** | |
|---|---|---|---|---|---|
| **C+7(♯11)** | 1 | ♭5 | ♯5 | ♭7 | |
| **D7(alt5)** | ♭7 | 3 | ♭5 | ♯5 | |
| **E9(alt5)** | ♯5 | 9 | 3 | ♭5 | |
| **F♯9(♭5)** | ♭5 | 1 | 9 | 3 | (F♯maj9♭5) |
| **A♭9** | 3 | ♭7 | 1 | 9 | |
| **B♭9(♯5)** | 9 | ♯5 | ♭7 | 1 | |

| | | | |
|---|---|---|---|
| ***C-6(11)** | [11 for 5] | = | F7 |
| | [11 for 3] | = | A-7♯5 |
| | [11 for R] | = | F9(no 5) |
| ***C-maj7(11)** | [11 for R] | = | G+7 |

* The inversions containing the 11th in the bass are weakest.

The tritone produced by the notes B and F (on the C-maj7(11) chord) forms an ambiguous or weak sound, since it is the guide tones of G7, C minor's V7 chord. The two inversions placing the tritone in the bottom of the voicing are weakest.

Seven new voicings will be introduced in this chapter:

| | | |
|---|---|---|
| **Cmaj7(♯11)** | [11 for 3] | {1 5 7 ♯11} |
| | [11 for R] | {3 5 7 ♯11} |
| **C6(♯11)** | [11 for 3] | {1 5 6 ♯11} |
| | [11 for R] | {3 5 6 ♯11} |
| **C-7♭5(11)** | [11 for R] | {♭3 ♭5 ♭7 11} |
| **C7(♯11)** | [11 for 3] | {1 5 ♭7 ♯11} |
| | [11 for R] | {3 5 ♭7 ♯11} |
| **C-maj7(11)** | [11 for 3] | {1 5 7 11} |
| | [11 for 5] | {1 ♭3 7 11} |

Note the above voicings that function for two different chords:

| | | | | | | |
|---|---|---|---|---|---|---|
| **Cmaj7(♯11)** | [11 for R] ⟶ | 3 | 5 | 7 | ♯11 | |
| | | **E** | **G** | **B** | **F♯** | |
| | | ♭3 | ♭5 | ♭7 | 11 | ⟵ C♯-7♭5(11) [11 for R] |

| | | | | | | |
|---|---|---|---|---|---|---|
| **C7(♯11)** | [11 for 3] ⟶ | 1 | 5 | ♭7 | ♯11 | |
| | | **C** | **G** | **B♭** | **F♯** | |
| | | 11 | 1 | ♭3 | 7 | ⟵ G-maj7(11) [11 for 5] |

Many of these new voicings create physical and harmonic problems within certain inversions. Consideration should be given to the desired sound and the appropriate context when using these inversions. The tritone can produce a unique, if not weak, sound when placed in the middle of the following voicings:

| | | |
|---|---|---|
| **Cmaj7(♯11)** | [11 for 3] | 7<br>♯11<br>1<br>5 |
| **C7(♯11)** | [11 for 3] | ♭7<br>♯11<br>1<br>5 |
| **C6(♯11)** | [11 for 3] | 6<br>♯11<br>1<br>5 |
| **C-maj7(11)** | [11 for 5] | ♭3<br>7<br>11<br>1 |

**maj7(♯11)**

**11 for 5** {1 3 7 ♯11} = maj7♭5

There are three applicable voicings

| | | |
|---|---|---|
| 3 | ♭5 | 7 |
| 7 | 1 | 3 |
| ♭5 | 7 | 1 |
| 1 | 3 | ♭5 |

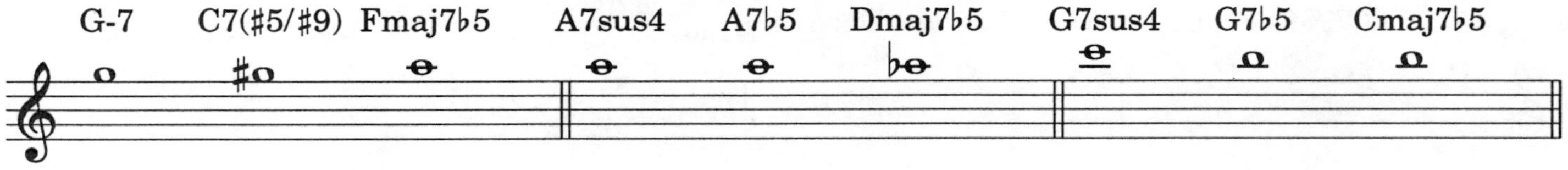


**11 for 3** {1 5 7 ♯11}

There are two applicable voicings:

| | |
|---|---|
| ♯11 | 7 |
| 7 | ♯11 |
| 5 | 1 |
| 1 | 5 |

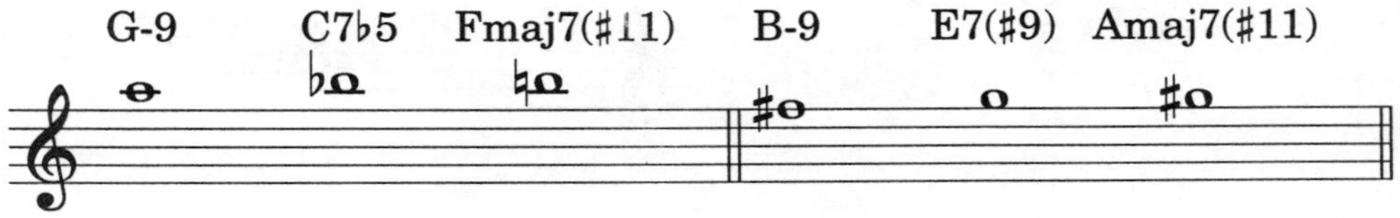


**11 for 1** {3 5 7 ♯11} Cmaj7(♯11) = C♯-7♭5(11)

There are three applicable voicings:

| | | |
|---|---|---|
| ♯11 | 5 | 7 |
| 7 | ♯11 | ♯11 |
| 5 | 7 | 3 |
| 3 | 3 | 5 |

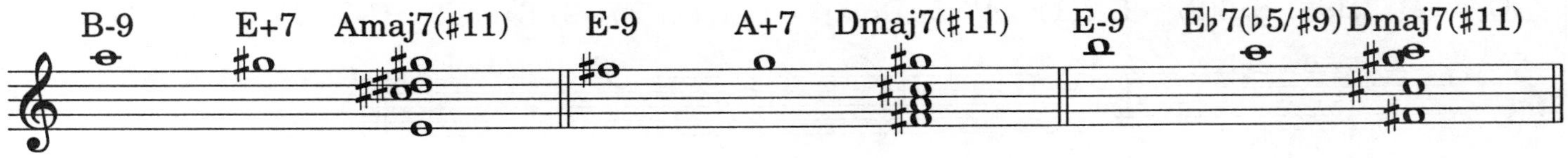

**maj6(♯11)**

**11 for 5** {1 3 6 ♯11} = maj6(♭5) C6(♭5) = A-6 / F♯-7♭5

There are four applicable voicings:

| | | | |
|---|---|---|---|
| 3 | ♭5 | 6 | 1 |
| 6 | 1 | 3 | ♭5 |
| ♭5 | 6 | 1 | 3 |
| 1 | 3 | ♭5 | 6 |

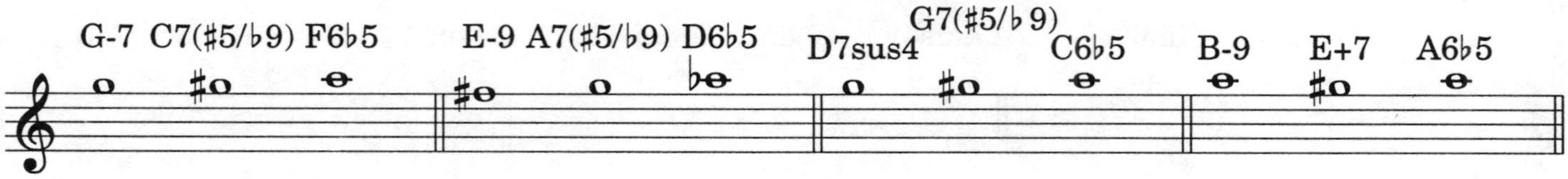


**11 for 3** {1 5 6 ♯11}

There are two applicable voicings:

| | |
|---|---|
| 6 | 1 |
| ♯11 | 5 |
| 1 | ♯11 |
| 5 | 6 |

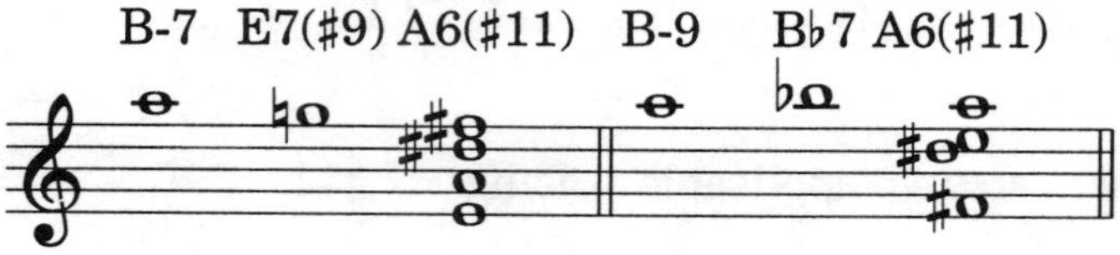


**11 for 1** {3 5 6 ♯11}

There are two applicable voicings:

| | |
|---|---|
| 6 | 5 |
| ♯11 | ♯11 |
| 3 | 6 |
| 5 | 3 |

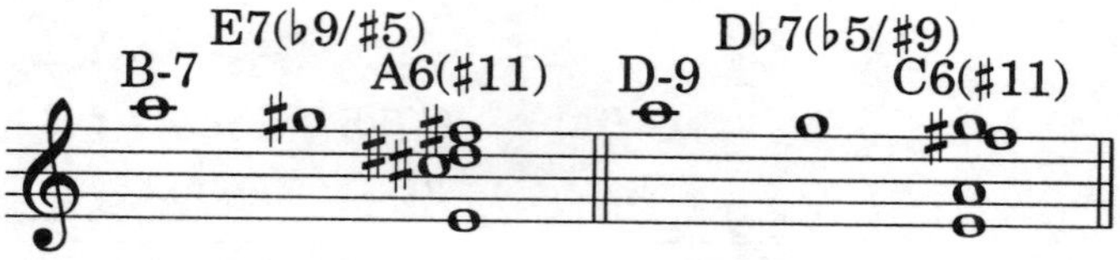


**min7(11)**

**11 for 5** {1 ♭3 ♭7 11} C-7(11) = F7sus4

All four inversions are applicable:

| | | | |
|---|---|---|---|
| ♭3 | 11 | ♭7 | 1 |
| ♭7 | 1 | ♭3 | 11 |
| 11 | ♭7 | 1 | ♭3 |
| 1 | ♭3 | 11 | ♭7 |

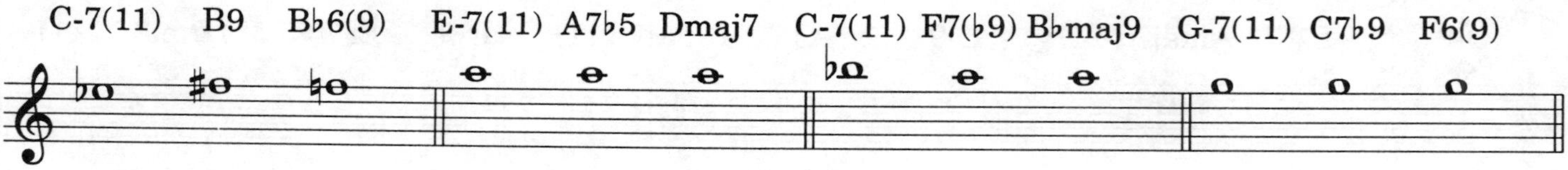


**11 for 3** {1 5 ♭7 11}C-7(11) = C7sus4

All four inversions are applicable:

| | | | |
|---|---|---|---|
| 11 | 5 | ♭7 | 1 |
| ♭7 | 1 | 11 | 5 |
| 5 | ♭7 | 1 | 11 |
| 1 | 11 | 5 | ♭7 |

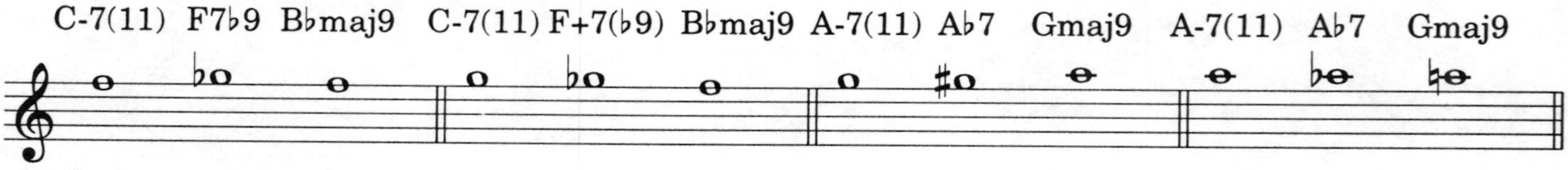

**11 for 1** {♭3 5 ♭7 11}C-7(11) = G-7(♯5)

All four inversions are applicable:

| | | | |
|---|---|---|---|
| 11 | 5 | ♭7 | ♭3 |
| ♭7 | ♭3 | 11 | 5 |
| 5 | ♭7 | ♭3 | 11 |
| ♭3 | 11 | 5 | ♭7 |

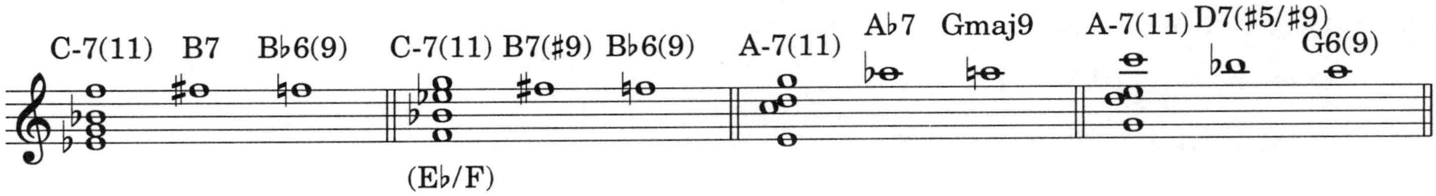


**min7♭5(11)** **11 for 5** not applicable

**11 for 3** {1 ♭5 ♭7 11}C-7♭5(11) = G♭maj7♭5

There are three applicable inversions:

| | | |
|---|---|---|
| 11 | ♭7 | 1 |
| ♭7 | 11 | ♭5 |
| ♭5 | 1 | 11 |
| 1 | ♭5 | ♭7 |

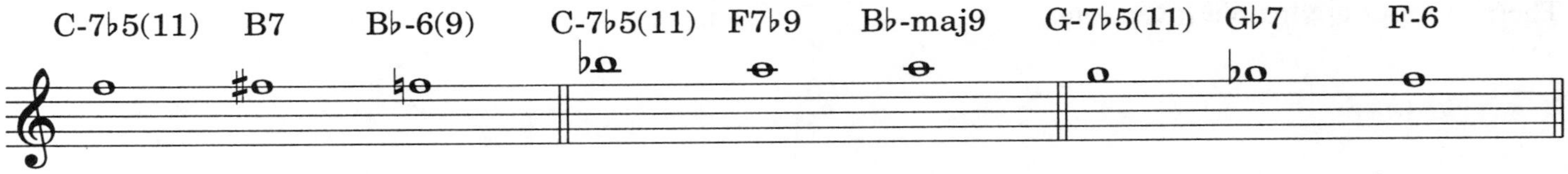


**11 for 1** {♭3 ♭5 ♭7 11}C-7♭5(11) = Bmaj7(♯11)

There are three applicable inversions:

| | | |
|---|---|---|
| 11 | ♭5 | ♭7 |
| ♭7 | 11 | 11 |
| ♭5 | ♭7 | ♭3 |
| ♭3 | ♭3 | ♭5 |

**min6(11)**

Tension 11 on a min6 chord produces a very strong IV chord sound in relation to the Imin6 chord:

| | | | |
|---|---|---|---|
| **C-6(11);** | 11 for 5 | = | F7 |
| | 11 for 3 | = | F(add9) (A-7♯5) |
| | 11 for 1 | = | F9 |

Those voicings containing the characteristic ♭3rd of the min6 chord might sound a little more complete than the 11 for 3 voicing {1 5 6 11}.

**11 for 5** {1 ♭3 6 11}

There are four applicable inversions:

| | | | |
|---|---|---|---|
| ♭3 | 11 | 6 | 1 |
| 6 | 1 | ♭3 | 11 |
| 11 | 6 | 1 | ♭3 |
| 1 | ♭3 | 11 | 6 |

**11 for 3** {1 5 6 11}

There are four applicable inversions:

| | | | |
|---|---|---|---|
| 11 | 5 | 6 | 1 |
| 6 | 1 | 11 | 5 |
| 5 | 6 | 1 | 11 |
| 1 | 11 | 5 | 6 |

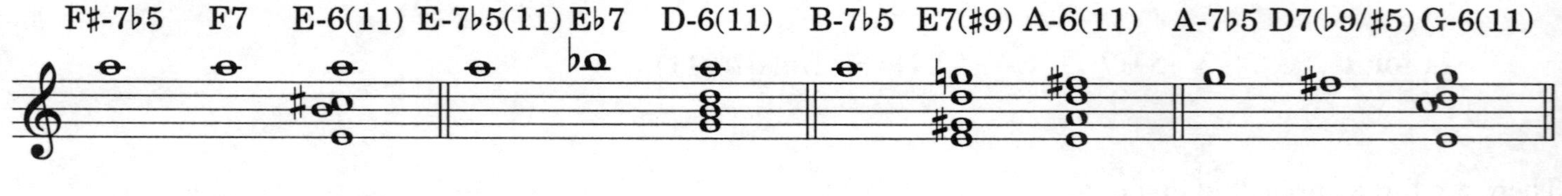


**11 for 1** {♭3 5 6 11}

There are four applicable inversions:

| | | | |
|---|---|---|---|
| 11 | 5 | 6 | ♭3 |
| 6 | ♭3 | 11 | 5 |
| 5 | 6 | ♭3 | 11 |
| ♭3 | 11 | 5 | 6 |

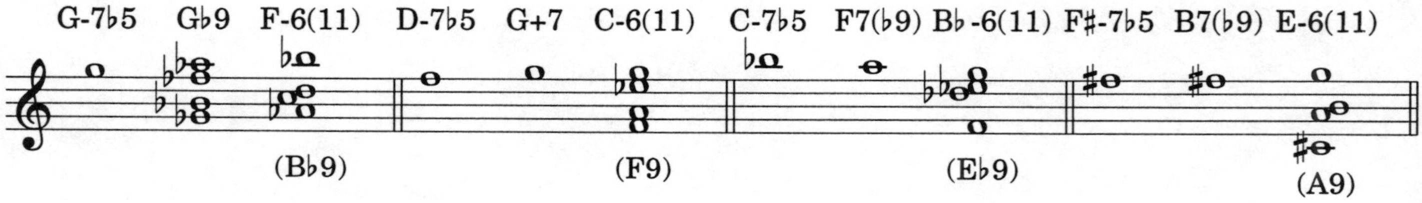

### minor maj7(11)

The tritone produced by the 11 and 7 of a minor maj7 type chord is also the guide-tones (3 and ♭7) of its V7 chord, producing a potentially ambiguous sound. The notes B and F are both 11 and 7 of C-maj7(11) and 3 and ♭7 of G7. The root and/or ♭3rd of the min maj7 chord are basic chord tones that are not common to its V7 chord and best support the 7 and 11 of the min.maj7 chord. This implies the {1 ♭3 7 11} voicing and is perhaps the strongest of the three different voicings introduced here. Of all the voicings used, those inversions placing the tritone (11 and 7) in the bottom are the weakest.

**11 for 5** {1 ♭3 7 11} C-maj7(11) = F7(♯11)

There are two applicable inversions:

| | |
|---|---|
| ♭3 | 7 |
| 7 | ♭3 |
| 11 | 1 |
| 1 | 11 |

**11 for 3** {1 5 7 11}

There are three applicable inversions:

| | | |
|---|---|---|
| 11 | 5 | 7 |
| 7 | 1 | 11 |
| 5 | 7 | 1 |
| 1 | 11 | 5 |

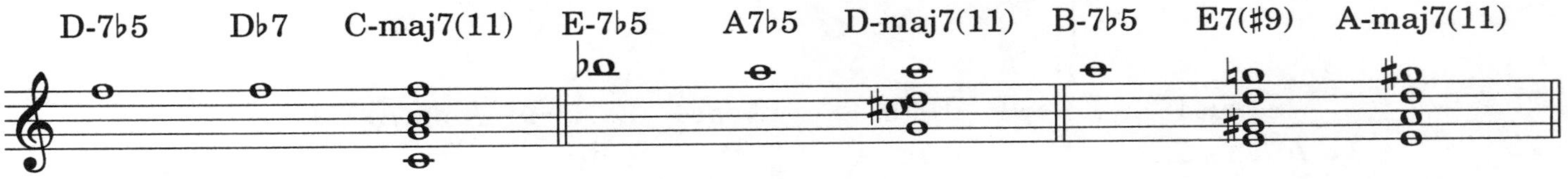


**11 for 1** {♭3 5 7 11} C-maj7(11) = G+7

There are four applicable inversions:

| | | | |
|---|---|---|---|
| 11 | 5 | 7 | ♭3 |
| 7 | ♭3 | 11 | 5 |
| 5 | 7 | ♭3 | 11 |
| ♭3 | 11 | 5 | 7 |

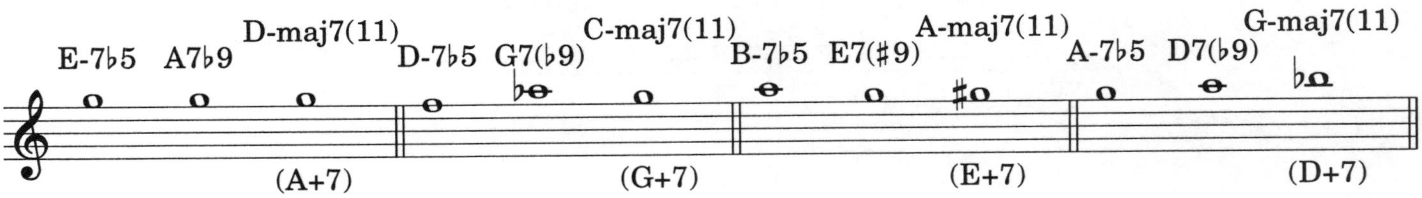

**dom7(♯11)** **11 for 5** {1 3 ♭7 ♯11} = dom7♭5

There are four applicable inversions:

| | | | |
|---|---|---|---|
| 3 | ♭5 | ♭7 | 1 |
| ♭7 | 1 | 3 | ♭5 |
| ♭5 | ♭7 | 1 | 3 |
| 1 | 3 | ♭5 | ♭7 |

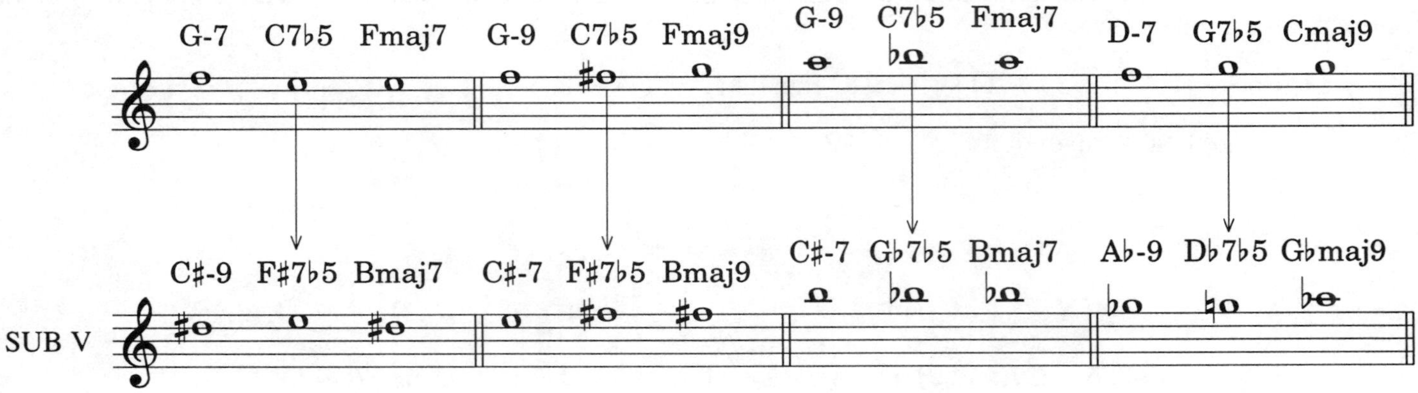


**11 for 3** {1 5 ♭7 ♯11} C7(♯11) = G-maj7(11)

There are two applicable inversions:

| | |
|---|---|
| ♯11 | ♭7 |
| ♭7 | ♯11 |
| 5 | 1 |
| 1 | 5 |

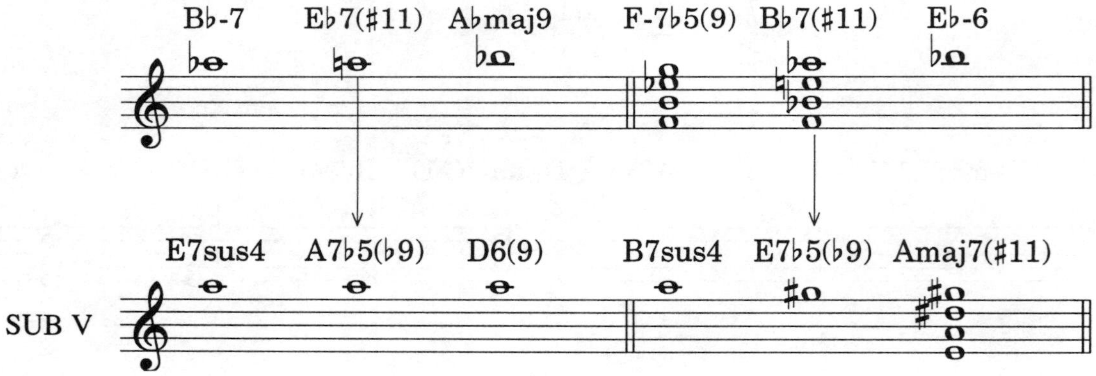


**11 for 1** {3 5 ♭7 ♯11} C7(♯11) = G♭7(♭9) {1 3 ♭7 ♭9}

There is one applicable voicing:

♯11
♭7
5
3

This is the same voicing as the 1st inversion of the ninth (no 5) voicing for a dom7(♭9):

1
3
♭9
♭7

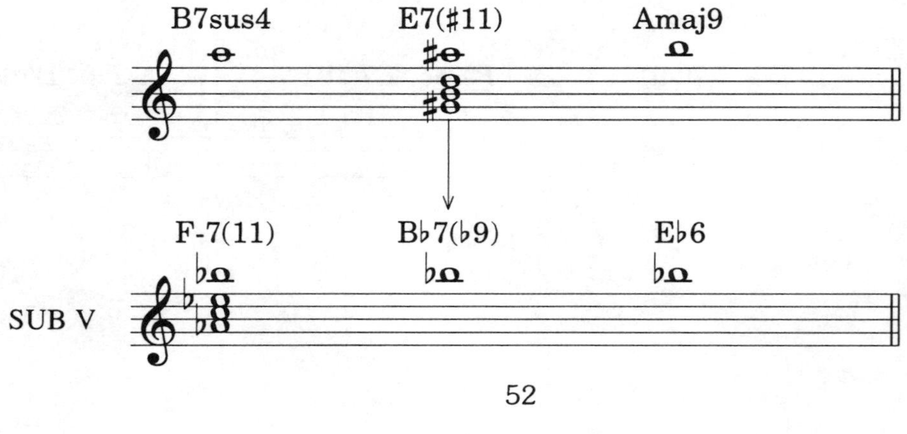

**dom7♯5(♯11) / dom7(alt5)** [**11 for 5** not applicable]

A unique chord in that 11 for 3 and 11 for 1 produce the same inversions found in the dom7(9) {1 3 ♭7 9} chord:

| | | | |
|---|---|---|---|
| C7(alt5); | 11 for 3 | = | A♭9 |
| | 11 for 5 | = | G♭9 |

**11 for 3** {1 ♯5 ♭7 ♯11}

There are four applicable inversions:

| | | | |
|---|---|---|---|
| ♯11 | ♯5 | ♭7 | 1 |
| ♭7 | 1 | ♯11 | ♯5 |
| ♯5 | ♭7 | 1 | ♯11 |
| 1 | ♯11 | ♯5 | ♭7 |

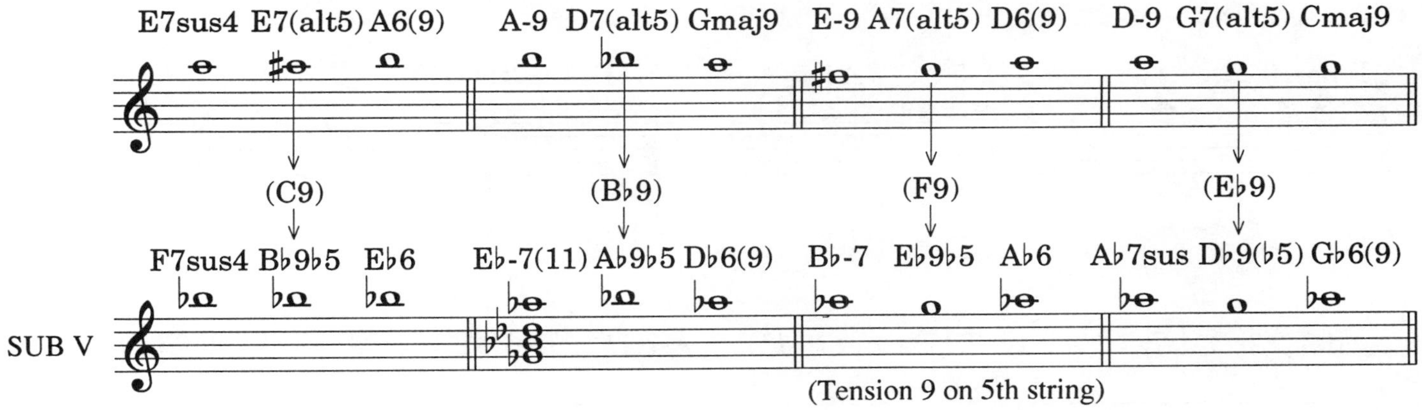


**11 for 1** {3 ♯5 ♭7 ♯11}

There are four applicable inversions:

| | | | |
|---|---|---|---|
| ♯11 | ♯5 | ♭7 | 3 |
| ♭7 | 3 | ♯11 | ♯5 |
| ♯5 | ♭7 | 3 | ♯11 |
| 3 | ♯11 | ♯5 | ♭7 |

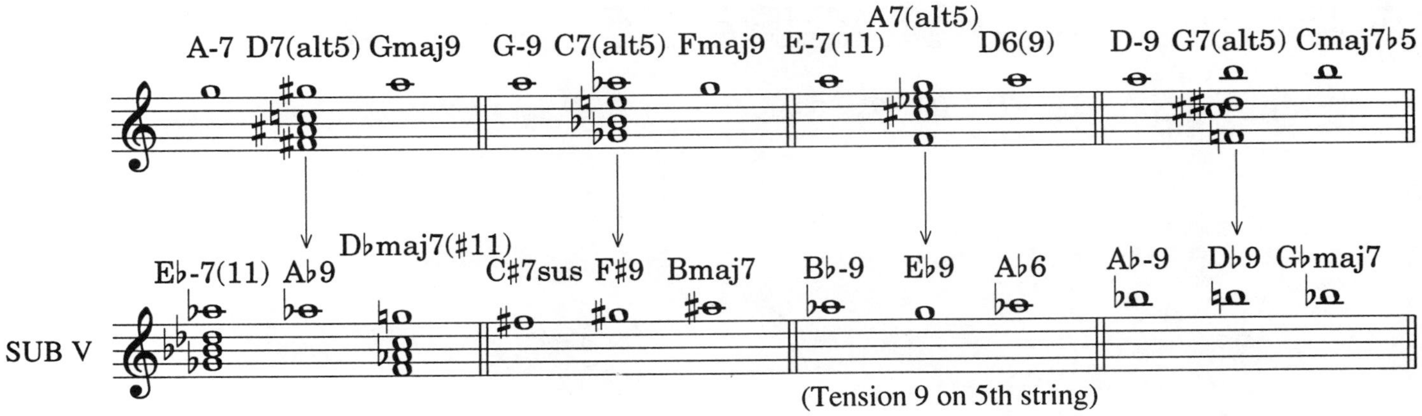


(**11 for 3 / 11 for 1** combinations):

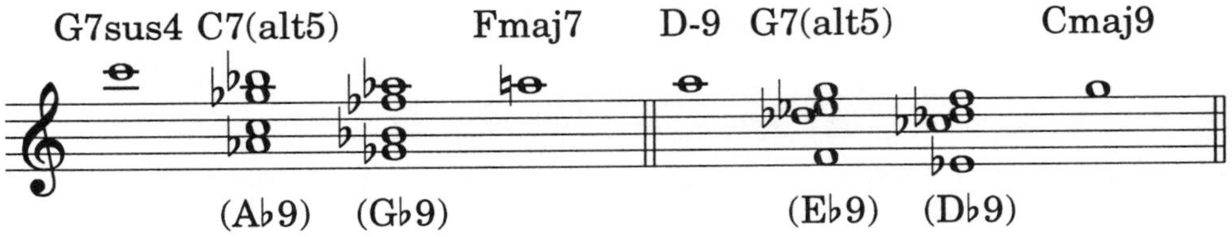

The following examples will use various eleventh chords over a typical "Jazz" or "II–V" blues form. Some unique non-drop 2 type voicings have been introduced in this section. They will be fully notated when used.

Drop 2 type voicings also give the option of substituting tension 11 for the 3rd or 5th of the chord. If the 5th is altered or voiced in the lead, tension 11 will substitute the 3rd. When either option is available, voice-leading and L.I.L. will determine which is best and will be fully notated when only one option is desired.

An additional voicing for the dom7♯5(♯11) or dom7(alt5) chord which was not presented earlier will be introduced here. This voicing has the ♯11th (or ♭5th) substituting the ♭7th; (1 3 ♭5 ♯5), and enharmonically produces a dom7♯5 chord: C7(alt5) (1 3 ♭5 ♯5) = A♭+7. This voicing will appear several times in the following example.

The following example transposes the "II–V" blues form to the key of "D." Note the contrary chromatic voice-leading of three voices from the D7(alt5) chord to the G9 chord and the two voices from the G9♭5 chord to the G-9 chord. Also note the parallel chromatic voice-leading of two voices from the C7♭5 chord to the F♯-7(11) chord, the B♭+7 chord to the E-7(11) chord, and the D6(9) chord to the B7(alt5) chord. Three voices move in parallel chromatic motion from the E-9 chord to the A7(alt5) chord.

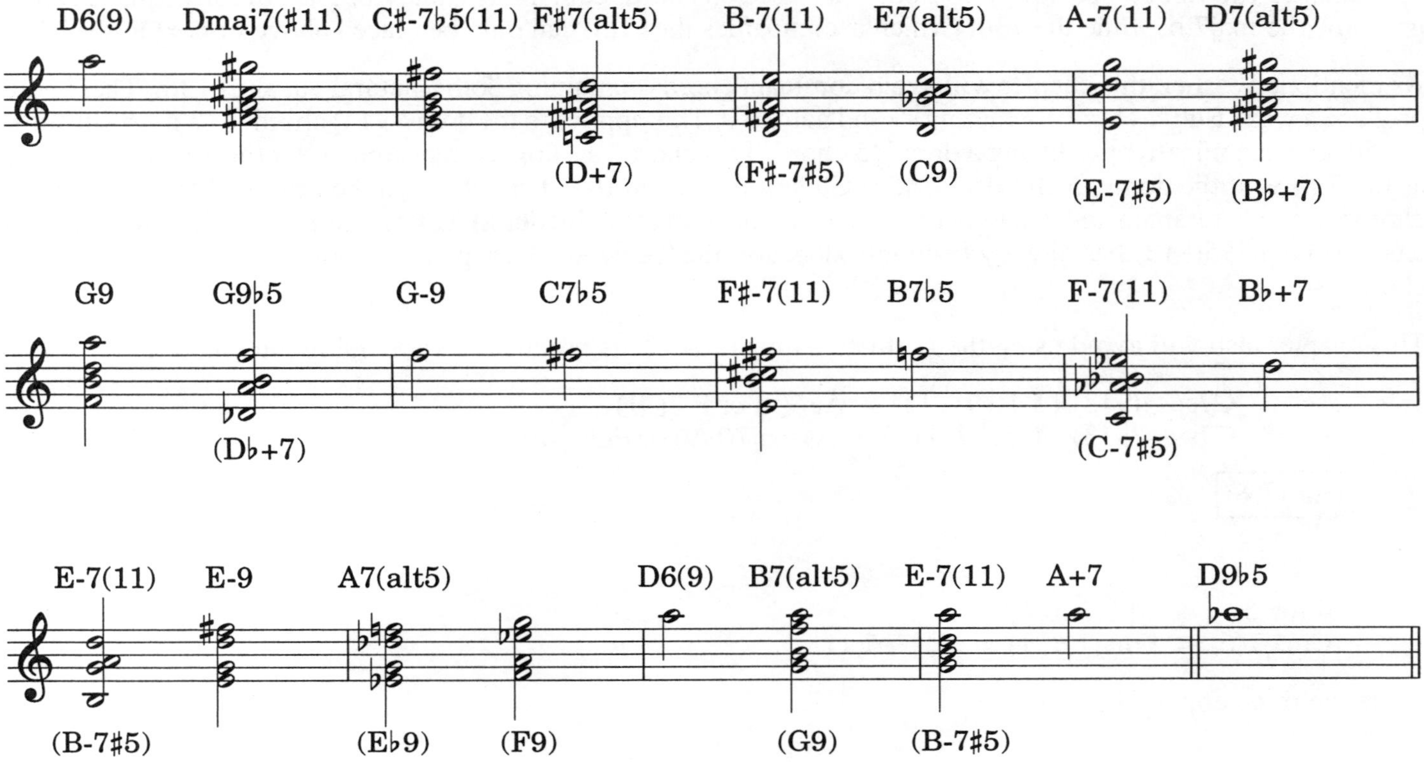

# Chapter 9.
## Tension 13

**13 for 5** or **1** {1 3 7 13} or {3 5 7 13} will be the tension substitution formula used in this chapter. The only exception will include one of the two new voicings introduced here. The dom7♭5(13) will introduce 13 for 3 {1 ♭5 ♭7 13}. These notes dictate a major 3rd even though it has been removed. The other new voicing introduced is the dom7sus4(13) {1 4 ♭7 13}. Note the 3rd inversion forms an upper-structure triad: F13(sus4) = B♭/E♭.

This chapter will refer to tension 13 as a 6th when used on chords containing a maj7th. The 6th can be placed above or below the maj7th, while the 13th (which accompanies the ♭7th) can only be placed above or next to the ♭7th.

As mentioned earlier, this chapter will avoid dominant chords containing both a natural 5th and ♭13th. These notes produce a weak Sub V chord containing ♭9 and natural 9. This applies to the dom7(♭13) chord. ♭13 must substitute the 5th enharmonically, producing a dom7♯5 chord. This chord has already appeared under the Tension 9 chapter as the Sub V of the dom9♭5 chords, C7♯5 = G♭9♭5. Its related II-V-I situation can be observed there. Dominant chords with a natural 5th and tension ♭13 will be examined in the **Additional Enharmonic Chordal Substitutions** chapter. Dom7♭5(♭13) has already been introduced in the **Tension 11** chapter as a dom7♯5(♯11) or dom7(alt5) chord.

This chapter also will avoid using the ♭13th on a dom7sus4. This produces a very ambiguous sound:

C7sus4(♭13) {1 4 ♭7 ♭13} = A♭6(9) or F-7(11)
C7sus4(♭13) {4 5 ♭7 ♭13} = A♭maj7(6/9) or Fm(11/9)

**maj7(6)**

**6 for 5** {1 3 6 7}
Cmaj7(6) = Fmaj7(♯11) = F♯-7♭5(11)

There are three applicable inversions:

| | | |
|---|---|---|
| 3 | 7 | 1 |
| 7 | 3 | 7 |
| 6 | 1 | 3 |
| 1 | 6 | 6 |

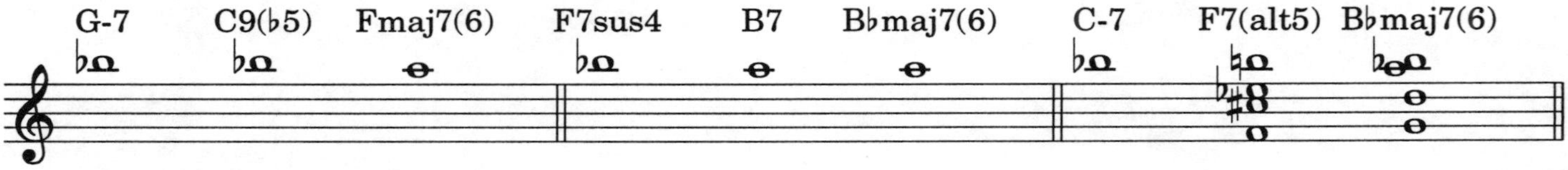

**6 for 1** {5 3 6 7}
Cmaj7(6) = Fmaj9(♭5) = G6(9){1 3 6 9}

There are four applicable inversions:

| | | | |
|---|---|---|---|
| 3 | 5 | 6 | 7 |
| 6 | 7 | 3 | 5 |
| 5 | 6 | 7 | 3 |
| 7 | 3 | 5 | 6 |

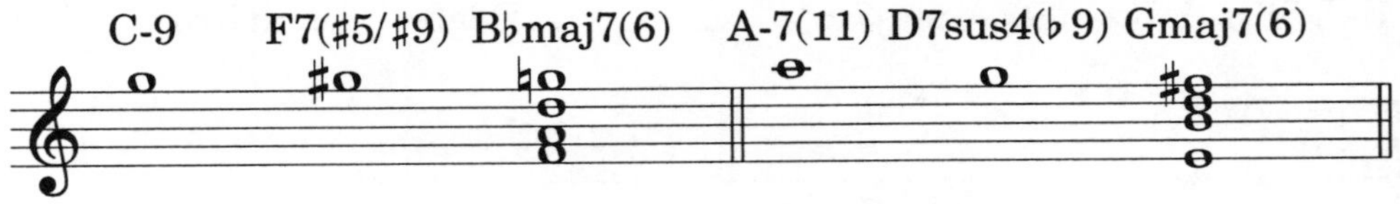


**maj7♭5(6)** (**6 for 5** not applicable)

**6 for 1** {3 ♭5 6 7} Cmaj7♭5(6) = B7sus4

There are four applicable inversions:

| | | | |
|---|---|---|---|
| 3 | ♭5 | 6 | 7 |
| 6 | 7 | 3 | ♭5 |
| ♭5 | 6 | 7 | 3 |
| 7 | 3 | ♭5 | 6 |

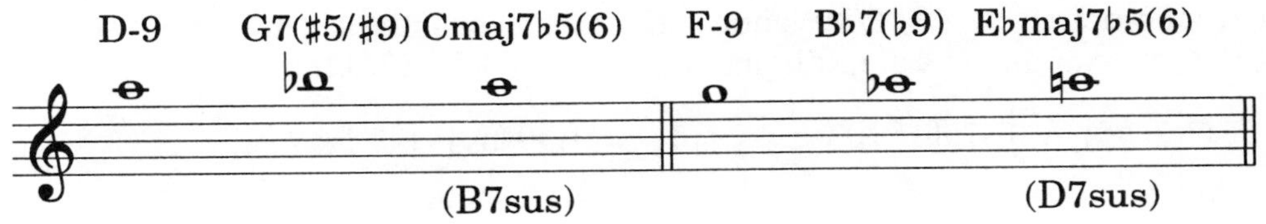


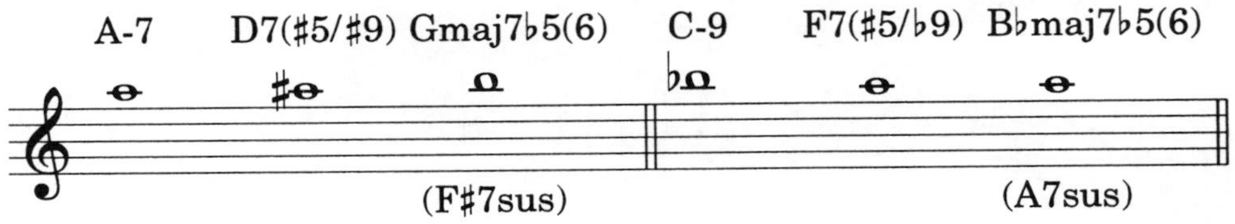

## min maj7(6)

**6 for 1** {♭3 5 6 7} C-maj7(6) = B+7

There are four applicable inversions:

| | | | |
|---|---|---|---|
| ♭3 | 5 | 6 | 7 |
| 6 | 7 | ♭3 | 5 |
| 5 | 6 | 7 | ♭3 |
| 7 | ♭3 | 5 | 6 |

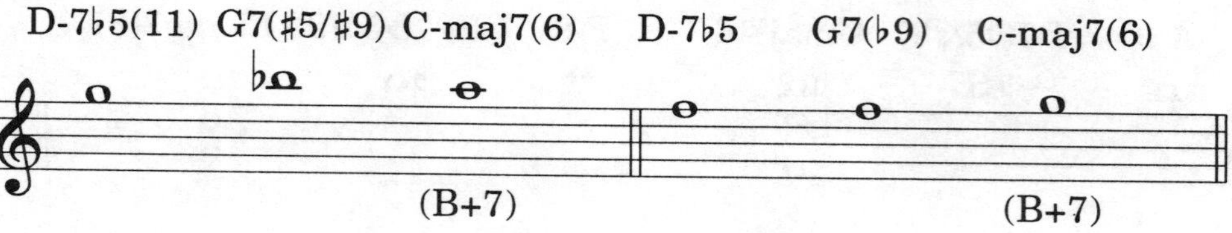


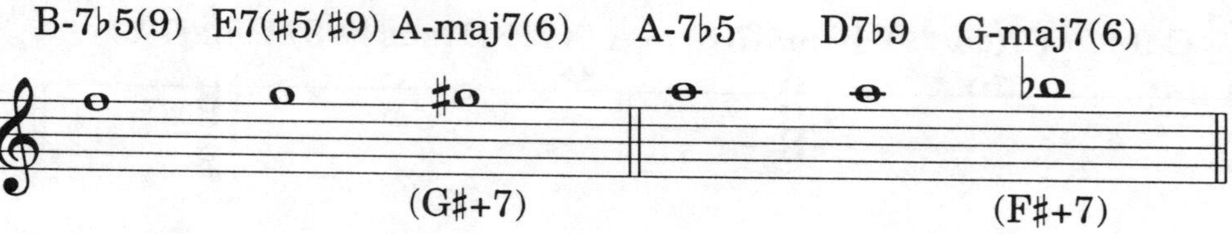


**6 for 5** {1 ♭3 6 7} C-maj7(6) = F7(♯11) = B7(♭9) {1 3 ♭7 ♭9)

There is one applicable voicing:

7
♭3
1
6

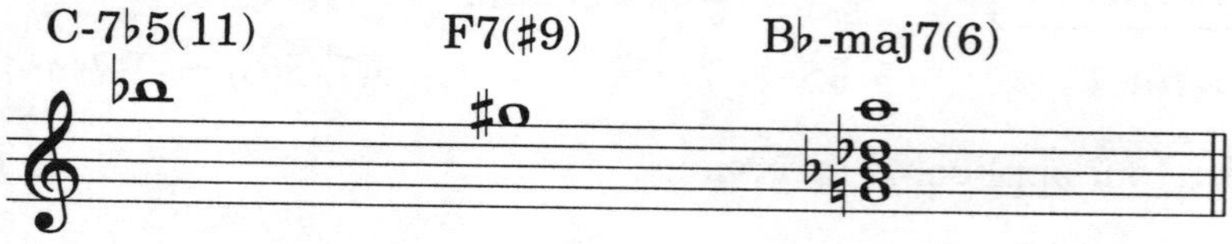


## min7♭5(♭13) / min7(alt5)

♭13 for ♭5 is not usually an appropriate substitution, since the ♭5th is an important characteristic chord tone. But in fact, the ♭13th tension on a minor chord does dictate an accompanying ♭5th chord tone. The only other possible chord sound would be a very incomplete dom7(♯5/♯9) chord. For this reason, the ♭13th for ♭5th substitution, {1 ♭3 ♭7 ♭13(♯5)} = min7♯5, will be examined as a mildly incomplete min7♭5(♭13) chord.

C-7(♯5) = F-7(11) {♭3 5 ♭7 11} = B♭9sus4 {1 4 ♭7 9}

There are four applicable inversions:

| | | | |
|---|---|---|---|
| 1 | ♭3 | ♯5 | ♭7 |
| ♯5 | ♭7 | 1 | ♭3 |
| ♭3 | ♯5 | ♭7 | 1 |
| ♭7 | 1 | ♭3 | ♯5 |

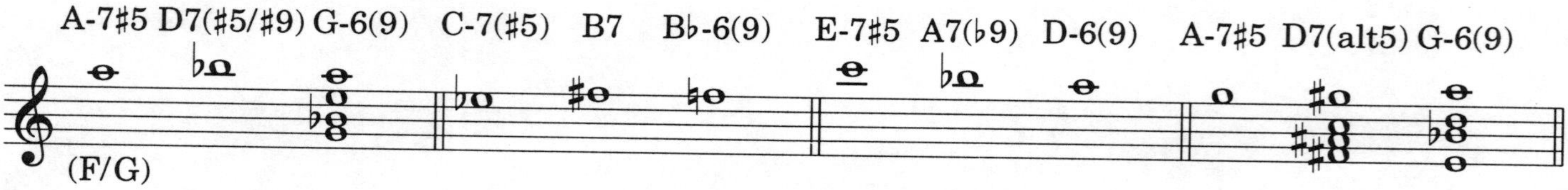

**♭13 for 1** {♭3 ♭5 ♭7 ♭13} or {♭3 ♭5 ♯5 ♭7}

C-7♭5(♭13) = G♭6(9) {1 3 6 9} = Emaj9♭5 = Bmaj7(6)

There are four applicable inversions:

| | | | |
|---|---|---|---|
| ♭3 | ♭5 | ♯5 | ♭7 |
| ♯5 | ♭7 | ♭3 | ♭5 |
| ♭5 | ♯5 | ♭7 | ♭3 |
| ♭7 | ♭3 | ♭5 | ♯5 |

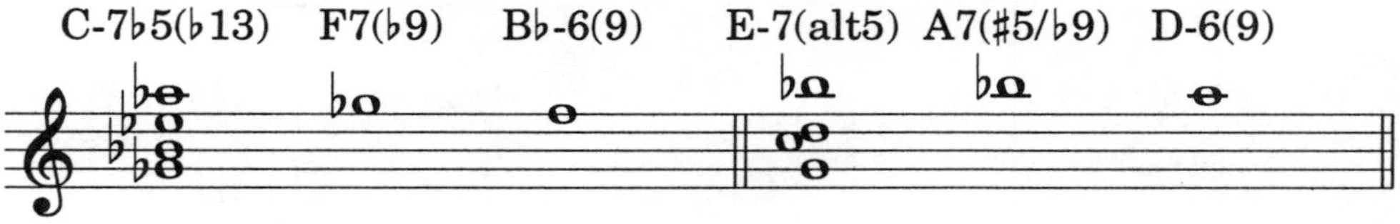


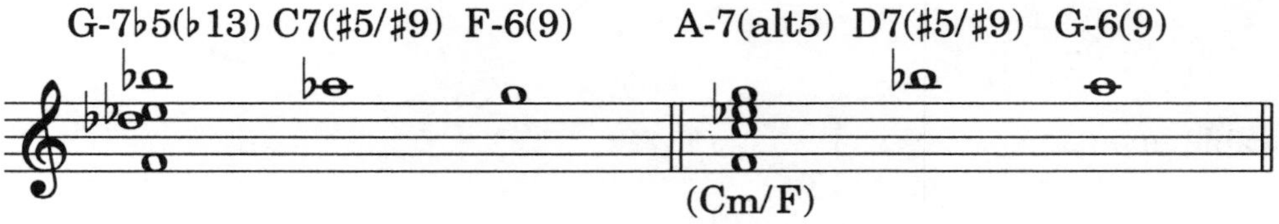


**dom7(13)**

**13 for 5** {1 3 ♭7 13} C7(13) = G♭7(♭5/♯9) = B♭maj9(♭5) {1 ♭5 7 9}

There are two applicable inversions:

| | |
|---|---|
| 3 | 1 |
| ♭7 | 13 |
| 13 | 3 |
| 1 | ♭7 |

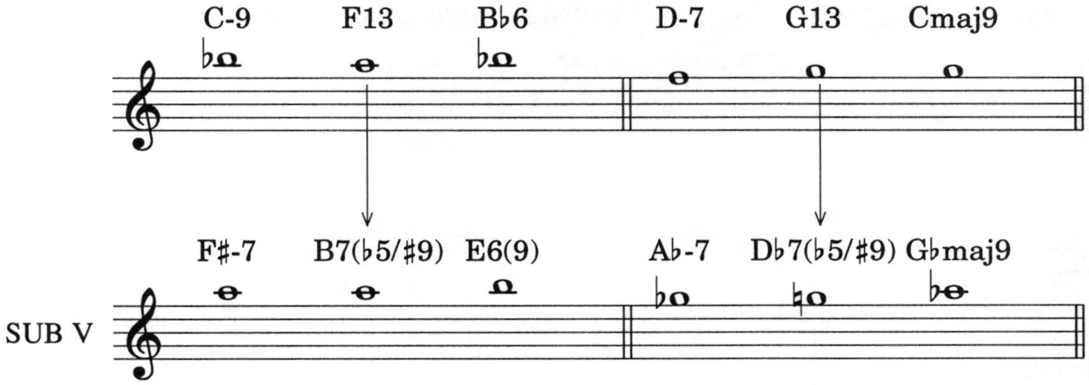


**13 for 1** {3 5 ♭7 13} C13 = G-6(9) {1 ♭3 6 9}

There is one applicable inversion:

13
3
♭7
5

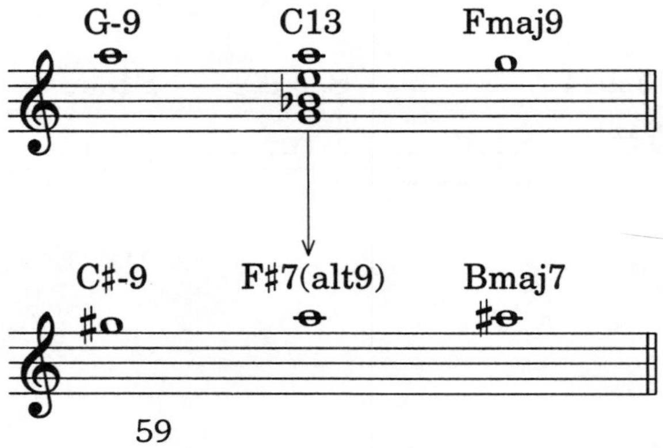


SUB V

**dom7♭5(13)** (**13 for 5** not applicable)

**13 for 1** {3 ♭5 ♭7 13} C13♭5 = G♭7(♯9) {1 3 ♭7 ♯9}

There is one applicable inversion:

| |
|---|
| 13 |
| 3 |
| ♭7 |
| ♭5 |

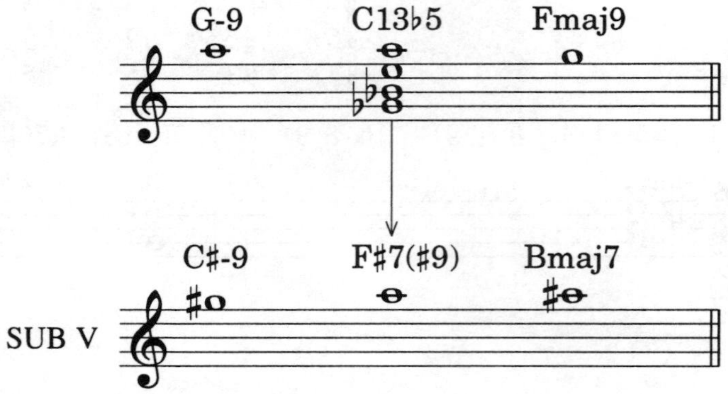


**13 for 3** {1 ♭5 ♭7 13}

There are two applicable inversions:

| | |
|---|---|
| 1 | ♭5 |
| 13 | ♭7 |
| ♭5 | 13 |
| ♭7 | 1 |

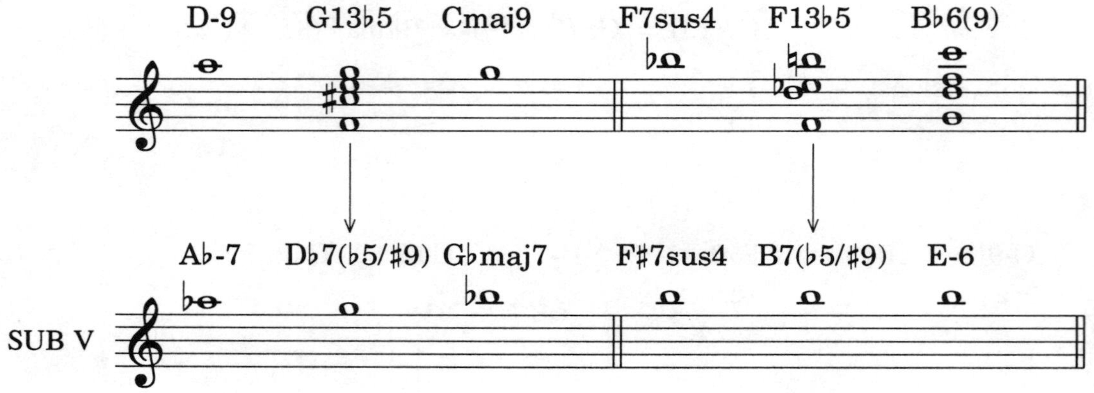


**dom7sus4(13)**

**13 for 5** {1 4 ♭7 13}

There are two applicable inversions:

| | |
|---|---|
| 4 | 1 |
| ♭7 | 13 |
| 13 | 4 |
| 1 | ♭7 |

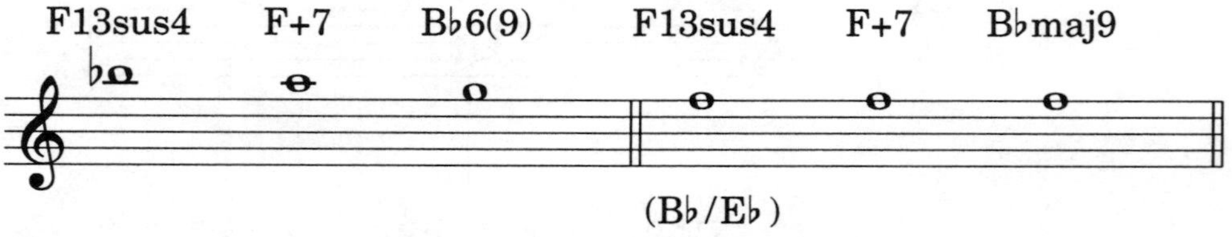

**13 for 1** {4 5 ♭7 13} C13sus4 = G-9 {1 ♭3 ♭7 9}

There are two applicable voicings:

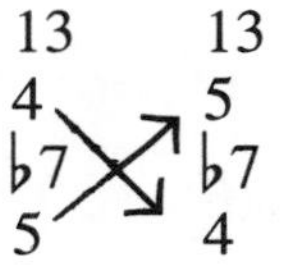


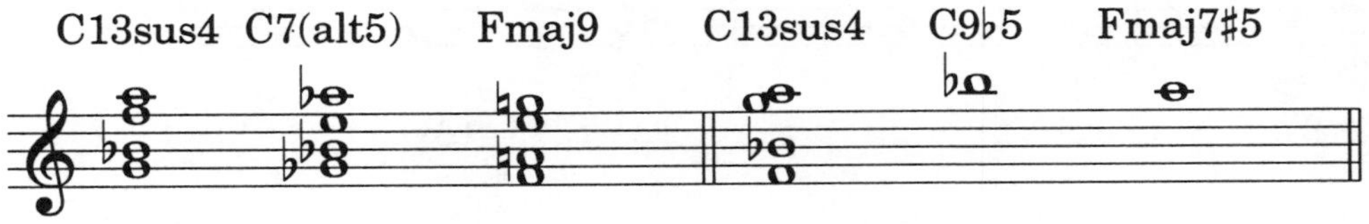


The following examples will use various thirteenth chords in a "Jazz" or "II-V" blues form. Note that the dom7♯5(♯11) or dom7(alt5) chords that were introduced in the past chapter appear again in this chapter as dom7♭5(♭13).

In the next example, note the multiple functions of the dom7♯5 and min7♯5 chords. Also note the different functions of the maj6(9) chord on the first three voicings. Finally, note the common lead tone on the last four bars. This "II-V" blues is in the key of "C."

# Chapter Ten.
## Two Tensions

This chapter will examine the three different two-tension combinations produced by tensions 9, 11, and 13: (9 & 13), (9 & 11), and (11 & 13). The preferred four-note voicings will include two tensions and the guide-tones, thus omitting the root and 5th. When a ♭5th or ♯5th is needed, the least needed guide-tone (usually the 3rd) will be removed.

Some of the most effective voicings place the guide-tones on the lower two strings (4th and 5th strings) and the tensions on the upper two strings (2nd and 3rd strings). The first and third inversions of drop 2 type voicings arrange their intervals in this matter, producing some of the most useful voicings in this chapter.

Since 9 and 13 are perhaps the most common tensions found together, this chapter will begin by examining them first, followed by (9 & 11) and (11 & 13).

### Tensions 9 and 13

Those chords containing a ♭5th and natural 13 tension will be examined enharmonically under the **Three Tensions** chapter as ♯11 and 13:

{9 ♯11 13} {♭9 ♯11 13} {♯9 ♯11 13}

Those dominant chords that contain both ♭5 and tension ♭13 will examine two different voicing formulas:

{3 ♭5 9 ♭13} and {♭5 ♭7 9 ♭13}

*The {♭5 ♭7 9 ♭13} formula will also be used as the min7♭5(♭13/9) voicing formula in this section.
This voicing will serve both subdominant and dominant functions in their following relative II-V-I examples.

Note the ninth (no 5) enharmonic substitution chords produced by the {3 ♭5 9 ♭13} formula:

C7♭5(♭13/9) = E9 {1 3 ♭7 9 }
C7♭5(♭13/♭9) = E6(9) {1 3 6 9 }
C7♭5(♭13/♯9) = Emaj7(9) {1 3 7 9 }

Additional enharmonic chord symbol notation could also be used to describe the above chords:

C7♭5(♭13/9): C+7(♯11/9) / C+7(9/♭5) / C9(♯11/♯5) / C9(♯5/♭5) / C9(alt5) / C9(♭13/♭5) / etc.
C7♭5(♭13/♭9): C+7(♯11/♭9) / C+7(♭9/♭5) / C7♭5(♭9/♯5) / C7(♭9/alt5) / C7(♭9/♯5/♭5) / etc.
C7♭5(♭13/♯9): C+7(♯11/♯9) / C+7(♯9/♭5) / C7♭5(♯9/♯5) / C7(♯9/alt5) / C7(♯9/♯5/♭5) / etc.

As discussed in the **Chord Symbol Notation** chapter, ♯11 and ♭13 will be avoided in chord symbol notation. Consequently, I recommend avoiding the following symbol descriptions of the above chords:

C7♭5(♭13/9): avoid C7(♭13/♯11/9) or C9(♭13/♯11)
C7♭5(♭13/♭9): avoid C7(♭13/♯11/♭9)
C7♭5(♭13/♯9): avoid C7(♭13/♯11/♯9)

Due to the incomplete nature and limited voicings, the natural 5th produces, {5 7 9 13} voicings will be avoided in this section. They will be examined later in the **Additional Enharmonic Chordal Substitutions** chapter.

With the exception of a dom7(♯9/13) chord, all of the voicings used in this section have been previously introduced as basic four-part (7th and 6th chords) or 9th chords. As was the case in the **Tension 13** chapter, a dom7sus4(♭13) chord with 9 or ♭9 will be avoided.

The following dom7 chords have already been introduced enharmonically in the **Tension 9** chapter. Their relative II-V-I examples can be observed there:

C7(♭13/9): C+7(9)
C7(♭13/♭9): C+7(♭9)
C7(♭13/♯9): C+7(♯9)

The following dom7 chords were introduced by their Sub V chords in the **Tension 9** chapter:

C7(13/9) = G♭+7(♯9)
C7(13/♭9) = G♭7(♯9)

**maj7(6/9)** **{3 7 6 9}** Cmaj7(6/9) = E7sus4

Avoiding tension 9 on the 5th string leaves three applicable voicings:

| | | |
|---|---|---|
| 6 | 7 | 9 |
| 9 | 3 | 6 |
| 7 | 9 | 3 |
| 3 | 6 | 7 |

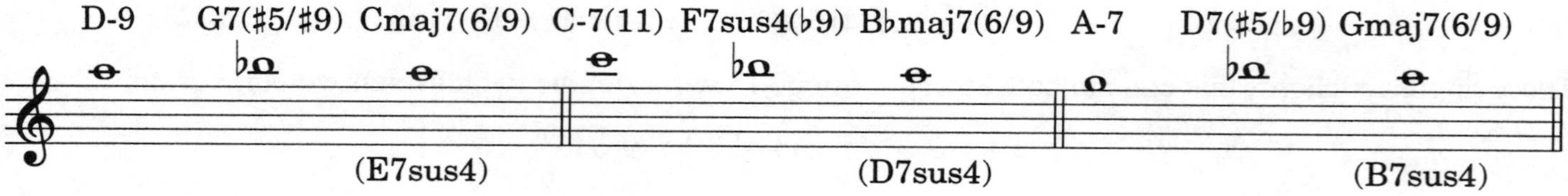


**min maj7(6/9)** **{♭3 7 6 9}** C-maj7(6/9) = B7♯9 {1 3 ♭7 ♯9}

There is one applicable inversion:

9
6
♭3
7

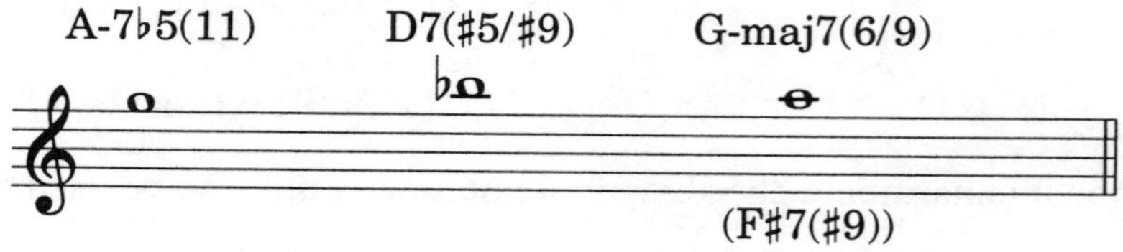


**min7♭5(♭13/9)** **{♭5 ♭7 9 ♭13}** C-7♭5(9/♭13) = B♭+7

Avoiding tension 9 on the 5th string leaves three applicable voicings:

| | | |
|---|---|---|
| ♭13 | ♭7 | 9 |
| 9 | ♭5 | ♭13 |
| ♭7 | 9 | ♭5 |
| ♭5 | ♭13 | ♭7 |

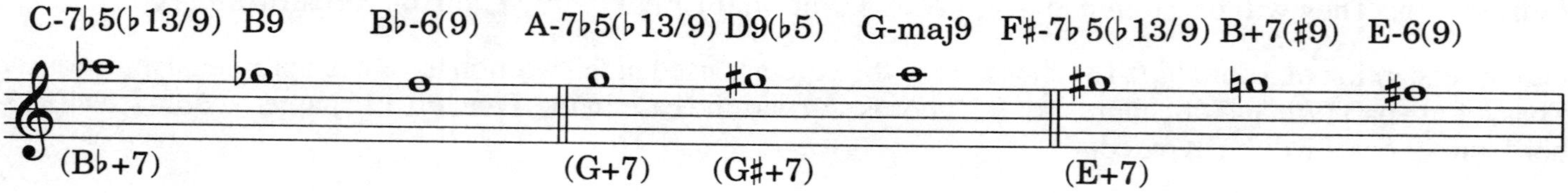

**dom7(♯9/13)** {3 ♭7 ♯9 13} There are two applicable voicings:

| | |
|---|---|
| 13 | ♯9 |
| ♯9 | 13 |
| ♭7 | 3 |
| 3 | ♭7 |

Only one example is needed, since the Sub V mirrors the original chord:

C13(♯9) = G♭13(♯9)

13............ A...............♯9

♯9............E♭............13

♭7............B♭............... 3

3........... E .............. ♭7

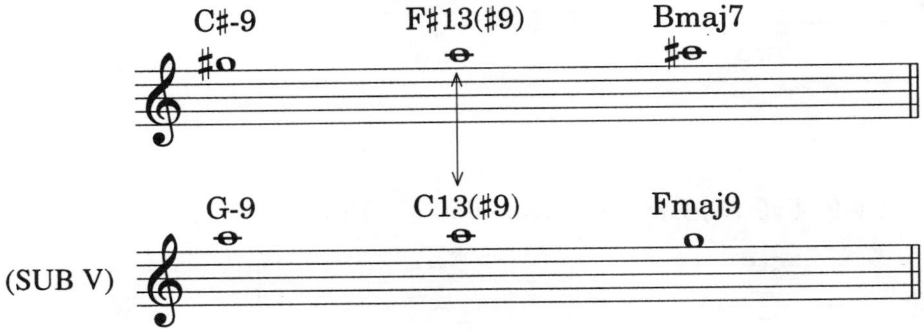


**dom7♭5(♭13/9)** [dom9(♯5/♭5)] or [dom9(alt5)]

**{♭5 ♭7 9 ♭13}** C7♭5(♭13/9) = B♭+7

Those voicings producing tension 9 on the 5th string will be avoided. However, the Sub V's of these voicings will be examined since ♭13(♯5) now appears in the bass.

Four applicable inversions:

| | | | |
|---|---|---|---|
| 9 | ♭5 | ♭13 | ♭7 |
| ♭13 | ♭7 | 9 | ♭5 |
| ♭5 | ♭13 | ♭7 | 9 |
| ♭7 | 9 | ♭5 | ♭13 |

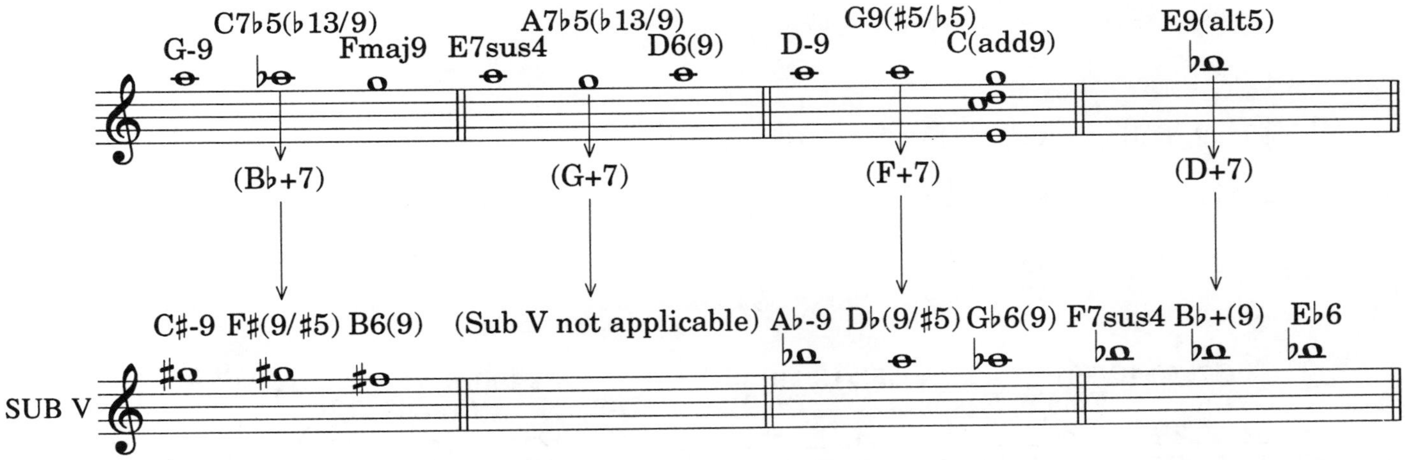

**{3 ♭5 9 ♭13}** C7♭5(♭13/9) = E9 {1 3 ♭7 9}

Four applicable inversions:

| | | | |
|---|---|---|---|
| ♭5 | ♭13 | 9 | 3 |
| 9 | 3 | ♭5 | ♭13 |
| ♭13 | 9 | 3 | ♭5 |
| 3 | ♭5 | ♭13 | 9 |

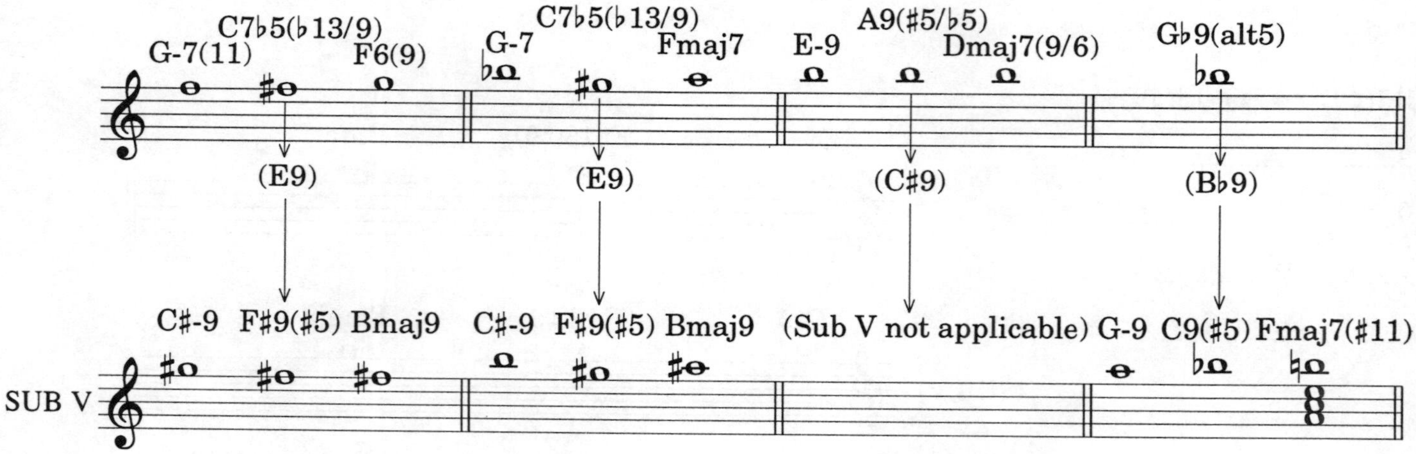


**dom7♭5(♭13/♭9)** [dom7(♭9/alt5)]

Those inversions containing tension ♭13 on the 5th string will omit their Sub V chords, which would subsequently contain tension 9 on the 5th string.

Note the fourth intervals produced by these tensions and the ♭5th:

C7♭5(♭13/♭9): ♭5 — G♭ ⟩ 4th

♭9 — D♭ ⟩ 4th

♭13 — A♭

**{♭5 ♭7 ♭9 ♭13}** C7♭5(♭13/♭9) = B♭-7(♯5)

Four applicable inversions:

| | | | |
|---|---|---|---|
| ♭9 | ♭5 | ♭13 | ♭7 |
| ♭13 | ♭7 | ♭9 | ♭5 |
| ♭5 | ♭13 | ♭7 | ♭9 |
| ♭7 | ♭9 | ♭5 | ♭13 |

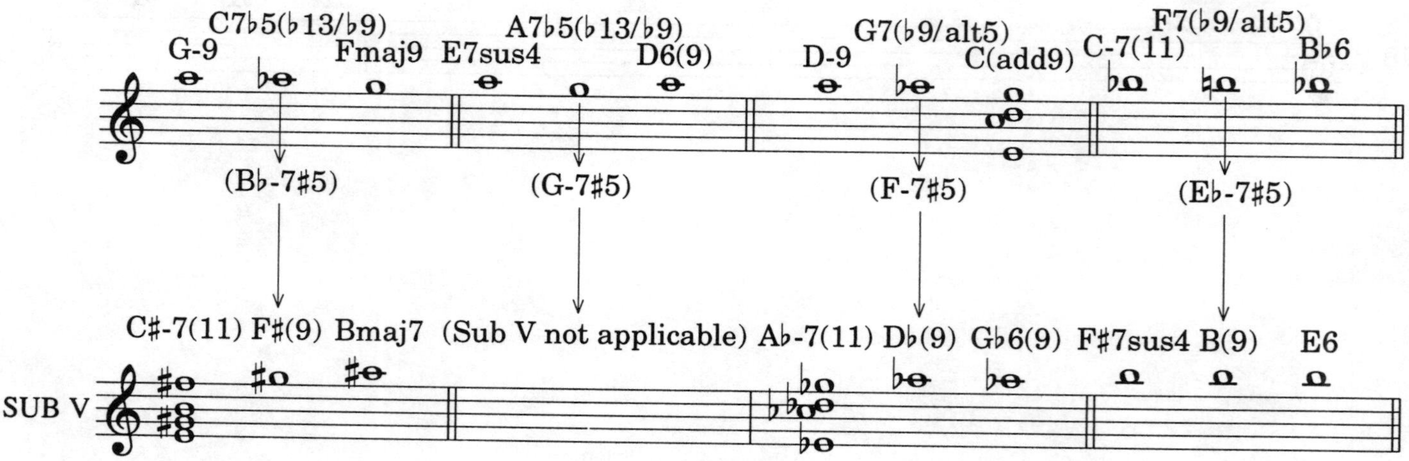

**{3 ♭5 ♭9 ♭13}** C7♭5(♭13/♭9) = E6(9) {1 3 6 9}

Four applicable inversions:

| | | | |
|---|---|---|---|
| ♭5 | ♭13 | ♭9 | 3 |
| ♭9 | 3 | ♭5 | ♭13 |
| ♭13 | ♭9 | 3 | ♭5 |
| 3 | ♭5 | ♭13 | ♭9 |

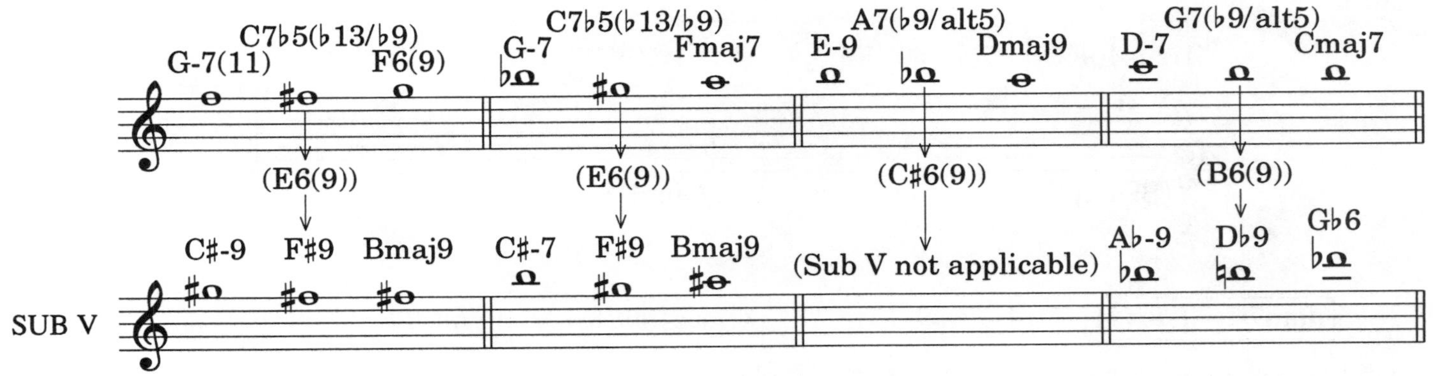


**dom7♭5(♭13/♯9)** [dom7(♯9/alt5)]

The voicing formula containing the ♭7th will be avoided due to the ambiguous sound produced. Without the third, the { ♭5 ♭7 ♯9 ♭13} voicing functions better as a min7♭5(♭13) { ♭3 ♭5 ♭7 ♭13} chord.

**{3 ♭5 ♯9 ♭13}** C7♭5(♭13/♯9) = Emaj9 { 1 3 7 9 }

Two applicable inversions:

| | |
|---|---|
| ♭5 | ♭13 |
| ♯9 | 3 |
| ♭13 | ♯9 |
| 3 | ♭5 |

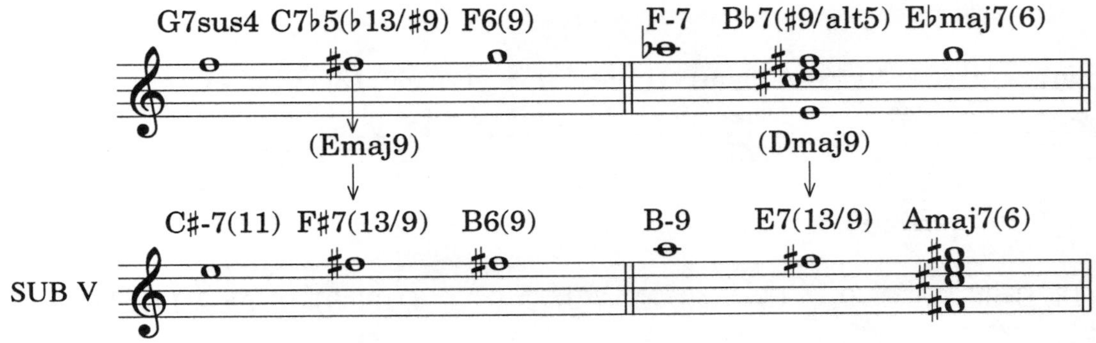

**dom7sus4(9/13)**  {4 ♭7 9 13}  C7sus4(9/13) = B♭maj7

Avoiding tension 9 on the 5th string leaves two applicable inversions:

| | |
|---|---|
| 13 | 9 |
| 9 | 13 |
| ♭7 | 4 |
| 4 | ♭7 |

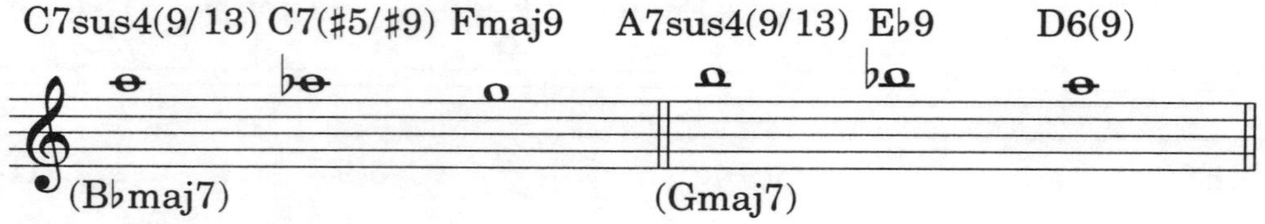


**dom7sus4(♭9/13)**  {4 ♭7 ♭9 13}  C7sus4(♭9/13) = B♭-maj7

Avoiding tension 9 on the 5th string leaves two applicable inversions:

| | |
|---|---|
| 13 | ♭9 |
| ♭9 | 13 |
| ♭7 | 4 |
| 4 | ♭7 |

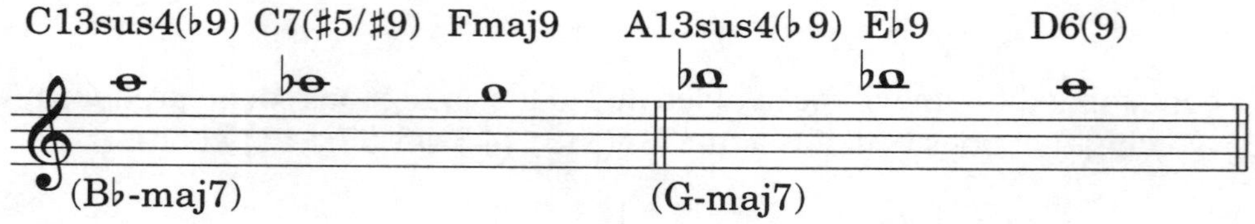


The following examples will use various chords containing tensions 9 and 13 in a II-V blues form. Chords introduced in past chapters will be included to enhance voice-leading. In this first example, note the same dominant voicings used on beats three and four in measures five and six.

In this next example, note the descending chromatic voices against a common lead voice in the last two measures.

This last example utilizes some of the dominant type chords that contain ♭5 and ♭13 { ♭5 9 ♭13}, { ♭5 ♭9 ♭13 }, { ♭5 ♯9 ♭13 }. In this example, ♭13 will be enharmonically substituted by ♯5, producing chord symbols containing { ♭5 ♯5} or (alt5). These versatile and interesting voicings present some unique chromatic and constant structure voice-leading possibilities. Additional examples of these dominant chord types can be found at the end of the **Three Tensions** chapter.

# Tensions 9 and 11

The two types of voicings used in this section follow the traditional drop 2 substitution formula: 9 for 1 {3 7 9 11} and 11 for 3 or 5 {5 7 9 11}. With the exception of the dom7(♯9/♯11) chord, all of these voicings have been introduced in previous chapters.

Those dom7 chords containing a ♯5 have already been introduced enharmonically under the **Tensions 9 and 13** section:

C+7(9/♯11) = C7♭5(♭13/9)
C+7(♭9/♯11) = C7♭5(♭13/♭9)
C+7(♯9/♯11) = C7♭5(♭13/♯9)

The following chords that have 9 for 1 and 11 for 5 {3 7 9 11} tension substitutions have been previously introduced enharmonically under the **Tension 9** chapter. Their relative II-V-I examples and Sub V chords can be found in that chapter.

Cmaj7(9/♯11) = Cmaj7♭5(9)
C7(9/♯11) = C7♭5(9)
C7(♭9/♯11) = C7♭5(♭9)
C7(♯9/♯11) = C7♭5(♯9)

Note the unique character of the maj6 and min6 chords with the addition of tensions 9 and 11. 6, 9, and 11 form a complete triad a whole step above the root of the original chord:

C6(9/♯11) forms a D major triad.
C-6(9/11) forms a D minor triad.

**maj7(9/♯11)** **{5 7 9 ♯11}** Cmaj7(9/♯11) = Gmaj7

Avoiding tension 9 on the 5th string leaves two applicable voicings:

| | |
|---|---|
| 7 | 9 |
| ♯11 | 5 |
| 9 | ♯11 |
| 5 | 7 |

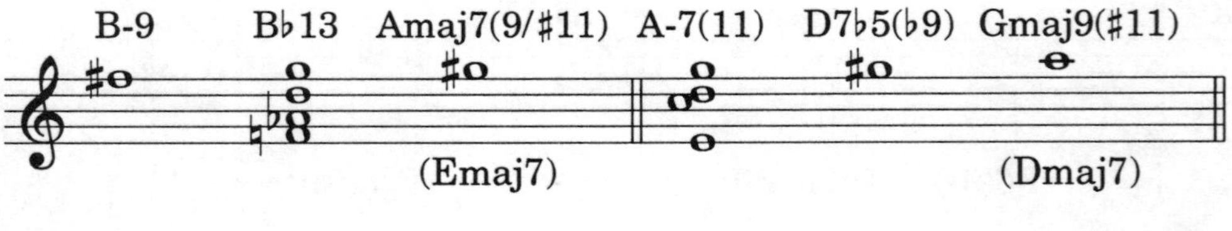


**maj6(9/♯11)** **{3 6 9 ♯11}** C6(9/♯11) (C6♭5(9)) = F♯-7♯5

Avoiding tension 9 on the 5th string leaves three applicable voicings:

| | | |
|---|---|---|
| ♯11 | 6 | 9 |
| 9 | 3 | ♯11 |
| 6 | 9 | 3 |
| 3 | ♯11 | 6 |

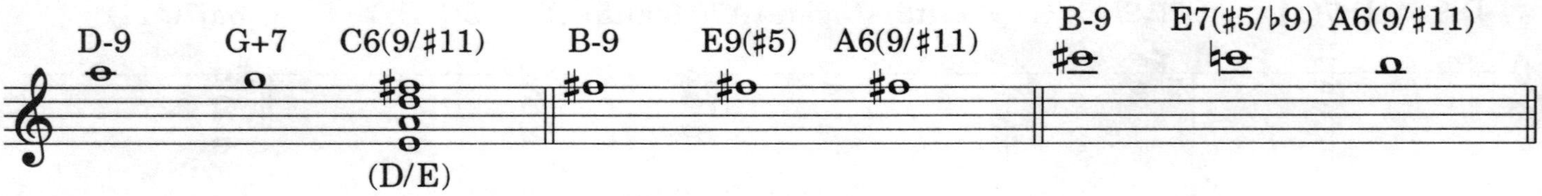

**{5 6 9 ♯11}** C6(9/♯11) = A13sus4 {1 4 ♭7 13}

There are two applicable inversions:

| | |
|---|---|
| 9 | 6 |
| 5 | ♯11 |
| ♯11 | 9 |
| 6 | 5 |

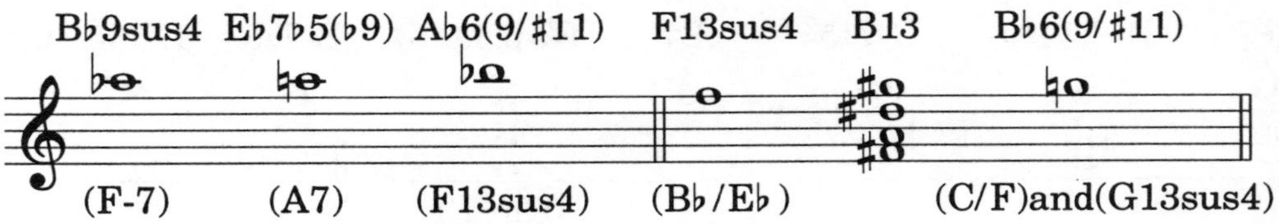


**min.maj7(11/9)**

As discussed in the **Tension 11** chapter under the min.maj7(11) chord, 11 and 7 produce the guide-tones (3 and ♭7) of its V7 chord, producing a potentially ambiguous sound. Tension 9 further complicates this by being a chord tone (the 5th) of its V7 chord. The weakest possible voicing {5 7 9 11} includes all of the basic chord tones {1 3 5 ♭7} of its V7 chord. This produces an extremely ambiguous sound and therefore will not be included in this section.

**{♭3 7 9 11}** C-maj7(11/9) = F13♭5

There are two applicable voicings:

| | |
|---|---|
| 11 | 7 |
| 9 | ♭3 |
| 7 | 9 |
| ♭3 | 11 |

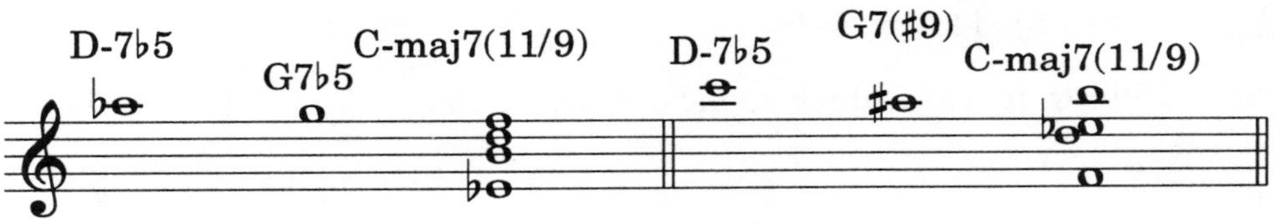


**min6(11/9)** **{♭3 6 9 11}** C-6(11/9) = B7♭5(♯9) / F13

There are two applicable inversions:

| | |
|---|---|
| 6 | 11 |
| ♭3 | 9 |
| 9 | 6 |
| 11 | ♭3 |

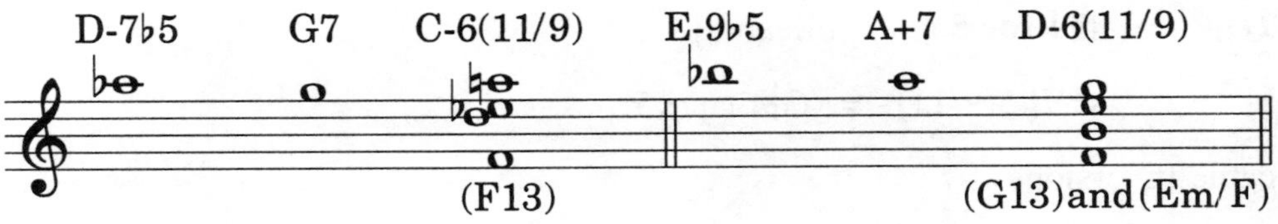

**{5 6 9 11}** C-6(11/9) = F6(9) {1 3 6 9}

Avoiding tension 9 on the 5th string leaves three applicable inversions:

| | | |
|---|---|---|
| 5 | 6 | 9 |
| 9 | 11 | 5 |
| 6 | 9 | 11 |
| 11 | 5 | 6 |

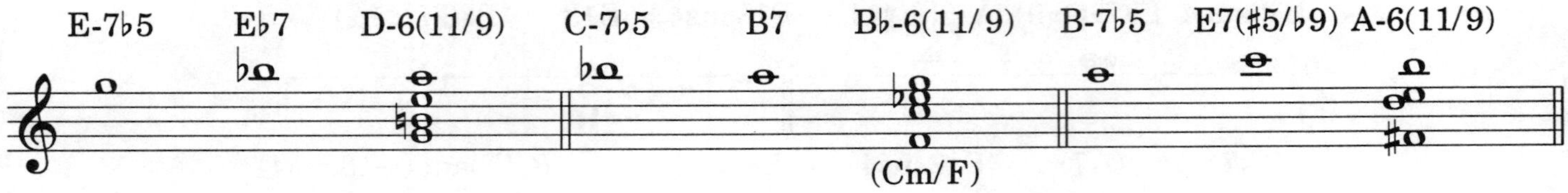


**min7(9/11)** **{♭3 ♭7 9 11}** C-7(9/11) = F13sus4 = A♭6(9/♯11)

There are two applicable inversions:

| | |
|---|---|
| ♭7 | 11 |
| ♭3 | 9 |
| 9 | ♭7 |
| 11 | ♭3 |

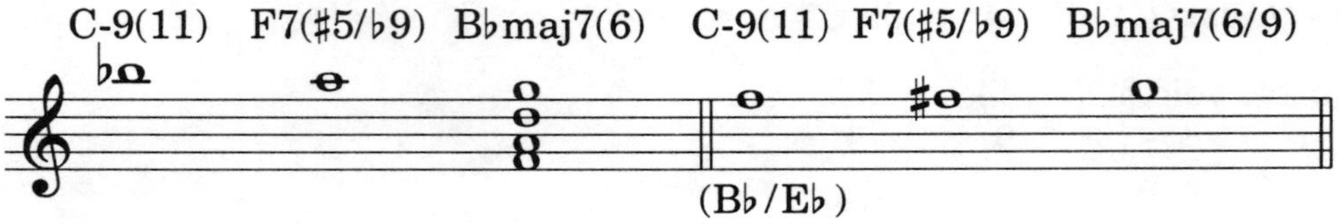


**{5 ♭7 9 11}** C-7(9/11) = G-7

Avoiding tension 9 on the 5th string leaves three applicable inversions:

| | | |
|---|---|---|
| 9 | ♭7 | 5 |
| 5 | 11 | 9 |
| 11 | 9 | ♭7 |
| ♭7 | 5 | 11 |

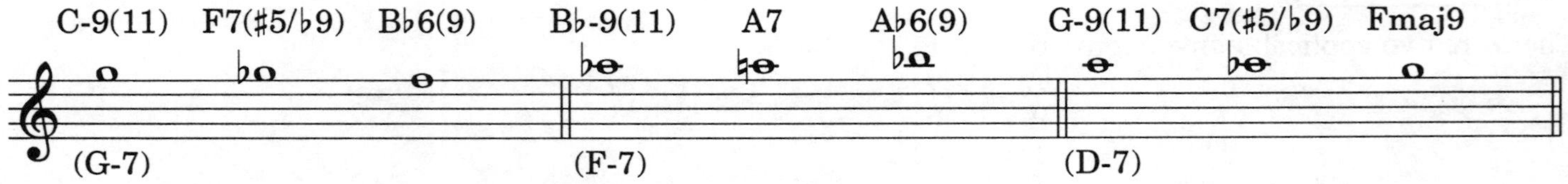


**min7♭5(9/11)** [**11 for 5** not applicable]

**{♭5 ♭7 9 11}** C-7♭5(9/11) = G♭maj7♯5

There are two applicable inversions:

| | |
|---|---|
| ♭7 | 9 |
| 11 | ♭5 |
| 9 | 11 |
| ♭5 | ♭7 |

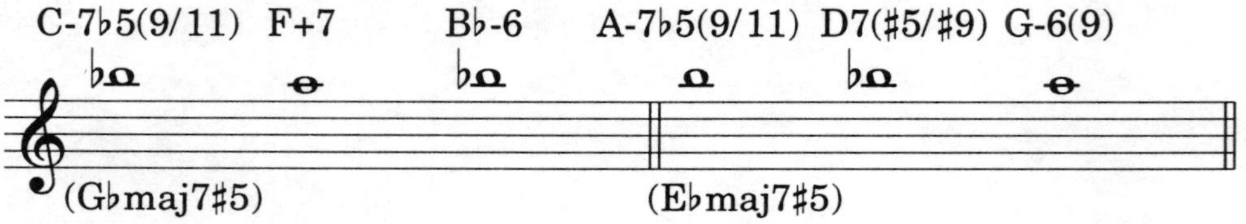

**dom7(9/♯11)**  {5 ♭7 9 ♯11}  C7(9/♯11) = G-maj7

There are three applicable voicings:

| | | |
|---|---|---|
| ♯11 | ♭7 | 9 |
| ♭7 | ♯11 | 5 |
| 5 | 9 | ♯11 |
| 9 | 5 | ♭7 |

Note that tension 9 is not available on the 5th string but becomes available on its Sub V chord as the ♯5th.

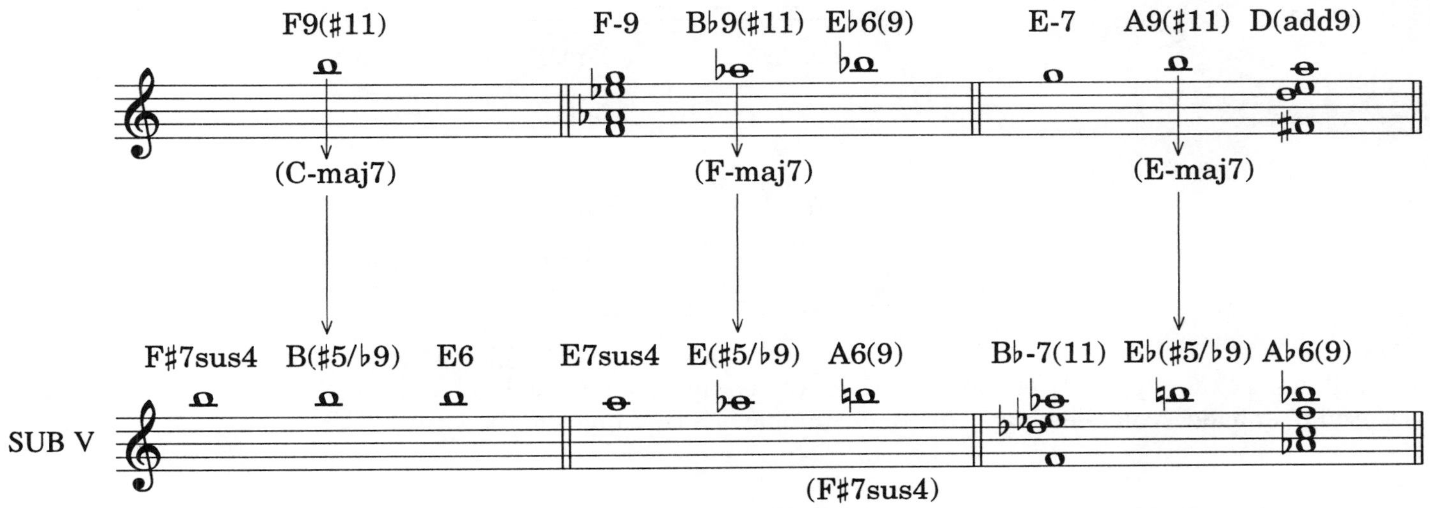


**dom7(♭9/♯11)**  {5 ♭7 ♭9 ♯11}  C7(♭9/♯11) = E♭7(♯9)

There are three applicable inversions:

| | | |
|---|---|---|
| ♯11 | ♭7 | ♭9 |
| ♭7 | ♯11 | 5 |
| 5 | ♭9 | ♯11 |
| ♭9 | 5 | ♭7 |

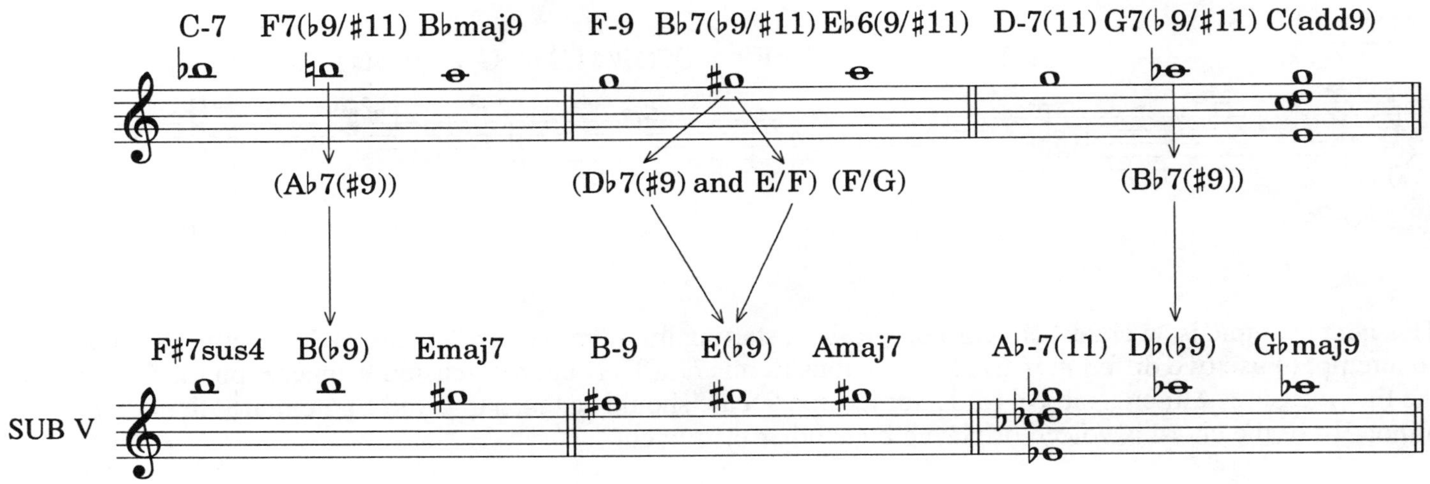

**dom7(♯9/♯11)** **{5 ♭7 ♯9 ♯11}**

Only two voicings are physically available, and one of these cannot be used due to the ♯9th tension being located on the 5th string. These voicings will reappear in the **Three Tensions** chapter, where both will be available.

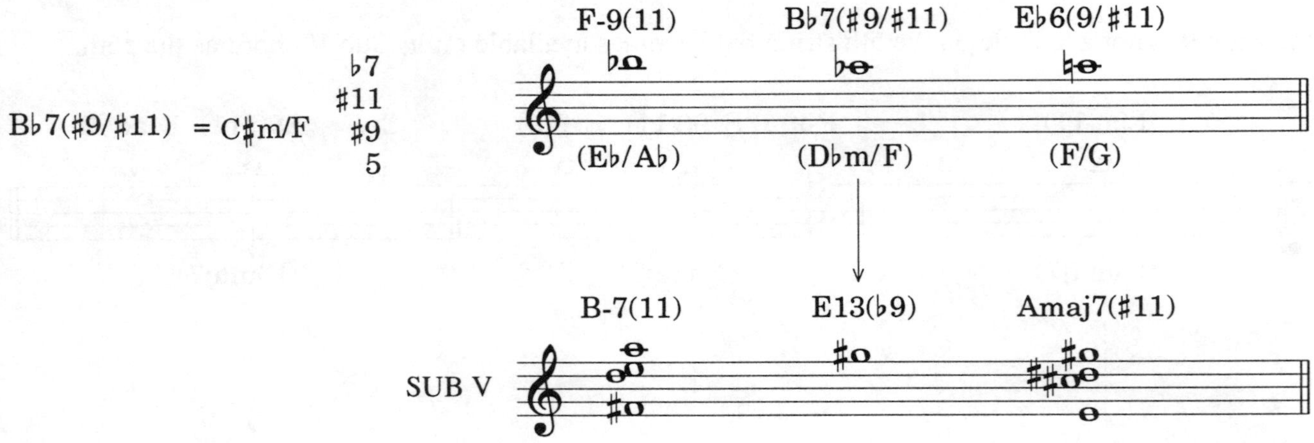


The following examples will use various chords containing tensions 9 and 11. Additional chords from past chapters are used to enhance voice-leading. This first example is a II-V blues in the key of "F."

This next example is an eight-bar chord progression starting in "A" minor and ending in the relative "C" major. In an attempt to use two different maj7♯5 inversions as min7♭5(9/11) chords, tension 9 appears on the 5th string in the first measure. Although above L.I.L. for tension 9, care should be taken to avoid a potential ♭9th interval if the minor 3rd of the chord is voiced or played by another instrument.

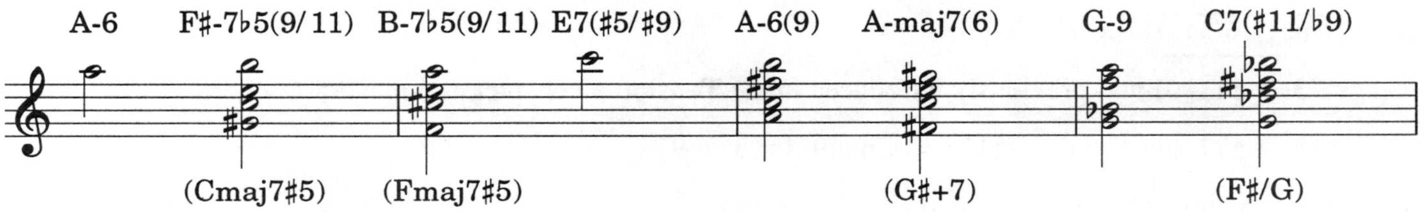


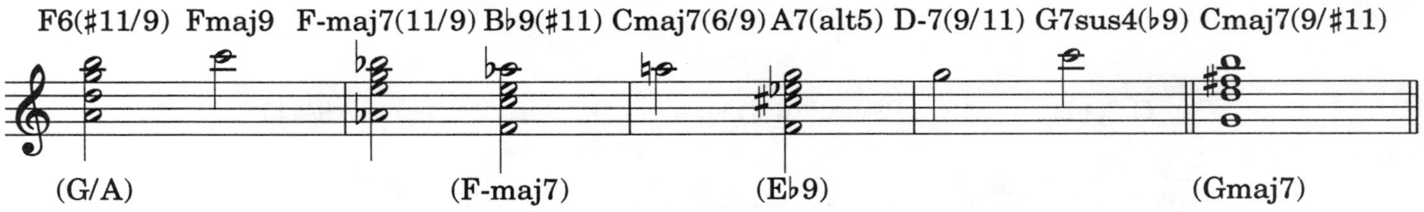


# Tensions 11 and 13

We are left with very few chords in this section, since most have been previously introduced enharmonically.

Only one dom7 voicing will be examined in this section: C7(♯11/13) {5 ♭7 ♯11 13}. The remaining dom7 chords were introduced earlier.

C7(♯11/13) {1 ♭7 ♯11 13} and {3 ♭7 ♯11 13} are examined as C7♭5(13) chords in the **Tension 13** chapter.

As discussed in the **Chord Symbol Notation** chapter, ♯11 and ♭13 should be avoided in the same chord symbol. If these notes are desired, dom7(♯11/♯5) voicings under the **Tensions 11** chapter will suffice.

The traditional drop 2 tension substitution formula [13 for 5] and [11 for 3] produces a very incomplete {1 7 11 13} voicing which will be omitted from this section. Instead, the more complete {3 7 11 13} and {5 7 11 13} voicings will be examined.

Only one new voicing is introduced in this section: ♭7<br>♭5 min7♭5(11/♭13)<br>11<br>♭13

This voicing is an inversion of the previously introduced maj7(9) {1 3 7 9} voicing:

3............♭7
1............♭5
7............11
9............♭13

The min7♭5(11/♭13) chord presents unique voicing possibilities, since any combination of the basic chord tones can accompany tensions 11 and ♭13:

| | | | |
|---|---|---|---|
| C-7♭5(11/♭13): | 1 ♭3 11 ♭13 | = | A♭6 / F-7 |
| | 1 ♭5 11 ♭13 | = | A♭13 |
| | 1 ♭7 11 ♭13 | = | A♭6(9) {1 3 6 9} |
| | ♭3 ♭5 11 ♭13 | = | B6(♯11) {3 5 6 ♯11} |
| | ♭3 ♭7 11 ♭13 | = | B♭7(sus4) |
| | ♭5 ♭7 11 ♭13 | = | G♭maj9 {1 3 7 9} |

Those voicings not containing the ♭7th could be examined as dim7 chords with tensions 11 and ♭13. This makes the ♭7th a rather characteristic note in this chord. Thus, the single most characteristic voicing would contain both the ♭5th and ♭7th {♭5 ♭7 11 ♭13}. This voicing, as well as the voicing containing the guide-tones {♭3 ♭7 11 ♭13} will be examined in this section. Students are encouraged to explore the remaining voicing types.

**maj7(6/♯11)**

**{3 7 ♯11 6}** was previously introduced in the **Tension 13** chapter as a maj7♭5(6) chord.

**{5 7 ♯11 6}** Cmaj7(6/♯11) = Gmaj9 {1 3 7 9}

There are two applicable inversions:

| | |
|---|---|
| 6 | 7 |
| ♯11 | 5 |
| 7 | ♯11 |
| 5 | 6 |

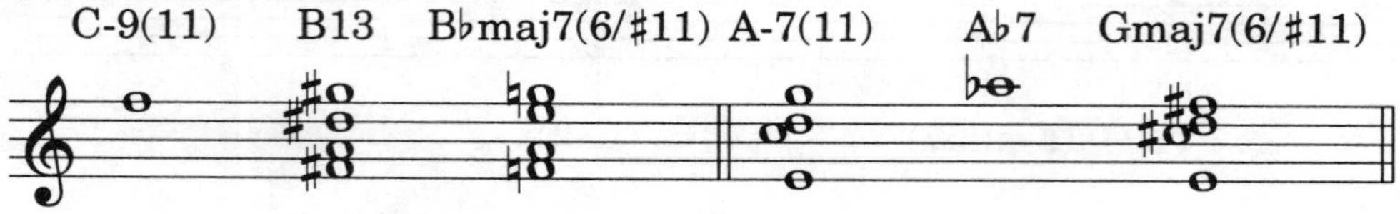


**min maj7(11/6)**

As discussed in the **Tension 11** chapter under the **min maj7(11)** chord, 11 and 7 produce the guide-tones (3 and 7) of its V7 chord, forming a potentially ambiguous sound. Also mentioned was the support the root and/or ♭3rd have on these ambiguous voicings. Of the two voicings displayed here, {♭3 7 11 6} appears to be the stronger, while {5 7 11 6} is quite ambiguous.

**{♭3 7 11 6}** C-maj7(6/11) = F7♭5 / B7♭5

Note: since F7♭5 = B7♭5, Cmin.maj7(6/11) = G♭min.maj7(6/11).

There are four applicable inversions:

| | | | |
|---|---|---|---|
| ♭3 | 11 | 6 | 7 |
| 6 | 7 | ♭3 | 11 |
| 11 | 6 | 7 | ♭3 |
| 7 | ♭3 | 11 | 6 |

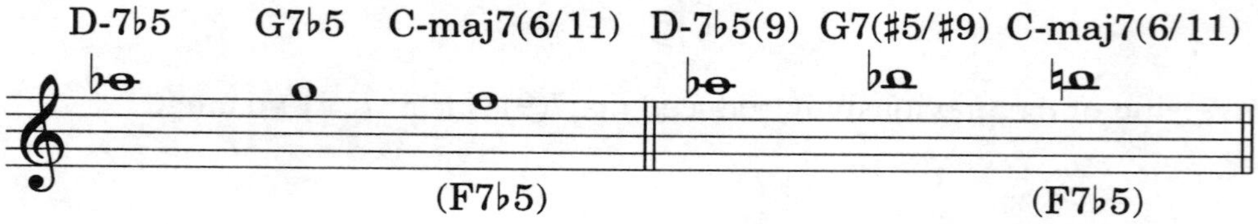


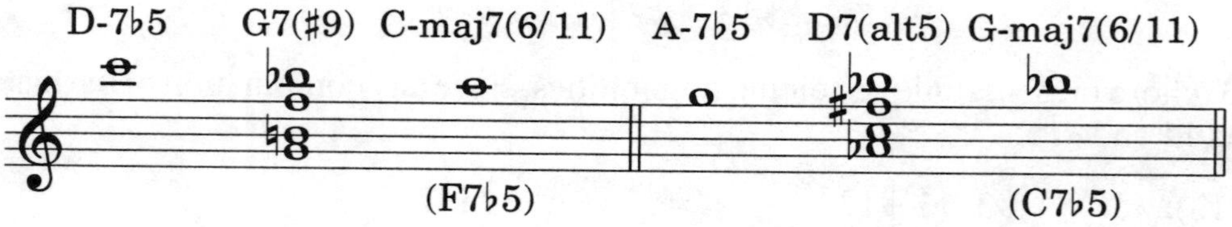


**{5 7 11 6}** C-maj7(6/11) = G9 {1 3 ♭7 9}

There are four applicable inversions:

| | | | |
|---|---|---|---|
| 11 | 5 | 6 | 7 |
| 6 | 7 | 11 | 5 |
| 5 | 6 | 7 | 11 |
| 7 | 11 | 5 | 6 |

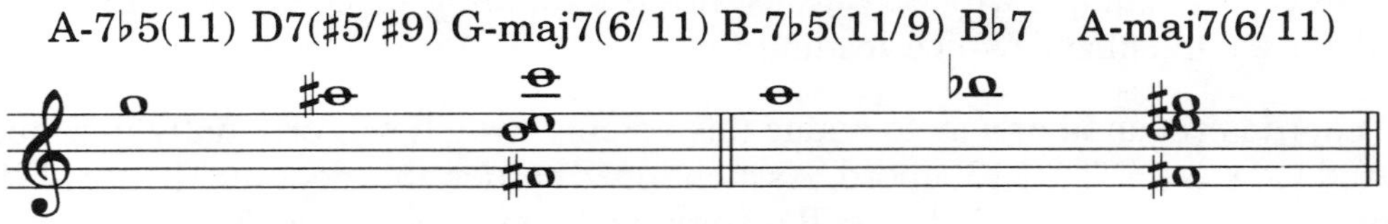


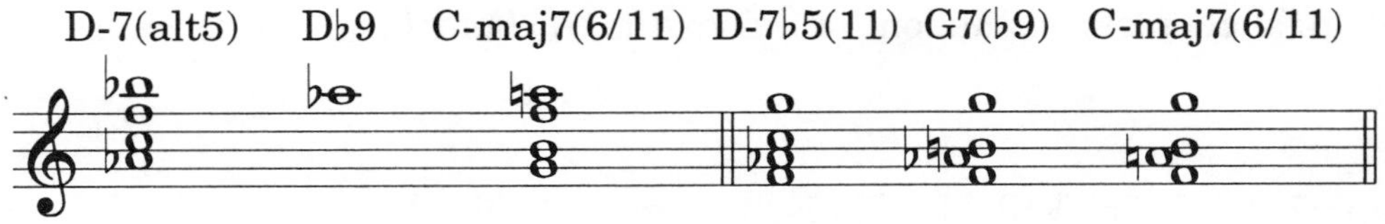


**dom7(♯11/13)** **{5 ♭7 ♯11 13}** C7(♯11/13) = G-maj9 {1 ♭3 7 9}

There is one applicable voicing:

13
♯11
♭7
5

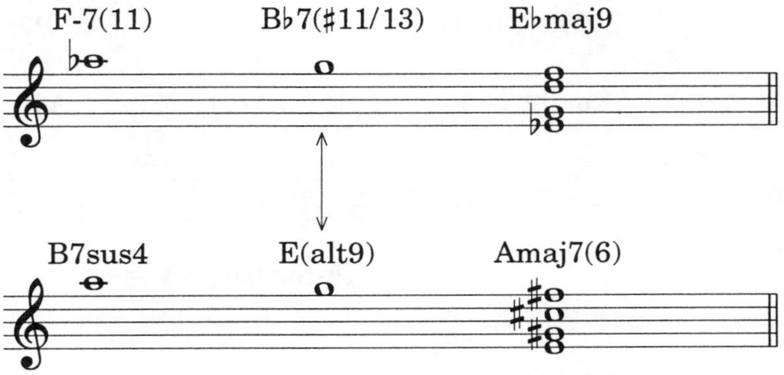


(SUB V)

**min7♭5(11/♭13)** **{♭5 ♭7 11 ♭13}** C-7♭5(11/♭13) = G♭maj9 {1 3 7 9}

There are two applicable inversions:

| | |
|---|---|
| ♭13 | ♭7 |
| 11 | ♭5 |
| ♭7 | 11 |
| ♭5 | ♭13 |

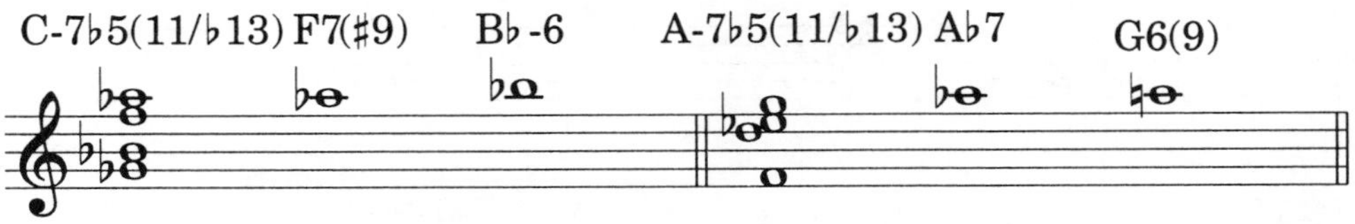


**{♭3 ♭7 11 ♭13}** C-7♭5(11/♭13) = B♭7(sus4)

Avoiding the potential ♭9th interval that could result by placing tension 11on the 5th string leaves three applicable inversions:

| | | |
|---|---|---|
| 11 | ♭7 | ♭3 |
| ♭7 | 11 | ♭13 |
| ♭13 | ♭3 | 11 |
| ♭3 | ♭13 | ♭7 |

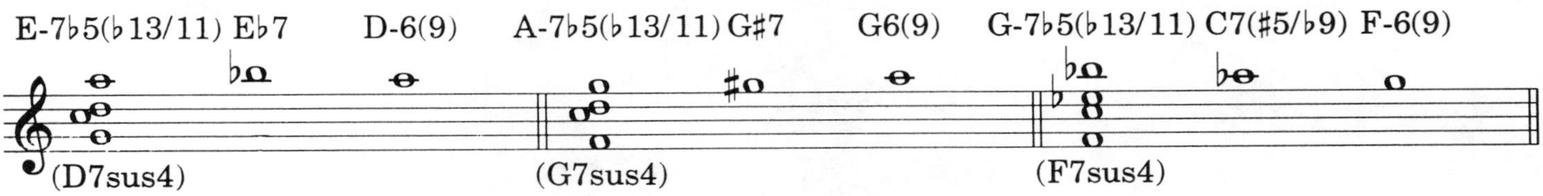

The following eight-measure example will use various chords containing tensions 11 and 13. Additional chords from past chapters are also used to enhance voice-leading.

The C7 (♯11/♭13) chord is yet another way to notate this voicing, which was originally introduced as a C+7 (♯11) or C7(alt5) chord and later as a C7♭5(♭13) chord. As mentioned earlier, this notation (♭13/♯11) in the same symbol has various and confusing implications. While still recommending its avoidance, it is included here for demonstrative purposes.

Also note the additional chordal substitution for a dom9(no 5) chord {1 3 ♭7 9} at the end of this exercise: C(♯11/9) = D9.

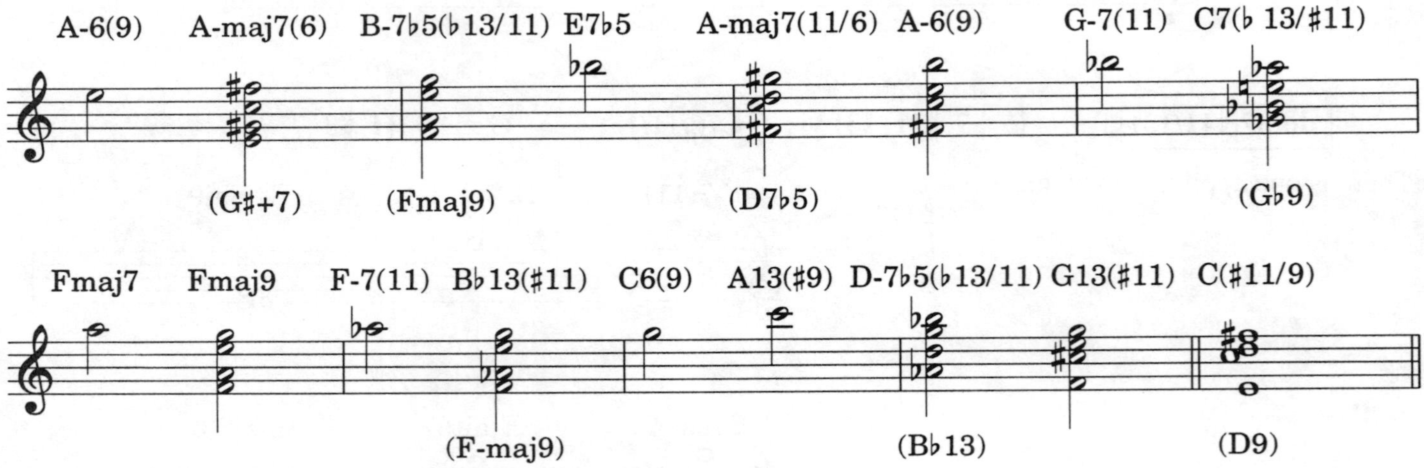


This next II-V blues example uses various chords from the past tension chapters. Also included are a couple of new functions in the second measure: G-maj9 {1 ♭3 7 9} = E-7♭5(11/9) and G-9 [1 ♭3 ♭7 9} = A7(♭9/♭13).

This example incorporates chromatic voice-leading to a greater degree than previous examples. Note the voice-leading motif in measures five and six is repeated in measures nine and ten and inverted in measures seven and eight. Also note the contrary chromatic voices in the last two measures.

# Chapter Eleven.
## Voice-Leading Chord Scales

Upon completion of <u>single</u> tension additions to the basic four-part chords, it is possible to voice-lead any note from any chord scale.

| | | | | | | |
|---|---|---|---|---|---|---|
| 1 | 2 | 3 | 4 | 5 | 6 | 7 |
| | (9) | | (11) | | (13) | |

The addition of two tensions often eases the physical difficulty (fingering) that some of the single tension voicings produce. Examples:

| **maj7(6)** | to | **maj7(9/6)** |
|---|---|---|
| 6 | | 6 |
| 1 | | 9 |
| 7 | | 7 |
| 3 | | 3 |

| **dom7(♯9)** | to | **dom7(♯9/♯5)** |
|---|---|---|
| ♯9 | | ♯9 |
| 5 | | ♯5 (♭13) |
| 3 | | 3 |
| ♭7 | | ♭7 |

The following are examples of harmonized chord scales. The "avoid notes" can be harmonized by standard *dominant*, *chromatic*, or *diatonic* approach techniques. These avoid notes are based on *traditional* jazz harmonic concepts and might be available in today's more contemporary music where an increased dissonance level is more accepted. These notes are in fact the more desired notes in *modal* music.

**maj7**

| | | | | | | | |
|---|---|---|---|---|---|---|---|
| (Ionian) | 5 | 6 | 7 | 1 | 9 | 3 | (11 is an avoid note) |
| (Gmaj7) | Gmaj9 | Gmaj7(9/6) | Gmaj7 | G6 | Gmaj9 | Gmaj7 | |

| | | | | | | | |
|---|---|---|---|---|---|---|---|
| (Lydian) | 5 | 6 | 7 | 1 | 9 | 3 | ♯11 |
| (Gmaj7) | Gmaj9 | G6 | Gmaj7♭5 | G6♭5 | Gmaj7(9/6) | Gmaj7♭5 | Gmaj9♭5 |

**min7**

| | | | | | | |
|---|---|---|---|---|---|---|
| (Dorian or Aeolian) (13 and ♭13 are avoid notes) | 5 | ♭7 | 1 | 9 | ♭3 | 11 |
| (G-7) | G-9 | G-7 | G-7 | G-9 | G-7(11) | G-7(11/9) |

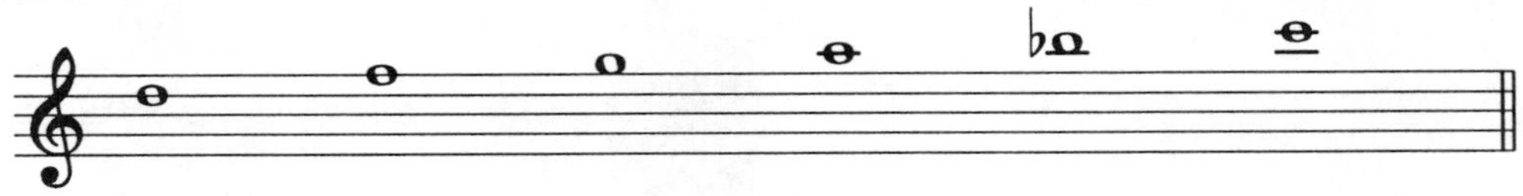

**min7♭5**

| | | | | | | | |
|---|---|---|---|---|---|---|---|
| (Locrian) | ♭5 | ♭13 | ♭7 | 1 | | ♭3 | 11 |
| (♭9 is an avoid note) | | | | | | | |
| (Locrian with natual 9) | ♭5 | ♭13 | ♭7 | 1 | 9 | ♭3 | 11 |
| (A-7♭5) | A-7♭5 | A-7♭5(♭13) | A-7♭5(11) | A-7♭5 | A-7♭5(9) | A-7♭5 | A-7♭5(11) |

*With the exception of the voicing containing the 9th, these voicings work in a pure Locrian situation as well.

**dom7**

| | | | | | | |
|---|---|---|---|---|---|---|
| (Mixolydian) | 5 | 13 | ♭7 | 1 | 9 | 3 (11 is an avoid note) |
| (G7) | G9 | G7(13/9) | G9 | G13 | G9 | G7 |

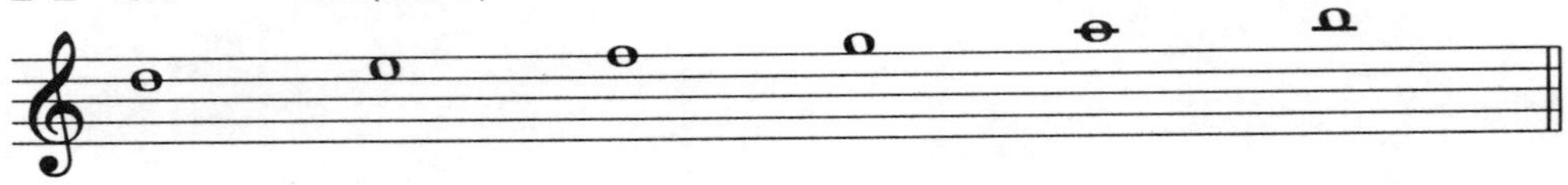

| | | | | | | | |
|---|---|---|---|---|---|---|---|
| (Lydian ♭7) | 5 | 13 | ♭7 | 1 | 9 | 3 | ♯11 |
| (G7) | G9 | G9(13) | G9♭5 | G13 | G9(13) | G7♭5 | G9♭5 |

(Mix. ♭9/♭13) (with addition of ♯9) (11 is an avoid note)

| | | | | | | | |
|---|---|---|---|---|---|---|---|
| | 5 | ♭13 | ♭7 | 1 | ♭9 | ♯9 | 3 |
| (G7) | G7(♭9) | G7(♯9/♯5) | G7(♭9) | G7♯5 | G7(♭9) | G7(♯9/♯5) | G7(♭9) |

| | | | | | | | |
|---|---|---|---|---|---|---|---|
| (altered) | ♭5 | ♯5 | ♭7 | 1 | ♭9 | ♯9 | 3 |
| (G7) | G7♭5(♯9) | G7♯5(♭9) | G+7 | G+7 | G7♭5(♭9) | G7♯5(♯9) | G+7 |

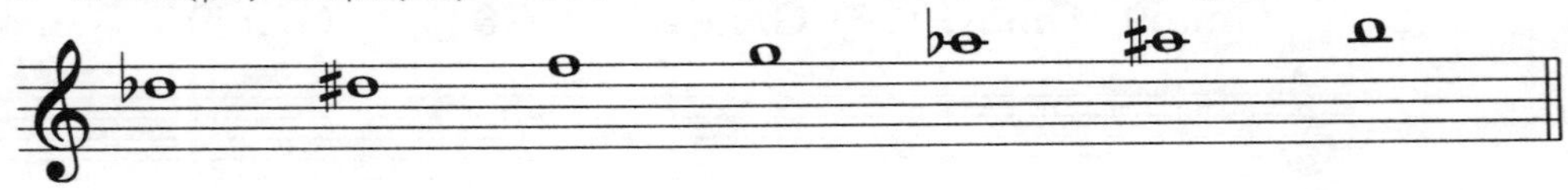

| | | | | | | |
|---|---|---|---|---|---|---|
| (whole-tone) | ♭5(♯11) | ♯5(♭13) | ♭7 | 1 | 9 | 3 |
| (G7) | G9♭5 | G9♯5 | G+7 | G+7 | G9♯5 | G7♭5 |

| | | | | | | | | |
|---|---|---|---|---|---|---|---|---|
| (dominant-diminished) | 5 | 13 | ♭7 | 1 | ♭9 | ♯9 | 3 | ♯11 |
| (G7) | G7(♯9) | G13(♯9) | G7(♭9) | G13 | G7(♭9) | G13(♯9) | G7♭5 | G7♭5(♯9) |

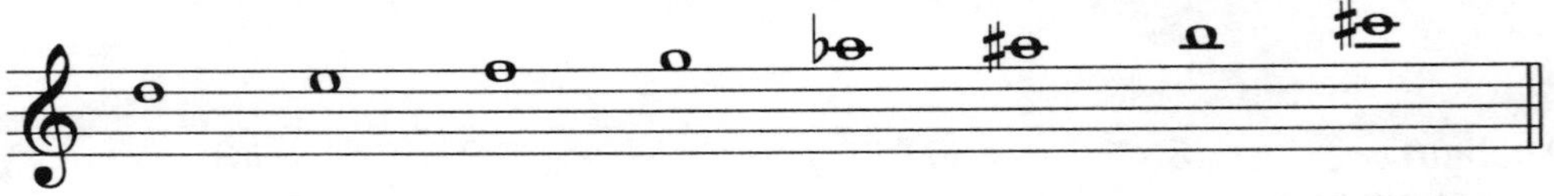

# Chapter Twelve.
## Three Tensions (9/11/13)

The past tension substitution formulas become inappropriate when dealing with three tensions on a four-note voicing. The approach used here will involve determining the most appropriate guide-tone or chord tone to accompany the three tensions. All of the three tension combinations presented in this chapter form complete triads:

| | | | | |
|---|---|---|---|---|
| 9 | ♯11 | 13 | — | major triad |
| 9 | 11 | 13 | — | minor triad |
| 9 | 11 | ♭13 | — | diminished triad |
| ♭9 | ♯11 | 13 | — | minor triad |
| ♯9 | ♯11 | 13 | — | diminished triad |

When these triads occur on the top three voices, they produce upper-structure triads over the basic or original chord.

As discussed earlier, ♯11 and ♭13 will be avoided in the same chord symbol. The following three-tension combinations (which do not produce basic triads) are enharmonically examined in the Tensions 9 and 13 chapter:

| | | |
|---|---|---|
| dom7(♭13/♯11/9) | = | dom7♭5(♭13/9) |
| dom7(♭13/♯11/♭9) | = | dom7♭5(♭13/♭9) |
| dom7(♭13/♯11/♯9) | = | dom7♭5(♭13/♯9) |

With the exception of the dom7(13/♯11/♭9) {1 ♭9 ♯11 13} and the dom7(13/♯11/♯9) {♭7 ♯9 ♯11 13} chords, all voicings have been previously introduced.

C7(13/♯11/♭9) {1 ♭9 ♯11 13 } = E♭7(13/♯11/♯9) { ♭7 ♯9 ♯11 13}

**maj7(9/♯11/13)**

The only characteristic voicing would have to contain the 7th {7 9 ♯11 13}. The {3 9 ♯11 13} and {5 9 ♯11 13} voicings have been previously introduced as maj6(9/♯11) chord voicings under the **Tensions 9 and 11** chapter. The remaining {1 9 ♯11 13} voicing, though incomplete, will be examined. Keep in mind that this voicing, lacking a 7th, could function as an incomplete dom7(9/♯11/13) chord as well.

Note the major triad formed by tensions 9, ♯11, and 13; Cmaj7(9/♯11/13) - tensions form a D major triad

**{7 9 ♯11 13}** Cmaj7(9/♯11/13) = B-7 / D6

Avoiding tension 9 on the 5th string leaves three applicable inversions:

| | | |
|---|---|---|
| 9 | 13 | 7 |
| 13 | 9 | ♯11 |
| ♯11 | 7 | 9 |
| 7 | ♯11 | 13 |

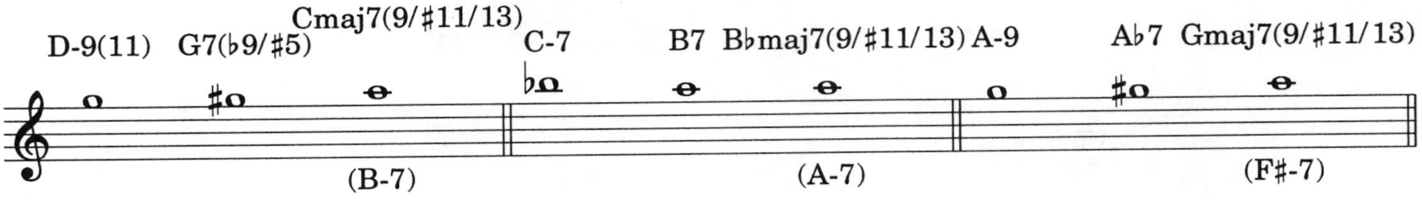

**{1 9 ♯11 13}** C(9/♯11/13) = D7

Avoiding tension 9 on the 5th string leaves three applicable inversions:

| | | |
|---|---|---|
| 9 | 13 | 1 |
| 13 | 9 | ♯11 |
| ♯11 | 1 | 9 |
| 1 | ♯11 | 13 |

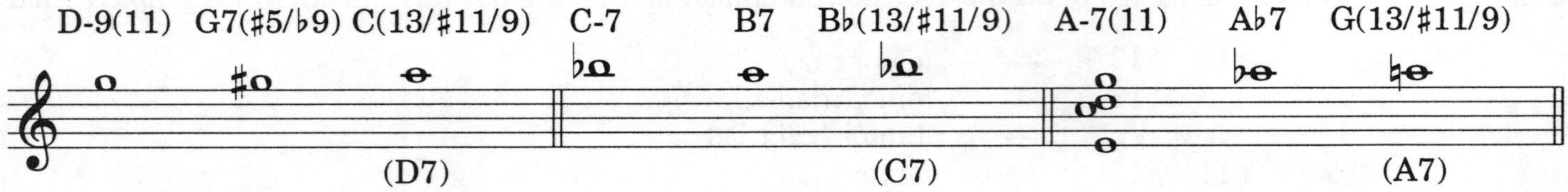


*These voicings will reappear in a dominant function under dom7(9/♯11/13).

**min.maj7(9/11/13)**

The most characteristic voicing contains the 7th {7 9 11 13}, yet it produces one of the more ambiguous sounds because these notes also form the V9 chord of the original minor chord. This dual (tonic/dominant) function can be a very confusing sound and should be used with care.

The {♭3 9 11 13} voicing (perhaps the best voicing using these three tensions} has been previously introduced as a min6(9/11) chord under the **Tensions 9 and 11** chapter. The {5 9 11 13} voicing was also introduced in that chapter as a min6(9/11) chord.

Note the minor triad formed by tensions 9, 11, and 13: C-maj7(9/11/13) – tensions form a D minor triad

Also note that those voicings not containing the 7th could have a ♭7th (modal dorian sound).

**{7 9 11 13}** C-maj7(9/11/13) = B-7♭5 / G9

Avoiding tension 9 on the 5th string leaves three applicable inversions:

| | | |
|---|---|---|
| 9 | 13 | 7 |
| 13 | 9 | 11 |
| 11 | 7 | 9 |
| 7 | 11 | 13 |

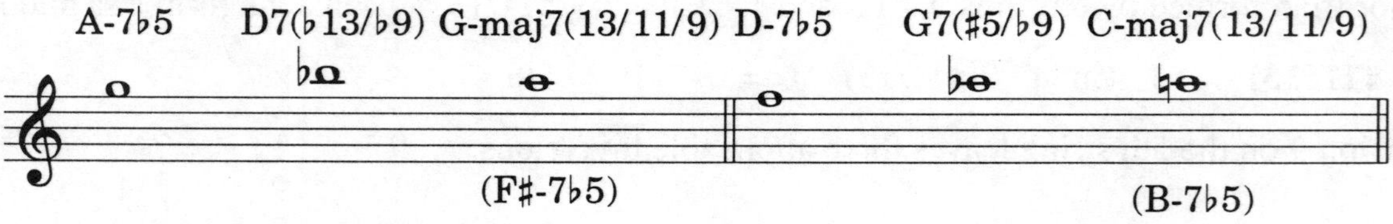


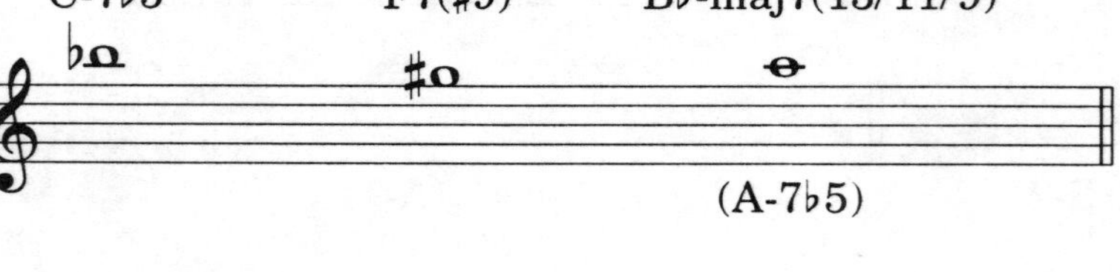

**{1 9 11 13}** C-maj7(9/11/13) = D-7

*Note that this voicing also could function as a dom7sus4(9/13) chord.

Avoiding tension 9 on the 5th string leaves three applicable inversions:

| | | |
|---|---|---|
| 9 | 13 | 1 |
| 13 | 9 | 11 |
| 11 | 1 | 9 |
| 1 | 11 | 13 |

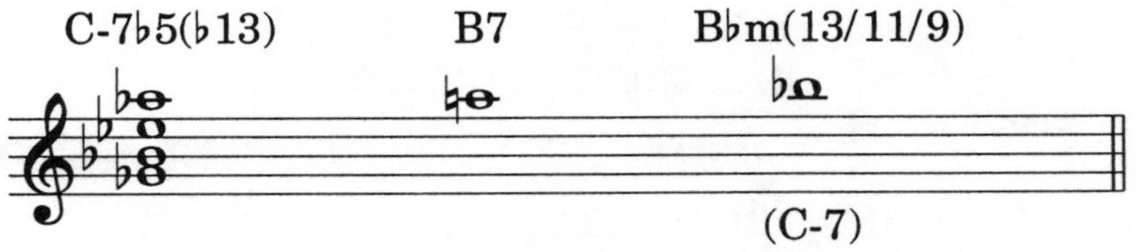


**min7♭5(9/11/♭13)**

The only characteristic voicing would contain the ♭5th {♭5 9 11 ♭13}. The remaining voicings will be examined, although less complete and producing some very ambiguous, if not weak, sounds. The tritone produced by tension 9 and ♭13 is partly responsible for this ambiguous sound.

Note that tensions 9, 11, and ♭13 produce a diminished triad; C-7♭5(9/11/♭13) – tensions form a D° triad

The two inversions containing 9 or 11 on the 5th string will be avoided.

**{♭5 9 11 ♭13}** C-7♭5(9/11/♭13) = A♭13(♭5)

There are two applicable inversions:

| | |
|---|---|
| ♭13 | 9 |
| 11 | ♭5 |
| 9 | 11 |
| ♭5 | ♭13 |

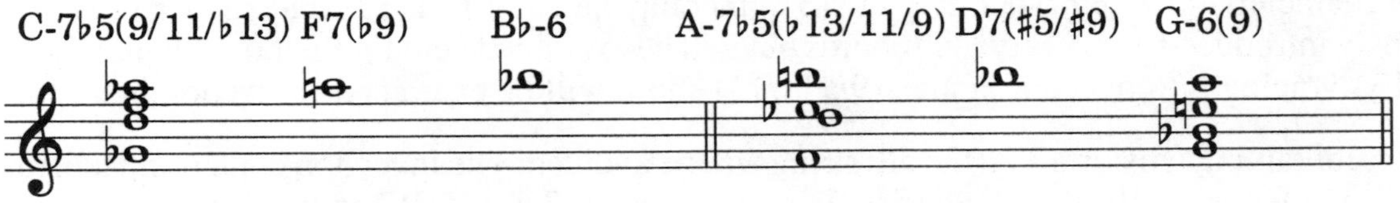

**{♭7 9 11 ♭13}** C-7♭5(9/11/♭13) = B♭7

There are two applicable inversions:

| | |
|---|---|
| 9 | ♭7 |
| ♭13 | 11 |
| 11 | 9 |
| ♭7 | ♭13 |

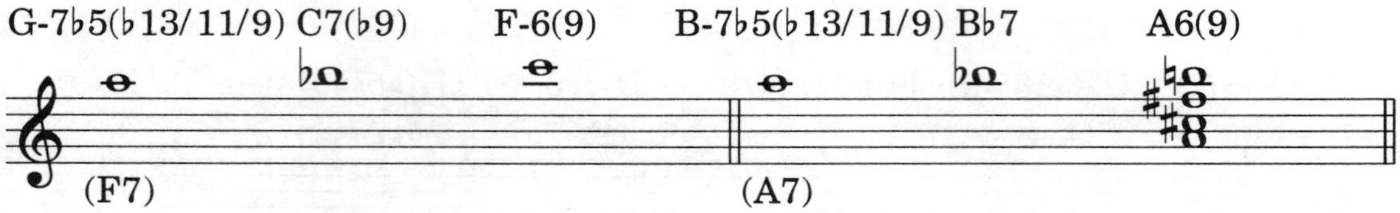


**{♭3 9 11 ♭13}** C-7♭5(9/11/♭13) = A♭6 (♯11) (1 5 6 ♯11)

There is one applicable inversion:

11
9
♭13
♭3

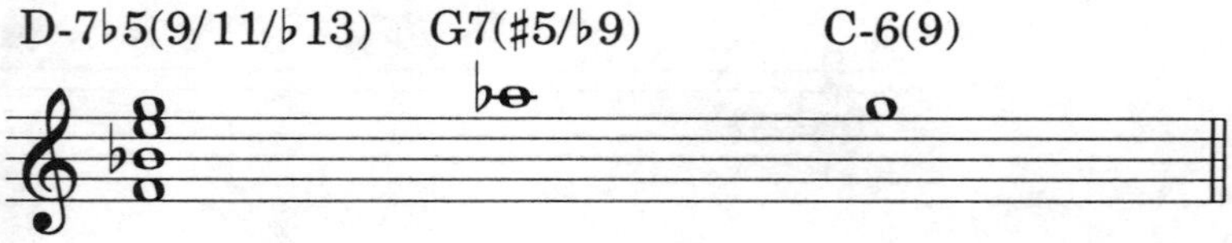


**{1 9 11 ♭13}** C-7♭5(9/11/♭13) = D-7♭5 / F-6

There are two applicable inversions:

| | |
|---|---|
| 9 | 1 |
| ♭13 | 11 |
| 11 | 9 |
| 1 | ♭13 |

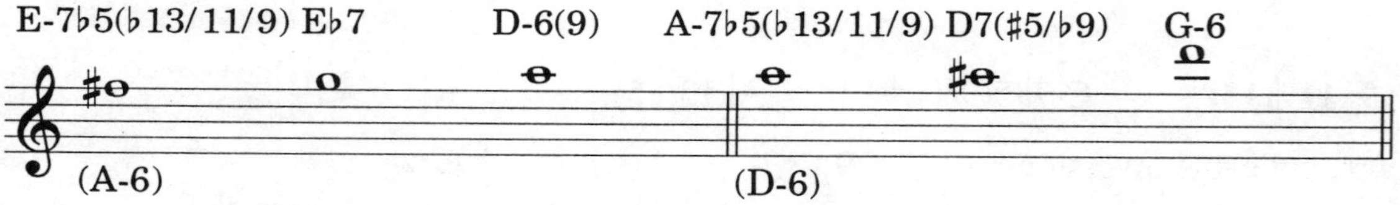


**dom7(9/♯11/13)**

There is one characteristic voicing {♭7 9 ♯11 13}. Incomplete {3 9 ♯11 13} and {5 9 ♯11 13} voicings have been previously introduced as maj6(9/♯11) chords but will be examined here for their dominant functions. Also, the {1 9 ♯11 13} voicing introduced as a maj7(9/♯11/13) chord will be examined for its dominant function.

The inversion containing tension 13 on the 5th string will be avoided. The inversion containing tension 9 on the 5th string will be avoided when the dom7 chord is functioning as a V7 chord. When the dom7 chord is functioning as a Sub V chord, the 9 on the 5th string will be allowed, since it is really functioning as a ♯5th on the V7 chord: (the 9th of G7 is the ♯5 of D♭7)

*Keep in mind that tensions 9, ♯11, and 13 on a dominant chord are most characteristic in a Sub V function.

Note the major triad formed by tensions 9, ♯11, and 13: C7(9/♯11/13) – tensions form a D major triad.

**{♭7 9 ♯11 13}** C7(9/♯11/13) = B♭maj7♯5

There are three applicable inversions:

| | | |
|---|---|---|
| ♯11 | 9 | 13 |
| ♭7 | 13 | 9 |
| 13 | ♯11 | ♭7 |
| 9 | ♭7 | ♯11 |

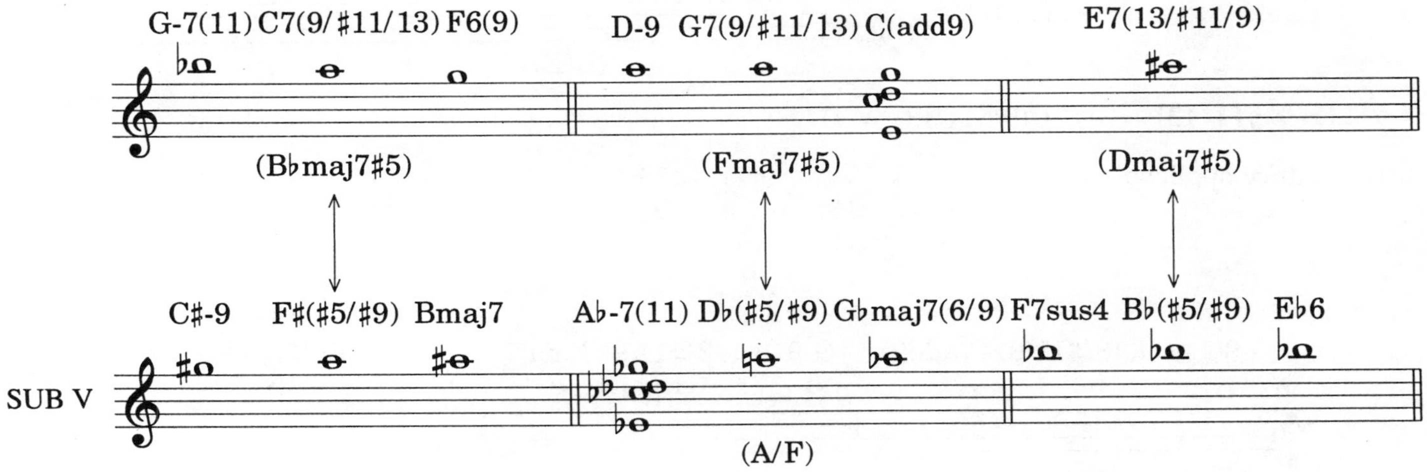


**{3 9 ♯11 13}** C(9/♯11/13) = F♯-7♯5 / C6(9/♯11)

There are three applicable inversions:

| | | |
|---|---|---|
| 3 | ♯11 | 13 |
| 13 | 9 | 3 |
| ♯11 | 13 | 9 |
| 9 | 3 | ♯11 |

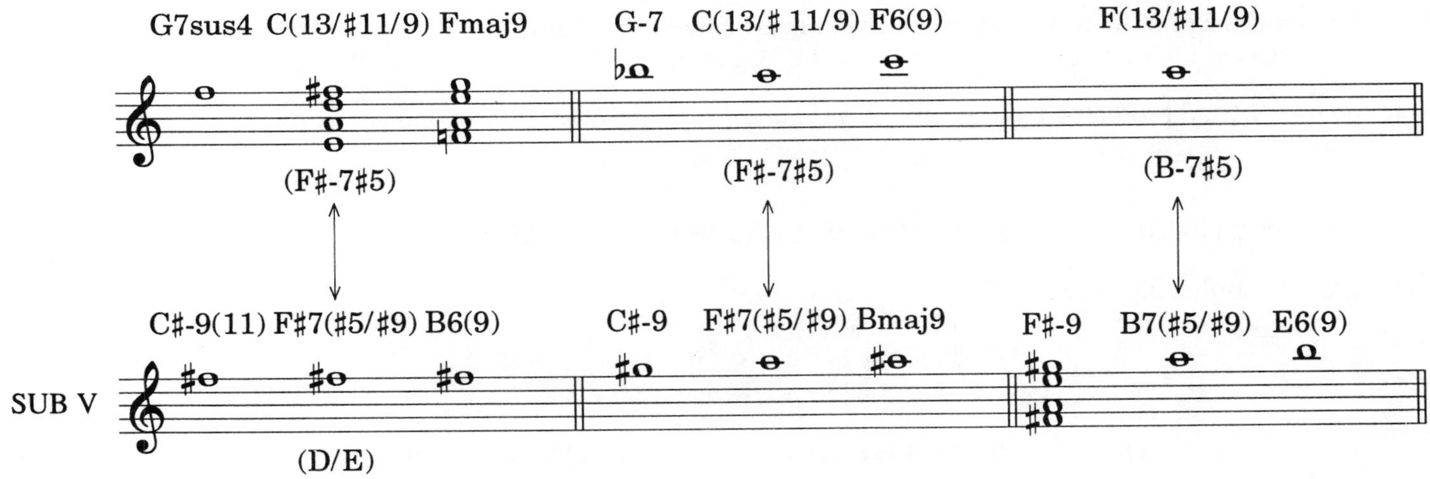

**{5 9 ♯11 13}**  C(9/♯11/13) = A13(sus4) / C6(9/♯11)

There is one applicable inversion:

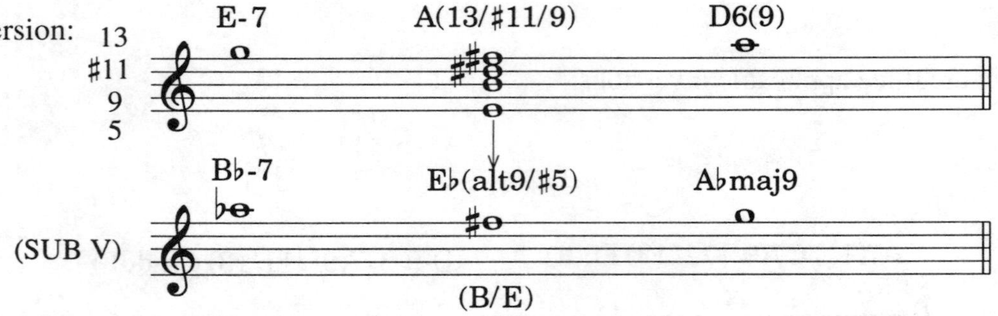


**{1 9 ♯11 13}**  C(9/♯11/13) = D7

There are three applicable inversions:

| | | |
|---|---|---|
| 9 | ♯11 | 13 |
| 13 | 1 | 9 |
| ♯11 | 13 | 1 |
| 1 | 9 | ♯11 |

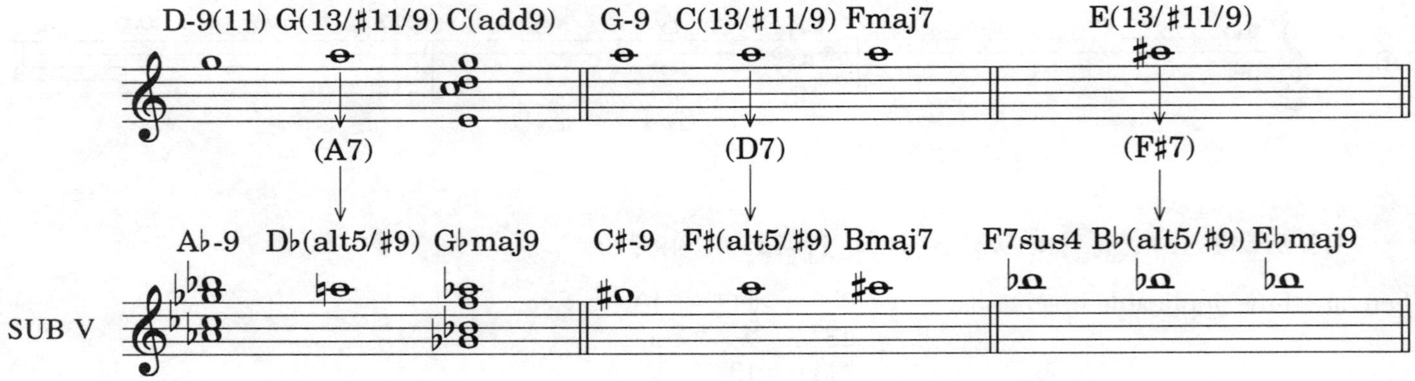


**dom7(♭9/♯11/13)**

The ♭9th dictates a dominant type chord allowing it to be the most characteristic note. This means the guide-tones will not be missed in voicings not containing them. Again, tension 13 will be avoided on the 5th string.

Note the minor triad produced by tensions ♭9, ♯11, and 13: C7(♭9/♯11/13) – tensions form an F♯ minor triad.

**{♭7 ♭9 ♯11 13}**  C7(♭9/♯11/13) = E♭7(♯9/♯11) {5 ♭7 ♯9 ♯11}

There are two applicable inversions:

| | |
|---|---|
| ♭9 | 13 |
| 13 | ♭9 |
| ♯11 | ♭7 |
| ♭7 | ♯11 |

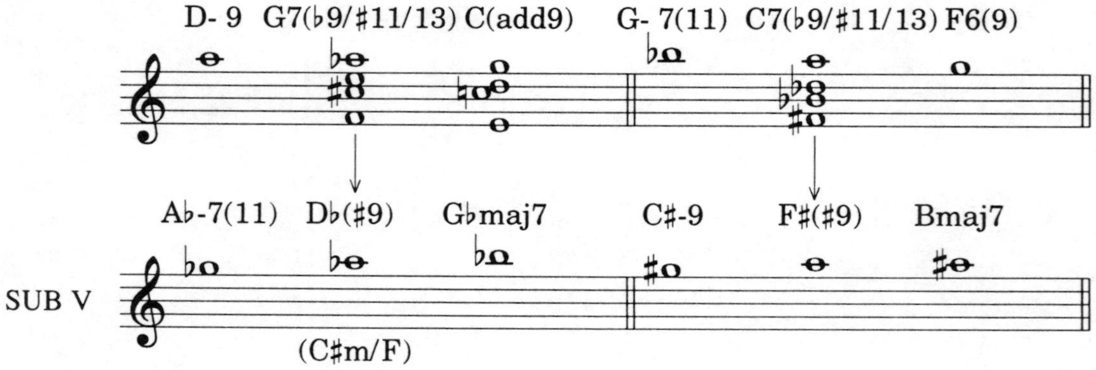

**{3 ♭9 ♯11 13}** C7(♭9/♯11/13) = F♯-7

Note that the Sub V chord forms a complete min7 chord, and when used in its related V7 situation, it has the ambiguous function of an incomplete V7(♯9) or V-7 chord.

There are three applicable inversions:

| | | |
|---|---|---|
| 3 | ♯11 | 13 |
| 13 | ♭9 | 3 |
| ♯11 | 13 | ♭9 |
| ♭9 | 3 | ♯11 |

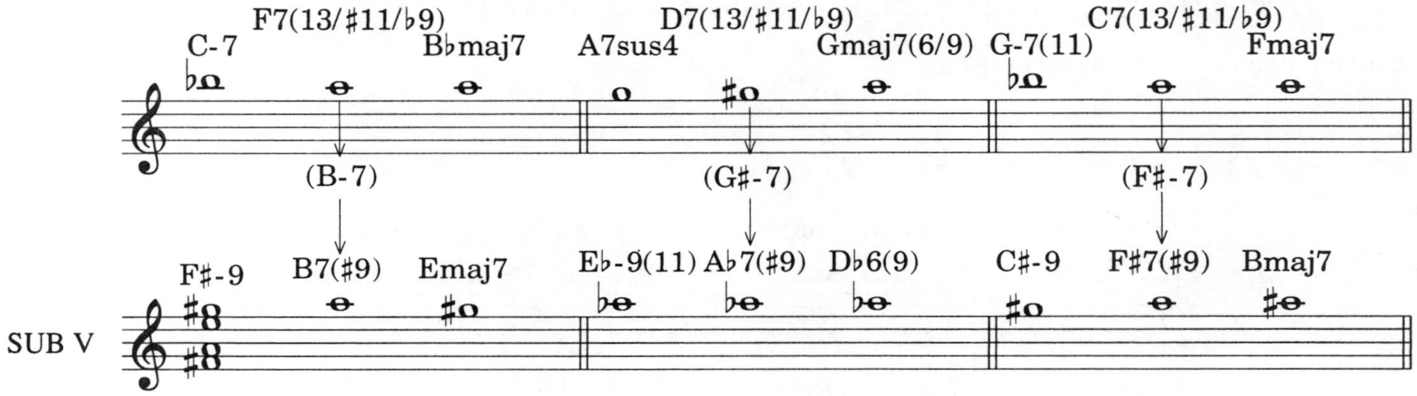


**{5 ♭9 ♯11 13}** C7(♭9/♯11/13) = A13 / E♭7♭5(♯9)

There is one applicable inversion:

13
♯11
♭9
5

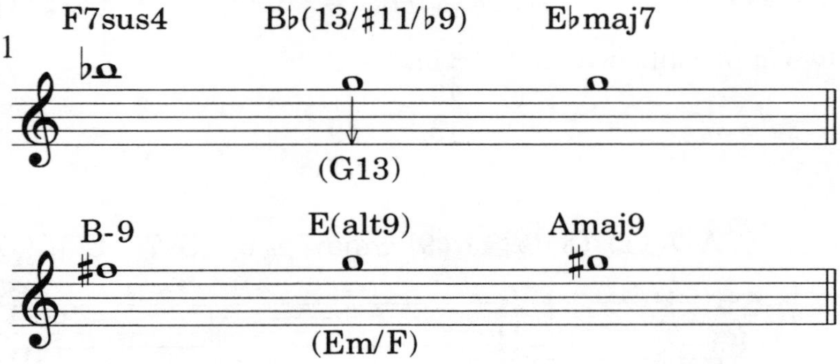


(SUB V)

**{1 ♭9 ♯11 13}** C(♭9/♯11/13) = E♭7(♯9/♯11/13) {♭7 ♯9 ♯11 13}

There are two applicable inversions:

| | |
|---|---|
| ♯11 | 13 |
| 1 | ♭9 |
| 13 | 1 |
| ♭9 | ♯11 |

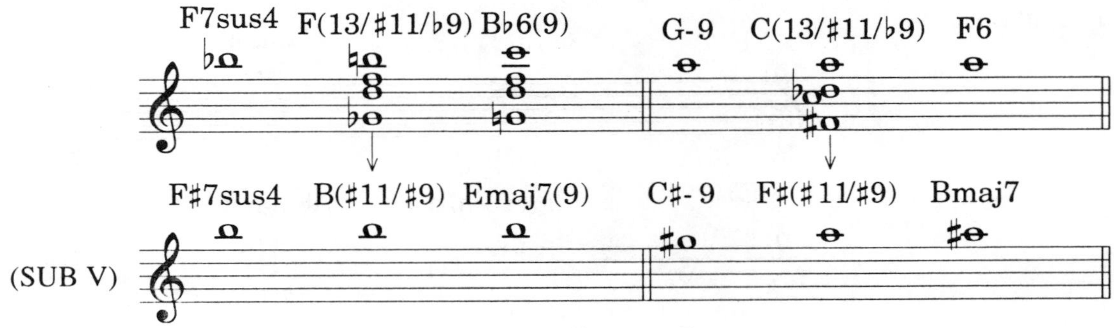

**dom7(♯9/♯11/13)**

The {1 ♯9 ♯11 13} voicing will be omitted due to the rather ambiguous sound produced by the complete dim7 chord formed: {1 ♯9 ♯11 13} = {1 ♭3 ♭5 ♭♭7}.

Those voicings that contain tension 13 or ♯9 on the 5th string will be omitted.

Note the diminished triad produced by tensions ♯9, ♯11, and 13: C7(♯9/♯11/13) - tensions form an E♭° triad.

**{♭7 ♯9 ♯11 13}** C7(♯9/♯11/13) = A7(♭9/♯11/13) {1 ♭9 ♯11 13}

There are two applicable inversions:

| | |
|---|---|
| ♯9 | 13 |
| 13 | ♯9 |
| ♯11 | ♭7 |
| ♭7 | ♯11 |

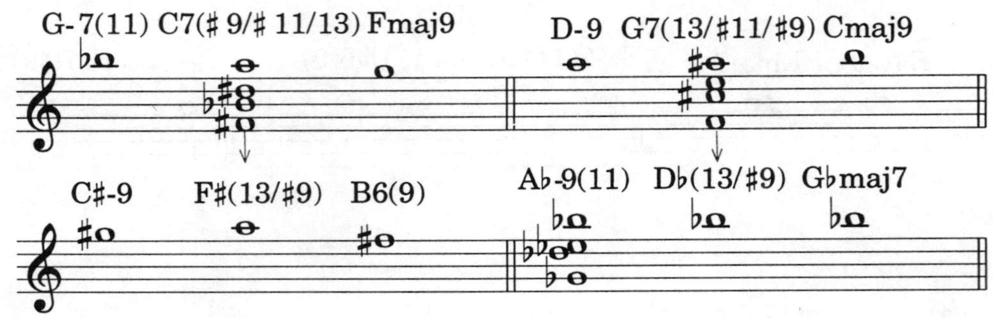


**{3 ♯9 ♯11 13}** C7(♯9/♯11/13) = A6(♯11) {1 5 6♯11}

There are two applicable inversions:

| | |
|---|---|
| ♯11 | 13 |
| ♯9 | 3 |
| 13 | ♯9 |
| 3 | ♯11 |

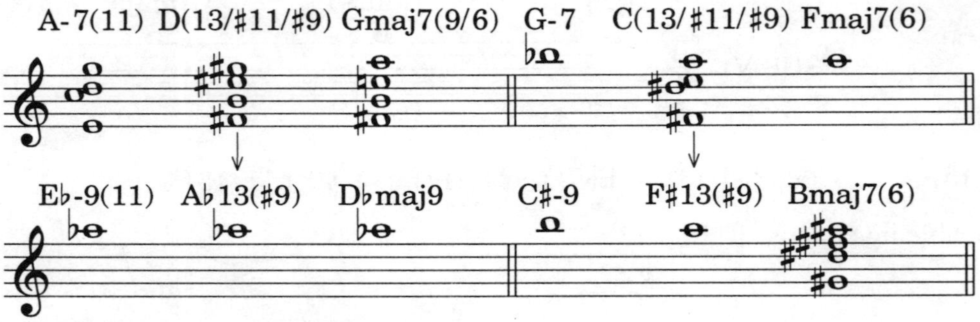


**{5 ♯9 ♯11 13}** C7(♯9/♯11/13) = A13♭5

There is one applicable inversion:

13
♯11
♯9
5

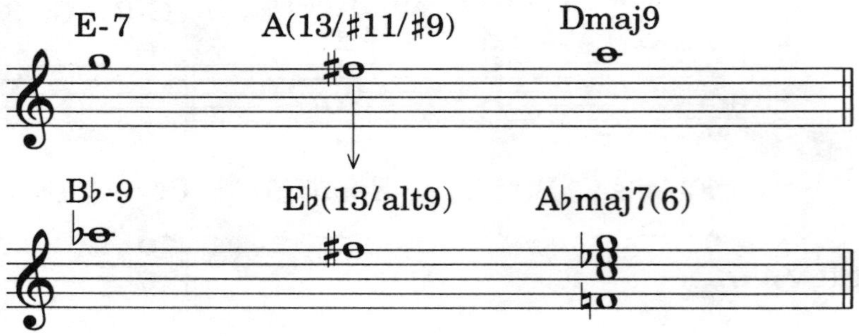

The following examples will use various chords containing tensions 9, 11, and 13. Additional chords from past chapters are also used to enhance voice-leading. Hybrid chords will be listed as they occur.

This first "II-V" blues example in the key of "F" contains some interesting chromatic voice-leading. In measure three, the top three voices contain contrary – chromatic motion while the bottom voice sustains. Measure four into measure five [F7(♭9/alt5) — B♭7(9/13)] contains a good example of contrary chromatic motion in all four voices; the top three voices ascend while the bottom voice descends. In measure eight to measure nine [D♭7(9/♯11/13) — Gm(add9)], the top three voices descend chromatically while the bottom voice sustains. In measure nine to measure ten, those same three voices again descend chromatically. Finally, note the chromatic constant structures produced by the last six chords.

*Note that the E-7♭5(9/11/♭13) voicing contains a major 7th width.

This next example also contains some interesting chromatic voice-leading as well as another chord voicing containing a major 7th width (F-9). In measure four to measure five [E♭7(♭9/alt5) — A♭6(9)], three voices descend chromatically while one middle voice ascends. In measure seven, again, three voices descend chromatically while one middle voice ascends. In measure seven to measure eight the top three voices contain minor triads which descend chromatically. Finally, note the same structures a whole step apart on the last two chords.

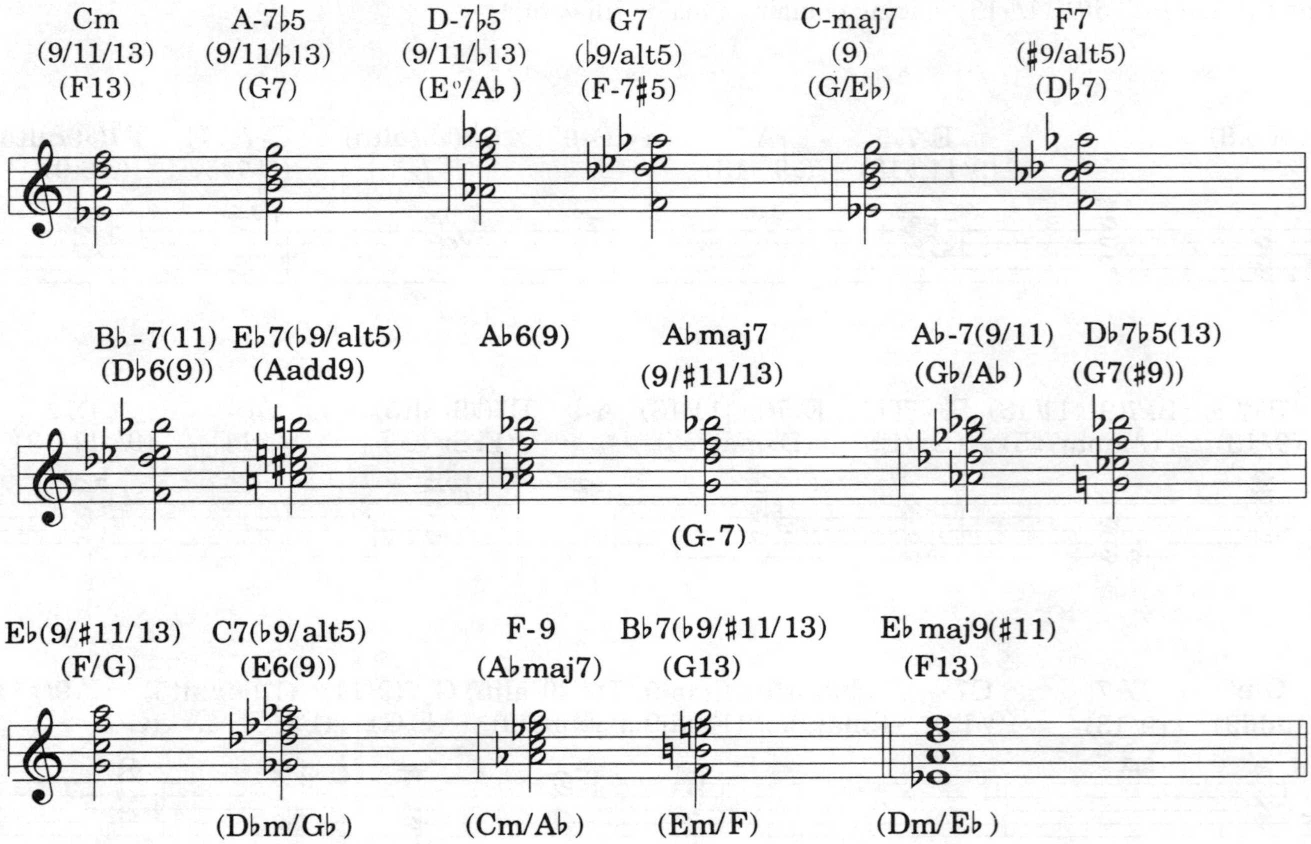

# Chapter Thirteen.
## Altered 9th Tensions (♭9 and ♯9) on Dom7 Chords

These dominant chords contain both tensions ♭9 and ♯9 in their voicings. Since tension ♭9 dictates the dom7 chord, voicings with and without the guide-tones will be examined. Some of the Sub V chords will produce very incomplete structures and should be used with care.

With the exception of the dom7(alt9/13) {3 ♭9 ♯9 13} chord, all of the voicings in this chapter have been previously introduced enharmonically. Those inversions placing tension ♯9 on the 5th string will be avoided. Those chords using tension 13 will avoid this tension on the 5th string as well.

### dom7(alt9)

The most characteristic voicing would include the guide-tones {3 ♭7 ♭9 ♯9}.

**{3 ♭7 ♭9 ♯9}** C7(alt9) = D♭-6(9) {1 ♭3 6 9}

There is one applicable inversion:

♯9
♭7
3
♭9

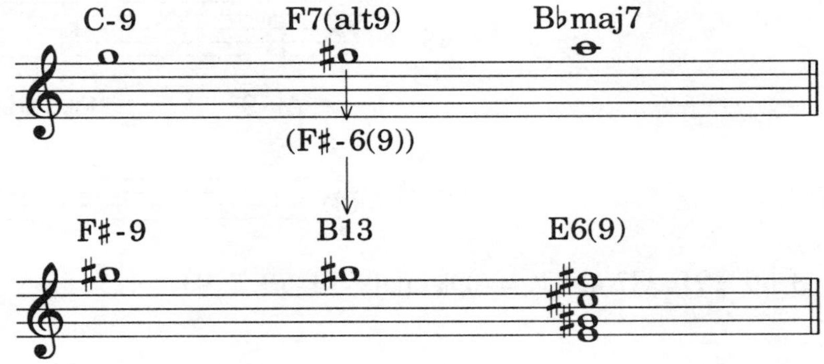


(Sub V)

**{1 ♭7 ♭9 ♯9}** C7(alt9) = G♭6(♯11) {3 5 6 ♯11}

There are two applicable inversions:

| | |
|---|---|
| ♯9 | ♭9 |
| 1 | 1 |
| ♭7 | ♯9 |
| ♭9 | ♭7 |

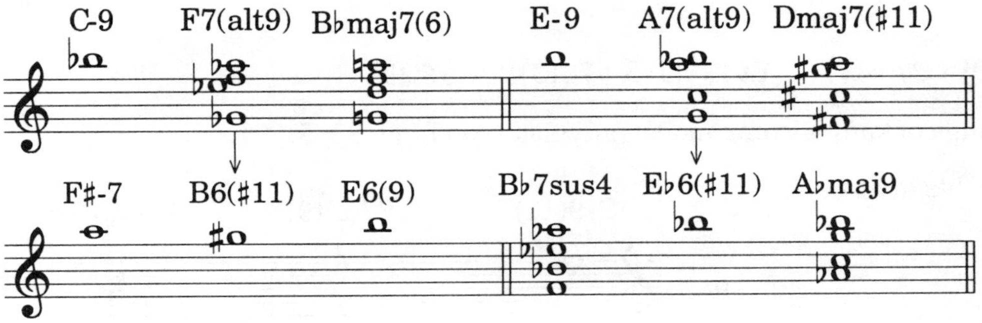


(Sub V)

**{5 ♭7 ♭9 ♯9}** C7(alt9) = E♭7

There are three applicable inversions:

| | | |
|---|---|---|
| ♯9 | ♭7 | ♭9 |
| ♭7 | ♯9 | 5 |
| 5 | ♭9 | ♯9 |
| ♭9 | 5 | ♭7 |

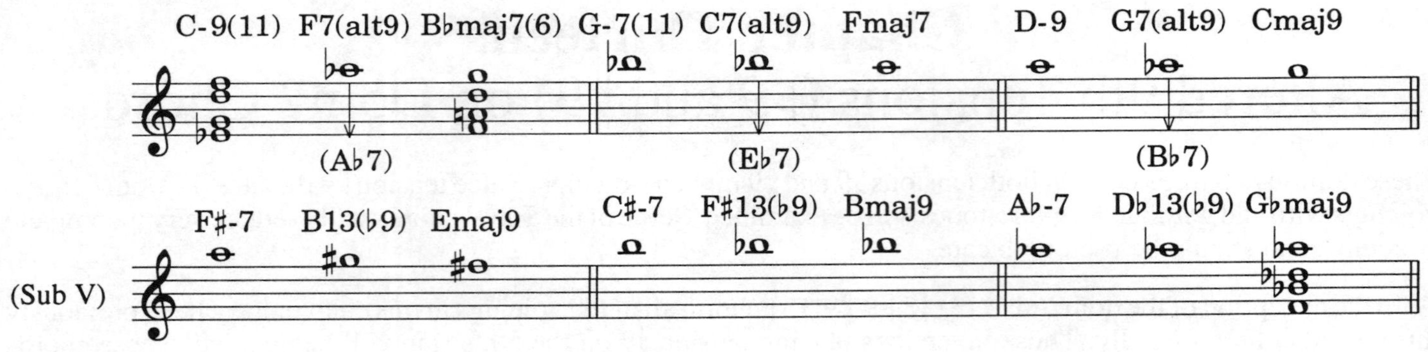


**{3 5 ♭9 ♯9}** C7(alt9) = E♭7(♭9) {1 3 ♭7 ♭9}

There is one applicable inversion:

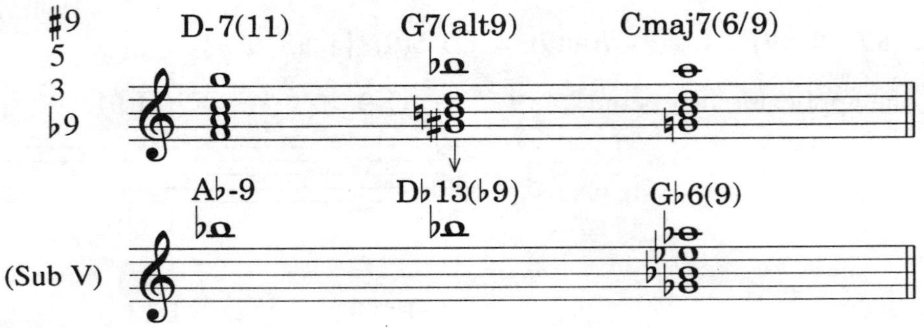


**{1 3 ♭9 ♯9}** C7(alt9) = D♭-maj9 {1 ♭3 7 9}

There is one applicable inversion:

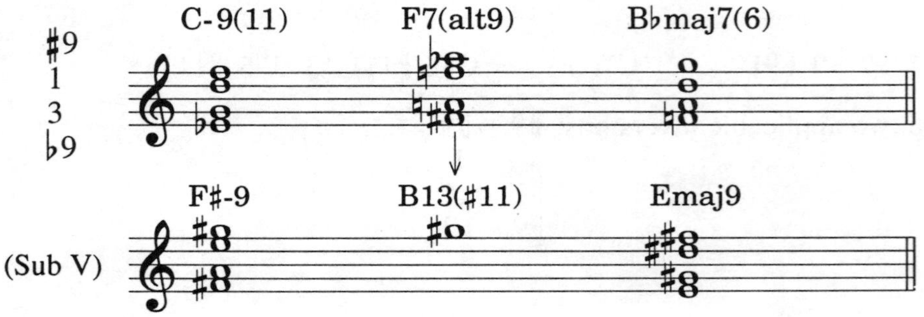


**{1 5 ♭9 ♯9}** C7(alt9) = E♭13 {1 3 ♭7 13} / A7♭5(♯9)

Note that this voicing contains a strong modal phrygian sound: {1 ♭3 5 ♭9}.

There is one applicable inversion:

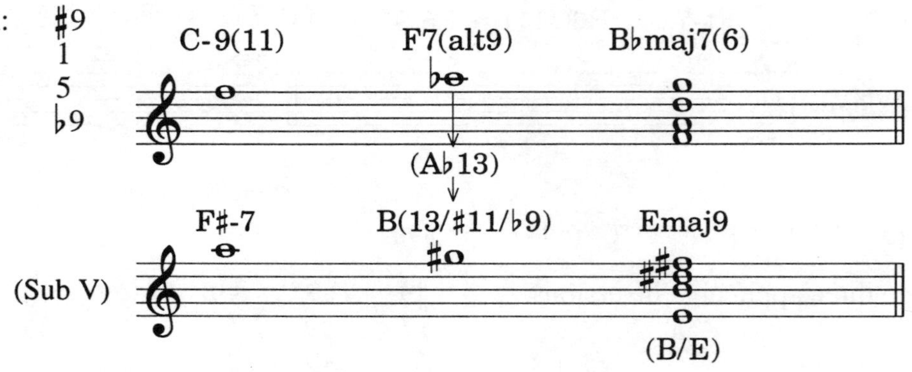

**dom7(alt9/♯11)**

**{♭7 ♭9 ♯9 ♯11}** C7(alt9/♯11) = E♭-7 / G♭6

There are three applicable inversions:

| | | |
|---|---|---|
| ♯9 | ♭7 | ♭9 |
| ♭7 | ♯9 | ♯11 |
| ♯11 | ♭9 | ♯9 |
| ♭9 | ♯11 | ♭7 |

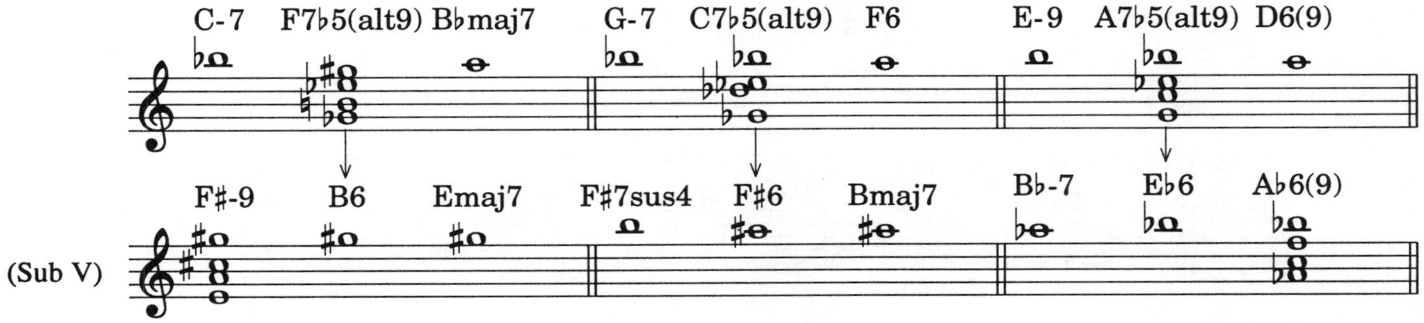


**{3 ♭9 ♯9 ♯11}** C7(alt9/♯11) = A6(♯11) {3 5 6 ♯11}

There are two applicable inversions:

| | |
|---|---|
| ♯11 | 3 |
| ♯9 | ♯9 |
| ♭9 | ♯11 |
| 3 | ♭9 |

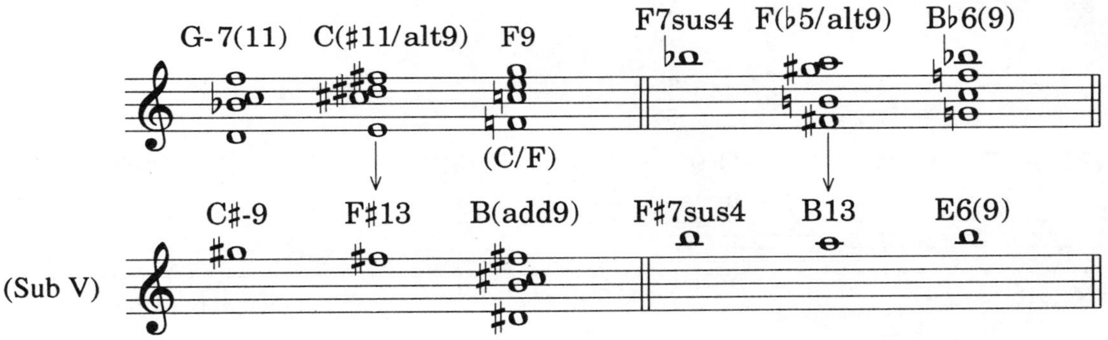


**{1 ♭9 ♯9 ♯11}** C7(alt9/♯11) = G♭6(♯11) {1 5 6 ♯11}

There is one applicable inversion:

♯9
1
♯11
♭9

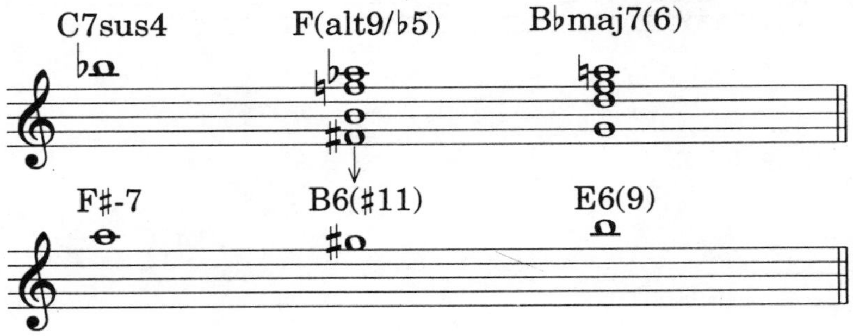


(Sub V)

**{5 ♭9 ♯9 ♯11}** C7(alt9/♯11) = E♭7(♯9) {1 3 ♭7 ♯9}

This voicing cannot be used, since the single available inversion has tension ♯9 on the 5th string.

**dom7(alt9/♭13)** [dom7♯5(alt9)]

**{3 ♭9 ♯9 ♭13}** C+7(alt9) = Amaj7(♯11) {3 5 7 ♯11}

There are three applicable inversions:

| | | |
|---|---|---|
| ♯9 | 3 | ♯5 |
| ♯5 | ♯9 | ♯9 |
| 3 | ♯5 | ♭9 |
| ♭9 | ♭9 | 3 |

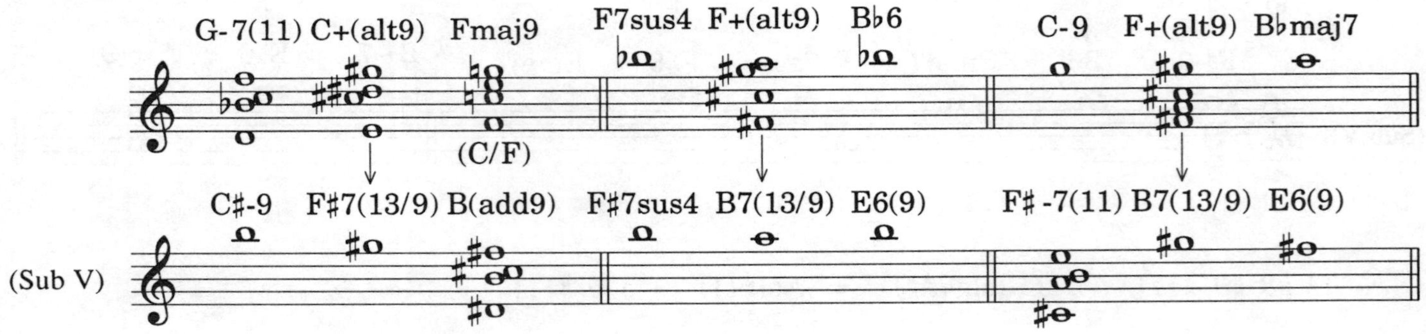


**{♭7 ♭9 ♯9 ♭13}** C+7(alt9) = E♭7sus4

There are three applicable inversions:

| | | |
|---|---|---|
| ♯9 | ♭7 | ♭9 |
| ♭7 | ♯9 | ♯5 |
| ♯5 | ♭9 | ♯9 |
| ♭9 | ♯5 | ♭7 |

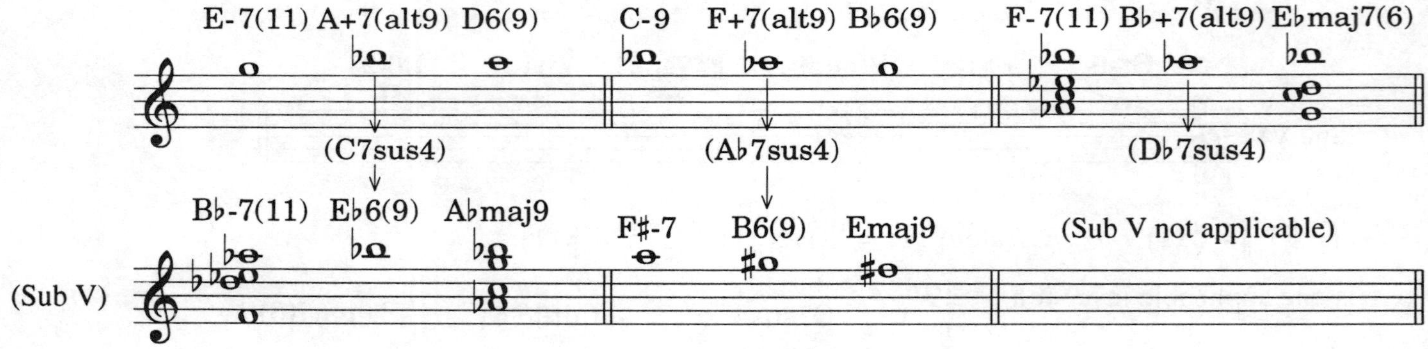

**{1 ♭9 ♯9 ♭13}** C7(alt9/♭13) = E♭13sus4

There is one applicable inversion: ♯9 1 ♭13 ♭9

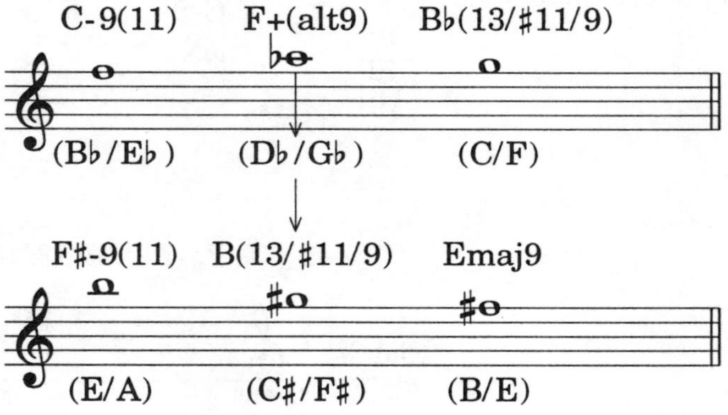


(SubV)

The {5 ♭9 ♯9 ♭13} voicing will be omitted, as was done in earlier chapters, due to the natural 5 and ♭13 it contains.

**dom7(alt9/13)**

{3 ♭9 ♯9 13}

There is one applicable inversion: ♯9 13 3 ♭9

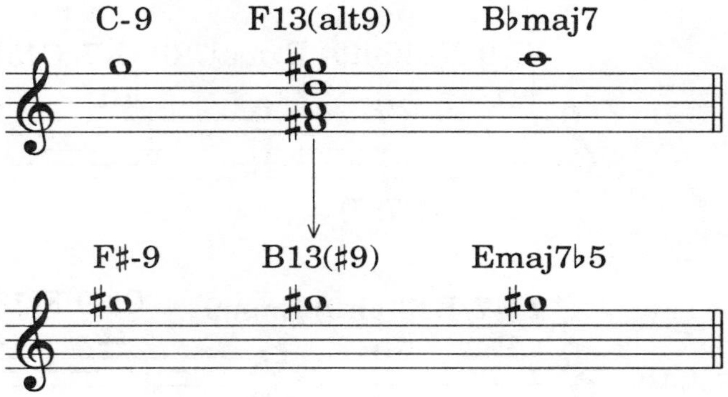


(SubV)

**{♭7 ♭9 ♯9 13}** C7(alt9/13) = E♭7(♯11) {1 5 ♭7 ♯11}

There is one applicable inversion: ♭9 13 ♯9 ♭7

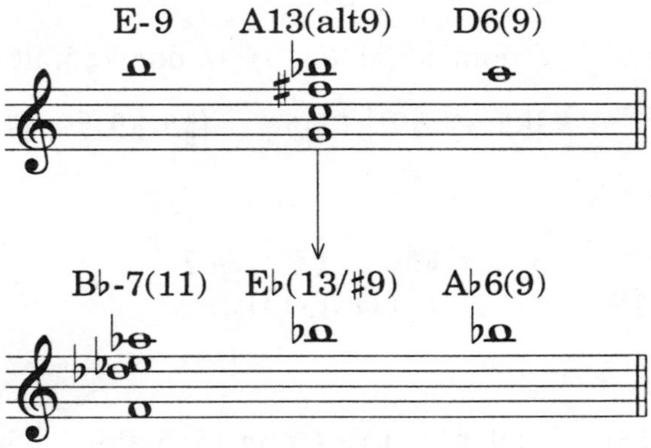


(Sub V)

**{1 ♭9 ♯9 13}** C13(alt9) = E♭13(♭5) {1 ♭5 ♭7 13}

There is one applicable inversion: ♯9 / 1 / 13 / ♭9

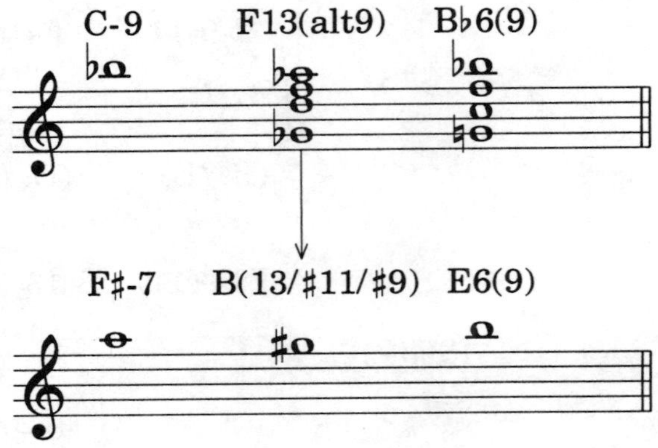


(Sub V)

**{5 ♭9 ♯9 13}** C13(alt9) = A7(♭5) / E♭7(♭5)

There are two applicable inversions:

| | |
|---|---|
| ♯9 | 13 |
| 13 | ♯9 |
| 5 | ♭9 |
| ♭9 | 5 |

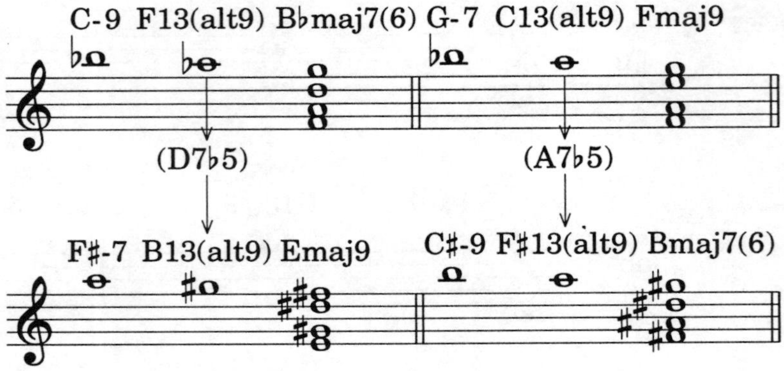


(Sub V)

The following dom7 chords have four tensions and no chord tones. These unique voicings imply specific chord scales and have several enharmonic spellings.

I. dom7(alt9/alt5) / dom7♭5(alt9/♭13) / dom7♯5(alt9/♯11) / dom7(♭9/♯9/♯11/♭13)

{♭5 ♯5 ♭9 ♯9} {♭5 ♭9 ♯9 ♭13} {♯5 ♭9 ♯9 ♯11}

These tensions imply the "altered" scale:

| | | | | | | |
|---|---|---|---|---|---|---|
| 1 | ♭2 | ♯2 | 3 | ♭5 | ♯5 | ♭7 |
| | (♭9) | (♯9) | | (♯11) | (♭13) | |

II. dom7(alt9/♯11/13) {♭9 ♯9 ♯11 13} / dom13♭5(alt9) {♭5 ♭9 ♯9 13}

These tensions imply the symmetrical "dominant diminished" scale:

| | | | | | | | |
|---|---|---|---|---|---|---|---|
| 1 | ♭2 | ♯2 | 3 | ♯4 | 5 | 6 | ♭7 |
| | (♭9) | (♯9) | | (♯11) | | (13) | |

**dom7(alt9/alt5)** C7(alt9/alt5) {♭9 ♯9 ♭5 ♯5} = A♭7sus4

There are three applicable inversions:

| | | |
|---|---|---|
| ♯9 | ♯5 | ♭9 |
| ♯5 | ♯9 | ♯11 |
| ♯11 | ♭9 | ♯9 |
| ♭9 | ♯11 | ♯5 |

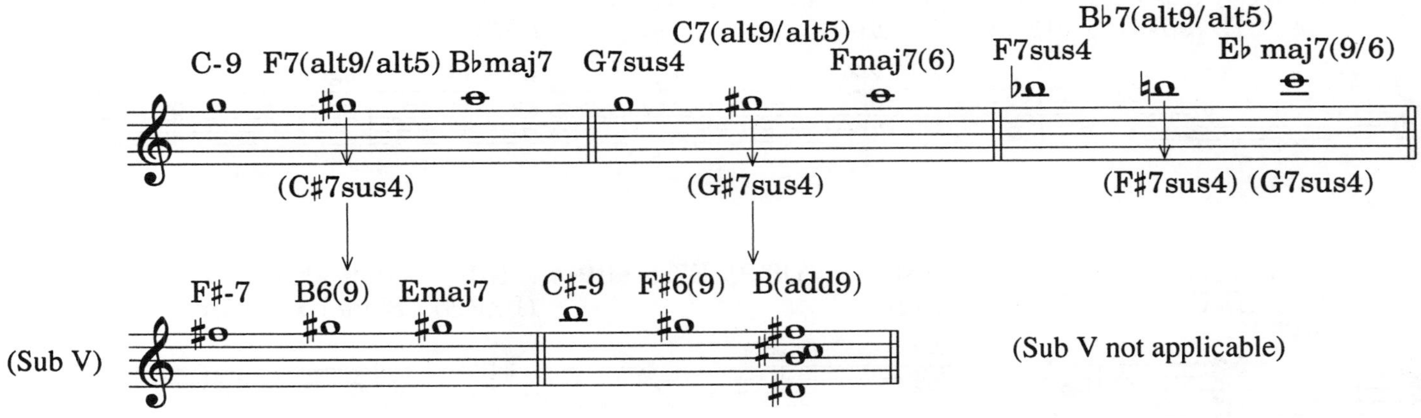


**dom7(alt9/♯11/13)** C13(♭5/alt9) {♭9 ♯9 ♯11 13} = E♭-7(♭5)

Avoiding inversions containing tensions ♯9 or 13 on the 5th string leaves two applicable inversions:

| | |
|---|---|
| ♯9 | 13 |
| 13 | ♯9 |
| ♯11 | ♭9 |
| ♭9 | ♯11 |

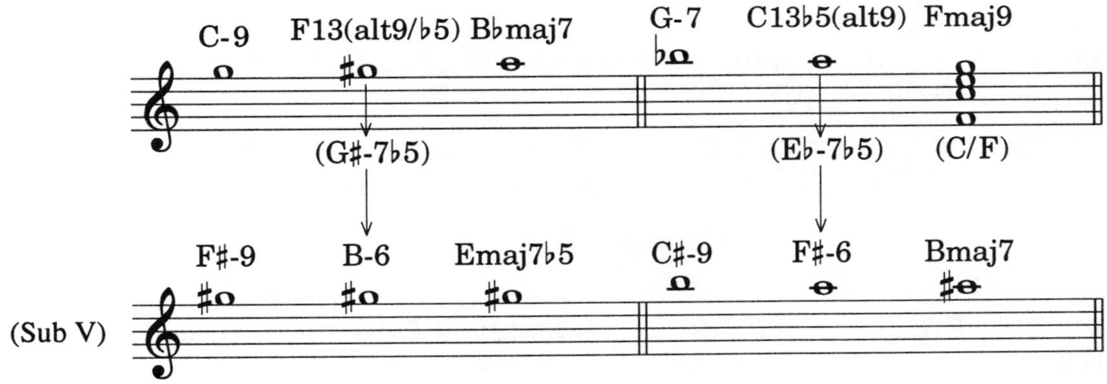


The following examples will use various dominant chords containing altered 9th tensions. Additional chords from past chapters also will be used to enhance voice-leading.

This first "II-V blues" example in the key of "D" contains some interesting constant structures and chromatic motion. The first two chord structures are repeated a whole step lower in the second measure. The E7(alt) structure in measure three is repeated a whole step higher in the following measure. The three chords starting in measure five contain one common tone while the top three voices descend chromatically. The B13(alt9) chord in measure seven has two common tones while the remaining voices move in contrary chromatic motion to the next chord. Measure eight's two chords share one common tone while the top three voices descend chromatically. Measure ten's A7(alt) chord has two voices ascending and two voices descending to the next chord. Finally, note the last three chords use the same structure descending chromatically.

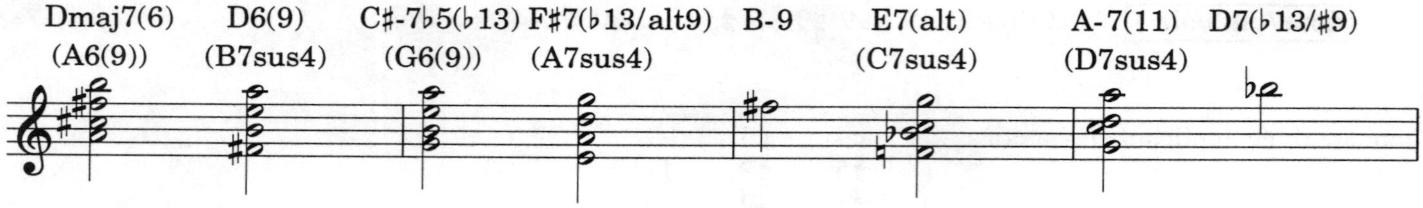


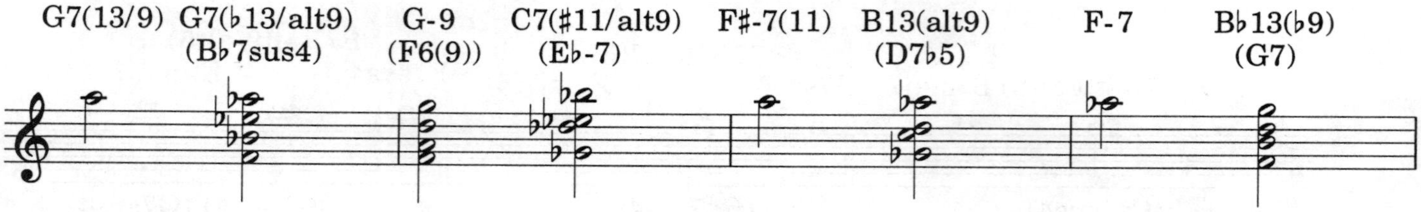

This next example in the key of "C" also contains some interesting voice-leading ideas. In the first measure, the top two voices sustain while the bottom two move in contrary chromatic motion. Note that only one voice moves (chromatically) in measures two and three on the C7(alt9) to A♭maj9 chords and A♭maj9 to G7(alt5/♯9) chords. Measure three's G7(alt5/♯9) chord sustains the lead tone while the remaining voices produce contrary chromatic motion to the C6(9) chord. Measure four's C7(alt) chord contains contrary chromatic motion between the top two voices ascending while the bottom two descend to the Fmaj7 chord. Finally, note the contrary motion between the top voice and bottom voices on the last two chords.

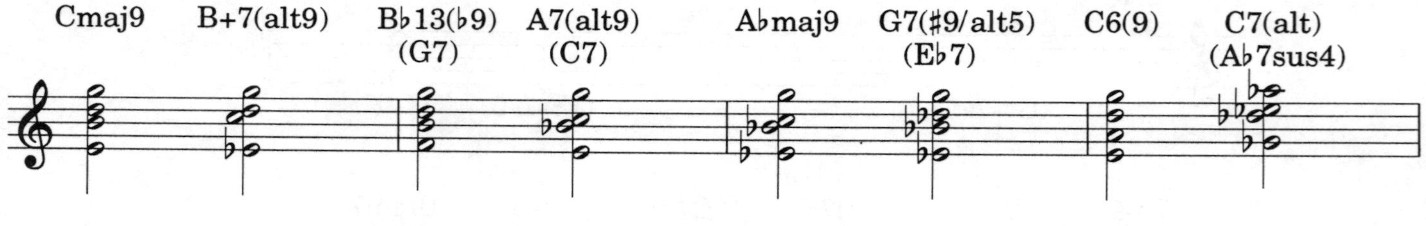


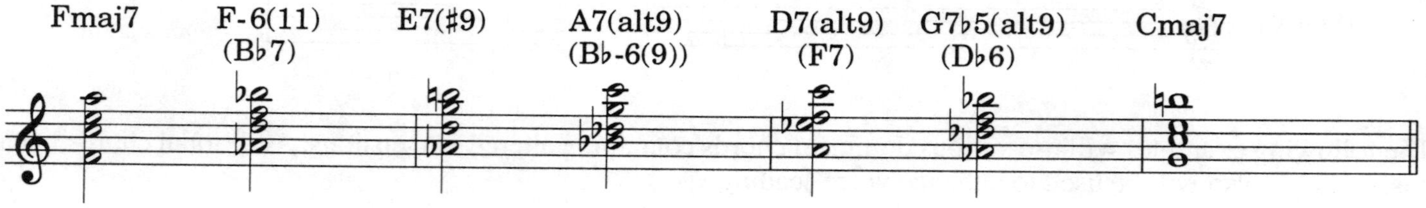

# Chapter Fourteen.
## Enharmonic Chordal Substitutions

The following chords (highlighted within boxes) appear in the order they were introduced in this text. Enharmonic substitutions for each one of these chords appear in the order they were introduced as well. Chords include the basic four-part chords and all the chords introduced in the tension chapters. To the left of each chord is the tension chapter where that chord can be found. Additional enharmonic substitutions of the same voicings that have not been introduced to this point will be examined in the **Additional Enharmonic Chordal Substitutions** chapter.

This chapter will include the Substitute Vth chord for each dom7 chord introduced as well as the most common relative major and minor situations. Some of the more incomplete voicings will receive additional notation for the same root to the right of that chord in parenthesis. A more in-depth and organized approach to relative major and minor chords can be found in the **Relative Major – Minor** chapter.

**major7**

| *Tension Chapter* | | | **C** | **E** | **G** | **B** |
|---|---|---|---|---|---|---|
| | | Cmaj7 | 1 | 3 | 5 | 7 |
| (9) | | A-9 | ♭3 | 5 | ♭7 | 9 |
| (9 & 13) | | D7sus4(13/9) | ♭7 | 9 | 4 | 13 |
| (9 & 11) | | Fmaj7(♯11/9) | 5 | 7 | 9 | ♯11 |

**major7♭5**

| *Tension Chapter* | | | **C** | **E** | **G♭** | **B** |
|---|---|---|---|---|---|---|
| | | Cmaj7♭5 | 1 | 3 | ♭5 | 7 |
| (9) | | A-6(9) | ♭3 | 5 | 6 | 9 |
| (9) | Sub V | A♭7♯5(♯9) | 3 | ♯5 | ♭7 | ♯9 |
| (9 & 13) | Sub V | D7(13/9) | ♭7 | 9 | 3 | 13 |
| (11) | | F♯-7♭5(11) | ♭5 | ♭7 | 1 | 11 |

**major7♯5**

| *Tension Chapter* | | | **C** | **E** | **G♯** | **B** |
|---|---|---|---|---|---|---|
| | | Cmaj7(♯5) | 1 | 3 | ♯5 | 7 |
| (9) | | A-maj7(9) | ♭3 | 5 | 7 | 9 |
| (9 & 11) | | F♯-7♭5(11/9) | ♭5 | ♭7 | 9 | 11 |
| (9 -11-13) | SubV | D7(13/♯11/9) | ♭7 | 9 | ♯11 | 13 |
| | SubV | A♭7(♯9/♯5) | 3 | ♯5 | 1 | ♯9 |

**minor7**

| | | | C | E♭ | G | B♭ | |
|---|---|---|---|---|---|---|---|
| | | C-7 | 1 | ♭3 | 5 | ♭7 | |
| | | E♭6 | 6 | 1 | 3 | 5 | |
| (9) | | A♭maj9 | 3 | 5 | 7 | 9 | |
| (9) | | F9sus4 | 5 | ♭7 | 9 | 4 | |
| (9 -11) | | F-7(9/11) | 5 | ♭7 | 9 | 11 | |
| (9-11-13) | | D♭maj7(9/♯11/13) | 7 | 9 | ♯11 | 13 | |
| (9-11-13) | | B♭-maj7(13/11/9) | 9 | 11 | 13 | 1 | [B♭7sus4(13/9)] |
| (9-11-13) | Sub V | F♯7(13/♯11/♭9) | ♯11 | 13 | ♭9 | 3 | |
| | | C7♯9 (C-7) | 1 | ♯9 | 5 | ♭7 | |
| (dom/alt9) | Sub V | A7♭5(alt9) | ♯9 | ♭5 | ♭7 | ♭9 | |
| | | E♭13 (E♭6) | 13 | 1 | 3 | 5 | |

**minor7♭5**

| | | | C | E♭ | G♭ | B♭ |
|---|---|---|---|---|---|---|
| | | C-7♭5 | 1 | ♭3 | ♭5 | ♭7 |
| | | E♭-6 | 6 | 1 | ♭3 | 5 |
| (9) | Sub V | A♭9 | 3 | 5 | ♭7 | 9 |
| (9) | | D7(♭9/♯5) | ♭7 | ♭9 | 3 | ♯5 |
| (9) | | F7sus4(♭9) | 5 | ♭7 | ♭9 | 4 |
| (11) | | G♭6(♯11) | ♯11 | 6 | 1 | 3 |
| (9 -11-13) | | D♭-maj7(9/11/13) | 7 | 9 | 11 | 13 |
| (9-11-13) | | B♭-7♭5(♭13/11/9) | 9 | 11 | ♭13 | 1 |
| (dom/alt9) | Sub V | A13♭5(alt9) | ♯9 | ♭5 | 13 | ♭9 |
| | | E♭13(♯9) (E♭-6) | 13 | 1 | ♯9 | 5 |

**minor7♯5**

| | | | C | E♭ | G♯ | B♭ | |
|---|---|---|---|---|---|---|---|
| | | C-7(♯5) | 1 | ♭3 | ♯5 | ♭7 | |
| (9) | | B♭9sus4 | 9 | 4 | ♭7 | 1 | |
| | Rel | B♭-7(9/11) | 9 | 11 | ♭7 | 1 | |
| | | D♭maj7(6/9) | 7 | 9 | 5 | 6 | |
| (11) | Rel | F-7(11) | 5 | ♭7 | ♭3 | 11 | |
| | | A♭(add9) | 3 | 5 | 1 | 9 | |
| (11) | | E♭-6(11) | 6 | 1 | 11 | 5 | (E♭13sus4) |
| (9 -13) | Sub V | D7♭5(♭13/♭9) | ♭7 | ♭9 | ♭5 | ♭13 | (D7(♭9/alt5)) |
| | | A♭9 | 3 | 5 | 1 | 9 | |
| (9-11) | | G♭6(♯11/9) | ♯11 | 6 | 9 | 3 | |
| (9 -11-13) | SubV | G♭13(♯11/9) | ♯11 | 13 | 9 | 3 | |
| | | C7(♯9/♯5) | 1 | ♯9 | ♯5 | ♭7 | |

**minor6** refer to **minor7♭5**

**major6** refer to **minor7**

**dom7**

| | | | C | E | G | B♭ | |
|---|---|---|---|---|---|---|---|
| | Sub V | C7 | 1 | 3 | 5 | ♭7 | |
| (9) | | F♯7(♭9/♭5) | ♭5 | ♭7 | ♭9 | 3 | |
| (11) | | G-6(11) | 11 | 6 | 1 | ♭3 | |
| (9-11-13) | Sub V | B♭7(13/♯11/9) | 9 | ♯11 | 13 | 1 | |
| | | E7♯5(♯11/♯9) | ♯5 | 1 | ♯9 | ♯11 | [E-7♭5(♭13)] |
| (9-11-13) | | B♭maj7(13/♯11/9) | 9 | ♯11 | 13 | 1 | [B♭6♭5(9)] |
| (9-11-13) | | D-7♭5(♭13/9/11) | ♭7 | 9 | 11 | ♭13 | |
| (dom/alt9) | Sub V | A7(alt9) | ♯9 | 5 | ♭7 | ♭9 | |
| | | E♭13(♭9) | 13 | ♭9 | 3 | 5 | |

**dom7♯5**

| | | | C | E | G♯ | B♭ | |
|---|---|---|---|---|---|---|---|
| | Sub V | C+7 | 1 | 3 | ♯5 | ♭7 | |
| (9) | | F♯7♭5(9) | ♭5 | ♭7 | 9 | 3 | |
| (9) | Sub V | B♭9(♭5) | 9 | ♭5 | ♭7 | 1 | [B♭-7♭5(9)] |
| (11) | | E7(alt5) | ♯5 | 1 | 3 | ♭5 | [E7♯5(♯11)] |
| (11) | | F-maj7(11) | 5 | 7 | ♭3 | 11 | |
| (13) | | D♭-maj7(6) | 7 | ♭3 | 5 | 6 | |
| (9-13) | | D-7♭5(♭13/9) | ♭7 | 9 | ♭5 | ♭13 | |
| (9-13) | Sub V | D7♭5(♭13/9) | ♭7 | 9 | ♭5 | ♭13 | [D9(♯5/♭5)] |
| | | A♭9(♯5) | 3 | ♯5 | 1 | 9 | |

**dom7♭5**

| | | | C | E | G♭ | B♭ |
|---|---|---|---|---|---|---|
| | Sub V | C7♭5 | 1 | 3 | ♭5 | ♭7 |
| | | F♯7♭5 | ♭5 | ♭7 | 1 | 3 |
| (9) | Sub V | A♭9(♯5) | 3 | ♯5 | ♭7 | 9 |
| (9) | | D9(♯5) | ♭7 | 9 | 3 | ♯5 |
| (11-13) | | G-maj7(11/6) | 11 | 6 | 7 | ♭3 |
| (11-13) | | D♭-maj7(11/6) | 7 | ♭3 | 11 | 6 |
| (dom/alt9) | Sub V | A13(alt9) | ♯9 | 5 | 13 | ♭9 |
| (dom/alt9) | | E♭13(alt9) | 13 | ♭9 | ♯9 | 5 |

**dom7sus4**

| | | | C | F | G | B♭ | |
|---|---|---|---|---|---|---|---|
| | | C7sus4 | 1 | 4 | 5 | ♭7 | |
| (9) | Rel | E♭6(9) | 6 | 9 | 3 | 5 | |
| (11) | | C-7(11) | 1 | 11 | 5 | ♭7 | |
| (11) | Rel | G-7(11) | 11 | ♭7 | 1 | ♭3 | |
| | | B♭6(9) | 9 | 5 | 6 | 1 | |
| (13) | | D♭maj7♭5(6) | 7 | 3 | ♭5 | 6 | |
| (9-13) | Rel | A♭maj7(9/6) | 3 | 6 | 7 | 9 | |
| | | F-7(11/9) | 5 | 1 | 9 | 11 | [F9sus4] |
| (11-13) | | D-7♭5(♭13/11) | ♭7 | ♭3 | 11 | ♭13 | |
| (dom/alt9) | Sub V | A+7(alt9) | ♯9 | ♯5 | ♭7 | ♭9 | |
| | | E♭13(9) | 13 | 9 | 3 | 5 | |
| | SubV | E7(alt9/alt5) | ♯5 | ♭9 | ♯9 | ♭5 | |
| | | B♭9(13) | 9 | 5 | 13 | 1 | |

**dimin.7**

| | | C | E♭ | G♭ | B♭♭ |
|---|---|---|---|---|---|
| | C°7 | 1 | ♭3 | ♭5 | ♭♭7 |
| | E♭°7 | ♭♭7 | 1 | ♭3 | ♭5 |
| | A°7 | ♭3 | ♭5 | ♭♭7 | 1 |
| | G♭°7 | ♭5 | ♭♭7 | 1 | ♭3 |
| (9) | D7(♭9) | ♭7 | ♭9 | 3 | 5 |
| (9) | F7(♭9) | 5 | ♭7 | ♭9 | 3 |
| (9) | A♭7(♭9) | 3 | 5 | ♭7 | ♭9 |
| (9) | B7(♭9) | ♭9 | 3 | 5 | ♭7 |

**minor (maj7)**

| | | | C | E♭ | G | B |
|---|---|---|---|---|---|---|
| | | C-maj7 | 1 | ♭3 | 5 | 7 |
| (9) | | A-7♭5(9) | ♭3 | ♭5 | ♭7 | 9 |
| (9-13) | | D7sus4(13/♭9) | ♭7 | ♭9 | 4 | 13 |
| (9-11) | Sub V | F7(♯11/9) | 5 | ♭7 | 9 | ♯11 |
| | | B7(♯5/♭9) | ♭9 | 3 | ♯5 | 1 |

**major7(9)**

9 for 1 / drop 2 {3 5 7 9}...refer to **minor7**

| | | | C | E | B | D | |
|---|---|---|---|---|---|---|---|
| (9) | Rel | Cmaj9 | 1 | 3 | 7 | 9 | |
| | | A-(11/9) | ♭3 | 5 | 9 | 11 | |
| (9-13) | Sub V | A♭7♭5(♭13/♯9) | 3 | ♭13 | ♯9 | ♭5 | [A♭7(♯9/alt5)] |
| | | D7(13/9) | ♭7 | 9 | 13 | 1 | |
| (11-13) | | Fmaj7(13/♯11) | 5 | 7 | ♯11 | 13 | |
| (11-13) | | F♯-7♭5(♭13/11) | ♭5 | ♭7 | 11 | ♭13 | |

**major7♭5(9)**

9 for 1 / drop 2 {3 ♭5 7 9} refer to **major6(9)**
Ninth(no3) {1 ♭5 7 9} refer to **dom7♭5(♯9)**

**minor maj7(9)**

9 for 1 / drop 2 {♭3 5 7 9} refer to **major7♯5**

| | | | C | E♭ | B | D |
|---|---|---|---|---|---|---|
| (9) | | C-maj9 | 1 | ♭3 | 7 | 9 |
| (11-13) | Sub V | F7(13/♯11) | 5 | ♭7 | ♯11 | 13 |
| (dom/alt9) | | B7(alt9) | ♭9 | 3 | 1 | ♯9 |

**minor7(9)**

9 for 1 / drop 2 {♭3 5 ♭7 9} refer to **major7**

| | | | C | E♭ | B♭ | D |
|---|---|---|---|---|---|---|
| (9) | Rel | C-9 | 1 | ♭3 | ♭7 | 9 |
| | | E♭maj7(6) | 6 | 1 | 5 | 7 |
| (13) | | F13sus4 | 5 | ♭7 | 4 | 13 |

**minor7♭5(9)**

9 for 1 / drop 2 {♭3 ♭5 ♭7 9} refer to **min. maj7**
Ninth(no3) { 1 ♭5 ♭7 9 } refer to **dom7♯5**

**major6(9)**

9 for 1 / drop 2 {3 5 6 9} refer to **dom7(sus4)**

| | | | **C** | **E** | **A** | **D** | |
|---|---|---|---|---|---|---|---|
| (9) | Rel | C6(9) | 1 | 3 | 6 | 9 | |
| (9) | | B♭maj7♭5(9) | 9 | ♭5 | 7 | 3 | |
| | | Am(11) | ♭3 | 5 | 1 | 11 | |
| (13) | Rel | Fmaj7(6) | 5 | 7 | 3 | 6 | |
| | | D-9 | ♭7 | 9 | 5 | 1 | (D9) |
| (13) | | F♯-7♭5(♭13) | ♭5 | ♭7 | ♭3 | ♭13 | |
| (9-13) | Sub V | A♭7♭5(♭13/♭9) | 3 | ♭13 | ♭9 | ♭5 | |
| | | D9 | ♭7 | 9 | 5 | 1 | |
| (9-11) | | G-6(11/9) | 11 | 6 | 9 | 5 | (G7sus4(13/9)) |

**minor6(9)**

9 for 1 / drop 2 {♭3 5 6 9} refer to **major7♭5**

| | | | **C** | **E♭** | **A** | **D** |
|---|---|---|---|---|---|---|
| (9) | | C-6(9) | 1 | ♭3 | 6 | 9 |
| (13) | Sub V | F13 | 5 | ♭7 | 3 | 13 |
| (dom/alt9) | | B7(alt9) | ♭9 | 3 | ♭7 | ♯9 |

**dom7(9)**

9 for 1 / drop 2 {3 5 ♭7 9} refer to **minor7♭5**

| | | | **C** | **E** | **B♭** | **D** | |
|---|---|---|---|---|---|---|---|
| (9) | Sub V | C9 | 1 | 3 | ♭7 | 9 | |
| (11) | (F♯+7(♯11)) | F♯7(alt5) | ♭5 | ♭7 | 3 | ♯5 | |
| (9) | Sub V | D7♯5(9) | ♭7 | 9 | ♯5 | 1 | |
| (9-13) | (A♭7♭5(♭13/9)) | A♭9(alt5) | 3 | ♯5 | 9 | ♭5 | |
| (11) | Sub V | E+7(♯11) | ♯5 | 1 | ♯11 | ♭7 | {E-7♭5(♭13)} |
| | | B♭9♭5 | 9 | ♭5 | 1 | 3 | {B♭maj9♭5} |
| (11) | | G-6(11) | 11 | 6 | ♭3 | 5 | |
| (11-13) | | F-maj7(11/6) | 5 | 7 | 11 | 6 | |

**dom7(♭9)**

9 for 1 / drop 2 {3 5 ♭7 ♭9} refer to **dimin.7**

| | | | **C** | **E** | **B♭** | **D♭** |
|---|---|---|---|---|---|---|
| (9) | Sub V | C7(♭9) | 1 | 3 | ♭7 | ♭9 |
| (11) | | F♯7(♯11) | ♯11 | ♭7 | 3 | 5 |
| (13) | | C♯-maj7(6) | 7 | ♭3 | 6 | 1 |
| (dom/alt9) | Sub V | A7(alt9) | ♯9 | 5 | ♭9 | 3 |
| | | E♭13(♭9) | 13 | ♭9 | 5 | ♭7 |

**dom7(♯9)** 9 for 1 / drop 2 {3 5 ♭7 ♯9}

| | | | **E** | **G** | **B♭** | **D♯** |
|---|---|---|---|---|---|---|
| (9) | Sub V | C7(♯9) | 3 | 5 | ♭7 | ♯9 |
| (9-13) | | F♯13(♭9) | ♭7 | ♭9 | 3 | 13 |
| (9-11) | Sub V | A7(♯11/♭9) | 5 | ♭7 | ♭9 | ♯11 |
| | | E♭(♭9) | ♭9 | 3 | 5 | 1 |

| | | *9th(no 5) voicing.......* | **C** | **E** | **B♭** | **D♯** |
|---|---|---|---|---|---|---|
| (9) | Sub V | C7(♯9) | 1 | 3 | ♭7 | ♯9 |
| (13) | | F♯13(♭5) | ♭5 | ♭7 | 3 | 13 |
| (9-13) | | D♭-maj7(6/9) | 7 | ♭3 | 6 | 9 |
| (dom/alt9) | Sub V | A7(♯11/alt9) | ♯9 | 5 | ♭9 | ♯11 |
| | | E♭13(♭9) | 13 | ♭9 | 5 | 1 |

**dom7♭5(9)** 9 for 1 / drop 2 {3 ♭5 ♭7 9} refer to **dom7♯5**
Ninth(no3) {1 ♭5 ♭7 9 } refer to **dom7♯5**

**dom7♭5(♭9)** 9 for 1 / drop 2 {3 ♭5 ♭7 ♭9} refer to **dom7**

9th (no3) chord voicing not available until triad over bass chapter:
C7(♭9/♭5) {1 ♭5 ♭7 ♭9} = G♭/C

**dom7♭5(♯9)** 9 for 1 / drop 2 {3 ♭5 ♭7 ♯9}

| | | | **E** | **G♭** | **B♭** | **D♯** |
|---|---|---|---|---|---|---|
| (9) | Sub V | C7(♯9/♭5) | 3 | ♭5 | ♭7 | ♯9 |
| (13) | | F♯13 | ♭7 | 1 | 3 | 13 |
| (9) | Rel | Emaj9♭5 | 1 | 9 | ♭5 | 7 |
| (9-11) | | C♯-6(11/9) | ♭3 | 11 | 6 | 9 |
| (11-13) | | B♭-7♭5(♭13/11) | ♭5 | ♭13 | 1 | 11 |
| (9-11-13) | Sub V | A7(13/♯11/♭9) | 5 | 13 | ♭9 | ♯11 |
| | | E♭7(alt9) | ♭9 | ♯9 | 5 | 1 |

**dom7♯5(9)** 9 for 1 / drop 2 {3 ♯5 ♭7 9} refer to **dom7♭5**
*Ninth with omitted 3rd chord voicing* {1 ♯5 ♭7 9} refer to **dom7(9)**

**dom7♯5(♭9)** 9 for 1 / drop 2 {3 ♯5 ♭7 ♭9} refer to **minor7♭5**
*Ninth with omitted 3rd chord voicing* not available.

**dom7♯5(♯9)** 9 for 1 / drop 2 {3 ♯5 ♭7 ♯9} refer to **major7♭5**
*Ninth with omitted 3rd chord voicing* not applicable: {1 ♯5 ♭7 ♯9} forms an incomplete dominant sound. This voicing will appear later in a dominant capacity.

**dom7sus4(9)**

9 for 1 / drop 2 {4 5 ♭7 9} refer to **minor7**
*Ninth(no5) voicing* {1 4 ♭7 9} refer to **minor7♯5**

**dom7sus4(♭9)**

9 for 1 / drop 2 {4 5 ♭7 ♭9} refer to **minor7♭5**

**major7(♯11)**

**11 for 5** {1 3 7 ♯11} refer to **major7♭5**

**11 for 3** {1 5 7 ♯11}; no enharmonic substitutions through the tension chapters. The relative minor forms a model dorian voicing:

| | **C** | **G** | **B** | **F♯** |
|---|---|---|---|---|
| Cmaj7♯11 | 1 | 5 | 7 | ♯11 |
| A-7(13/9) | ♭3 | ♭7 | 9 | 13 |

| | | **11 for 1** {3 5 7 ♯11} | **E** | **G** | **B** | **F♯** |
|---|---|---|---|---|---|---|
| (11) | | Cmaj7(♯11) | 3 | 5 | 7 | ♯11 |
| (11) | | C♯-7♭5(11) | ♭3 | ♭5 | ♭7 | 11 |
| (13) | Rel | Gmaj7(6) | 6 | 1 | 3 | 7 |
| | | Em(9) | 1 | ♭3 | 5 | 9 |
| (dom/alt9) | Sub V | E♭+7(alt9) | ♭9 | 3 | ♯5 | ♯9 |
| | | A7(13/9) | 5 | ♭7 | 9 | 13 |

**major6(♯11)**

**11 for 5** {1 3 6 ♯11} refer to **minor7♭5**

| | | **11 for 3** {1 5 6 ♯11} | **C** | **G** | **A** | **F♯** | |
|---|---|---|---|---|---|---|---|
| (11) | | C6(♯11) | 1 | 5 | 6 | ♯11 | |
| (9-11-13) | | E-7♭5(♭13/11/9) | ♭13 | ♭3 | 11 | 9 | |
| (9-11-13) | Sub V | E♭7(13/♯11/♯9) | 13 | 3 | ♯11 | ♯9 | |
| | | A7(13/♯9) | ♯9 | ♭7 | 1 | 13 | (A-7(13)) |
| (dom/alt9) | Sub V | F♯7(♯11/alt9) | ♯11 | ♭9 | ♯9 | 1 | |
| | | C13(♯11) | 1 | 5 | 13 | ♯11 | |

| | | **11 for 1** {3 5 6 ♯11} | **E** | **G** | **A** | **F♯** |
|---|---|---|---|---|---|---|
| (11) | | C6(♯11) | 3 | 5 | 6 | ♯11 |
| (11-13) | | C♯-7♭5(♭13/11) | ♭3 | ♭5 | ♭13 | 11 |
| (dom/alt9) | Sub V | E♭7♭5(alt9) | ♭9 | 3 | ♭5 | ♯9 |
| | | A13 | 5 | ♭7 | 1 | 13 |
| (dom/alt9) | Sub V | F♯7(alt9) | ♭7 | ♭9 | ♯9 | 1 |
| | | C13(♯11) | 3 | 5 | 13 | ♯11 |

**minor7(11)**

**11 for 5** {1 ♭3 ♭7 11} refer to **dom7sus4**
**11 for 3** {1 5 ♭7 11} refer to **dom7sus4**
**11 for 1** {♭3 5 ♭7 11} refer to **minor7♯5**

**minor6(11)**

**11 for 5** {1 ♭3 6 11} refer to **dom7**
**11 for 1** {♭3 5 6 11} refer to **dom9**

**minor maj7(11)**

**11 for 5** {1 ♭3 7 11} refer to **dom7(♯11)** {1 5 ♭7 ♯11}
**11 for 3** {1 5 7 11} *unique...no substitutes*
**11 for 1** {♭3 5 7 11} refer to **dom7♯5**

**dom7(♯11)**

**11 for 5** {1 3 ♭7 ♯11} refer to **dom7♭5**

| | | **11 for 3** {1 5 ♭7 ♯11} | **C** | **G** | **B♭** | **F♯** |
|---|---|---|---|---|---|---|
| (11) | Sub V | C7(♯11) | 1 | 5 | ♭7 | ♯11 |
| | | F♯7(♭9/♭5) | ♭5 | ♭9 | 3 | 1 |
| (11) | | G-maj7(11) | 11 | 1 | ♭3 | 7 |
| (dom/alt9) | Sub V | A13(alt9) | ♯9 | ♭7 | ♭9 | 13 |
| | | E♭13(♯9) | 13 | 3 | 5 | ♯9 |

**11 for 1** {3 5 ♭7 ♯11} refer to **dom7(♭9)**

**dom7♯5(♯11)**

**11 for 3** {1 ♯5 ♭7 ♯11} refer to **dom9**
**11 for 1** {3 ♯5 ♭7 ♯11} refer to **dom9**

**major7(6)**

**6 for 5** {1 3 6 7} refer to **major7(♯11)**
**6 for 1** {3 5 6 7} refer to **major6(9)**

**major7♭5(6)**

**6 for 1** {3 ♭5 6 7} refer to **dom7sus4**

**minor maj7(6)**

**6 for 5** {1 ♭3 6 7} refer to **dom7(♯11)**
**6 for 1** {♭3 5 6 7} refer to **dom7♯5**

**minor7♭5(♭13)**

**13 for 5** {1 ♭3 ♭7 ♭13} refer to **minor7♯5**
**13 for 1** {♭3 ♭5 ♭7 ♭13} refer to **maj6(9)**

**dom7(13)**

**13 for 5** {1 3 ♭7 13} refer to **dom7♭5(♯9)**
**13 for 1** {3 5 ♭7 13} refer to **min6(9)**

**dom7♭5(13)**

**13 for 1** {3 ♭5 ♭7 13} refer to **dom7(♯9)**

| | | **13 for 3** {1 ♭5 ♭7 13} | **C** | **G♭** | **B♭** | **A** |
|---|---|---|---|---|---|---|
| (13) | Sub V | C13♭5 | 1 | ♭5 | ♭7 | 13 |
| | | F♯7(♯9/♭5) | ♭5 | 1 | 3 | ♯9 |
| (9-11) | | G-maj7(11/9) | 11 | 7 | ♭3 | 9 |
| (9-11-13) | | E-7♭5(♭13/11/9) | ♭13 | 9 | ♭5 | 11 |
| (9-11-13) | Sub V | E♭7(13/♯11/♯9) | 13 | ♯9 | 5 | ♯11 |
| (dom/alt9) | | A13(alt9) | ♯9 | 13 | ♭9 | 1 |

**dom7sus4(13)**

**13 for 1** {4 5 ♭7 13} refer to **minor7(9)**

| | | **13 for 5** {1 4 ♭7 13} | **C** | **F** | **B♭** | **A** |
|---|---|---|---|---|---|---|
| (13) | | C13sus4 | 1 | 4 | ♭7 | 13 |
| (9-11) | Rel | G-7(11/9) | 11 | ♭7 | ♭3 | 9 |
| | | B♭maj9 | 9 | 5 | 1 | 7 |
| (9-11) | | E♭6(♯11/9) | 6 | 9 | 5 | ♯11 |
| (9-11-13) | Sub V | E♭7(13/♯11/9) | 13 | 9 | 5 | ♯11 |
| (dom/alt9) | | A+7(alt9) | ♯9 | ♯5 | ♭9 | 1 |

**major7(9/6)**

{3 7 9 6} refer to **dom7sus4**

**minor maj7(9/6)**

{♭3 6 7 9} refer to **dom7(♯9)**

**minor7♭5(♭13/9)**

{♭5 ♭7 9 ♭13} refer to **dom7♯5**

**dom7(13/9)**

{3 ♭7 9 13} refer to **maj7♭5**

**dom7(13/♭9)**

{3 ♭7 ♭9 13} refer to **dom7(♯9)**

**dom7(13/♯9)**

| | | {3 ♭7 ♯9 13} | **E** | **B♭** | **D♯** | **A** |
|---|---|---|---|---|---|---|
| (9-13) | Sub V | C13(♯9) | 3 | ♭7 | ♯9 | 13 |
| (9-13) | | F♯13(♯9) | ♭7 | 3 | 13 | ♯9 |

**dom7(♭13) with 9, ♭9,or ♯9**

refer to **dom7♯5** with **9, ♭9, or ♯9**

**dom7♭5(13) with 9, ♭9, or ♯9**

refer to three tensions as **dom7** with:
**(9/♯11/13), (♭9/♯11/13), or (♯9/♯11/13)**

**dom7♭5(♭13/9)**

{3 ♭5 9 ♭13} refer to **dom7(9)** {1 3 ♭7 9 }
{♭5 ♭7 9 ♭13} refer to **dom7(♯5)**

**dom7♭5(♭13/♭9)**

{3 ♭5 ♭9 ♭13} refer to **maj6(9)** {1 3 6 9 }
{♭5 ♭7 ♭9 ♭13} refer to **min7(♯5)**

**dom7♭5(♭13/♯9)**

{3 ♭5 ♯9 ♭13} refer to **maj7(9)** {1 3 7 9 }

**dom7sus4(13/9)**

{4 ♭7 9 13} refer to **major7**

**dom7sus4(13/♭9)**

{4 ♭7 ♭9 13} refer to **minor maj7**

**major7(♯11/9)**

{3 7 9 ♯11} refer to **major7♭5(9)**
{5 7 9 ♯11} refer to **major7**

**major6(♯11/9)**

{3 6 9 ♯11} refer to **minor7♯5**
{5 6 9 ♯11} refer to **dom7sus4(13)**

**minor maj7(11/9)**

{♭3 7 9 11} refer to **dom7♭5(13)**

**minor6(11/9)**

{♭3 6 9 11} refer to **dom7♭5(♯9)**
{5 6 9 11} refer to **maj6(9)**

**minor7(11/9)**

{♭3 ♭7 9 11} refer to **dom7sus4(13)**
{5 ♭7 9 11} refer to **minor7**

**minor7♭5(11/9)**

{♭5 ♭7 9 11} refer to **major7♯5**

**dom7(♯11/9)**

{3 ♭7 9 ♯11} refer to **dom7♭5(9)**
{5 ♭7 9 ♯11} refer to **minor maj7**

**dom7(♯11/♭9)**

{3 ♭7 ♭9 ♯11} refer to **dom7♭5(♭9)**
{5 ♭7 ♭9 ♯11} refer to **dom7(♯9)**

**dom7(♯11/♯9)**

{3 ♭7 ♯9 ♯11} refer to **dom7♭5(♯9)**

| {5 ♭7 ♯9 ♯11} | | | G | B♭ | D♯ | F♯ |
|---|---|---|---|---|---|---|
| (9-11) | Sub V | C7(♯11/♯9) | 5 | ♭7 | ♯9 | ♯11 |
| | | F♯13(♭9) | ♭9 | 3 | 13 | 1 |
| (9-11-13) | Sub V | A7(13/♯11/♭9) | ♭7 | ♭9 | ♯11 | 13 |
| | | E♭(♯9) | 3 | 5 | 1 | ♯9 |

**major7(♯11/6)**

{3 7 ♯11 6} refer to **major7♭5(6)**
{5 7 ♯11 6} refer to **major7(9)** {1 3 7 9}

**minor maj7(11/6)**

{♭3 7 11 6} refer to **dom7♭5**
{5 7 11 6} refer to **dom7(9)** {1 3 ♭7 9}

**dom7(13/♯11)**

{3 ♭7 ♯11 13} refer to **dom7♭5(13)**
{5 ♭7 ♯11 13} refer to **minor maj7(9)**

**minor7♭5(♭13/11)**

{♭3 ♭7 11 ♭13} refer to **dom7sus4**
{♭5 ♭7 11 ♭13} refer to **major7(9)**

**major7(13/♯11/9)**

{7 9 ♯11 13} refer to **minor7**
{1 9 ♯11 13} refer to **dom7**
{3 9 ♯11 13} refer to **major6(♯11/9)**
{5 9 ♯11 13} refer to **major6(♯11/9)**

**minor maj7(13/11/9)**

{7 9 11 13} refer to **minor7♭5**
{1 9 11 13} refer to **minor7**
{♭3 9 11 13} refer to **minor6(11/9)**
{5 9 11 13} refer to **minor6(11/9)**

**minor7♭5(♭13/11/9)**

{1 9 11 ♭13} refer to **minor 7♭5**
{♭3 9 11 ♭13} refer to **major 6(♯11)**
{♭5 9 11 ♭13} refer to **dom13(♭5)**
{♭7 9 11 ♭13} refer to **dom7**

**dom7(13/♯11/9)**

{1 9 ♯11 13} refer to **dom7**
{3 9 ♯11 13} refer to **minor7♯5**
{5 9 ♯11 13} refer to **dom7sus4(13)**
{♭7 9 ♯11 13} refer to **major7♯5**

**dom7(13/♯11/♭9)**

{3 ♭9 ♯11 13} refer to **minor7**
{5 ♭9 ♯11 13} refer to **dom7♭5(♯9)**
{♭7 ♭9 ♯11 13} refer to **dom7(♯11/♯9)** {5 ♭7 ♯9 ♯11}

| | | {1 ♭9 ♯11 13} | **C** | **D♭** | **F♯** | **A** |
|---|---|---|---|---|---|---|
| (9-11-13) | Sub V | C7(13/♯11/♭9) | 1 | ♭9 | ♯11 | 13 |
| | | F♯(♯11/♯9) | ♯11 | 5 | 1 | ♯9 |
| (9-11-13) | Sub V | E♭7(13/♯11/♯9) | 13 | ♭7 | ♯9 | ♯11 |
| | | A13(♯9) | ♯9 | 3 | 13 | 1 |

**dom7(13/♯11/♯9)**

{1 ♯9 ♯11 13} not applicable
{3 ♯9 ♯11 13} refer to **major 6(♯11)**
{5 ♯9 ♯11 13} refer to **dom13(♭5)**
{♭7 ♯9 ♯11 13} refer to **dom7(13/♯11/♭9)**

**dom7(alt9)**

{3 ♭7 ♭9 ♯9} refer to **minor6(9)** {1 ♭3 6 9}
{1 ♭7 ♭9 ♯9} refer to **major6(♯11)** {3 5 6 ♯11}
{5 ♭7 ♭9 ♯9} refer to **dom7**
{3 5 ♭9 ♯9} refer to **dom7(♯11)** {3 5 ♭7 ♯11}
{1 3 ♭9 ♯9} refer to **minor maj7(9)** {1 ♭3 7 9}
{1 5 ♭9 ♯9} refer to **dom7♭5(♯9)**

**dom7(♯11/alt9)**

{♭7 ♭9 ♯9 ♯11} refer to **minor7**
{3 ♭9 ♯9 ♯11} refer to **major6(♯11)** {3 5 6 ♯11}
{1 ♭9 ♯9 ♯11} refer to **major6(♯11)** {1 5 6 ♯11}
{5 ♭9 ♯9 ♯11} refer to **dom7(♯9)** {1 3 ♭7 ♯9}

**dom7(♭13/alt9)**

{3 ♭9 ♯9 ♭13} refer to **major7(♯11)**
{♭7 ♭9 ♯9 ♭13} refer to **dom7sus4**
{1 ♭9 ♯9 ♭13} refer to **dom13sus4**
{5 ♭9 ♯9 ♭13} not applicable

**dom7(13/alt9)**

{1 ♭9 ♯9 13} refer to **dom13(♭5)**
{5 ♭9 ♯9 13} refer to **dom7♭5**
{♭7 ♭9 ♯9 13} refer to **dom7(♯11)** {1 5 ♭7 ♯11}

| | | | **E** | **D♭** | **D♯** | **A** | |
|---|---|---|---|---|---|---|---|
| | | {3 ♭9 ♯9 13} | | | | | |
| (dom/alt9) | Sub V | C13(alt9) | 3 | ♭9 | ♯9 | 13 | |
| | | F♯13(♯9) | ♭7 | 5 | 13 | ♯9 | (F♯-13) |

**dom7(alt9/alt5)**

{♭9 ♯9 ♭5 ♯5} refer to **dom7sus4**

**dom7(13/♯11/alt9)**

{♭9 ♯9 ♯11 13} refer to **minor7♭5**

# Chapter Fifteen.
## Additional Enharmonic Chordal Substitutions

Up to this point, our enharmonic chordal substitutions have been produced by tension additions, dominant Sub V chords, and relative major and minor chords. By relaxing some of the rules established through the tension addition chapters, additional chordal substitution possibilities can be added to our previously established voicings. Though some of these substitutions will produce "incomplete" voicings, they might prove more effective in certain situations than a more complete chord voicing.

Along with these incomplete voicings, two additional voicing types that were previously omitted will be examined; dominant 7th chords with a natural 5th and tension ♭13, though its Sub V will not be examined, and tensions 9 & 11 on a min7♯5 chord.

At the end of this chapter the "incomplete" Sub V chords that were produced by their Sub V relation to the dominant chords presented in the tension addition chapters will be displayed.

**major 7♭5**

| | C | E | G♭ | B |
|---|---|---|---|---|
| Cmaj7♭5 | 1 | 3 | ♭5 | 7 |
| E9(♭13) | ♭13 | 1 | 9 | 5 |
| Bsus4(♭9) | ♭9 | 4 | 5 | 1 |

**major 7♯5**

| | C | E | G♯ | B |
|---|---|---|---|---|
| Cmaj7(♯5) | 1 | 3 | ♯5 | 7 |
| E7(♭13) | ♭13 | 1 | 3 | 5 |
| B13sus4(♭9) | ♭9 | 4 | 13 | 1 |

**minor 7**

| | C | E♭ | G | B♭ | |
|---|---|---|---|---|---|
| C-7 | 1 | ♭3 | 5 | ♭7 | |
| G-7♯5(11) | 11 | ♯5 | 1 | ♭3 | |
| B♭7sus4(13/9) | 9 | 4 | 13 | 1 | {B♭-maj7(13/11/9)} |

**dom7♯5**

| | C | E | G♯ | B♭ |
|---|---|---|---|---|
| C7♯5 | 1 | 3 | ♯5 | ♭7 |
| E♭13sus4(♭9) | 13 | ♭9 | 4 | 5 |

**dom7♭5**

| | | C | E | G♭ | B♭ | |
|---|---|---|---|---|---|---|
| | C7♭5 | 1 | 3 | ♭5 | ♭7 | |
| | B♭9(alt5) | 9 | ♭5 | ♯5 | 1 | (B♭-7♭5(♭13/9)) |
| | E9(alt5) | ♯5 | 1 | 9 | ♭5 | (E-7♭5(♭13/9)) |

**major7(9)**

| | | C | E | B | D |
|---|---|---|---|---|---|
| | Cmaj9 | 1 | 3 | 7 | 9 |
| | E7(♭13) | ♭13 | 1 | 5 | ♭7 |

**minor maj7(9)**

| | | C | E♭ | B | D |
|---|---|---|---|---|---|
| | C-maj9 | 1 | ♭3 | 7 | 9 |
| Sub V | D13(♭9) | ♭7 | ♭9 | 13 | 1 |
| | A♭7(♯11/♯9) | 3 | 5 | ♯9 | ♯11 |
| | A-7♭5 | ♭3 | ♭5 | 9 | 11 |

**minor7(9)**

| | | C | E♭ | B♭ | D | |
|---|---|---|---|---|---|---|
| | C-9 | 1 | ♭3 | ♭7 | 9 | |
| Sub V | D7(♭9/♯5) | ♭7 | ♭9 | ♯5 | 1 | |
| | A♭9(♯11) | 3 | 5 | 9 | ♯11 | (A♭(♯11/9)) |

**major6(9)**

| | | C | E | A | D |
|---|---|---|---|---|---|
| | C6(9) | 1 | 3 | 6 | 9 |
| | E-7♯5(11) | ♯5 | 1 | 11 | ♭7 |

**minor6(9)**

| | | C | E♭ | A | D |
|---|---|---|---|---|---|
| | C-6(9) | 1 | ♭3 | 6 | 9 |
| Sub V | D7(♭9) | ♭7 | ♭9 | 5 | 1 |
| | A♭7(♯11/♭9) | 3 | 5 | ♭9 | ♯11 |
| | A-7♭5(11) | ♭3 | ♭5 | 1 | 11 |
| | E♭maj7♭5(6) | 6 | 1 | ♭5 | 7 |

**dom7(♭9)**

| | | C | E | B♭ | D♭ |
|---|---|---|---|---|---|
| | C7(♭9) | 1 | 3 | ♭7 | ♭9 |
| | B♭-7♭5(9) | 9 | ♭5 | 1 | ♭3 |

**dom7(♯9)**

| | C | E | B♭ | D♯ |
|---|---|---|---|---|
| C7(♯9) | 1 | 3 | ♭7 | ♯9 |
| A♭7(♭13/9) | 3 | ♭13 | 9 | 5 |
| B♭-7♭5(11/9) | 9 | ♭5 | 1 | 11 |

**dom7♭5(♯9)**

| | E | G♭ | B♭ | D♯ |
|---|---|---|---|---|
| C7(♯9/♭5) | 3 | ♭5 | ♭7 | ♯9 |
| A♭9(♭13) | ♭13 | ♭7 | 9 | 5 |

**major 7(♯11)**

| | C | G | B | F♯ |
|---|---|---|---|---|
| Cmaj7(♯11) | 1 | 5 | 7 | ♯11 |
| B7(♭13/♭9) | ♭9 | ♭13 | 1 | 5 |

| | E | G | B | F♯ |
|---|---|---|---|---|
| Cmaj7(♯11) | 3 | 5 | 7 | ♯11 |
| F♯7sus4(♭9) | ♭7 | ♭9 | 4 | 1 |

**major 6(♯11)**

| | C | G | A | F♯ |
|---|---|---|---|---|
| C6(♯11) | 1 | 5 | 6 | ♯11 |
| G-maj7(11/9) | 11 | 1 | 9 | 7 |
| B7(♭13/♭9) | ♭9 | ♭13 | ♭7 | 5 |

| | | E | G | A | F♯ | |
|---|---|---|---|---|---|---|
| | C6(♯11) | 3 | 5 | 6 | ♯11 | |
| Relative | Em(11/9) | 1 | ♭3 | 11 | 9 | (E-7♭5(11/9)) |
| | Gmaj7(9/6) | 6 | 1 | 9 | 7 | (G-maj7(9/6)) |

**minor maj7(11)**

| | | C | G | B | F | |
|---|---|---|---|---|---|---|
| | C-maj7(11) | 1 | 5 | 7 | 11 | |
| | E7(♭13/alt9) | ♭13 | ♯9 | 5 | ♭9 | |
| | A-7♯5(9) | ♭3 | ♭7 | 9 | ♯5 | |
| Sub V | B7(♭9/alt5) | ♭9 | ♯5 | 1 | ♭5 | |
| | F9(♯11) | 5 | 9 | ♯11 | 1 | {F(♯11/9)} |

**dom7(♯11)**

| | C | G | B♭ | F♯ |
|---|---|---|---|---|
| C7(♯11) | 1 | 5 | ♭7 | ♯11 |
| E-7♭5(♭13/9) | ♭13 | ♭3 | ♭5 | 9 |

| | E | G | B♭ | F♯ |
|---|---|---|---|---|
| C7(♯11) | 3 | 5 | ♭7 | ♯11 |
| E-7♭5(9) | 1 | ♭3 | ♭5 | 9 |

**dom7♭5(13)**

| | C | G♭ | B♭ | A |
|---|---|---|---|---|
| C13(♭5) | 1 | ♭5 | ♭7 | 13 |
| D7(♭13) | ♭7 | 3 | ♭13 | 5 |

**dom7sus4 (13)**

| | C | F | B♭ | A |
|---|---|---|---|---|
| C13sus4 | 1 | 4 | ♭7 | 13 |
| D7(♭13/♯9) | ♭7 | ♯9 | ♭13 | 5 |

**dom7(13/♯9)**

| | | E | B♭ | D♯ | A |
|---|---|---|---|---|---|
| Sub V | C13(♯9) | 3 | ♭7 | ♯9 | 13 |
| | F♯13(♯9) | ♭7 | 3 | 13 | ♯9 |
| Sub V | E♭7(♯11/♭9) | ♭9 | 5 | 1 | ♯11 |
| | A7(♯11/♭9) | 5 | ♭9 | ♯11 | 1 |

**dom7(13/♯11/♭9)**

| | C | D♭ | F♯ | A |
|---|---|---|---|---|
| C7(13/♯11/♭9) | 1 | ♭9 | ♯11 | 13 |
| F7(♭13/♭9) | 5 | ♭13 | ♭9 | 3 |

**dom7(13/alt9)**

| | | E | D♭ | D♯ | A | |
|---|---|---|---|---|---|---|
| | C13(alt9) | 3 | ♭9 | ♯9 | 13 | |
| | E-maj7(11/6) | 1 | 6 | 7 | 11 | |
| | D♭-7♯5(9) | ♭3 | 1 | 9 | ♯5 | |
| Sub V | E♭7(♭9/♭5) | ♭9 | ♭7 | 1 | ♭5 | |
| | A7(♯11) | 5 | 3 | ♯11 | 1 | (A(♯11)) |

# Incomplete Sub V Chords

This is a list of the dominant Substitute V chords that were introduced in the tension chapters by only their Sub V relation and not by tension additions. Some of these voicings appear quite incomplete and might not prove very useful in dominant situations. The list will be in order of the Sub V's appearance through the tension chapters and will include the original dominant chords that produced the Sub V chords and the original chords that introduced the voicings.

| | Sub V Chord | Original Dom Chord | Original Chord |
|---|---|---|---|
| 1 | C7(alt5) {1 3 ♭5 ♯5} | F♯9(♭5) {1 ♭5 ♭7 9} | A♭+7 |
| 2 | C7♭5(♭9) {1 3 ♭5 ♭9} | F♯7(♯11) {1 5 ♭7 ♯11} | F♯7(♯11) |
| 3 | C7♭5(9) {1 3 ♭5 9} | F♯+7(♯11) {1 ♯5 ♭7 ♯11} | D9 {1 3 ♭7 9} |
| 4 | C7♭5(♯9) {1 3 ♭5 ♯9} | F♯13(♭5) {1 ♭5 ♭7 13} | F♯13(♭5) |
| 5 | C9(♯5) {1 3 ♯5 9} | F♯7♭5(♭13/9) {♭5 ♭7 9 ♭13} | E+7 |
| 6 | C9(♯5) {1 ♯5 ♭7 9} | F♯7♭5(♭13/9) {3 ♭5 9 ♭13} | B♭9 {1 3 ♭7 9} |
| 7 | C9 {1 3 5 9} | F♯7♭5(♭13/♭9) {♭5 ♭7 ♭9 ♭13} | E-7(♯5) |
| 8 | C9 {1 5 ♭7 9} | F♯7♭5(♭13/♭9) {3 ♭5 ♭9 ♭13} | B♭6(9) {1 3 6 9} |
| 9 | C7(13/9) {1 ♭7 9 13} | F♯7♭5(♭13/♯9) {3 ♭5 ♯9 ♭13} | B♭maj9 {1 3 7 9} |
| 10 | C+7(♭9) {1 3 ♯5 ♭9} | F♯7(9/♯11) {5 ♭7 9 ♯11} | D♭-maj7 |
| 11 | C7(♭9) {1 3 5 ♭9} | F♯7(♭9/♯11){5 ♭7 ♭9 ♯11} | A7(♯9) {3 5 ♭7 ♯9) |
| 12 | C13(♭9) {1 3 ♭9 13} | F♯7(♯9/♯11) {5 ♭7 ♯9 ♯11} | F♯7(♯9/♯11) |
| 13 | C7(♯5/♯9) {1 3 ♯5 ♯9} | F♯7(9/♯11/13) {♭7 9 ♯11 13} | Emaj7♯5 |
| 14 | C7(♯5/♯9) {1 ♭7 ♯5 ♯9} | F♯7(9/♯11/13) {3 9 ♯11 13} | C-7(♯5) |
| 15 | C7(♯9/alt5) {1 ♭5 ♯5 ♯9} | F♯7(9/♯11/13) {1 9 ♯11 13} | A♭7 |
| 16 | C7(♯9) {1 5 ♭7 ♯9} | F♯7(♭9/♯11/13) {3 ♭9 ♯11 13} | C-7 |
| 17 | C7(♯11/♯9) {1 5 ♯9 ♯11} | F♯7(♭9/♯11/13) {1 ♭9 ♯11 13} | F♯7(♭9/♯11/13) |
| 18 | C7(♯9) {1 3 5 ♯9} | F♯7(♭9/♯11/13) {♭7 ♭9 ♯11 13} | A7(♯11/♯9) {5 ♭7 ♯9 ♯11} |
| 19 | C13(♯9) {1 3 ♯9 13} | F♯7(♯9/♯11/13) {♭7 ♯9 ♯11 13} | E♭7(♭9/♯11/13) {1 ♭9 ♯11 13} |
| 20 | C13(♯9) {1 ♭7 ♯9 13} | F♯7(♯9/♯11/13) {3 ♯9 ♯11 13} | E♭6(♯11) {1 5 6 ♯11} |
| 21 | C13(♭9) {3 5 ♭9 13} | F♯7(alt9) {5 ♭7 ♭9 ♯9} | A7 |
| 22 | C13(♯11) {3 5 ♯11 13} | F♯7(alt9) {1 ♭7 ♭9 ♯9} | C6(♯11) {3 5 6 ♯11} |
| 23 | C13(♭9) {5 ♭7 ♭9 13} | F♯7(alt9) {3 5 ♭9 ♯9} | E♭7(♯11) {3 5 ♭7 ♯11} |
| 24 | C13 {1 3 5 13} | F♯7(alt9/♯11) {♭7 ♭9 ♯9 ♯11} | A-7 / C6 |
| 25 | C13 {1 5 ♭7 13} | F♯7(alt9/♯11) {3 ♭9 ♯9 ♯11} | E♭6(♯11) {3 5 6 ♯11} |
| 26 | C13(♯11) {1 5 ♯11 13} | F♯7(alt9/♯11) {1 ♭9 ♯9 ♯11} | C6(♯11) {1 5 6 ♯11} |
| 27 | C13(♭9) {1 5 ♭9 13} | F♯7(alt9/♯11) {5 ♭9 ♯9 ♯11} | A7(♯9) {1 3 ♭7 ♯9} |
| 28 | C7(13/9) {5 ♭7 9 13} | F♯7(alt9/♭13) {3 ♭9 ♯9 ♭13} | E♭maj7(♯11) {3 5 7 ♯11} |
| 29 | C7(13/9) {3 5 9 13} | F♯7(alt9/♭13) {♭7 ♭9 ♯9 ♭13} | A7sus4 |
| 30 | C7(13/♯9) {3 5 ♯9 13} | F♯13(alt9) {♭7 ♭9 ♯9 13} | A7(♯11) {1 5 ♭7 ♯11} |
| 31 | C7(13/♯9) {5 ♭7 ♯9 13} | F♯13(alt9) {3 ♭9 ♯9 13} | F♯13(alt9) |
| 32 | C7(13/9) {1 5 9 13} | F♯7(alt9/alt5) {♭5 ♯5 ♭9 ♯9} | D7sus4 |
| 33 | C7(13/♯9) {1 5 ♯9 13} | F♯13(alt9/♯11) {♭9 ♯9 ♯11 13} | A-7♭5 |

All of these Sub V chords can be found in a II - V - I situation placed under the original dominants.

# Chapter Sixteen.
## Relative Major-Minor

In this chapter both the relative major to minor (and vice-versa) and the relative minor to minor 7♭5 (and vice-versa) will be examined:

C major to A minor (A minor to C major)
C minor to A minor7♭5 (A minor 7♭5 to C minor)

The following chord types with tension additions will be explored:

1) **major 7/major 7♭5** and **major 6/major 6♭5** relative to minor: Cmaj7/Cmaj7♭5 and C6/C6♭5 relative to A minor.

The relative minor of major chords containing natural 5th and ♯11 form a "dorian" minor (♭7 & 13) which will be examined in a later section.

2) **minor 7** relative to major: C-7 relative to E♭ major.

3) **minor 6** relative to both major and minor 7♭5: C-6 relative to E♭major and A-7♭5.

4) **minor 7♭5** relative to minor: C-7♭5 relative to E♭ minor.

5) **minor maj7** relative to minor 7♭5: C-maj7 relative to A-7♭5.

With the exception of the drop 2 C-maj7(9), which is relative to E♭maj7♯5, the minor(maj7) chords' relation to major chords will be avoided, since the majority of these chords would produce tensions on a major 7♯5 chord.

Those relative chords that were not displayed in the tension chapters will receive asterisks and an example of a II-V-I situation at the end of this chapter. Chords are listed as they were introduced in this text. Some of the relative voicings are so incomplete that they can have more than one function in relation to the root of the chord. When this happens, the additional function will be listed in parentheses.

**Four-part 7th & 6th Chords (Drop 2);**

Cmaj7.............*relative to*.......A-7(9)

Cmaj7♭5................................A-6(9)

Cmaj7♯5................................A-maj7(9)

C6........................................ A-7

C-7.......................................E♭6

C-6....................................... E♭6♭5 or E♭6(♯11) and A-7♭5

C-maj7..................................A-7♭5(9)

C-7♭5.................................. E♭-6

| *Original Voicing* | **Tension 9** |
|---|---|
| | **Cmaj9;** |
| E-7 / G6 | drop 2 {3 5 7 9} *relative* to A-7(11/9) {5 ♭7 9 11} (A9sus4)<br>{1 3 7 9} *relative* to Am(11/9) {♭3 5 9 11} * |
| | **Cmaj9♭5;** |
| D6(9) {1 3 6 9}<br>A♭7♭5(♯9) | drop 2 {3 ♭5 7 9} *relative* to A-6(11/9) {5 6 9 11} (A7sus4(9/13))<br>{1 ♭5 7 9} *relative* to A-6(11/9) {♭3 6 9 11} |
| | **C6(9);** |
| (A7sus4)<br>B♭maj9♭5 | drop 2 {3 5 6 9} *relative* to A-7(11) {1 5 ♭7 11} (A7sus4)<br>{1 3 6 9} *relative* to Am(11) {1 ♭3 5 11} * |
| | **C-7(9);** |
| E♭maj7 | drop 2 {♭3 5 ♭7 9} *relative* to E♭maj7 {1 3 5 7}<br>{1 ♭3 ♭7 9} *relative* to E♭maj7(6) {1 5 6 7} * |
| | **C-6(9);** |
| E♭maj7♭5 | drop 2 {♭3 5 6 9} *relative* to E♭maj7♭5 {1 3 ♭5 7}<br>*relative* to A-7♭5(11) {1 ♭5 ♭7 11}<br>{1 ♭3 6 9} *relative* to E♭maj7♭5(6) {1 ♭5 6 7} *<br>*relative* to A-7♭5(11) {1 ♭3 ♭5 11} * |
| | **C-maj7(9);** |
| E♭maj7♯5 | drop 2 {♭3 5 7 9} *relative* to E♭maj7♯5<br>*relative* to A-7♭5(11/9) {♭5 ♭7 9 11}<br>{1 ♭3 7 9} *relative* to A-7♭5(11/9) {♭3 ♭5 9 11} * |
| | **C-7♭5(9);** |
| E♭-maj7<br>D+7 | drop 2 {♭3 ♭5 ♭7 9} *relative* to E♭-maj7 {1 ♭3 5 7}<br>{1 ♭5 ♭7 9} *relative* to E♭-maj7(6) {♭3 5 6 7} |

| *Original Voicing* | **Tension 11** |
|---|---|
| | **Cmaj7(♯11);** |
| | **11 for 5** = Cmaj7♭5 under **Four-part 7th & 6th Chords** |
| | ♯11 and 5 not applicable |
| | **C6(♯11);** **11 for 5** = C6♭5 |
| | C6♭5 *relative to* A-6 |
| | ♯11 and 5 not applicable |
| | **C-7(11);** |
| C7sus4 | {1 5 ♭7 11} *relative to* E♭6(9) {3 5 6 9} |
| F7sus4 | {1 ♭3 ♭7 11} *relative to* E♭6(9) {1 5 6 9} * |
| G-7(♯5) | {♭3 5 ♭7 11} *relative to* E♭(add9) {1 3 5 9} * |
| | **C-6(11);** |
| A-7(♯5) | {1 5 6 11} *relative to* E♭6(9/♯11) {3 ♭5 6 9} |
| | *relative to* A-7(♯5) {1 ♭3 ♯5 ♭7} |
| F9{1 3 ♭7 9} | {♭3 5 6 11} *relative to* E♭(9/♭5) {1 3 ♭5 9} * |
| | *relative to* A-7♭5(♭13) {1 ♭5 ♭13 ♭7} * |
| F7 | {1 ♭3 6 11} *relative to* E♭(9/♯11/13) {1 ♭5 6 9} |
| | *relative to* A-7♭5(♭13) {1 ♭3 ♭5 ♭13} * |
| | **C-maj7(11);** |
| | {1 5 7 11} *relative to* A-7♯5(9) {♭3 ♯5 ♭7 9} * |
| G+7 | {♭3 5 7 11} *relative to* A-7♭5(♭13/9) {♭5 ♯5 ♭7 9} (A9(alt5)) |
| F7(♯11) | {1 ♭3 7 11} *relative to* A-7♭5(♭13/9) {♭3 ♭5 ♯5 9} * |
| {1 5 ♭7 ♯11} | |
| | **C-7♭5(11);** |
| G♭maj7♭5 | {1 ♭5 ♭7 11} *relative to* E♭-6(9) {♭3 5 6 9} |
| Bmaj7(♯11) | {♭3 ♭5 ♭7 11} *relative to* E♭m(9) {1 ♭3 5 9} * |

| *Original Voicing* | |
|---|---|
| | **Tension 13** |
| | **Cmaj7(6)** |
| Fmaj7(♯11) | {1 3 6 7} *relative to* A-(add9) {1 ♭3 5 9} * |
| G6(9) {1 3 6 9} | {3 5 6 7} *relative to* A-9 {1 5 ♭7 9} (A9) * |
| | **Cmaj7♭5(6)** |
| B7sus4 | {3 ♭5 6 7} *relative to* A-6(9) {1 5 6 9} * refer to **maj6(9)** {1 5 6 9} |
| | **C-maj7(6)** |
| F7(♯11) | {1 ♭3 6 7} *relative to* A-7♭5(9) {1 ♭3 ♭5 9} * |
| B+7 | {♭3 5 6 7} *relative to* A-7♭5(9) {1 ♭5 ♭7 9} |
| | **C-7♭5(♭13)** |
| C-7(♯5) | {1 ♭3 ♯5 ♭7} *relative to* E♭-6(11) {1 5 6 11} (E♭13sus4) |
| G♭6(9) {1 3 6 9} | {♭3 ♭5 ♯5 ♭7} *relative to* E♭m(11) {1 ♭3 5 11} * |
| | **Tension 9 &13** |
| | **Cmaj7(13/9)** |
| E7sus4 | {3 7 9 6} *relative to* A-7(11/9) {1 5 9 11} (A9sus4) * |
| | **Cmaj7♭5(13/9)** |
| | refer to **Cmaj7(13/♯11/9)** under **Tensions 9, 11, & 13** |
| | **C-maj7(6/9)** |
| B7(♯9) {1 3 ♭7 ♯9} | {♭3 7 9 6} *relative to* A-7♭5(11/9) {1 ♭5 9 11} * |
| | **C-7♭5(♭13/9)** |
| B♭+7 | {♭5 ♭7 9 ♭13} *relative to* E♭-maj7(11) {♭3 5 7 11} |

| *Original Voicing* | | |
|---|---|---|
| | **Tension 9 &11** | |
| | **Cmaj7(♯11/9)** | |
| | | **♯11 for 5** = Cmaj9♭5 under **Tension 9** |
| | | **♯11 with 5** not applicable |
| | **C6(♯11/9)** | (**♯11 for 5** = C6♭5(9)) |
| (F♯-7(♯5)) | | {3 ♭5 6 9} *relative to* A-6(11) {1 5 6 11} (A13sus4) |
| | | {1 ♭5 6 9} under **Tensions 9, 11, & 13** |
| | **C-7(11/9)** | |
| F13sus4 | | {♭3 ♭7 9 11} *relative to* E♭maj9 {1 5 7 9} * |
| B♭6 / G-7 | | {5 ♭7 9 11 } *relative to* E♭maj9 {3 5 7 9} |
| | **C-6(11/9)** | |
| | | {1 6 9 11} refer to **C-maj7(13/11/9)** |
| B7♭5(♯9) | | {♭3 6 9 11} *relative to* E♭maj9♭5 {1 ♭5 7 9} |
| | | *relative to* A-7♭5(♭13/11) {1 ♭5 ♯5 11} * |
| F6(9) {1 3 6 9} | | {5 6 9 11} *relative to* E♭maj9♭5 {3 ♭5 7 9} |
| | | *relative to* A-7♯5(11) {1 ♯5 ♭7 11} * |
| | **C-maj7(11/9)** | |
| F13♭5 | | {♭3 7 9 11} *relative to* A-7♭5(♭13/11/9) {♭5 9 11 ♭13} |
| | **C-7♭5(11/9)** | |
| G♭maj7♯5 | | {♭5 ♭7 9 11} *relative to* E♭-maj9 {♭3 5 7 9} |
| | **Tension 11&13** | |
| | **C-maj7(11/6)** | |
| F7♭5 | | {♭3 7 6 11} *relative to* A-7♭5(♭13/9) {1 ♭5 ♯5 9} * |
| G9 {1 3 ♭7 9} | | {5 7 6 11 } *relative to* A-7♯5(9) {1 ♯5 ♭7 9} * |
| | **C-7♭5(♭13/11)** | |
| G♭maj9 {1 3 7 9} | | {♭5 ♭7 11 ♭13} *relative to* E♭m(11/9) {♭3 5 9 11} * |
| B♭7sus4 | | {♭3 ♭7 11 ♭13} *relative to* E♭m(11/9) {1 5 9 11} (E♭sus4(9)) * |

| *Original Voicing* | **Tensions 9, 11, &13** |
|---|---|
| | **Cmaj7(13/♯11/9)** |
| | {5 9 ♯11 13} is not applicable |
| B-7 | {7 9 ♯11 13} *relative to* A-6(11/9) {1 6 9 11} |
| D7 | {1 9 ♯11 13 } *relative to* A-6(11) {1 ♭3 6 11} |
| | {3 9 ♯11 13 } under **Tension 9 & 11** as C6(♯11/9) |
| | **C-maj7(13/11/9)** |
| B-7♭5 / D-6 | {7 9 11 13} *relative to* A-7♯5(11/9) {1 ♯5 (♭13) 9 11} |
| D-7 | {1 9 11 13 } *relative to* A-7♯5(11) {1 ♭3 ♯5 11} * |
| | *relative to* E♭maj7(13/♯11/9) {7 9 ♯11 13} |
| | **C-7♭5(♭13/11/9)** |
| A♭13(♭5) | {♭5 9 11 ♭13} *relative* to E♭-maj7(11/9) {♭3 7 9 11} |

The new relative chords that have been discovered, (and received asterisks), will now be displayed in various II V I examples. These chords will be grouped into three different categories: major, minor, and minor7♭5. The relative chord or chords will be listed as well as the original chord to first introduce that voicing.

The following is an organized list of the relative chords that will be examined, showing the order in which they will appear and any multiple functions they might have.

| **MAJOR** | | | **Functions** |
|---|---|---|---|
| 1 | major (add9) | {1 3 5 9} | dom7(9) / maj7(9) |
| 2 | major♭5 (add9) | {1 3 ♭5 9} | dom7♭5(9) / maj7♭5(9) |
| 3 | maj7(9) | {1 5 7 9} | maj7(9) / min. maj7(9) |
| 4 | maj6(9) | {1 5 6 9} | maj6(9) / min6(9) |
| 5 | maj7(6) | {1 5 6 7} | maj7(6) / min. maj7(6) |
| 6 | maj7♭5(6) | {1 ♭5 6 7} | maj7♭5(6) only |
| 7 | maj7(6/9) | {1 6 7 9} | maj7(6/9) / min. maj7(6/9) |

| **MINOR** | | | **Functions** |
|---|---|---|---|
| 1 | minor(add9) | {1 ♭3 5 9} | min7(9) / min. maj7(9) / min6(9) |
| 2 | minor(add11) | {1 ♭3 5 11} | min7(11)/min. maj7(11)/min6(11) |
| 3 | minor(9/11) | {♭3 5 9 11} | min7(9/11)/min.maj7(9/11)/min6(9/11) |
| 4 | minor(9/11) | {1 5 9 11} | same as above plus dom9sus |
| 5 | minor(9/11) | {1 ♭3 9 11} | min7(9/11)/min.maj7(9/11)/min6(9/11) |
| 6 | minor 7(9) | {1 5 ♭7 9} | min7(9) / dom7(9) |
| 7 | min.maj7(9/11) | {1 7 9 11} | min.maj7(9/11)only |
| 8 | min.maj7(6/11) | {1 6 7 11} | min.maj7(6/11)only |

| **MINOR 7♭5** | | | **Functions** |
|---|---|---|---|
| 1 | min7♭5(9) | {1 ♭3 ♭5 9} | min7♭5(9) only |
| 2 | min7♭5(11) | {1 ♭3 ♭5 11} | min7♭5(11) only |
| 3 | min7♭5(9/11) | {1 ♭5 9 11} | min7♭5(9/11) only |
| 4 | min7♭5(9/11) | {♭3 ♭5 9 11} | min7♭5(9/11) only |
| 5 | min7♭5(♭13) | {1 ♭5 ♭7 ♭13} | min7♭5(♭13)/dom7(alt5) |
| 6 | min7♭5(♭13) | {1 ♭3 ♭5 ♭13} | min7♭5(♭13) / dom7(♯9/alt5) |
| 7 | min7♭5(♭13/9) | {♭3 ♭7 9 ♭13} | min7♭5(♭13/9)only |
| 8 | min7♭5(♭13/9) | {♭3 ♭5 9 ♭13} | min7♭5(♭13/9)only |
| 9 | min7♭5(♭13/9) | {1 ♭5 9 ♭13} | min7♭5(♭13/9)/ dom9(alt5) |
| 10 | min7♭5(♭13/9) | {1 ♭7 9 ♭13} | min7♭5(♭13/9)/ dom9+ |
| 11 | min7♭5(♭13/9) | {1 ♭3 9 ♭13} | min7♭5(♭13/9)only |
| 12 | min7♭5(♭13/11) | {1 ♭5 11 ♭13} | min7♭5(♭13/11)only |
| 13 | min7♭5(♭13/11) | {1 ♭7 11 ♭13} | min7♭5(♭13/11)only |
| 14 | min7♭5(♭13/11) | {1 ♭3 11 ♭13} | min7♭5(♭13/11)only |

**major(add9)** {1 3 5 9}

C(add9) relative to A-7(11) (♭3 5 ♭7 11}
*original* chord E-7♯5

Avoiding tension 9 on the 5th string leaves three applicable inversions:

| | | |
|---|---|---|
| 9 | 1 | 5 |
| 5 | 3 | 9 |
| 3 | 9 | 1 |
| 1 | 5 | 3 |

**major ♭5(add9)** {1 3 ♭5 9}

C(9/♭5) relative to A-6(11) (♭3 5 6 11}
*original* chord D9 {1 3 ♭7 9}

Avoiding tension 9 on the 5th string leaves three applicable inversions:

| | | |
|---|---|---|
| ♭5 | 9 | 1 |
| 9 | ♭5 | 3 |
| 1 | 3 | 9 |
| 3 | 1 | ♭5 |

**maj7(9)** {1 5 7 9}

Cmaj7(9) relative to A-7(11/9) {♭3 ♭7 9 11}
*original* chord D13sus4 {1 4 ♭7 13}

Avoiding tension 9 on 5th string leaves only one applicable inversion:

9
7
5
1

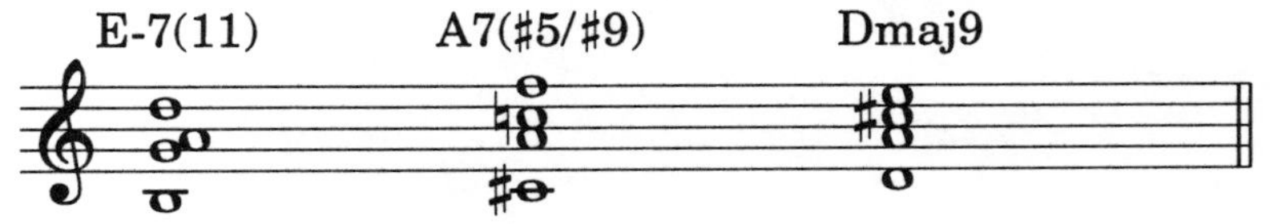


**maj6(9)** {1 5 6 9} (min6(9))

C6(9) relative to A-7(11) {1 ♭3 ♭7 11} ; C-6(9) relative to E♭maj7♭5(6) {3 ♭5 6 7}
*original chord* D7sus4

Avoiding tension 9 on the 5th string leaves three applicable inversions:

| | | |
|---|---|---|
| 6 | 1 | 9 |
| 9 | 5 | 6 |
| 1 | 9 | 5 |
| 5 | 6 | 1 |

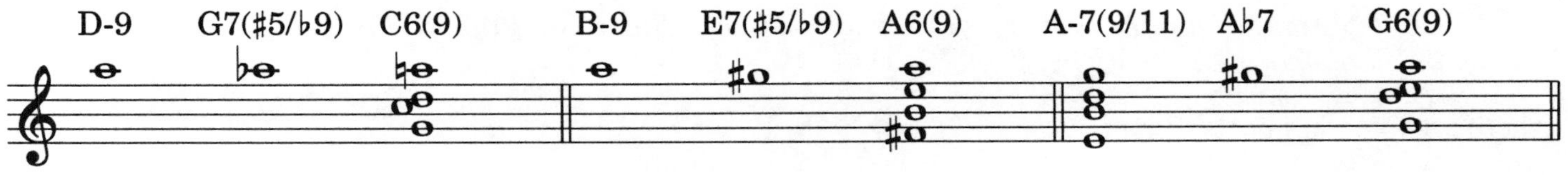


**maj7(6)** {1 5 6 7}

Cmaj7(6) relative to A-9 {1 ♭3 ♭7 9}
*original chord* A-9

There is one applicable inversion:

7
5
1
6

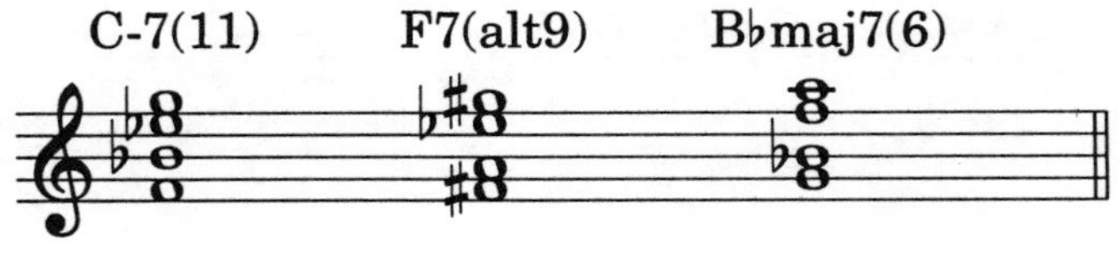

**maj7♭5(6)** {1 ♭5 6 7}

Cmaj7♭5(6) relative to A-6(9) {1 ♭3 6 9}
*original chord* A-6(9)

There is one applicable inversion:

7
♭5
1
6

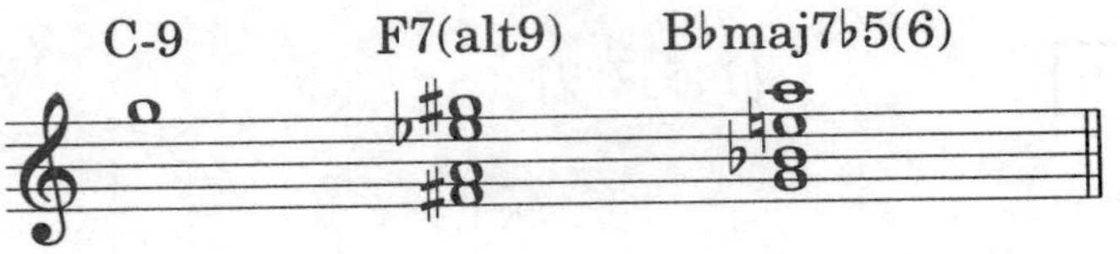


**maj7(6/9)** {1 6 7 9}

Cmaj7(6/9) relative to A-(11/9) {1 ♭3 9 11}
*original chord* F6(♯11) {3 5 6 ♯11}

There are two applicable inversions:

| | |
|---|---|
| 9 | 1 |
| 7 | 7 |
| 6 | 9 |
| 1 | 6 |

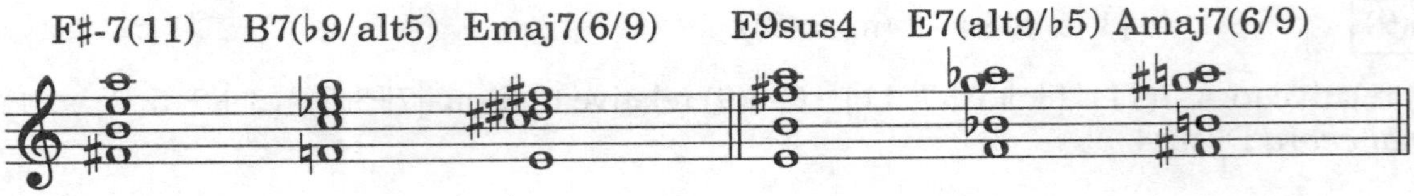


*Note: The above E9sus4 voicing is introduced in the **New Voicings** chapter.

**minor(add9)** {1 ♭3 5 9}

Cm(add9) relative to A-7♭5(11) {♭3 ♭5 ♭7 11} and E♭maj7(6) {1 3 6 7}
*original chord* A♭maj7(♯11) {3 5 7 ♯11}

There are three applicable inversions:

| | | |
|---|---|---|
| ♭3 | 9 | 5 |
| 9 | 5 | 9 |
| 5 | ♭3 | 1 |
| 1 | 1 | ♭3 |

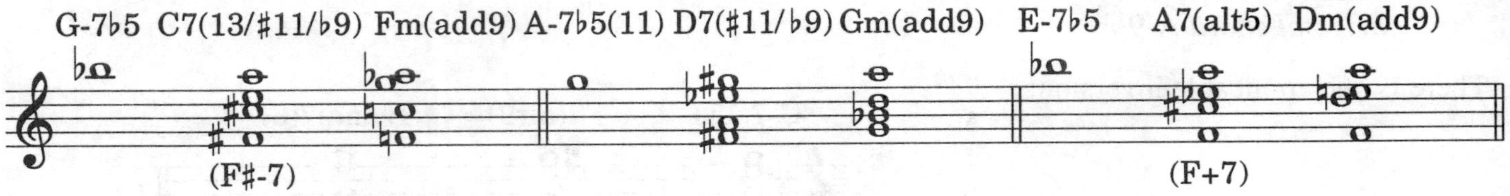

**minor(add11)** {1 ♭3 5 11}

Cm(add11) relative to E♭6(9) {1 3 6 9} and A-7♭5(♭13) {♭3 ♭5 ♭7 ♭13}
*original chord* E♭6(9)

There are four applicable inversions:

| | | | |
|---|---|---|---|
| 11 | 5 | ♭3 | 1 |
| 1 | ♭3 | 5 | 11 |
| 5 | 1 | 11 | ♭3 |
| ♭3 | 11 | 1 | 5 |

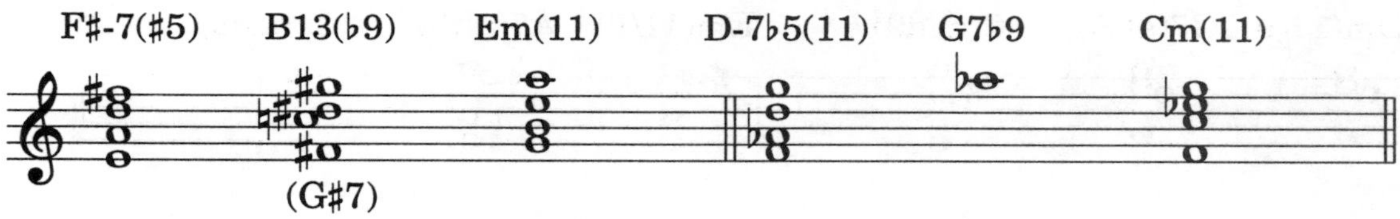


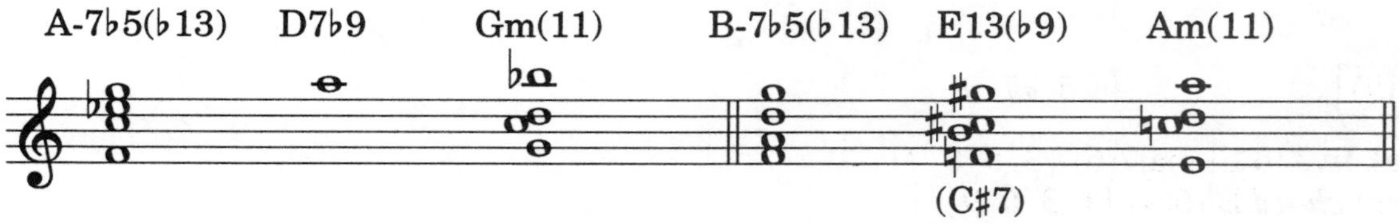


**minor(11/9)** {♭3 5 9 11}

Cm(11/9) relative to E♭maj9 {1 3 7 9} and A-7♭5(♭13/11) {♭5 ♭7 11 ♭13}
*original chord* E♭maj9

There are two applicable inversions:

| | |
|---|---|
| 11 | 5 |
| 9 | ♭3 |
| 5 | 9 |
| ♭3 | 11 |

**minor(11/9)** {1 5 9 11}

Cm(11/9) relative to E♭maj7(6/9) {3 6 7 9} and A-7♭5(♭13/11) {♭3 ♭7 11 ♭13}
*original chord* G7sus4

Avoiding tension 9 on the 5th string leaves three applicable inversions:

| | | |
|---|---|---|
| 1 | 9 | 5 |
| 11 | 5 | 9 |
| 9 | 11 | 1 |
| 5 | 1 | 11 |

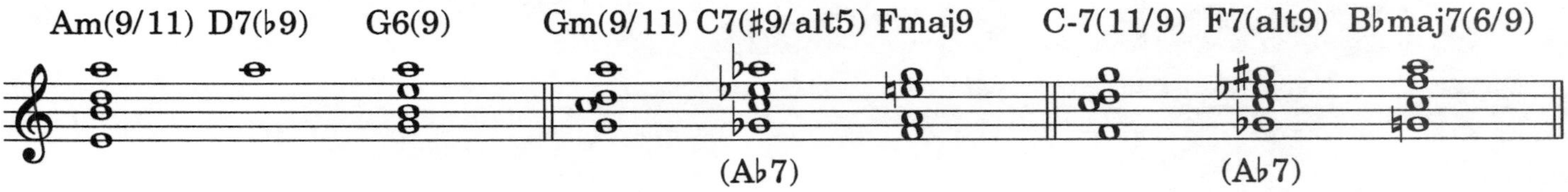

**minor(11/9)** {1 ♭3 9 11}

Cm(11/9) relative to E♭maj7(6/9) {1 6 7 9}
*original chord* A♭6(♯11) {3 5 6 ♯11}

There are two applicable inversions:

| | |
|---|---|
| 11 | ♭3 |
| 9 | 9 |
| 1 | 11 |
| ♭3 | 1 |

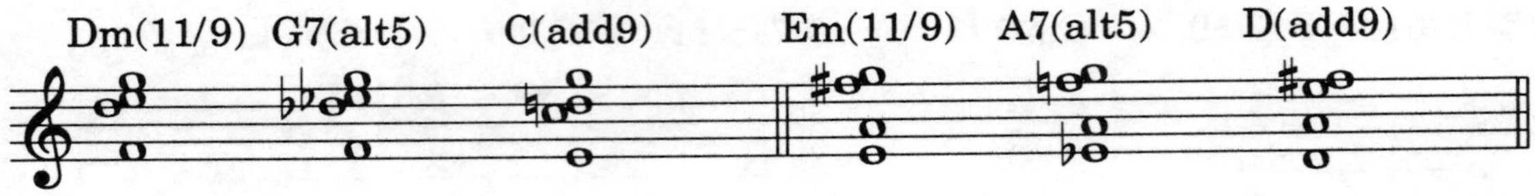


*Note: The above A7(alt5) and D(add9) voicings are introduced in the **New Voicings** chapter.

**min7(9)** {1 5 ♭7 9}

C-9 relative to E♭maj7(6) {3 5 6 7}
*original chord* B♭6(9) {1 3 6 9}

Avoiding tension 9 on the 5th string leaves three applicable inversions:

| | | |
|---|---|---|
| 1 | 9 | ♭7 |
| 5 | ♭7 | 9 |
| 9 | 5 | 1 |
| ♭7 | 1 | 5 |

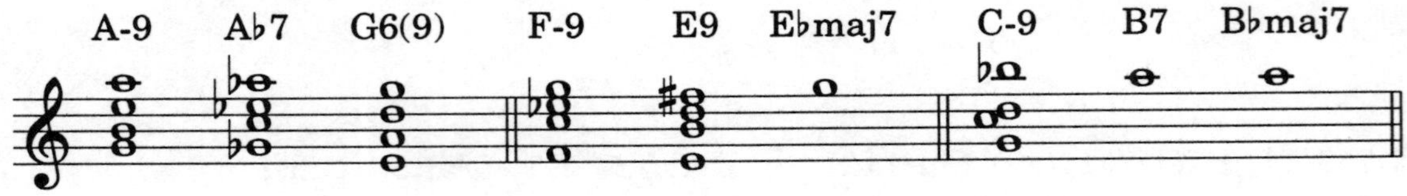


**min. maj7(9/11)** {1 7 9 11}

C-maj7(9/11) relative to A-7♭5(♭13/11/9) {♭3 9 11 ♭13}
*original chord* F6(♯11) {1 5 6 ♯11}

Avoiding tension 9 on the 5th string leaves only one applicable inversion:

| |
|---|
| 9 |
| 7 |
| 11 |
| 1 |

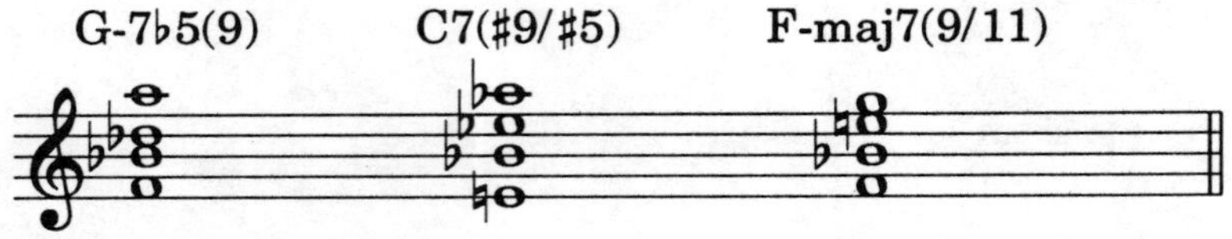

**min. maj7(6/11)** {1 6 7 11}

C-maj7(6/11) relative to A-7♭5(♭13/9) {1 ♭3 9 ♭13}
*original chord* A♭13(alt9) {3 ♭9 ♯9 13}

There is only one applicable inversion:

7
11
1
6

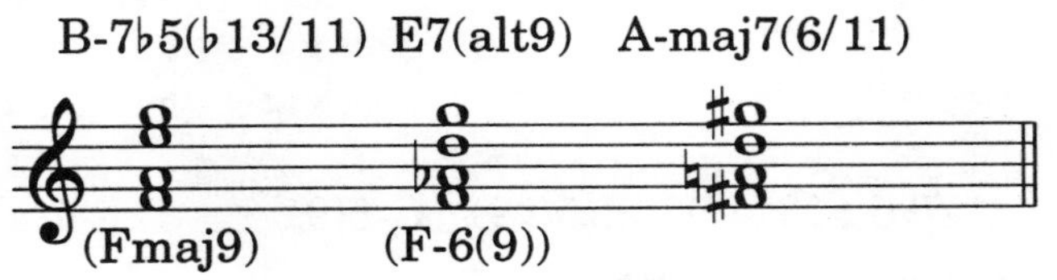


**min7♭5(9)** {1 ♭3 ♭5 9}

C-7♭5(9) relative to E♭-maj7(6) {1 ♭3 6 7}
*original chord* A♭7(♯11) {3 5 ♭7 ♯11}

There is only one applicable inversion:

9
♭5
♭3
1

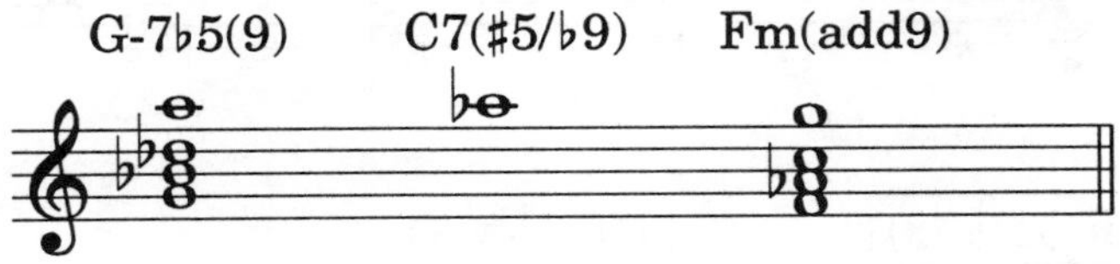


**min7♭5(11)** {1 ♭3 ♭5 11}

C-7♭5(11) relative to E♭-6(9) {1 ♭3 6 9}
*original chord* E♭-6(9)

There is only one applicable inversion:

11
1
♭5
♭3

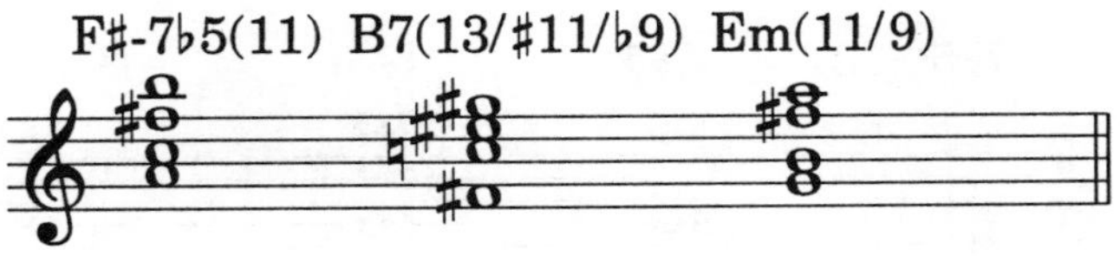


**min7♭5(11/9)** {1 ♭5 9 11}

C-7♭5(11/9) relative to E♭-maj7(6/9) {♭3 6 7 9}
*original chord* D7(♯9) {1 3 ♭7 ♯9}

There is only one available inversion, and unfortunately this one has tension 9 on the 5th string:

11
1
♭5
9

**min7♭5(11/9)** {♭3 ♭5 9 11}

C-7♭5(11/9) relative to E♭-maj9 {1 ♭3 7 9}
*original chord* E♭-maj9

There is only one applicable inversion:

11
9
♭5
♭3

**min7♭5(♭13)** {1 ♭5 ♭7 ♭13}

C-7♭5(♭13) relative to E♭-6(11) {♭3 5 6 11}
*original chord* A♭9 {1 3 ♭7 9}

There are four applicable inversions:

| | | | |
|---|---|---|---|
| ♭7 | 1 | ♭5 | ♭13 |
| ♭5 | ♭13 | ♭7 | 1 |
| 1 | ♭5 | ♭13 | ♭7 |
| ♭13 | ♭7 | 1 | ♭5 |

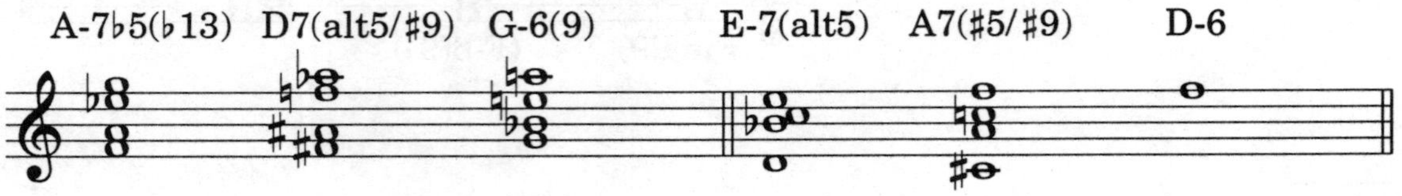


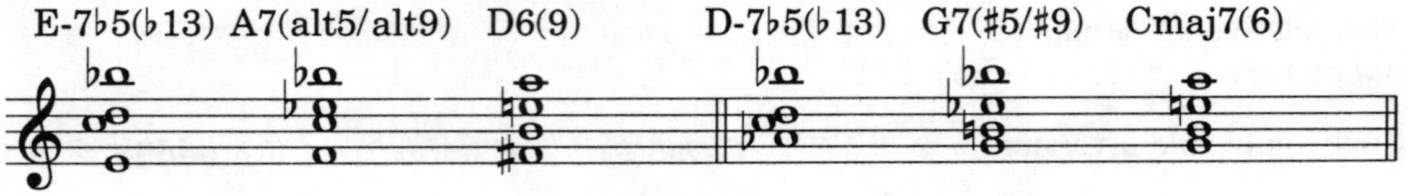


**min7♭5(♭13)** {1 ♭3 ♭5 ♭13}

C-7♭5(♭13) relative to E♭-6(11) {1 ♭3 6 11}
*original chord* A♭7

There are four applicable inversions:

| | | | |
|---|---|---|---|
| ♭13 | 1 | ♭5 | ♭3 |
| ♭3 | ♭5 | 1 | ♭13 |
| 1 | ♭3 | ♭13 | ♭5 |
| ♭5 | ♭13 | ♭3 | 1 |

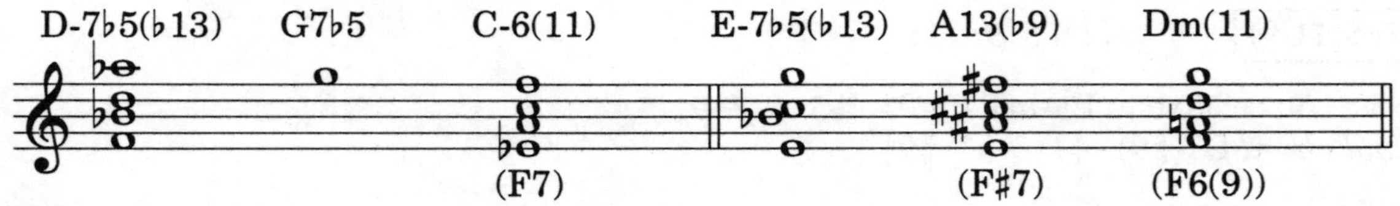


**min7♭5(♭13/9)** {♭3 ♭7 9 ♭13} (min7♯5(9))

C-7♭5(♭13/9) relative to E♭-maj7(11) {1 5 7 11}
*original chord* E♭-maj7(11)

There are three applicable inversions:

| | | |
|---|---|---|
| 9 | ♭7 | ♭13 |
| ♭13 | ♭3 | 9 |
| ♭3 | 9 | ♭7 |
| ♭7 | ♭13 | ♭3 |

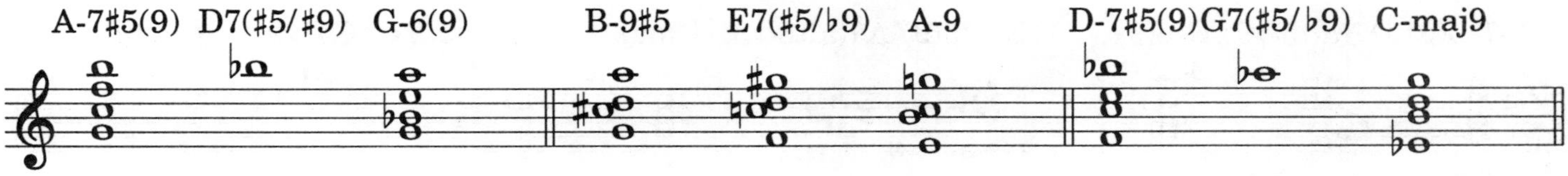


**min7♭5(♭13/9)** {♭3 ♭5 9 ♭13}

C-7♭5(♭13/9) relative to E♭-maj7(11) {1 ♭3 7 11}
*original chord* A♭7(♯11) {1 5 ♭7 ♯11}

There are two applicable inversions:

| | |
|---|---|
| ♭5 | 9 |
| 9 | ♭5 |
| ♭13 | ♭3 |
| ♭3 | ♭13 |

**min7♭5(♭13/9)** {1 ♭5 9 ♭13}

C-7♭5(♭13/9) relative to E♭-maj7(6/11) {♭3 7 6 11}
*original chord* A♭7♭5 / D7♭5

Note: Since the original chord mirrors the same chord a tritone away, it applies to any substitution chords of the original chord:

| | | |
|---|---|---|
| A♭7♭5 | = | D7♭5 |
| E♭-maj7(6/11) | = | A-maj7(6/11) |
| C-7♭5(♭13/9) | = | F♯-7♭5(♭13/9) |

Avoiding tension 9 on the 5th string leaves three applicable inversions:

| | | |
|---|---|---|
| 1 | ♭13 | 9 |
| ♭5 | 9 | ♭13 |
| 9 | 1 | ♭5 |
| ♭13 | ♭5 | 1 |

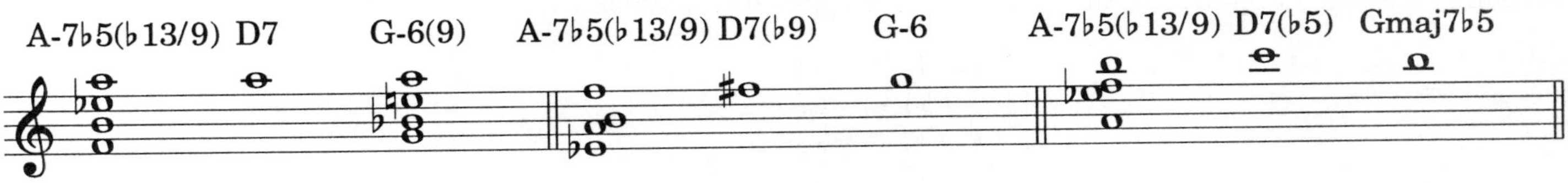


**min7♭5(♭13/9)** {1 ♭7 9 ♭13} (min9♯5)

C-7♭5(♭13/9) relative to E♭-maj7(11/6) {5 7 6 11}
*original chord* B♭9 {1 3 ♭7 9}

Avoiding tension 9 on the 5th string leaves three applicable inversions:

| | | |
|---|---|---|
| 1 | 9 | ♭7 |
| ♭13 | ♭7 | 9 |
| 9 | ♭13 | 1 |
| ♭7 | 1 | ♭13 |

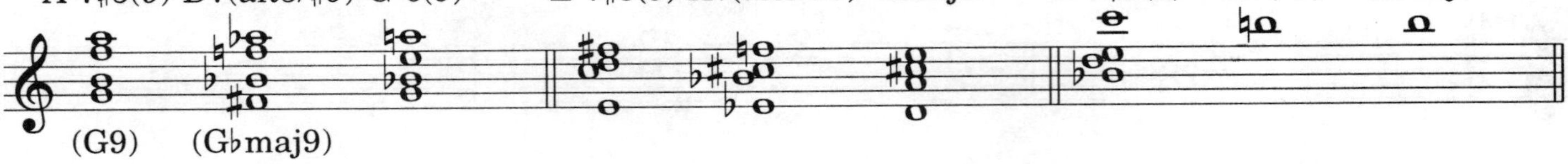


**min7♭5(♭13/9)** {1 ♭3 9 ♭13} (min7♯5(9))

C-7♭5(♭13/9) relative to E♭-maj7(11/6) {1 6 7 11}
*original chord* B13(alt9) {3 ♭9 ♯9 13}

There is only one applicable inversion:

| |
|---|
| 9 |
| ♭13 |
| ♭3 |
| 1 |

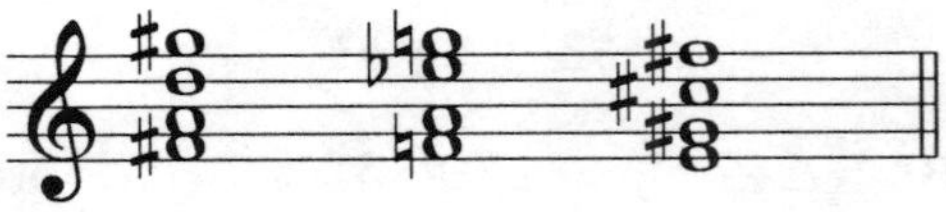


**min7♭5(♭13/11)** {1 ♭5 11 ♭13}

C-7♭5(♭13/11) relative to E♭-6(11/9) {♭3 6 9 11}
*original chord* D7♭5(♯9) / A♭13

There are two applicable inversions:

| | |
|---|---|
| ♭13 | 1 |
| 11 | ♭5 |
| 1 | 11 |
| ♭5 | ♭13 |

**min7♭5(♭13/11)** {1 ♭7 11 ♭13} (min7♯5(11))

C-7♭5(♭13/11) relative to E♭-6(11/9) {5 6 9 11}
*original chord* A♭6(9) {1 3 6 9}

Avoiding tension 11 on the 5th string leaves three applicable inversions:

| | | |
|---|---|---|
| ♭7 | 1 | 11 |
| 11 | ♭13 | ♭7 |
| 1 | 11 | ♭3 |
| ♭13 | ♭7 | 1 |

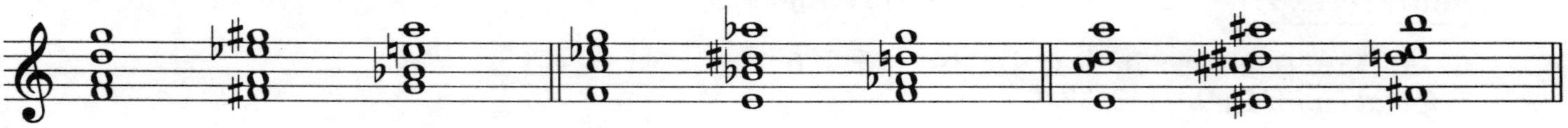

**min7♭5(♭13/11)** {1 ♭3 11 ♭13} (min7♯5(11))

C-7♭5(♭13/11) relative to E♭-maj7(13/11/9) {1 9 11 13} or E♭-6(11/9) {1 6 9 11}
*original chord* F-7

Avoiding tension 11 on the 5th string leaves three applicable inversions:

| | | |
|---|---|---|
| 1 | ♭3 | 11 |
| 11 | ♭13 | 1 |
| ♭3 | 11 | ♭13 |
| ♭13 | 1 | ♭3 |

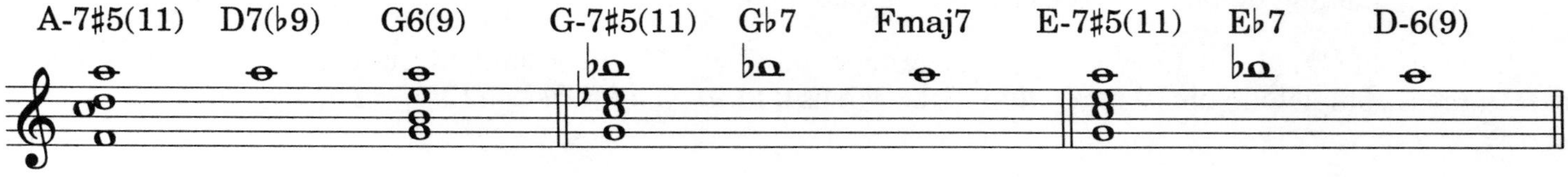

# Chapter Seventeen.
## Additional Substitutions in II-V-I Examples

After removing all of the chords that were examined in the **Relative Major-Minor** chapter, only dominant type chords remain in the **Additional Enharmonic Chordal Substitutions** chapter. These can be organized into three different groups:

1) Dominant chords with ♭13 and natural 5 (no Sub V's).
2) Dominant sus4 chords with ♭9 (no Sub V's).
3) Remaining dominant chords (including Sub V's).

The dom7sus4(13/9) {1 4 9 13} voicing (original chord min7 / maj6) will be omitted, due to the ambiguity produced by forming a complete I6 chord in relation to the V7sus4(13/9) chord: C7sus4(13/9) = F6.

**dom7(♭13)**

**{1 3 5 ♭13}** C7(♭13) = A♭maj7♯5

There are three applicable inversions:

| | | |
|---|---|---|
| 3 | 5 | 1 |
| ♭13 | 1 | 5 |
| 5 | ♭13 | 3 |
| 1 | 3 | ♭13 |

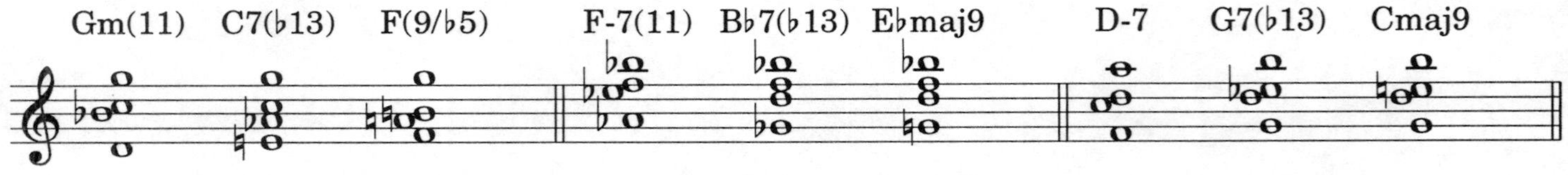


**{1 5 ♭7 ♭13}** C7(♭13) = A♭maj9 {1 3 7 9}

There are two applicable inversions:

| | |
|---|---|
| ♭7 | 1 |
| 5 | ♭13 |
| 1 | 5 |
| ♭13 | ♭7 |

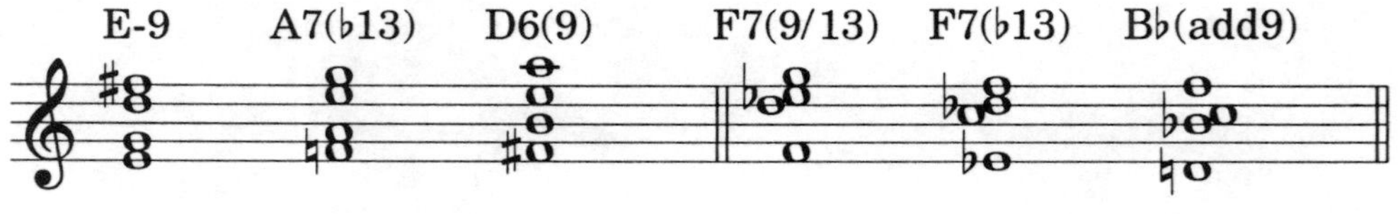


**{3 5 ♭7 ♭13}** C7(♭13) = B♭13(♭5) {1 ♭5 ♭7 13}

There are two applicable inversions:

| | |
|---|---|
| ♭7 | 3 |
| 5 | ♭13 |
| 3 | 5 |
| ♭13 | ♭7 |

**dom7(♭13/9)**

**{1 5 9 ♭13}** C9(♭13) = A♭maj7(♭5)

There are two applicable inversions:

| | |
|---|---|
| 9 | 1 |
| ♭13 | 5 |
| 5 | 9 |
| 1 | ♭13 |

**{3 5 9 ♭13}** C9(♭13) = E7(♯9) {1 3 ♭7 ♯9}

There is one applicable inversion:

5
9
♭13
3

**{5 ♭7 9 ♭13}** C9(♭13) = E7♭5(♯9) / B♭13

There are two applicable inversions:

| | |
|---|---|
| ♭7 | 9 |
| 5 | ♭13 |
| 9 | 5 |
| ♭13 | ♭7 |

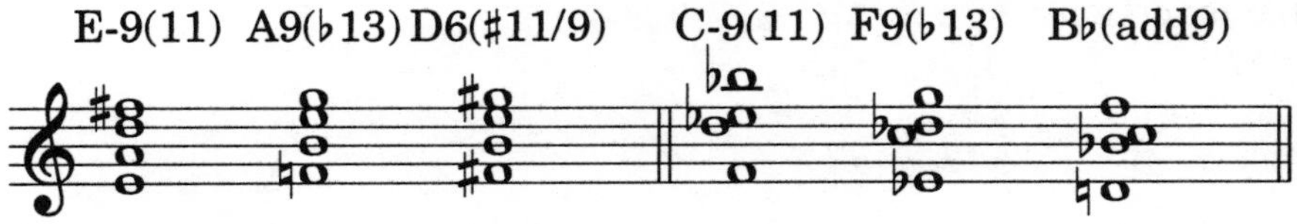


**dom7(♭13/♭9)**

**{1 5 ♭9 ♭13}** C7(♭13/♭9) = D♭maj7(♯11) {1 5 7 ♯11}

There are two applicable inversions:

| | |
|---|---|
| 5 | 1 |
| 1 | 5 |
| ♭13 | ♭9 |
| ♭9 | ♭13 |

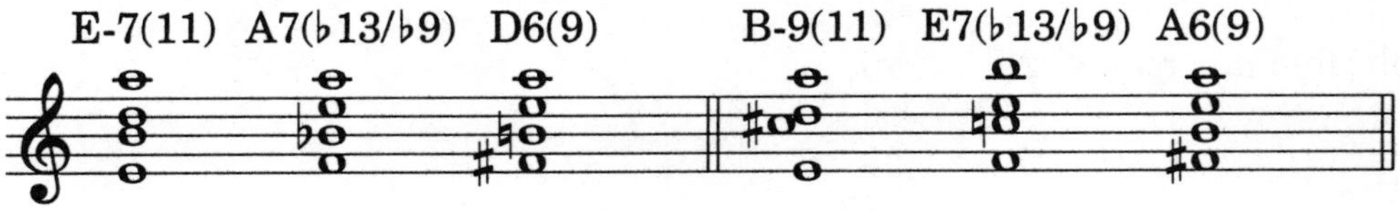

**{5 ♭7 ♭9 ♭13}** C7(♭13/♭9) = D♭6(♯11) {1 5 6 ♯11}

There are two applicable inversions:

| | |
|---|---|
| ♭7 | ♭9 |
| 5 | ♭13 |
| ♭9 | 5 |
| ♭13 | ♭7 |

**{3 5 ♭9 ♭13}** C7(♭13/♭9) = G7(13/♯11/♭9) {1 ♭9 ♯11 13}

There are two applicable inversions:

| | |
|---|---|
| 3 | ♭9 |
| ♭13 | 5 |
| 5 | 3 |
| ♭9 | ♭13 |

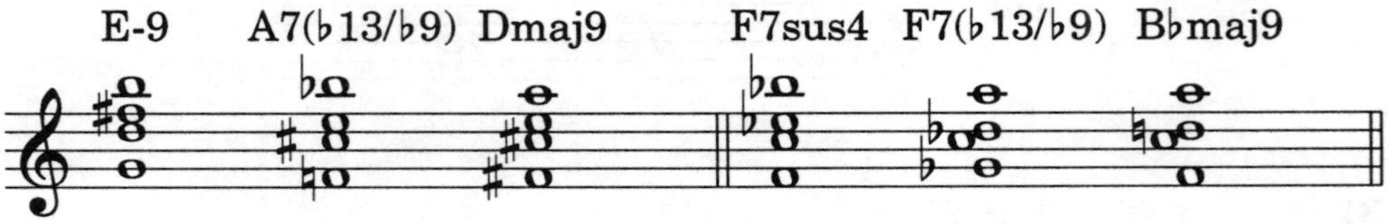


**dom7(♭13/♯9)**

**{5 ♭7 ♯9 ♭13}** C7(♭13/♯9) = B♭13sus4 {1 4 ♭7 13}

There are two applicable inversions:

| | |
|---|---|
| ♭7 | ♯9 |
| 5 | ♭13 |
| ♯9 | 5 |
| ♭13 | ♭7 |

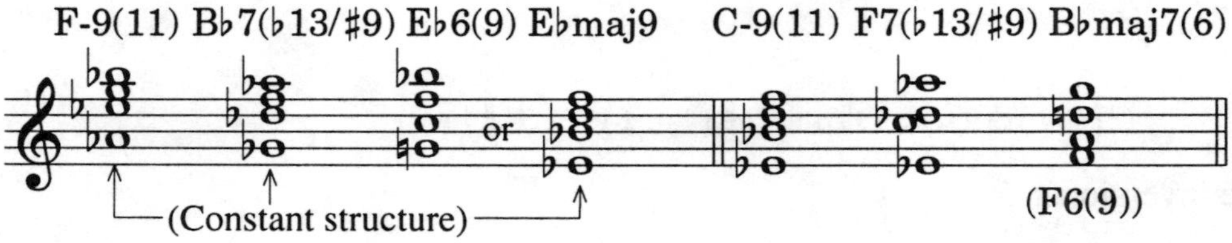


**dom7(♭13/alt9)**

**{5 ♭9 ♯9 ♭13}** C7(♭13/alt9) = A♭-maj7(11) {1 5 7 11}

There are two applicable inversions:

| | |
|---|---|
| ♯9 | ♭9 |
| ♭13 | 5 |
| 5 | ♯9 |
| ♭9 | ♭13 |

**dom7sus4(♭9)**

**{1 4 5 ♭9}** C7sus4(♭9) = D♭maj7(♭5)

There are three applicable inversions:

| | | |
|---|---|---|
| 4 | 5 | 1 |
| 1 | ♭9 | 4 |
| 5 | 1 | ♭9 |
| ♭9 | 4 | 5 |

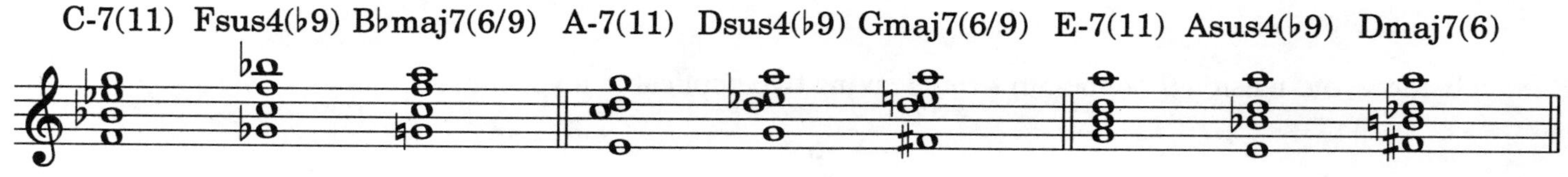


**{1 4 ♭7 ♭9}** C7sus4(♭9) = G♭maj7(♯11) {3 5 7 ♯11}

There are three applicable inversions:

| | | |
|---|---|---|
| 1 | 4 | ♭9 |
| 4 | 1 | 1 |
| ♭9 | ♭7 | 4 |
| ♭7 | ♭9 | ♭7 |

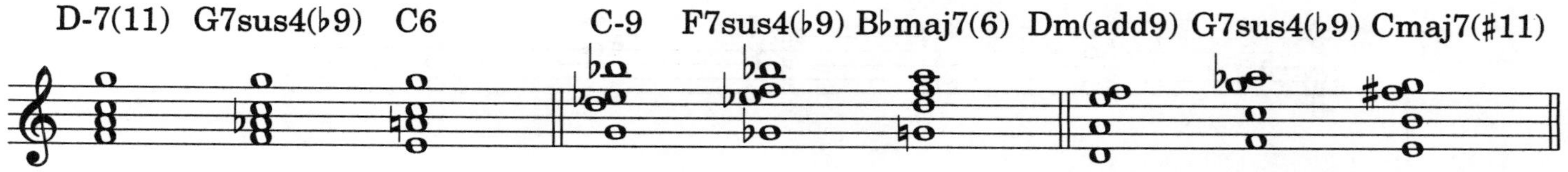


(Constant structure)

**dom13sus4(♭9)**

**{1 4 ♭9 13}** C13sus4(♭9) = D♭maj7♯5

Avoiding tension 13 on the 5th string leaves two applicable inversions:

| | |
|---|---|
| 4 | 13 |
| 1 | ♭9 |
| 13 | 1 |
| ♭9 | 4 |

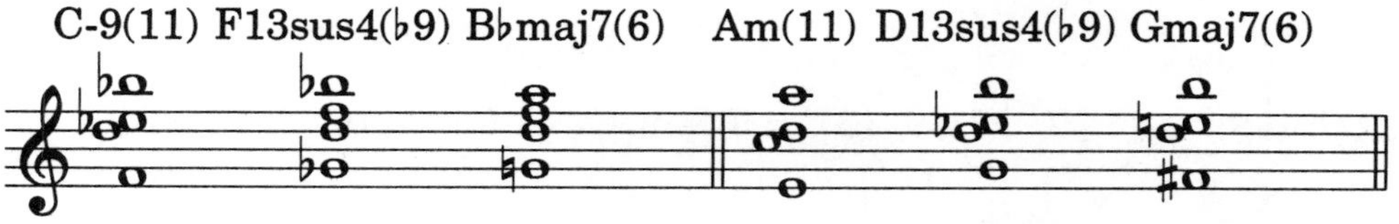


**{4 5 ♭9 13}** C13sus4(♭9) = A+7

Avoiding tension 13 on the 5th string leaves three applicable inversions:

| | | |
|---|---|---|
| 4 | 5 | 13 |
| 13 | ♭9 | 4 |
| 5 | 13 | ♭9 |
| ♭9 | 4 | 5 |

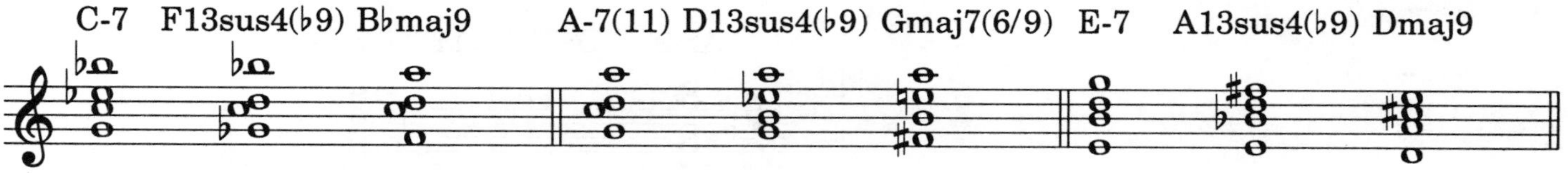

**dom9(alt5)**

**{1 ♭5 ♯5 9}**

Sub V — C9(alt5) { 1 ♭5 ♯5 9 } = D7♭5 / A♭7♭5

↓ ↓ ↓ ↓

F♯9(alt5) { ♭5 1 9 ♯5 }

Remember to avoid tension 9 on the 5th string leaving two applicable inversions:

| | |
|---|---|
| ♯5 ⟶ 9 | 1 ⟶ ♭5 |
| 9 ⟶ ♯5 | ♭5 ⟶ 1 |
| 1 ⟶ ♭5 | 9 ⟶ ♯5 |
| ♭5 ⟶ 1 | ♯5 ⟶ 9 |

Note: This voicing also was used in the **Relative Major-Minor** chapter as a **min7♭5(♭13/9)** chord {1 ♭5 9 ♭13}.

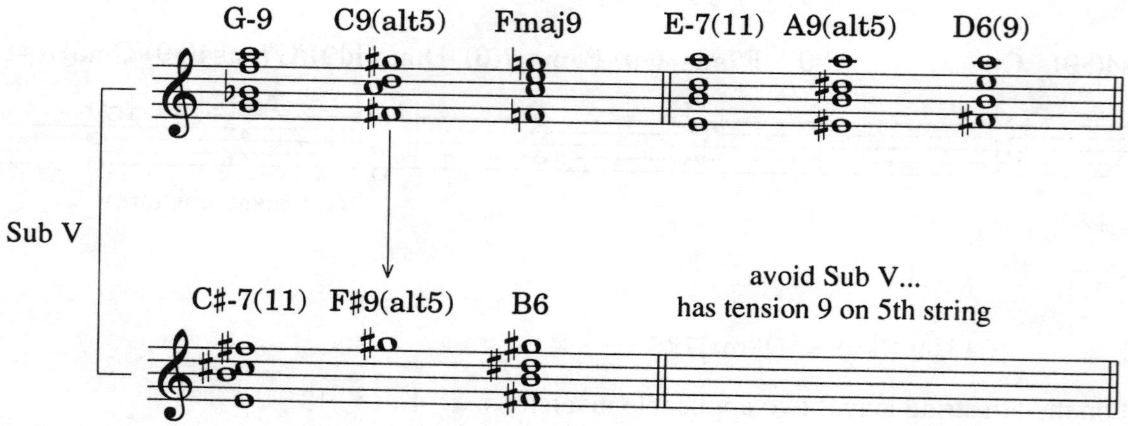


**dom13(♭9) / dom7(♯11/♯9)**
**{1♭7♭9 13} / {3 5♯9♯11}**

Sub V — C13(♭9) { 1 ♭7 ♭9 13} = B♭-maj9 {1 ♭3 7 9}

↓ ↓ ↓ ↓

F♯7(♯11/♯9) {♯11 3 5 ♯9}

There is one applicable inversion:

1 ⟶ ♯11

13 ⟶ ♯9

♭9 ⟶ 5

♭7 ⟶ 3

**dom7(♭9/♯5) / dom9(♯11)**
**{1♯5 ♭7 ♭9} / {3 5 9♯11}**

Sub V ——— C7(♭9/♯5)  { 1 ♯5 ♭7 ♭9 } = B♭-9 {1 ♭3 ♭7 9}

↓ ↓ ↓ ↓

F♯9(♯11)  {♯11 9 3 5}

There is one applicable inversion:

1 ⟶ ♯11
♯5 ⟶ 9
♭9 ⟶ 5
♭7 ⟶ 3

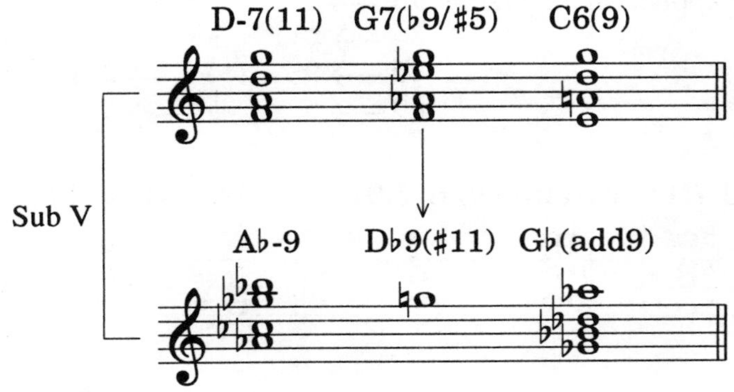


*Note*: The **dom9(♯11)** voicing could have a *lydian* function since no 7th is present:

{3 5 9 ♯11} C(♯11/9) = Cmaj9(♯11). The following II-V-I example displays the Lydian function:

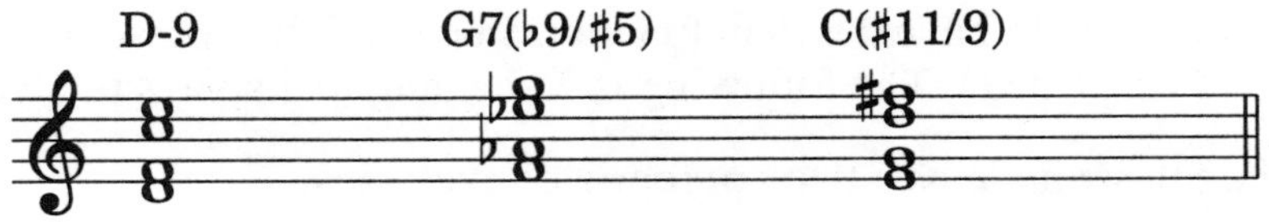


**dom7(♭9) / dom7(♯11/♭9)**
**{1 5♭7♭9} / {3 5♭9♯11}**

Sub V ——— C7(♭9).......... { 1 5 ♭7 ♭9 } = B♭-6(9) {1 ♭3 6 9}

↓ ↓ ↓ ↓

F♯7(♯11/♭9)  {♯11 ♭9 3 5 }

There is one applicable inversion:

1 ⟶ ♯11
5 ⟶ ♭9
♭9 ⟶ 5
♭7 ⟶ 3

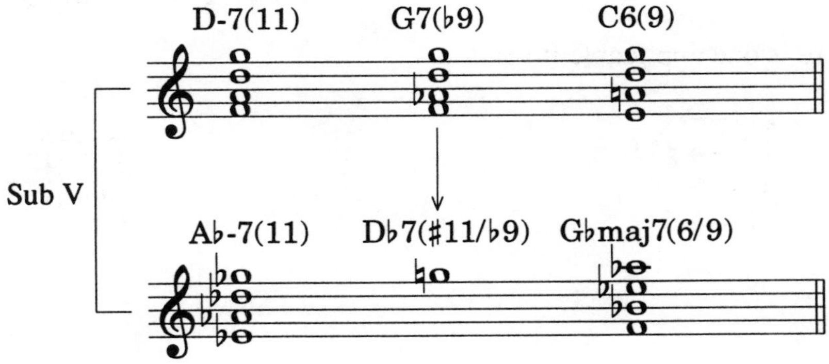

**dom7(♭9/alt5) / dom9(♯11)**
**{1 ♭5 ♯5 ♭9} / {1 5 9 ♯11}**

Sub V — C7(♭9/alt5) { 1 ♭5 ♯5 ♭9 } = D♭-maj7(11) {1 5 7 11}

↓ ↓ ↓ ↓

F♯9(♯11) {♯11 1 9 5 }

There are three applicable inversion:

| | | |
|---|---|---|
| ♭5 ⟶ 1 | ♯5 ⟶ 9 | 1 ⟶ ♯11 |
| 1 ⟶ ♯11 | ♭9 ⟶ 5 | ♭5 ⟶ 1 |
| ♯5 ⟶ 9 | 1 ⟶ ♯11 | ♭9 ⟶ 5 |
| ♭9 ⟶ 5 | ♭5 ⟶ 1 | ♯5 ⟶ 9 |

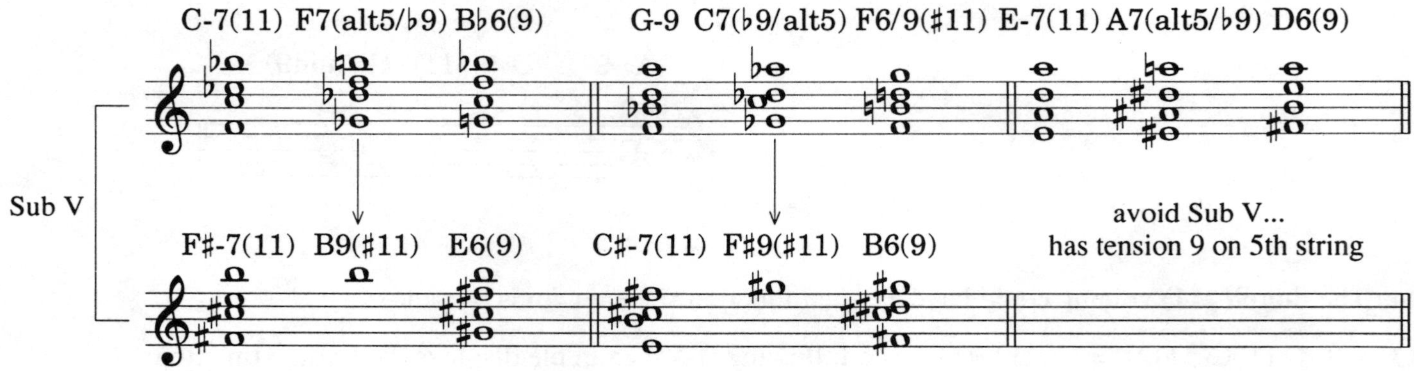


Note: The **dom9(♯11)** voicing could have a lydian function since no 7th is present:
{1 5 9 ♯11} C(♯11/9) = Cmaj9(♯11). The following II-V-I example displays the lydian function.

Avoiding tension 9 on the 5th string leaves two appropriate inversions.

**dom7(♯11/♭9)**
**{ 1 5 ♭9 ♯11 }**

Sub V — C7(♯11/♭9) {1 5 ♭9 ♯11 } = A13(♯9)/E♭13(♯9) {3 ♭7 ♯9 13}

↓ ↓ ↓ ↓

F♯7(♯11/♭9) {♯11 ♭9 5 1 }

There is one applicable inversion:

♯11 ⟶ 1
1 ⟶ ♯11
5 ⟶ ♭9
♭9 ⟶ 5

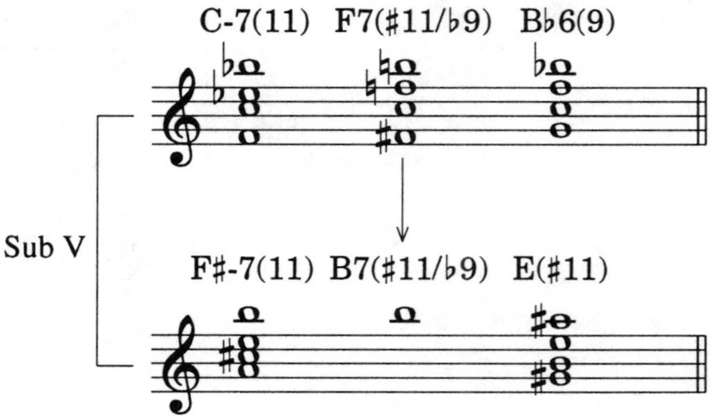

**dom7(♭9/♭5) / dom7(♯11)**
**{1 ♭5 ♭7 ♭9} / {1 3 5 ♯11}**

Sub V — C7(♭9/♭5) {1 ♭5 ♭7 ♭9} = A13(alt9) {3 ♭9 ♯9 13} There is one applicable inversion:

↓ ↓ ↓ ↓

Sub V — F♯7(♯11) {♯11 1 3 5}

1 → ♯11
♭5 → 1
♭9 → 5
♭7 → 3

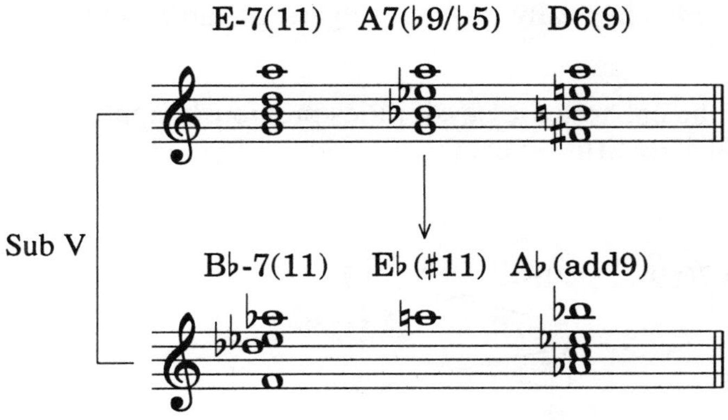


Note: The **dom7(♯11)** voicing could have a lydian function, since no 7th is present:
{1 3 5 ♯11} C(♯11) = Cmaj7(♯11)
The E(♯11) chord under **dom7(♯11/♭9)** presents this function.

# Chapter Eighteen.
## New Voicings

By examining all of the possible interval combinations that are physically available within the established framework (9, ♭10, 10, 11, and ♯11) on the middle four strings of the guitar, (excluding doublings and ♭9th intervals), we see that the vast majority of these voicings already have been introduced in the tension chapters.

With the exception of one voicing, the few remaining interval combinations physically available within this framework appear to be inversions of the ninth (no 3) or ninth (no 5) chord voicings introduced in the **Tension 9** chapter or drop 3 type voicings, both of which produce some physically difficult fingerings and potential voice-leading problems when integrated with drop 2 voicings.

Low Interval Limits allowing, these voicings offer all of the enharmonic possibilities previously applied to their chord tones and tensions under the **Enharmonic Chordal Substitution** chapters.

**Ninth (no 5) Chord Inversions:**

| dom7(9) | | | dom 7(♯9) | | |
|---|---|---|---|---|---|
| | 9 | 3 | | ♯9 | ♭7 |
| | ♭7 | ♭7 | | ♭7 | ♯9 |
| | 3 | 9 | | 3 | 1 |
| | 1 | 1 | | 1 | 3 |

The following ninth (no 3) or ninth (no 5) chord voicings can be produced by using the same inversion formula:

| | |
|---|---|
| 9 | 9 |
| 7 | 1 |
| 3 | 3 |
| 1 | 7 |

| **dom7(9)** | | **dom7(♯9)** | | **maj6(9)** | |
|---|---|---|---|---|---|
| | 9 | | ♯9 | | 9 |
| | 1 | | 1 | | 1 |
| | 3 | | 3 | | 3 |
| | ♭7 | | ♭7 | | 6 |

| **min7(9)** | | **dom7sus4(9)** | | **dom7♭5(9)** | |
|---|---|---|---|---|---|
| | 9 | | 9 | | 9 |
| | 1 | | 1 | | 1 |
| | ♭3 | | 4 | | ♭5 |
| | ♭7 | | ♭7 | | ♭7 |

The following drop 3 type voicings are physically available on the middle four strings:

| **dom7** | | **dom7♭5** | | **min7♭5** | |
|---|---|---|---|---|---|
| | 3 | | 3 | | ♭3 |
| | 1 | | 1 | | 1 |
| | 5 | | ♭5 | | ♭5 |
| | ♭7 | | ♭7 | | ♭7 |

| | | | |
|---|---|---|---|
| **dom7♯5** | 1<br>♭7<br>3<br>♯5 | **min7♯5** | 1<br>♭7<br>♭3<br>♯5 |
| **dom7sus4** | ♭7<br>5<br>1<br>4 | **min.maj7(11)** | 7<br>5<br>1<br>11 |

Obvious enharmonic substitutions:

| | | |
|---|---|---|
| ♭3 - 1 | 1 - 3 | 7 - ♯11 |
| 1 - 6 | ♭7 - 9 | 5 - 9 |
| ♭5 - ♭3 | ♭3 - 5 | 1 - 5 |
| ♭7 - 5 | ♯5 - 1 | 11 - 1 |

The final voicing introduced in this chapter is unique in that its chordal structure has not yet been introduced. This voicing also affords only one "legitimate" chord, although a couple of "progressive" enharmonic chordal substitutions will be offered.

| Interval | Note | | Degree |
|---|---|---|---|
| major 3rd | D♯ | → | 5 |
| perfect 5th | B | → | ♯9 |
| major 3rd | E | → | ♭13 |
| | C | → | 3 |

A♭7(♭13/♯9)

Additional possible enharmonic chordal substitutes:

Cmaj7(♯9) {1 3 7 ♯9}  A-9(♯11) {♭3 5 9 ♯11}

This voicing also might imply an incomplete polychord. The bottom two notes form a major 3rd interval, suggesting the root and third of an incomplete major triad, while the top two notes also form a major 3rd interval, suggesting a major triad a half-step below or major 7th above the bottom structure:

D♯
B
E
C

implies a B major triad over a C major triad: <u>B</u> / C

# Chapter Nineteen.
## Enharmonic Substitutions of Ninth Chords with omitted third or fifth

The ninth (no 3) and ninth (no 5) chord voicings introduced in the **Tension 9** chapter produce some of the most interesting and useful enharmonic chordal substitutions. Some of these chords have so many substitutions that it is possible to find one voicing that will satisfy all three basic harmonic functions:

| | | | | | | |
|---|---|---|---|---|---|---|
| Cmaj9<br>{1 3 7 9} | = | Am(11/9)<br>{♭3 5 9 11} | / | F♯-7♭5(♭13/11)<br>{♭5 ♭7 11 ♭13} | / | A♭7(alt5/♯9)<br>{3 ♭5 ♯5 ♯9} |

| **Tonic** | **Sub-Dominant** | **Dominant** |
|---|---|---|
| Am(11/9) | B-7♭5(♭13/11) | E7(alt5/♯9) |
| (Cmaj9) | (Fmaj9) | (A♭maj9) |

It is commonly referred to as "constant structure harmonic motion" when moving one voicing around to satisfy different chords. This concept will be examined in more detail in the later chapter appropriately titled **Constant Structure Harmonic Motion**.

The following list will include all of the ninth chords with omitted 3rd or 5th and their enharmonic substitutions.

**Cmaj9** Am(11/9) / Fmaj7(13/♯11) / F♯-7♭5(♭13/11) / A♭7(alt5/♯9) / D9(13) / E7(♭13)
{1 3 7 9}

**Cmaj9(♭5)** A♭7♭5(♯9) / D13 / A-6(11/9) / F♯-7♭5(♭13/11) / F13(♯11/♭9) / B7(alt9)/E9(♭13)
{1 ♭5 7 9}

**C-maj9** F13(♯11) / B7(alt9) / D13(♭9) / A♭7(♯11/♯9) / A-7♭5(11/9)
{1 ♭3 7 9}

**C-9** E♭maj7(6) / F13sus4 / D7(♭9/♯5) / A♭9(♯11)
{1 ♭3 ♭7 9}

**C-9♭5/ C9♭5** D7♯5 / A♭9(♭5) / F♯7(alt5) / G-maj7(11) / E♭-maj7(6) / E-7♭5(♭13/9)/ E9(alt5) / B♭9+ / F13sus4(♭9)
{1 ♭5 ♭7 9}

**C6(9)** Am(11) / B♭maj9(♭5) / Fmaj7(6) / D-9 /F♯-7(alt5) / G-6(11/9) / A♭7(alt5/♭9) / D9 / E-7♯5(11)
{1 3 6 9}

**C-6(9)** F13 / B7(alt9) / D7(♭9) / A♭7(♯11/♭9) / A-11♭5 / E♭maj7(6/♭5)
{1 ♭3 6 9}

**C9** G♭7(alt5) /D9+ /A♭9(alt5) /E7(alt5) /B♭9(♭5) /G-6(11) /F-maj7(11/6) /B♭(9/♭5) /E-7(alt5)/D-7♯5(9)
{1 3 ♭7 9}

**C7(♭9)** G♭7(♯11) / D♭-maj7(6) / E♭13(♭9) / A7(alt9) / B♭-7♭5(9)
{1 3 ♭7 ♭9}

**C7(♯9)** G♭13(♭5) / D♭-maj7(6/9) / A7(alt9/♯11) / E♭13(♭9) / A♭9(♭13) / B♭-7♭5(11/9)
{1 3 ♭7 ♯9}

**C9(♭5)** refer to **C-9(♭5)** above

**C9(♯5)** refer to **C9** above (C9 = D9♯5)
{1 ♯5 ♭7 9}

**C9sus4** D-7♯5 / G-7(11) / B♭(add9) / F-6(11) / A♭6(9/♯11) / A♭13(♯11/9) / D7(♯9/♯5) / E7(alt5/♭9) / B♭9
{1 4 ♭7 9}

The following "blues" progression will use ninth (no 3) or ninth (no 5) chord voicings to substitute each chord. The original chord changes are above the stave while the ninth chord substitutes are below in parentheses.

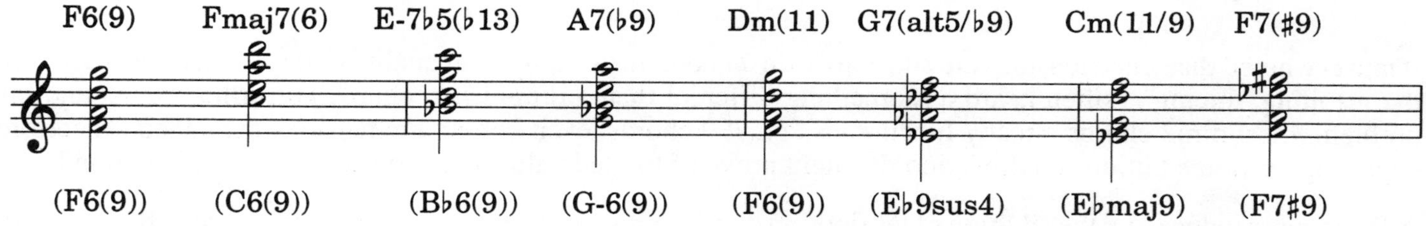


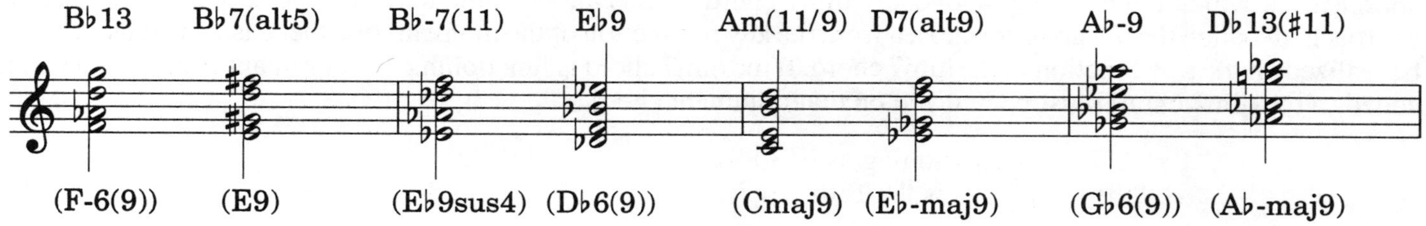

# Chapter Twenty.
## Tension Additions on Diminished 7th Chords

It must be noted that when tensions are added to a dim7 chord, the symmetrical quality of the chord is destroyed and the resulting voicing is often heard as something different than a diminished chord. To further compound this problem, most dim7 chords already function as dom7♭9 chords, even before any tensions are added. Therefore, exploring tension additions on dim7 chords might prove of limited value and is presented with this in mind.

All voicings produced by the addition of tensions on dim7 chords have been previously introduced enharmonically as dominant chords with various combinations of tensions ♭9, ♯9, ♯11, and 13. Further examination of these tensions will be performed under the **Symmetrical Dominant Substitutions** chapter.

There are basically two approaches to the addition of tensions on diminished 7th chords. The first is the symmetrical approach, in which a whole step above any dim7 chord tone is an available tension. The second is the diatonic approach, in which the tensions are chosen from the key or function of the moment. In either case, the tensions must be realized on the true function of the dim7 chord. If the dim7 chord is functioning as a dominant chord, the tensions added to the dim7 chord must be realized on that dominant chord:

C°7(9) is functioning as F13(♭9)...
the 9th of C°7 is the 13th of F7(♭9).

In contrast, if the dim7 chord has no dominant function, and instead is functioning as a "tonic-diminished" or chromatically descending diminished, the tensions should be realized on that dim7 chord. Upon further examination of the symmetrical approach to tension addition on dim7 chords, we see tensions 7, 9, 11, and ♭13 appearing a whole step above the chord tones. Combining chord tones and tensions produces the traditional symmetrical diminished scale;

| 1 | 2 | ♭3 | 4 | ♭5 | ♯5(♭13) | 6(♭♭7) | 7 | 8 |
|---|---|---|---|---|---|---|---|---|
| | 1 | 1/2 | 1 | 1/2 | 1 | 1/2 | 1 | 1/2 |

Tension ♭13 will be used instead of its enharmonic ♯5 spelling, which might appear confusing within a diminished context (augmented 5th on a diminished chord), although ♯5 does, in fact, describe this tone's relation to the scale more accurately, since the natural 5th might be implied by ♭13. Within this chapter, ♭13 will not imply natural 5.

Note that the major 7th appears as a tension above the ♭♭7 chord tone. When the major 7th is added to a dim7 chord, it is commonly referred to as a "dim.maj7" "or "tonic diminished" chord.

Since dim7 chords duplicate themselves through minor 3rd inversions, be aware of tension additions on all four relative dim7 chords:

<u>no</u> tensions C°7 = E♭°7 = F♯°7 = A°7
<u>one</u> tension C°maj7 = E♭°7(b13) = F♯°7(11) = A°7(9)
<u>two</u> tensions C°maj7(9) = E♭°maj7(♭13) = F♯°7(♭13/11) = A°7(11/9)
<u>two</u> tensions C°maj7(11) = E♭°7(♭13/9) = F♯°maj7(11) = A°7(♭13/9)
<u>three</u> tensions C°maj7(11/9) = E♭°maj7(♭13/9) = F♯°maj7(♭13/11) = A°7(♭13/11/9)

Note that if all four tensions (7, 9, 11, and ♭13) are used in a four note voicing, a complete dim7 chord is formed a whole step above the original dim7 chord:

C°maj7(♭13/11/9) = D°7

Since a dim7 chord commonly functions as a dom7(♭9) chord a half-step below any dim7 chord tone, tensions added to the dim7 chord should be realized on all four relative dom7(♭9) chords:

| | | | | | | | |
|---|---|---|---|---|---|---|---|
| no diminished tensions | C°7 | = | E♭°7 | = | F♯°7 | = | A°7 |
| | B7(♭9) | = | D7(♭9) | = | F7(♭9) | = | A♭7(♭9) |
| one diminished tension | C°maj7 | = | E♭°7(♭13) | = | F♯°7(11) | = | A°7(9) |
| | B(♭9) | = | D13(♭9) | = | F7(♯11/♭9) | = | A♭7(♯9) |
| two diminished tensions | C°maj7(9) | = | E♭°maj7(♭13) | = | F♯°7(♭13/11) | = | A°7(11/9) |
| | B(♯9) | = | D13(♭9) | = | F13(♯11/♭9) | = | A♭7(♯11/♯9) |
| two diminished tensions | C°maj7(11) | = | E♭°7(♭13/9) | = | F♯°maj7(11) | = | A°7(♭13/9) |
| | B(♯11/♭9) | = | D13(♯9) | = | F(♯11/♭9) | = | A♭13(♯9) |
| three diminished tensions | C°maj7(11/9) | = | E♭°maj7(♭13/9) | = | F♯°maj7(♭13/11) | = | A°7(♭13/11/9) |
| | B(♯11/♯9) | = | D(13/♯9) | = | F(13/♯11/♭9) | = | A♭7(13/♯11/♯9) |

Note the dominant tensions (♭9, ♯9, ♯11, 13) formed by the symmetrical diminished scale. By combining these dominant tensions and chord tones, the symmetrical dominant diminished scale is produced:

1 ♭2 ♯2 3 ♯4 5 6 ♭7 8

1/2 – 1 – 1/2 – 1 – 1/2 – 1 – 1/2 – 1

This scale and subsequent chords will be examined further in the **Symmetrical Dominant Substitutions** chapter.

All substitute chords produced by the addition of tensions 7, 9, 11 and ♭13 on a dim7 chord are either dominant and/or hybrid chords and have been previously introduced as dominant chords with various combinations of tensions ♭9, ♯9, ♯11, 13;

**One tension;** C°maj7 = E♭°7(♭13) = F♯°7(11) = A°7(9)
First introduced as a **dom7(♯9)** (A♭7(♯9)) chord. One inversion forms the hybrid chord B/C.

**Two tensions;** C°maj7(9) = E♭°maj7(♭13) = F♯°7(♭13/11) = A°7(11/9)
First introduced as a **dom7(♯11/♯9)** (A♭7(♯11/♯9)) chord. Two inversions form two different hybrid chords, B/D and Bm/D♯.

**Two tensions**; C°maj7(11) = E♭°7(♭13/9) = F♯°maj7(11) = A°7(♭13/9)

First introduced as a **dom13(♯9)** (A♭13(♯9) / D13(♯9)) chord.

**Three tensions;** C°maj7(11/9) = E♭°maj7(♭13/9) = F♯°maj7(♭13/11) = A°7(♭13/11/9)
First introduced as a **dom7(♭9/♯11/13)** (F(13/♯11/♭9) {1 ♭9 ♯11 13}) chord. One inversion forms the hybrid chord Bm/F.

The diatonic approach to tension additions on a dim7 chord can form different tensions depending on the key or function of the dim7 chord. In the key of C, C♯°7 (♯I°7) would have tensions 7 (C), ♭9 (D), ♭11 (F), and ♭13 (A), which are derived from the key of C. Since ♯I°7 usually functions as a dominant V7♭9/II chord (A7(♭9)), the C♯°7 tensions should be realized on A7(♭9): ♯9 (C), 11 (D), ♭13 (F), root (A).

The following chart might be helpful in determining the "function" of a dim7 chord. A diminished chord will either have a dominant function or its own diminished function. If there is no clear dominant function, the dim7 chord will assume its own function of tonic diminished (I°7) or descending chromatic diminished (♭III°7 / ♭V°7).

Keep in mind, since one dim7 chord equals three other dim7 chords, there are only three different dim7 chords possible:

1) C°7 = E♭°7 = F♯°7 = A°7
2) C♯°7 = E°7 = G°7 = B♭°7
3) D°7 = F°7 = A♭°7 = B°7

The following chart is relative to the key of the moment:

1) VII°7 = II°7 = IV°7 = ♯V°7
   dominant functions; V7(♭9) - of - VI, or V7(♭9)

2) ♭VII°7 = ♯I°7 = III°7 = V°7
   dominant functions; V7(♭9) - of - II, or V7(♭9) - of - IV

3) VI°7 = I°7 = ♭III°7 = ♭V°7
   (♯II°7) (♯IV°7)
   dominant functions; V7(♭9) - of - III, or V7(♭9) - of - V
   / Tonic Diminished (I°7)
   / Chromatic descending diminished (♭III°7 / ♭V°7)

In the key of C:

1) B°7 = D°7 = F°7 = G♯°7
   dominant functions; E7(♭9) / G7(♭9)

2) B♭°7 = C♯°7 = E°7 = G°7
   dominant functions; A7(♭9) / C7(♭9)

3) A°7 = C°7 = E♭°7 = G♭°7
   (D♯°7) (F♯°7)
   dominant functions; B7(♭9) / D7(♭9)
   / Tonic Diminished (C°7) (C°maj7)
   / Chromatic descending diminished (E♭°7 / G♭°7)

# Chapter Twenty-One.
## Constant Structure Harmonic Motion

The **Enharmonic Chordal Substitution** chapters present many different chord types and functions within a single chord. It is subsequently possible to harmonize a progression of different chord types and functions with a single chord type. If only *one* inversion of this single chord is used while harmonizing a progression, it would be referred to as "constant structure harmonic motion."

The following example uses a maj6(9) (1 3 6 9) chord to harmonize the original chord progression (written in parenthesis).

| | | | | | | | | |
|---|---|---|---|---|---|---|---|---|
| G6(9) | D♭6(9) | C6(9) | B6(9) | B♭6(9) | D♭6(9) | F6(9) | D♭6(9) | C6(9) |
| (Cmaj7) | (A7) | (D-7) | (G7) | (E-7♭5) | (A7) | (D-7) | (G7) | (C) |

Although this approach can go "outside" of the original harmonic functions, often by symmetrical motion of one voicing, the approach here will be to satisfy the original functions through the use of their enharmonic substitutional possibilities. Dominant chords offer some *symmetrical* constant structure possibilities that will be examined in the following chapter. Obviously, this concept will often compromise voice-leading, but this can be accepted when the harmonic structure never varies. Voice-leading is at its best between varied structures.

Those chords found to have the most substitutions and varied functions perform best in a constant structure approach. The following chords will be examined for their most common substitutions and functions, and each will be placed in a number of II-V-I situations to display their different functions. Those chords that can satisfy all three basic functions have the best constant structure possibilities.

**Major7♭5**

Cmaj7♭5 = A-6(9) = F♯-7♭5(11) = D7(13/9) = A♭7(♯9♯5)

| | | | | |
|---|---|---|---|---|
| Tonic Function | 1) D-7 | G7 | Cmaj7♭5 (Lydian) | |
| | 2) B-7♭5 | E7 | Cmaj7♭5 {A-6(9)} (Minor) | |
| | 3) G7 | A7 | Cmaj7♭5 {D7(13/9)} (Blues) | |
| Sub-Dominant Function | 1) Cmaj7♭5 {F♯-7♭5(11)} | B7 | Em | |
| Dominant Function | 1) A-7 | Cmaj7♭5 {D7(13/9)} | Gmaj7 | |
| | 2) E♭-7 | Cmaj7♭5 {A♭7(♯9♯5)} | D♭maj7 | |

Multi-Function (Constant Structure)

| | | |
|---|---|---|
| 1) Cmaj7♭5 {F♯-7♭5(11)} | E♭maj7♭5 {B7(♯9♯5)} | Gmaj7♭5 {E-6(9)} |
| 2) Fmaj7♭5 {G7(13/9)} | D♭maj7♭5 {A7(♯9♯5)} | Cmaj7♭5 {D7(13/9)} |

**Minor7♭5**

C-7♭5 = E♭-6 = G♭6(♭5) = A♭9 = D7(♭9♯5)

| | | | | |
|---|---|---|---|---|
| Tonic Function | 1) A♭-7 | D♭7 | C-7♭5 {G♭6(♭5)} (Lydian) | |
| | 2) F-7♭5 | B♭7 | C-7♭5 {E♭-6} (Minor) | |
| | 3) D♭7 | E♭7 | C-7♭5 {A♭9} (Blues) | |
| Sub-Dominant Function | 1) C-7♭5 | F7 | B♭m | |
| Dominant Function | 1) A-7 | C-7♭5 {D7(♭9♯5)} | Gmaj7 | |
| | 2) E♭-7 | C-7♭5 {A♭9} | D♭maj7 | |

Multi-Function (Constant Structure)

| | | |
|---|---|---|
| 1) C-7♭5 | E♭-7♭5 | G-7♭5 |
| | {F7(♭9♯5)} | {B♭-6} |
| 2) F-7♭5 | D♭-7♭5 | C-7♭5 |
| {D♭9} | {E♭7(♭9♯5)} | {A♭9} |

**Minor7♯5**

C-7♯5 = A♭(add9) = F-7(11) = D♭maj7(6/9) = B♭9sus4 or B♭-7(11/9) = D7(♭9/alt5) = C7(♯9/♯5)<u>no3</u>

| | | | | |
|---|---|---|---|---|
| Tonic Function | 1) B♭-7 | E♭7 | C-7♯5 {A♭(add9)} | |
| | 2) E♭-7 | A♭7 | C-7♯5 {D♭maj7(6/9)} | |
| | 3) G-7♭5 | C7 | C-7♯5 {F-7(11)} | |
| Sub-Dominant Function | 1) C-7♯5 {F-7(11)} | | B♭7 | E♭maj7 |
| | 2) C-7♯5 | | F7 | B♭m |
| | 3) C-7♯5 {B♭-7(11/9)} | | E♭7 | A♭6 |
| Dominant Function | 1) A-7 | C-7♯5 {D7(♭9/alt5)} | G6 | |
| | 2) G-7 | C-7♯5 {C7(♯9/♯5)} | F6 | |
| | 3) F-7 | C-7♯5 {B♭9sus4} | E♭6 | |

Multi-Function (Constant Structure)

| | | |
|---|---|---|
| 1) C-7♯5 | A♭-7♯5 | G-7♯5 |
| {F-7(11)} | {B♭7(♭9/alt5)} | {E♭(add9)} |
| 2) C-7♯5 | E♭-7♯5 | F-7♯5 |
| {C-7♭5(♭13)} | {F7(♭9/alt5)} | {B♭-7(11)} |

**Dom7♯5**

C7♯5 = D♭-maj7(6) = F-maj7(11) = B♭-7♭5(9) or B♭7♭5(9) = D7(9/alt5) = E7(alt5) = A♭7♯5(9) = G♭7♭5(9)

| | | | | |
|---|---|---|---|---|
| Tonic Function | 1) E♭-7♭5 | A♭7 | C7♯5{D♭-maj7(6)} | |
| | 2) G-7♭5 | C7 | C7♯5{F-maj7(11)} | |
| Sub-Dominant Function | 1) C7♯5{B♭-7♭5(9)} | E♭7 | A♭m | |
| Dominant Function | 1) B-7 | C7♯5{E7(alt5)} | Amaj7 | |
| | 2) A-7 | C7♯5{D7(9/alt5)} | G6 | |
| | 3) F-7 | C7♯5{B♭7♭5(9)} | E♭6 | |
| | 4) E♭-7 | C7♯5{A♭7♯5(9)} | D♭6 | |
| | 5) C♯-7 | C7♯5{F♯7♭5(9)} | B6 | |

Multi-Function (Constant Structure)

1) C7♯5 {B♭-7♭5(9)} — B7♯5 {E♭7(alt5)} — E♭7♯5 {A♭-maj7(11)} .........or.......... G7♯5 {A♭-maj7(6)}

**Dom7sus4**

C7sus4=B♭6(9)=G-7(11)=E♭6(9)=C-7(11)=A♭maj7(9/6)=F-7(11/9) or F9sus4=A7♯5(alt9)=E7(alt9/alt5)

| | | | | |
|---|---|---|---|---|
| Tonic Function | 1) C-7 | F7 | C7sus4{B♭6(9)} | |
| | 2) F-7 | B♭7 | C7sus4{E♭6(9)} | |
| | 3) B♭-7 | E♭7 | C7sus4{A♭maj7(9/6)} | |
| | 4) A-7♭5 | D7 | C7sus4{G-7(11)} | |
| Sub-Dominant Function | 1) C7sus4{G-7(11)} | C7 | F6 | |
| | 2) C7sus4{C-7(11)} | F7 | B♭6 | |
| | 3) C7sus4{F-7(11/9)} | B♭7 | E♭6 | |
| Dominant Function | 1) E-7 | C7sus4{A7♯5(alt9)} | D6 | |
| | 2) B-7 | C7sus4{E7(alt9/alt5)} | A6 | |
| | 3) C-7 | C7sus4{F9sus4} | B♭6 | |

Multi-Function (Constant Structure)

1) C7sus4 {G-7(11)} — E♭7sus4 {C7♯5(alt9)} — D7sus4 {F6(9)}

2) C7sus4 {C-7(11)} — C♯7sus4 {F7(alt9/alt5)} — D7sus4 {B♭maj7(9/6)}

**Major7(9) [1 3 7 9]**

Cmaj7(9) = A-(11/9) = F♯-7♭5(♭13/11) = D7(13/9) = A♭7(♯9/alt5)

| | | | | |
|---|---|---|---|---|
| Tonic Function | 1) D-7 | G7 | Cmaj7(9) | |
| | 2) B-7♭5 | E7 | Cmaj7(9){A-(11/9)} | |
| | 3) G7 | A7 | Cmaj7(9){D7(13/9)} | (Blues) |
| Sub-Dominant Function | 1) Cmaj7(9){A-(11/9)} | D7 | G6 | |
| | 2) Cmaj7(9){F♯-7♭5(♭13/11)} | B7 | Em | |

| | | | |
|---|---|---|---|
| Dominant Function | 1) A-7 | Cmaj7(9){D7(13/9)} | G6 |
| | 2) E♭-7 | Cmaj7(9){A♭7(♯9/alt5)} | D♭6 |

Multi-Function (Constant Structure)

| | | |
|---|---|---|
| 1) Cmaj7(9) | F♯maj7(9) | Gmaj7(9) |
| {A-(11/9)} | {D7(♯9/alt5)} | |
| 2) Cmaj7(9) | E♭maj7(9) | Gmaj7(9) |
| {F♯-7♭5(♭13/11)} | {B7(♯9/alt5)} | {E-(11/9)} |
| 3) Fmaj7(9) | D♭maj7(9) | Cmaj7(9) |
| {G7(13/9)} | {A7(♯9/alt5)} | {D7(13/9)} |

**Major6(9) [1 3 6 9]**

C6(9) = Am(11) = Fmaj7(6) = B♭maj7♭5(9) = D-9 or D9 = F♯-7♭5(♭13) = A♭7(♭9/alt5)

| | | | |
|---|---|---|---|
| Tonic Function | 1) D-7 | G7 | C6(9) |
| | 2) B-7♭5 | E7 | C6(9){Am(11)} |
| | 3) G-7 | C7 | C6(9){Fmaj7(6)} |
| | 4) E-7♭5 | A7 | C6(9){D-9} |
| | 5) C-7 | F7 | C6(9){B♭maj7♭5(9)} |

| | | | |
|---|---|---|---|
| Sub-Dominant Function | 1) C6(9){Am(11)} | D7 | G6 |
| | 2) C6(9){F♯-7♭5(♭13)} | B7 | Em |
| | 3) C6(9){D-9} | G7 | C6 |

| | | | |
|---|---|---|---|
| Dominant Function | 1) A-7 | C6(9){D9} | G6 |
| | 2) E♭-7 | C6(9){A♭7(♭9/alt5)} | D♭6 |

Multi-Function (Constant Structure)

| | | |
|---|---|---|
| 1) C6(9) | F♯6(9) | D6(9) |
| {Am(11)} | {D7(♭9/alt5)} | {Gmaj7(6)} |
| 2) C6(9) | E♭6(9) | G6(9) |
| {F♯-7♭5(♭13)} | {B7(♭9/alt5)} | {Em(11)} |

**Dom7(9) [1 3 ♭7 9]**

C7(9) = G-6(11) = B♭(9/♭5) = E-7♭5(♭13) or E7(alt5) = F♯7(alt5) = D7♯5(9) = A♭7(9/alt5)

| | | | |
|---|---|---|---|
| Tonic Function | 1) A-7♭5 | D7 | C9{G-6(11)} |
| | 2) C-7 | F7 | C9{B♭(9/♭5)} |

| | | | |
|---|---|---|---|
| Sub-Dominant Function | 1) C9{E-7♭5(♭13)} | A7 | Dm |

| | | | |
|---|---|---|---|
| Dominant Function | 1) B-7 | C9{E7(alt5)} | A6 |
| | 2) C♯-7 | C9{F♯7(alt5)} | B6 |
| | 3) A-7 | C9{D7♯5(9)} | G6 |
| | 4) E♭-7 | C9{A♭7(9/alt5)} | D♭6 |

Multi-Function (Constant Structure)

| | | | |
|---|---|---|---|
| 1) C9 | E♭9 | G9....... or........ | E9 |
| {E-7♭5(♭13)} | {A7(alt5)} | {D-6(11)} | {D(9/♭5)} |

When only one inversion is used in the multi-function examples, it is considered a "constant structure" approach to the progression. If different inversions of the same chord are used, the constant structure sound is lost, but voice-leading improves and the "sound" of using one chord type remains. This might half-jokingly be referred to as "constant chord type structures."

The following is an example of the two approaches discussed on the Dom7(9) chord's multi-function progression:

**C9** [E-7♭5(♭13)] **E♭9** [A7(alt5)] **G9** [D-6(11)]

1) (Constant Structure)

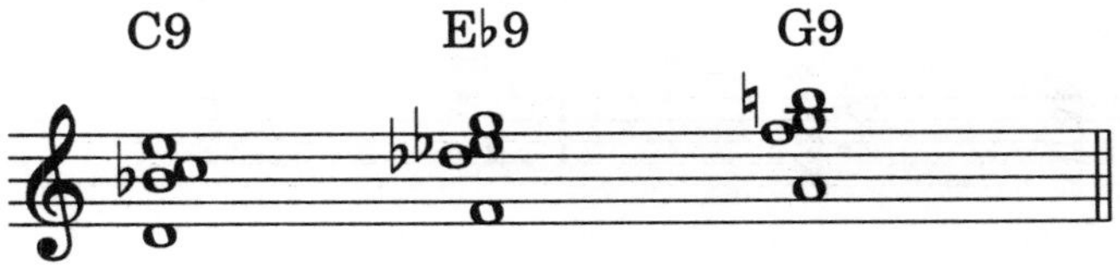


2) (Constant Chord Type {different inversions})

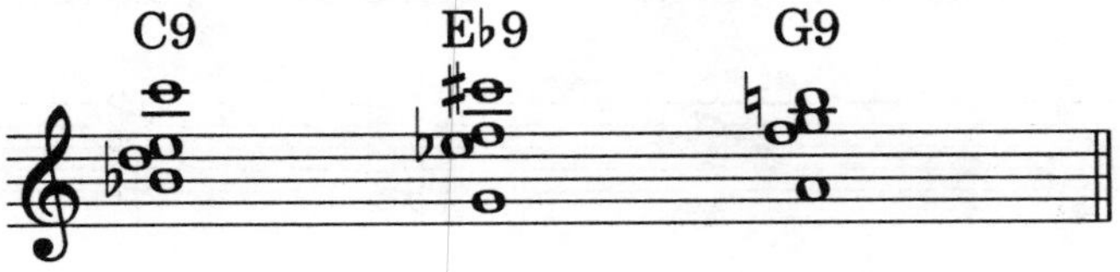


At this point, special attention should be given to the *minor* II-V-I cadences that appeared in the multi-function examples. It might have been noted, (as in the above example), that a certain interval pattern was evolving between the II, V, and I chords. By establishing one chord voicing that will satisfy all three functions, it can be moved a minor third from the II to the V and a major third from the V to the I:

**E-7♭5**.....(minor third).......**G-7♭5**.......(major third).......**B-7♭5**
II-7♭5 {E-7♭5} V7 {A7(♭9/♯5)} Im {D-6}

*Any* chord that will satisfy the II-7♭5 chord, with or without available tensions, can be moved through this interval pattern to produce a complete *minor* II-V-I cadence.

The following is a list of some of the most obvious chords that could function as min7♭5 chords;

**F♯-7♭5(9)** = A-maj7....... A♭7♯5
**F♯-7♭5(11)** = Cmaj7♭5.... A-6(9) [1 ♭3 6 9]....Fmaj7(♯11) [3 5 7 ♯11]
**F♯-7♭5(♭13)** = D7....D9 [1 3 ♭7 9]......C6(9) [1 3 6 9]
**F♯-7♭5(11/9)** = Cmaj7♯5.....A-maj7(9) [1 ♭3 7 9]......A-maj7(9) [♭3 5 7 9]
**F♯-7♭5(♭13/9)** = E7♯5
**F♯-7♭5(♭13/11)** = Cmaj7(9) [1 3 7 9]......D13 & A♭7(♯9/♭5).......E7sus4.......F6(♯11) [3 5 6 ♯11]

Each one of these chords will satisfy all three minor cadence chords (II-7♭5, V7, and I-) and each one can be moved through the interval pattern to establish a constant structure *minor* II V I cadence. In relation to their present roots, they will function as F♯-7♭5, A♭7, and A minor chords.

Application of these concepts would make it possible to harmonize an entire song with just two or three chord types. The following is an example of a typical "two-five blues" harmonized with just three chords; dom7sus4, maj6(9) [1 3 6 9], and dom7(9) [1 3 ♭7 9]. Their inversions will aid in some harmonic variety and voice-leading, while integrated with constant structure phrases.

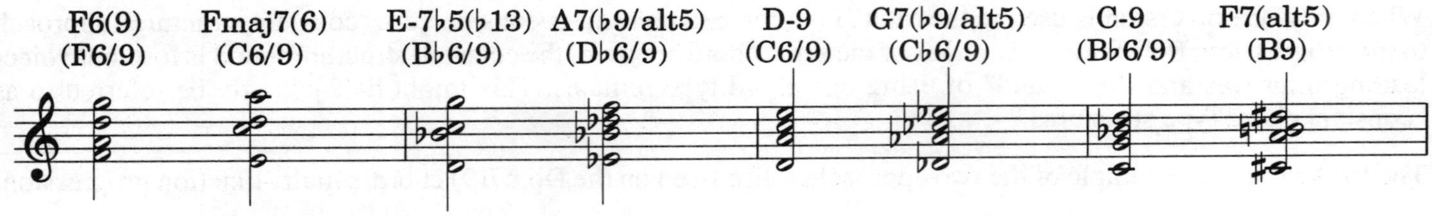


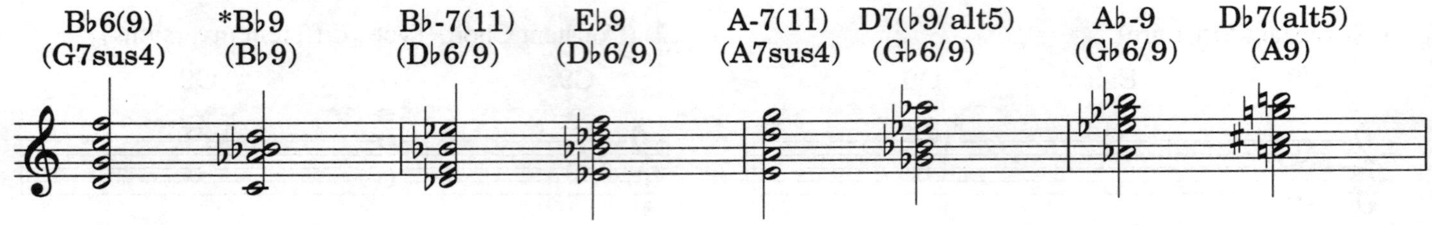


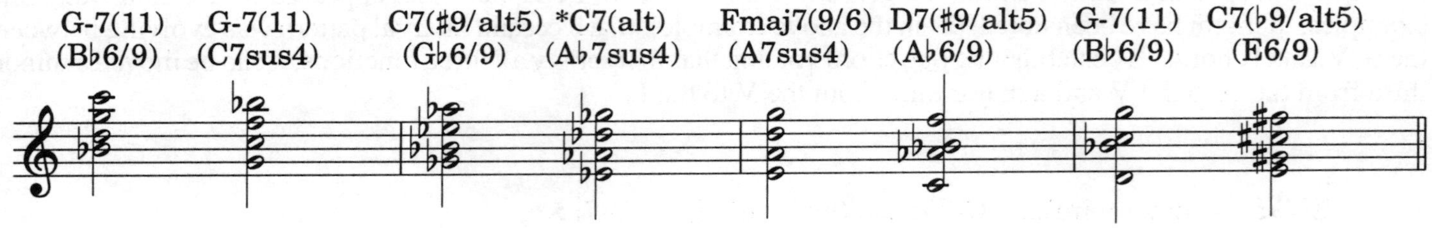

* L.I.L. violations on <u>weak</u> half of measure.

Here are some additional *minor* II - V - I cadences with two different chord types moving through the "minor third-major third" interval pattern;

1)

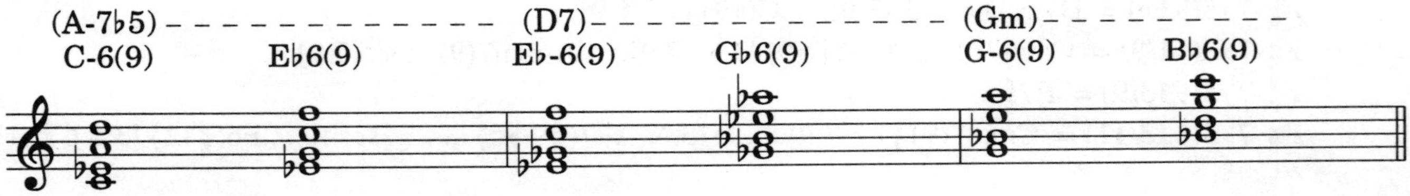


2)

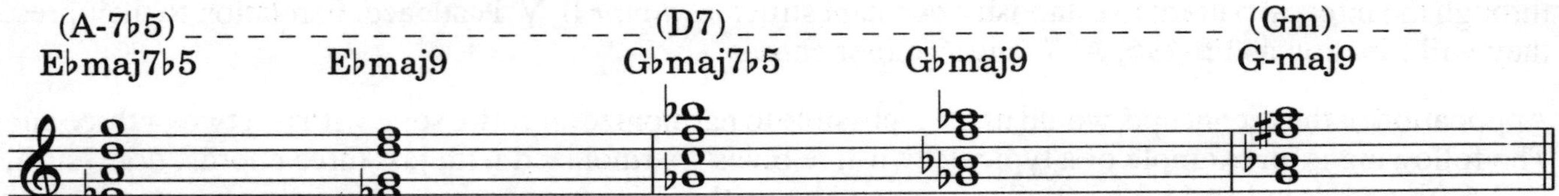


3)

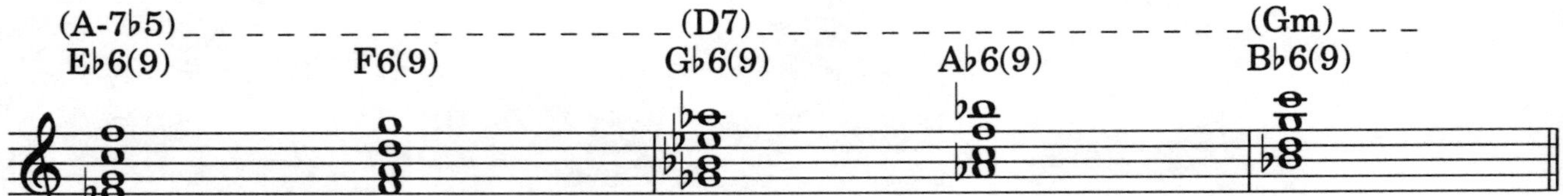

4) 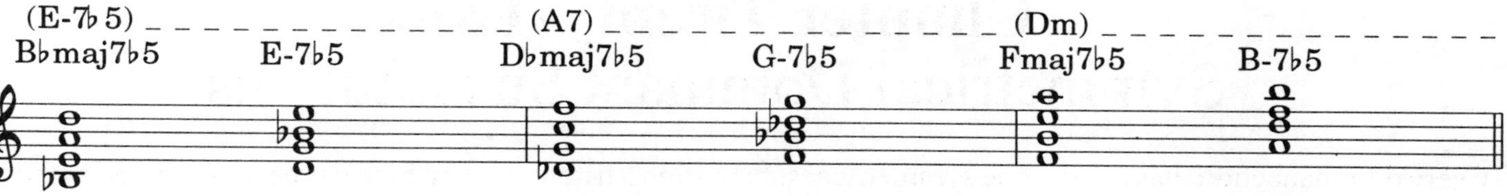


5) 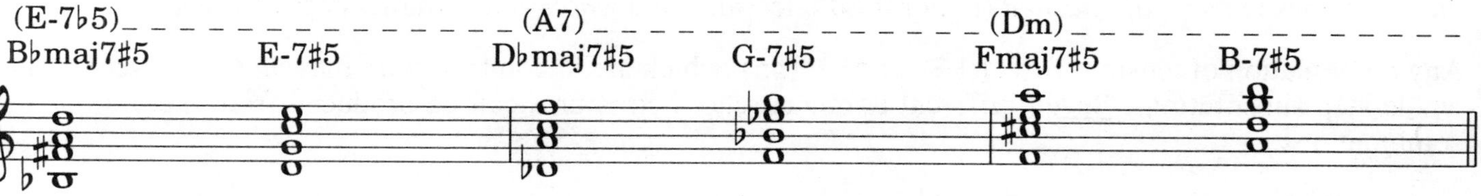


"Major" cadences;

1) (II-7 – V7 – I);

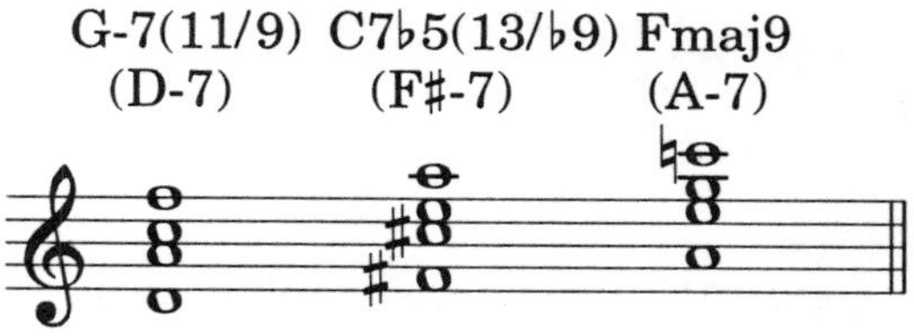


2) (I – VI7 – II-7 – V7 – I);

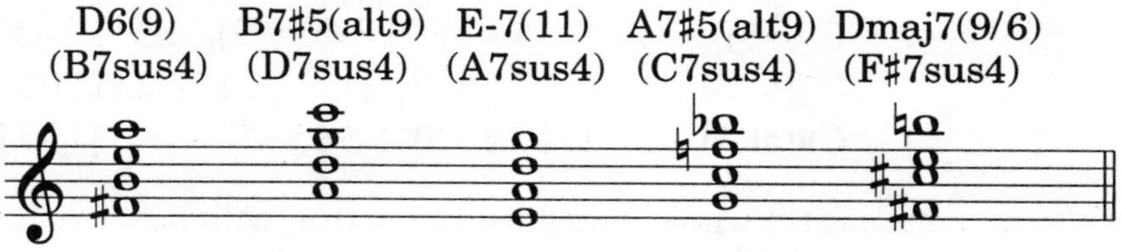

# Chapter Twenty-Two.
## Symmetrical Dominant Substitutions

Every dominant chord has at least one symmetrical substitution a tritone away which has been presented as the "Sub V" chord. Specific tension combinations derived from the *whole-tone* or *diminished* scales can be placed on a dominant chord which can then be moved symmetrically ("constant structure harmonic motion") in accordance with those tensions chosen; *diminished* (minor third intervals), and *whole-tone* (whole-step intervals).

Any combination of tensions 9, ♯11(♭5), and ♭13(♯5), which are in common with the *whole-tone* scale, can have whole-step substitutions. <u>Seven</u> different dominant chord structures can be produced from the various tension combinations;

C7♯5 C7♭5 C9(no5) [1 3 ♭7 9] C9(♯5) C9(♭5) C7(alt5) C9(alt5)

Note that it is perhaps more appropriate to refer to ♯11 and ♭13 as ♭5 and ♯5, since ♯11 and ♭13 could imply a natural 5th.

Three different voicing possibilities exist for each of the last four chords;

**C9(♯5)**...........[3 ♯5 ♭7 9], [1 ♯5 ♭7 9], and [1 3 ♯5 9]
**C9(♭5)**...........[3 ♭5 ♭7 9], [1 ♭5 ♭7 9], and [1 3 ♭5 9]
**C7(alt5)**.........[3 ♭5 ♯5 ♭7], [1 ♭5 ♯5 ♭7], and [1 3 ♭5 ♯5]
**C9(alt5)**.........[3 ♭5 ♯5 9], [♭5 ♯5 ♭7 9], and [1 ♭5 ♯5 9]

When examining the whole-step substitutions for each chord, we find only <u>three</u> different interval combinations exist for four-note voicings within the whole-tone scale;

| | | | | | | |
|---|---|---|---|---|---|---|
| **1)** | C7♭5<br>[1 3 ♭5 ♭7] | D9(♯5)<br>[3 ♯5 ♭7 9] | E9(alt5)<br>[1 ♭5 ♯5 9] | F♯7♭5<br>[1 3 ♭5 ♭7] | A♭9(♯5)<br>[3 ♯5 ♭7 9] | B♭9(alt5)<br>[1 ♭5 ♯5 9] |
| **2)** | C7♯5<br>[1 3 ♯5 ♭7] | D9(alt5)<br>[♭5 ♯5 ♭7 9] | E7(alt5)<br>[1 3 ♭5 ♯5] | F♯9(♭5)<br>[3 ♭5 ♭7 9] | A♭9(♯5)<br>[1 3 ♯5 9] | B♭9(♭5)<br>[1 ♭5 ♭7 9] |
| **3)** | C9<br>[1 3 ♭7 9] | D9(♯5)<br>[1 ♯5 ♭7 9] | E7(alt5)<br>[1 ♭5 ♯5 ♭7] | F♯7(alt5)<br>[3 ♭5 ♯5 ♭7] | A♭9(alt5)<br>[3 ♭5 ♯5 9] | B♭9(♭5)<br>[1 3 ♭5 9] |

Note the symmetrical *Sub V* chords in the first example;

C7♭5=F♯7♭5 D9(♯5)=A♭9(♯5) E9(alt5)=B♭9(alt5)

Also note those voicings missing a third could function as min7♭5 chords, and the B♭9(♭5); [1 3♭5 9], could function as a B♭maj7♭5(9) chord.

Any combination of tensions ♭9, ♯9, ♯11, and 13, which are in common with the symmetrical *dominant* diminished scale (1 ♭2 ♯2 3 ♯4 5 6 ♭7 8), can have minor third substitutions. <u>Fifteen</u> different dominant chord structures can be produced from the various tension combinations;

*Single* Tension;

1) C7(♯11) or C7♭5 2) C7(♭9) 3) C7(♯9) 4) C7(13)

*Two* Tensions;

5) C7(♯11/♭9) 6) C7(♯11/♯9) 7) C7(13/♯11) 8) C7(13/♭9)
9) C7(13/♯9) 10) C7(alt9)

*Three* Tensions;

11) C7(♯11/alt9) 12) C7(13/alt9) 13) C7(13/♯11/♭9) 14) C7(13/♯11/♯9)

*Four* Tensions;

15) C7(13/♯11/alt9)

Note that all those chords containing a ♯11th tension could be accompanied by a natural 5th, or function enharmonically as a ♭5th. Also note the dom7♭5 is the only chord that can function in the whole-tone system *and* the diminished system.

Unlike the whole-tone scale, the diminished scale offers *many* different dominant chord types with very few reappearing under a new chord type. The following will attempt to organize the various dominant tension combinations and their related symmetrical substitutions over four-note structures.

*Single* tension combinations;

1) **C7♭5;**

**[1 3♭5♭7]** = E♭13(alt9) [5♭9♯9 13] = F♯7♭5 [1 3♭5♭7] = A13(alt9) [5♭9♯9 13]

**C7(♯11);**

**[3 5♭7♯11]** = E♭7(alt9) [3 5♭9♯9] = F♯7(♭9) [1 3♭7♭9] = A13(♭9) [5♭7♭9 13]
**[1 5♭7♯11]** refer to E♭7(♯11) under **C13(alt9) [♭7♭9♯9 13]**
**[1 3♭7♯11]** refer to **C7♭5**
**[1 3 5♯11]** refer to A(♯11) under **C13(alt9) [3♭9♯9 13]**

2) **C7(♭9);**

**[3 5♭7♭9]** = E♭7(♭9) = F♯7(♭9) = A7(♭9)
**[1 3♭7♭9]** refer to F♯7(♭9) under **C7(♯11)**
**[1 5♭7♭9]** refer to E♭7(♭9) under **C7(alt9)**
**[1 3 5♭9]** refer to E♭(♭9) under **C7(♯9)**

3) **C7(♯9);**

**[3 5♭7♯9]** = E♭ (♭9) [1 3 5♭9] = F♯13(♭9) [3♭7♭9 13] = A7(♯11/♭9) [5♭7♭9♯11]
**[1 3♭7♯9]** refer to F♯7(♯9) under **C13(♯11)**
**[1 5♭7♯9]** refer to E♭7(♯9) under **C7(♯11/alt9) [♭7♭9♯9♯11]**
**[1 3 5♯9]** refer to F♯(♯9) under **C13(♯11/♭9) [♭7♭9♯11 13]**

4) **C13;**

**[1 3♭7 13]** = E♭13(♯11/♭9) [5♭9♯11 13] = F♯7(♯9/♭5) [3♭5♭7♯9] = A7(alt9) [1 5♭9♯9]
**[3 5♭7 13]** refer to F♯13 under **C7(alt9)**
**[1 5♭7 13]** refer to F♯13 under **C7(♯11/alt9) [3♭9♯9♯11]**
**[1 3 5 13]** refer to F♯13 under **C7(♯11/alt9) [♭7♭9♯9♯11]**

*Two* tension combinations;

5) **C7(♯11/♭9);**

**[3 ♭7 ♭9 ♯11]** = E♭7(alt9) **[5 ♭7 ♭9 ♯9]** = F♯7 [1 3 5 ♭7] = A13(♭9) [3 5 ♭9 13]
**[1 ♭7 ♭9 ♯11]** refer to E♭7(♯11/♭9) under **C13(alt9) [3 ♭9 ♯9 13]**
**[5 ♭7 ♭9 ♯11]** refer to A7(♯11/♭9) under **C7(♯9)**
**[1 3 ♭9 ♯11]** refer to A7(♯11/♭9) under **C13(alt9) [♭7 ♭9 ♯9 13]**
**[1 5 ♭9 ♯11]** refer to E♭7(♯11/♭9) or A7(♯11/♭9) under **C13(♯9)**
**[3 5 ♭9 ♯11]** refer to A7(♯11/♭9) under **C7(alt9)**

6) **C7(♯11/♯9);**

**[3 5 ♯9 ♯11]** = E♭7(alt9) [1 3 ♭9 ♯9] = F♯13(♭9) [1 ♭7 ♭9 13] = A13(♯11) [5 ♭7 ♯11 13]
**[3 ♭7 ♯9 ♯11]** refer to F♯7(♯9/♭5) under **C13**
**[1 ♭7 ♯9 ♯11]** refer to E♭7(♯11/♯9) under **C13(♯11/alt9)**
**[5 ♭7 ♯9 ♯11]** refer to E♭7(♯11/♯9) under **C13(♯11/♭9) [♭7 ♭9 ♯11 13]**
**[1 3 ♯9 ♯11]** refer to A7(♯11/♯9) under **C13(alt9) [1 ♭9 ♯9 13]**
**[1 5 ♯9 ♯11]** refer to F♯7(♯11/♯9) under **C13(♯11/♭9) [1 ♭9 ♯11 13]**

7) **C13(#11);**

**[3 ♭7 ♯11 13]** = E♭7(♯11/alt9) [5 ♭9 ♯9 ♯11] = F♯7(♯9) [1 3 ♭7 ♯9] = A13(♭9) [1 5 ♭9 13]
**[1 ♭7 ♯11 13]** refer to E♭13(♯11) under **C13(alt9) [1 ♭9 ♯9 13]**
**[1 3 ♯11 13]** refer to A13(♯11) under **C13(♯11/alt9)**
**[1 5 ♯11 13]** refer to F♯13(♯11) under **C7(♯11/alt9) [1 ♭9 ♯9 ♯11]**
**[3 5 ♯11 13]** refer to A13(♯11) under **C7(♯11/alt9) [3 ♭9 ♯9 ♯11]**
**[5 ♭7 ♯11 13]** refer to A13(♯11) under **C7(♯11/♯9)**

8) **C13(♭9);**

**[3 ♭7 ♭9 13]** refer to F♯13(♭9) under **C7(♯9)**
**[1 ♭7 ♭9 13]** refer to F♯13(♭9) under **C7(♯11/♯9)**
**[5 ♭7 ♭9 13]** refer to A13(♭9) under **C7(♯11)**
**[1 3 ♭9 13]** refer to A13(♭9) under **C13(♯11/♭9) [♭7 ♭9 ♯11 13]**
**[1 5 ♭9 13]** refer to A13(♭9) under **C13(♯11)**
**[3 5 ♭9 13]** refer to A13(♭9) under **C7(♯11/♭9)**

9) **C13(♯9);**

**[3 ♭7 ♯9 13]** = E♭7(♯11/♭9) [1 5 ♭9 ♯11] = F♯13(♯9) [3 ♭7 ♯9 13] = A7(♯11/♭9) [1 5 ♭9 ♯11]
**[1 ♭7 ♯9 13]** refer to E♭13(♯9) under **C7(♯11/alt9) [1 ♭9 ♯9 ♯11]**
**[5 ♭7 ♯9 13]** refer to F♯13(♯9) under **C13(alt9) [3 ♭9 ♯9 13]**
**[1 3 ♯9 13]** refer to A13(♯9) under **C13(♯11/♭9) [1 ♭9 ♯11 13]**
**[1 5 ♯9 13]** refer to F♯13(♯9) under **C13(♯11/alt9)**
**[3 5 ♯9 13]** refer to F♯13(♯9) under **C13(alt9) [♭7 ♭9 ♯9 13]**

10) **C7(alt9);**

**[3 ♭7 ♭9 ♯9]** = E♭7(♭9) [1 5 ♭7 ♭9] = F♯13 [3 5 ♭7 13] = A7(♯11/♭9) [3 5 ♭9 ♯11]
**[1 ♭7 ♭9 ♯9]** refer to E♭7(alt9) under **C7(♯11/alt9) [3 ♭9 ♯9 ♯11]**
**[5 ♭7 ♭9 ♯9]** refer to E♭7(alt9) under **C7(♯11/♭9)**
**[1 3 ♭9 ♯9]** refer to E♭7(alt9) under **C7(♯11/♯9)**
**[1 5 ♭9 ♯9]** refer to A7(alt9) under **C13**
**[3 5 ♭9 ♯9]** refer to E♭7(alt9) under **C7(♯11)**

*Three* tension combinations;

11) **C7(♯11/alt9);**

**[♭7 ♭9 ♯9 ♯11]** = E♭7(♯9) [1 5 ♭7 ♯9] {E♭-7} = F♯13 [1 3 5 13] {F♯6} = A13(♯11/♭9) [3 ♭9 ♯11 13]
**[3 ♭9 ♯9 ♯11]** = E♭7(alt9) [1 ♭7 ♭9 ♯9] = F♯13 [1 5 ♭7 13] = A13(♯11) [3 5 ♯11 13] {A6(♯11)}
**[1 ♭9 ♯9 ♯11]** = E♭13(♯9) [1 ♭7 ♯9 13] = F♯13(♯11) [1 5 ♯11 13] {F♯6(♯11)} = A13(♯11/♯9) [3 ♯9 ♯11 13]
**[5 ♭9 ♯9 ♯11]** refer to E♭7(♯11/alt9) under **C13(♯11)**

12) **C13(alt9);**

**[3 ♭9 ♯9 13]** = E♭7(♯11/♭9) [1 ♭7 ♭9 ♯11] = F♯13(♯9) [5 ♭7 ♯9 13] = A(♯11) [1 3 5 ♯11]
**[♭7 ♭9 ♯9 13]** = E♭7(♯11) [1 5 ♭7 ♯11] = F♯13(♯9) [3 5 ♯9 13] = A7(♯11/♭9) [1 3 ♭9 ♯11]
**[1 ♭9 ♯9 13]** = E♭13(♯11) [1 ♭7 ♯11 13] = F♯13(♯11/♯9) [5 ♯9 ♯11 13] = A7(♯11/♯9) [1 3 ♯9 ♯11]
**[5 ♭9 ♯9 13]** refer to E♭13(alt9) under **C7♭5**

13) **C13(♯11/♭9);**

**[1 ♭9 ♯11 13]** = E♭13(♯11/♯9) [♭7 ♯9 ♯11 13] = F♯7(♯11/♯9) [1 5 ♯9 ♯11] = A13(♯9) [1 3 ♯9 13]
**[♭7 ♭9 ♯11 13]** = E♭7(♯11/♯9) [5 ♭7 ♯9 ♯11] = F♯(♯9) [1 3 5 ♯9] = A13(♭9) [1 3 ♭9 13]
**[5 ♭9 ♯11 13]** refer to E♭13(♯11/♭9) under **C13**
**[3 ♭9 ♯11 13]** refer to A13(♯11/♭9) under **C7(♯11/alt9) [♭7 ♭9 ♯9 ♯11]**

14) **C13(♯11/♯9);**

**[3 ♯9 ♯11 13]** refer to A13(♯11/♯9) under **C7(♯11/alt9) [1 ♭9 ♯9 ♯11]**
**[5 ♯9 ♯11 13]** refer to F♯13(♯11/♯9) under **C13(alt9) [1 ♭9 ♯9 13]**
**[♭7 ♯9 ♯11 13]** refer to E♭13(♯11/♯9) under **C13(♯11/♭9) [1 ♭9 ♯11 13]**
**[1 ♯9 ♯11 13]** is enharmonically the same as C°7; 1 ♭3(♯9) ♭5(♯11) ♭♭7(13), therefore C13(♯11/♯9) = E♭13(♯11/♯9) = F♯13(♯11/♯9) = A13(♯11/♯9).

*Four* tension combinations;

15) **C13(♯11/alt9);**

**[♭9 ♯9 ♯11 13]** = E♭7(♯11/♯9) [1 ♭7 ♯9 ♯11] {E♭-7♭5} = F♯13(♯9) [1 5 ♯9 13] {F♯-6} = A13(♯11) [1 3 ♯11 13] {A6♭5}

Note, with the exclusion of the dom7♭9 and the dom13(♯11/♯9), the symmetrical Sub V chords in the dom7♭5 and dom13(♯9) chords;

C7♭5 = F♯7♭5..............................E♭13(alt9) = A13(alt9)
C13(♯9) = F♯13(♯9).....................E♭7(♯11/♭9) = A7(♯11/♭9)

Also note those incomplete voicings that contain dual functions;

Under **C7(♯11/alt9);**

E♭7(♯9) [1 5 ♭7 ♯9] = E♭-7
F♯13 [1 3 5 13] = F♯6
A13(♯11) [3 5 ♯11 13] = A6(♯11)
E♭13(♯9) [1 ♭7 ♯9 13] = E♭-7(13) {Modal Dorian}
F♯13(♯11) [1 5 ♯11 13] = F♯6(♯11)

Under **C13(alt9);**

F♯13(♯9) [5 ♭7 ♯9 13] = F♯-7(13) {Modal Dorian}
A(♯11) [1 3 5 ♯11] = A7(♯11) or Amaj7(♯11)

Under **C13(♯11/♯9);** [1 ♯9 ♯11 13] = C°7

Under **C13(♯11/alt9);** E♭7(♯11/♯9) = E♭-7♭5 F♯13(♯9) = F♯-6 A13(♯11) = A6♭5

The following II - V - I examples will present a *single* voicing in all of its relative symmetrical dominant functions.

1) Whole-tone (dom7♭5);

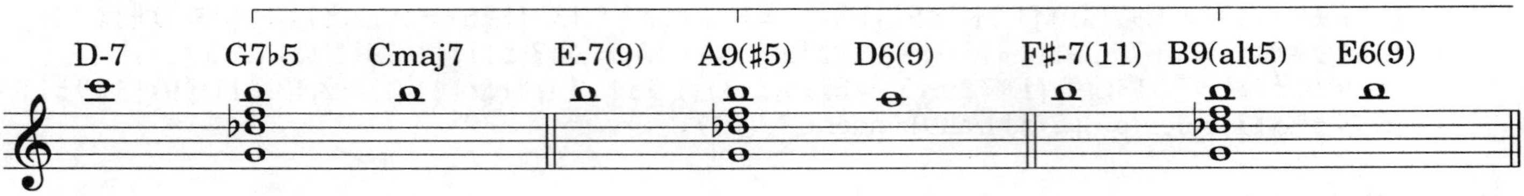


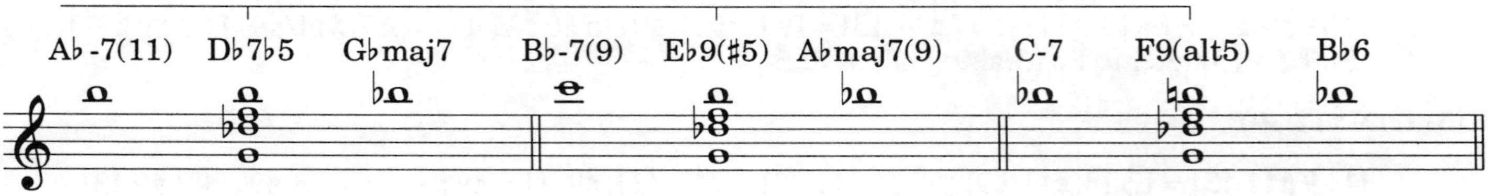


2) Diminished {dom13(♭9)};

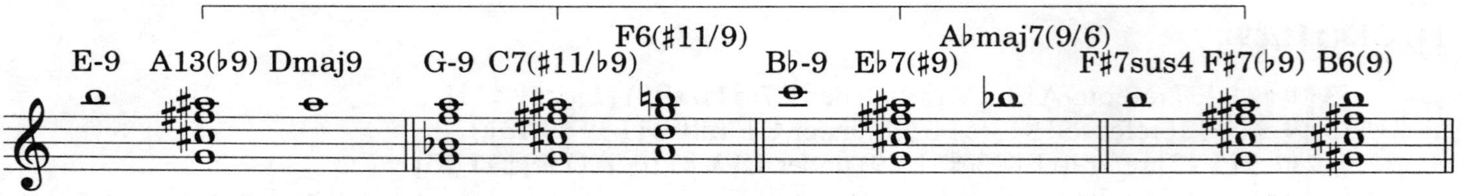


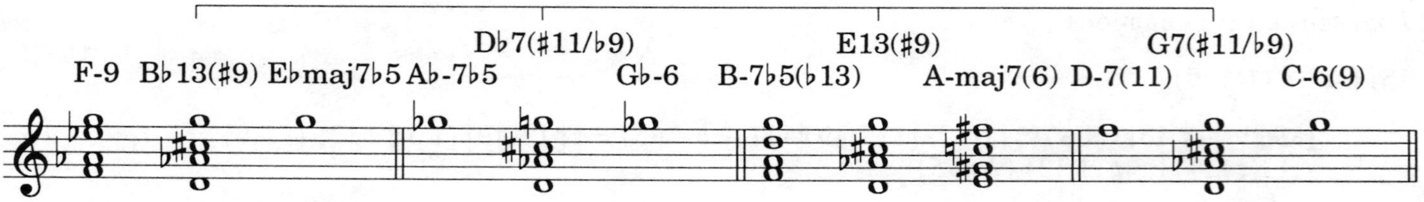


The following II - V - I examples will move one voicing symmetrically, "constant structure harmonic motion," over a single dominant chord.

1) Whole-tone (dom7♯5);

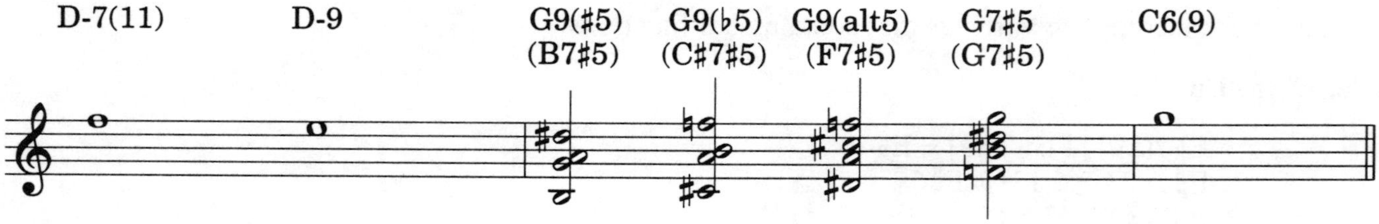


2) Diminished {dom13(♭9)};

# Chapter Twenty-Three.
## Altered Dominant

As was presented earlier in the **Dominant Substitute V Chord** chapter, altered or "alt" on a dominant chord refers to the fifth and ninth being flatted *and* raised; (♭5,♯5) and (♭9,♯9). Adding the root and guide tones to these altered notes produces an "altered" scale or seventh mode of the "real" or "jazz" melodic minor scale;

| | | | | | | | |
|---|---|---|---|---|---|---|---|
| 1 | ♭2 | ♯2 | 3 | ♭5 | ♯5 | ♭7 | 8 |
| | (♭9) | (♯9) | | (♯11) | (♭13) | | |

Observing the altered dominant scale from its *Sub V* shows a "natural" dominant scale, (or "Mixolydian" mode), with ♯11. This scale is often referred to as the "Lydian♭7" scale or fourth mode of the "Jazz" melodic minor scale;

| | | | | | | | | |
|---|---|---|---|---|---|---|---|---|
| C Melodic Minor.................. | C | D | E♭ | F | G | A | B | C |
| F Lydian♭7............................ | 5 | 6 | ♭7 | 1 | 2 | 3 | ♯4 | 5 |
| B Altered............................... | ♭2 | ♯2 | 3 | ♭5 | ♯5 | ♭7 | 1 | ♭2 |

Tension ♯9(♯2) and ♯5 (sometimes referred to as ♭13) appear to be the most "characteristic" altered chord tones or tensions since they are also tensions 9(2) and 13(6) on their relative Sub V chord.

The following lists the different dominant chords and tension combinations that have been presented and could be used as "altered" chords;

1) Basic 7th chords; dom7♯5 dom7♭5

2) Single tension chapters;

**Tension 9;** dom7♯5(♭9) dom7♭5(♭9) dom7♯5(♯9) dom7♭5(♯9)
**Tension 11;** dom7♯5(♯11) or dom7(alt5)

3) Two tension chapters;

**Tensions 9 & 13;** dom7♭5(♭13/♭9) or (♭9/alt5) dom7♭5(♭13/♯9) or (♯9/alt5)

4) **Altered 9th Tensions on Dom7th Chords;**

dom7(alt9/no5) dom7♭5(alt9) dom7♯5(alt9) dom7(alt9/alt5)

The altered dominant contains a unique and characteristic property in the placement of parallel voicings a whole-step apart on the ♭5th and ♯5th of the original altered chord. By placing either major triads, dom7ths, or dom9th chords on these notes, an altered "upper-structure" sound is produced;

**G7(alt);** (♭5th) - D♭, D♭7, or D♭9 (♯5th) - E♭, E♭7, or E♭9

Realize each chords relation to the original altered chord;

| | | | | | | | | | | | |
|---|---|---|---|---|---|---|---|---|---|---|---|
| D♭........... | 1 | 3 | 5 | ♭7 | 9 | E♭........ | 1 | 3 | 5 | ♭7 | 9 |
| G7(alt)..... | ♭5 | ♭7 | ♭9 | 3 | ♯5 | G7(alt).. | ♯5 | 1 | ♯9 | ♭5 | ♭7 |

Note the <u>sixteen</u> different dom9th voicings produced by using *all* four "drop 2" [3 5 ♭7 9] and *all* four "ninth (no 5)" [1 3 ♭7 9] chord inversions on <u>*both*</u> D♭9 and E♭9.

Two additional structures, major(add9) and dom9(no3), can be placed on the ♭5th and ♯5th of an altered chord as well. These structures could be viewed from perhaps a more familiar enharmonic root;

D♭(add9) = F-7♯5 E♭(add9) = G-7♯5 D♭9(no3) = B6(9) [1 3 6 9] E♭9(no3) = D♭6(9) [1 3 6 9]

Root relation to G altered; ♭VII-7♯5 I-7♯5 III6(9) ♭V6(9)

Notice three of the above voicings have *three* altered tensions while G-7♯5 has two. Also note G-7♯5 and D♭6(9) contain the "characteristic" ♯5 and ♯9 altered tensions, while F-7♯5 and B6(9) have the *same* three tensions; (♭5, ♯5, and ♭9).

| | | | | | | | | | |
|---|---|---|---|---|---|---|---|---|---|
| G-7♯5; | G | B♭ | D♯ | F | D♭6(9); | D♭ | F | B♭ | E♭ |
| **G7(alt)**............... | 1 | **♯9** | **♯5** | ♭7............................... | | ♭5 | ♭7 | **♯9** | **♯5** |
| F-7♯5; | F | A♭ | C♯ | E♭ | B6(9); | B | D♯ | G♯ | C♯ |
| **G7(alt)**............. | ♭7 | **♭9** | **♭5** | **♯5**................................ | | 3 | **♯5** | **♭9** | **♭5** |

Additional *non-symmetrical* structures built off the ♭5th and ♯5th of the dominant altered could include the triad plus any remaining altered notes;

(G alt); D♭(♯11) [1 3 5 ♯11] D♭6 [1 3 5 6] E♭(add4) [1 3 4 5] E♭(♭13) [1 3 5 ♭13]

These triads could place their additional notes in the bottom voice producing some interesting hybrid structures that could be used as G altered voicings;

D♭/G D♭/B♭ (B♭-7) E♭/A♭ E♭/B

* Bottom voice should not violate L.I.L. for G altered.

Notice the B note is the only non-triadic note for <u>both</u> D♭ and E♭ triads. This note might function as an interesting pedal under these two triads; D♭/B - E♭/B.

The following examples combine the altered upper-structure concepts introduced here with past altered voicings;

1) (D-7)- - - - - - - - - - - - - (G7altered)- - - - - - - - - - - - - - - - (C)

D9sus4 F6(9) D♭9 B♭7sus4 E♭9 B6(9) C(add9)

2) (G7altered) - - - - - - - - - - - - - - - - - - - - - - - - - - - - (C)

E♭9 D♭6(9) D♭9 B6(9) Cmaj7(9)

3) (G7altered) - - - - - - - - - - - - - - - - - - - - - - - - - - - - (C)

D♭7 D♭6(9) F-7♯5 B♭7sus4 Cmaj7(9)

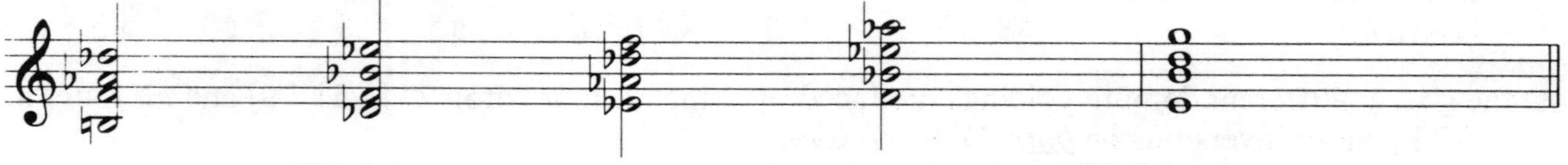

4) (G7alt) - - - - - (G7alt) - - - - -

D-9 E♭9 D♭9 Cmaj7 D-9 D♭9 E♭9 Cmaj7

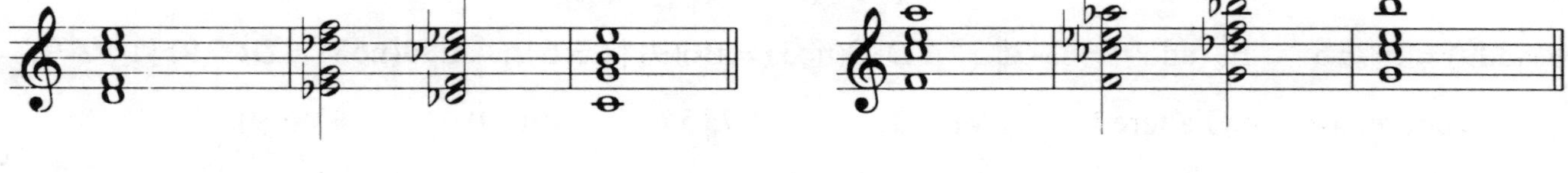

The following altered voicings include some "constant structure motion" ideas;

1) (D-9) (G7alt) – – – – (Cmaj7(♯11/9))
C6(9) B6(9) D♭6(9) D6(9)

2) (D-7(11/9)) (G7alt) – – – – (C(13/♯11/9)
E-7♯5 G-7♯5 F-7♯5 F♯-7♯5

3) (C-7(11)) (F7alt) – – – – – (B♭ (add9))
G-7♯5 F-7♯5 E♭-7♯5 D-7♯5

# Chapter Twenty-Four.
## Approach Voicings

Three basic approach techniques, referred to as "diatonic," "chromatic," and "dominant," can be applied to voicings that are used to introduce established chords.

*Diatonic* approach voicings are relative to the key or mode of the moment, and usually resolve to the chord being approached by diatonic step. These voicings can often be viewed as diatonic extensions of the previous voicing, (displayed in the following example).

(C-7) - - - - - - - - - - - - - (F7)
C-7(11) D-7(11) F7(13/9)

*Dominant* approach uses voicings that have a dominant relation to the chord being approached;

(C-7) - - - - - - - - - - - - (F7)
C-7(9) C7(♭9) F13(♭9)

*Chromatic* approach uses voicings that are the *same* as the chord being approached, a half-step above or below that chord. This could be considered chromatic "constant structure" motion.

(C-7) - - - - - - - - - - - - - - (F7)
C-7(11) E13 or G♭13 F13

Note the above G♭13 chord could also be considered a *dominant* approach voicing. Chromatic approach voicings have additional possibilities that will be examined later in this chapter.

As noted above, approach voicings can often have two and, in rare cases, three approach functions in one voicing;

"Chromatic" <u>and</u> "dominant" approach functions in *one* voicing;

(G7) - - - - - - - - - - - - - (C)
G7(♯9) G7♯5(alt9) C6(9)

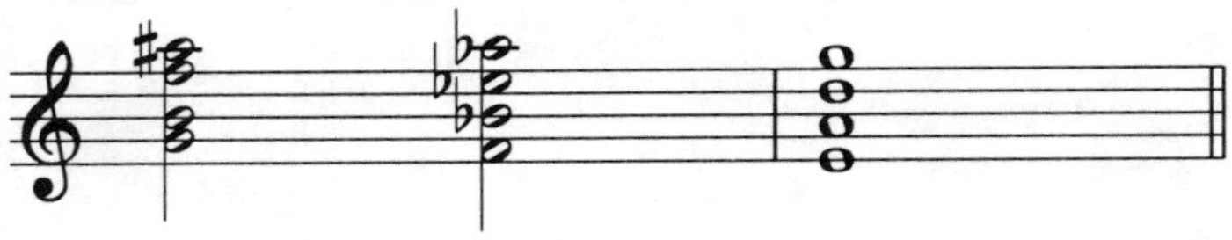

Note the above approach voicing could also have an additional "diatonic" function; (diatonic to G altered scale).

"Dominant" and "diatonic" approach functions in *one* voicing;

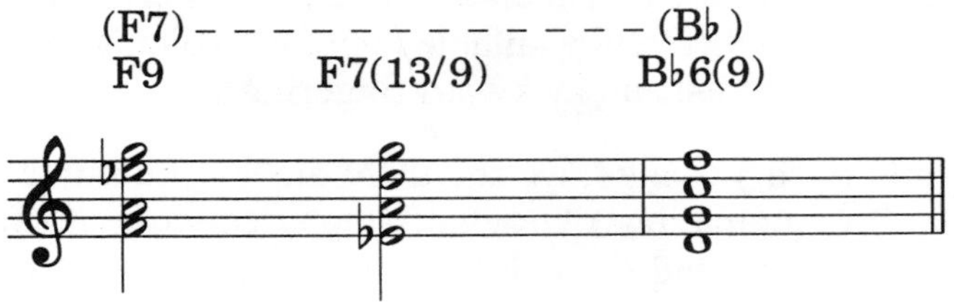


"Diatonic" and "chromatic" approach functions in *one* voicing;

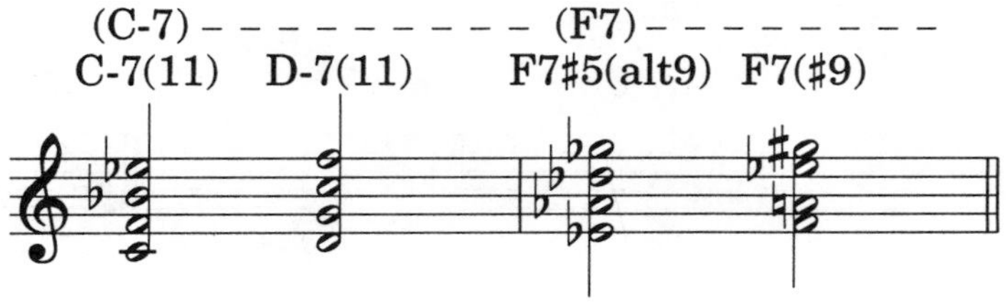


The usual and perhaps most effective placement of an approach voicing is on the weak area of the harmonic rhythm where traditional rules such as "Low Interval Limits" can more easily be violated. In the previous examples, the approach voicing was placed on the weak half of the measure; beats 3 & 4.

Some of the most effective uses of approach voicings are found in "stagnant" harmonic situations. Here, the harmonic color and variety these approach techniques offer can enhance an existing "basic" progression or vamp.

In the following chord progression, which was taken from a common "standard" tune, each chord receives the duration of eight beats, producing a somewhat stagnant harmonic situation. By the addition of approach voicings, the progression receives more harmonic variety and motion. The *original* chords are in parenthesis.

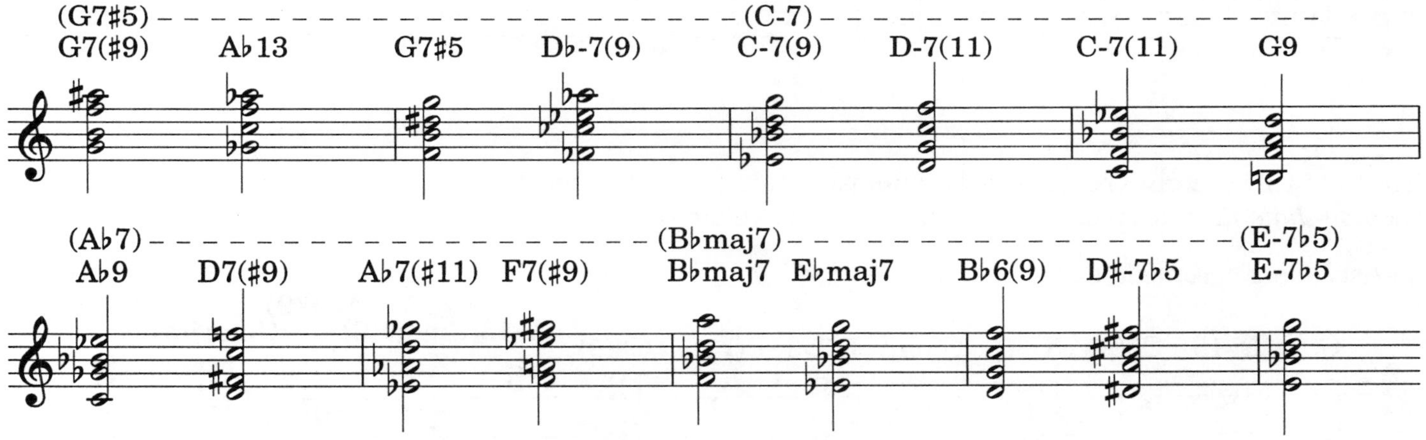


The following is an example of using *only* chromatic approach voicings on the beginning of the *same* "standard" tune.

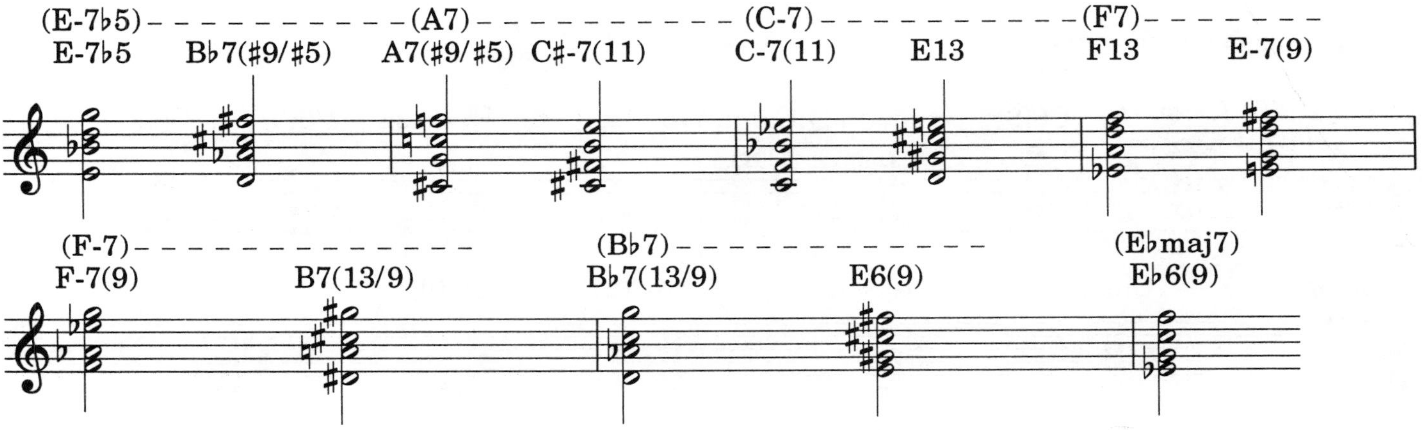

Many different voicings could *chromatically* approach a single chord when the various combinations of above and below half-step resolutions to that chord are considered. In fact, considering all possible chromatic resolutions to a four-note structure produces fourteen different available approach voicings to that structure, although some will be omitted due to ♭9th intervals, doublings, and awkward fingerings.

In examining these fourteen approach voicings, we see there are four possible combinations of three half-steps ascending and *one* descending, six combinations of *two* half-steps ascending and *two* half-steps descending, and four combinations of *one* half-step ascending and *three* descending.

The following examples display nine different chromatic approach voicings to the "drop 2" root inversion Cmaj7 chord. The remaining five approach voicings were omitted due to ♭9th intervals, doublings, or awkward fingerings.

1) *Three* half-steps ascending and *one* descending;

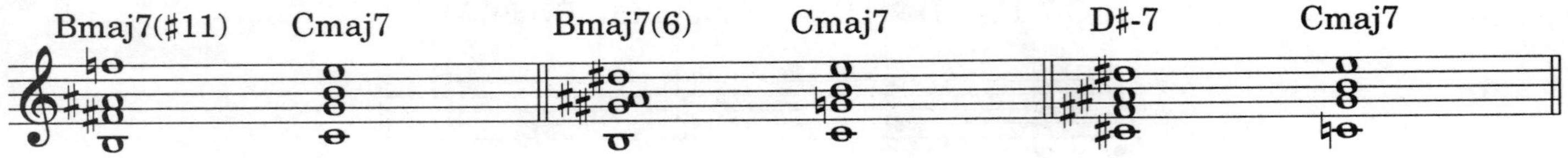


2) *Two* half-steps ascending and *two* descending;

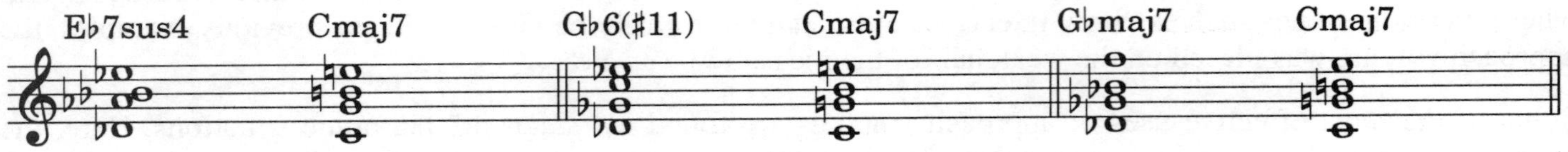


3) *One* half-step ascending and *three* descending;

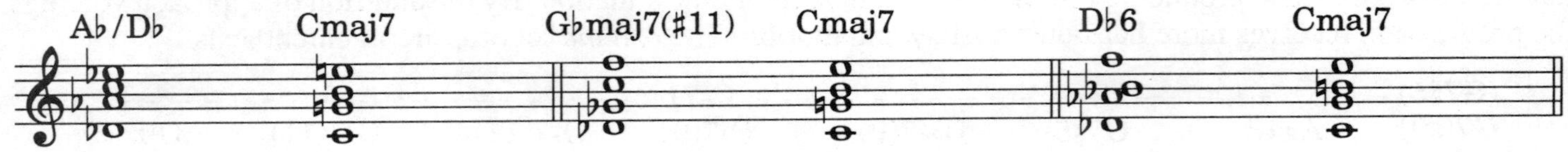


The following exercises harmonize the chromatic scale, (ascending and descending), with a Cmaj7 type chord, while the *non-diatonic* notes receive chromatic approach voicings.

1) Ascending chromatic line;

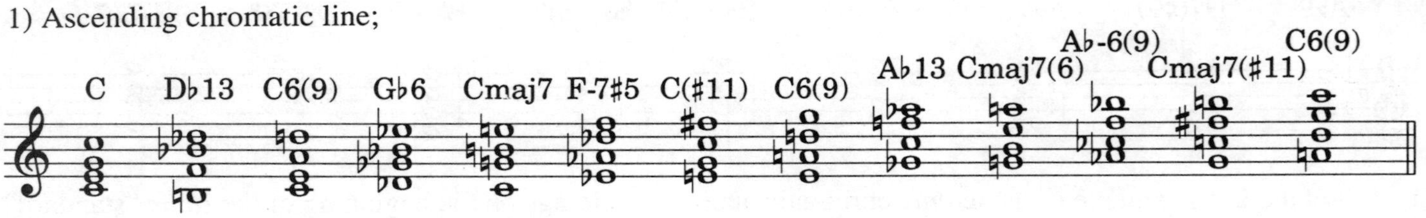


2) Descending chromatic line;

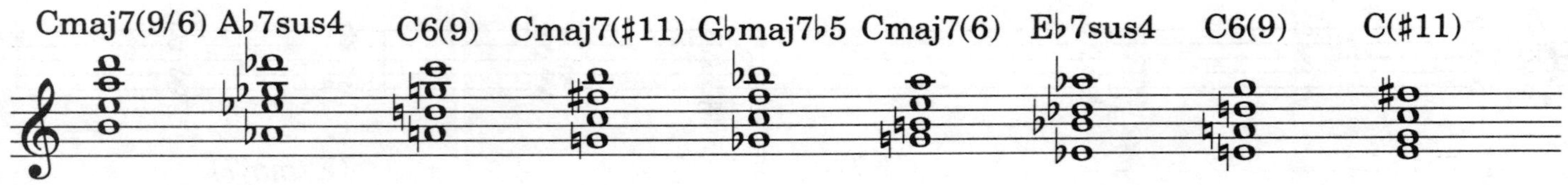


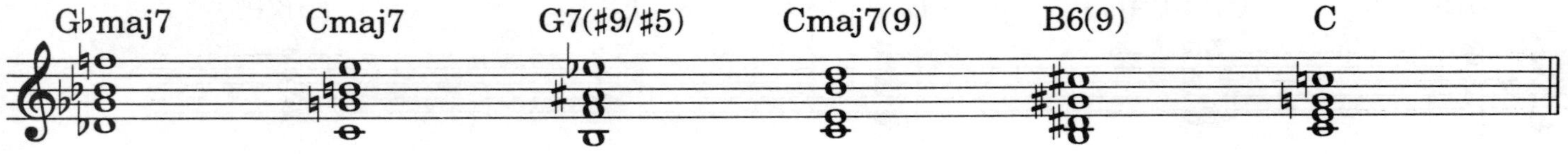

Chromatic approach voicings could also involve *one* common tone while the remaining three tones resolve in various chromatic combinations. Thirty-two potential approach voicings can be produced from these combinations! While one note remains common; four different chromatic approach voicings are produced by three ascending half-steps, four more voicings produced by three descending half-steps, twelve more voicings produced by two ascending and one descending half-steps, and twelve more by two descending and one ascending half-steps. Of course ♭9th intervals, doublings, and awkward fingerings will omit quite a few voicings, (although some doublings will be occasionally used).

The following examples display twenty-four of these chromatic approach voicings, (with some doublings), to the drop 2, root inversion, Cmaj7 chord. Common tones will be darkened for reference.

1) Three half-steps ascending;

2) Three half-steps descending;

3) Two half-steps descending and one ascending;

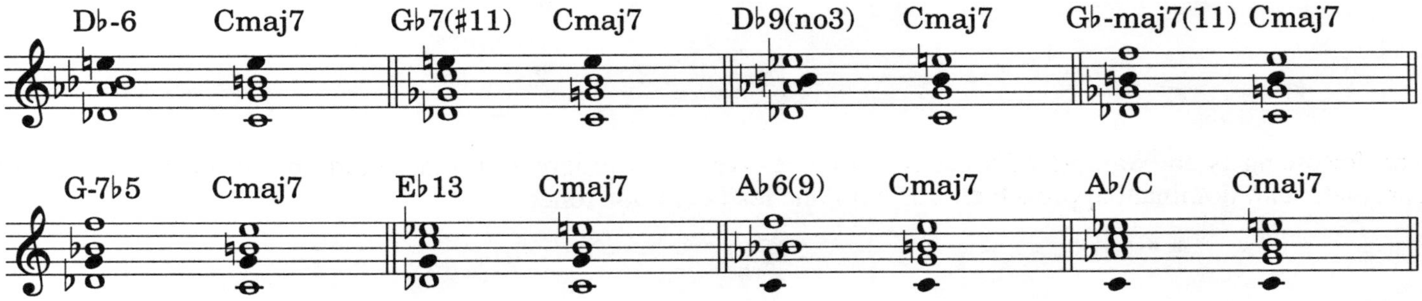


4) Two half-steps ascending and one descending;

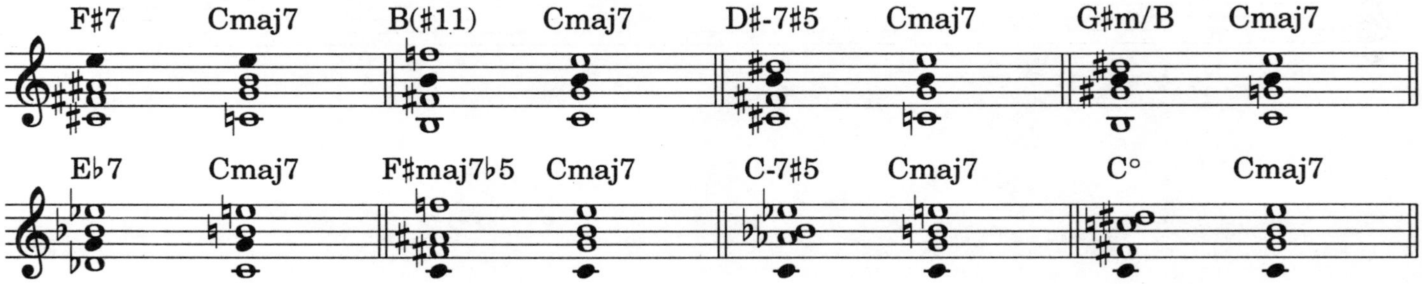

Two or three common tones in chromatic approach voicings are possible, but begin to destroy the "approach" quality of these voicings. Some of these voicings will be explored along with additional concepts in the **Chromatic Guidelines** chapter.

The following example uses the *three* chromatic-*one* common tone approach voicings on the beginning of a "standard" chord progression;

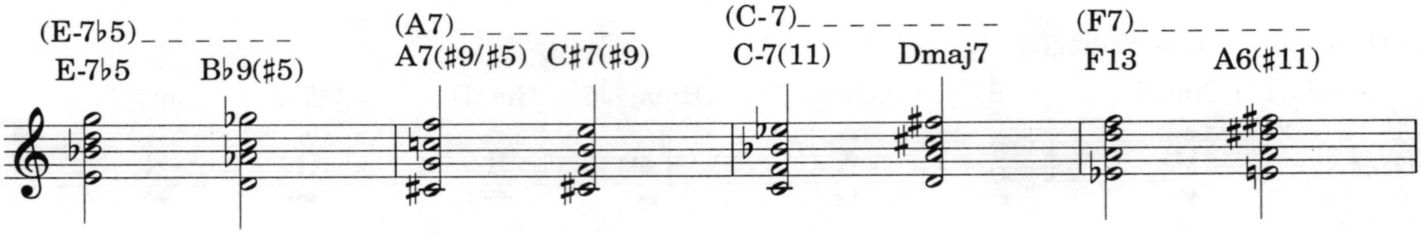


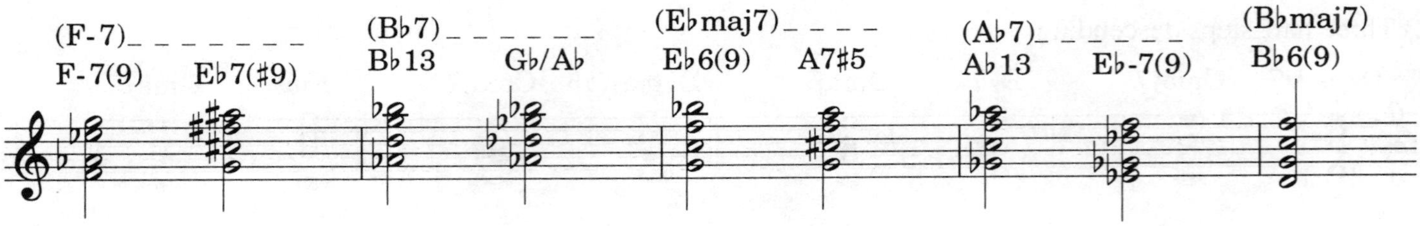


The following is an example of a backward cycle-five chord progression that could be considered a chain of chromatic and dominant approach chords with one lead common tone;

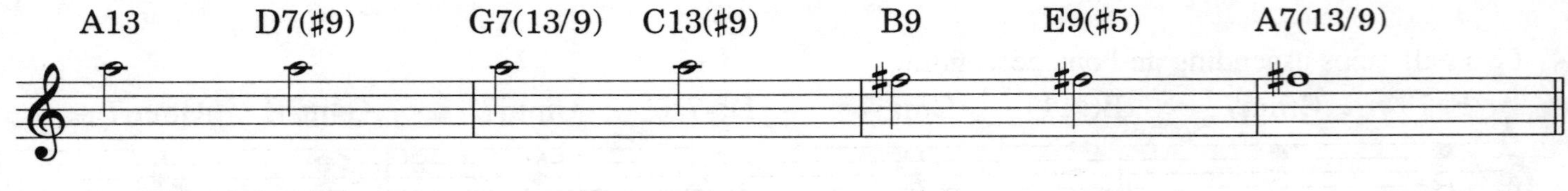

The following "F Blues" uses a variety of chromatic approach chords with the emphasis again on a lead common tone. Voicings not fully notated are drop 2 type voicings;

# Chapter Twenty-Five.
## Fourth Voicings

There are five basic fourth-type voicings available to the middle four strings of the guitar. The following will list each voicing as well as the initial chord type to first introduced it. Additional enharmonic chordal uses for each voicing can be found in the appropriate **Enharmonic Chordal Substitution** chapter containing these chords.

1) **C**... 4th..... **F**........ 4th..... **B♭**..... 4th..... **E♭** (perfect fourths) {F7sus4}

2) **C**.. ♯4th.....**F♯**..... 4th..... **B**....... 4th..... **E** (one tritone) {Cmaj7♭5}

3) **C**... 4th..... **F....** ♯4th.....**B**. ...... 4th..... **E** (one tritone) {Fmaj7(♯11)}

4) **C**... 4th..... **F**........ 4th..... **B♭**... ♯4th.....**E** (one tritone) {F-maj7(11)}

5) **C**.. ♯4th.....**F♯**........4th..... **B**...... ♯4th.....**E♯** (two tritones) {D13(♯9) or A♭13(♯9)}

Of course different inversions of the above chords are available, but do not contain *all* fourth intervals as do the specific inversions listed.

When all or most of the voicings used in a comping situation are fourth voicings, a contemporary and sometimes "modal" sound is produced. It is also common to find a good deal of chromatic and diatonic approach chords using fourth type voicings in this contemporary environment. Occasional fourth voicings can and do appear in many different styles, but a contemporary "quartal" sound can only be produced by using many fourth voicings. Fourth voicings can be found in "modal" or "diatonic" situations, and each requires a different approach.

**Modal** music, where many fourth voicings are commonly found, does not contain the traditional "avoid" or weak notes that are commonly found in diatonic harmonies. In fact, many of the avoid notes in diatonic harmonies are the desired "characteristic" notes in modal music. The incomplete or ambiguous nature of fourth voicings seem to enhance this modal sound. It is certainly easier to play many different fourth voicings in a modal situation, where every voicing is available, than it is in a diatonic situation where voicings that contain avoid notes should be omitted or placed on weak harmonic rhythms. Of course in many diatonic situations there are places where the harmony can be stagnant, allowing for a temporary modal approach to those harmonies.

When trying to make the majority of voicings in a **Diatonic** situation fourth-type voicings, a difficult irony is produced by the need for many voicings to clarify harmonic function, (often two or more incomplete fourth voicings are needed to clarify one chords function), and a consequent reduction in voicings due to diatonic avoid notes. Often a compromise between these two problems is needed to harmonize "changes" with fourth type voicings. Perhaps the "need" for harmonic clarification in diatonic progressions could be reduced and "avoid notes" could be accepted more often.

The following will examine fourth voicings by diatonically moving them through specific scales and determining their modal and applicable diatonic uses.

### MAJOR SCALE

Modally, all seven of the fourth voicings produced here will be available to any one of the seven major scale modes.

Fourth voicings in **C major scale**, (or any of its seven relative modes);

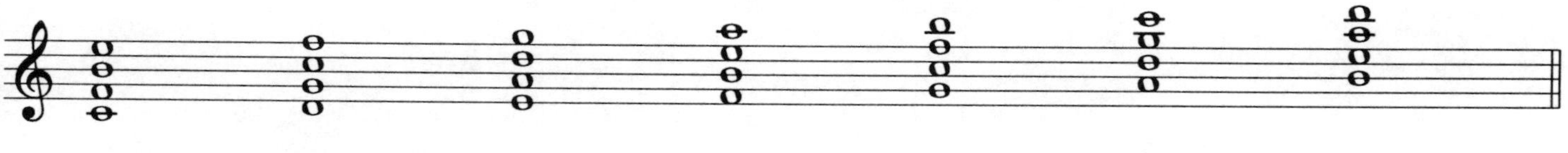

Note that four of the five basic fourth-type voicings originally presented are contained in the major scale.

A unique and contemporary chord symbol notation depicting the different modes has recently evolved and appears quite different from traditional chord symbol notation since many of the characteristic modal tensions are "avoid notes" in traditional harmony. The following modal chord symbols are not uncommon in today's music.

| | |
|---|---|
| *Ionian;* | maj(add4) |
| *Dorian;* | min13 or min7(13) |
| *Phrygian;* | min(♭9) or sus4(♭9) or min(11/♭9) |
| *Lydian;* | maj7(♯11) |
| *Mixolydian;* | dom7(add11) or dom7(add4) |
| *Aeolian;* | min(add♭13) |
| *Locrian;* | min7♭5(♭9) |

Descriptive modal chord symbols have also become quite common;

**C (lydian)** = Cmaj7(♯11) and possible tensions 9 and 13(6)
**C (dorian)** = C-7(13) and possible tensions 9 and 11
**C (phrygian)** = Cno3rd(11/♭9) or Cmin(♭9) and possible tensions 11 and ♭13
**C (aeolian)** = Cmin(add♭13) and possible tensions 9 and 11

These symbols which are most common in modal music have also found there way into diatonic tunes, modifying many of the basic harmonic functions by the use of traditional avoid notes. Contemporary diatonic tunes often contain modal approaches to some or all of their harmonies. It is not uncommon to find a II-7(13), V7(add11), or II-7♭5(♭9) chord in today's diatonic progressions. Although these chords can involve many different types of voicings, fourth voicings still play a major role in supporting their "modal" sounds.

Its worth noting at this time that the dorian mode is the *relative* minor of the lydian mode, allowing past maj7(♯11) and maj6(♯11) voicings (with or without available tensions 9 and 13) to function as dorian voicings. As an example, Cmaj7(♯11) [1 5 7 ♯11] = A-7(13/9) [♭3 ♭7 9 13].

The following will examine one of the fourth voicings established in "C major" and apply some of the relative modes and consequent chord notations.

| Fourth voicing; | **G.....** | **C.....** | **F......** | **B** | |
|---|---|---|---|---|---|
| 1) D dorian........................... | 11..... | ♭7...... | ♭3...... | 13 ...... | D-7(13/9) |
| 2) E phrygian....................... | ♭3..... | ♭13..... | ♭9....... | 5 ...... | Em(♭13/♭9) |
| 3) F lydian............................ | 9........ | 5........ | 1..... | ♯11 ..... | F(♯11/9) |
| 4) G mixolydian.................... | 1...... | 11...... | ♭7....... | 3 ....... | G7(add11) |
| 5) A aeolian.......................... | ♭7...... | ♭3..... | ♭13....... | 9........ | A-7(♭13/9) |
| 6) B locrian........................... | ♭13..... | ♭9..... | ♭5........ | 1........ | B-7♭5(♭13/♭9) |

Additional dominant possibilities of above voicing;

G7(add11) - G mixolydian♭9/♭13 (C harmonic minor)
B7(♭9/alt5) E7(♭13/alt9)

Diatonic applications of fourth voicings usually involves finding one or more "safe" voicings, (no avoid notes and clear harmonic function), to begin and end with while the other voicings containing avoid notes and incomplete structures are used in between. It is also common to find "chromatic approach" voicings and/or "symmetrical constant structure" voicings in between or linking these "safe" voicings. The following examples will present some of these diatonic ideas with fourth voicings over typical II - V - I chord cadences.

This first example uses <u>only</u> diatonic fourth voicings in the key of "C ", ending on C lydian.

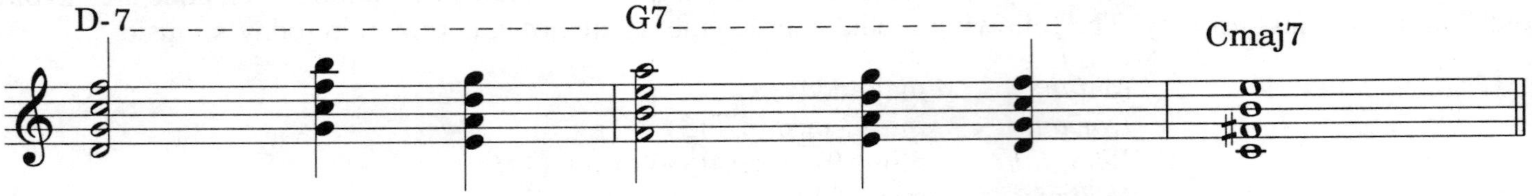


This next example introduces chromatic approach voicings to the diatonic fourth voicings.

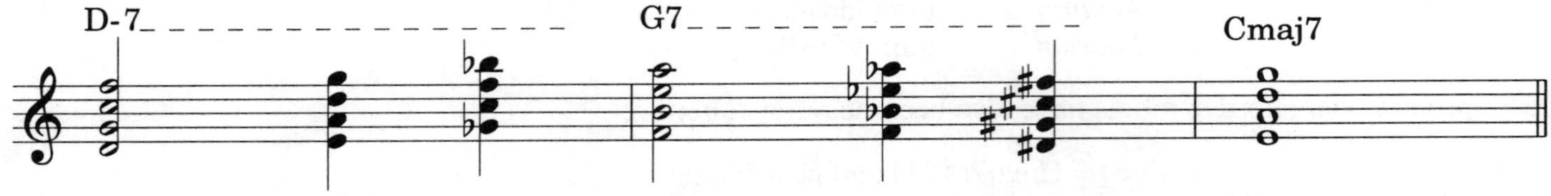


The following examples will examine symmetrical constant structure fourth voicings in different II V I situations. Some of these examples will present a *major7th* note on a dom7 chord; a very unique and contemporary sound.

#1) Whole-steps;

a)
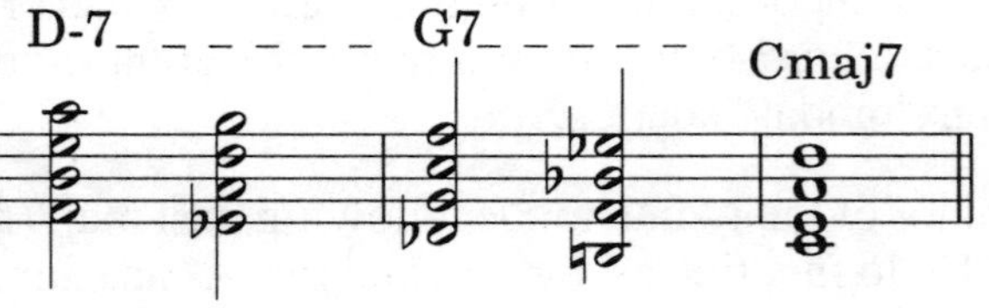


b)
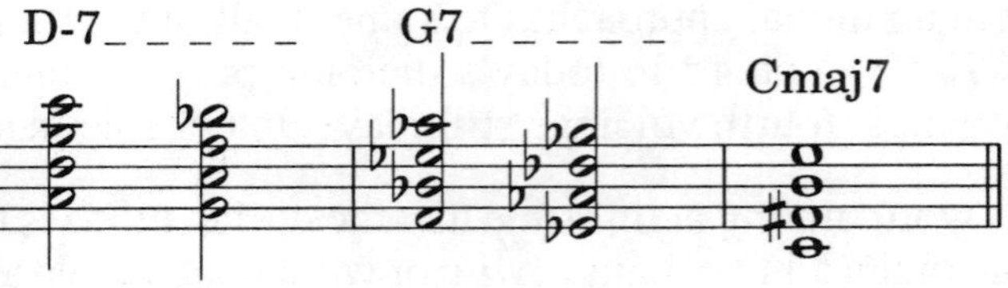


c)
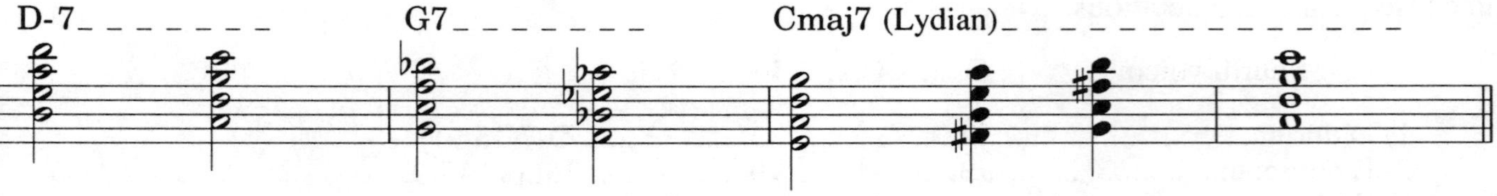


#2) Symmetrical diminished, (whole-half-whole-half);

a)
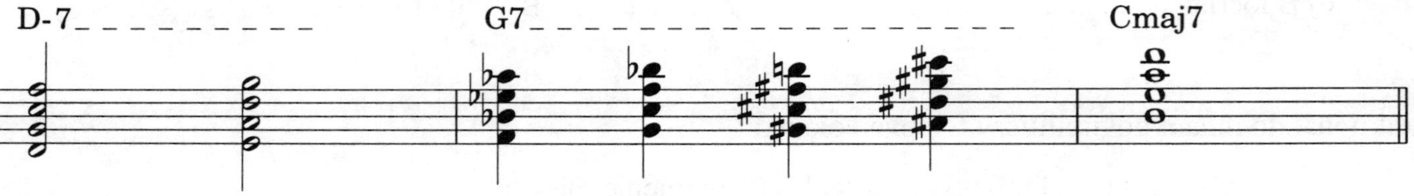


b)

#3) Minor thirds;

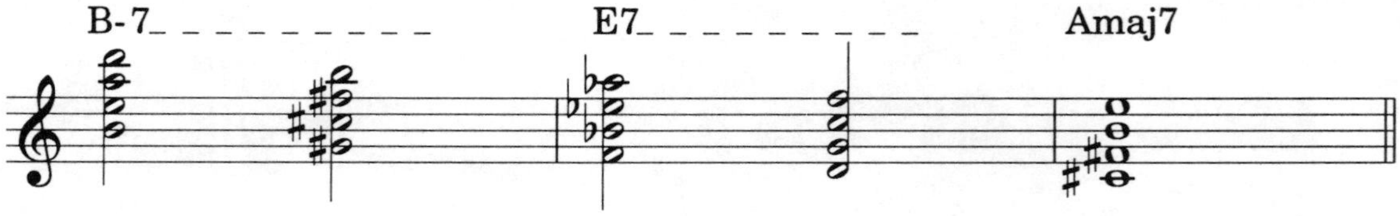

The major scale modes also have some altered dominant possibilities that can be examined. There are four major scales; E♭, A♭, D♭, and G♭, which produce altered dominant tensions on a G7 chord. The following will enharmonically realize the notes of each major scale in relation to the G7 chord.

| | | | | | | | |
|---|---|---|---|---|---|---|---|
| E♭ major scale (G phrygian)..G | A♭ | B♭ | C | D | E♭ | F |
| G7 chord................................1 | ♭9 | ♯9 | 4 | 5 | ♭13 | ♭7 |
| A♭ major scale (G locrian).....G | A♭ | B♭ | C | D♭ | E♭ | F |
| G7 chord................................1 | ♭9 | ♯9 | 4 | ♭5 | ♯5 | ♭7 |
| D♭ major scale........................G♭ | A♭ | B♭ | C | D♭ | E♭ | F |
| G7 chord................................7 | ♭9 | ♯9 | 4 | ♭5 | ♯5 | ♭7 |
| G♭ major scale........................G♭ | A♭ | B♭ | C♭ | D♭ | E♭ | F |
| G7 chord................................7 | ♭9 | ♯9 | 3 | ♭5 | ♯5 | ♭7 |

Note the potential problems with A♭ and D♭ major scales. The 11th and ♭5th in the same voicing strongly suggest a min7♭5 chord, and the 11th and natural 7th produce dominant guide-tones a half-step above the original guide-tones.

The following lists those fourth voicings that are in common with *more* than one of the above major scales. Of special note is the B♭7sus4 or F-7(11) voicing which is in common with *all* four scales.

D♭ and G♭ major scales share the voicing; A♭7sus4 [E♭, A♭, D♭, G♭]
E♭ and A♭ major scales share the voicing; C7sus4 [G, C,F, B♭]
A♭, D♭, and G♭ major scales share the voicing; E♭7sus4 [B♭, E♭, A♭, D♭]
E♭, A♭, and D♭ major scales share the voicing; F7sus4 [C, F, B♭, E♭]
E♭, A♭, D♭, and G♭ major scales share the voicing; B♭7sus4 [F, B♭, E♭, A♭]

The following II V I examples will examine all four altered dominant sounds presented.

1) E♭ major (G phrygian);

(Note the following D-7 voicings are the same as those voicings under G7 transposed up a minor third)

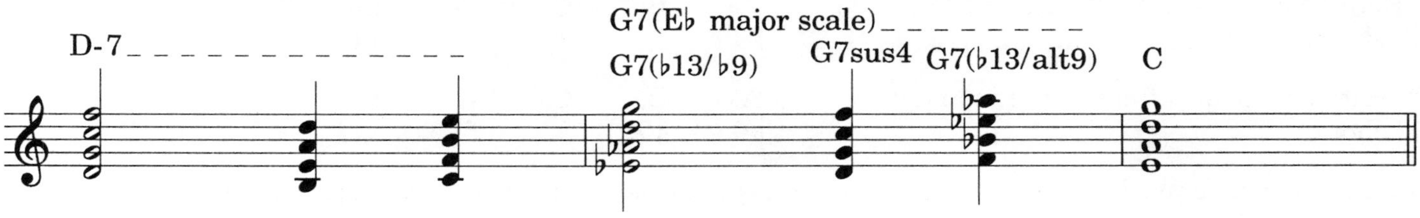


2) A♭ major (G locrian);

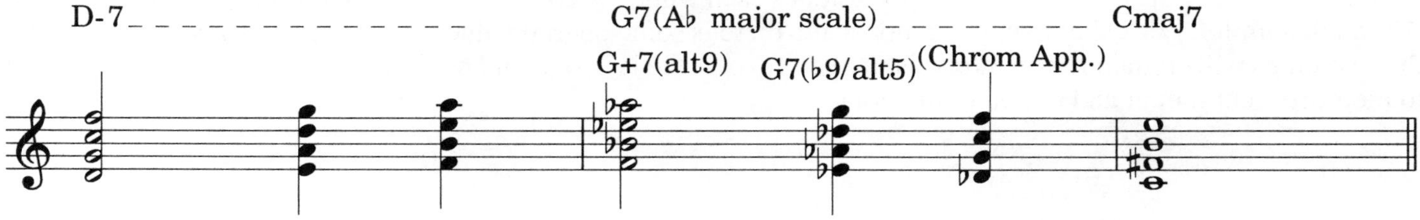

3) D♭ major;

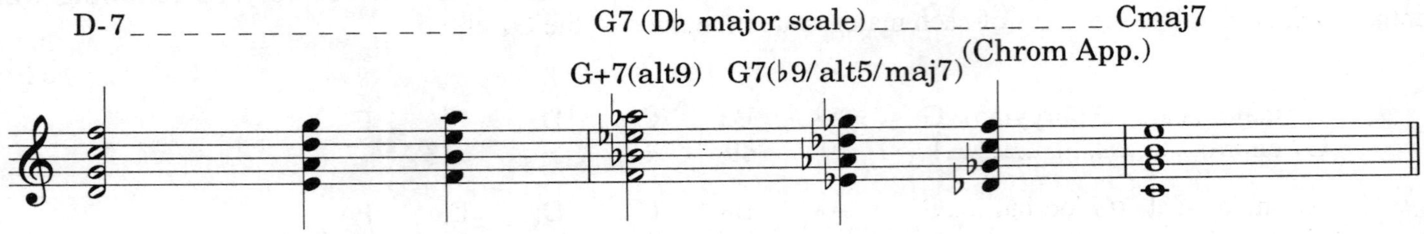


Note the chromatic motion of each voice in the above approach chord; three voices descend while the 4th-string voice ascends in approaching Cmaj7.

4) G♭ major;

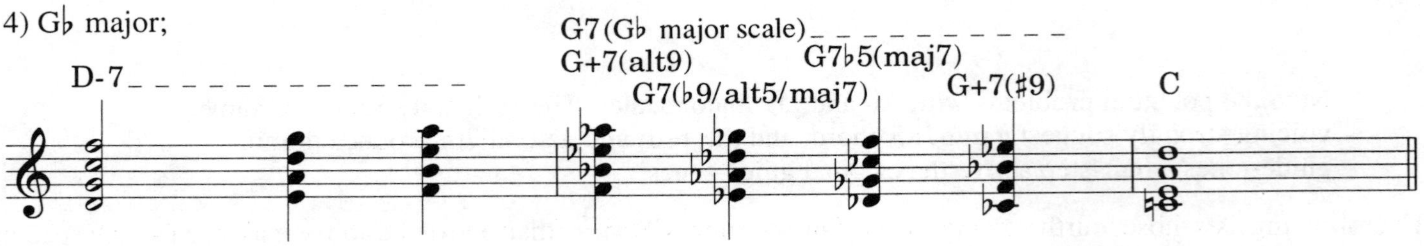


Although the major scale offers the most diverse uses of fourth voicings in a modal or diatonic situation, other scales can be examined for their potential use in quartal harmony. The remaining seven-tone diatonic scales, (without consecutive half-steps), are the *melodic* minor, *harmonic* minor, and *harmonic* major. Primary interest will be placed on the examination of the melodic minor and its modes, as well as the third mode of the harmonic major. The harmonic minor will be omitted due to its limited modal uses and problematic "avoid notes." The useful *fifth* mode of the harmonic minor (Mixolydian♭9/♭13) can be substituted by the third mode of the harmonic major which, unlike the harmonic minor, has no avoid notes. Both modes are dominant modes and commonly function on a V7 of a minor chord.

The following modes are related to a G7 chord;

| | | | | | | | | |
|---|---|---|---|---|---|---|---|---|
| C Harmonic minor (from its fifth mode); | G | A♭ | B | C | D | E♭ | F | G |
| G7 chord................................................ | 1 | ♭9 | 3 | 4 | 5 | ♭13 | ♭7 | 1 |
| E♭ Harmonic major (from its third mode); | G | A♭ | B♭ | C♭ | D | E♭ | F | G |
| G7 chord................................................ | 1 | ♭9 | ♯9 | 3 | 5 | ♭13 | ♭7 | 1 |

Students are encouraged to examine and experiment with the additional harmonic major and minor modes.

Unlike the major scale, the melodic minor and harmonic major cannot maintain fourth intervals on each degree of their scales. When attempting to construct fourth voicings on each degree, a major third interval is produced on those voicings containing the ♭3rd and natural 7th in the melodic minor, and the major 3rd and ♭6th in the harmonic major. In addition, both of these scales contain two tritones each while, by comparison, the major scale contains only one. Although admittedly weaker than the major scale, there is some quartal value to these scales since the majority of their voicings will contain fourth intervals. In their favor is the lack of avoid notes, making more voicings available to their different modal and diatonic functions.

## MELODIC MINOR SCALE

Examination of this scale and its modes will include the *same* intervals ascending and descending, commonly referred to as the "jazz" or "real" melodic minor scale. With the exception of the fifth mode, there are no avoid notes in the melodic minor modes, allowing use of any one of the fourth voicings produced. The 4th degree of the fifth mode is the *only* avoid note.

Diatonic use of the *second* mode will be omitted due to its "unstable" nature. This mode has limited harmonic use with the possible exception of a modal II-7 chord in an established melodic minor key, or as a modal I minor chord; (Dorian ♭9). This mode does contain a valuable "melodic" relation to its parallel *dominant* chord;

| | | | | | | | | |
|---|---|---|---|---|---|---|---|---|
| D dorian ♭9................ | D | E♭ | F | G | A | B | C | D |
| D7 chord.................... | 1 | ♭9 | ♯9 | 4 | 5 | 13 | ♭7 | 8 |

Unfortunately, the dorian ♭9th mode appears rather unstable "harmonically" in supporting its parallel dominant sound.

C Melodic minor scale harmonized in fourths;

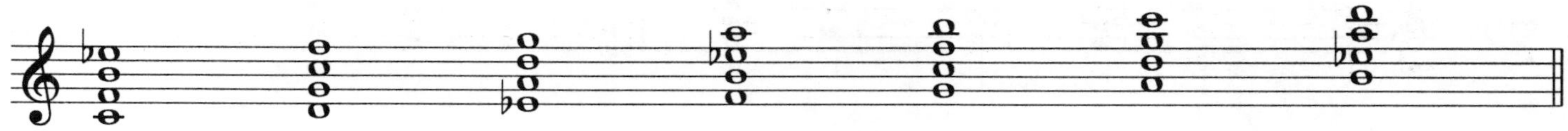

*Note the major third interval in the above voicings containing E♭ and B.

The following will examine <u>each</u> above fourth voicing, from left to right, in relation to the available modes.

First mode (C melodic minor);
C-maj7(11) C-(11/9) C-6(9) C-maj7(11/6) C-maj7(11) C-6(9) C-maj7(9/6)
* Note the 9th is in the bass, (L.I.L. violation), on the second voicing.

Third mode (E♭ Lydian augmented);
E♭+(9/6) E♭maj7(9/6) E♭maj7♭5 E♭+(♯11/9) E♭+(9/6) E♭maj7♭5(6) E♭maj7(alt5)

Fourth mode (F Lydian ♭7);
F7(♯11) F6(9) F7(13/9) F7♭5 F(♯11/9) F6(9) F7♭5(13)

Fifth mode (G Mixolydian ♭13);
G7(♭13/add4) G7sus4 G9(♭13) G9(♭13) G7(add4) G9sus4 G9(♭13)

Sixth mode (A Locrian-natural 9);
A-7♭5(♭13/9) A-7♯5(11) A-7♭5(11) A-7♭5(♭13/9) A-7♯5(9) A-7(11) A-7♭5(11/9)
* Note the 9th is in the bass, (L.I.L. violation), on the last voicing.

Seventh mode (B altered);
B7♭5(♭9) B7(alt9/alt5) B7♯5(♯9) B7♭5 B7(♭9/alt5) B7(alt9/♯5) B7(♯9)
* Note the ♯9th is in the bass, (L.I.L. violation), on the second voicing.

The *fourth* and *seventh* modes offer the best and most common use of these voicings in a diatonic situation;

Lydian ♭7 is common on dominant Sub V chords.
Altered is common on dominant V7 chords.

The *first* and *sixth* modes also offer some common diatonic uses;

Melodic minor is common on I and IV minor chords.
Locrian-natural 9 is common on min7♭5 chords.

The *third* and *fifth* modes are not quite as common as the above modes, but offer some interesting uses nonetheless;

Lydian augmented is useful on a Imaj7♯5 chord.
Mixolydian ♭13 is useful on a V7 chord, (commonly V7 of II-7).

The following examples will examine the four most common melodic minor modes in their related diatonic functions.

♯1)

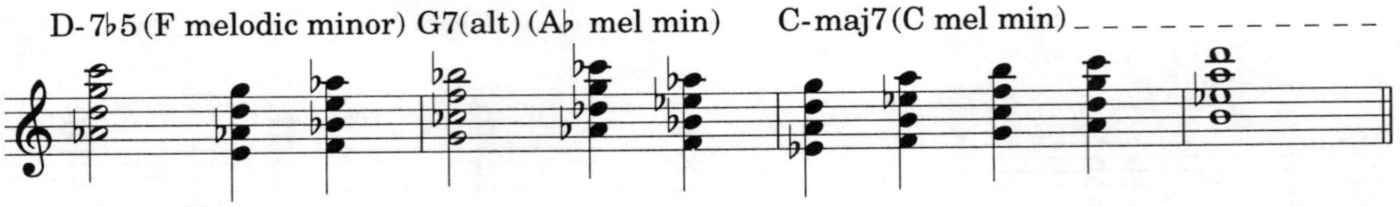


♯2)

♯3)

♯4)

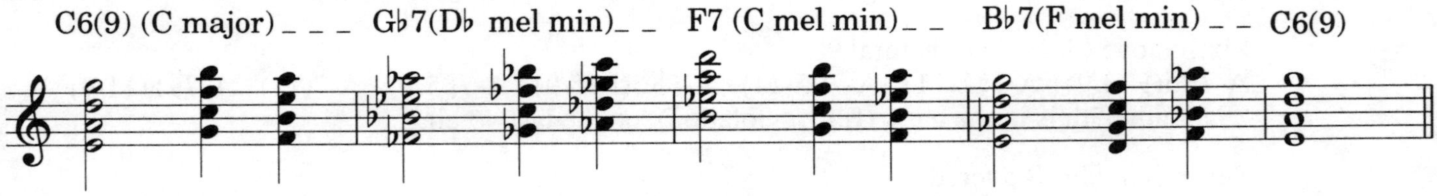

## HARMONIC MAJOR SCALE

C Harmonic major scale harmonized in fourths;

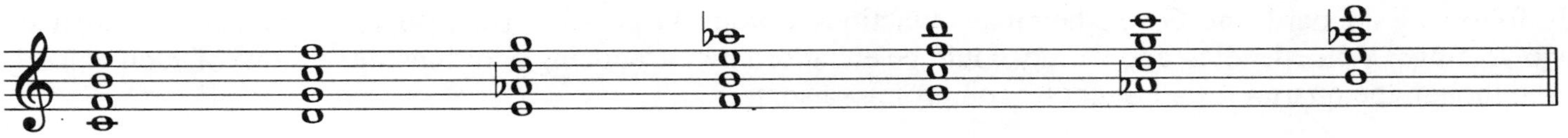

*Note the major third interval in those voicings containing E and A♭.

Only the *third* mode will be examined in this chapter. The following will relate each above voicing, from left to right, to this dominant mode:

E7(♭13/♭9)    E7(♭13/alt9)    E7(♯9)    E(♭9)    E7(♭13/alt9)    E7(♭13/♯9)    E7

The most common function of this mode is on the V7 chord of a minor chord, although it could also resolve to a major chord. Both resolutions are displayed in the following example.

F♯-7♭5 (F♯ locrian)    B7 (G harmonic major) _ _    Em (E dorian) _ _ _ _ _    E7 (C harmonic major)

A-7    D7 (B♭ harmonic major) _ _ _ _    Gmaj7

The following summarizes the modes and related fourth voicings available to a single dominant chord;

**G7 Chord;**

| | | | | | | | |
|---|---|---|---|---|---|---|---|
| Major scale dominant modes; | | | | | | | |
| G Mixolydian (C major); | 1 | 9 | 3 | 11 | 5 | 13 | ♭7 |
| G Phrygian (E♭ major); | 1 | ♭9 | ♯9 | 11 | 5 | ♭13 | ♭7 |
| G Locrian (A♭ major); | 1 | ♭9 | ♯9 | 11 | ♭5 | ♯5 | ♭7 |
| G Altered/natural7 (D♭ major); | 7 | ♭9 | ♯9 | 11 | ♭5 | ♯5 | ♭7 |
| G Altered/natural7 (G♭ major); | 7 | ♭9 | ♯9 | 3 | ♭5 | ♯5 | ♭7 |
| Melodic minor dominant modes; | | | | | | | |
| G Mixolydian ♭13 (C melodic minor); | 1 | 9 | 3 | 11 | 5 | ♭13 | ♭7 |
| G Lydian ♭7 (D melodic minor); | 1 | 9 | 3 | ♯11 | 5 | 13 | ♭7 |
| G Altered (A♭ melodic minor); | 1 | ♭9 | ♯9 | 3 | ♭5 | ♯5 | ♭7 |
| Harmonic major dominant mode; | | | | | | | |
| G Mixolydian ♭13/alt9 (E♭ harmonic major); | 1 | ♭9 | ♯9 | 3 | 5 | ♭13 | ♭7 |

Out of the five different fourth type voicings originally introduced, only one; D13(♯9)/A♭13(♯9), has not appeared in the scales presented. This voicing will be included in the following example of a "standard" tune harmonized with fourth voicings. Both of its dominant functions will be used; D13(♯9)/A♭13(♯9) and B7(♯11/♭9)/F7(♯11/♭9).

Originally presented in the **Constant Structure Harmonic Motion** chapter, note the multiple functions of the F7sus4 and Cmaj7♭5 fourth voicings presented in the beginning of this chapter, and their subsequent varied use in the following standard tune. Given their many functions, it would be possible to harmonize an entire song with these two voicings. Voice-leading and variety could be enhanced by introducing additional inversions of each voicing, even though the quartal sound might be compromised some.

In the following "standard" tune, all different approach chords, chord patterns, and modal sections will be labeled. Be sure to realize, with the exception of certain approach chords, what chord tones and tensions each fourth voicing produces on the original chords. Also note the "B" section has single chords sustaining for two measures, allowing them to be approached as temporary modal modulations with a specific scale for each chord voiced in fourths.

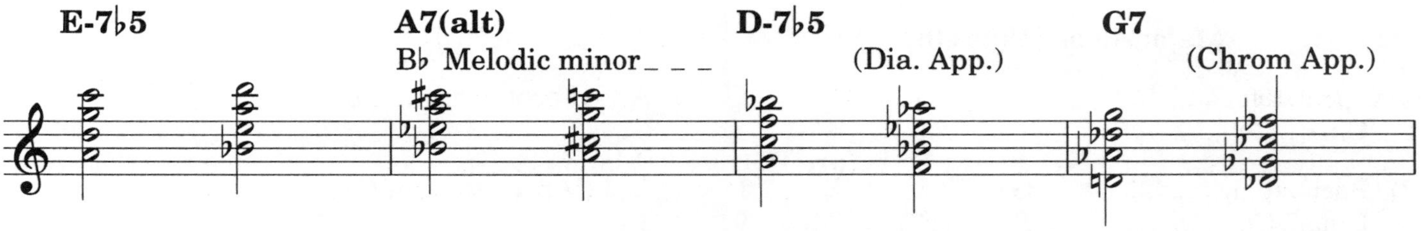


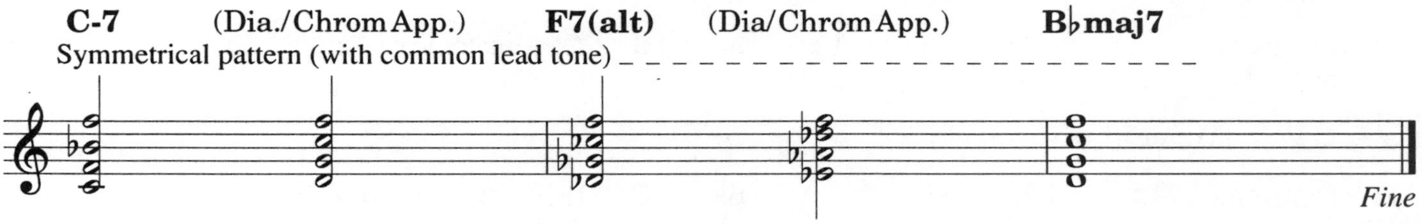


## PENTATONIC SCALE

Although seven-tone scales probably offer the most useful applications of four-note quartal voicings, the traditional pentatonic scale; (1 2 3 5 6), has some quartal qualities worth examining. Unlike seven-tone scales, this pentatonic scale contains no half-steps. Since the half-step is often the source of "avoid" or weak notes in diatonic harmonies, the pentatonic scale might offer some voicing alternatives to seven-tone scale voicings.

While fourth voicings are constructed by skipping every *two* notes in a seven-tone scale; **(1)**-2-3-**(4)**-5-6-**(7)**-8-9-**(10)**-11-12-**(13)**, etc., pentatonic fourth voicings are produced by skipping every *other* note; **(1)**-2-**(3)**-5-**(6)**-8-**(9)**-10-**(12)**-13-**(15)**, etc.

The following voicings are constructed off each degree of the pentatonic scale. Notice that *two* of these structures are complete fourth voicings while the remaining *three* structures contain <u>two</u> fourth intervals and <u>one</u> major third.

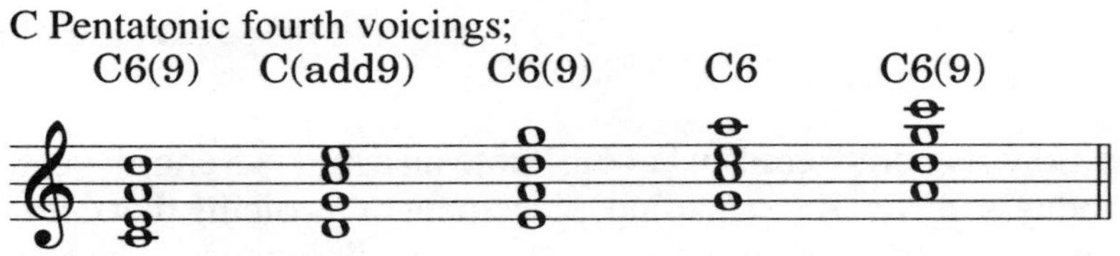


Although the major third interval does compromise the quartal sound to some degree, the majority of fourth intervals produce an overall satisfactory quartal sound. What is equally, if not more important to their quartal value is the strong and descriptive "pentatonic sound" these structures contain when at least two, and preferably more, are used as chordal substitutions. Further more, this pentatonic scale can often reflect the different music styles it is commonly used in such as "country," "rock," and "blues." These styles can be "heard" or implied by using several of the voicings produced by the pentatonic scale as substitute voicings.

The following relates D♭ major pentatonic to B♭ minor, (D♭'s "relative" minor), and G Altered;

| | | | | | | |
|---|---|---|---|---|---|---|
| D♭ Pentatonic......... | D♭ | E♭ | F | A♭ | B♭ | (possible D♭ "country" sound) |
| B♭ minor................ | ♭3 | 4 | 5 | ♭7 | 1 | (possible B♭ "rock" or "blues" sound) |
| G Altered............... | ♭5 | ♯5 | ♭7 | ♭9 | ♯9 | |

When two or more of the five possible D♭ pentatonic voicings are used as G7(alt) voicings, a "duality" of sound is produced. D♭ major or B♭ minor are clearly "heard" while G altered is also "heard." It might also be possible to "hear" two styles at the same time; D♭ "country" or B♭ "rock" against the dark "jazzy" G altered.

The following will list the possible pentatonic scales, (and subsequent voicings), that can be used as substitutes for the <u>four</u> "basic" chord groups.

**Major7th or Major6th;**

| | | | | | | |
|---|---|---|---|---|---|---|
| 1) C pentatonic........... | C | D | E | G | A | (I pentatonic of C) |
| Cmaj7/C6.............. | 1 | 2 | 3 | 5 | 6 | |
| 2) G pentatonic........... | G | A | B | D | E | (V pentatonic of C) |
| Cmaj7/C6.............. | 5 | 6 | 7 | 9 | 3 | |
| 3) D pentatonic.......... | D | E | F♯ | A | B | (II pentatonic of C) |
| Cmaj7/C6............. | 9 | 3 | ♯11 | 6 | 7 | |

**Minor7th;**

| | | | | | | |
|---|---|---|---|---|---|---|
| 1) E♭ pentatonic......... | E♭ | F | G | B♭ | C | (♭III pentatonic of C minor) |
| C-7....................... | ♭3 | 11 | 5 | ♭7 | 1 | |
| 2) B♭ pentatonic......... | B♭ | C | D | F | G | (♭VII pentatonic of C minor) |
| C-7........................ | ♭7 | 1 | 9 | 11 | 5 | |
| 3) F pentatonic........... | F | G | A | C | D | (IV pentatonic of C minor) |
| C-7........................ | 11 | 5 | 13 | 1 | 9 | |
| (C-6 or C-maj7)........ | 11 | 5 | 6 | 1 | 9 | |

**Minor7♭5;**

| | | | | | | |
|---|---|---|---|---|---|---|
| 1) A♭ pentatonic......... | A♭ | B♭ | C | E♭ | F | (♭VI pentatonic of C-7♭5) |
| C-7♭5................... | ♭13 | ♭7 | 1 | ♭3 | 11 | |
| 2) D♭ pentatonic........ | D♭ | E♭ | F | A♭ | B♭ | (♭II pentatonic of C-7♭5) |
| C-7♭5................... | ♭9 | ♭3 | 11 | ♭13 | ♭7 | |
| 3) G♭ pentatonic......... | G♭ | A♭ | B♭ | D♭ | E♭ | (♭V pentatonic of C-7♭5) |
| C-7♭5................... | ♭5 | ♭13 | ♭7 | ♭9 | ♭3 | |

Note that tension ♭9 is traditionally considered an "avoid" note on a min7♭5 chord, yet it is not uncommon to appear as an available tension in today's music. Keep in mind, placement of a voicing that contains this tension on the weak harmonic rhythm of a measure or phrase would produce the least dissonance. The most "characteristic" ♭5th tone is contained in only *one* pentatonic which also includes the ♭9th.

**Dominant 7th;**

The following pentatonics will be organized into <u>three</u> groups depicting their differences and possible applications.

**Group I;**

| | | | | | | |
|---|---|---|---|---|---|---|
| 1) C pentatonic..... | C | D | E | G | A | (I pentatonic of C7) |
| C7........................ | 1 | 9 | 3 | 5 | 13 | |
| 2) G♭ pentatonic.... | G♭ | A♭ | B♭ | D♭ | E♭ | (♭V pentatonic of C7) |
| C7.......................... | ♭5 | ♯5 | ♭7 | ♭9 | ♯9 | |

**Group II;**

| | | | | | | |
|---|---|---|---|---|---|---|
| 1) F pentatonic....... | F | G | A | C | D | (IV pentatonic of C7sus4) |
| C7sus4.................. | 4 | 5 | 13 | 1 | 9 | |
| 2) B♭ pentatonic...... | B♭ | C | D | F | G | (♭VII pentatonic of C7sus4) |
| C7sus4.................... | ♭7 | 1 | 9 | 4 | 5 | |
| 3) D♭ pentatonic...... | D♭ | E♭ | F | A♭ | B♭ | (♭II pentatonic of C7sus4) |
| C7sus4.................... | ♭9 | ♯9 | 4 | ♭13 | ♭7 | |

**Group III;**

| | | | | | | |
|---|---|---|---|---|---|---|
| 1) E pentatonic..... | E | F♯ | G♯ | B | C♯ | (III pentatonic of C7) |
| C7........................ | 3 | ♭5 | ♯5 | 7 | ♭9 | |
| 2) B pentatonic...........B | | C♯ | D♯ | F♯ | G♯ | (VII pentatonic of C7) |
| C7........................ | 7 | ♭9 | ♯9 | ♭5 | ♯5 | |

The first group includes the two most commonly used pentatonics in a dominant capacity; C pentatonic - "natural" tensions, and G♭ pentatonic - "altered" tensions.

The second group includes those pentatonics most commonly used on dom7sus4 chords; B♭ pentatonic - C9sus4, F pentatonic - C9sus4(13), and D♭ pentatonic - C7sus4(♭13/alt9). In an appropriate situation and with care, it might be possible to use these pentatonics against a dom7 chord without the suspended 4th. The D♭ pentatonic, which contains altered tensions, is probably the best choice for this application.

The third group includes two different pentatonics that contain altered tensions and a major 7th. The B pentatonic appears most characteristically altered of the two, supporting the major 7th with *all* the altered tensions; (♭5, ♯5, ♭9, ♯9). Again, this is a "progressive" sound that should be used in an appropriate context.

Note those pentatonics that contain dual functions;
(C pent. - Cmaj7 or C7), (B♭ pent. - C7sus4 or C-7), (F pent. - C7sus4 or C-6),
(D♭ pent. - C7sus4 or C-7♭5), and (G♭ pent. - C7 or C-7♭5).

The following examples will present the pentatonic voicings discovered in various *Tonic, Sub-dominant,* and *Dominant* capacities. Be sure to realize the tensions imposed on the basic 7th chords by these pentatonic voicings. In more musical applications, these voicings would most likely appear within isolated phrases over an entire song form.

These first two examples present pentatonic voicings over major and minor II V I cadences. Note in both examples the dominant chords use the typical "altered" sound by selecting pentatonic voicings a tritone away.

1) Minor II-V-I cadence;

**B-7♭5** _ _ _ _ _ _ _ _ _ _ _ _ **E7** _ _ _ _ _ _ _ _ _ _ _ _ _ **A-7** _ _ _ _ _ _ _ _ _ _ _ _ _

**(F pent)** **(G pent)** **(B♭ pent)** _ _ _ _ _ _ _ _ _ _ **(C pent)** **(G pent)**

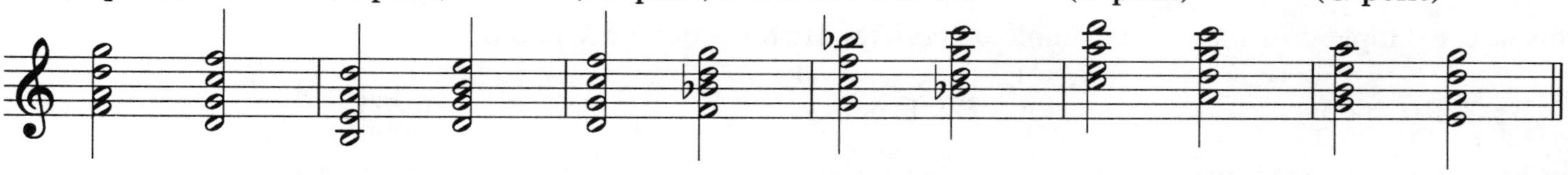

2) Major II-V-I cadence;

**B-7** _ _ _ _ _ _ _ _ _ _ _ _ **E7** _ _ _ _ _ _ _ _ _ _ _ _ _ **Amaj7** _ _ _ _ _ _ _ _ _ _ _ _ _

**(D pent)** **(A pent)** **(B♭ pent)** _ _ _ _ _ _ _ _ _ _ **(E pent)** _ _ _ _ _ _ _ _ _ _ _ _ _

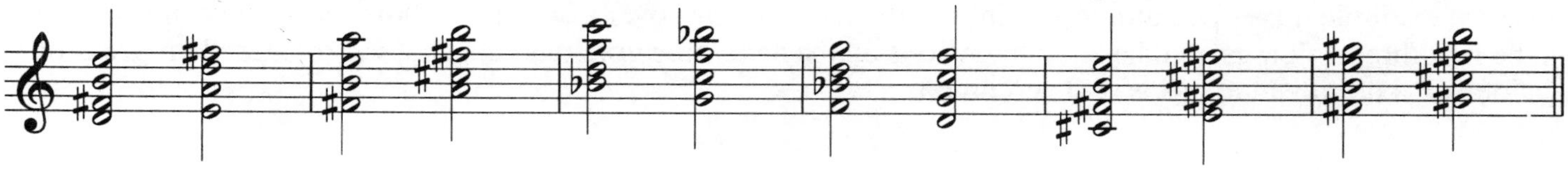

The next examples present the *four* different pentatonics that produce altered tensions on dominant chords;
**C7(alt);** G♭ pent. (♭V), D♭ pent. (♭II), B pent.(VII), and E pent.(III)

Note the chromatically ascending pentatonics over these first four II V I examples. The first two examples use the ♭Vth pentatonic on the dominant chords while the last two use the VIIth.

1) **D-7**(C pent) **G7**(C♯ pent) **Cmaj7**(D pent)

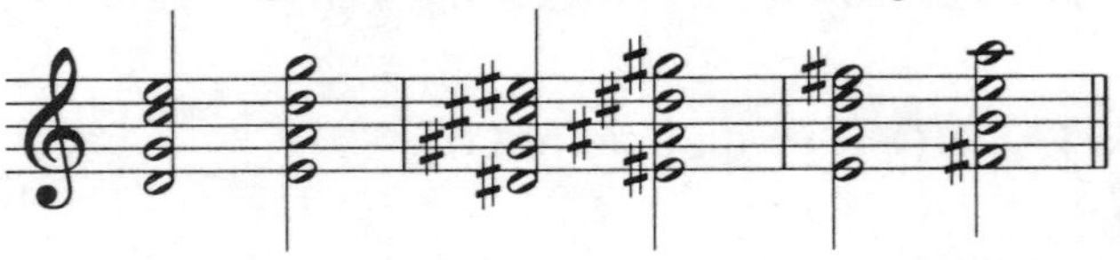

2) **F-7**(E♭ pent) **B♭7**(E pent) **E♭maj7**(F pent)

3) **D-7**(F pent) **G7**(F♯ pent) **Cmaj7**(G pent)

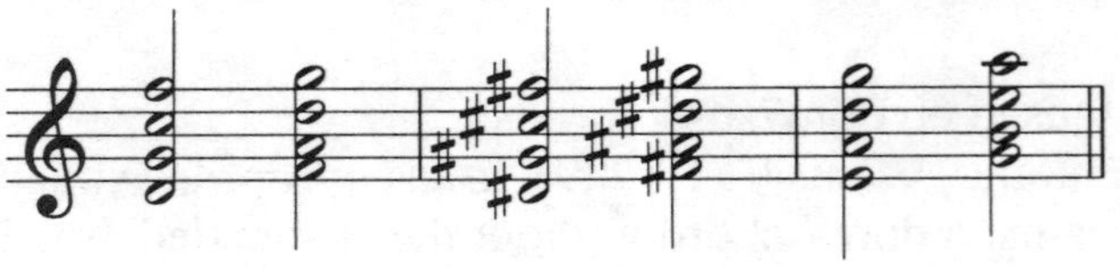

4) **B-7**(D pent) **E7**(E♭ pent) **Amaj7**(E pent)

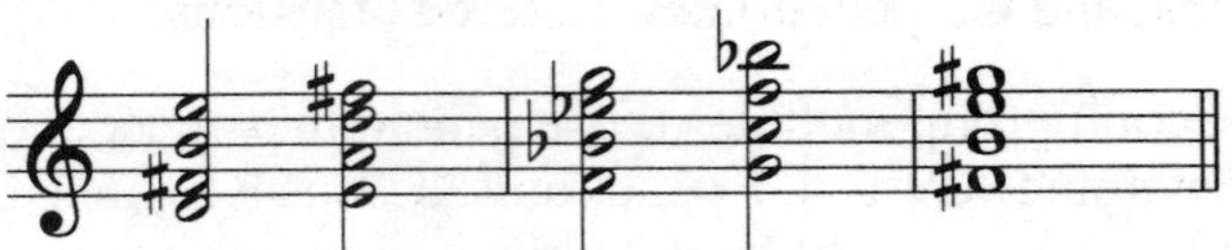

This next example uses the ♭II pentatonic on the dominant chord.

**D-7**(F pent) **G7**(A♭ pent) **Cmaj7** (D pent)

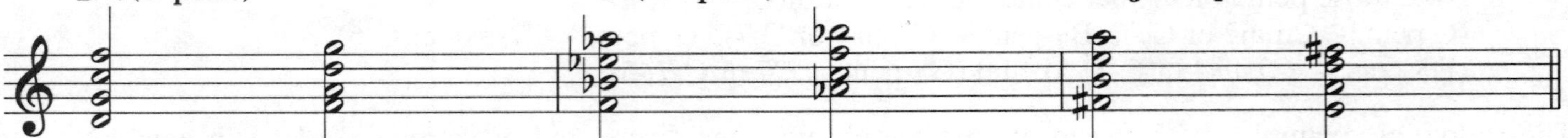

This next example uses the III pentatonic on the dominant chord.

**G-7**(B♭ pent) **C7** (E pent) **F6(9)** (F pent)

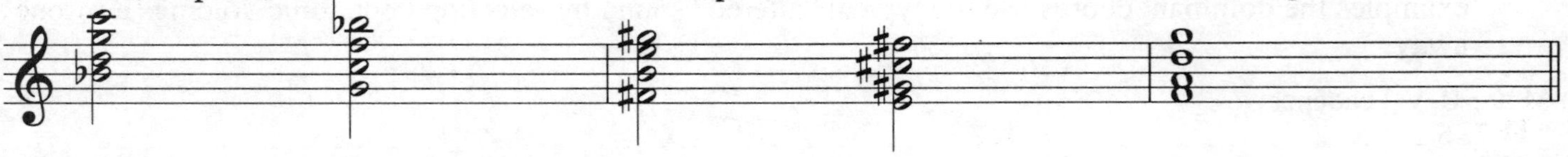

This next example uses the ♭V pentatonic on *both* the II chord <u>and</u> the V chord.

**F♯-7♭5** (C pent) **B7** (F pent) **E-7(11)**

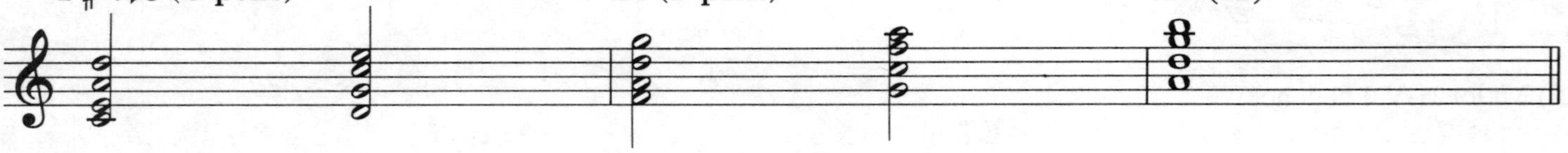

This next example mixes pentatonic voicings with other voicings over a dominant chord. Note the natural tensions on the first three voicings and the altered tensions on the next three voicings. This natural to altered progression of tensions on a dominant chord is quite common.

**C7** _ _ _ _ _ _ _ _ _ _ _ _ _ _ _ _ _ _ _ _ _ _ _ _ _ _ _ _ _ _ _ **F6(9)**

C9 _ _ _ _ _ _ _ _ _ _ _ _ _ _ _ _ G♭ pent _ _ _ _ _ _ _ _ _ _ _ _

This next example will notate the lead voice only. The complete voicings can be derived from the pentatonics listed.

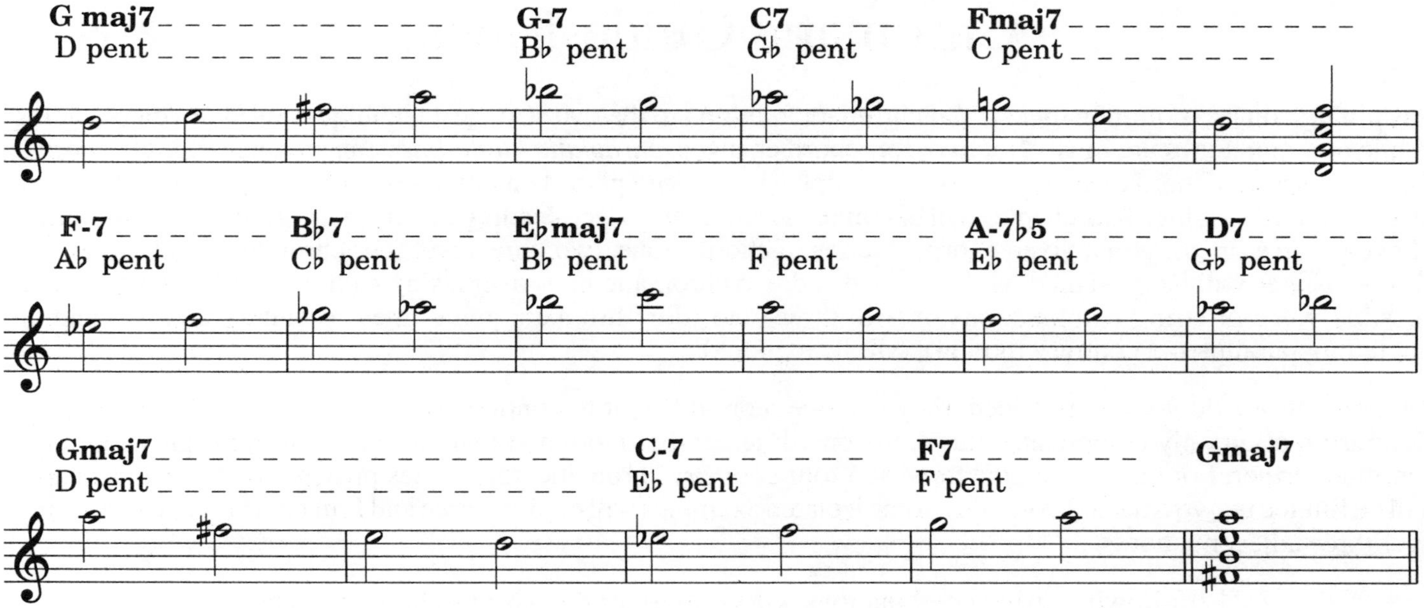


This last example mixes pentatonic voicings and *fourth* voicings in a "II-V Blues" form. Since the "effect" of pentatonics requires two or more voicings from one pentatonic scale, it will be lost in many of these II-V patterns, although the voicings used *are* in common with pentatonic voicings. Note the *ascending* whole-step fourth voicing pattern produced in measures eight and nine, while the same pattern *descends* in measures eleven and twelve.

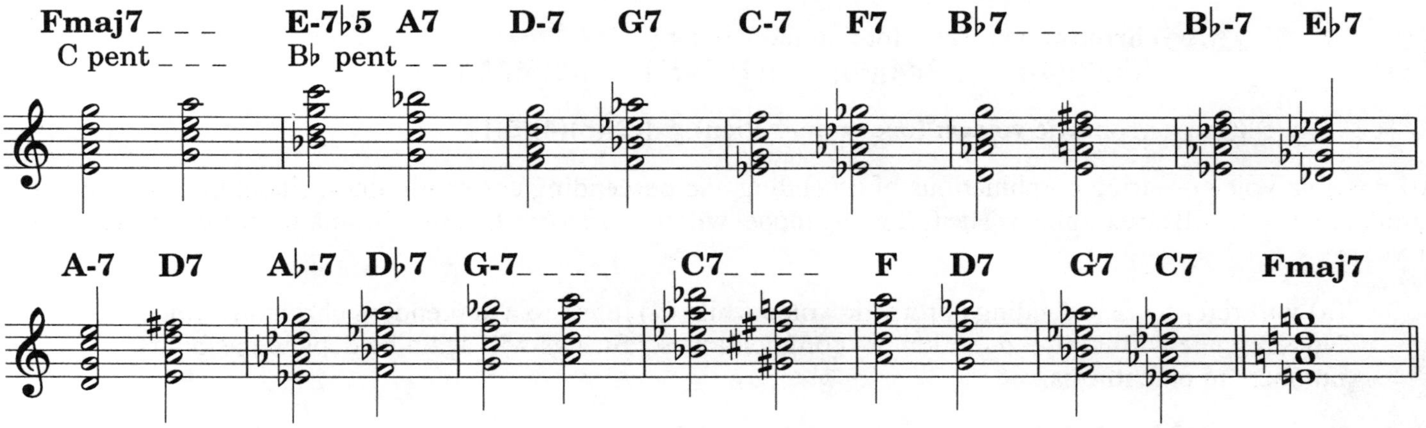


Measures eleven and twelve would maintain the descending whole-step fourth voicing pattern on the *top* three strings if "guide-tones" placed in the lower voice were desired to clarify the harmony;

# Chapter Twenty-Six.
## Chromatic Guide-Lines

Sustaining voices, (common tones), and chromatic motion are the two strongest techniques used in voice-leading. While common tones are most effective over chord changes, *chromatic guide-lines* can enhance a single chord as well as a series of chord changes. Up to now, emphasis has been placed on voice-leading the *top* note or 2nd string of every chord voicing. This chapter will examine the chromatic voice-leading or chromatic guide-line possibilities of every voice or string in a given chord or series of chords. One, two, three, and four chromatic guide-lines over chord changes will be presented while just one and two chromatic lines over a single chord will be examined. All possible voice or string combinations of two, three, and four chromatic guide-lines ascending and descending, (including parallel and contrary motion), will be explored.

As more chromatic voices are added, they become more difficult to continue over a series of different voicings. Contrary motion only complicates this situation while parallel motion and an obliging chord progression might continue further. For this reason, the three and four *contrary* chromatic guide-lines presented later in this chapter will be limited to <u>two</u> adjacent voicings. Some isolated examples will explore three and four contrary chromatic lines over <u>three</u> adjacent chords.

The following string combinations will be used for the various chromatic lines; (strings will be notated as bold numbers in parenthesis).

**<u>One</u> chromatic voice:** (four combinations); **[(2)] [(3)] [(4)] [(5)]**

**<u>Two</u> chromatic voices:** (six combinations);
**[(2)(3)] [(2)(4)] [(2)(5)] [(3)(4)] [(3)(5)] [(4)(5)]**

**<u>Three</u> chromatic voices:** (four combinations);
**[(2)(3)(4)] [(3)(4)(5)] [(2)(3)(5)] [(2)(4)(5)]**

**<u>Four</u> chromatic voices:** (one combination); **[(2)(3)(4)(5)]**

All possible voice or string combinations of ascending and descending chromatic lines, (including contrary and parallel motion), will be examined. The following model will be used to portray the chromatic motion of each string or voice;

**(a)** will refer to an <u>ascending</u> chromatic voice while **(d)** refers to a <u>descending</u> chromatic voice. No reference will imply *no* motion or "common tones." Strings will again be depicted as bold numbers in parenthesis.

Example; **(2a)(3d)(4d)(5a)**, would depict the 2nd and 5th strings ascending chromatically while the 3rd and 4th strings descend chromatically.

The following model dictates the chromatic motion over the three different voicings in the accompanying musical example;

**(2d) (3a) (4a) (5)**

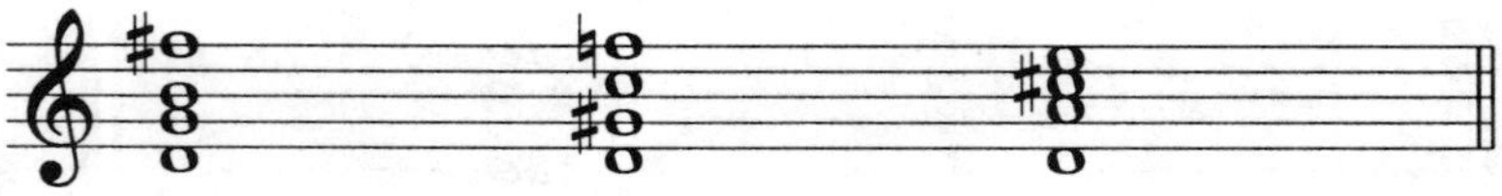

The following will examine all possible combinations of chromatic motion in a four-note structure:

**1) One chromatic voice;**

Two different directions; ascending and descending, for each string gives <u>eight</u> different possible chromatic lines.

**2) Two chromatic voices;**

Four different direction combinations for each of the six two-string combinations gives a total of twenty-four different possible chromatic lines.

Parallel;

**[(2a)(3a)] [(2a)(4a)] [(2a)(5a)] [(3a)(4a)] [(3a)(5a)] [(4a)(5a)]**
**[(2d)(3d)] [(2d)(4d)] [(2d)(5d)] [(3d)(4d)] [(3d)(5d)] [(4d)(5d)]**

Contrary;

**[(2a)(3d)] [(2a)(4d)] [(2a)(5d)] [(3a)(4d)] [(3a)(5d)] [(4a)(5d)]**
**[(2d)(3a)] [(2d)(4a)] [(2d)(5a)] [(3d)(4a)] [(3d)(5a)] [(4d)(5a)]**

**3) Three chromatic voices;**

Eight different direction combinations for each of the four three-string combinations gives a total of thirty-two different possible chromatic lines.

Parallel;

**[(2a)(3a)(4a)] [(3a)(4a)(5a)] [(2a)(3a)(5a)] [(2a)(4a)(5a)]**
**[(2d)(3d)(4d)] [(3d)(4d)(5d)] [(2d)(3d)(5d)] [(2d)(4d)(5d)]**

Contrary, (Two parallel/one contrary);

**[(2a)(3d)(4d)] [(3a)(4d)(5d)] [(2a)(3d)(5d)] [(2a)(4d)(5d)]**
**[(2d)(3a)(4a)] [(3d)(4a)(5a)] [(2d)(3a)(5a)] [(2d)(4a)(5a)]**

**[(2d)(3d)(4a)] [(3d)(4d)(5a)] [(2d)(3d)(5a)] [(2d)(4d)(5a)]**
**[(2a)(3a)(4d)] [(3a)(4a)(5d)] [(2a)(3a)(5d)] [(2a)(4a)(5d)]**

**[(2d)(3a)(4d)] [(3d)(4a)(5d)] [(2d)(3a)(5d)] [(2d)(4a)(5d)]**
**[(2a)(3d)(4a)] [(3a)(4d)(5a)] [(2a)(3d)(5a)] [(2a)(4d)(5a)]**

**4) Four chromatic voices;**

A total of sixteen different direction combinations and chromatic lines are possible.

Parallel;

**[(2a)(3a)(4a)(5a)] [(2d)(3d)(4d)(5d)]**

Contrary, (Three parallel/one contrary);

**[(2a)(3d)(4d)(5d)] [(2d)(3a)(4d)(5d)]**
**[(2d)(3a)(4a)(5a)] [(2a)(3d)(4a)(5a)]**

**[(2d)(3d)(4a)(5d)] [(2d)(3d)(4d)(5a)]**
**[(2a)(3a)(4d)(5a)] [(2a)(3a)(4a)(5d)]**

Contrary, (Two parallel ascending/two parallel descending);

**[(2d)(3d)(4a)(5a)] [(2d)(3a)(4a)(5d)] [(2d)(3a)(4d)(5a)]**
**[(2a)(3a)(4d)(5d)] [(2a)(3d)(4d)(5a)] [(2a)(3d)(4a)(5d)]**

*Remember the 5th string has the additional problem of L.I.L., omitting some of the line possibilities available to the other strings.

While observing the chromatic guide-line possibilities <u>on</u> or <u>through</u> different chord types, it becomes obvious that *dominant* chords contain the most chromatic possibilities. This will be most evident in the examples showing chromatic lines over a <u>single</u> chord. A chord progression containing many dominant chords will also yield more chromatic line possibilities than one with less dominant chord types.

In the following examples, before preparing an entire exercise, begin first by isolating and playing <u>just</u> the chromatic voices. This will allow you to better "hear" the quality and motion the lines have to offer. It might also be beneficial to record the chromatic guide-lines and play them back while performing the entire exercise.

This chapter will begin with the examination of <u>one</u> and <u>two</u> chromatic voices on a <u>single</u> chord voicing. But for a few isolated examples, (some of which will be presented at the end of these single chord examples), <u>three</u> and <u>four</u> chromatic guide-lines over a single chord will not be included. This many chromatic voices on a single four-note chord can begin to lose or compromise the function of that chord.

In the following examples, an occasional non-functional voicing might appear. When this occurs, it can simply be considered a "chromatic approach" to the next functional voicing. The following example will demonstrate;

**<u>One</u> chromatic guide-line on a <u>single</u> chord**

The following rhythms are arbitrary and it might be most effective to attack the full voicing with *each* chromatic note. "Chromatic approach" voicings are put in parenthesis.

1) 2nd string <u>ascending</u>;

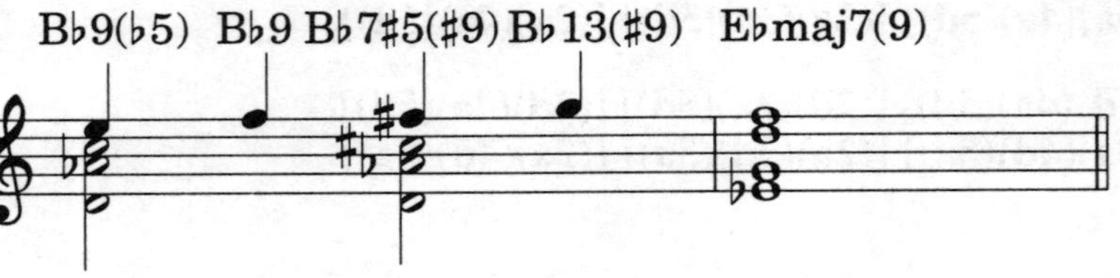


2) 2nd string <u>descending</u>; a)

b)

3) 3rd string descending;

4) 3rd string ascending;

5) 4th string ascending;

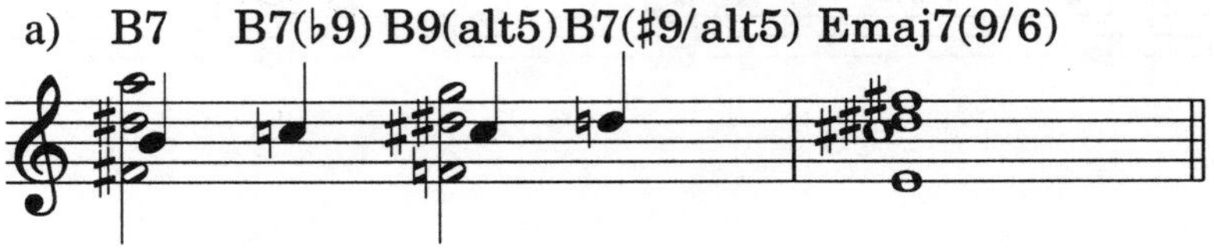

6) 4th string descending;

7) 4th string ascending *and* descending;

8) 5th string ascending;

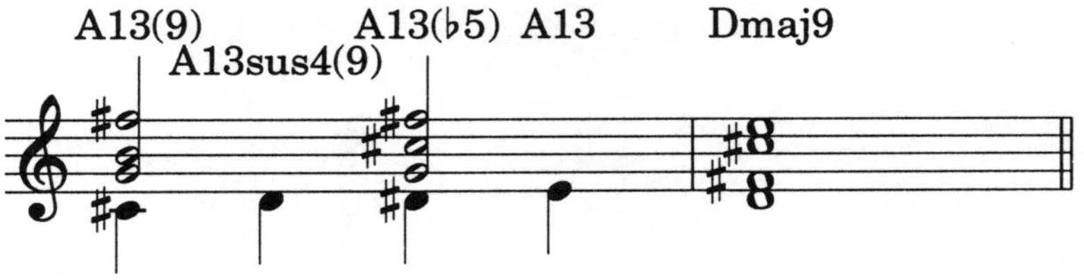

9) 5th string <u>descending</u>;

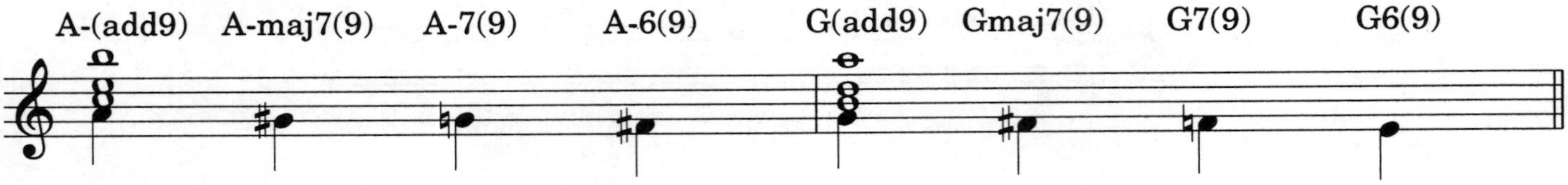


The following example will demonstrate *ascending* and *descending* on one string <u>and</u> one chord;

The following examples will demonstrate different string or voice combinations of <u>one</u> chromatic guide-line;

## Two chromatic guide-lines on a single chord

After playing each of the following twelve examples, prepare their chromatic guide-lines in the *reverse* direction for all twenty-four possible line combinations for two chromatic voices in a four-note structure. A new target or ending chord might be needed when lines are reversed. Before examining the following twelve examples, two examples of reversed guide-lines and new target chords are given;

Parallel chromatic motion, **[(2a)(3a)]**;

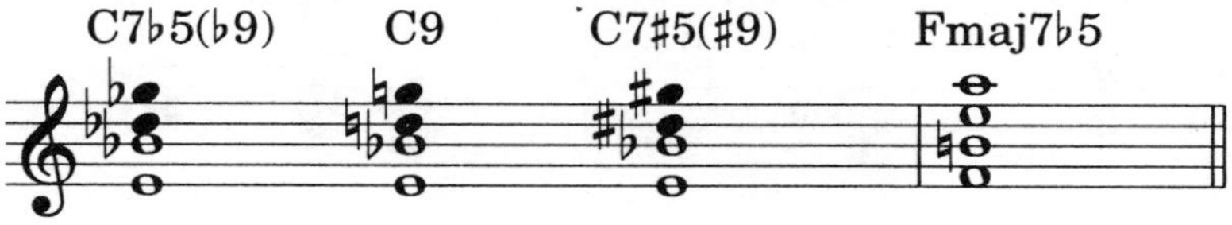


The above example in reverse direction, **[(2d)(3d)]**, with new ending chord;

Contrary chromatic motion, **[(2d)(3a)]** ;

The above example in reverse direction, **[(2a)(3d)]**, with new ending chord;

The following twelve examples display two chromatic guide-lines on a single chord;

1) Parallel, **[(2d)(3d)]**;

2) Contrary, **[(2a)(3d)]**;

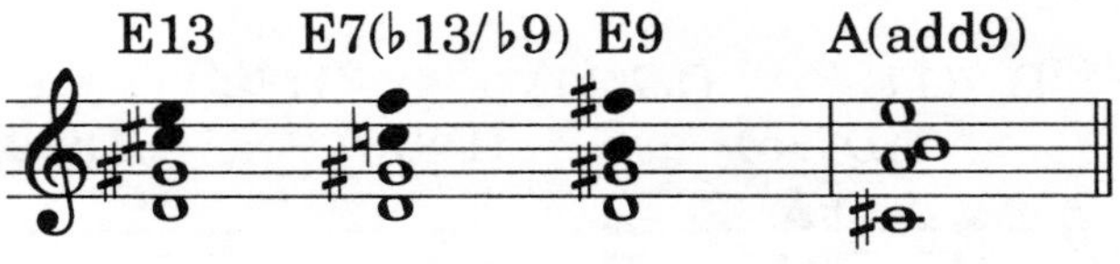


3) Parallel, **[(3d)(4d)]**;

4) Contrary, **[(3d)(4a)]**;

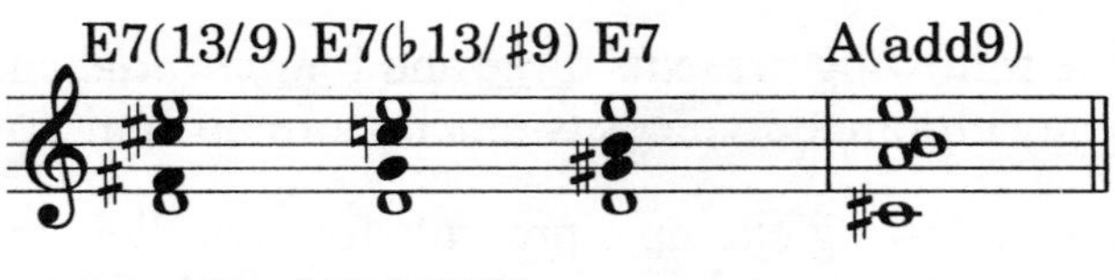


5) Parallel, **[(4d)(5d)]** ;

6) Contrary, **[(4a)(5d)]**;

7) Parallel, **[(2d)(4d)]**;

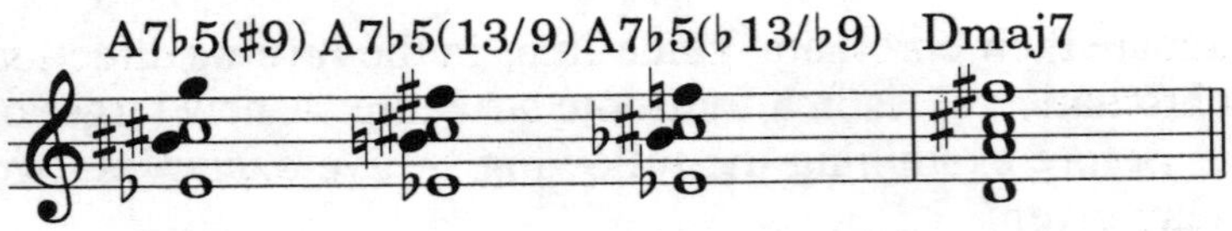


8) Contrary, **[(2a)(4d)]**;

9) Parallel, **[(3a)(5a)]**;

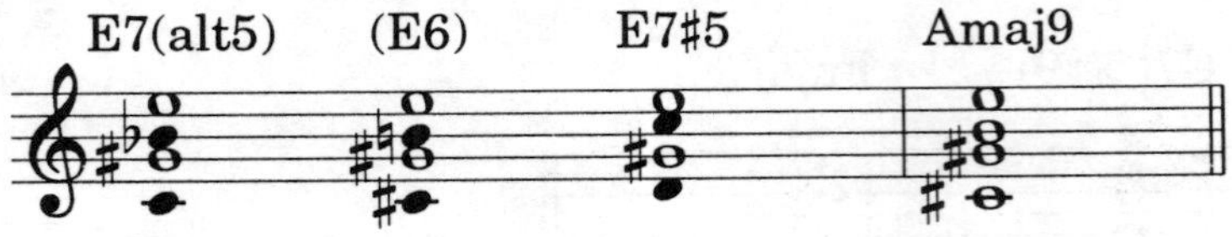


10) Contrary, **[(3a)(5d)]**;

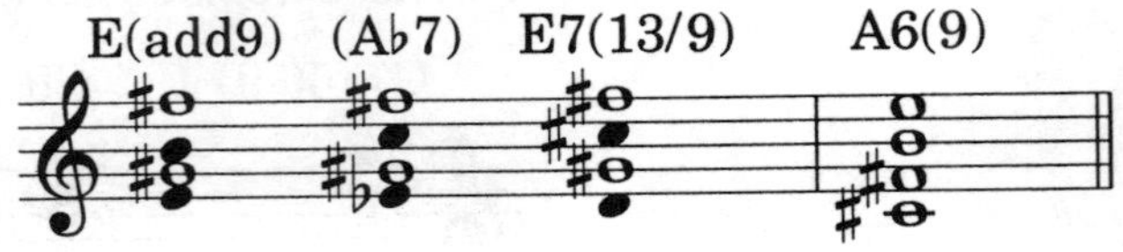


11) Parallel, **[(2d)(5d)]**;

12) Contrary, **[(2a)(5d)]**;

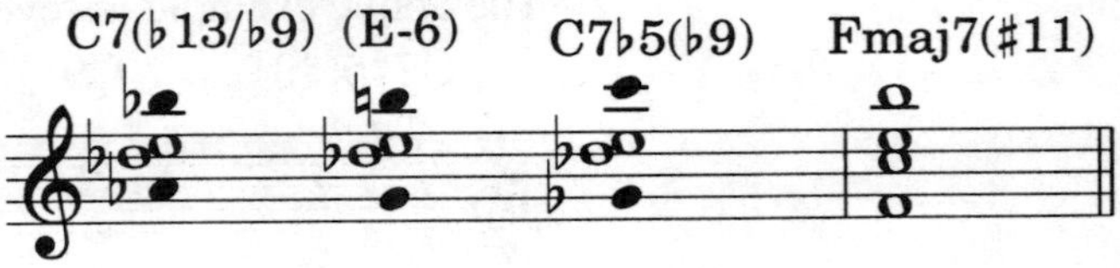


The following example uses different combinations of strings or voices *and* parallel or contrary motion with two chromatic guide-lines;

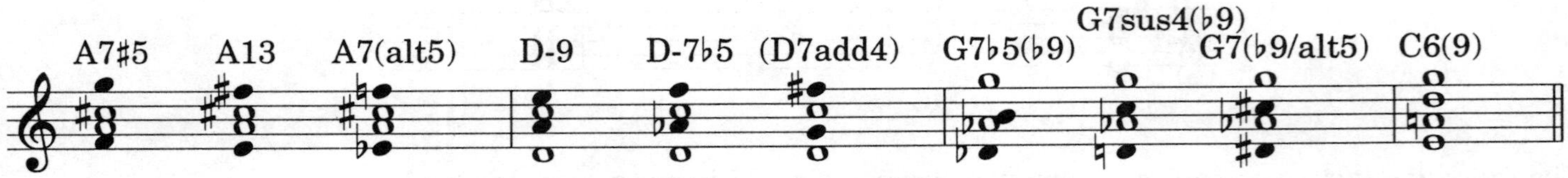


The following example combines ascending and descending chromatic motion on any one of two strings over a single chord;

The following presents three and four *parallel* chromatic guide-lines on a single chord. *Contrary* motion with this many chromatic voices is much more difficult to extend over three or more different voicings on a single chord.

The following example presents four parallel chromatic voices on a single chord, and requires a chord that when transposed up or down a whole-step, will still function on the original chord. The chords in between function as chromatic approach chords.

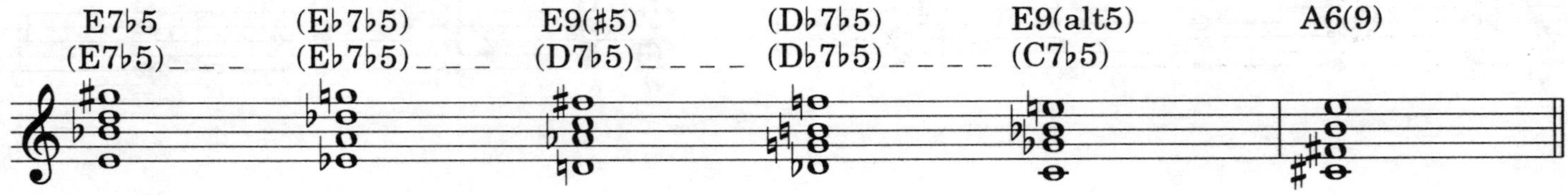

The following is an example of three parallel chromatic voices;

## CHROMATIC GUIDE-LINES OVER CHORD CHANGES

In this half of the chapter chromatic voices will be examined over chord changes, beginning with II V I chord cadences and followed by more extended musical examples.

Three and four chromatic voices present some unique problems. *Contrary* motion with this many voices is difficult to extend over three or more chord voicings. For this reason, the contrary motion examples for *three* and *four* chromatic voices will be combined into a single II V I example; II(three voices) - V(four voices) - I. Some isolated examples of three or four contrary chromatic voices over the entire II V I cadence will appear later in this chapter. *Parallel* motion for three or four chromatic voices will be attempted over a complete II V I cadence.

Three and four chromatic guide-lines will share some voicing cadences with a few of those previously introduced in the **Chromatic Approach Voicings** chapter. The primary difference between "chromatic guide-lines" and "chromatic approach voicings" over chord changes is the guide-line must be aware of chord function while the approach voicings need not. If a functional chord with three or four chromatic guide-lines cannot be found, a chromatic approach chord with no function could be used to continue a desired chromatic motion.

### One chromatic guide-line in a chord progression

The following II V I examples present the same chromatic line on each string or voice;

Descending chromatic line;

1)
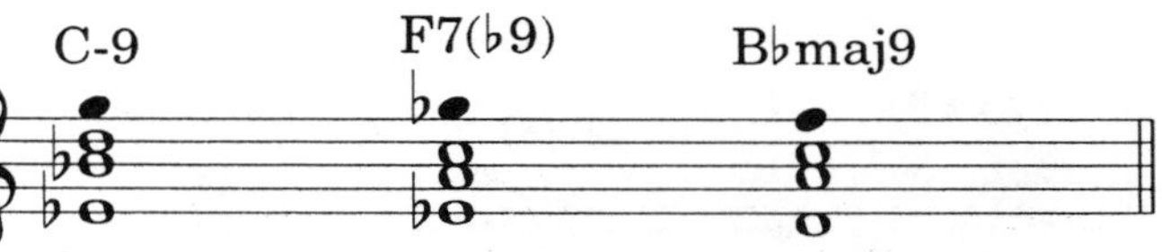


2)
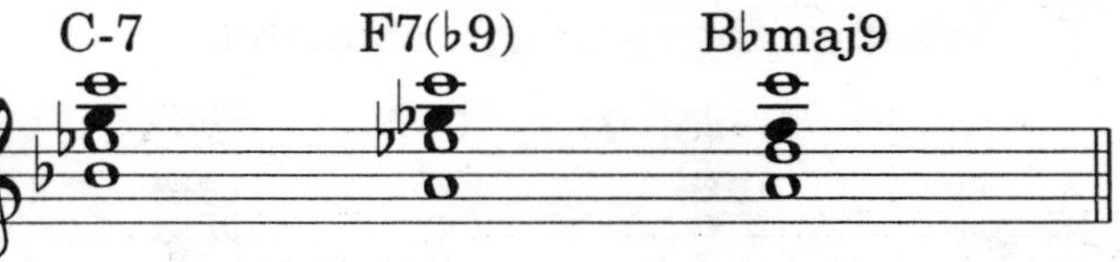


3)
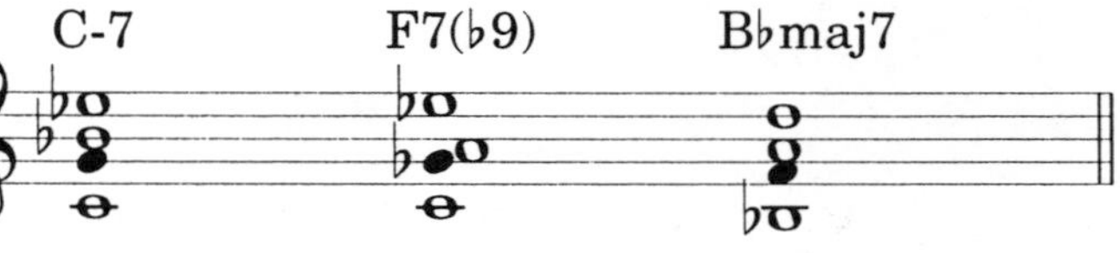


4)
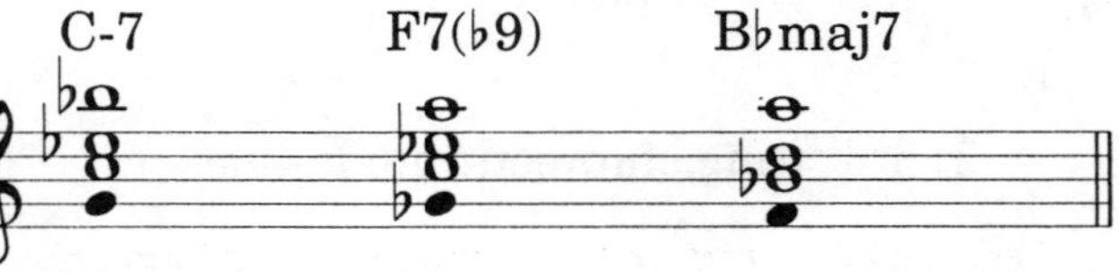


Ascending chromatic line;

1)
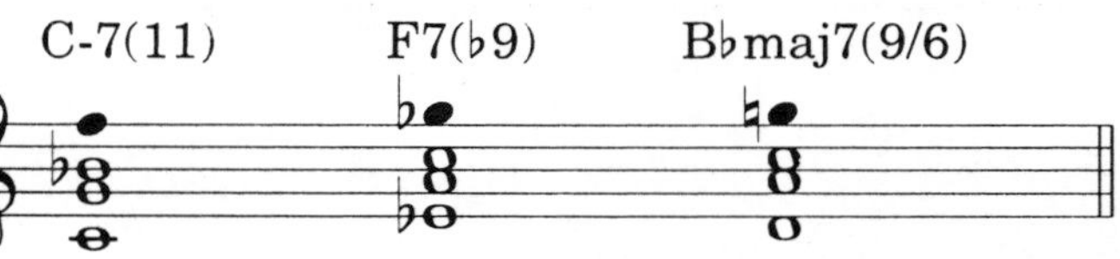


2)
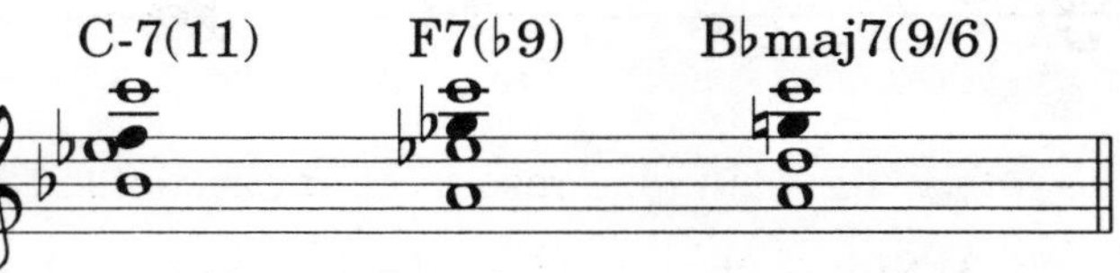


3)
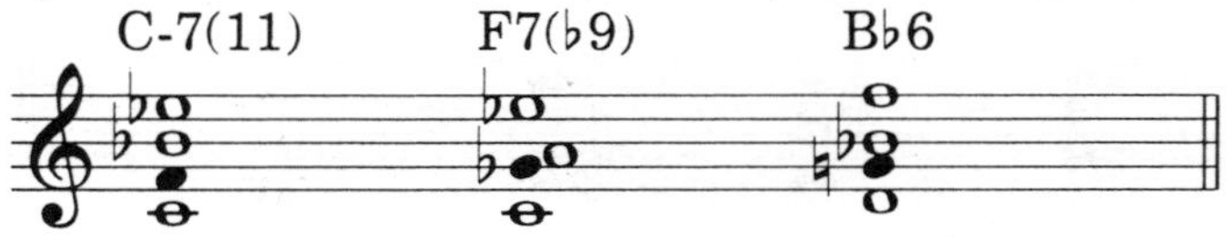


4)
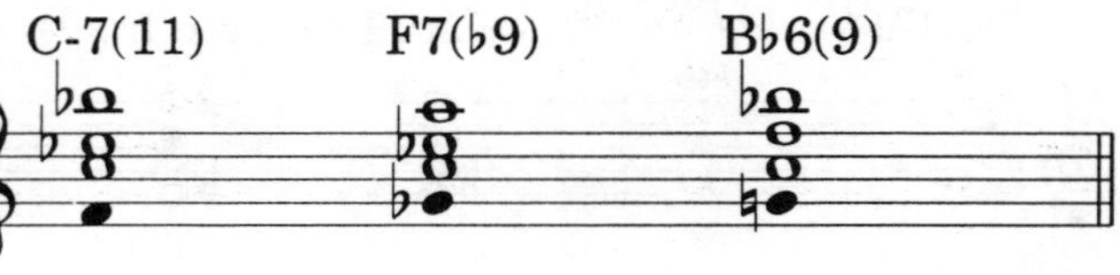

The following example presents an extended *descending* chromatic guide-line on the 4th string;

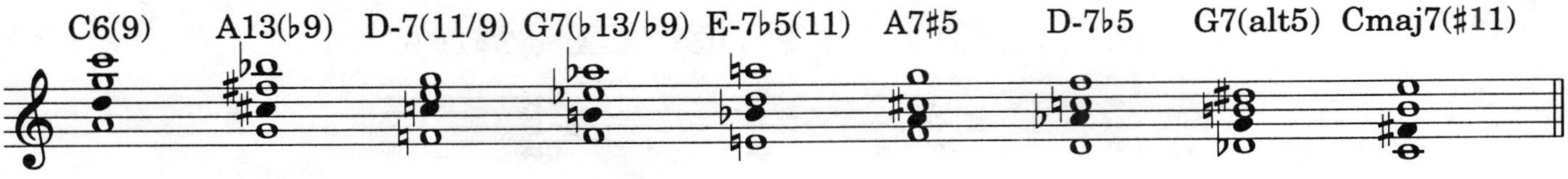


Using the same chromatic line in the above example on various strings or voices establishes an interesting way to "pull-together" chords that are *not* voice-leading to each other. This chromatic guide-line acts like a thread holding these leaping voicings together:

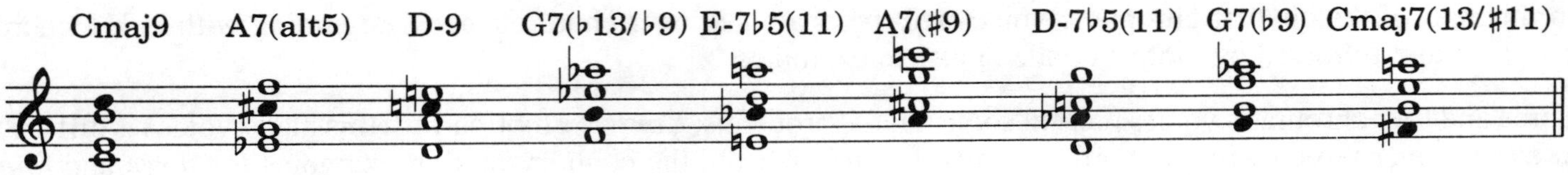


The following is an example of octavely displacing every other note of the above chromatic guide-line. Note the interesting line pattern produced on the top voice.

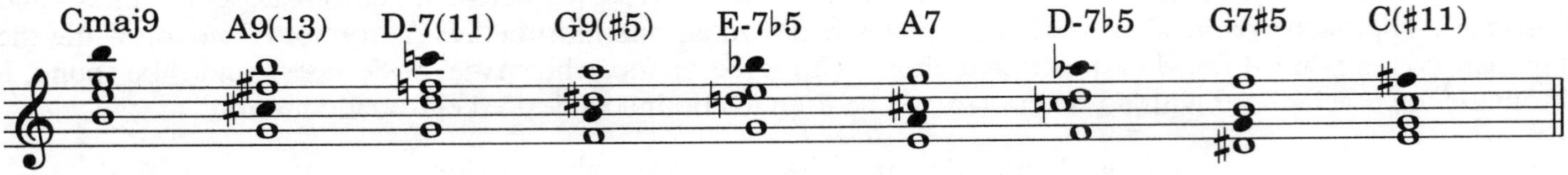


The following examples present a chromatic guide-line that ascends and descends on *one* string or voice, and finally on *three* strings or voices;

1) 4th string chromatic guide-line;

2) 3rd string chromatic guide-line;

3) Single chromatic guide-line continued through the 2nd, 3rd, and 4th strings;

## <u>Two</u> chromatic guide-lines in a chord progression

The following examples will present all <u>twenty-four</u> possible combinations of <u>two</u> chromatic guide-lines over a II V I chord cadence. Many of these examples will also contain additional chromatic voices, some of which might reappear in the sections containing *three* or *four* chromatic voices. Some exercises might also contain more than one example of two chromatic voices. The following example will display <u>three</u> different two-chromatic guide-line combinations, **[(4a)(5d)] [(2d)(4a)] [(2d)(5d)];**

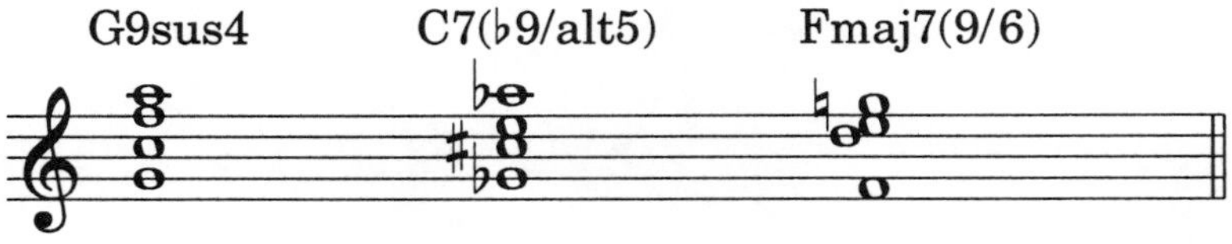


In two of the following contrary motion examples, **[(3a)(4d)]** and **[(2d)(4a)]**, a progressive new approach to dominant resolution is introduced. In these examples, the chords that are substituting the original V7 chords, (Fmaj7♯5 for F7 and Emaj7 for C7), contain the <u>major 7th</u> of those original V7 chords. The Emaj7 chord could be considered a "chromatic approach voicing" or an altered C7 chord with natural 7; (3 ♯5 7 ♯9), while the Fmaj7♯5 chord is a direct parallel substitute for F7; (Vmaj7♯5).

The "reason" natural 7 appears to function in a V7 capacity is its chromatic resolution tendency to the natural 5th of the I chord; The natural 7, (B), of C7 resolves to the natural 5th, (C), of F. This chromatic resolution is characteristic of "altered" V7 chords, and is probably why the natural 7 functions best *with* altered tensions; (♭9 ♯9 ♭5 ♯5), if tensions are desired.

Notice how above and below chromatic approach notes to a *major* triad include the <u>guide-tones</u>, <u>altered tensions</u>, and <u>major7th</u> of that triads V7 chord; (E, G♭) (G♯, B♭) (B, D♭) are half-steps above and below an F major triad (F) (A) (C). Realize these notes on a C7 chord, (F's V7 chord);

**C7**................. 3(E)........ ♭5(G♭) ...... ♯5(G♯) ...... ♭7(B♭)...... 7(B)....... ♭9(D♭)

*Natural 7 on dominant chords should be used in an appropriate context where this contemporary sound is desired.

Two chromatic voices *ascending* in <u>parallel</u> motion;

1)

2)

3)

4)

5)

6)

Two chromatic voices *descending* in parallel motion;

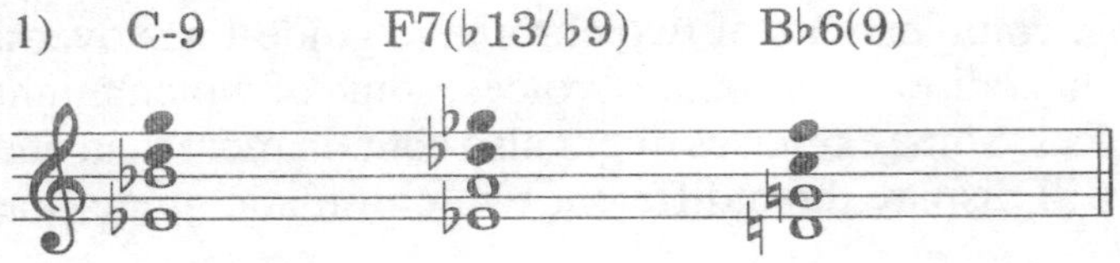


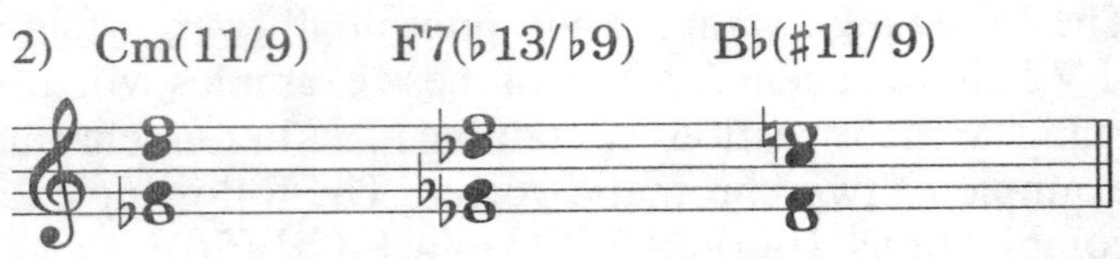


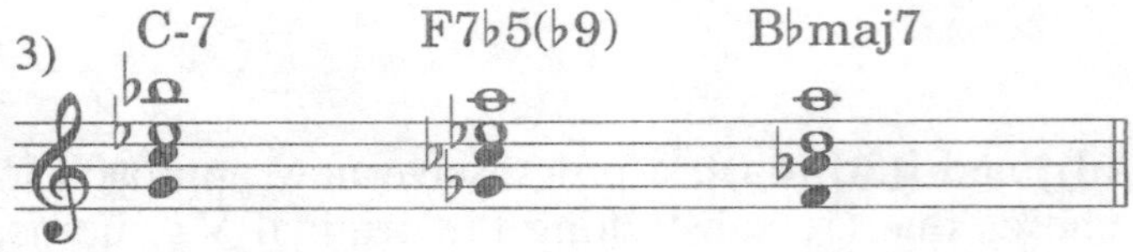


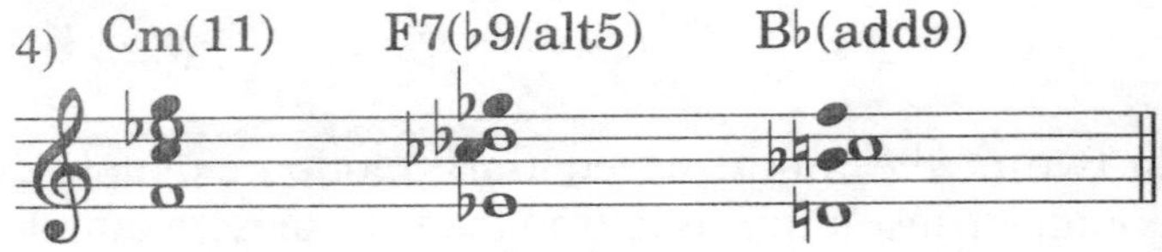


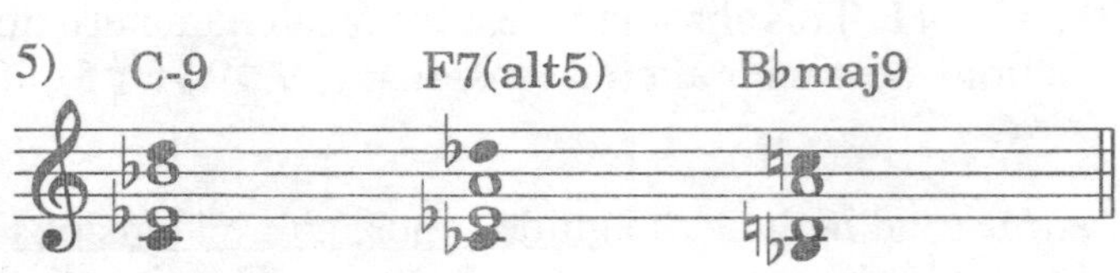


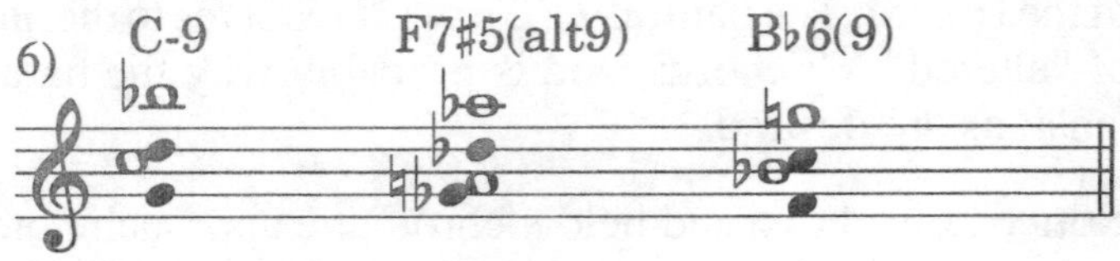


Two chromatic voices in *contrary* motion, (upper voice ascends/lower voice descends);

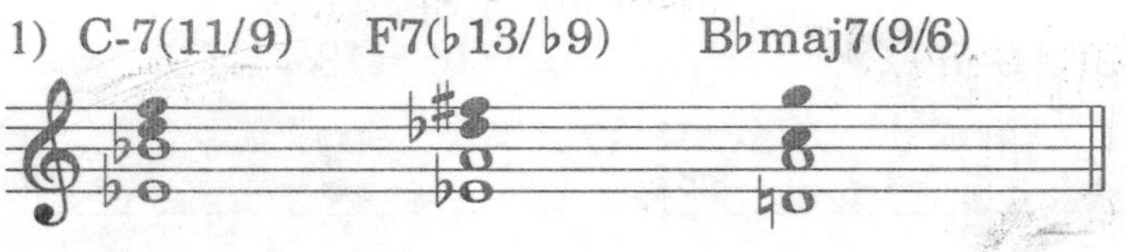


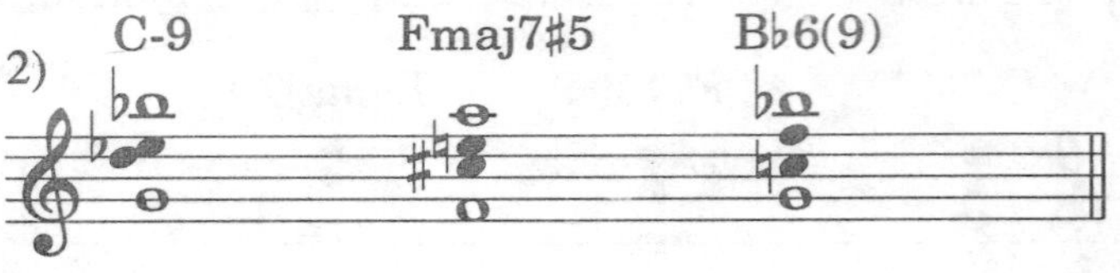


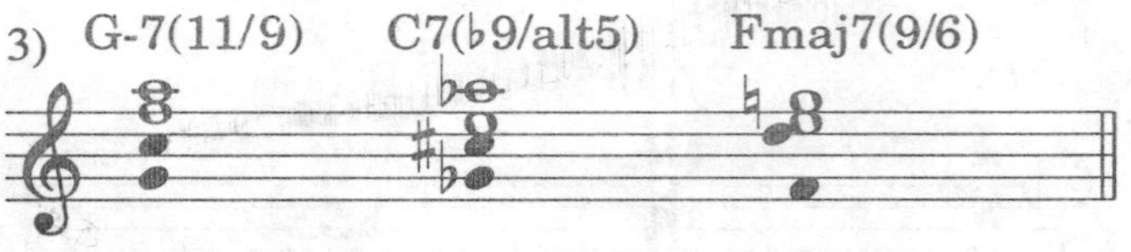


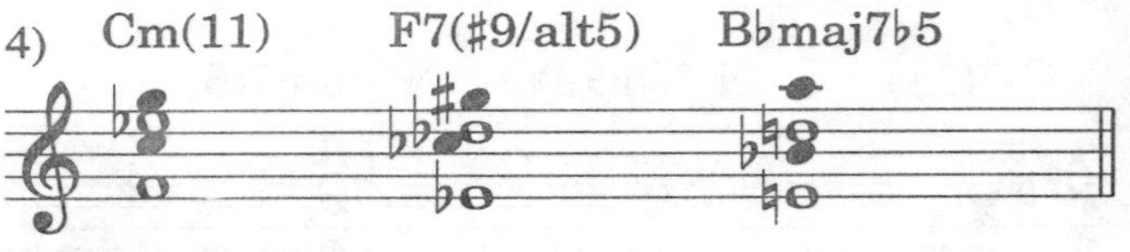


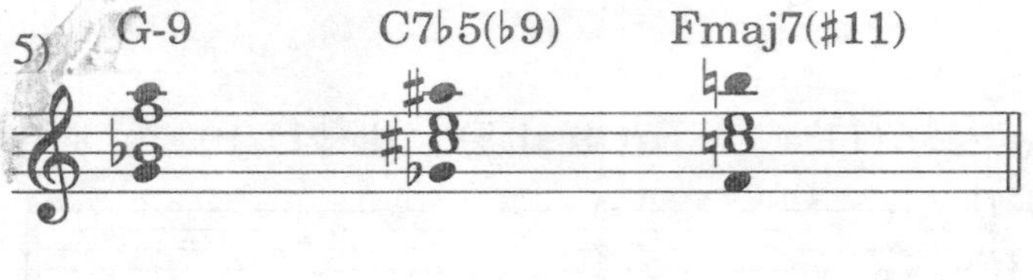


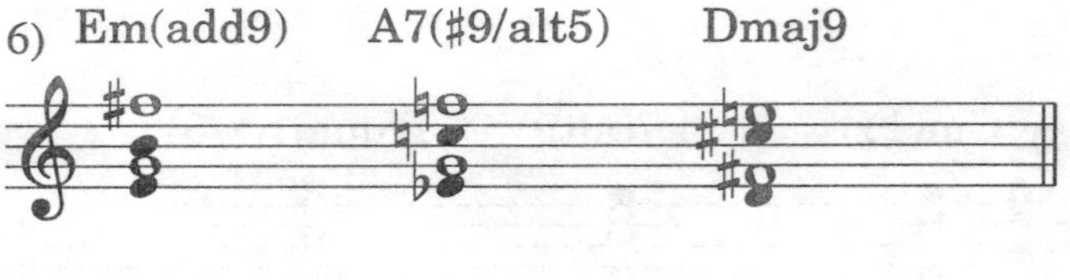

Two chromatic voices in *contrary* motion, (upper voice descends/lower voice ascends);

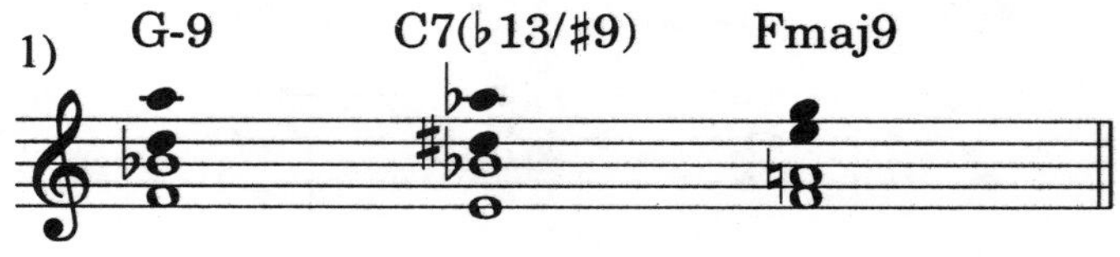


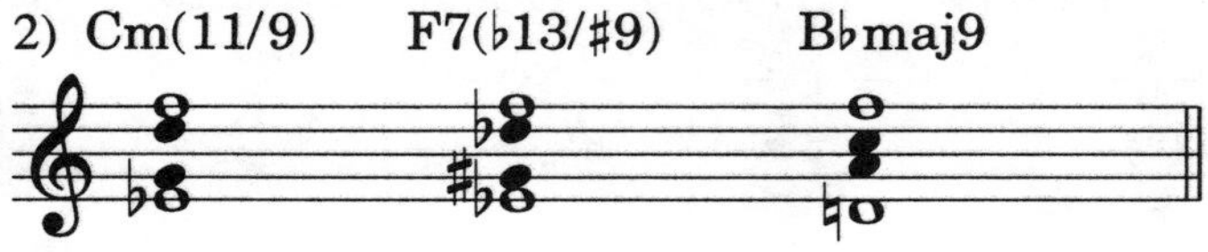

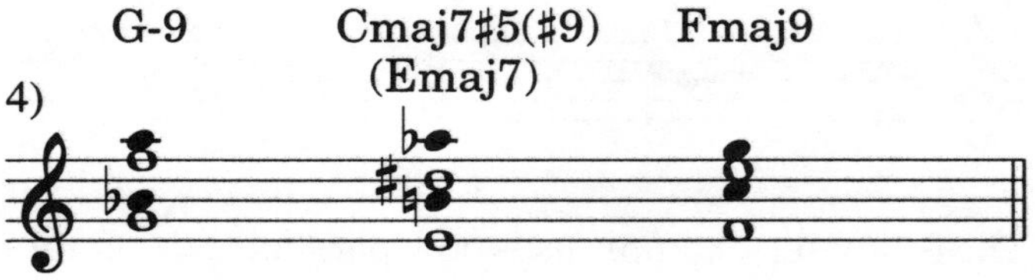

Applying two chromatic guide-lines over an extended chord progression introduces problems the single chromatic line did not offer. This is especially true of two contrary chromatic lines over an extended progression.

The following example uses two parallel chromatic guide-lines over an extended progression;

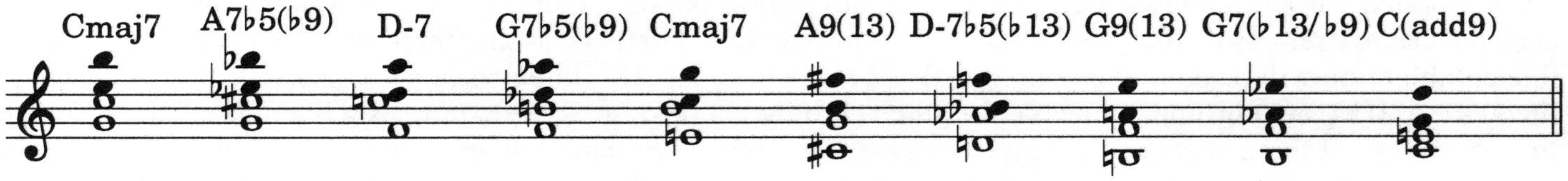


The following two examples use contrary motion between two chromatic voices over an extended progression. The lines must change strings or voices to continue their chromatic motion. Before displaying these examples, it should be noted that there are only two possible contrary chromatic lines over extended chord progressions;

| | | | | | | | | | | |
|---|---|---|---|---|---|---|---|---|---|---|
| 1) Ascend................ | B | C | C♯ | D | D♯ | E | F | F♯ | G | G♯ |
| Descend.............. | B | B♭ | A | A♭ | G | G♭ | F | E | E♭ | D |
| Interval................. | 1 | 2 | 3 | ♭5 | ♯5 | ♭7 | 8 | 9 | 10 | ♯11 |

| | | | | | | | | | |
|---|---|---|---|---|---|---|---|---|---|
| 2) Ascend............. | C | C♯ | D | D♯ | E | F | F♯ | G | G♯ |
| Descend............ | B | B♭ | A | A♭ | G | G♭ | F | E | E♭ |
| Interval........... | ♭2 | ♭3 | 4 | 5 | 6 | 7 | ♭9 | ♭10 | 11 |

Note the doubling or octave (8) in the first example and the ♭9th interval in the second example. If either line is to continue chromatically, it must include these intervals. The following example containing the ♭9th interval is *supported* by a hybrid chord.

1) (Asterisk denotes octave doubling)

2) (Asterisk denotes ♭9th interval)

The following example uses both parallel and contrary motion while also ascending and descending in one chromatic voice;

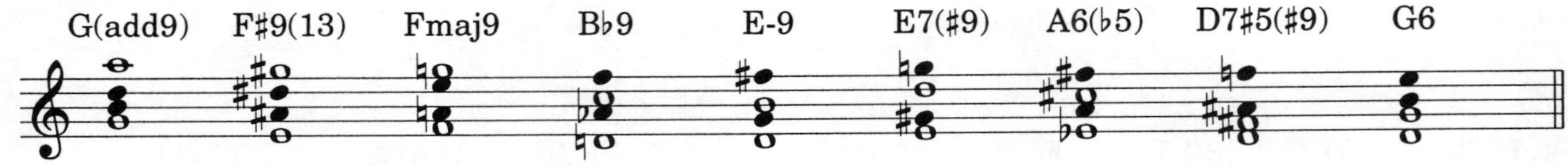


## **<u>Three</u> and <u>four</u> chromatic guide-lines in a chord progression**

Three and four chromatic guide-lines have a total of <u>forty-eight</u> different string and motion combinations. *Three* chromatic lines have <u>eight parallel</u> and <u>twenty-four contrary</u> combinations while *four* chromatic lines have <u>two parallel</u> and <u>fourteen contrary</u> combinations.

As mentioned earlier, applying only *one* of the thirty-eight possible contrary combinations over *more* than two chords can be extremely difficult and in some cases impractical. For this reason, a three and a four contrary chromatic line combination will be combined into <u>one</u> II V I chord cadence; II - (three chromatic lines) - V - (four chromatic lines) - I, or II - (four chromatic lines) - V - (three chromatic lines) - I. Some examples will contain four chromatic lines between all three cadence chords. Of course, each four-chromatic line example contains at least <u>one</u> three-chromatic line example within it. Applying a *variety* of the thirty-eight possible contrary chromatic combinations would be possible over an extended chord progression, and some examples will be presented later in this section.

The eight <u>parallel</u> examples for *three* chromatic voices will be examined over the entire II V I cadence. The descending parallel example for *four* chromatic voices will be included in the <u>contrary</u> motion examples. The ascending parallel example for *four* chromatic voices will not be included, but can easily be examined by finding one chord that when moved chromatically functions for each chord of the II V I cadence;

1)

| II | V | I |
|---|---|---|
| D7sus4 | E♭7sus4 | E7sus4 |
| [D-7(11)] | [G7(alt9/alt5)] | [Cmaj7(9/6)] |

2)

| II | V | I |
|---|---|---|
| C6(9) | D♭6(9) | D6(9) |
| [D-9] | [G7(♯9/alt5)] | [Cmaj7(♯11/9)] |

Some of these examples will produce physically awkward fingerings, and should be relocated to the top four strings if physically more available there.

<u>Descending</u> parallel chromatic motion in *three* voices on a four-note structure;

1)

2)
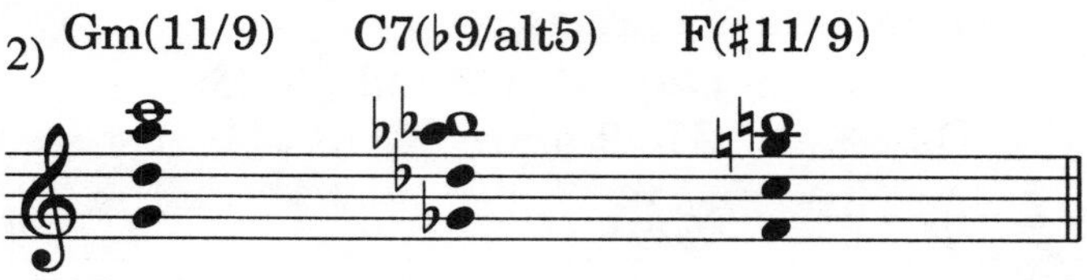


3)
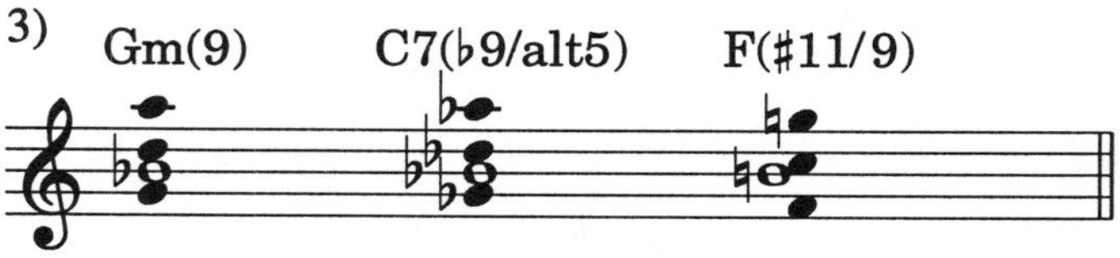


4)

<u>Ascending</u> parallel chromatic motion in *three* voices on a four-note structure;

1)

2)

3)
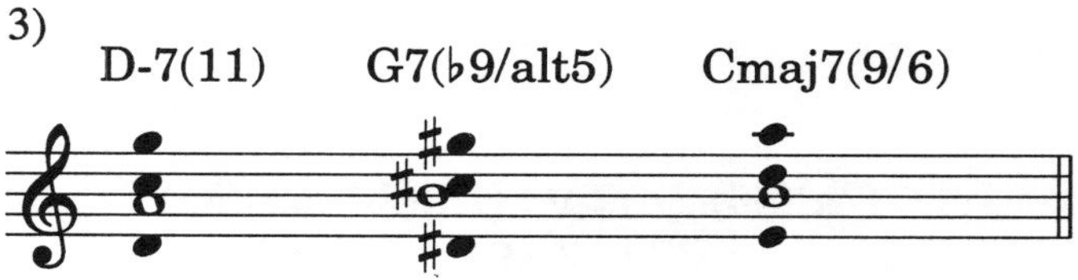


4)

The following is an example of parallel "indirect" chromatic motion using three voices. (Note the doubling);

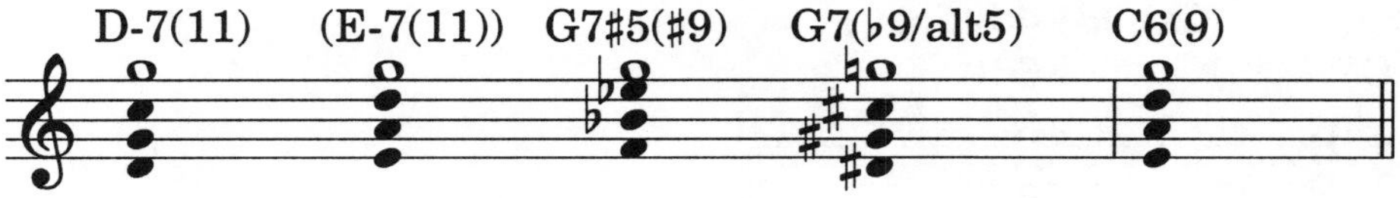


**<u>Contrary</u> chromatic motion in three and four voices**

The following examples will include three <u>and</u> four chromatic guide-lines, but will be organized in accordance with *three* chromatic lines, since they contain twenty-four different combinations while four chromatic lines contain only fourteen combinations. Reference to individual four-line combinations will be organized and presented immediately following these examples.

## *TWO* CHROMATIC LINES DESCEND WHILE *ONE* ASCENDS, (TWELVE COMBINATIONS)

1) 2nd, 3rd, and 4th strings;

a) II - **(2d)(3d)(4a)** - V - **(2a)(3d)(4d)(5a)** - I

D-9 G7(♭9/alt5) C(13/♯11/9)

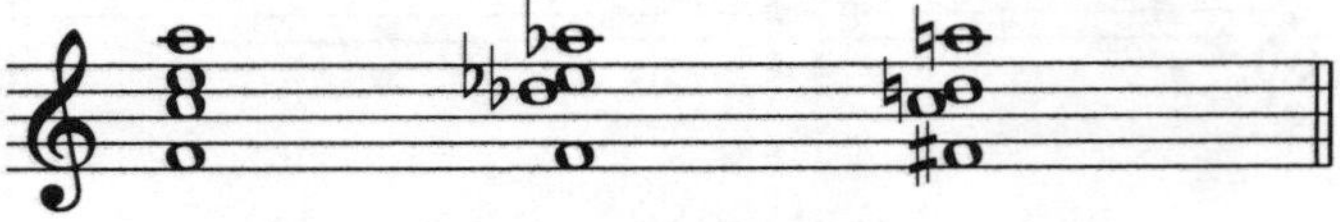

b) II - **(2a)(3d)(4d)** - V - **(2d)(3d)(4a)(5a)** - I

D-9 G7(♯9/♯5) C(13/♯11/9)

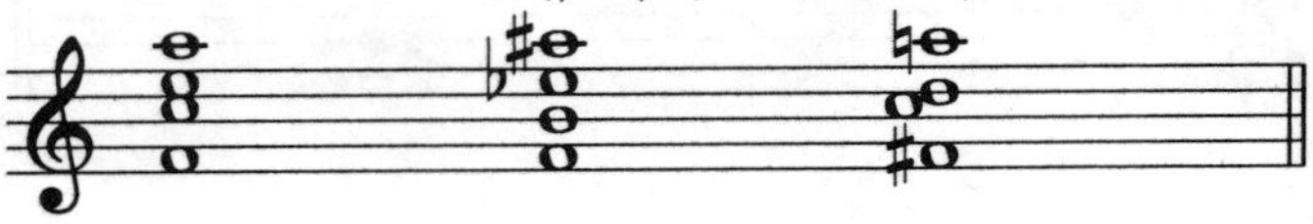

c) II - **(2d)(3a)(4d)** - V - **(2d)(3d)(4a)(5d)** - I

D-7 G7(♭9/♯5) C(add9)

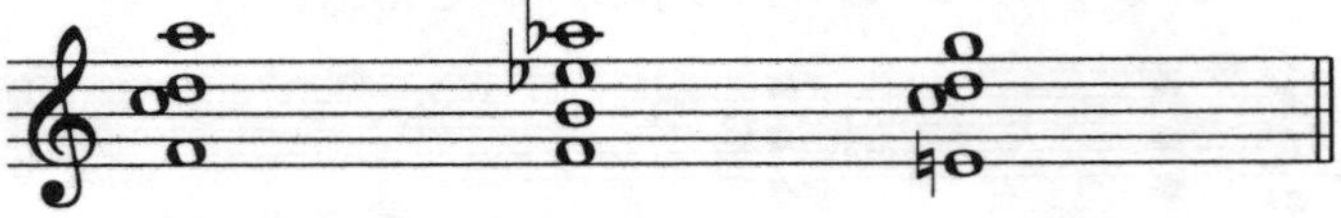

2) 3rd, 4th, and 5th strings;

a) II - **(3d)(4d)(5a)** - V - **(2d)(3a)(4d)(5a)** - I

E-7 A7♯5(♭9) D(♯11)

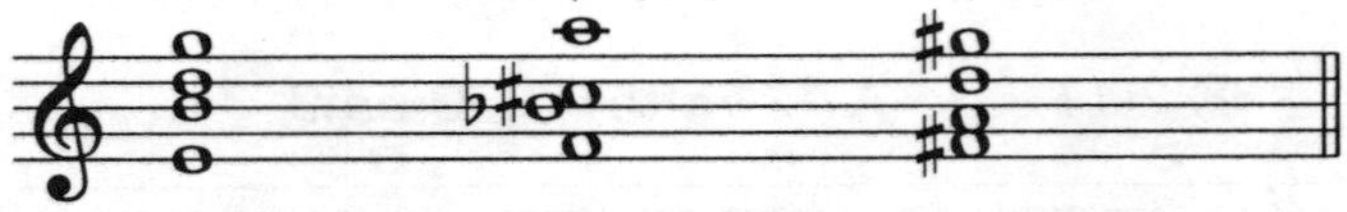

b) II - **(2d)(3a)(4d)(5d)** - V - **(3a)(4d)(5d)** - I

D-9 D♭7 Cmaj7(♯11)

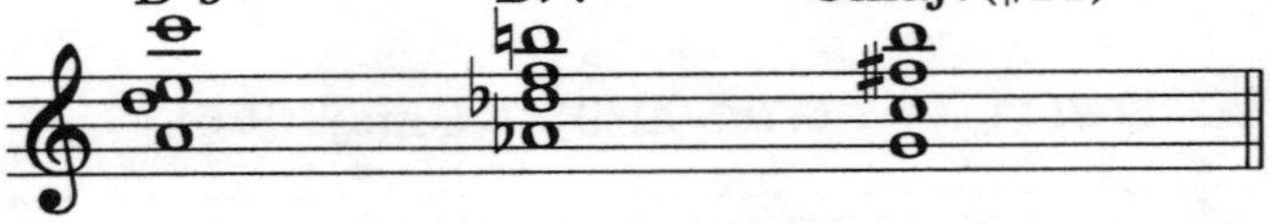

c) II - **(2a)(3d)(4a)(5d)** - V - **(3d)(4a)(5d)** - I

D9sus4 D♭7 C7(13/9)

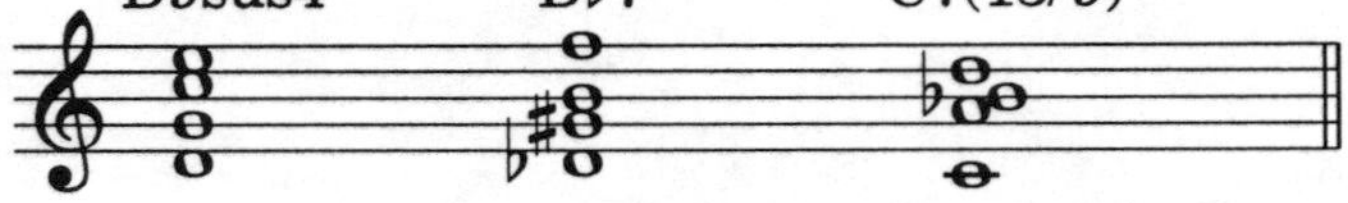

3) 2nd, 3rd, and 5th strings;

a) II - **(2d)(3d)(5a)** - V - **(2d)(3a)(4a)(5d)** - I

G-9 C7(♭9/alt5) F(13/♯11/9)

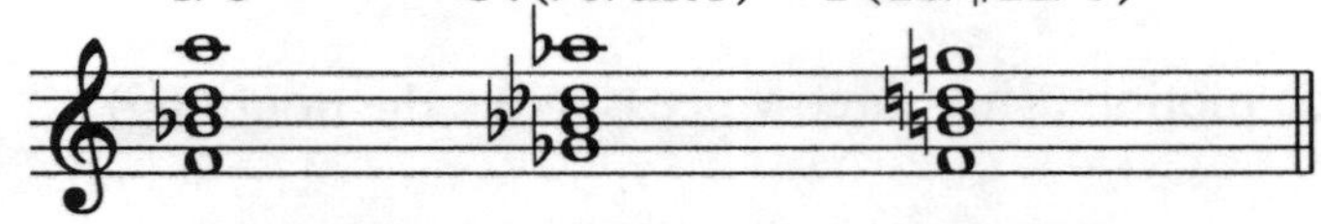

b) II - **(2a)(3d)(5d)** - V - **(2d)(3d)(4d)(5a)** - I

G-7 C7(♭13/♭9) F(add9)

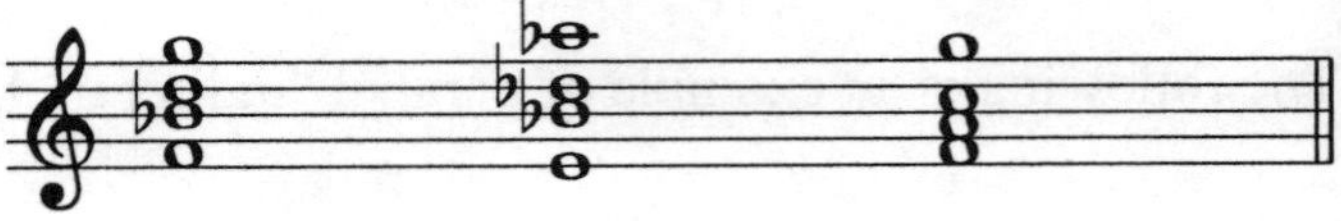

c) II - **(2d)(3a)(5d)** - V - **(2a)(3d)(4d)(5a)** - I

G-7 C7♭5(♯9) F6(9)

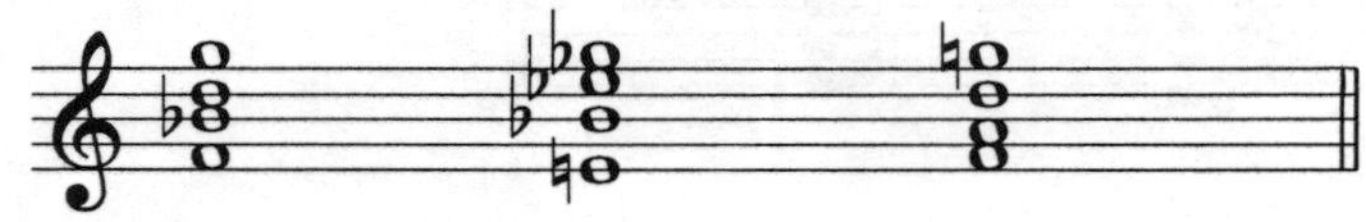

4) 2nd, 4th, and 5th strings;

a) II - **(2d)(4d)(5a)** - V - **(3d)(4d)(5d)** - I

C-7(11) F7♭5(♭9) B♭maj7

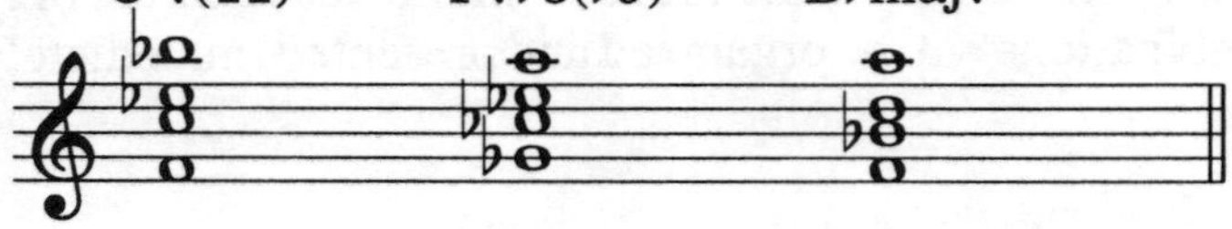

b) II - **(2a)(4d)(5d)** - V - **(2a)(4a)(5a)** - I

C-7(11/9) F7(♭9/alt5) B♭6(9)

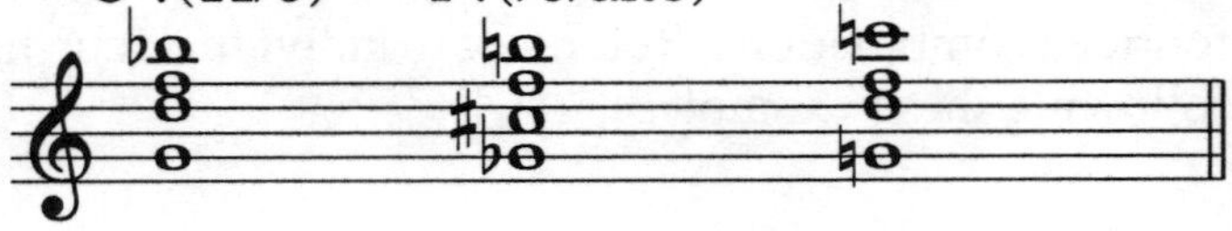

c) II - **[(2d)(4a)(5d)](3d)** - V - **(2a)(3d)(4a)(5a)**- I

G-9 C7♭5(♭9) F(♯11/9)

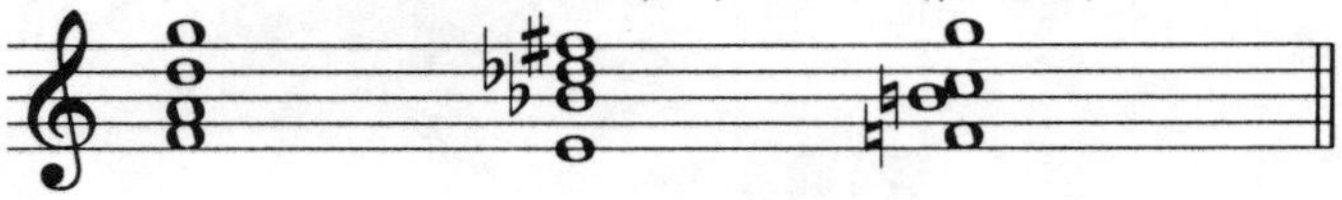

## *TWO* CHROMATIC LINES <u>ASCEND</u> WHILE *ONE* <u>DESCENDS</u>, (TWELVE COMBINATIONS)

1) 2nd, 3rd, and 4th strings;

a) II - **(2a)(3d)(4a)** - V - **(2a)(3d)(4d)(5d)** - I

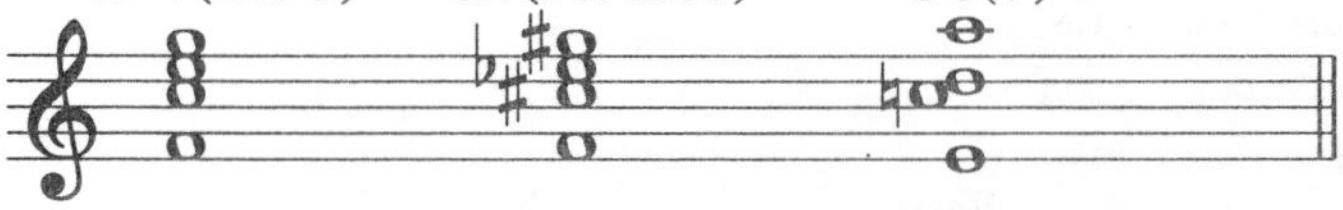


b) II - **(2d)(3a)(4a)** - V - **(2d)(3d)(4d)(5d)** - I

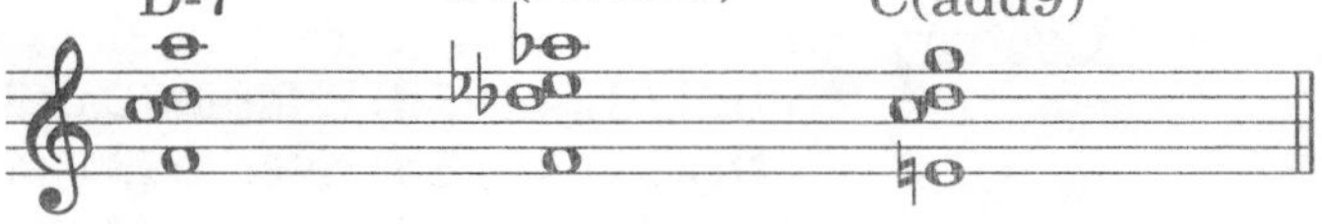


c) II - **(2a)(3a)(4d)** - V - **(2a)(3d)(4a)(5d)** - I

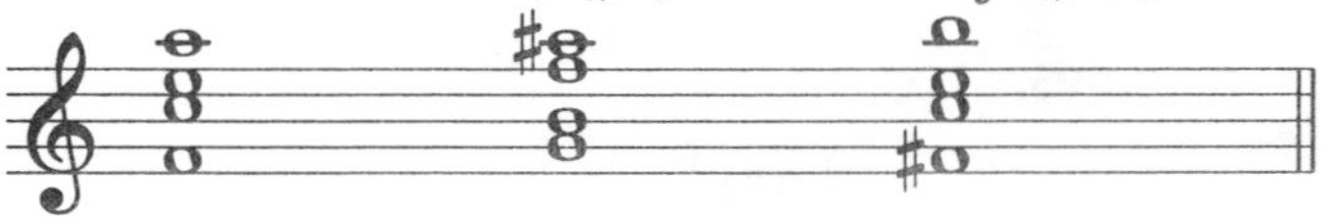


2) 3rd, 4th, and 5th strings;

a) II - **[(3a)(4a)(5d)](2d)** - V - **(2a)(3a)(4d)(5a)** - I

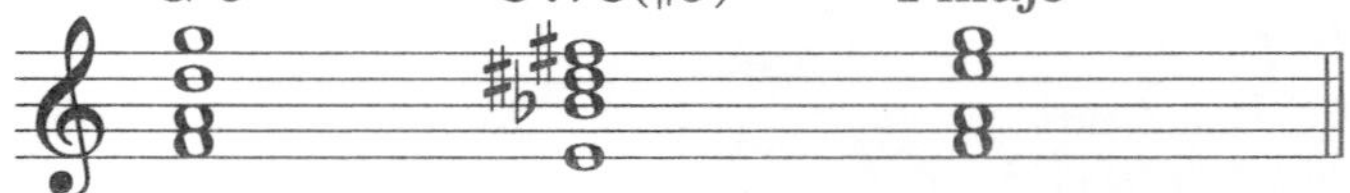


b) II - **[(3d)(4a)(5a)](2a)** - V - **(2a)(3a)(4d)(5a)** - I

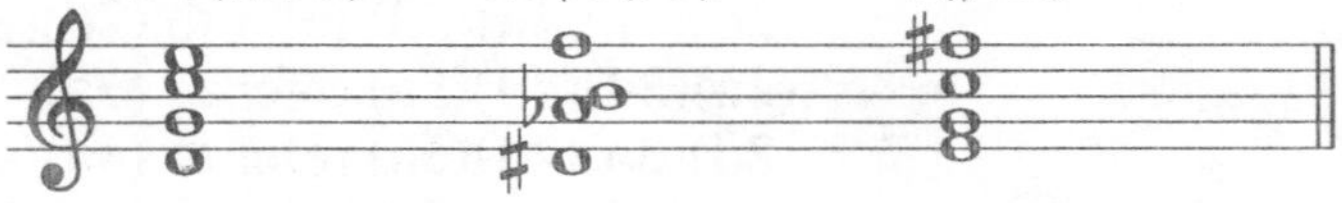


c) II - **[(3a)(4d)(5a)](2a)** - V - **(2a)(3d)(4d)(5a)** - I

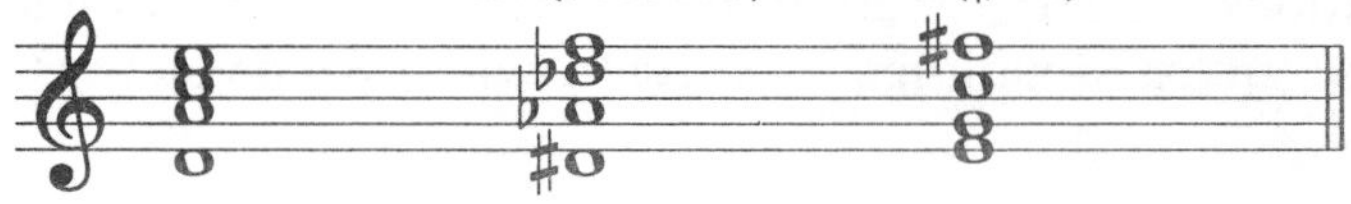


3) 2nd, 3rd, and 5th strings;

a) II - **(2a)(3a)(5d)** - V - **(2d)(3a)(4a)(5a)** - I

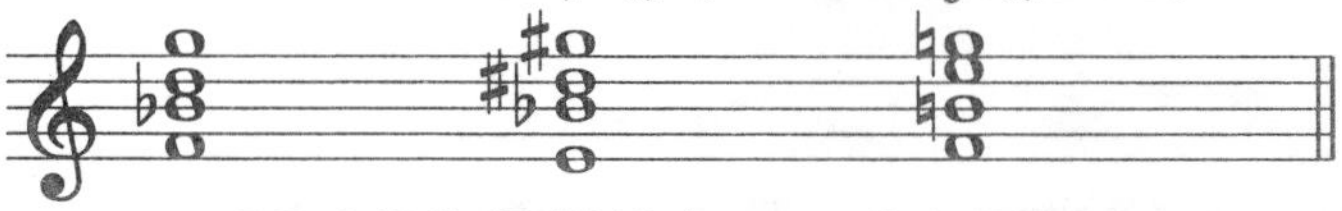


b) II - **(2d)(3a)(5a)** - V - **(2a)(3a)(4a)(5d)** - I

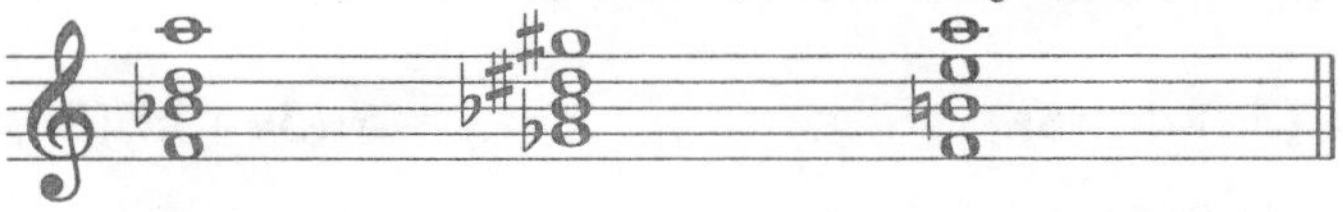


c) II - **[(2a)(3d)(5a)](4a)** - V - **(2a)(3d)(4a)(5d)** - I

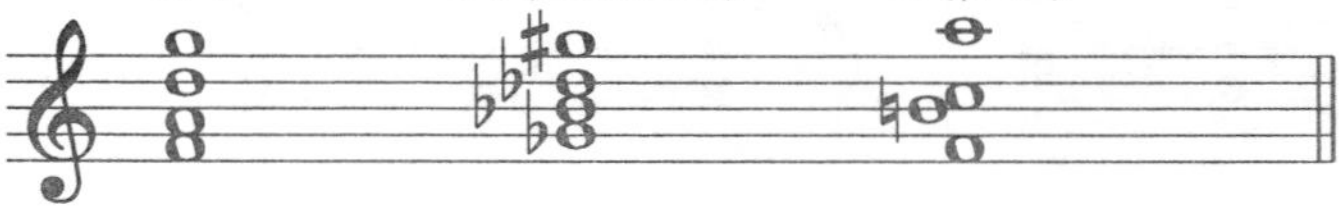


4) 2nd, 4th, and 5th strings;

a) II - **[(2a)(4a)(5d)](3a)** - V - **(2d)(3d)(4d)** - I

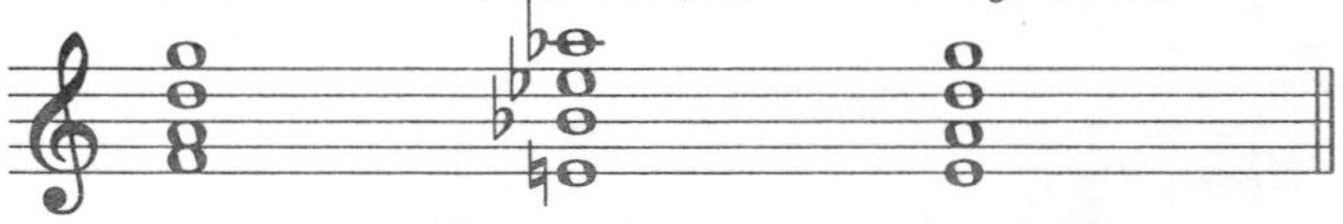


b) II - **(2d)(4a)(5a)** - V - **(3d)(4d)(5d)** - I

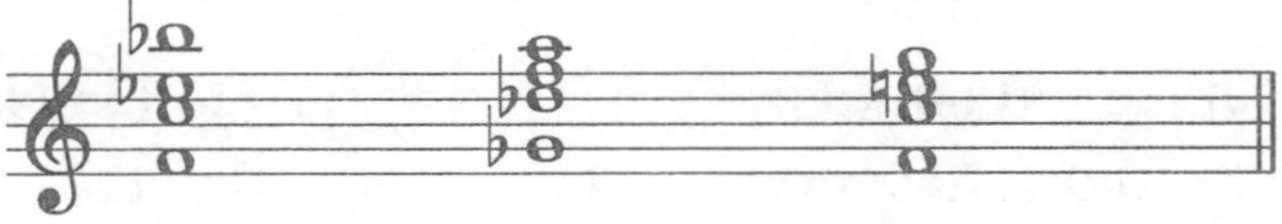


c) II - **(2a)(4d)(5a)** - V - **(2a)(3a)(4d)(5d)** - I

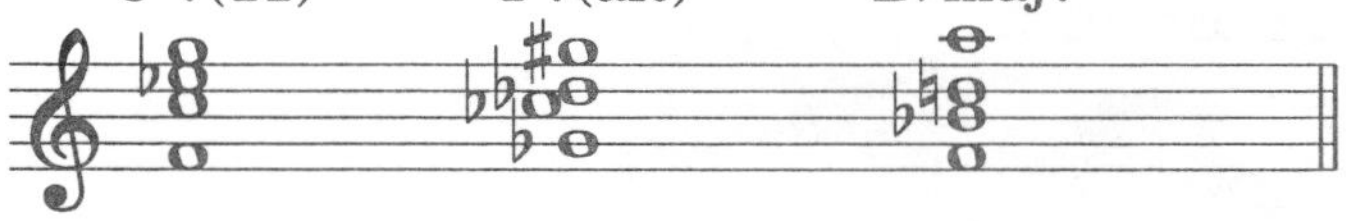

The following will organize the *four* chromatic guide-line examples already presented for easy individual reference. Each of the fourteen four-line combinations will be listed along with the three-line combination it can be found under.

1) *Four* descending chromatic lines; **(2d)(3d)(4d)(5d)** refer to **(2d)(3a)(4a)**

2) Contrary; *three* descending chromatic lines while *one* ascends;
**(2a)(3d)(4d)(5d)** refer to **(2a)(3d)(4a)**
**(2d)(3a)(4d)(5d)** refer to **(3a)(4d)(5d)**
**(2d)(3d)(4a)(5d)** refer to **(2d)(3a)(4d)**
**(2d)(3d)(4d)(5a)** refer to **(2a)(3d)(5d)**

3) Contrary; *three* ascending chromatic lines while *one* descends;
**(2d)(3a)(4a)(5a)** refer to **(2a)(3a)(5d)**
**(2a)(3d)(4a)(5a)** refer to **(2d)(4a)(5d)**
**(2a)(3a)(4d)(5a)** refer to **(3a)(4a)(5d)**
**(2a)(3a)(4a)(5d)** refer to **(2d)(3a)(5a)**

4) Contrary; *two* ascending and *two* descending chromatic lines;
**(2d)(3d)(4a)(5a)** refer to **(2a)(3d)(4d)**
**(2a)(3a)(4d)(5d)** refer to **(2a)(4d)(5a)**
**(2d)(3a)(4a)(5d)** refer to **(2d)(3d)(5a)**
**(2a)(3d)(4d)(5a)** refer to **(3a)(4d)(5a)**
**(2d)(3a)(4d)(5a)** refer to **(3d)(4d)(5a)**
**(2a)(3d)(4a)(5d)** refer to **(2a)(3a)(4d)**

The following three and four contrary chromatic line combinations extend over the entire II V I cadence. Additional string and motion combinations are possible, but in many cases require "doublings" or seventh-width sized voicings. Some of the following examples will include such voicings.

1) **(2a)(3d)(4a);**

Cm(11/9) F7♯5(alt9) B♭maj7(9/6)

2) **(2a)(3d)(4d);**

Dm(add9) G7(♭9/alt5) C(♯11)

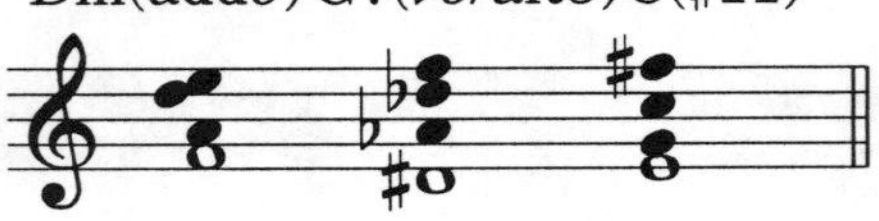

3) **(2d)(3a)(4d);**

A-7(11/9) D7(♭9/alt5) G6(9)

4) **(3a)(4d)(5a);**

D-7(11) G7(♭9/alt5) C(♯11/9)

5) **(3a)(4d)(5d);**

C-9 B7 B♭maj7(♯11)

6) **(2d)(3a)(5d);**

E-9 A7(♯9/alt5) Dmaj9

7) **(2a)(4d)(5a);**

E-9 A7♯5(♭9) Dmaj7(♯11)

8) **(2a)(4d)(5d);**

C-9 F7♯5(alt9) B♭maj7(♯11/9)

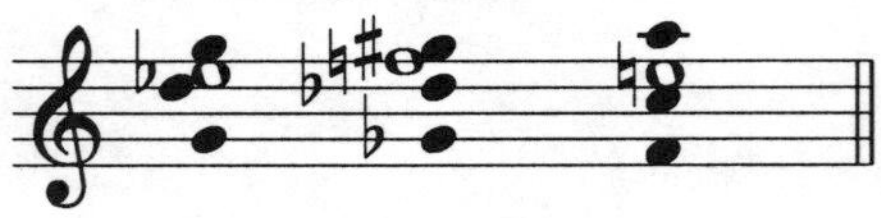

9) **(2a)(3a)(4d)(5a);**

D-9 G7(♭9/alt5) C(♯11/9)

10) **(2a)(3d)(4d)(5a);**

D-9 G7(♭9/alt5) C(♯11)

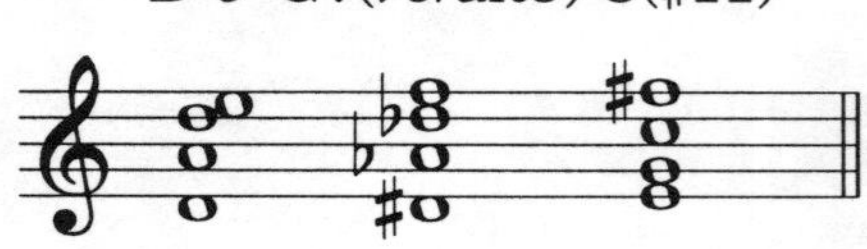

11) **(2d)(3a)(4a)(5d);**

Gm(11/9) C7(alt) Fmaj7(9/6)

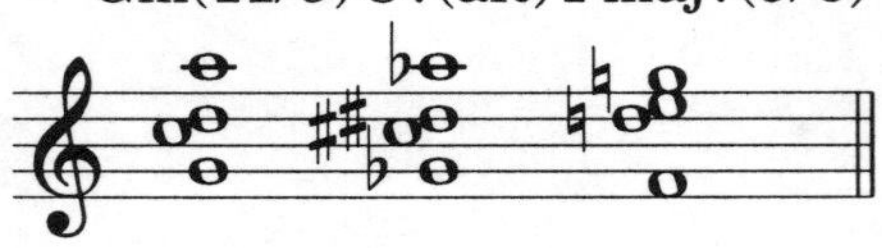

The following example uses three chromatic guide-lines with a <u>single</u> common tone over an extended chord progression;

Fmaj9 D7♭5(♭9) Gm(11/ 9) C7♯5(♯9) Fmaj7(♯11) D7(♭9/alt5) Gm(11/9) C7(♭9/alt5) F6(9)

The following example uses three and four chromatic guide-lines over an extended progression;

B♭maj9 G7♭5(♭9) C7(♭9) F7♯5(♭9) D7♭5 G7♯5 C7(alt5) F7♭5 B♭(add9)

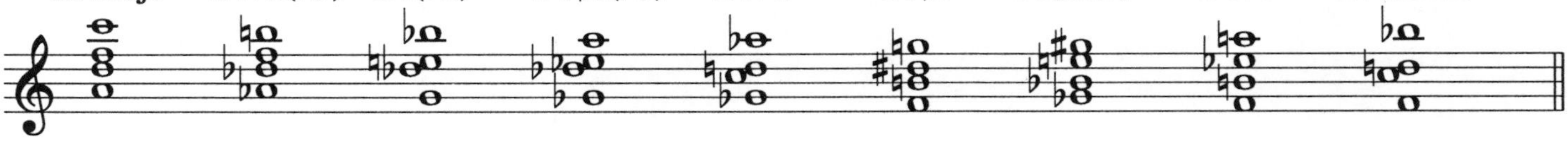

The remaining examples are II V I cadences that contain a variety of chromatic guide-line combinations.

1) Top two voices descend chromatically while bottom two voices have *indirect* chromatic motion;

D-7 G7(alt) Cmaj7

2) II - **(2d)(3d)(4d)** - V - **(2d)(3a)(4a)(5a)** - I ;

D-7 G7(♭9/alt5) C(add9)

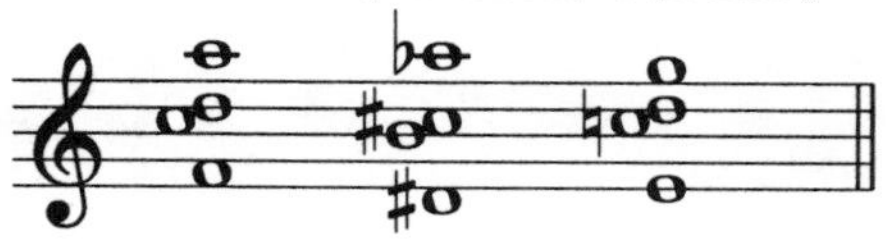

3) II - **(3a)(4d)** - V - **(3a)(4a)(5d)** - I ;

D-7(11) G7♭5(♭9) C6(9)

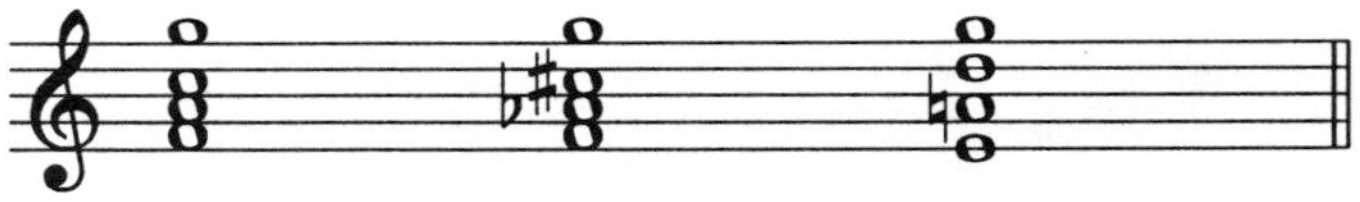

4) II - **(3d)(4a)** - V - **(3d)(4a)(5d)** - I ;

Dm(11/9) G7♯5(♯9) Cmaj9

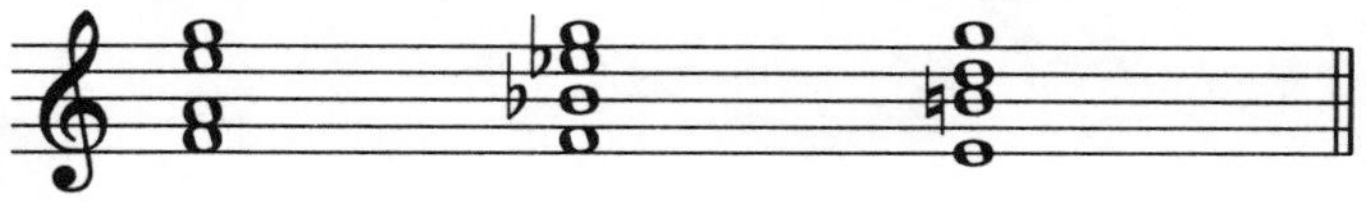

5) II - **(2d)(3d)(4d)** - V ;

D-7 G13(♭9) (E7) Cmaj9

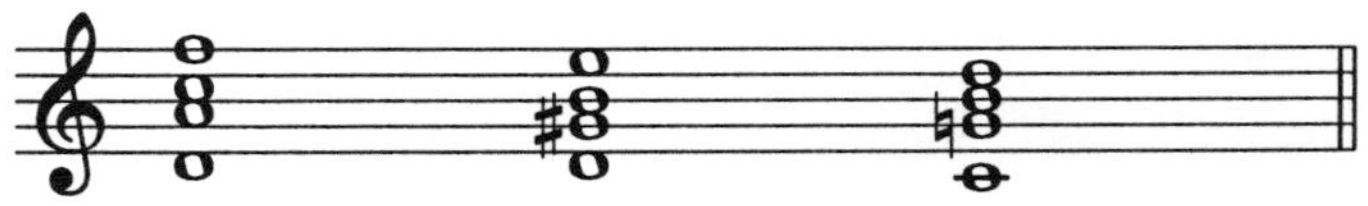

6) II - **(2a)(3a)(4a)** - V - **(2a)(3a)(4d)(5a)** - I ;

G-7(11/9) (D-7) C7♭5(♭9) (G♭7) F6(9)

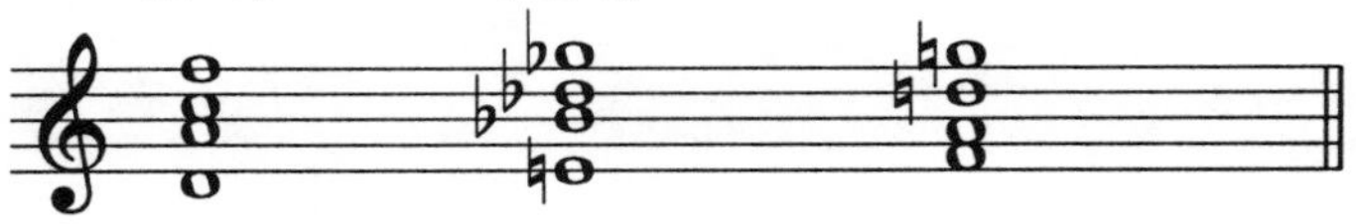

7) **(2d)(3d)(4a)(5d);**

G9sus4 C7(♭9/alt5) F9(13)

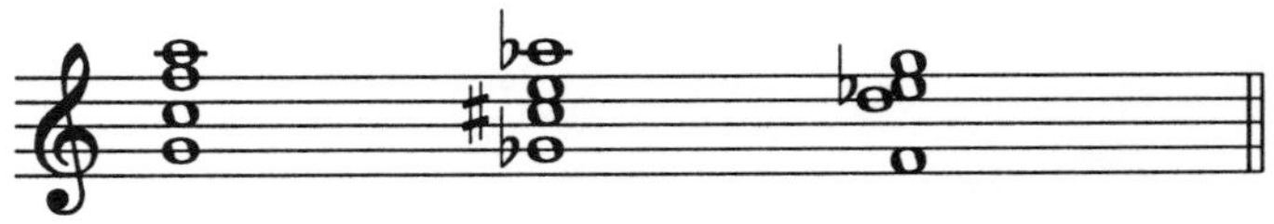

8) II - **(3d)(5d)** - V - **(2a)(5d)** - I ;

G-7 C9(alt5) Fmaj7(6)

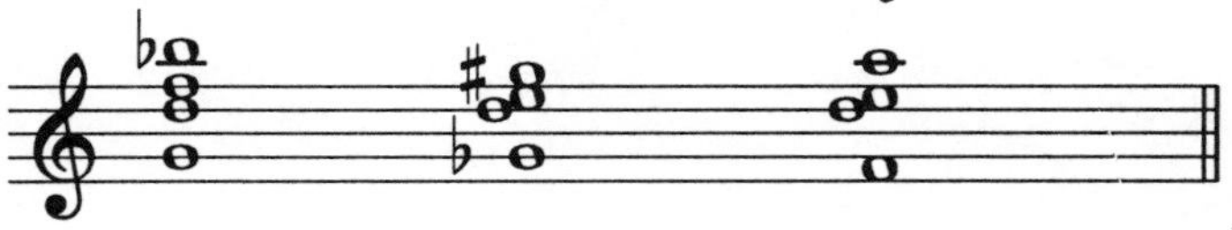

9) V - **(3a)(4a)(5a)** - I ;

D-7♯5(11) B♭6(9) G7(♯11/♭9) C-6(9)

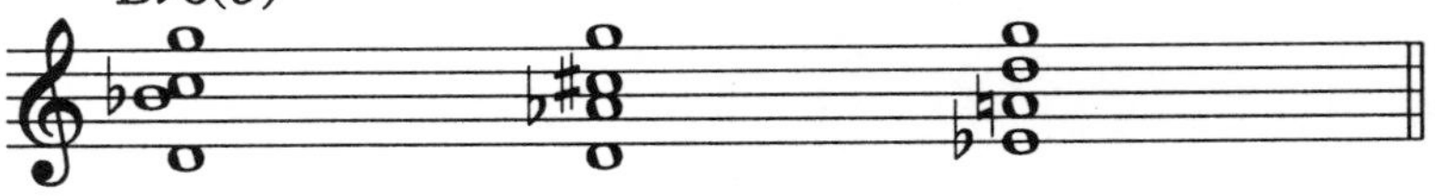

Although the following exercise contains some three and four chromatic guide-line examples, the most interesting element is the contrary motion produced by the top voice and the chord roots. Since some of the drop 2 type voicings contain no root, sing or record-and-playback the roots while playing the exercise.

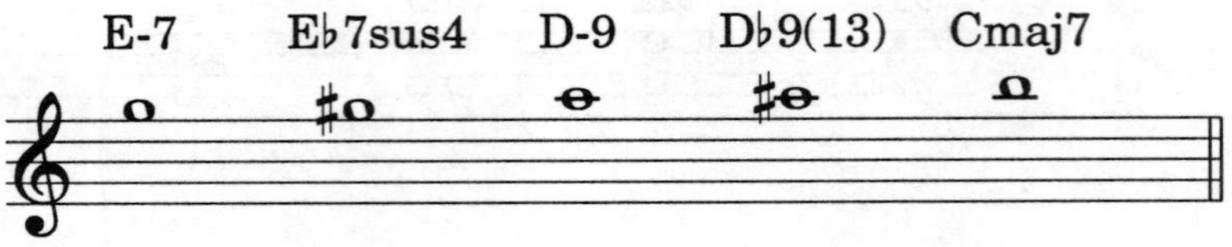

# Chapter Twenty-Seven.
## Triad over Bass Voicings

This chapter will explore all inversions of major and minor triads on the 2nd, 3rd, and 4th strings while non-triadic notes are placed on the 5th string. Omitting the three notes of the triad being used leaves *nine* possible bass notes underneath the triad. The following will organize these bass notes *intervallically* in relation to *one* major or minor triad;

♭2 2 ♭3 or 3 4 ♯4 ♭6 6 ♭7 7

Above in relation to C major and C minor triads;

| | | | | | | | | |
|---|---|---|---|---|---|---|---|---|
| C/D♭ | C/D | C/E♭ | C/F | C/F♯ | C/A♭ | C/A | C/B♭ | C/B |
| Cm/D♭ | Cm/D | Cm/E | Cm/F | Cm/F♯ | Cm/A♭ | Cm/A | Cm/B♭ | Cm/B |

The following will organize major and minor triads *intervallically* in relation to one bass note;

♭2 2 ♭3 3 ♯4 5 ♭6 or 6 ♭7 7

Above in relation to a C bass note;

| | | | | | | | | |
|---|---|---|---|---|---|---|---|---|
| D♭/C | D/C | E♭/C | E/C | F♯/C | G/C | A/C | B♭/C | B/C |
| D♭m/C | Dm/C | E♭m/C | Em/C | F♯m/C | Gm/C | A♭m/C | B♭m/C | Bm/C |

The above chords consist of both *hybrid* chords and 7th chord inversions. The *five* chords containing the bass notes; ♭2, 2, ♭3 or 3, 4, and ♯4 of the given triad are hybrid chords while the remaining *four* chords containing the bass notes; ♭6, 6, ♭7, and 7 of the given triad are specific inversions, (root and third inversions), of 7th chords. The following lists the 7th chord inversions;

| | | | |
|---|---|---|---|
| C/A♭ = A♭maj7♯5 | C/A = A-7 | C/B♭ = C7 | C/B = Cmaj7 |
| Cm/A♭ = A♭maj7 | Cm/A = A-7♭5 | Cm/B♭ = C-7 | Cm/B = C-maj7 |

With the exception of those containing ♭9th intervals, all of these structures, (hybrid chords and 7th chord inversions), have been previously introduced as specific inversions of different chords. The following will show the first chord that introduced each *hybrid* structure, (minus those structures containing ♭9th intervals);

| | | |
|---|---|---|
| C/D♭ = A7(♯9) | C/D = E-7♯5 | C/F = G13(sus4) |
| Cm/D♭ = A7♭5(♯9) | Cm/E = F♯7(13/♯11/♭9) | Cm/F = E♭6(9)[1 3 6 9] |

In past chapters, those voicings containing ♭9th intervals were avoided. Because of the unique sound of *hybrid* chords and *upper-structure triads* , the ♭9th interval will be made available to them in this chapter. Since these structures often imply *two* different sounds or chords within *one* voicing, the ♭9th interval produces less dissonance than it usually does on a "singular" harmonic structure. The following hybrid chords and 7th chord inversions contain ♭9th intervals;

C/E♭ C/F♯ C/B Cm/D Cm/F♯ Cm/B

It is interesting to note that of the *eighteen* major and minor structures presented;

Six are 7th chord inversions, (minus ♭9th intervals);
C/A♭ C/A C/B♭ Cm/A♭ Cm/A Cm/B♭

Six are hybrid chords, (minus ♭9th intervals);
C/D♭ C/D C/F Cm/D♭ Cm/E Cm/F

Six are structures containing ♭9th intervals;
C/E♭ C/F♯ C/B Cm/D Cm/F♯ Cm/B

Again, because of the unique sound these structures contain, <u>and</u> the limit of available voicings within this text's framework, the outside voicing width of a *major 7th* will be included. This might pose some voice-leading problems when integrated with *drop 2* voicing widths, but the "sound" and "style" will often circumvent a temporary lack of voice-leading. The width of a ♭7th will still be avoided.

There are <u>six</u> different structures that contain a major 7th width on <u>one</u> of their inversions;

*Cm/D♭ will be omitted due to the awkward fingering produced on the middle four strings of the guitar. This voicing is quite comfortable on the top four strings.

The following views the remaining five structures containing a major 7th width from a common bass note;

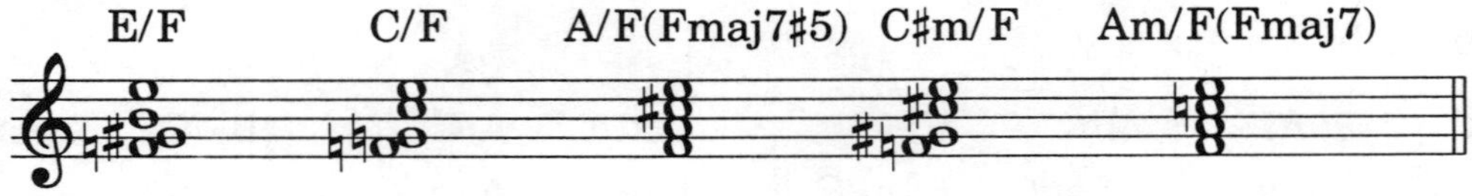


Four structures; C/A, Cm/A, Cm/A♭, and Cm/B♭, will be omitted from the eighteen major and minor structures presented due to their limited use in a hybrid or upper-structure environment. These structures lack the "dual" quality the remaining structures contain, and seem to demand their "singular" identity;

C/A = A-7 Cm/A = A-7♭5 Cm/A♭ = A♭maj7 Cm/B♭ = C-7 or E♭6

They may reappear as triad-over-bass structures when these specific inversions are desired. Triad-over-bass notation may also be more appropriate when the surrounding chords are notated that way as well. The following is an example of the triad-over-bass notation being most appropriate;

| | | | | | | |
|---|---|---|---|---|---|---|
| C/F | E/F | G/E | F♯/E | F/D | E/D | Em/C |
| | | (E-7) | | (D-7) | | (Cmaj7) |

We now have a total of <u>fourteen</u> structures that will be examined in this chapter;

| | | | | | | | |
|---|---|---|---|---|---|---|---|
| **C/D♭** | **C/D** | **C/E♭** | **C/F** | **C/F♯** | **C/A♭** | **C/B♭** | **C/B** |
| **Cm/D♭** | **Cm/D** | **Cm/E** | **Cm/F** | **Cm/F♯** | **........................** | | **Cm/B** |

The following inversions for each structure will be used;

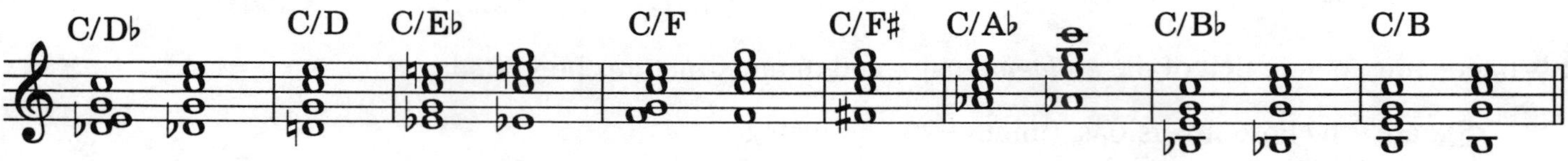


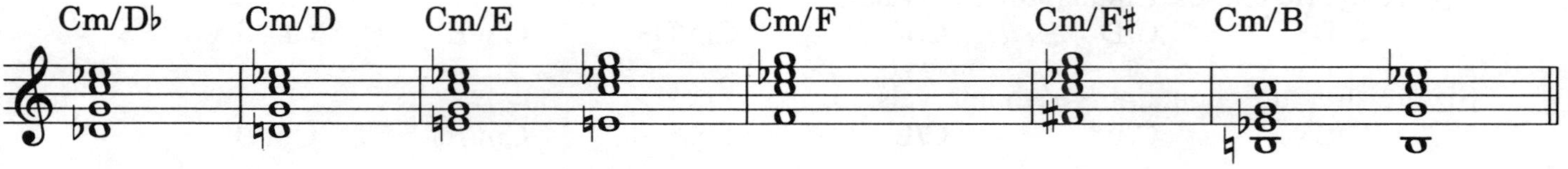

This section will begin by examining each structure as a root inversion chord. This will produce a few rather incomplete chords as well as some structures that are best used in a "modal" context.

Major;

| | | |
|---|---|---|
| **C/D♭** = D♭°maj7 | **C/D** = D9(sus4) | **C/E♭** = E♭13(♭9) |
| **C/F** = Fmaj7(9) or F-maj7(9) | **C/F♯** = F♯7♭5(♭9) or F♯-7♭5(♭9) | |
| **C/A♭** = A♭maj7♯5 | **C/B♭** = B♭(13/♯11/9) | **C/B** = Bsus4(♭13/♭9) or B phrygian |

Minor;

| | | |
|---|---|---|
| **Cm/D♭** = D♭maj7♭5(9) | **Cm/D** = D7sus4(♭9) | **Cm/E** = E°maj7(♭13) or E-maj7(♭13) |
| **Cm/F** = F9 or F-9 | **Cm/F♯** = F♯(13/♯11/♭9) | **Cm/B** = B(♭13/♭9) |

Although considering the bass note as the root produces some interesting chords, the most useful chords are often found on different roots *other* than the bass note. This concept introduces the "dual" quality these structures offer and begins examination of true *upper-structure triads;* triads over 7th chords. When a different root other than the bass note and triad is chosen, a chord is implied underneath the triad and the bass note now becomes a chord tone or tension on this lower chord structure and is subject to that structures *Low Interval Limits.* Since the chosen root is not part of the voicing, it should be recorded-and-played-back or sung while playing the voicing in order to hear the function of the voicing in relation to the root.

The following hybrid chord is examined for its upper-structure possibilities;

| **C/F**.......................... | F | C | E | G | | |
|---|---|---|---|---|---|---|
| *(Assumed root)* | \| | \| | \| | \| | *(Singular-structure)* | *(Upper-structure)* |
| D........................ | ♭3 | ♭7 | 9 | 11 | D-7(11/9) | C over D-7 |
| G........................ | ♭7 | 4 | 13 | 1 | G13sus4 | C over G7sus4 |
| B♭...................... | 5 | 9 | ♯11 | 13 | B♭(13/♯11/9) | C over B♭maj7 or B♭7 |
| E........................ | ♭9 | ♯5 | 1 | ♯9 | E7(alt9/♯5) | C over E7(♭9) |
| A........................ | ♭13 | ♯9 | 5 | ♭7 | A7(♭13/♯9) | C over A7(♭13) |

Again, it is important to know what the bass note is in relation to each new root. The above structures range, (F located on the 5th string), will satisfy L.I.L. for all of the new roots listed. If this structure were placed lower, for example F/B♭, L.I.L. would allow only the new root that produced the 5th in the bass; E♭(13/♯11/9), and of course the root inversion B♭maj7(9).

The following will examine all the new root possibilities, (minus those structures containing ♭9th intervals), each structure will afford. Only the root inversion, which has already been presented, will be used on structures containing a ♭9th interval.

The following structures, minus the C/F structure already presented, will be examined;

C/A♭ C/B♭ C/D C/D♭ Cm/D♭ Cm/E Cm/F

The root inversions, which have also been examined, will be included in the following models as well.

| **C/A♭**................ | A♭ | C | E | G | | |
|---|---|---|---|---|---|---|
| *(Assumed root)* | \| | \| | \| | \| | *(Singular-structure)* | *(Upper-structure)* |
| A♭.................... | 1 | 3 | ♯5 | 7 | A♭maj7♯5 | C over A♭ |
| F..................... | ♭3 | 5 | 7 | 9 | F-maj7(9) | C over F-maj7 |
| D..................... | ♭5 | ♭7 | 9 | 11 | D-7♭5(11/9) | C over D-7♭5 |
| E..................... | 3 | ♯5 | 1 | ♯9 | E7(♯9/♯5) | C over E7 |
| B♭.................... | ♭7 | 9 | ♯11 | 13 | B♭7(13/♯11/9) | C over B♭7 |
| G..................... | ♭9 | 4 | 13 | 1 | G13sus4(♭9) | C over G7sus4(♭9) |
| C..................... | ♭13 | 1 | 3 | 5 | C7(♭13) | C over ♭13 |

| **C/D**................. | D | C | E | G | | |
|---|---|---|---|---|---|---|
| *(Assumed root)* | | | | | *(Singular-structure)* | *(Upper-structure)* |
| D.................... | 1 | ♭7 | 9 | 4 | D9sus4 | C over Dsus4 |
| E.................... | 9 | ♯5 | 1 | ♭3 | E-7♯5 | C over E-7♭5 |
| A.................... | 11 | ♭3 | 5 | ♭7 | A-7(11) | C over A-11 |
| C.................... | 9 | 1 | 3 | 5 | C(add9) | C over 9 |
| G.................... | 5 | 4 | 13 | 1 | G13sus4 or G-6(11) | C over G7sus4 or Gm |
| B♭.................. | 3 | 9 | ♯11 | 13 | B♭(13/♯11/9) | C over B♭maj7 or B♭7 |
| F.................... | 6 | 5 | 7 | 9 | Fmaj7(9/6) | C over F6 or F-6 |
| F♯.................. | ♯5 | ♭5 | ♭7 | ♭9 | F♯7(♭9/alt5) | C over F♯7♭5 |
| A♭.................. | ♭5 | 3 | ♯5 | 7 | A♭maj7(alt5) | C over A♭maj7♭5 |

| **C/D♭**.............. | D♭ | C | E | G | | |
|---|---|---|---|---|---|---|
| *(Assumed root)* | | | | | *(Singular-structure)* | *(Upper-structure)* |
| D♭.................. | 1 | 7 | ♭3 | ♭5 | D♭°(maj7) | C over D♭° |
| A.................... | 3 | ♯9 | 5 | ♭7 | A7(♯9) | C over A7 |
| E♭.................. | ♭7 | 13 | ♭9 | 3 | E♭13(♭9) | C over E♭7 |
| C ................... | ♭9 | 1 | 3 | 5 | C7(♭9) | C over ♭9 |
| G♭.................. | 5 | ♯11 | ♭7 | ♭9 | G♭7(♯11/♭9) | C over G♭7 |

| **C/B♭**.............. | B♭ | C | E | G | | |
|---|---|---|---|---|---|---|
| *(Assumed root)* | | | | | *(Singular-structure)* | *(Upper-structure)* |
| B♭.................. | 1 | 9 | ♯11 | 13 | B♭(13/♯11/9) | C over B♭maj7 or B♭7 |
| A.................... | ♭9 | ♯9 | 5 | ♭7 | A7(alt9) | C over A7(♭9) |
| A♭.................. | 9 | 3 | ♯5 | 7 | A♭maj7♯5(9) | C over A♭maj9 |
| G.................... | ♭3 | 11 | 6 | 1 | G-6(11) | C over Gm |
| G♭.................. | 3 | ♯11 | ♭7 | ♭9 | G♭7(♯11/♭9) | C over G♭7 |
| F.................... | 11 | 5 | 7 | 9 | F-maj7(11/9) | C over Fm(11) |
| E.................... | ♭5 | ♭13 | 1 | ♭3 | E-7♭5(♭13) | C over E-7♭5 |
| E.................... | ♭5 | ♭13 | 1 | ♭3 | E°(♭13) | C over E° |
| E.................... | ♭5 | ♯5 | 1 | ♯9 | E7(♯9/alt5) | C over E7♭5 |
| E♭.................. | 5 | 13 | ♭9 | 3 | E♭13(♭9) | C over E♭7 |
| D.................... | ♭13 | ♭7 | 9 | 11 | D-7♭5(♭13/11/9) | C over D-7♭5(♭13) |
| D♭.................. | ♭♭7(6) | 7 | ♭3 | ♭5 | D♭°maj7 | C over D♭°7 |
| C.................... | ♭7 | 1 | 3 | 5 | C7 | C over ♭7 |

| **Cm/D♭**........... | D♭ | C | E♭ | G | | |
|---|---|---|---|---|---|---|
| *(Assumed root)* | | | | | *(Singular-structure)* | *(Upper-structure)* |
| D♭.................. | 1 | 7 | 9 | ♭5 | D♭maj7♭5(9) | Cm over D♭maj7 |
| A.................... | 3 | ♯9 | ♭5 | ♭7 | A7♭5(♯9) | Cm over A7 |
| E♭.................. | ♭7 | 13 | 1 | 3 | E♭13 | Cm over E♭7 |
| B♭.................. | ♭3 | 9 | 11 | 6 | B♭-6(11/9) | Cm over B♭m |
| G.................... | ♭5 | 11 | ♭13 | 1 | G-7♭5(♭13/11) | Cm over G-7♭5 |
| C.................... | ♭9 | 1 | ♯9 | 5 | C7(alt9) | Cm over ♭9 |
| G♭.................. | 5 | ♯11 | 13 | ♭9 | G♭7(13/♯11/♭9) | Cm over G♭7 |
| F.................... | ♭13 | 5 | ♭7 | 9 | F9(♭13) | Cm over F7(♭13) |

| **Cm/F**.............. | F | C | E♭ | G | | |
|---|---|---|---|---|---|---|
| *(Assumed root)* | I | I | I | I | *(Singular-structure)* | *(Upper-structure)* |
| F..................... | 1 | 5 | ♭7 | 9 | F9 or F-9 | Cm over F7 or F-7 |
| E♭................... | 9 | 6 | 1 | 3 | E♭6(9) | Cm over E♭(add9) |
| C..................... | 11 | 1 | ♭3 | 5 | Cm(11) | Cm over 11 |
| A♭................... | 6 | 3 | 5 | 7 | A♭maj7(6) | Cm over A♭6 |
| D♭................... | 3 | 7 | 9 | ♯11 | D♭maj7(♯11/9) | Cm over D♭maj7 |
| B♭................... | 5 | 9 | 4 | 13 | B♭7sus4(13/9) | Cm over B♭7sus4 |
| B♭................... | 5 | 9 | 11 | 6 | B♭-6(11/9) | Cm over B♭m |
| G..................... | ♭7 | 11 | ♭13 | 1 | G-7♭5(♭13/11) | Cm over G-7♭5 |
| A..................... | ♭13 | ♭3 | ♭5 | ♭7 | A-7♭5(♭13) | Cm over A-7♯5 |
| A..................... | ♯5 | ♯9 | ♭5 | ♭7 | A7(♯9/alt5) | Cm over A7♯5 |
| B..................... | ♭5 | ♭9 | 3 | ♯9 | B7(♭9/alt5) | Cm over B7♭5 |

| **Cm/E**.............. | E | C | E♭ | G | | |
|---|---|---|---|---|---|---|
| *(Assumed root)* | I | I | I | I | *(Singular-structure)* | *(Upper-structure)* |
| E..................... | 1 | ♭13 | 7 | ♭3 | E°maj7(♭13) | Cm over E° |
| E..................... | 1 | ♭13 | 7 | ♭3 | E-maj7(♭13) | Cm over Em |
| A..................... | 5 | ♯9 | ♯11 | ♭7 | A7(♯11/♯9) | Cm over A7 |
| C..................... | 3 | 1 | ♯9 | 5 | C7(♯9) | Cm over Cmajor |
| E♭................... | ♭9 | 13 | 1 | 3 | E♭13(♭9) | Cm over E♭7 |
| F♯................... | ♭7 | ♯11 | 13 | ♭9 | F♯7(13/♯11/♭9) | Cm over F♯7 |

We have now completed isolating any one hybrid structure or 7th chord inversion and examining all the enharmonic chordal functions it contains. Another approach, (and perhaps more useful), would start with a basic 7th chord and determine all the upper-structure triads and consequent hybrid voicings and 7th chord inversions it would contain. After establishing a desired upper-structure triad over a basic 7th chord, construction of different hybrid chords and 7th chord inversions is possible by using the chord tones and tensions of the basic 7th chord below the established upper-structure triad.

The following will examine the different hybrid chords and 7th chord inversions produced from the most common upper-structure triads over the most basic 7th chords. II - V - I chord cadence examples will display each hybrid and 7th chord inversion discovered. All examples will use a common "C" root for the basic 7th chords. If this key produces L.I.L. problems, (tension 9 in the bass for example), that exercise will be transposed to satisfy L.I.L. Although listed, the "obvious" 7th chord inversions will not receive II - V - I examples. Also listed will be all the structures that contain a ♭9th interval, while only their root inversions will receive a II - V - I example. Additional inversions containing the ♭9th interval will be examined under the *dominant* chord examples. Since dominant chords generally contain dissonance by their nature, the ♭9th interval is more readily accepted on these chords. The ♭9th interval might be easier to accept on *tonic* or *sub-dominant* functions if the surrounding chords contain similar triad-over-bass voicings.

*Some of the following examples will have already been presented in part or whole under previous chapters.

The available *upper-structure triads* to any single 7th chord type will be notated in *Roman Numerals*. Immediately following the triads numeral, in parenthesis, will be the tensions or chord tones that upper-structure triad forms on the original 7th chord. For example; Vm (5 ♭7 9)..... is a Gm upper-structure triad over a C7 chord and it contains the 5th(G), ♭7th(B♭), and 9th(D) of C7.

## MAJOR 7th CHORD

Available Upper-Structure Triads; II (9 ♯11 13) V (5 7 9) VIIm (7 9 ♯11)

**1)** II over Imaj7; D over Cmaj7

Chord tones in bass; **D/C** (D7) **D/E** **D/G** **D/B** (B-7)
Tensions cannot appear in bass because they are already contained in upper-structure triad.

a) D-9 G7(♯9/alt5) **D/C** C6(♯11/9)

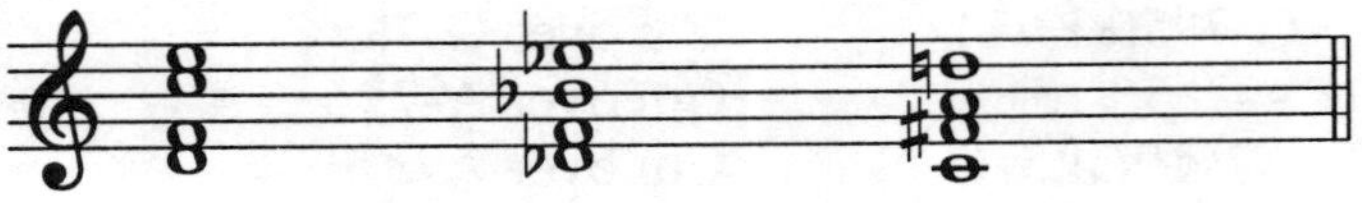

b) D-7(11) G+7(♭9) **D/E** C6(♯11/9)

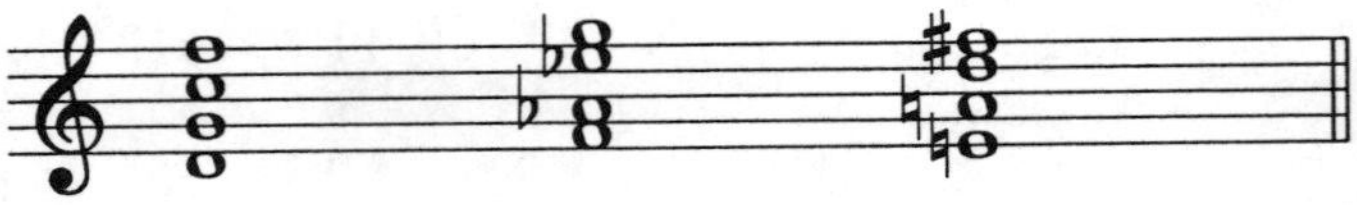

c) D-9(11) C/F G+7(♯9) E♭/F **D/G** C6(♯11/9)

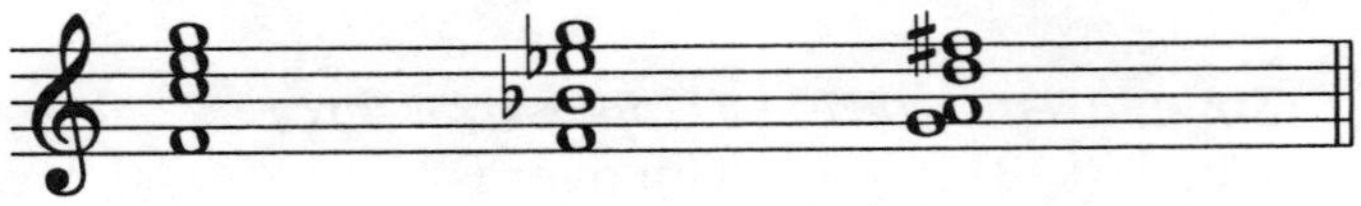

d) G-7(11) F♯7 F♯/E **G/E** Fmaj7(13/♯11/9)

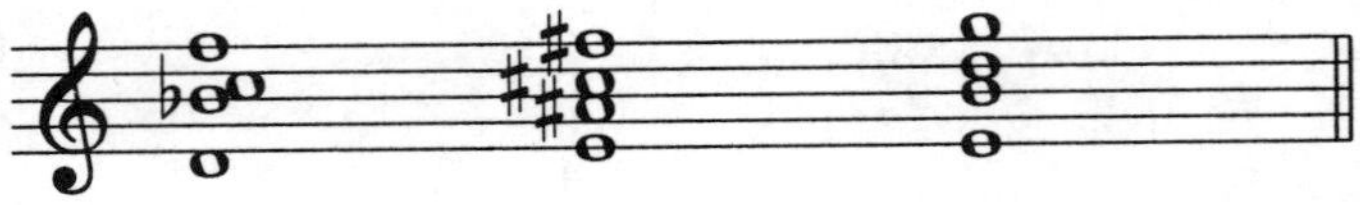

**2)** V over Imaj7; G over Cmaj7

Chord tones in bass; **G/C** **G/E** (E-7 or Cmaj9)
Tensions in bass; **G/A** **G/F♯** (♭9th interval)

a) D-9 Gmaj7(alt5) B/D♭ **G/C** Cmaj9

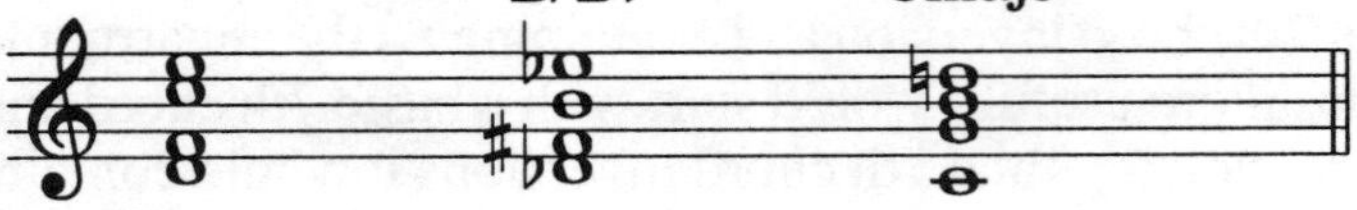

b) D-7(11) F/G G7(alt9) **G/A** Cmaj7(9/6)

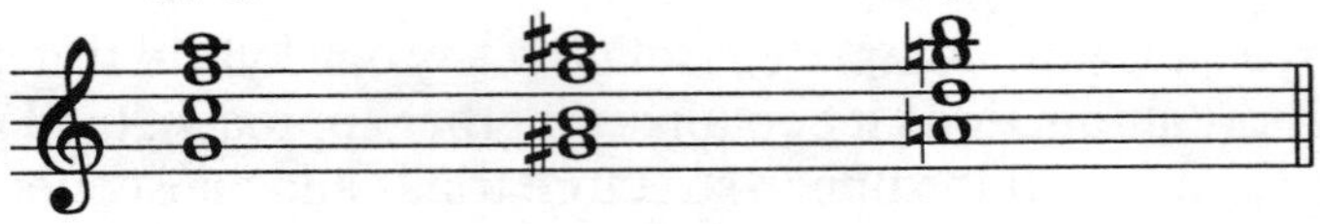

* Note the maj7th on the above V7 chord. This will be further examined under the dom7 chords in this chapter.

**3)** VIIm over Imaj7; Bm over Cmaj7

Chord tones in bass; **Bm/C** **Bm/E** **Bm/G** (Gmaj7)
Tensions in bass; **Bm/A** (B-7)

a) D-9 G7(♯9/alt5) **Bm/C** Cmaj9(♯11)

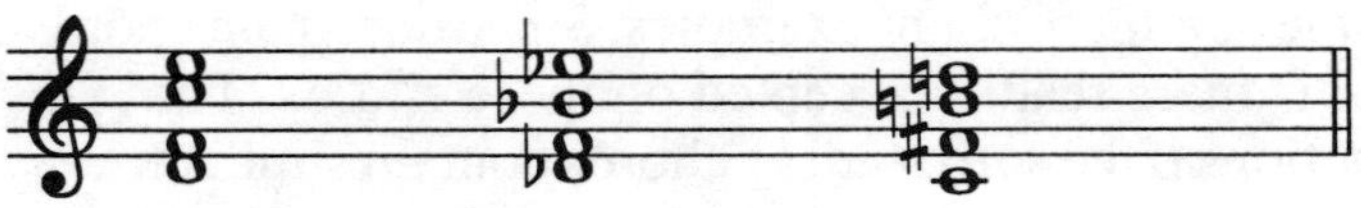

b) D-9 G+7 **Bm/E** Cmaj9(♯11)

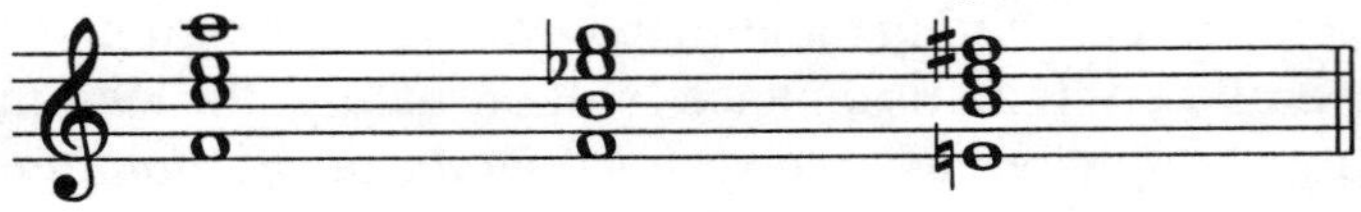

c) D-9 Fmaj7 G7sus4(♭9) **Bm/G**(Cmaj9♯11) Gmaj7

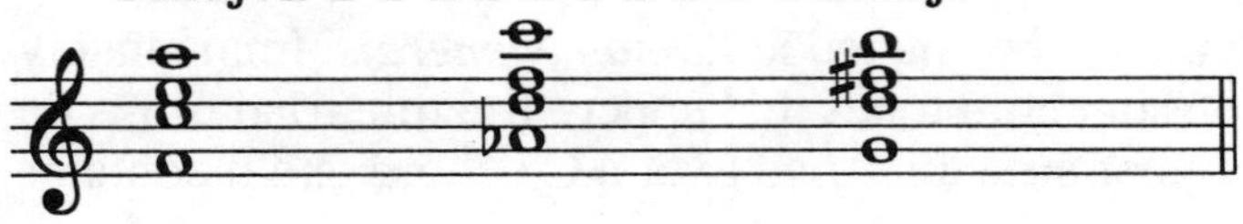

d) D-7(11) G7sus4(♭9) **Bm/A** Cmaj7(13/♯11/9)

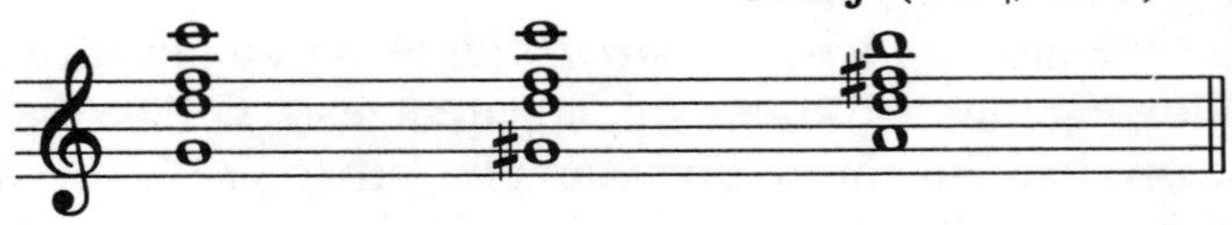

## MINOR 7th CHORD

Available Upper-Structure Triads; IV (11 13 1) {dorian} IIm (9 11 13) {dorian} ♭VII (♭7 9 11) Vm (5 ♭7 9)

**1)** IV over I-7; F over C-7

Chord tones in bass; **F/E♭** (F7) **F/G** **F/B♭**
Tension 9 in the bass will be avoided due to the potential *♭9th interval.*

This complete structure; F major triad over C-7, produces a specific modal dorian chord. When isolating the three possible triad-over-bass voicings, only the one containing the ♭7th in the bass (F/B♭) *dictates* a modal dorian voicing.

a) D-7(11) G13(♭9) E/D **F/E♭** C-6(11)

b) D-7♭5 G13(♭9) E/F **F/G** C-6(11)

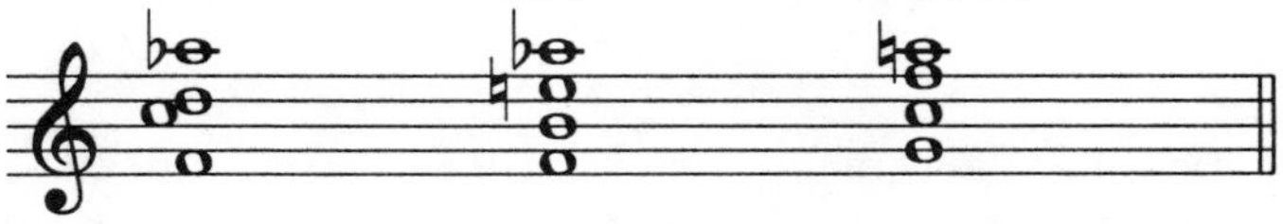

c) A-7♭5(♭13) Cm/F D7♭5(♭9) A♭/G♭ **C/F** G-7(13/11)

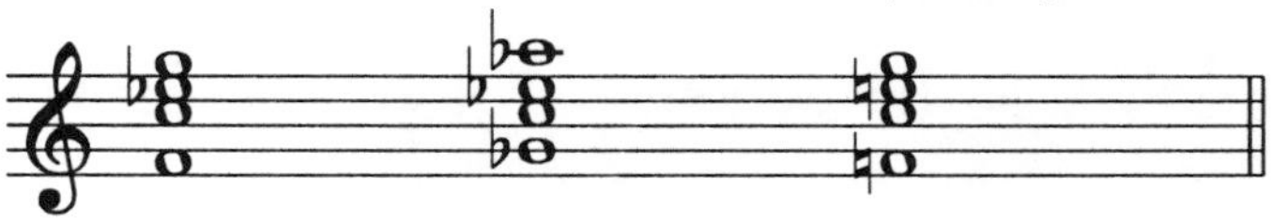

**2)** ♭VII over I-7; B♭ over C-7

Chord tones in bass; **B♭/C** **B♭/E♭** **B♭/G** (G-7)
Tensions in bass; **B♭/A** {dorian} (contains ♭9th interval)

a) D-9 G+7(♯9) **B♭/C** C-9(11)

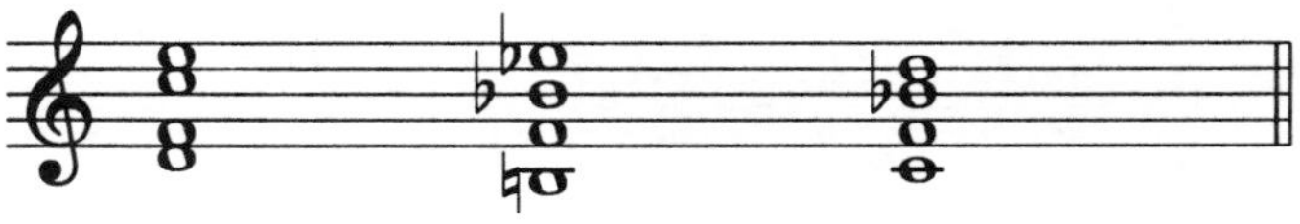

b) D-9(11) C/D G7(♭9/alt5) A♭m/D♭ **B♭/E♭** C-9(11)

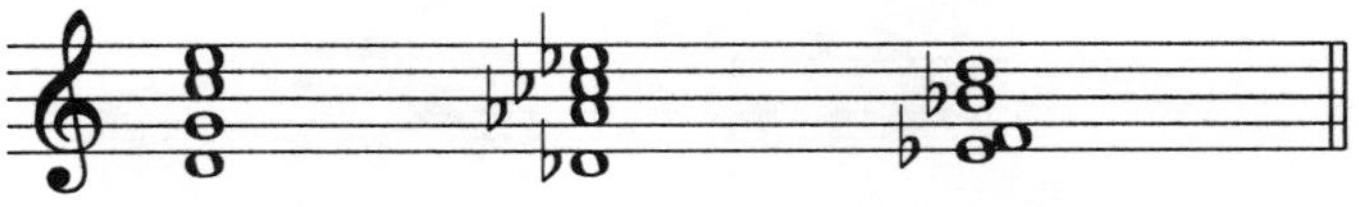

c) D-7♭5 G7(♭9) **B♭/G**(C-9(11))

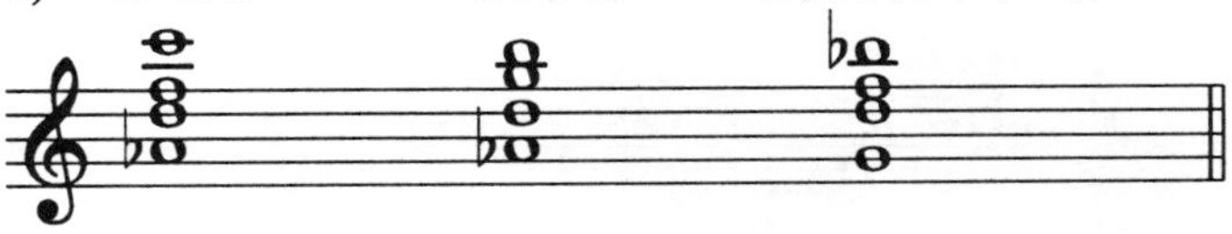

**3)** IIm over I-7; Dm over C-7

Chord tones in bass; **Dm/C** (D-7) **Dm/E♭** **Dm/G** **Dm/B♭** (B♭maj7)
Tensions are not available in bass.

a) F♯-7♭5(11) B+7(♭9) **F♯m/E** Em(13/11/9)

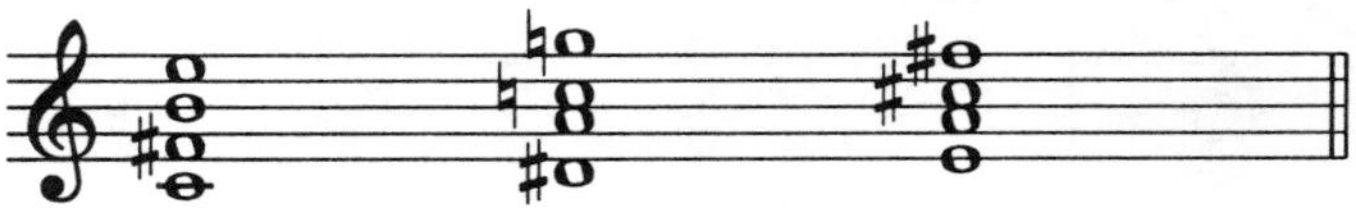

b) D-7♭5(11) G7(♯11/♭9) **Dm/E♭** Cm(13/11/9)

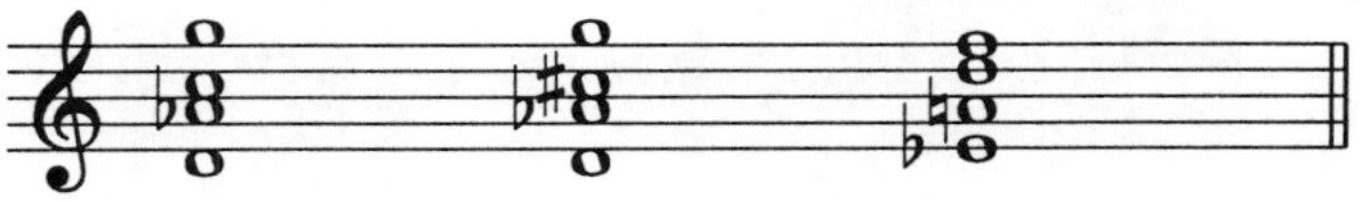

c) D-7♭5 G7(alt9) B♭7 **Dm/G** Cm(13/11/9)

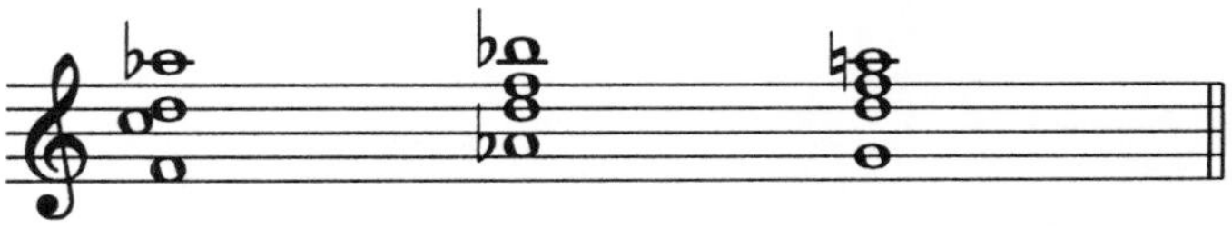

d) A-7♭5(♭13) F9 D+7(♯9) B♭/G♭ **Am/F** G-7(13/11/9)

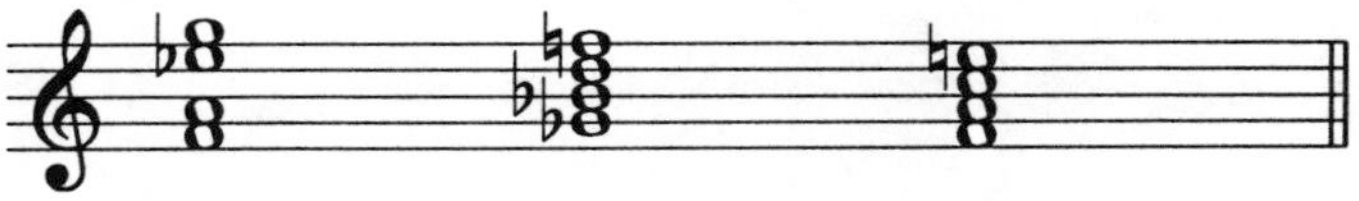

**4)** Vm over I-7; Gm over C-7

| | | |
|---|---|---|
| Chord tones in bass; | **Gm/C** | **Gm/E♭** (E♭maj7 or C-9) |
| Tensions in bass; | **Gm/F** (G-7) | **Gm/A** {dorian} (contains ♭9th interval) |

a) D-9(11) / C/D — G7(alt5) / E♭+7 — **Gm/C** / C-9

b) D-9 — G+7(♭9) — **Gm/F** / C-9(11)

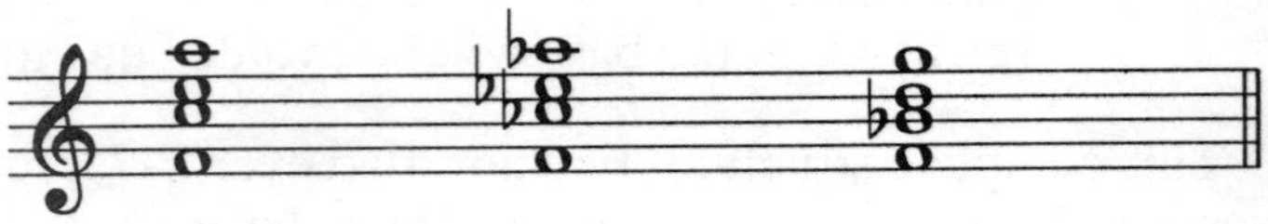

## MINOR 7♭5 CHORD

Tension ♭9 on a min7♭5 chord will be introduced for the first time. It <u>must</u> be used in an appropriate context. Tensions ♭9, natural 9, and 11 will be avoided in the bass. Tensions 9 and 11 produce potential ♭9th intervals when placed in the bass.

| | | | |
|---|---|---|---|
| <u>Available Upper-Structure Triads;</u> | ♭VII (♭7 9 11) | ♭VI (♭13 1 ♭3) | IVm (11 ♭13 1) |
| (contain ♭9th interval); | ♭II (♭9 11 ♭13) | ♭V (♭5 ♭7 ♭9) | ♭VIIm (♭7 ♭9 11) |

**1)** ♭VII over I-7♭5; B♭ over C-7♭5

| | | | |
|---|---|---|---|
| Chord tones in bass; | **B♭/C** | **B♭/E♭** | **B♭/G♭** (most characteristic) |
| Tensions in bass; | **B♭/A♭** (B♭7) | | |

a) **B♭/C** / C-7♭5(11/9) — F13(♭9) / D/C — B♭m(11) / D♭6(9)

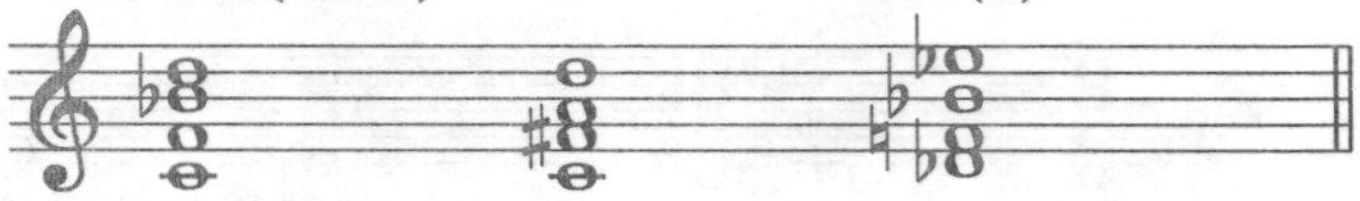

b) **B♭/E♭** / C-7♭5(11/9) — F7(♭9/alt5) / B/D♭ — B♭-6(11/9) / Cm/D♭

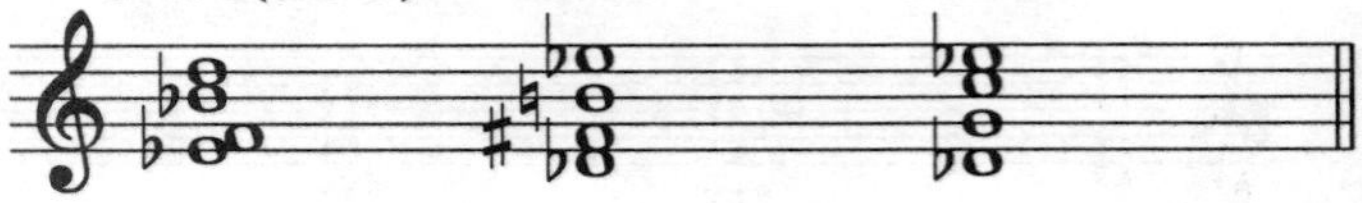

c) **B♭/G♭** / C-7♭5(11/9) — F+(♭9) / G♭-maj7 — B♭-9(11) / F-7

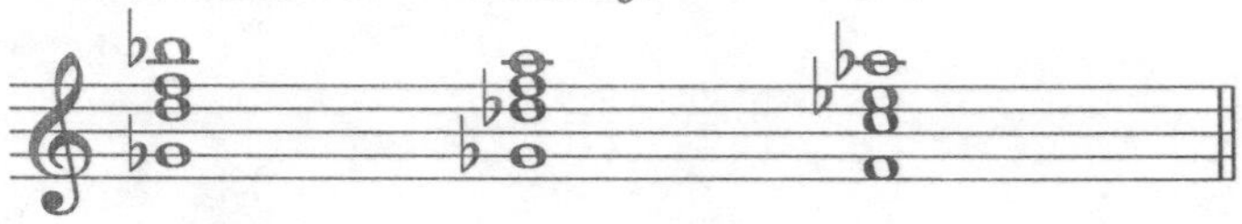

d) **B♭/A♭** / C-7♭5(♭13/11/9) — F+7(♭9) — B♭-9

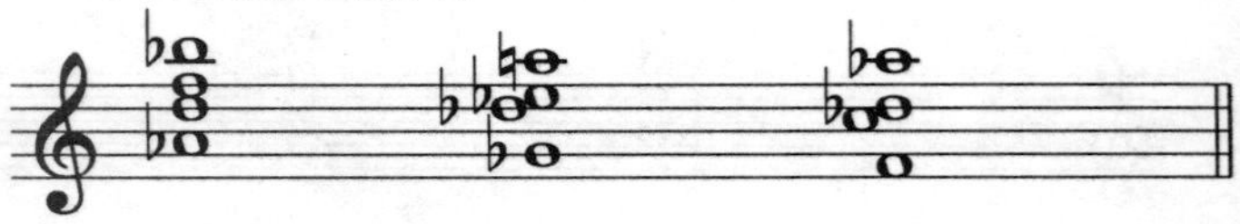

**2)** ♭VI over I-7♭5; A♭ over C-7♭5

| | | |
|---|---|---|
| Chord tones in bass; | **A♭/G♭** (G♭7) | **A♭/B♭** |
| Tensions not available in bass | | |

a) **A♭/G♭** / C-7♭5(♭13) — F+7(♭9) — B♭-9(11)

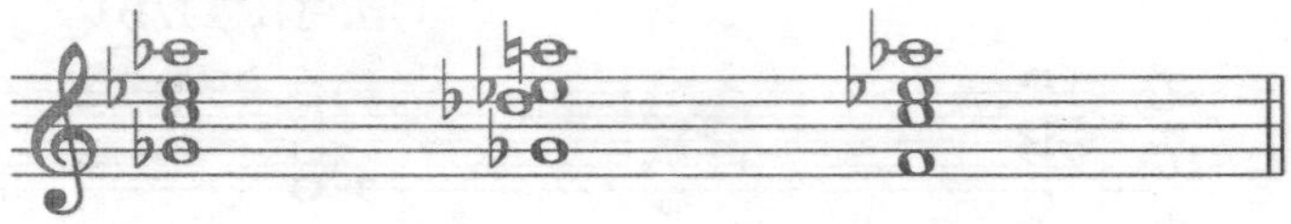

b) **E♭/F** / G-7♭5(♭13) — C+7(♯9) — F-maj9

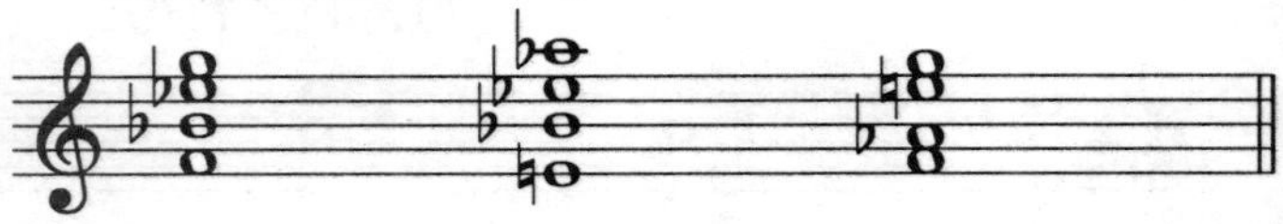

**3)** IVm over I-7♭5; Fm over C-7♭5

Chord tones in bass; **Fm/E♭** (F-7) **Fm/G♭** **Fm/B♭**
Tensions not available in bass

a) **Fm/E♭** F7♭5(♭9) B♭-maj9
C-7♭5(♭13/11) B7 F/D♭

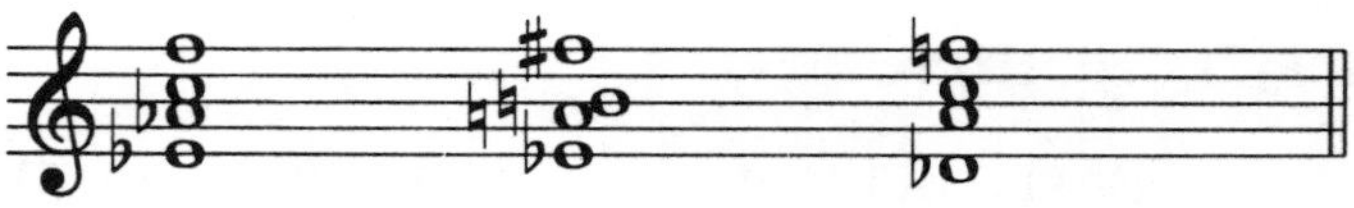

b) **Fm/G♭** F13(♭9) B♭-6(9)
C-7♭5(♭13/11) D/E♭

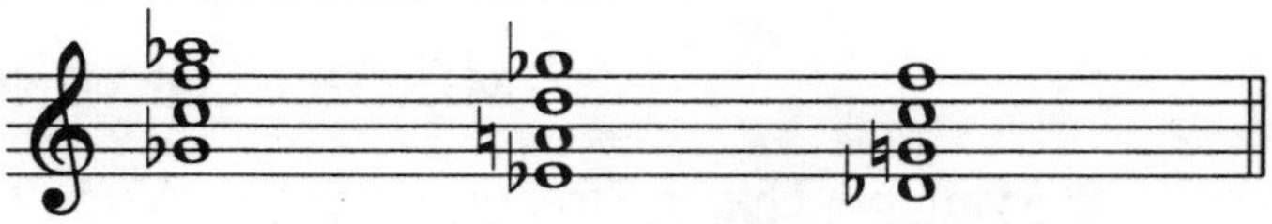

c) **Cm/F** C+7(♯9) F-6
G-7♭5(♭13/11) A♭/E

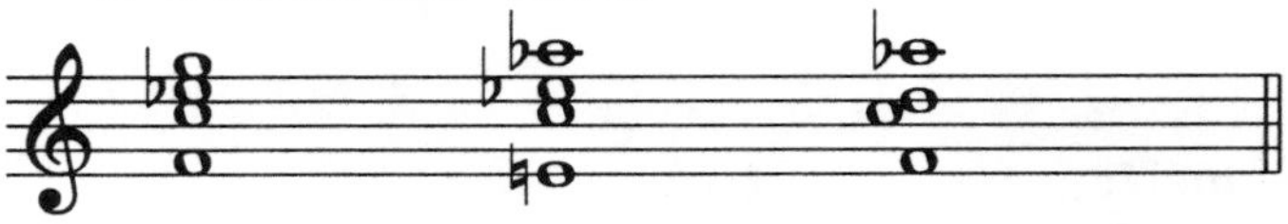

**4)** ♭II over I-7♭5; D♭ over C-7♭5

Chord tones in bass; **D♭/C** **D♭/E♭** **D♭/G♭** **D♭/B♭** (B♭-7)

a) **G♭/F** B♭7(♯9) E♭-maj7
F-7♭5(♭13/11/♭9) B♭m/D

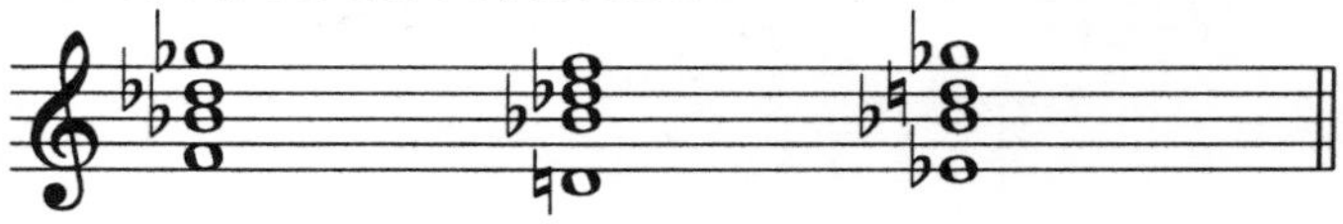

b) **D♭/E♭** F7♭5(♭9) B♭-6(9)
C-7♭5(♭13/11/♭9) B(♯11)

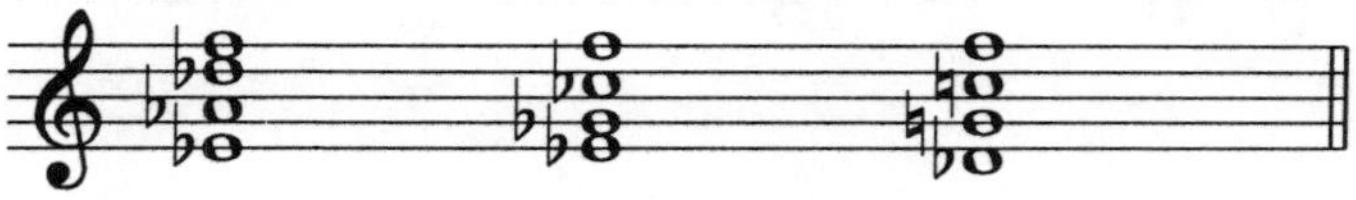

c) **D♭/G♭** F(♭9) B♭-6
C-7♭5(♭13/11/♭9) F/G♭

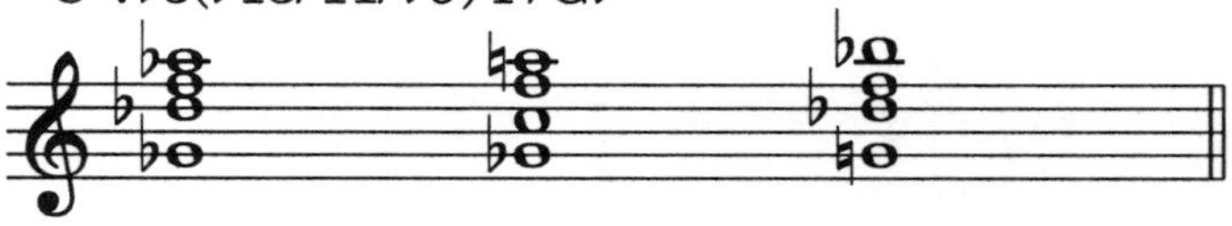

d) **G♭/E♭** B♭+7(♯9) E♭-6
F-7♭5(♭13/11/♭9) G♭/D

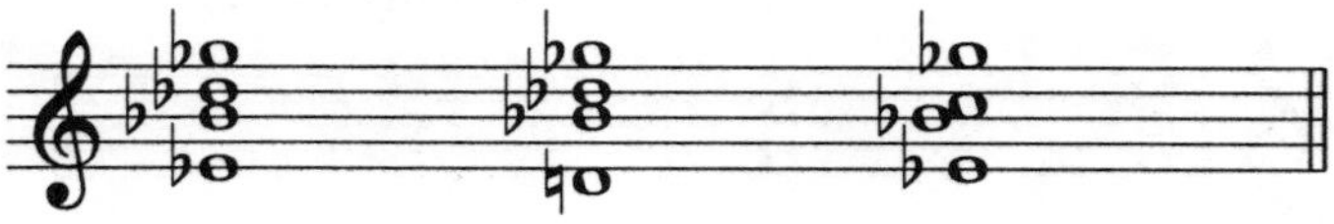

**5)** ♭V over I-7♭5; G♭ over C-7♭5

Chord tones in bass; **G♭/C** **G♭/E♭** (E♭-7)
Tensions in bass; **G♭/A♭**

a) **G♭/C** F13(♭9) B♭m(11)
C-7♭5(♭9) D/C

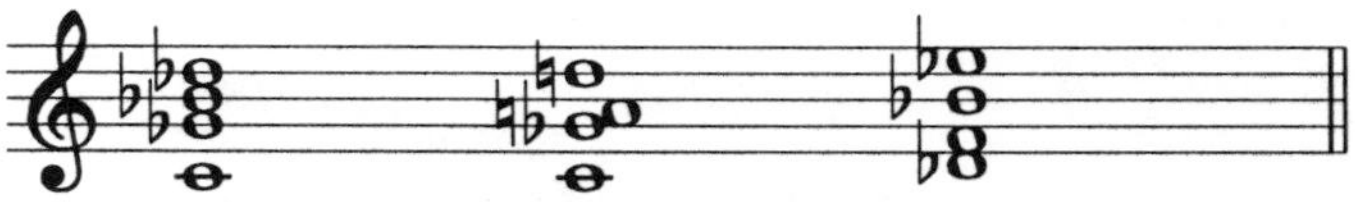

b) **G♭/E♭** F7♭5 B♭-maj9
C-7♭5(♭9) F/D♭

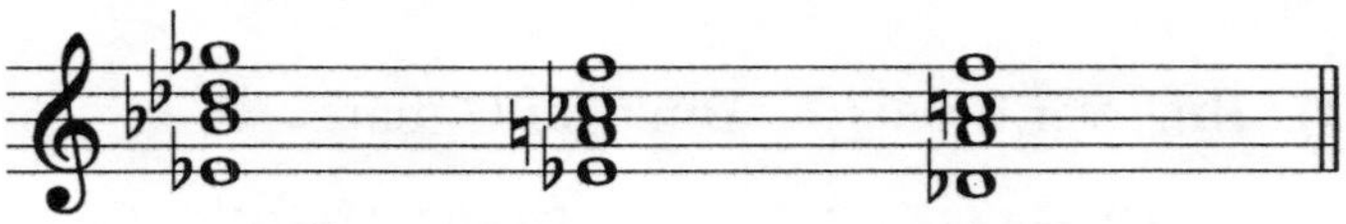

c) **G♭/A♭** F7(♭9) B♭-7(11)
C-7♭5(♭13/♭9)

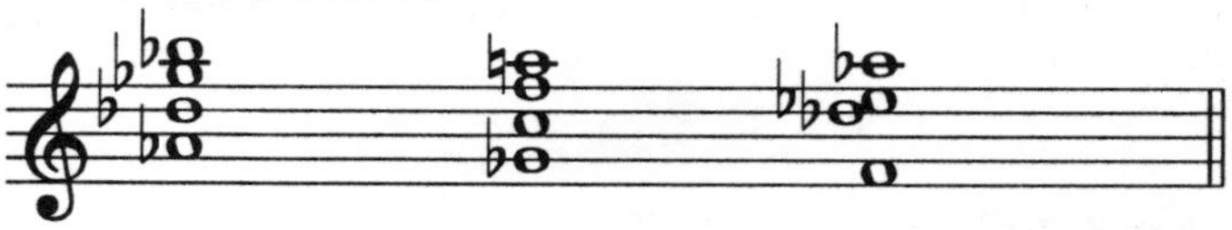

**6)** ♭VIIm over I-7♭5; B♭m over C-7♭5

Chord tones in bass; **B♭m/C** **B♭m/E♭** **B♭m/G♭** (G♭maj7)
Tensions in bass; **B♭m/A♭** (B♭-7)

a) **B♭m/C** F7(alt5) B♭-7
C-7♭5(11/♭9) C♯+7

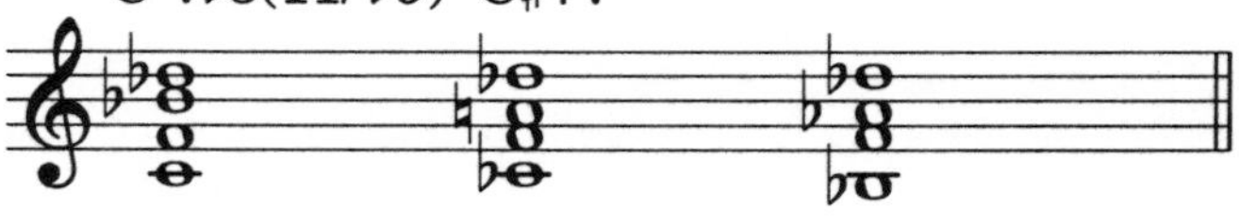

b) **B♭m/E♭** F+7 B♭-9(11)
C-7♭5(11/♭9) A♭/D♭

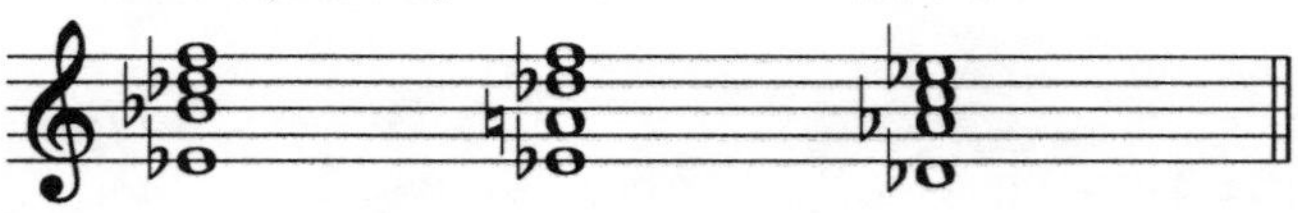

c) **B♭m/G♭** F13(♭9) B♭-6
C-7♭5(11/♭9) D/F

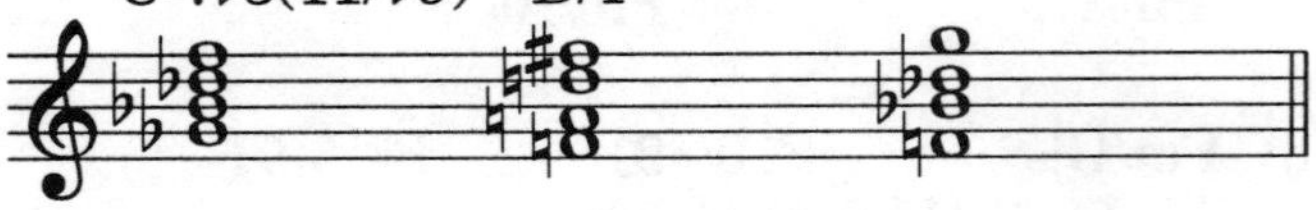

d) **Gm/F** D7(♭9/alt5) G-6(9)
A-7♭5(♭13/11/♭9)

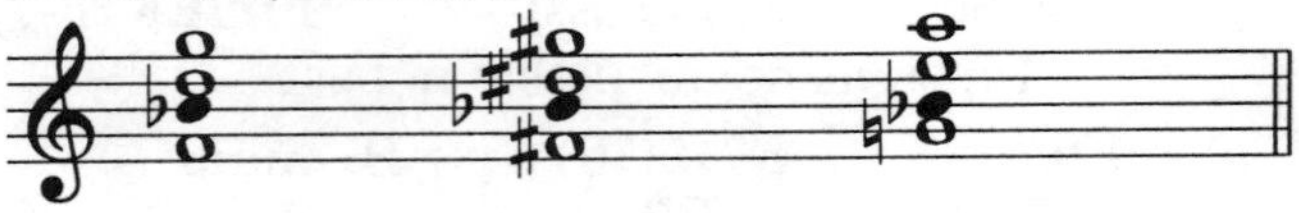

**MINOR 6 and MINOR (maj7) CHORDS**

<u>Available Upper-Structure Triads;</u> V (5 7 9) IV (11 6{13} 1) IIm (9 11 13{6})

* Tension 9 in bass will be avoided.

**1)** V over I-6; G over C-6

Chord tones in bass; **G/C** **G/E♭** (E♭maj7♯5) **G/A**
Tensions in bass; **G/F** (G7).....As was done in the ***Tensions 9 & 11*** chapter, this structure will be avoided as a C-maj7(11/9) chord due to its "ambiguous" function.

a) D-7♭5 G7(alt5) **G/C**
E♭+7 C-maj9

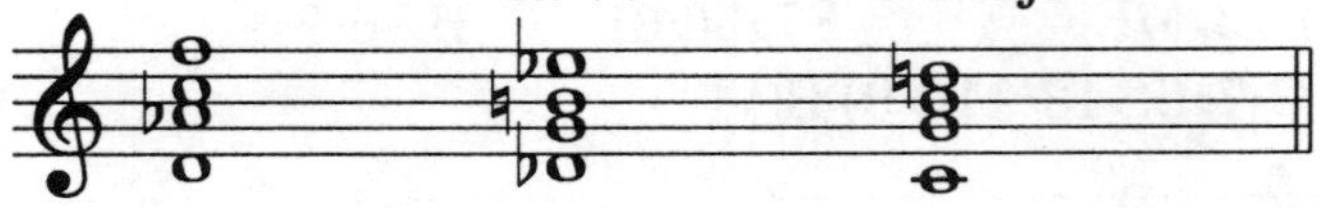

b) D-7♭5(9) G7(♭9/alt5) **G/E♭**
E+7 A♭m/D♭ C-maj9

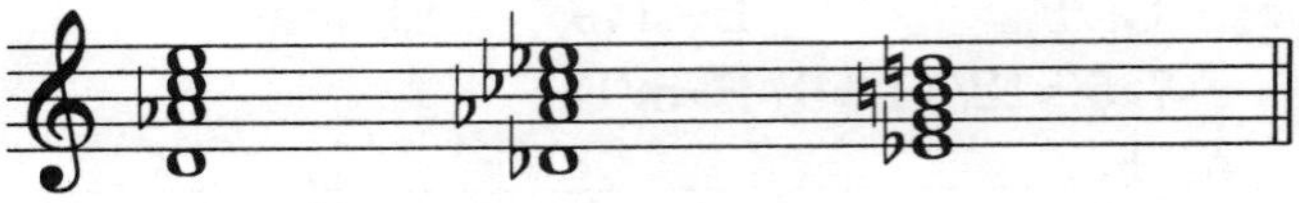

c) B-7♭5(11) E+7(alt9) **E/F♯**
C/F A-maj7(9/6)

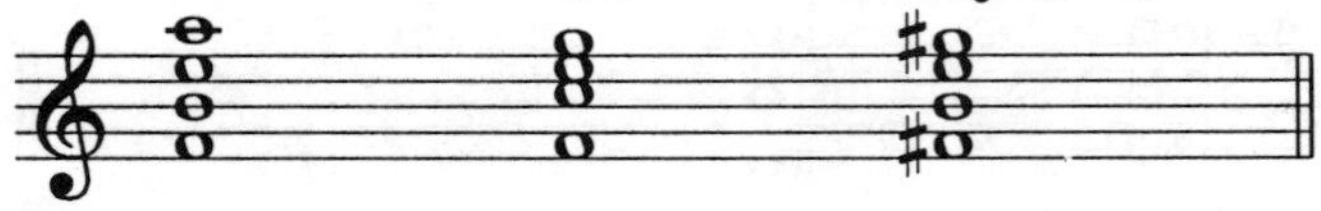

**2)** IV over I-maj7; F over C-maj7

Chord tones in bass; **F/E♭** and **F/G** examples can be found under "**MINOR 7th CHORD**" in this chapter. **F/B** contains a ♭9th interval and will not be examined for its C minor function. It is examined for its min7♭5 and dom7 functions under those chord headings.

**3)** IIm over I-maj7; Dm over C-maj7

Chord tones in bass; **Dm/C**, **Dm/E♭**, and **Dm/G** examples can be found under "**MINOR 7th CHORD**" in this chapter. **Dm/B** (B-7♭5) will be presented, but will be transposed to **Am/F♯**. Like the previous structure **G/F**, which was being used as a C-maj7(11/9) chord, **Am/F♯** produces an amiguous function when used as a G-maj7(13/11/9) chord, forming G minor's complete V9 chord; (D9).

A-7♭5 D+7(♯9) **Am/F♯**(G-maj7(13/11/9))

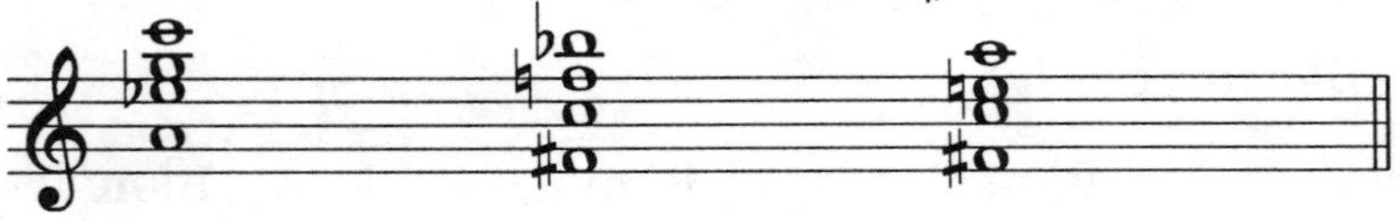

## DOMINANT 7th CHORD

Available *Major* Upper-Structure Triads;

II ♭III *III ♭V ♭VI VI *VII

Available *Minor* Upper-Structure Triads;

♭IIm ♭IIIm ♭Vm Vm *♭VIm VIm

*These triads contain the *major* 7th of the original dom 7 chord and will be supported by *altered* tensions.

Tensions ♯9 and 13 will be avoided in the bass while tension 9 *will* appear in the bass.
Tension 9 in the bass should be used cautiously.

As mentioned earlier, different inversions containing the ♭9th interval will be examined on dominant chords with a V7 function. The following is a list of those structures containing the ♭9th interval and functioning as a "C7" chord;

Major; **E♭/G♭** **E/G** **E/B♭** **F♯/C** **A♭/G** **A/C** **B/B♭**
Minor; **D♭m/C** **D♭m/G** **G♭m/C** **Gm/F♯** **A♭m/G** **A♭m/B♭**

Note that only three major and three minor structures are used;

| | | | |
|---|---|---|---|
| 1) Major triad over ♭3rd; | E♭/G♭ | E/G | A/C |
| 2) Major triad over ♭5th; | E/B♭ | F♯/C | |
| 3) Major triad over 7th; | A♭/G | B/B♭ | |
| 1) Minor triad over 7th; | D♭m/C | Gm/F♯ | A♭m/G |
| 2) Minor triad over ♭5th; | D♭m/G | G♭m/C | |
| 3) Minor triad over 9th; | A♭m/B♭ | | |

**1)** II over I7; D over C7 (Tensions not available in bass)

Chord tones in bass; **D/C** (D7) **D/E** **D/G** **D/B♭** (B♭maj7♯5)

Tensions 9, ♯11, and 13 appear most commonly on *Sub V* chords in a dominant capacity. The following examples will use these tensions on V7 chords, producing an interesting if not unexpected V7 sound.

a) A/D — B-9(11) F♯/E — E7(13/♯11/9) B/E — Amaj7(13/ ♯11/9)

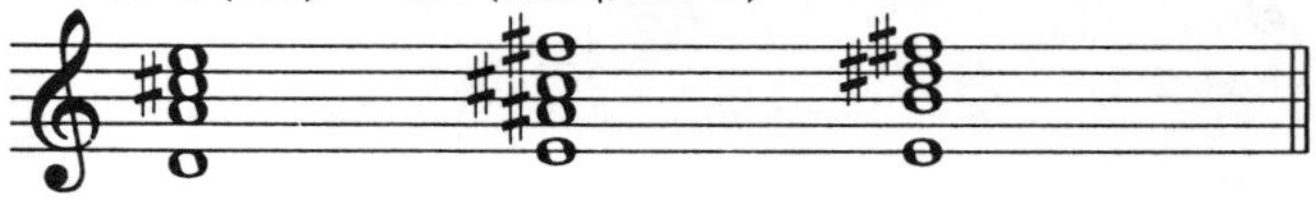

b) G-7(11) D/E — C7(13/♯11/9) C/F — Fmaj9

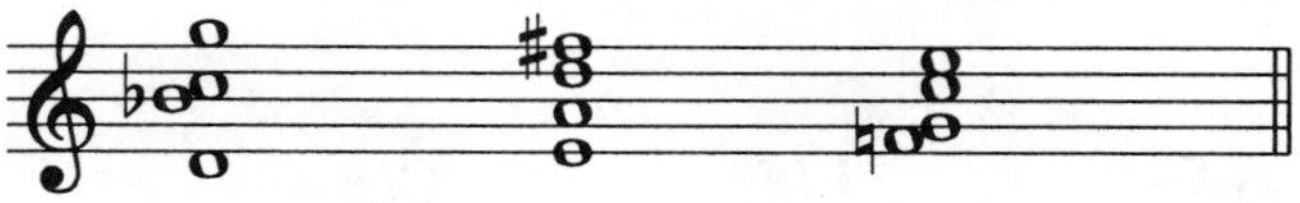

c) D/G — E-9(11) B/E — A7(13/♯11/9) A/D — Dmaj9

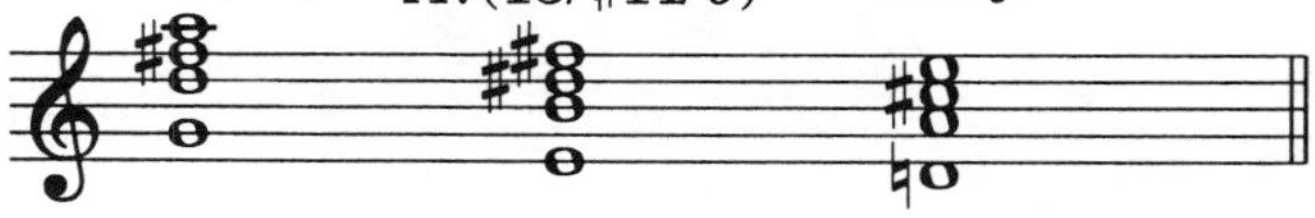

d) D-9 A/F — G7(13/♯11/9) C(add9)

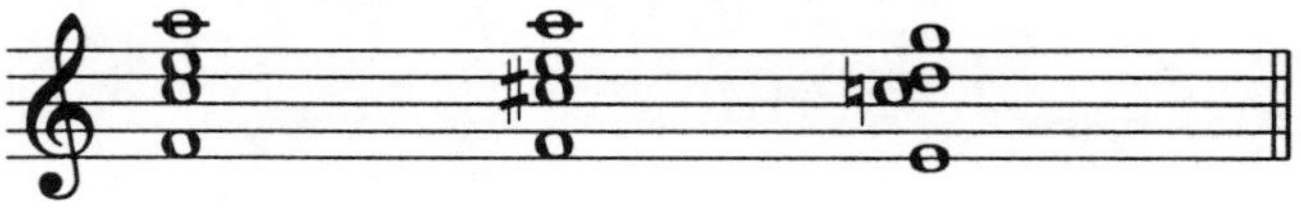

**2)** ♭III over I7; E♭ over C7

| | | | |
|---|---|---|---|
| Chord tones in bass; | **E♭/C** (C-7) | **E♭/E** | |
| Tensions in bass; | **E♭/D♭** (E♭7) | **E♭/A♭** | **E♭/G♭** (contains ♭9th interval) |

a) C-9 — **A♭/F** F7(♯9) — B♭maj7

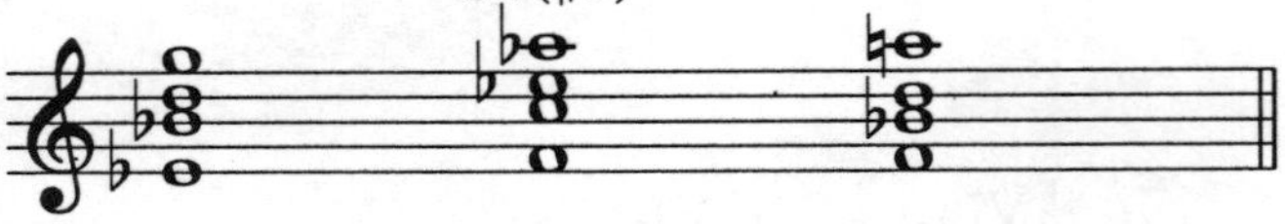

b) F/B♭ G-9(11) — **E♭/E** C7(♯9) — C/F Fmaj9

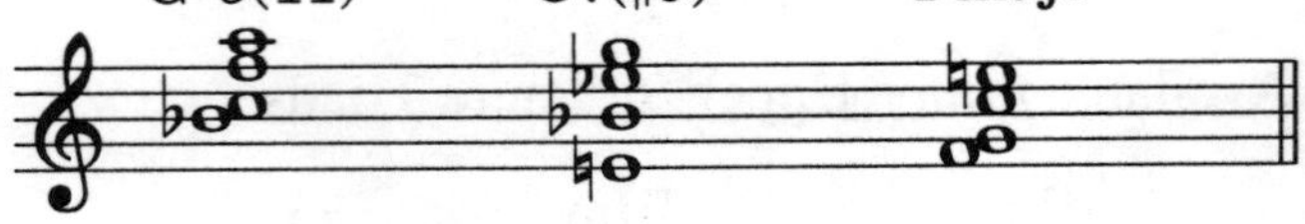

c) C-9 — **A♭/G♭** F7(alt9) — B♭maj9

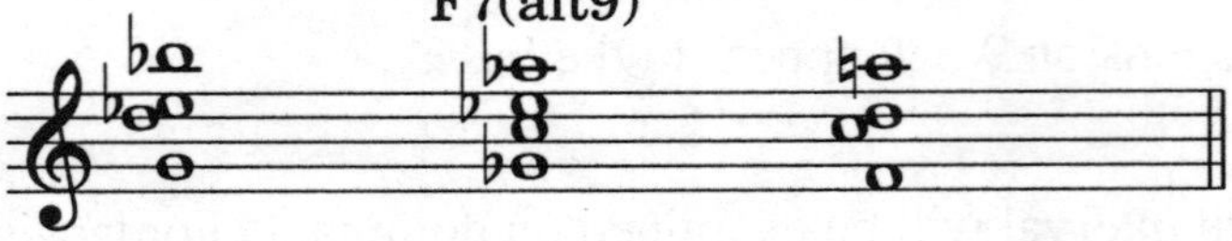

d) D/G E-9(11) — **C/F** A7(♭13/♯9) — **E/F♯** D(13/♯11/9)

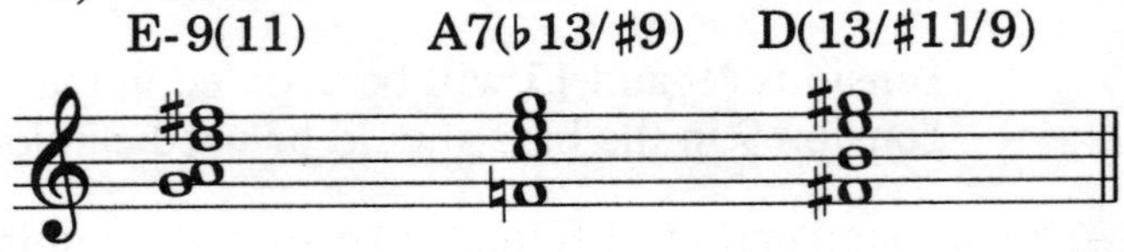

e) F/G G-9(11) — **E♭/G♭** C7(♯11/♯9) — C/F Fmaj9

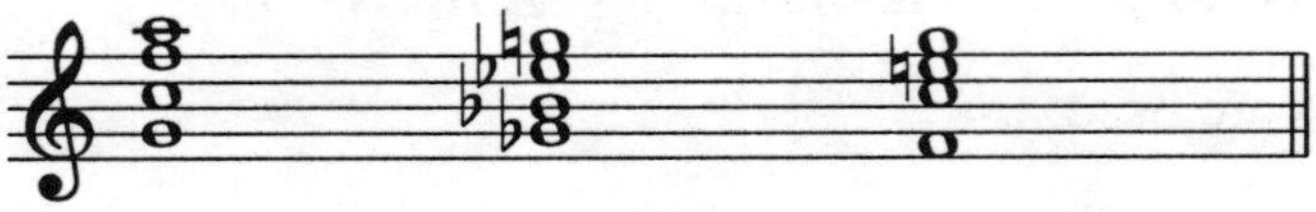

**3)** III over I7; E over C7

| | | | |
|---|---|---|---|
| Chord tones in bass; | **E/C** (Cmaj7♯5) | **E/G** | **E/B♭** |
| Tensions in bass; | **E/D♭** (D♭-7) | **E/F♯** | |

a) C/F D-9(11) — **B/G** Gmaj7♯5 — D/G C(13/♯11/9)

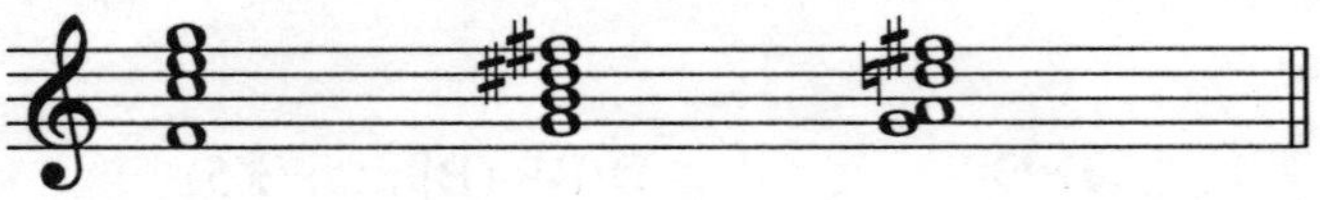

b) G-9 — **E/G** C7(♭13/maj7) — C/F Fmaj9

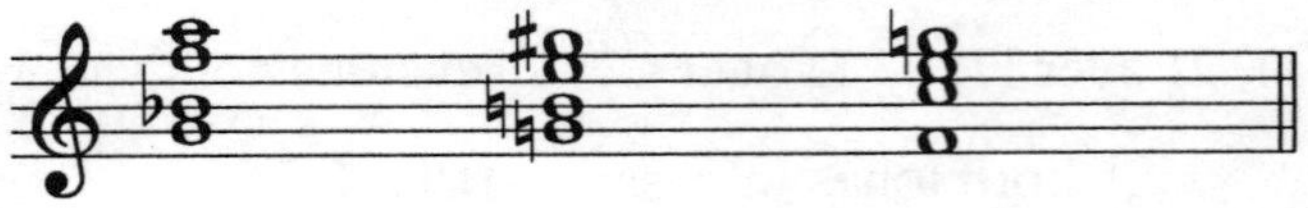

c) C/F D-9(11) — **B/F** G+7(maj7) — C(add9)

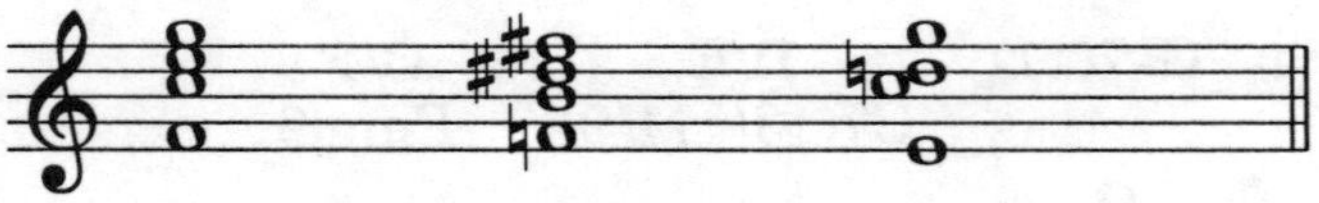

d) C-9(11) — **A/F♯** F+7(♭9/maj7) — F/G B♭maj9(6)

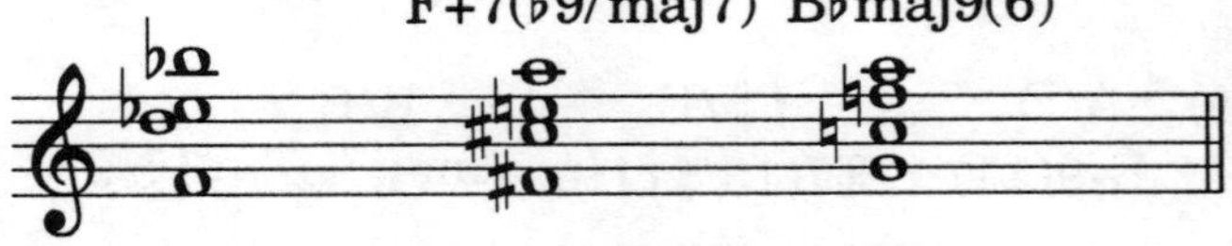

e) G-9 — **E/F♯** C7alt5(maj7) — C/F Fmaj9

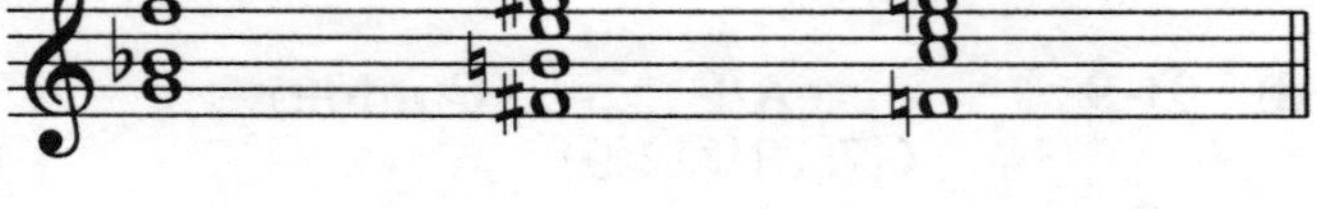

**4)** ♭V over I7; G♭ over C7

Chord tones in bass; **G♭/C** **G♭/E** (G♭-7) **F♯/G**
Tensions in bass; **F♯/G♯**

a) B♭/E♭ **B/F** C/F
C-9(11) F7♭5(♭9) B♭(13/♯11/9)

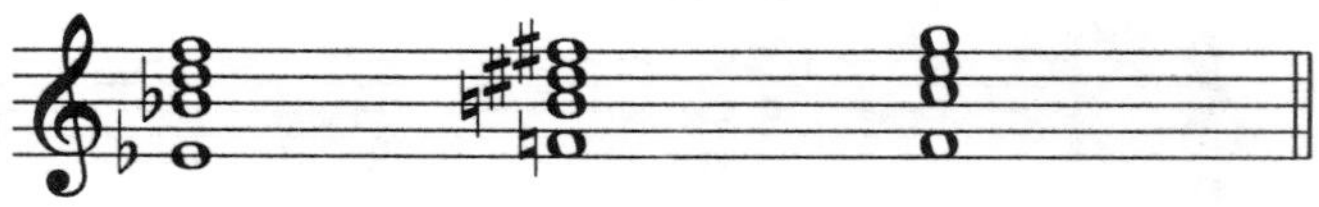

b) G-7(11) **F♯/E** F6(9)
C7♭5(♭9)

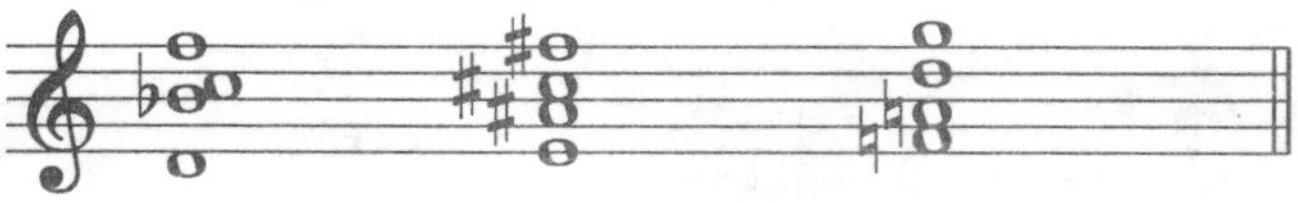

c) G-7(11) **G♭/G** F6(9)
C7(♯11/♭9)

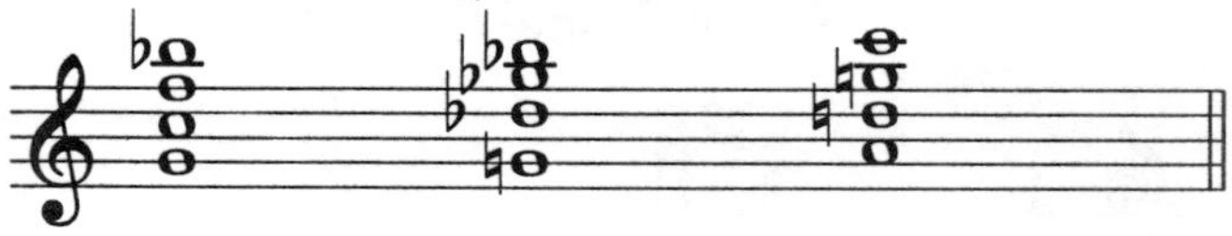

d) F/G **F♯/G♯** G/A
G-9(11) C7(♭9/alt5) F(13/♯11/9)

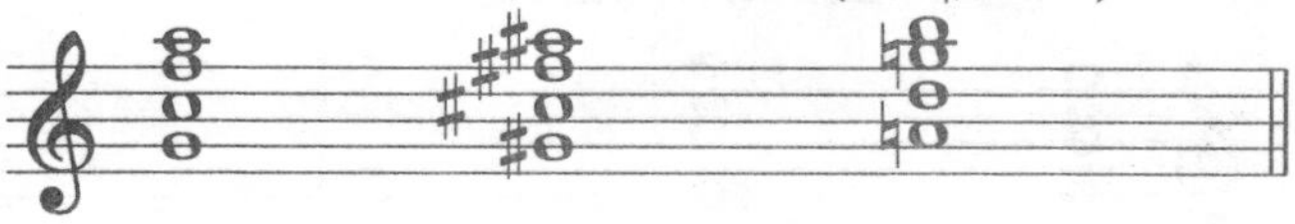

**5)** ♭VI over I7; A♭ over C7

Chord tones in bass; **A♭/E** (Emaj7♯5) **A♭/G** **A♭/B♭**
Tensions in bass; **A♭/D♭** **A♭/G♭** (A♭7)

a) F/D **A♭/E** C/F
G-9(11) C+7(♯9) Fmaj9

b) B♭/G **A♭/G** C/F
G-7 C7(♭13/♯9) Fmaj9

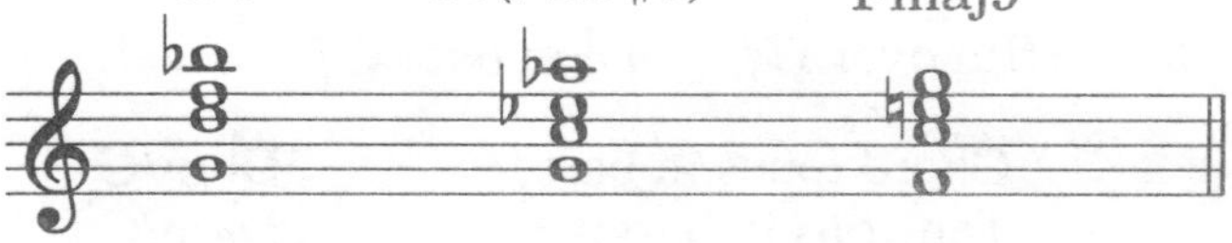

c) C/F **E♭/F** G/E
D-9(11) G+7(♯9) Cmaj9

d) C/F **E♭/A♭** D/G
D-9(11) G+7(alt9) C(13/♯11/9)

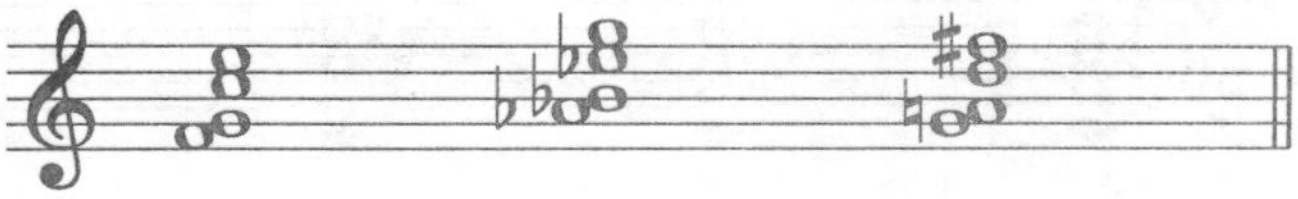

e) F/G **A♭/G♭** C/F
G-9(11) C7(♯9/alt5) Fmaj9

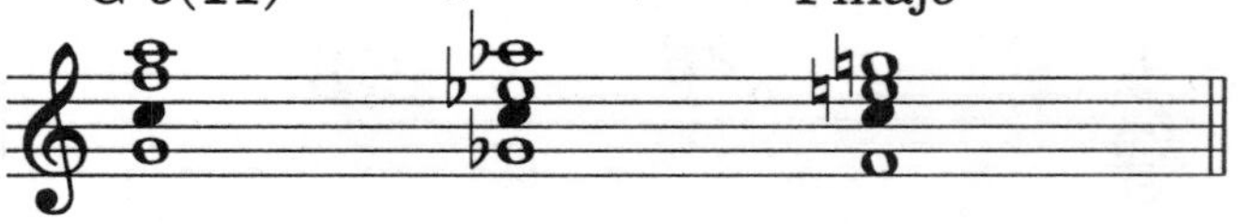

**6)** VI over I7; A over C7

Chord tones in bass; **A/C** **A/G** (A7) **A/B♭**
Tensions in bass; **A/F♯** (F♯-7)

a) B♭/C **A/C** Fmaj9/C
G-7(11) C13(♭9)

b) B♭/G **A/G** C/F
G-7 C13(♭9) Fmaj9

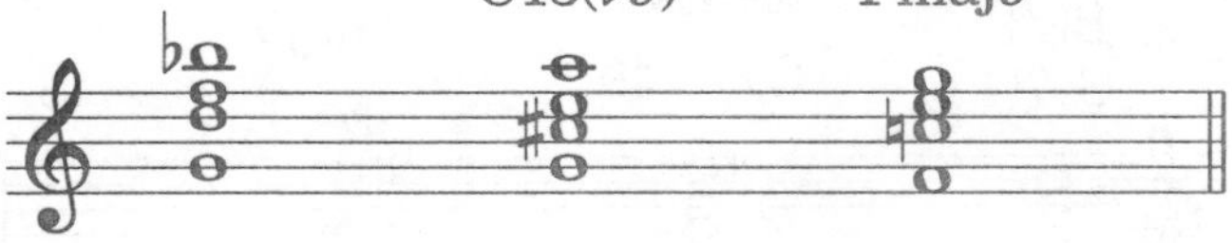

c) C/A♭ **E/F** G/E♭
D-7♭5(11/9) G13(♭9) C-maj9

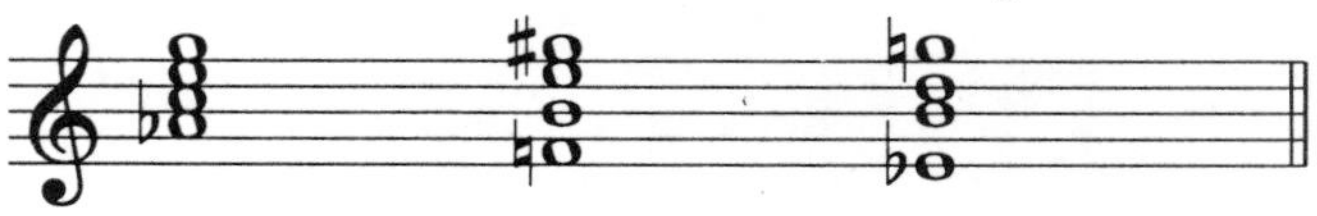

d) G-7(11) **A/F♯** Fmaj9(6)
C7♭5(13/♭9)

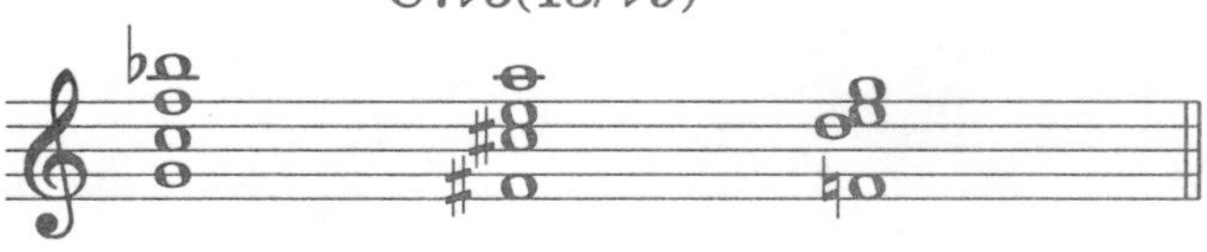

**7)** VII over I7; B over C7

Chord tones in bass; **B/C** **B/E** **B/G** **B/B♭**
Tensions in bass; **B/C♯** **B/G♯** (G♯-7)

a) B♭/C **B/C** C/F
G-7(11) C°maj7 Fmaj9

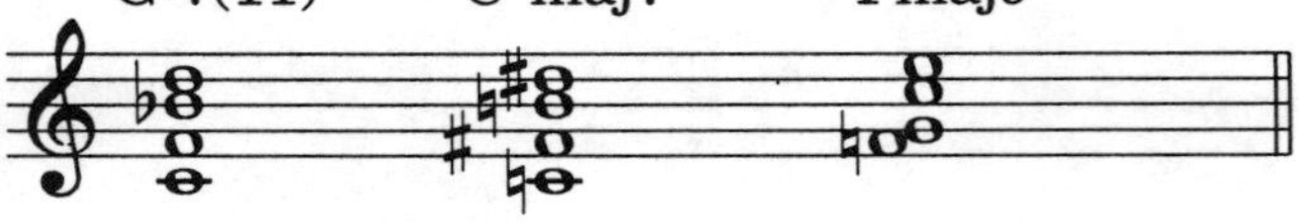

b) G-9 **B/E** Fmaj9
Cmaj7(♯11/♯9)

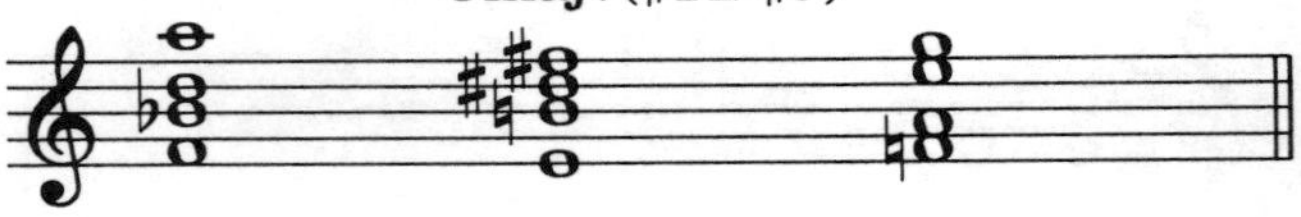

c) G/E **A♭/E** D6(9)
E-7 Amaj7(♯11/♯9)

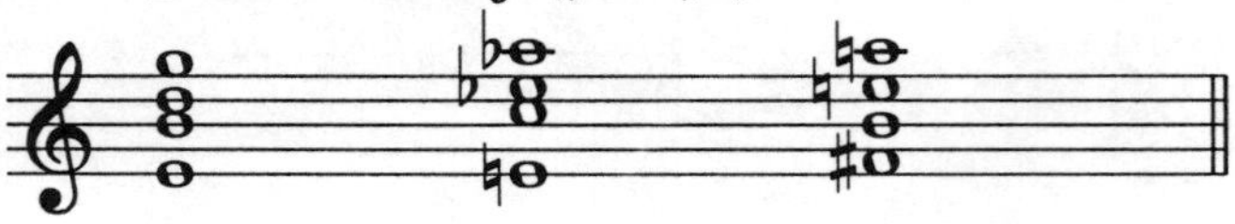

d) D-7(11) **F♯/F** G/E
G7♭5(♯9/maj7) Cmaj9

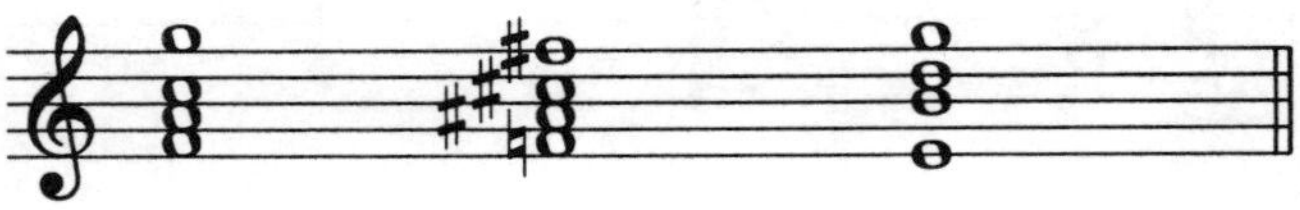

e) E♭/F **E/F♯** F/G
C-7(11) F7♭5(alt9/maj7) B♭maj9(6)

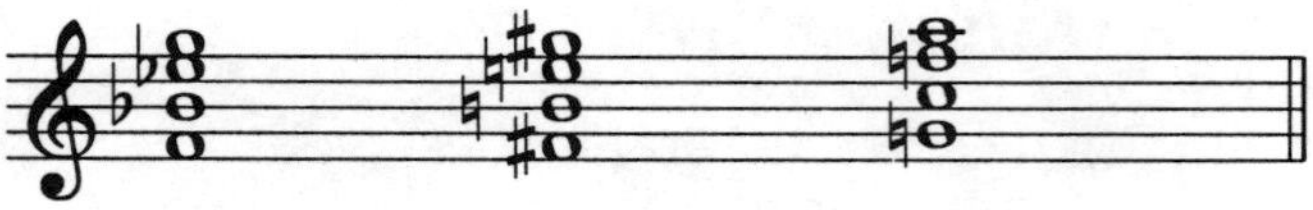

f) G/E **A♭/F** A/F♯
E-7 Amaj7(♯9/alt5) Dmaj9

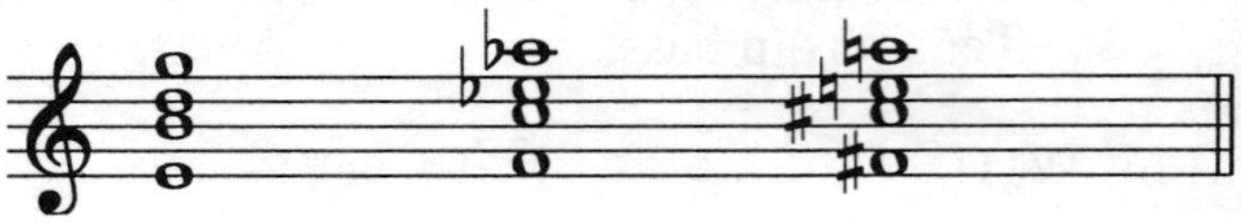

**8)** ♭IIm over I7; D♭m over C7

Chord tones in bass; **D♭m/C** **D♭m/G** **D♭m/B♭** (B♭-7♭5)
Tensions in bass; **D♭m/G♭**

a) B♭/C **D♭m/C** Fmaj7(6)
G-7(11) C+7(♭9) C6(9)

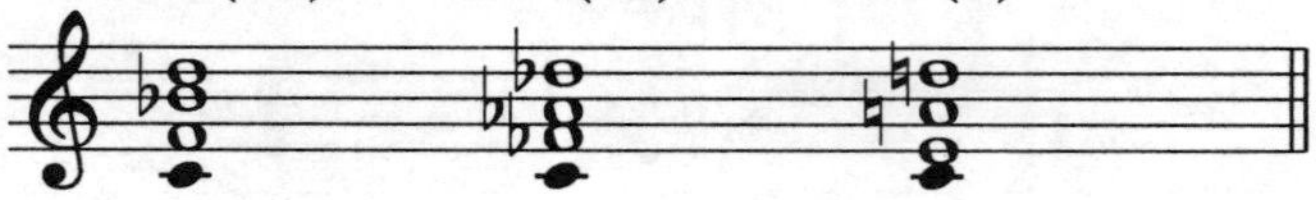

b) Dm/G **D♭m/G** C/F
G-9 C7(♭13/♭9) Fmaj9

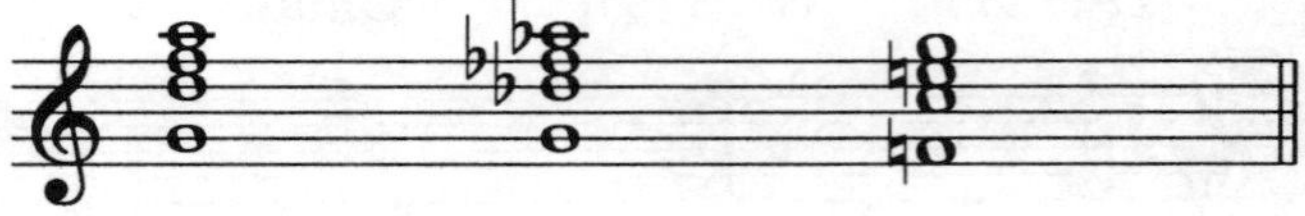

c) C+7 **G♯m/F** B+7
D-7♭5(♭13/9) G+7(♭9) C-maj7(6)

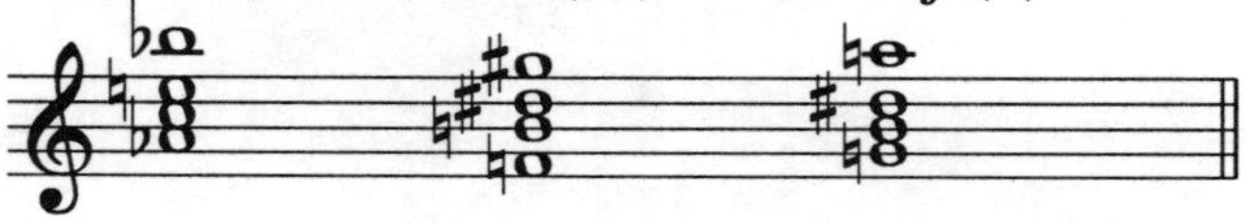

d) F/G **D♭m/G♭** Fmaj9(6)
G-9(11) C7(♭9/alt5)

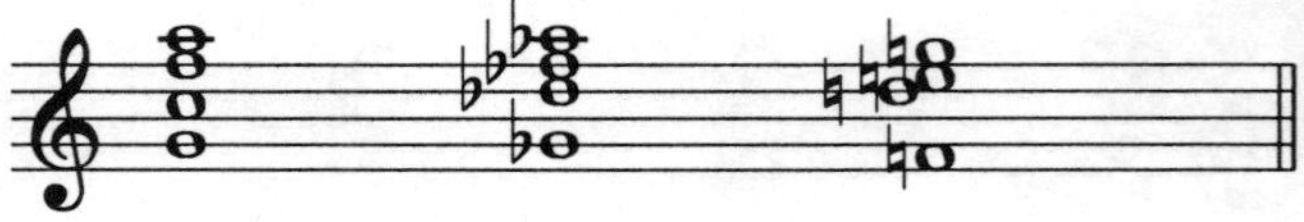

**9)** ♭IIIm over I7; E♭m over C7

Chord tones in bass; **E♭m/C** (C-7♭5) **E♭m/E** **E♭m/G**
Tensions in bass; **E♭m/D♭** (E♭-7) **E♭m/A♭**

a) B♭/C **E♭m/C** Fmaj9
G-7(11) C7♭5(♯9)

b) E♭7 **E♭m/E** E7(♯9)
G-7♭5(♭13) C7♭5(♯9) F-maj9(6)

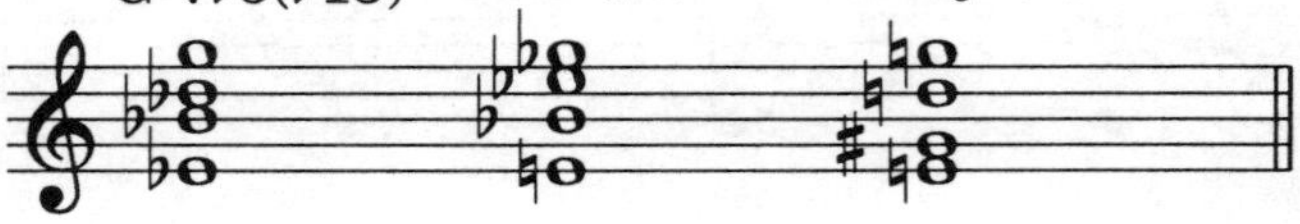

c) F/D D-7 — **B♭m/D** G7(♯11/♯9) — G/E Cmaj9

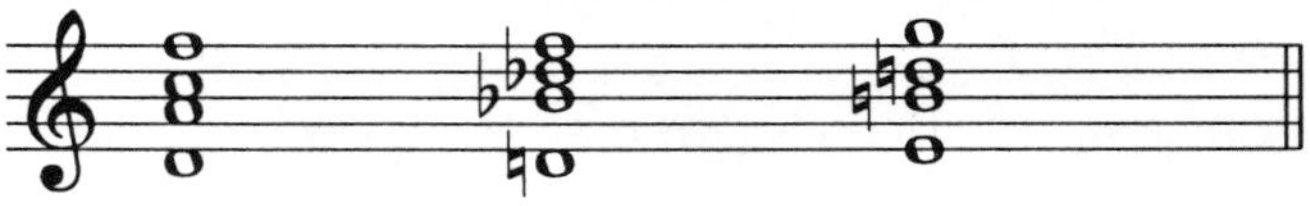

d) C-9 — **A♭m/G♭** F7♭5(alt9) — B♭maj7

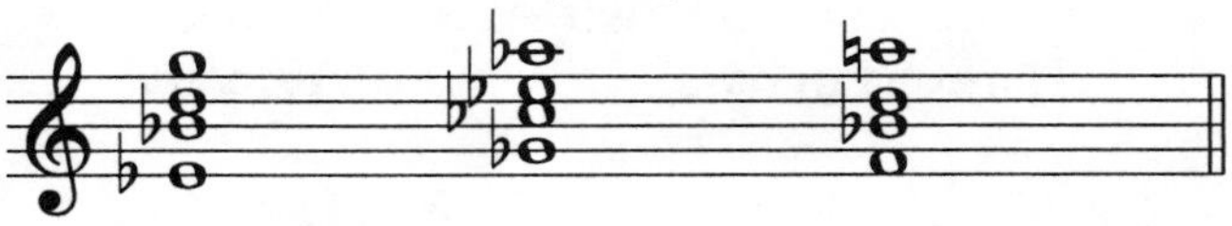

e) Am/D D-9 — **B♭m/E♭** G7(♯9/ alt5) — Bm/E Cmaj9(♯11)

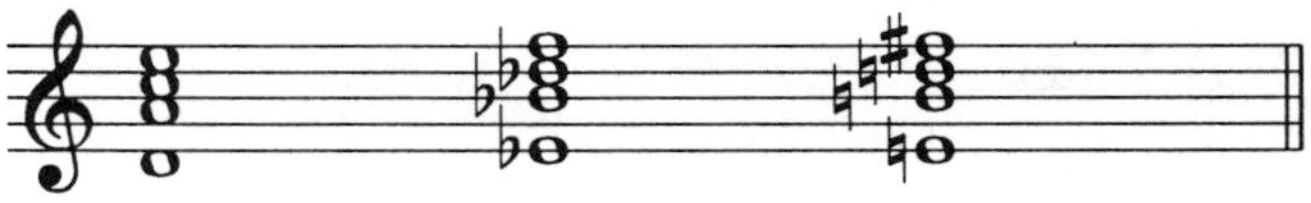

**10)** ♭Vm over I7; G♭m over C7 (Tensions not available in bass)

Chord tones in bass; **G♭m/C** **F♯m/E** (F♯-7) **F♯m/G** **G♭m/B♭**

a) B♭/C G-7(11) — **F♯m/C** C7♭5(13/♭9) — Dm/C F6

b) G-7(11) — **F♯m/E** C7(13/♯11/♭9) — F-6(9)

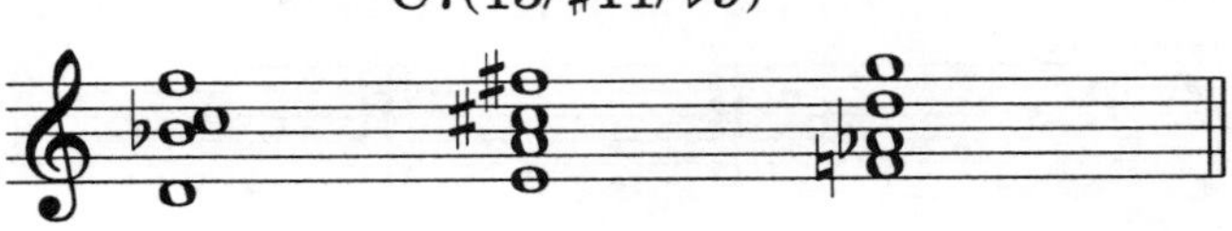

c) Dm/G G-9 — **F♯m/G** C7(13/♯11/♭9) — F(add9)

d) C/F D-9(11) — **D♭m/F** G7(13/♯11/♭9) — C(add9)

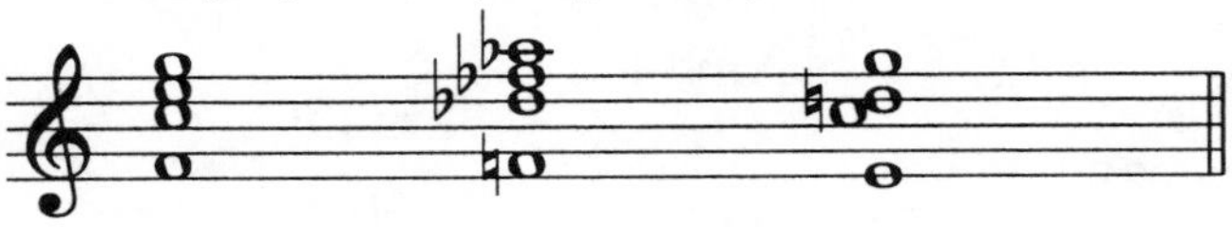

*Note the contrary chromatic motion in the above example "b)"; **(2a)(3a)(4d)**, and above example "c)"; **(3a)(4d)**.

**11)** Vm over I7; Gm over C7

Chord tones in bass; **Gm/C** **Gm/E** (E-7♭5 or C9)
Tensions in bass; **Gm/F♯** **Gm/A♭**

a) B♭/E♭ C-9(11) — **Cm/F** F9 — B♭maj7

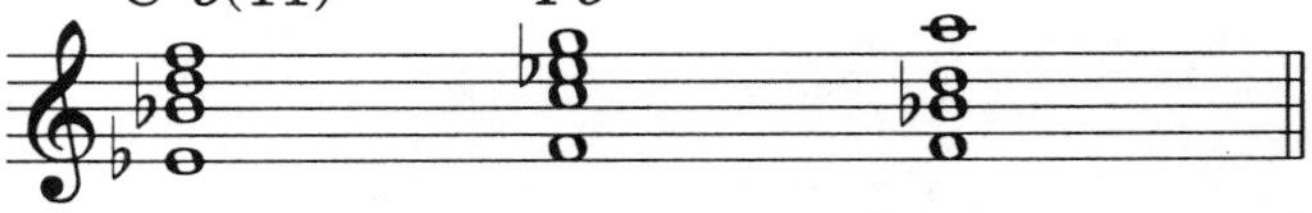

b) Gm/F G-7 — **Gm/F♯** C9(♯11) — G/F F(13/♯11/9)

c) G6(9) Em(11) — **Em/F** A9(♭13) — E/F♯ D(13/♯11/9)

**12)** ♭VIm over I7;   A♭m over C7

Chord tones in bass;   **A♭m/C**   **A♭m/E** (Emaj7)   **A♭m/G**   **A♭m/B♭**
Tensions in bass;   **A♭m/D♭**   **A♭m/G♭** (A♭-7)

a) Gm/C   **A♭m/C**   Am/D
G-7(11)   Cmaj7♯5(♯9)   Fmaj7(6)

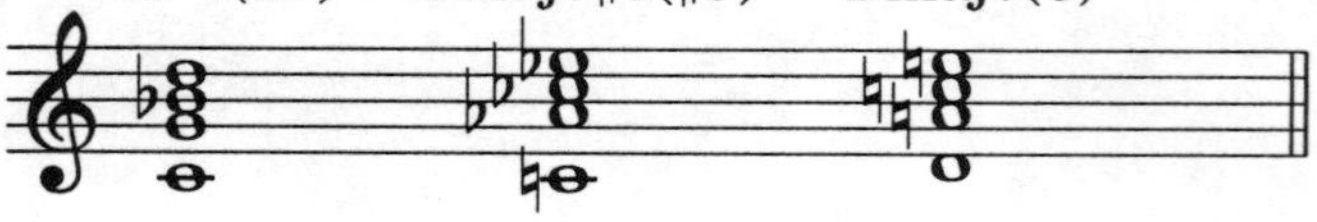

b) G-9   **A♭m/E**   C/F
Cmaj7♯5(♯9)   Fmaj9

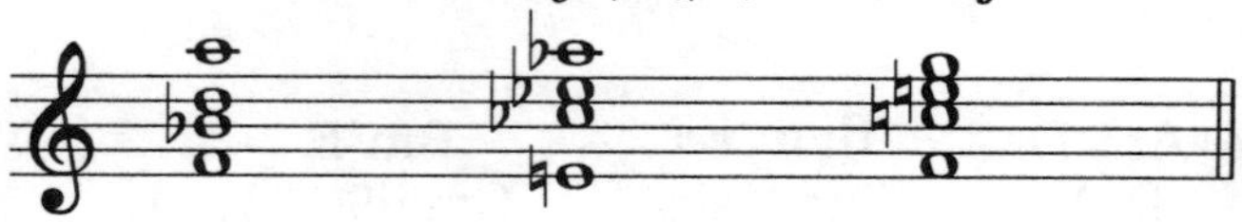

c) Gm(add9)   **A♭m/G**   C/F
Cmaj7(♭13/ ♯9)   Fmaj9

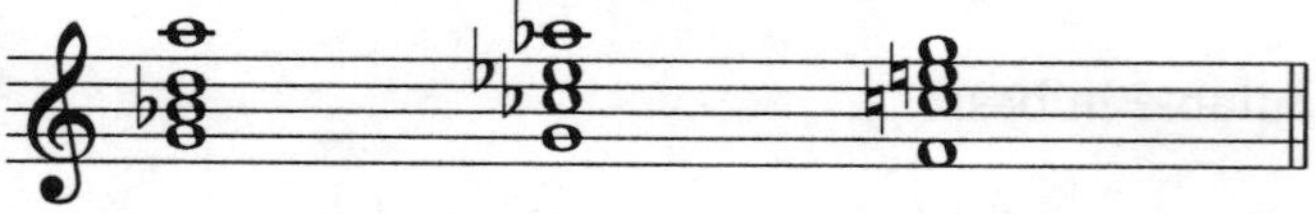

d) D-7(11)   **E♭m/F**   C6(9)
G+7(♯9/ maj7)

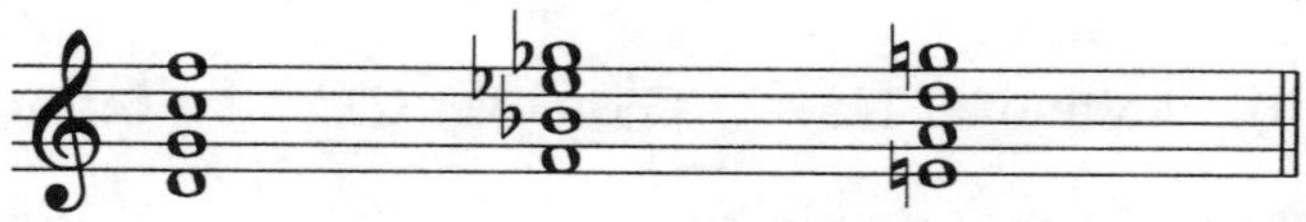

e) Gm(11/9)   **A♭m/D♭**   C/D
C+7(alt9/maj7)   Fmaj9(6)

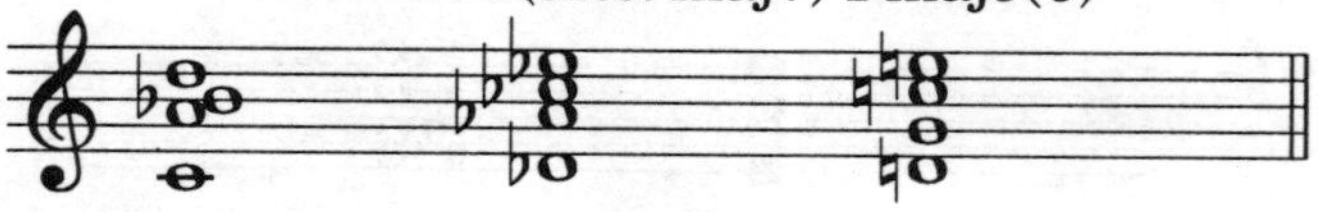

f) Gm(add9)   **A♭m/G♭**   Am/F
Cmaj7(♯9/alt5)   Fmaj7

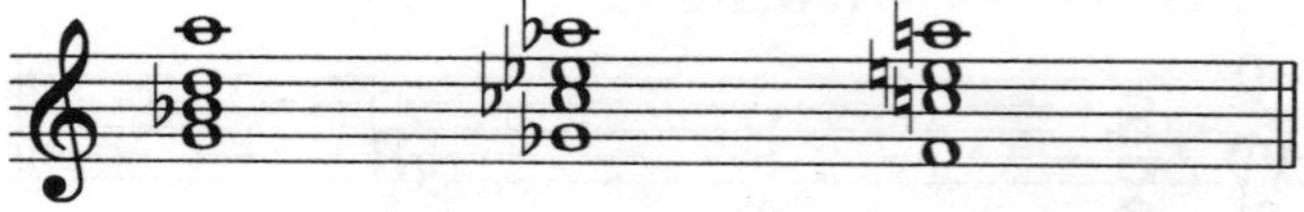

**13)** VIm over I7;   Am over C7

Chord tones in bass;   **Am/G** (A-7 or C6)   **Am/B♭**
Tensions in bass;   **Am/D♭**   **Am/F♯** (F♯-7♭5)

a) G-7(11)   **Am/G**   C/F
C6   Fmaj9

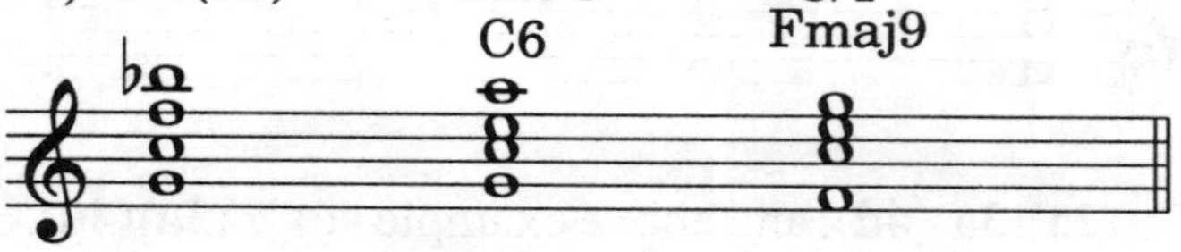

b) Gm/A♭   **Em/F**   Dm/E♭
D-7♭5(♭13/11)   G13   Cm(13/11/9)

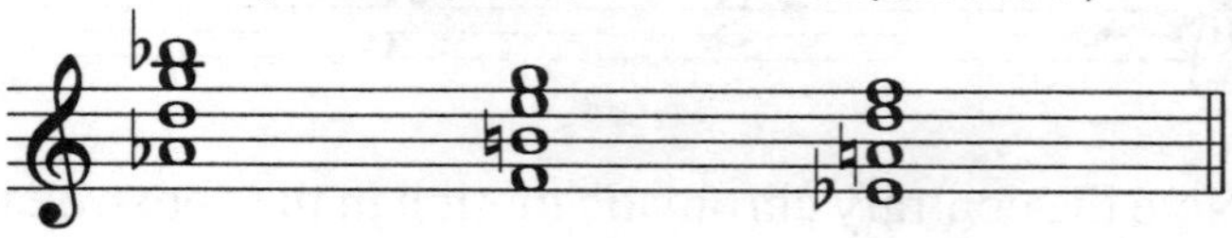

c) C-7(11)   **Dm/G♭**   C/F
F13(♭9)   B♭(13/♯11/9)

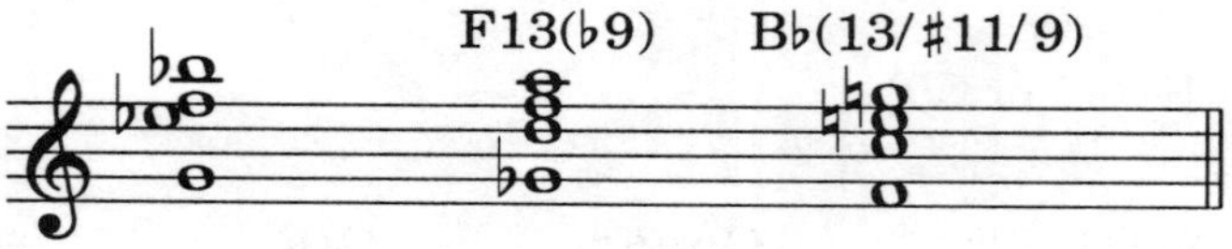

d) G-7(11)   **Am/F♯**   C/F
C6(♭5)   Fmaj9

## DOM 7sus4 CHORD

Available Upper-Structure Triads;

♭II (♭9 11 ♭13)   IV (11 13 1)   ♭VII (♭7 9 11)   IIm (9 11 13)   ♭VIIm (♭7 ♭9 11)

**1)** ♭II over I7sus4;   D♭ over C7sus4   (Tensions not available in bass)

Chord tones in bass;   **D♭/C** (D♭maj7)   **D♭/B♭** (B♭-7)   **D♭/G** (contains ♭9th interval)

a) B♭/C   **D♭/C**   C6(9)
G-7(11)   C7sus4(♭13/♭9)   Fmaj7(6)

b) Am/F   **A♭/F**   C(add9)
D-9   G7sus4(♭13/♭9)

c) Dm/G   **D♭/G**   C/F
G-9   C7sus4(♭13/♭9)   Fmaj9

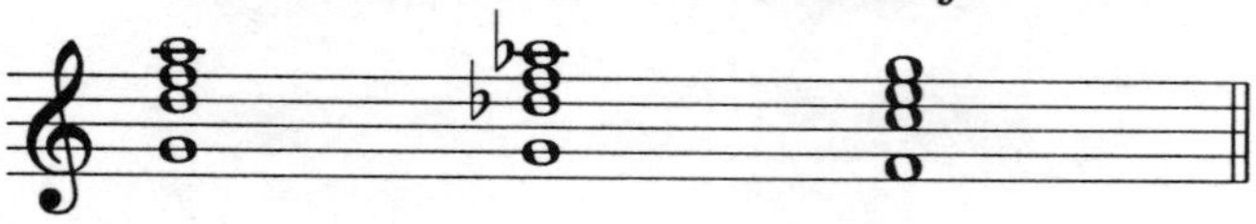

*Note parallel chromatic motion in above example "b," **(2d)(3d)**.

**2)** IV over I7sus4; F over C7sus4

Chord tones in bass; **F/G** **F/B♭**
Tensions in bass; **F/D** (D-7) **F/D♭** (D♭maj7♯5)

a) B♭/G **F/G** C/F
G-7 C13sus4 Fmaj9

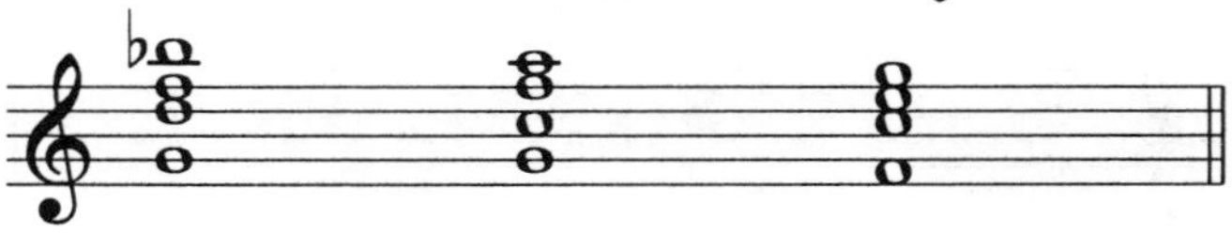

b) Am/D **C/F** G/E
D-9 G13sus4 Cmaj9

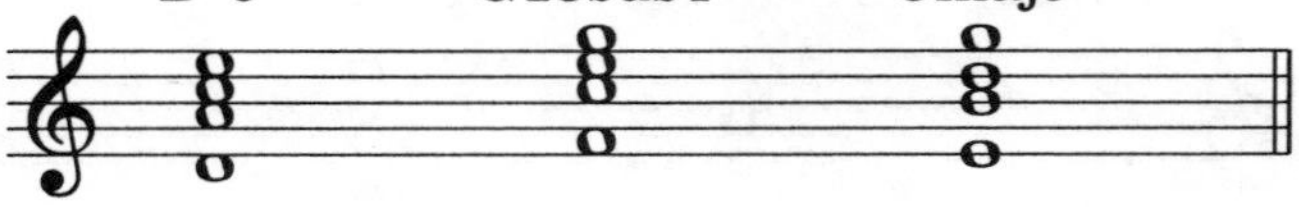

c) Cm(11) **B♭/G** F/G
F9sus4(13) B♭maj9(6)

d) C/F **C/A♭** D/G
D-9(11) G13sus4(♭9) C(13/♯11/9)

**3)** ♭VII over I7sus4; B♭ over C7sus4

Chord tones in bass; **B♭/C** **B♭/G** (G-7)
Tensions in bass; **B♭/A♭** (B♭7)

a) G/C **C/D** D/G
A-9(11) D9sus4 Gmaj9

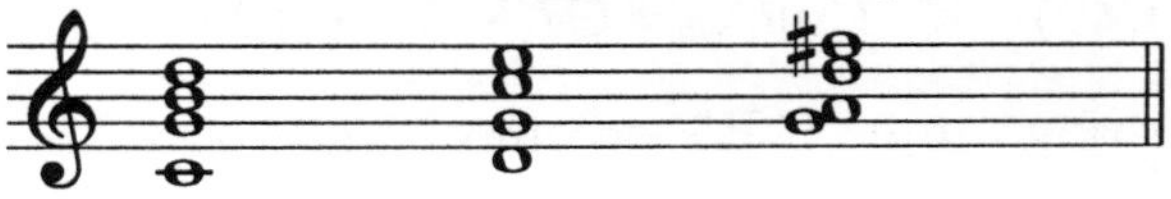

b) F/B♭ **B♭/G** A/F C/F
G-9(11) C9sus4 Fmaj7♯5 Fmaj9

c) D/G **G/F** A/F♯
E-9(11) A9sus4(♭13) Dmaj9

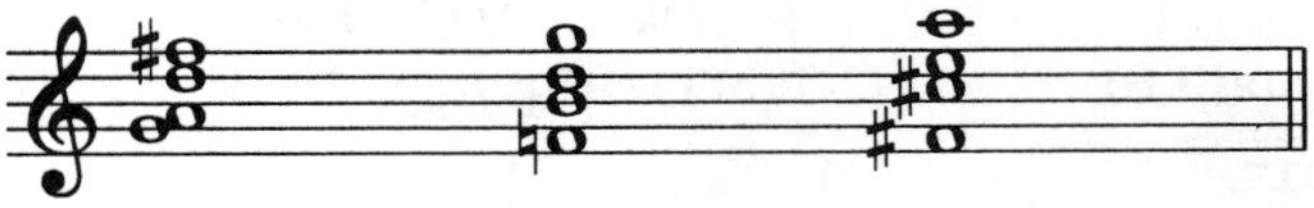

**4)** IIm over I7sus4; Dm over C7sus4 (Tensions not available in bass)

Chord tones in bass; **Dm/C** (D-7) **Dm/G** **Dm/B♭** (B♭maj7)

a) B♭/C **Dm/C** C6(9)
G-7(11) C9sus4(13) Fmaj7(6)

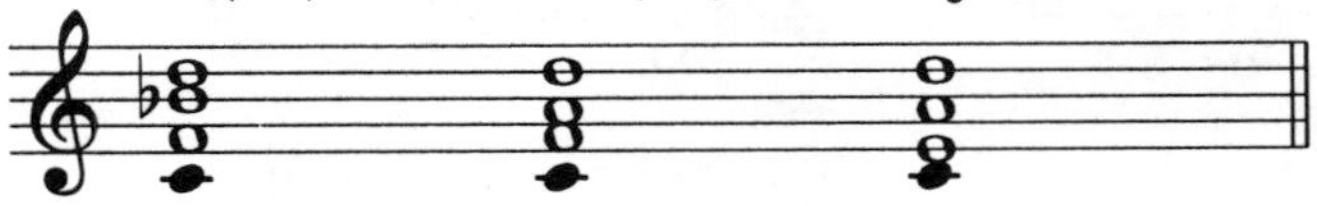

b) B♭6(9) **Dm/G** C/F
G-7(11) C9sus4(13) Fmaj9

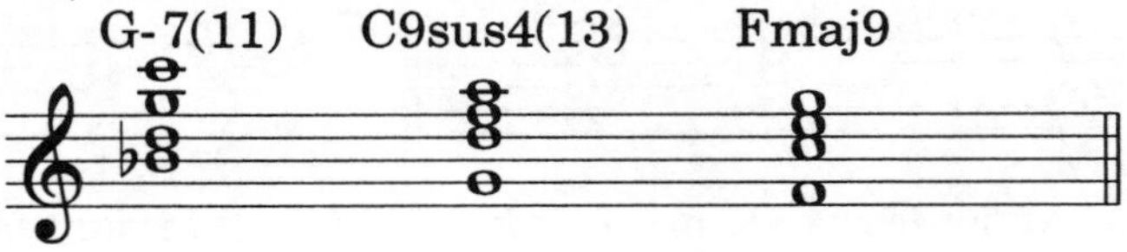

c) G7sus4 **Am/F** G/E
D-7(11) G9sus4(13) Cmaj9

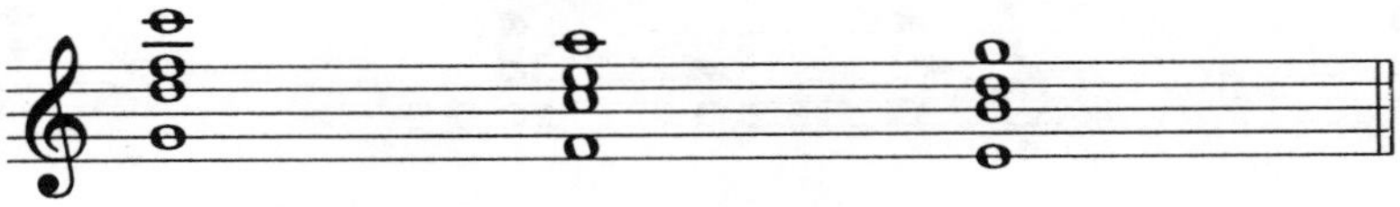

**5)** ♭VIIm over I7sus4;  B♭m over C7sus4

Chord tones in bass; **B♭m/C**  **B♭m/G** (G-7♭5)
Tensions in bass; **B♭m/A♭** (B♭-7 or D♭6)

a) D/E **Dm/E** E/C♯
B-7(11) E7sus4(♭9) Amaj9

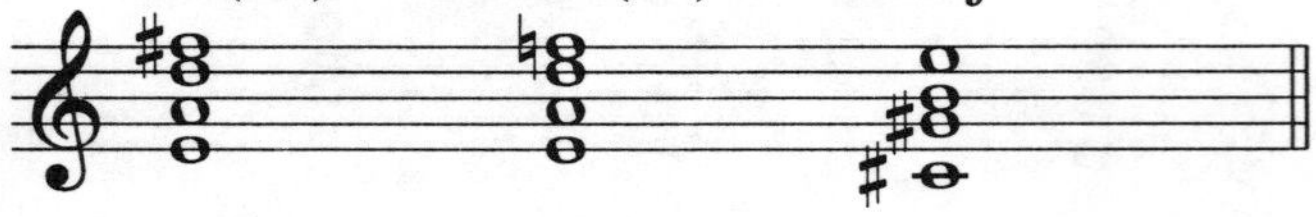

b) G-7(11) **B♭m/G** Fmaj7
C7sus4(♭9)

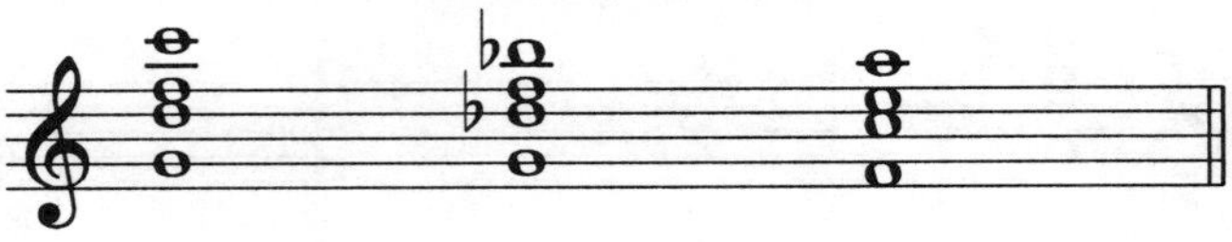

c) G(add9) **Gm/F** C♯7sus4
E-7(11) A7sus4(♭13/♭9) Dmaj7(♯11/6)

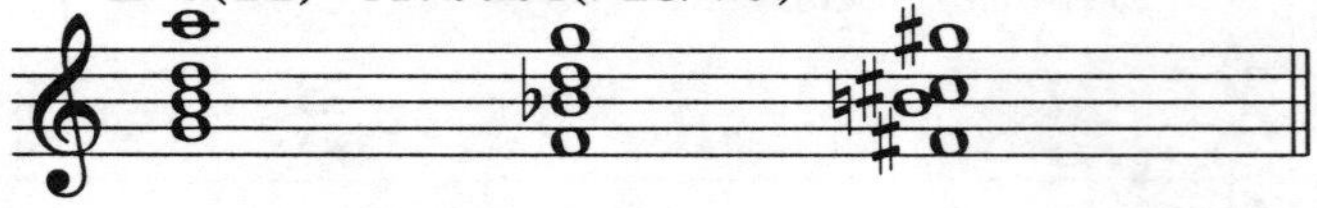

## TRIADS over TENSIONS

An additional approach to the use of triad-over-bass structures as "upper-structure triads" would be to consider the triad to be the root or original chord with tensions placed in the bass. This approach will be applied to dominant type chords only since it has very limited use on other chord types.

The following structures will receive II-V-I examples. They are presented here as substitute structures for a C7 chord;

(Major); **C/D♭** = C7(♭9)  **C/D** = C9  **C/E♭** = C7(♯9)  **C/F♯** = C7(♯11)  **C/A♭** = C7(♭13) {A♭maj7♯5}
(Minor); **Cm/D♭** = C7(alt9)  **Cm/E** = C7(♯9)  **Cm/F♯** = C7(♯11/♯9)  **Cm/A♭** = C7(♭13/♯9) {A♭maj7}

*Tension ♯9 will be temporarily allowed on the 5th string for the **C/E♭** structure.

1) Major triad over ♭9;

B♭/G **F/G♭** C/F
C-9(11) F7(♭9) B♭6(♯11/9)

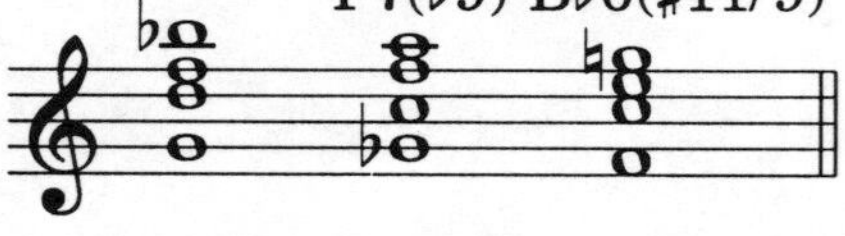

2) Major triad over 9;

E♭/F **F/G** D7sus4
C-7(11) F9 B♭maj9(6)

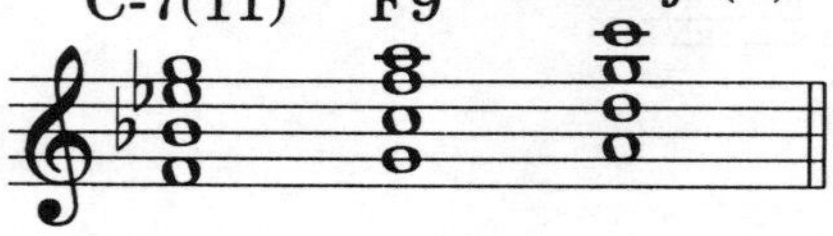

3) Major triad over ♯9;

B♭/G♭ **F/A♭** B♭m/G
C-7♭5(11/9) F7(♯9) B♭-6

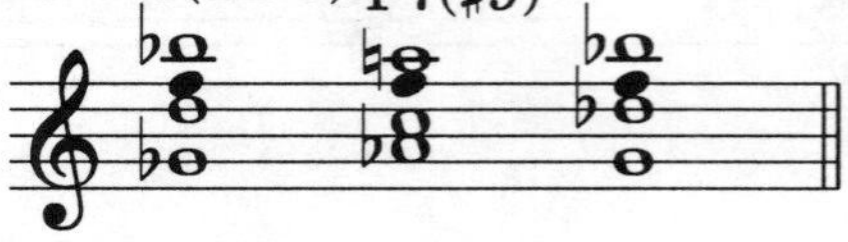

4) Major triad over ♯11;

Dm/G **C/G♭** G/F
G-9 C7(♯11) F(13/♯11/9)

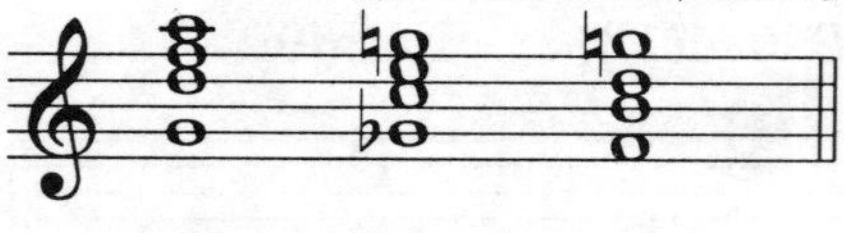

5) Major triad over ♭13;

G/E **A/F** C♯m/F♯
E-7 A7(♭13) Dmaj9(♯11)

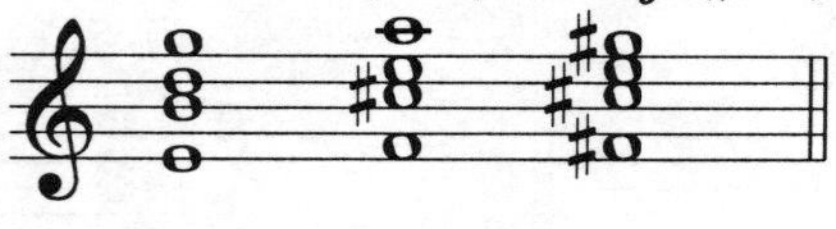

6) Minor triad over ♭9;

E♭/F **Fm/G♭** F/G
C-7(11) F7(alt9) B♭maj9(6)

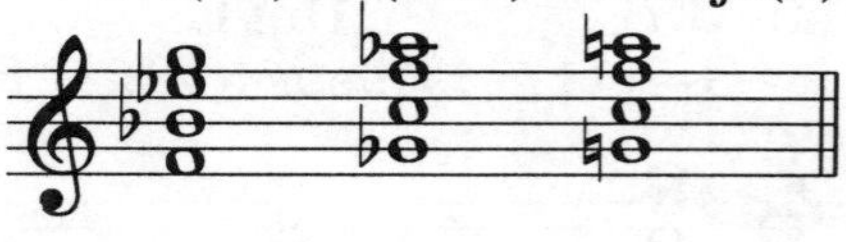

7) Minor triad over major 3rd;

G-7(11) **Cm/E** C/F
C7(♯9) Fmaj9

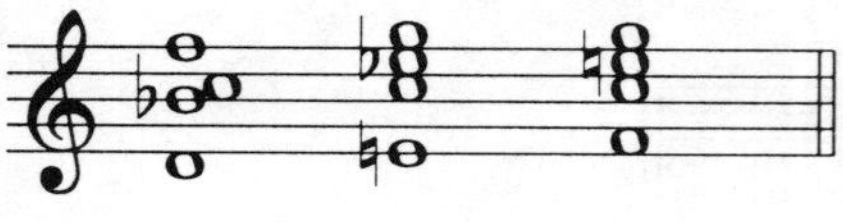

8) Minor triad over ♯11;

G-7(11) **Cm/F♯** C/F
C7(♯11/♯9) Fmaj9

9) Minor triad over ♭13;

G6(9) **Am/F** A/F♯
E-7(11) A7(♭13/♯9) Dmaj9

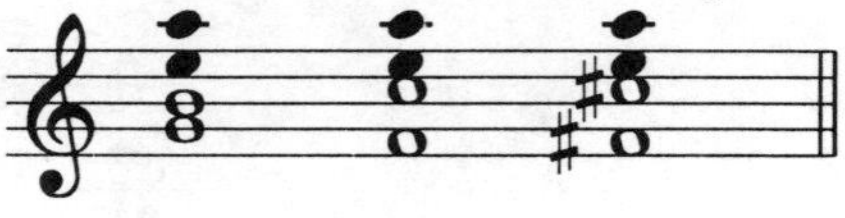

## TRIADS over BASS ARPEGGIOS

The following exercises can help establish the "dual" harmonic sound inherent in upper-structure triads over basic 7th chords, which can be hard to establish with just one four-note structure. By assigning different chord tones of a basic 7th chord under a single upper-structure triad, the complete 7th chord can be "heard" along with the complete upper-structure triad. Moreover, by alternating between the bass and triad while ascending through the different structures in tempo, the basic 7th chord can be heard independently of the upper-structure triad.

Those structures that can form consecutive *thirds* or *fourths* in the bass, which in turn forces inversions on the upper-structure triad, work best in these exercises.

The following structures have been transposed to more comfortably "fit" on the middle four strings.

1) C over B♭maj7;

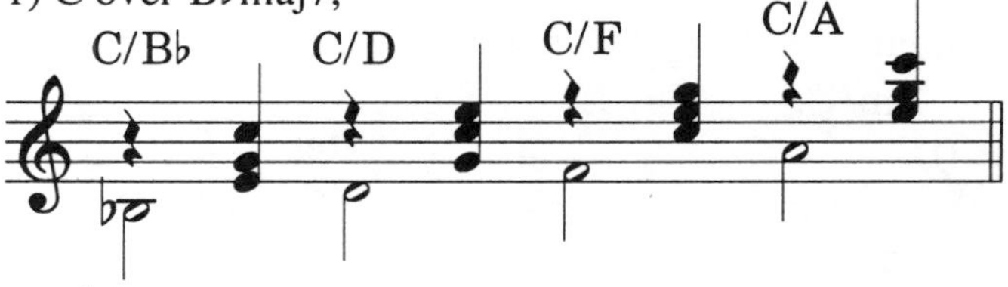


2) Bm over Cmaj7;

3) B♭ over C-7;

4) Dm over C-7;

5) Dm over C-maj7;

6) B♭ over C-7♭5;

7) D♭ over C-7♭5;

8) G♭ over C-7♭5, (G♭/A♭);

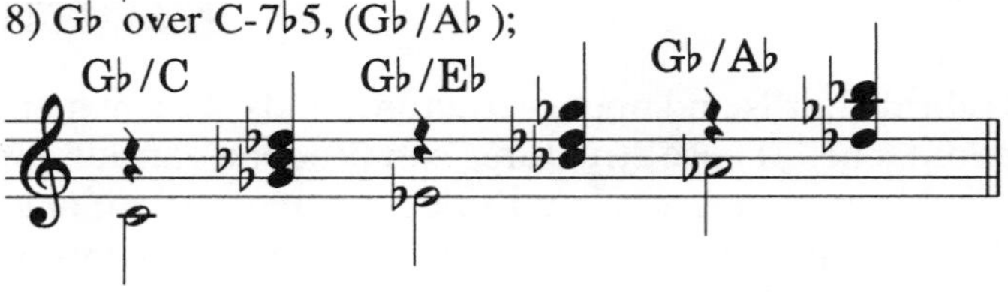


9) B♭m over C-7♭5;

### DOMINANT CHORDS

1) D over C7;

2) E♭ over C7, (E♭ over C+);

3) D over B♭7, (D over E(♭5));

4) F♯ over C7;

5) F over A7 (♭9), (F over C♯°7);

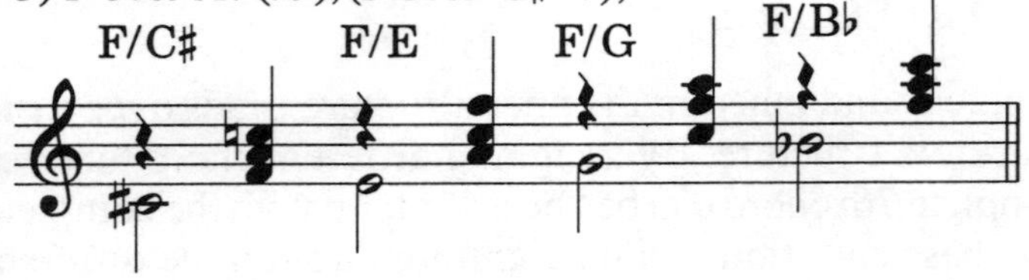


6) A over B♭7;

7) E♭m over C7;

8) Fm over B7;

9) Gm over C7, (Gm over C+);

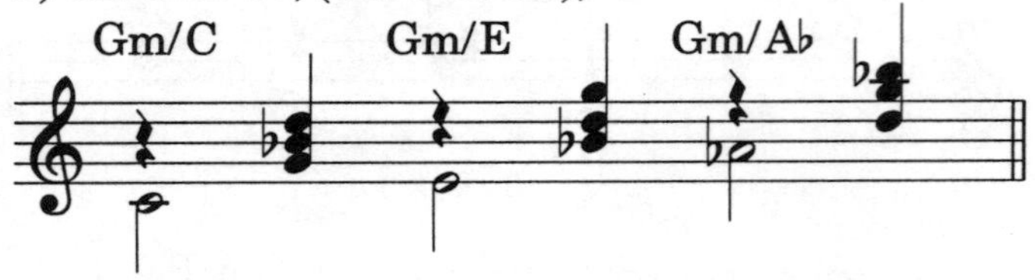


10) Fm over A7(♭9), (Fm over C♯°7);

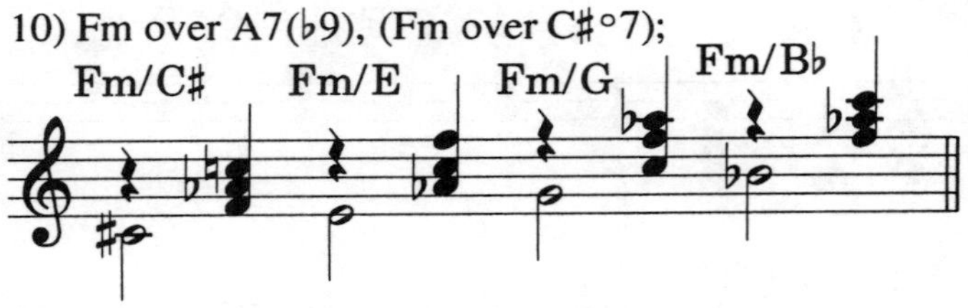


The following exercise uses the triad as the root or original chord while tensions are used in the bass. Note the tensions form their own *lower-structure* triad.

The following structures are functioning as "C" dominant voicings; (Cm over D♭m) = C7(♭13/alt9)

## SYMMETRICAL MOTION

Hybrid chords and upper-structure triads present a unique "marriage" between *diatonic* and *symmetrical* harmonic approaches. These structures can produce various symmetrical harmonies and line-patterns that have little regard for diatonic functions and rules, or they can enhance a functional chord progression without compromising its diatonic integrity. The following examples will present some different ideas that will incorporate one or both of these approaches through the use of triad-over-bass structures.

### PEDALS

While either the bass or the triad sustains, the other can move symmetrically or diatonically. The following examples will present symmetrical triadic motion while the bass sustains.

1) Triads move in minor thirds;

2) Triads move in whole-steps;

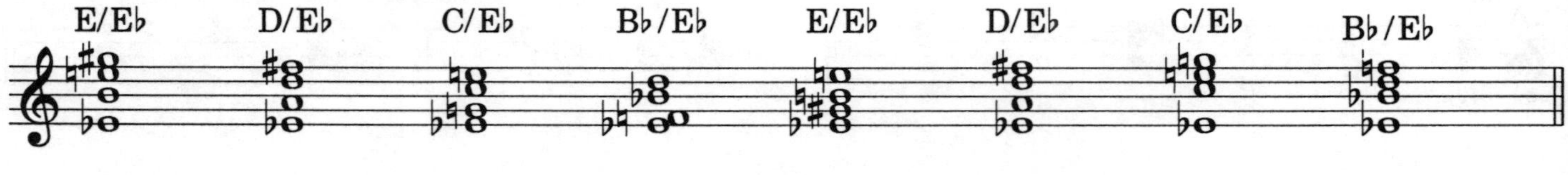

3)Triads move in major thirds;

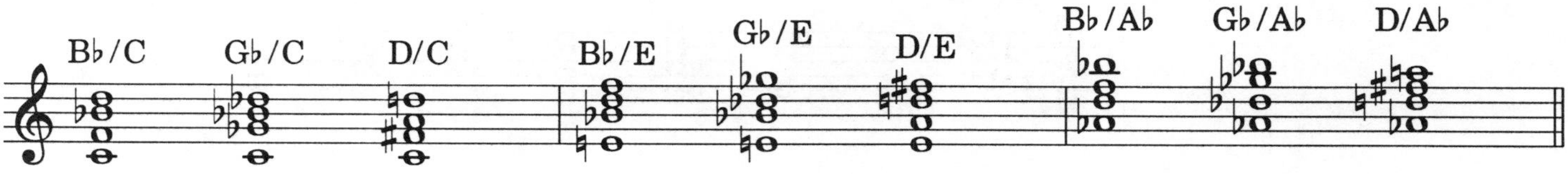


4) Triads move chromatically;

5) Triads move in "cycle-four";

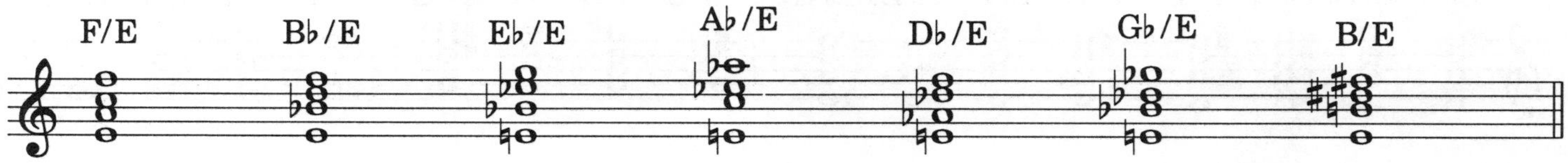


The following examples present symmetrical bass motion while the triad sustains. Although the triad remains the same, different inversions will be used for harmonic variety and motion.

1) Bass moves in minor thirds;

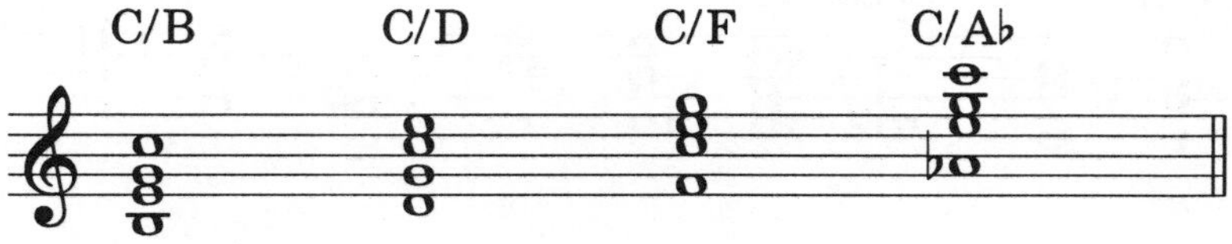


2) Bass moves in whole-steps;

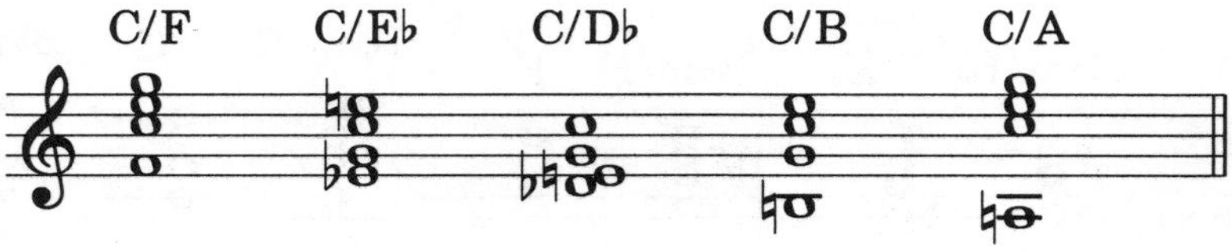


3) Bass moves in major thirds;

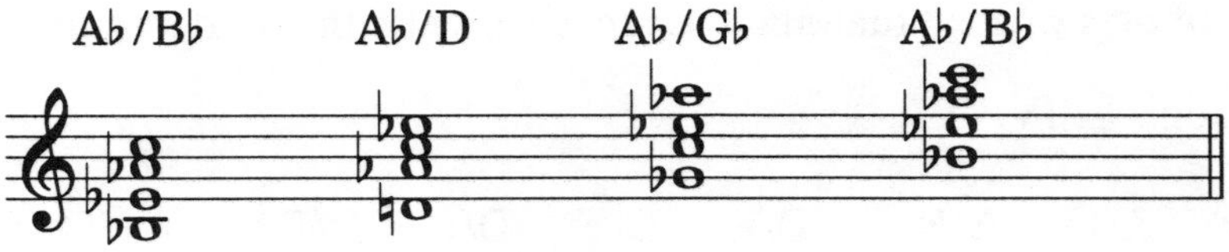


4) Bass moves chromatically;

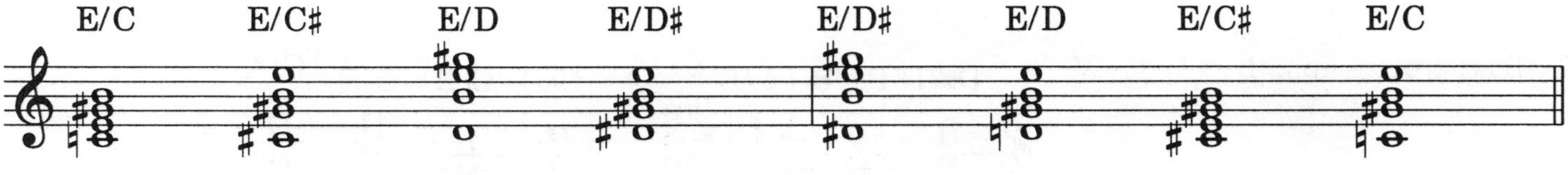

5) Bass moves in "cycle-four";

## DIATONIC MOTION

The following examples will present diatonic triadic motion while the bass sustains. If a diatonic bass note is chosen, it will usually reappear in one of these basic progression's triads, producing a doubled note or an octave. For this reason, at least two examples for each progression will be presented; one containing a *diatonic* bass note and one containing a *non-diatonic* bass note.

1) Triadic progression; I - IV - V - I

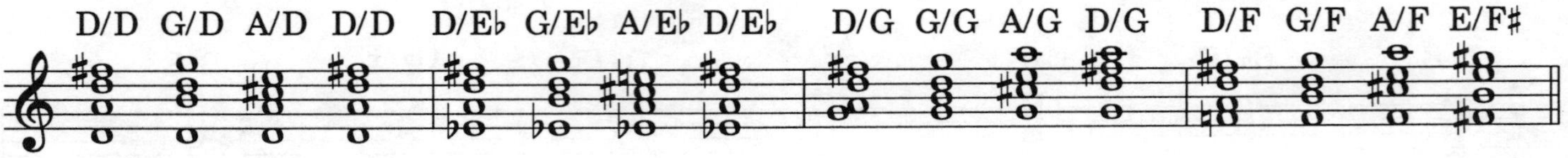


2) Triadic progression; I - II - III - IV

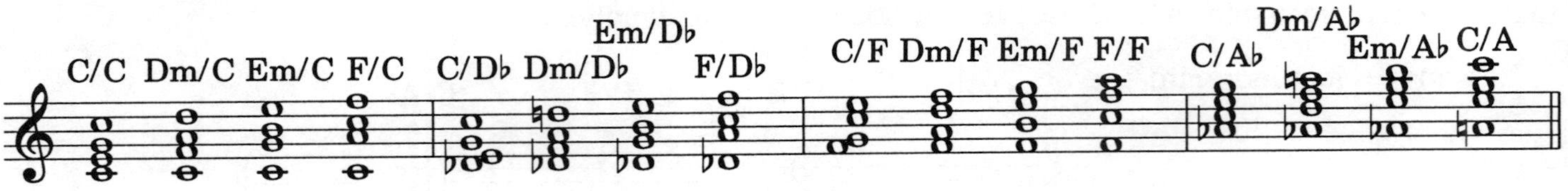


3) Triadic progression; IV - I

The following examples present diatonic bass motion while the triad sustains.

1) Bass progression; I - IV - V

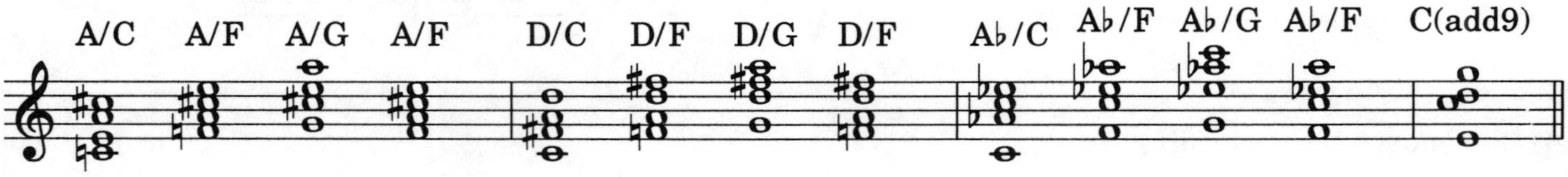


2) Bass progression; I - VI - II - V

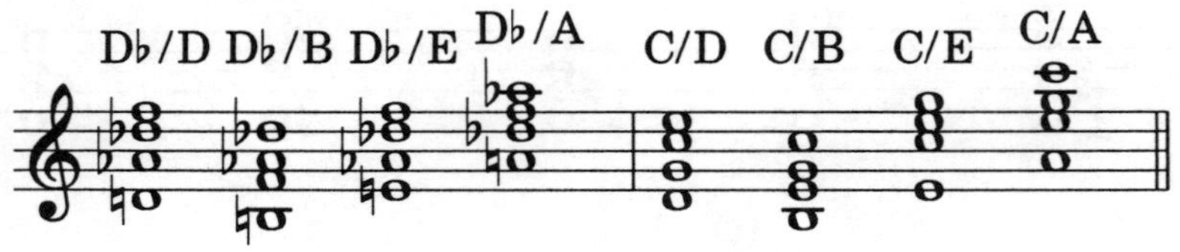

## CONTRARY MOTION

Different symmetrical and diatonic patterns can be introduced to both the upper-structure triads and bass at the *same* time. Obviously this can produce many different combinations of which some will be presented here. Some of the most successful patterns will produce *contrary* motion between the bass and the triads.

The following examples will combine different <u>symmetrical</u> patterns.

1) Contrary chromatic motion;

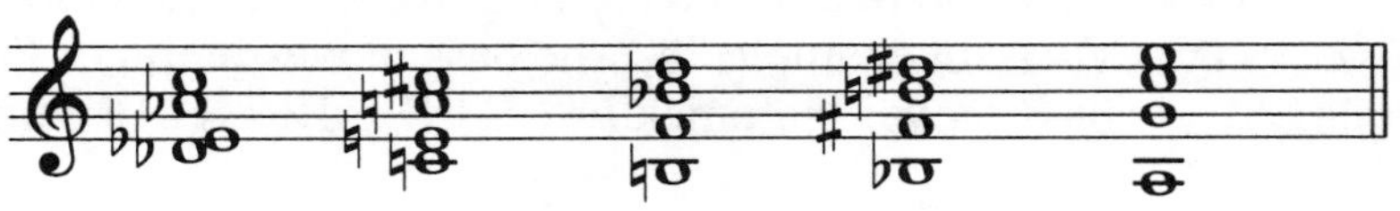


2) Contrary whole-step motion;

In example "a," the <u>roots</u> of the triads ascend while the actual voicings (different inversions) descend. Use of different inversions are required to physically stay on the middle four strings. In example "b," the triads ascend using the *same* inversion while the bass descends requiring the use of the <u>6th</u> string on the last two voicings.

a)

b)

3) Contrary minor-third motion;

4) Contrary fifth motion; (triads move in cycle-four while bass moves in cycle-five)

5) Triads move in cycle-four while bass ascends chromatically; (this example combines *two* of the previous symmetrical examples)

The following examples will combine different <u>diatonic</u> patterns.

1) Bass moves I - IV - V - I while triads move V - I - IV - V ;

2) Triads move I - IV - V - I while the bass uses *three* different progressions in *three* different keys;
**a)** I - II - III - IV in "C", **b)** I - VI - II - V in "A♭", and **c)** I - ♭VII - ♭VI - V in "F".

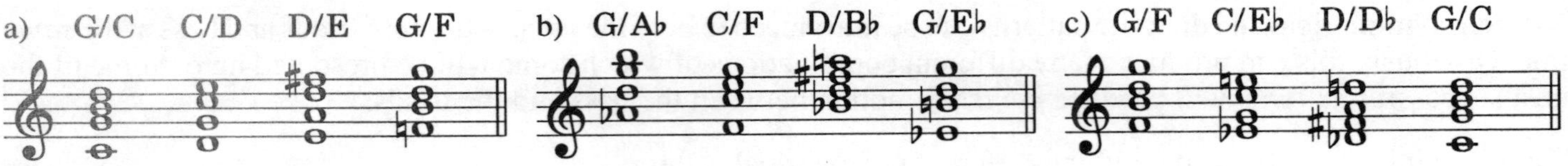


3) The following examples mix symmetrical and diatonic patterns. In example "a," the bass moves chromatically while the triads move I - IV - V - I. In example "b," the bass moves in minor thirds while the triads move I - V - IV - V - I. In example "c," the bass moves diatonically ( V - IV - III - II - I ) while the triads move in minor thirds.

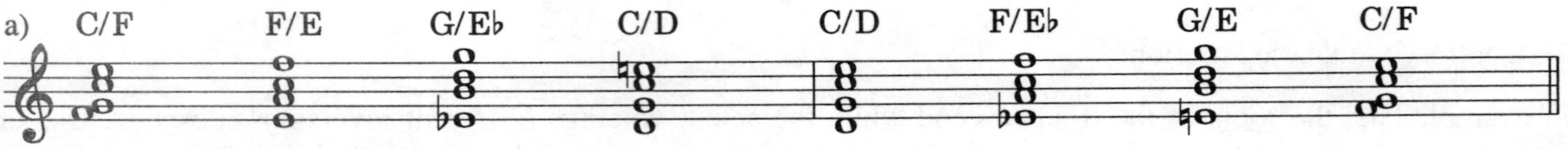


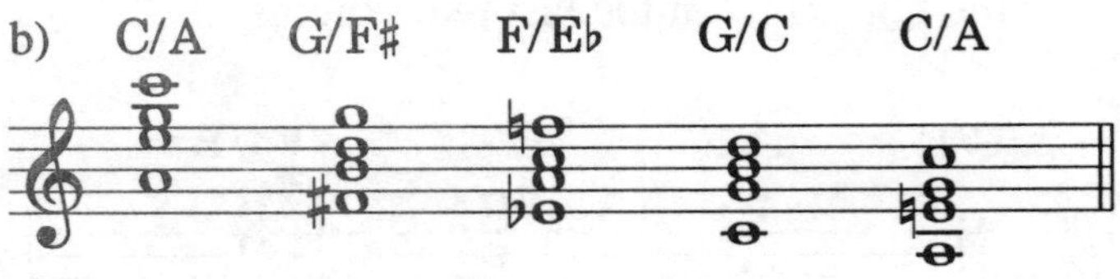

4) The following example uses no particular patterns, but concentrates instead on contrary motion between triad roots and bass;

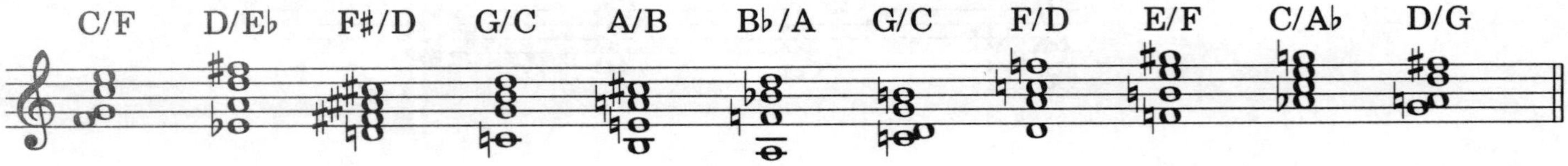


## "UNAVAILABLE" HALF-STEPS

As has been stated and in many cases presented, established harmonic rules, (i.e. ♭9th intervals and L.I.L.), can often be relaxed when using triad-over-bass structures. This is especially evident in dominant functions where *any* note can be "justified." In fact, all but four ( ♭9 - 9, 9 - ♯9, 3 - 4, and ♯5 - 6 ) of the twelve possible half-steps have been used in a dominant function. The following examples will attempt to use these remaining four half-steps in a dominant capacity. Verbal justification will be given to each half-step, but the contrary chromatic motion used to resolve each one is perhaps the best justification.

1) ♭9 and natural 9 might be available together because they are the 5th and ♭13th respectively on their *Sub V* chord.

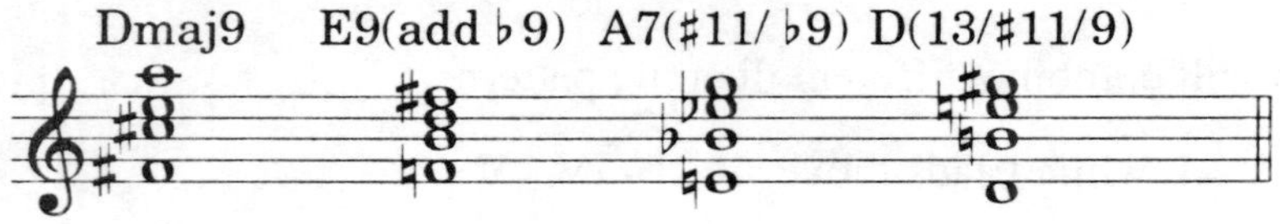

2) Natural 9 with ♯9 might be available because of the “Blues” sound they possess together.

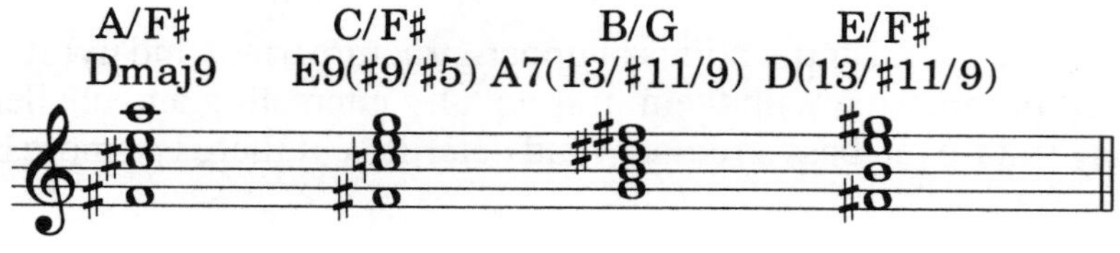


3) ♯5 with 6(13) might be available because they are 9 and ♯9 respectively on their *Sub V* chord.

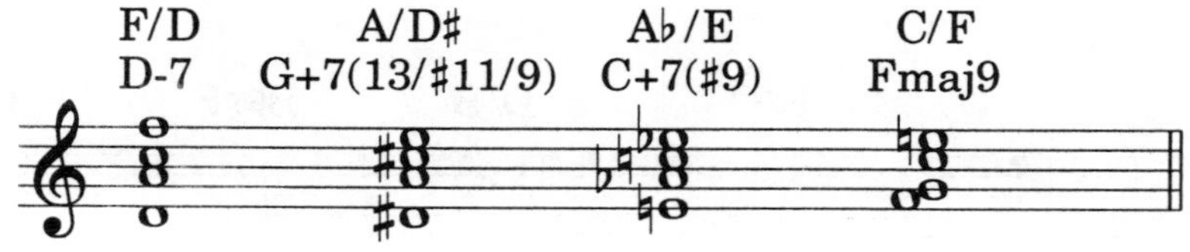


4) The 3rd and 4th are available together because the 4th is simply tension 11 on a dom7 chord. They are also ♭7 and natural 7 respectively on their *Sub V* chord; (natural 7 on a dominant chord was introduced earlier). The 3rd with the 4th on a dom7 chord is not an uncommon sound in today’s “jazz” or “pop” idioms.

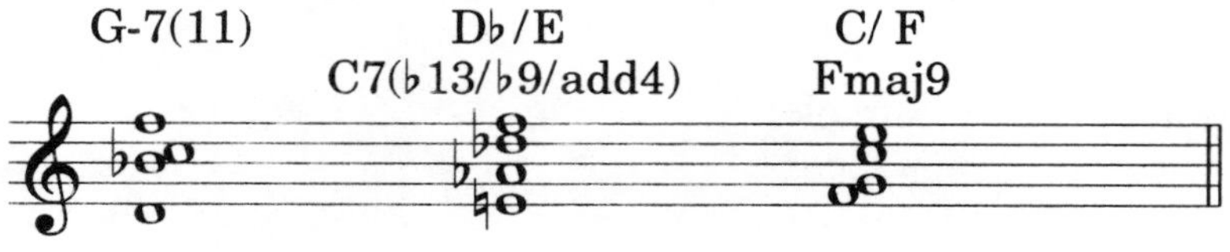


**DOUBLINGS**

In some situations the doubling of a note an octave higher might be necessary to continue the desired chordal or voice-leading ideas. Chromatic motion and “pedals” can often produce the need for *doublings*.

1) The following example contains doublings in order to continue the desired chordal ideas over a bass pedal;

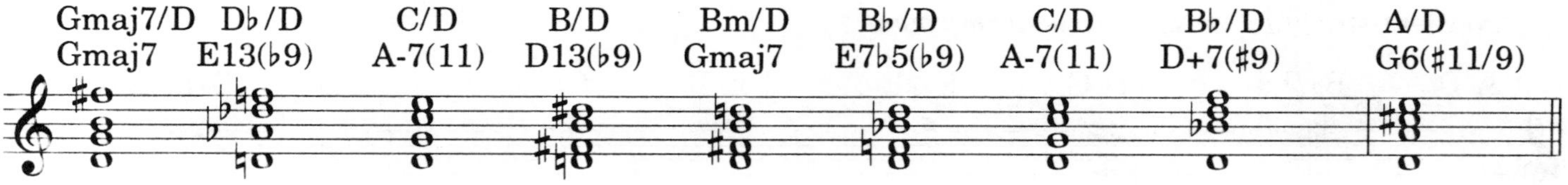


2) The following example contains doublings in order to continue the chord pattern;

3) In the following II - V - I example, the contrary chromatic motion dictates the need for a doubling on the V chord;

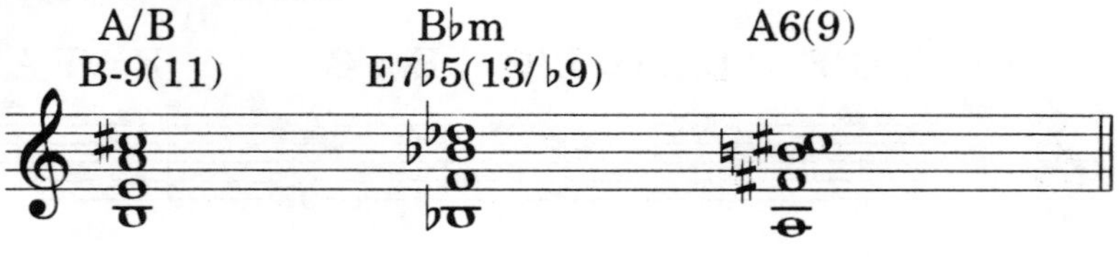

## REHARMONIZATION

Some of the most interesting and useful applications of upper-structure triads and hybrid chords is in *reharmonizing* or substituting a basic chord progression with them. It is equally interesting and challenging to analyze a piece of music which contains many triad-over-bass structures and determine if there is a more basic harmonic progression hidden beneath.

1) The following triad-over-bass progression is a *reharmonization* or substitution for the basic chord progression immediately following it. Could you have realized the *basic progression* if presented with the triad-over-bass progression only ?

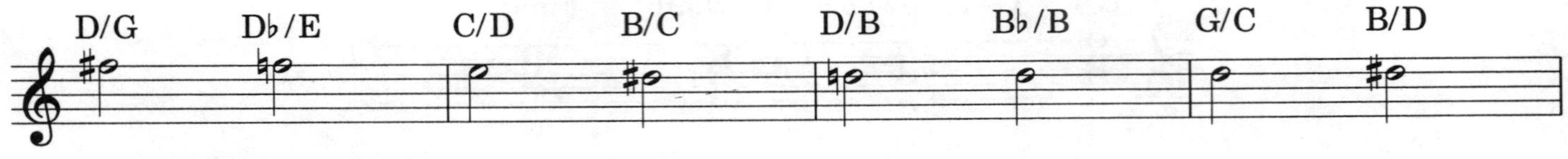


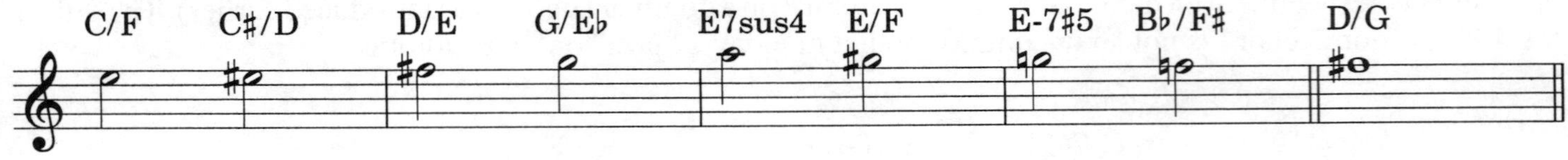


Basic (hidden) progression of above example;

‖ Gmaj7 E7 | A-7 D7 | B-7 E7 | A-7 D7 |

| D-7 G7 | Cmaj7 F7 | B-7 E7 | A-7 D7 | Gmaj7 ‖

*The above basic progression is the "A" section in "Rhythm Changes."

2) The following example is another triad-over-bass *reharmonization* of "Rhythm Changes" in the key of "D." This example takes more liberties by introducing the natural 7th on two dominant chords. Also note the "constant-structure" motion in the *turnaround.*

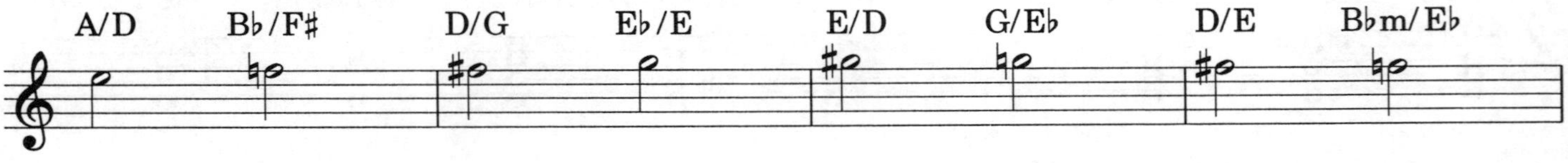


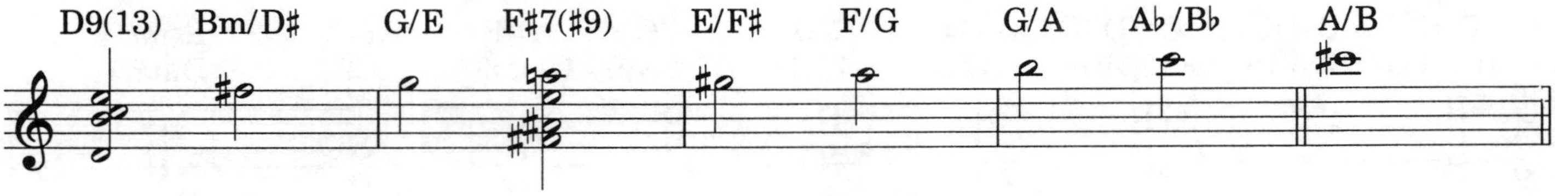


3) The following example is a <u>minor</u> I - VI - II - V cadence in the key of "E minor."

4) The following is an example of "constant-structure" motion through the use of triad-over-bass structures.

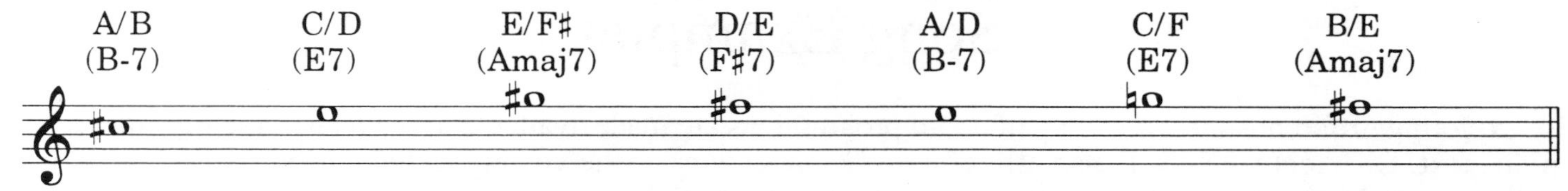


Continued interest in hybrid chords and upper-structure triads should include, and almost demands, examination of additional string sets and widths as well as augmented and diminished triads over various bass notes. Even the middle four strings lend themselves to further examination of triads plus an unrelated note. This chapter has dealt only with triads <u>over</u> an unrelated note. The unrelated note could be located on the <u>2nd</u> string (lead note over triad), or on the <u>3rd</u> or <u>4th</u> strings (<u>open</u> triads with an unrelated note in the middle).

The following "standard" tune has been harmonized with triad-over-bass structures. Included are examples of a diminished and an augmented triad over a bass note. The *original* chords appear above the triad-over-bass structures in **bold** type.

# Chapter Twenty-Eight.
## Song Examples

By exploring different songs, a variety of chord progressions are made available to the many voicings introduced in this text. Different songs will also afford various applications of the voicing techniques introduced including *modal* harmonies, *triad-over-bass* structures, *approach chord* voicings, and *constant-structure* motion. Each song will afford a variety of tempos with individual skills dictating what is "comfortable." Those songs containing many different approach voicings might demand quicker tempos allowing for a smoother and faster resolution of their chordal dissonance.

The following song examples will include "standard" jazz and pop tunes, "modern" jazz compositions, modal tunes, blues, "rhythm changes," and originals. Some of the examples can be played with the melodies of those songs and will be noted as such. Some examples also contain various rhythms to enhance the voicings. Additional rhythm applications and suggestions that could be applied to these songs are contained in the following chapter appropriately entitled **Rhythm**. Each song example will state the original basic chord progression in **bold** symbols over the top of each stave. A harmonized voice-lead rendition of these original chords will appear immediately below.

### Song Example - #1

(A majority of these voicings *will* work with the melody)

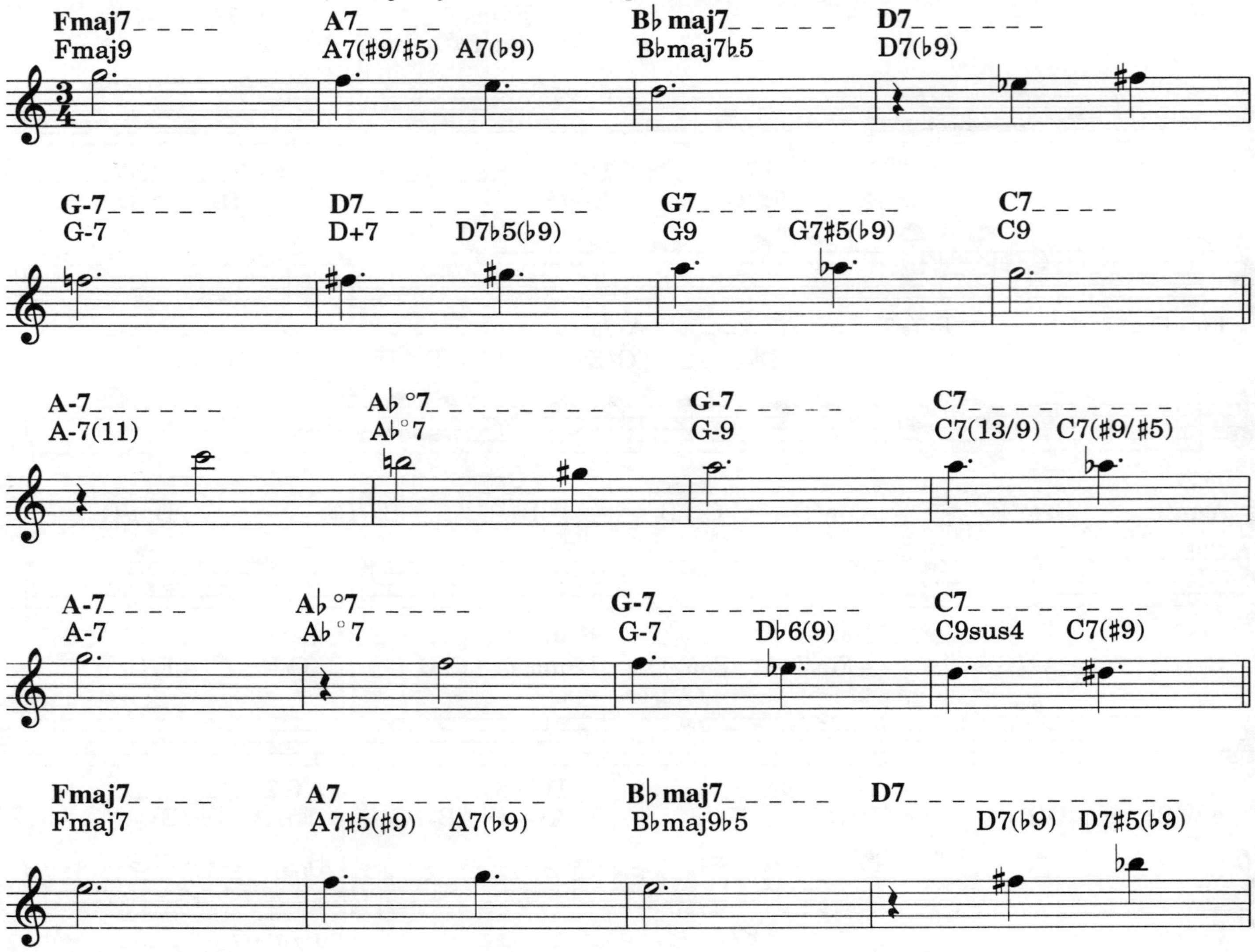

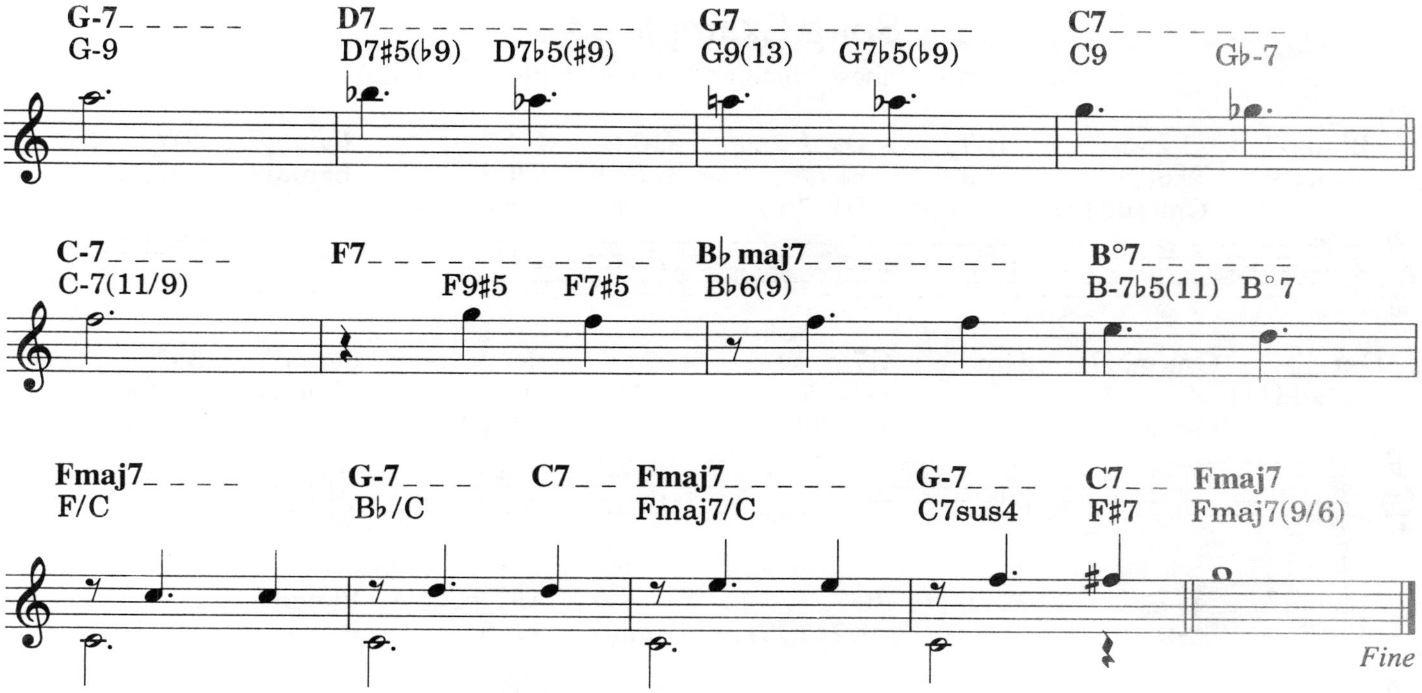
G-7 D7 G7 C7
G-9 D7♯5(♭9) D7♭5(♯9) G9(13) G7♭5(♭9) C9 G♭-7
C-7 F7 B♭ maj7 B°7
C-7(11/9) F9♯5 F7♯5 B♭6(9) B-7♭5(11) B°7
Fmaj7 G-7 C7 Fmaj7 G-7 C7 Fmaj7
F/C B♭/C Fmaj7/C C7sus4 F♯7 Fmaj7(9/6)
Fine

# Song Example - #2

(A majority of these voicings *will* work with the melody)

*Fine*

# Song Example - #3

The following example is a "minor blues." The nature of this "stagnant" or sustaining harmony lends itself well to modal voicings and various approach techniques. Note the constant fourth structure being moved chromatically in the first five measures.

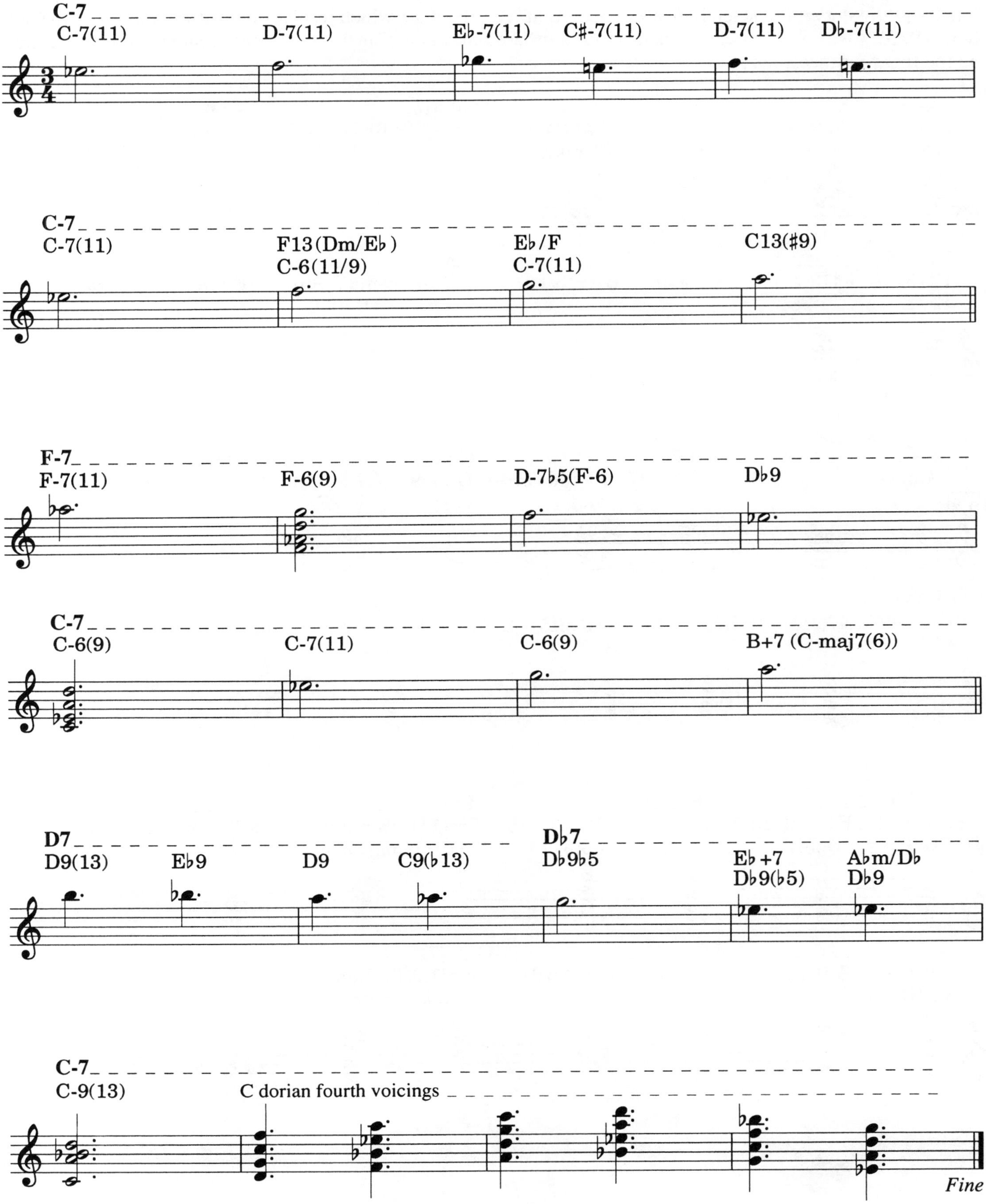

# Song Example - #4

The following example makes liberal use of dominant approach techniques in reharmonizing the basic progression. This allows for a "colorful" dominant cycle-five approach to each chord, enhancing the "predictable" diatonic progression. It is not uncommon in "jazz" to make the II-7 or II-7♭5 chord a dominant chord; II7 or (V7 of V).

Note the ♭9th interval in the tenth measure of section "A," (E♭/F♯), which resolves in contrary motion to the next chord, (D/G). Also note the use of "constant structure harmonic motion" in the first three measures of the "B" section, and the first four measures of the "C" section.

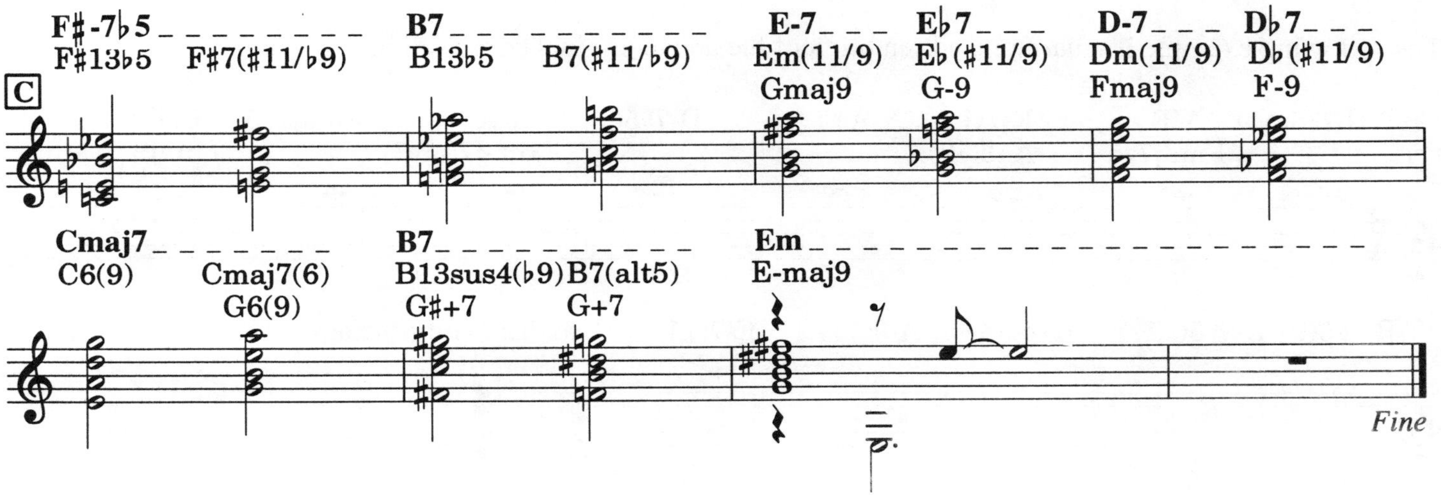


# Song Example - #5

This next example is an original composition. The original chords and melody will be given first, followed by a harmonized rendition that can be performed *with* the original melody or chords.

The basic chord progression on this piece is much more progressive and "modern" sounding than the basic chord progressions in the previous pieces. Care must be taken to not over-harmonize such pieces for fear of losing rather than "embellishing" their original sound.

"SOMEONE WHO LISTENS" © 1974 Bret Willmott

The following example is a harmonized rendition of the above original composition;

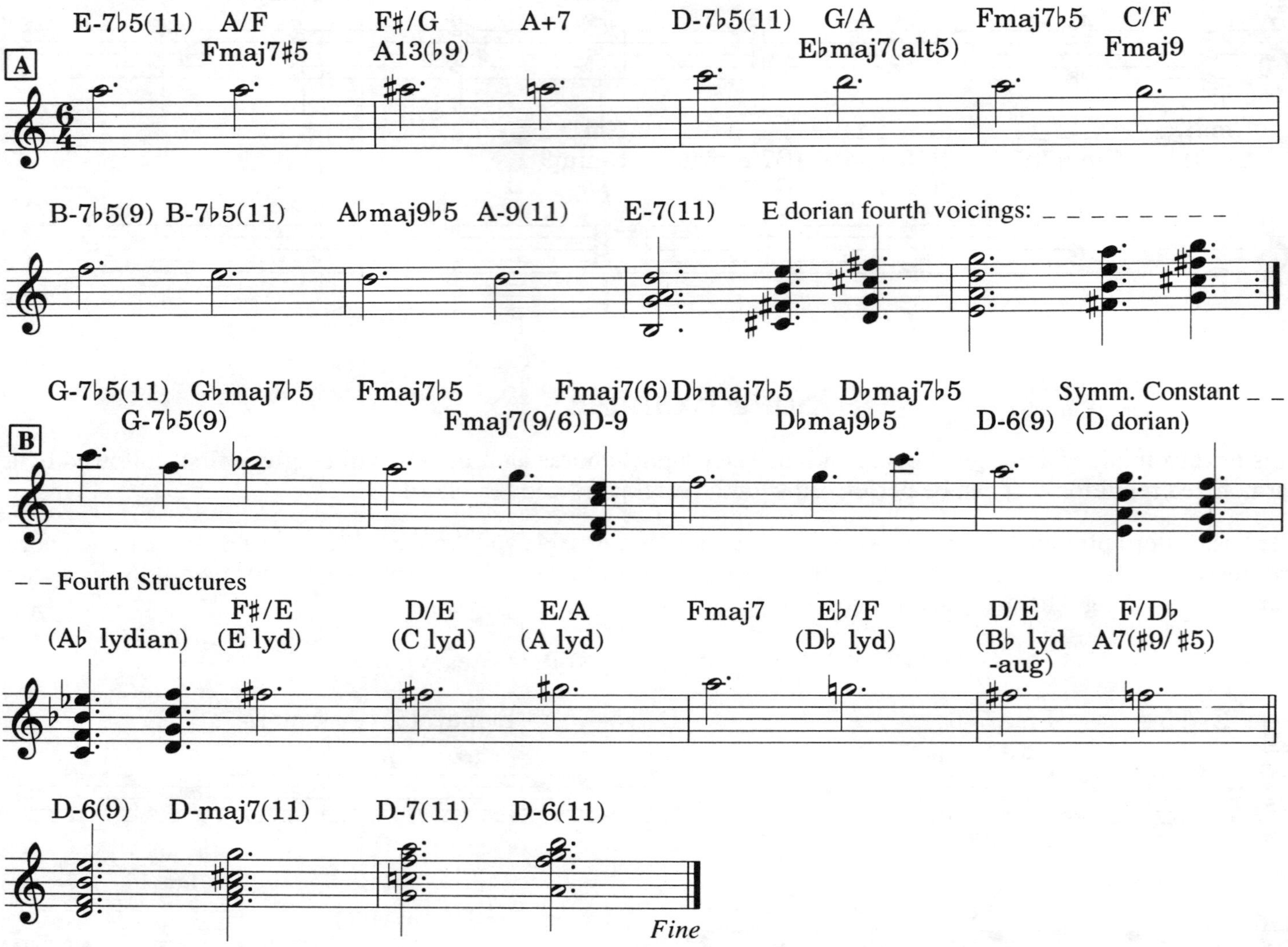


## Song Example - #6

This next example is a popular jazz form referred to as "rhythm changes." Note the chromatically descending major triads in the first two measures. Also note the chromatically descending bottom voices under a sustaining lead voice in measures 7 through 12 in the "A" section. The top two voices in measures 1 and 2 of the "B" section move in contrary chromatic motion while measures 3 and 4 move in opposite contrary chromatic motion. Note the use of chromatic approach chords in measures 5 and 6 of the "B" section. Finally, note the top voice in the first two measures of section "C" spells a D♭ maj7 chord, while in measures 3 and 4 the top voice spells a Cmaj7 chord, and finally a D-7♭5 chord in measures 5 and 6.

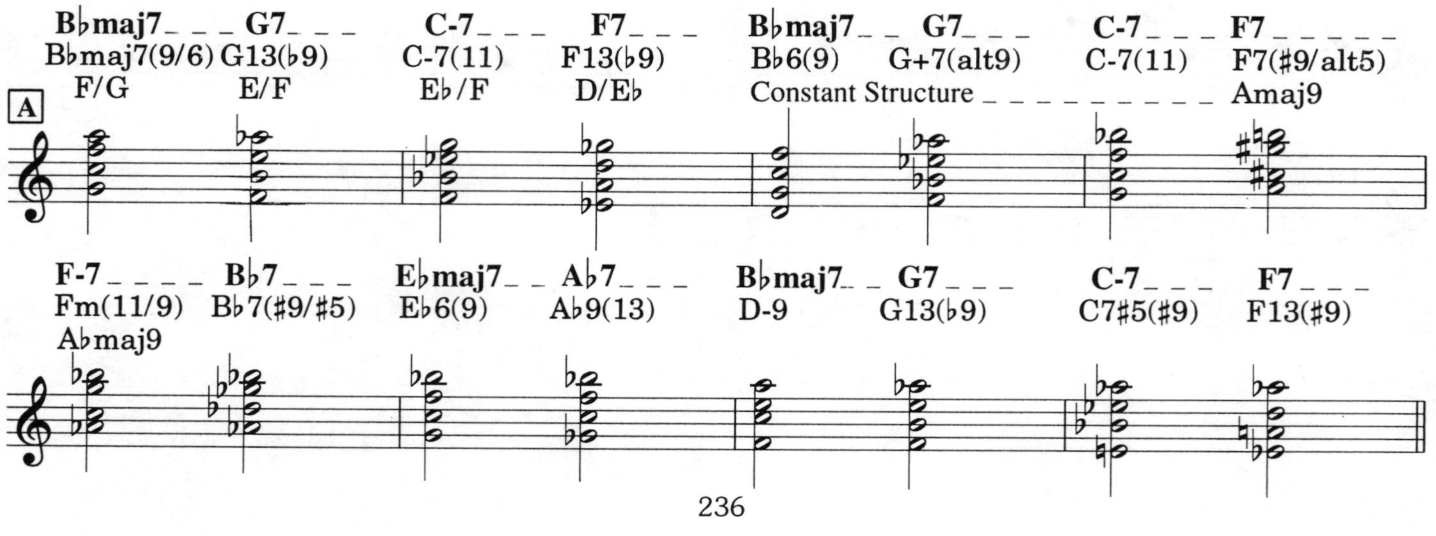

A 9
B♭maj7 G7 C-7 F7 B♭maj7 G7 C-7 F7
B♭13(♯9) G13 C7(♯9) F9(13) B♭maj9 G7♭5(♭9) C-7(11) F7♭5(♭9)
F-7 B♭7 E♭maj7 A♭7 C-7 F7 B♭maj7
F-7(11) B♭7♭5(♭9) E♭6(9) A♭9(♯11) C-7(11) F+7(♯9) B♭maj7
E♭-maj7 Amaj7♯5
B
D7 G7
D7(♭13) D+7(♭9) D9 D7♭5(♯9) G13 G7(♭13/♭9) G9 G7(♯9/♯5)
B♭maj7♯5
C7 F7
C9(13) B9(13) C7 E9(13) F13 F7(alt9) F7♭5(♯9) F7(alt)
F13 A♭13 B13
C
B♭maj7 G7 C-7 F7 B♭maj7 G7 C-7 F7
B♭maj7(9/ 6) G13(♭9) C-9(11) F7(alt5) B♭maj9 G9(13) C-9 F9(♯11)
F-7 B♭7 E♭maj7 A♭7 C-7 F7 B♭maj7
F-9 B♭7♭5 E♭maj9 A♭9(♯11) C-7(11) F+7(alt9) B♭6(9)
Fine

# Song Example - #7

The following is another "standard" tune. Note the top two voices moving in contrary chromatic motion in measures 6 and 7 of section "A." In the "D" section the min7♭5 voicings are repeated a <u>minor third</u> up for the dominant chords. Also note in this section the lead voice ascends while the chord roots descend. Note the tonic diminished substitutes for the ending B♭maj7 chord. Finally, note the top voice over the last two bars forms a B♭ Blues scale.

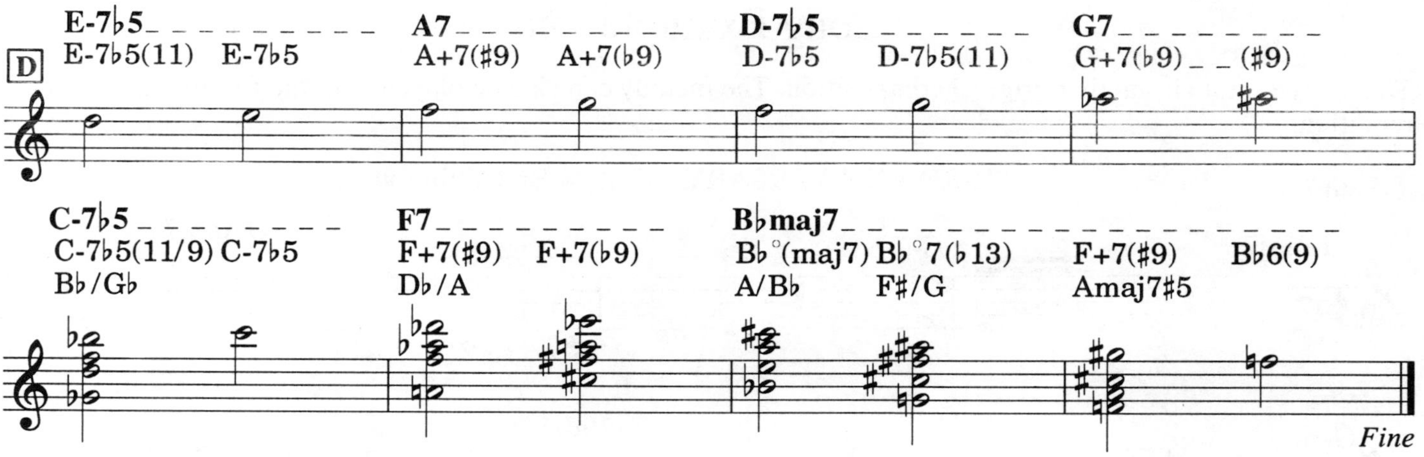
D
E-7♭5
E-7♭5(11) E-7♭5
A7
A+7(♯9) A+7(♭9)
D-7♭5
D-7♭5 D-7♭5(11)
G7
G+7(♭9) (♯9)
C-7♭5
C-7♭5(11/9) C-7♭5
B♭/G♭
F7
F+7(♯9) F+7(♭9)
D♭/A
B♭maj7
B♭°(maj7) B♭°7(♭13) F+7(♯9) B♭6(9)
A/B♭ F♯/G Amaj7♯5
Fine

# Song Example - #8

This last example is another original composition. The melody can also be played with the following harmonized rendition.

(Latin) "THIRD ANNIVERSARY" © 1974 Bret Willmott

The following is a harmonized rendition of the above composition. Note the use of "constant structure harmonic motion" in the second half of this piece.

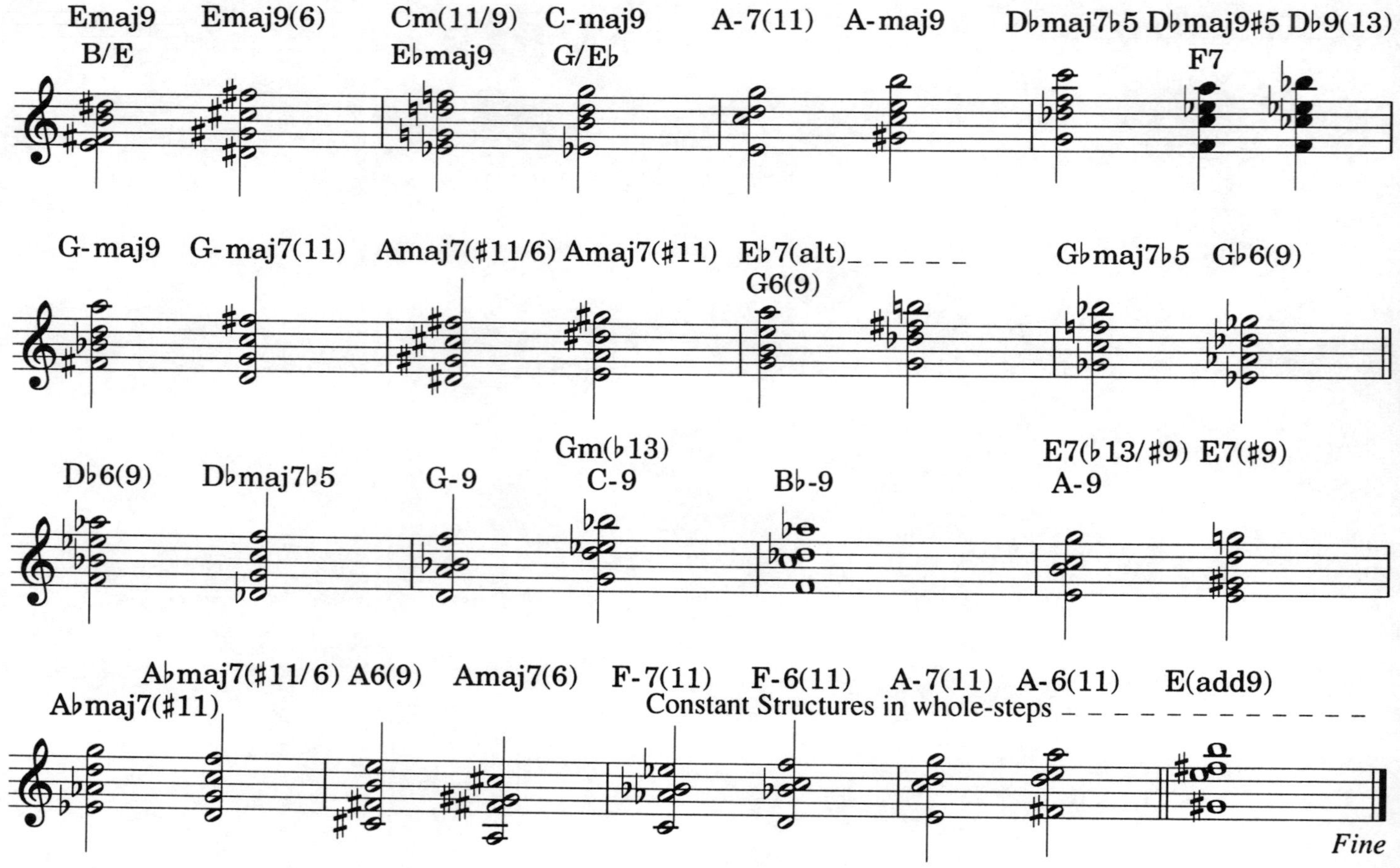

# Chapter Twenty-Nine.
## Rhythm

All the voicings and harmonic knowledge presented in this text would be wasted without the same attention given to *rhythm.* I think most musicians would prefer few and/or simple voicings with a rhythmic "groove" accompanying a soloist or melody than many complicated voicings with no rhythmic sense. Although this text will not undertake the many rhythmic styles, tempos, time-signatures, and concepts needed to use with these voicings, I still feel the need to stress their importance and deserving attention. Most of the voicings in this text were displayed with little or no rhythm. A few simple rhythmic ideas or suggestions will be presented here that could enhance those existing exercises or songs.

By the addition of quarter or eighth note anticipations and delays, an exercise or song becomes more rhythmically active. The following are just some of the possible anticipation and delay combinations over two measures of half notes in 4/4.

1)

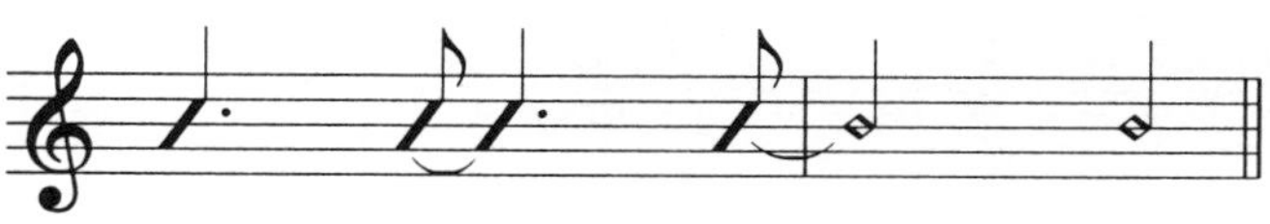

2)

3)

4)

5)

6)

7)

8)

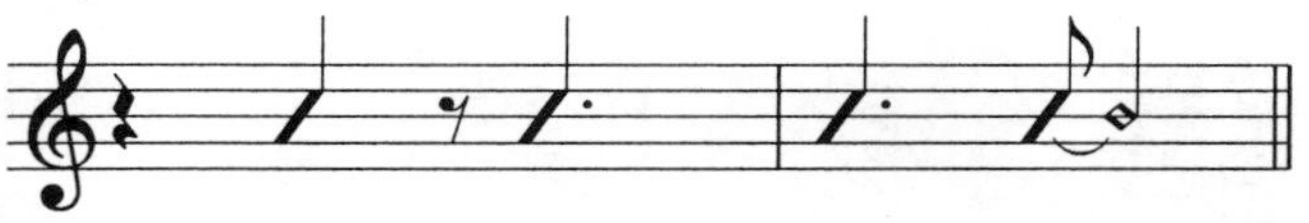

A couple of concepts unique to the guitar could also be used to enhance the voicings presented in this text. The first involves sliding into or away from a voicing chromatically. This is usually accomplished rhythmically with as little as a grace note and often with eighth or quarter notes. This concept enhances both the "sound" of the voicing as well as emphasizing its rhythmic placement. The second concept is a percussive technique achieved by muting the strings and strumming different rhythms after a voicing is sounded. These techniques are more or less applicable depending on the specific styles of music.

Another very important concept for comping in today's jazz or pop idioms is *silence.* What you don't play is often the best thing to play. An interesting and valuable exercise would be to omit certain voicings in the exercises and songs presented in this book. In those exercises or songs harmonizing the half-note in 4/4, try first omitting the *second* chord in each measure; (beats 3 and 4). This retains the *strongest* chord sound of the measure. Next try omitting the *first* chord of each measure; (beats 1 and 2). This retains the *weakest* chord sound of the measure. Finally try different chord omission combinations; like alternating between two half-note voicings and two half-note rests, or two half-note voicings and one half-note rest, etc. Also remember to add different rhythms to these chord omission exercises. Omitting voicings actually increases the different rhythmic possibilities and allows for more rhythmic creativity. Also note how voice-leading is broken by the omission of different chords. At first this might appear to be a problem, but the missing lines can often be "heard" through the silence. As many jazz artists are aware, it's what you hear while your not playing that is important. The following examples will display and suggest various chord omissions to existing exercises.

The following is another example of the half-note being harmonized. Note the use of symmetrical and modal chord patterns as well as chromatic and/or dominant approach voicings.

By removing various voicings and applying different rhythms to the above example, an interesting "comping" rendition of this chord progression can be produced.

In the following example, the first four measures of the *above* example have the second voicing in each bar removed. The next four measures have removed the first voicing in each bar. The next *six* bars remove every third voicing while the final three bars remain the same with only some rhythmic variation.

Note that several chromatic approach voicings have been added to the above example.

As mentioned earlier, different voicing omissions and rhythmic interpretations should be developed and applied to each exercise and musical example presented in this text. In the following example, try superimposing the displayed four-bar chord omission pattern over the *first* II - V blues example introduced at the end of the **Tension 9** chapter.

*Four-bar chord omission pattern;*

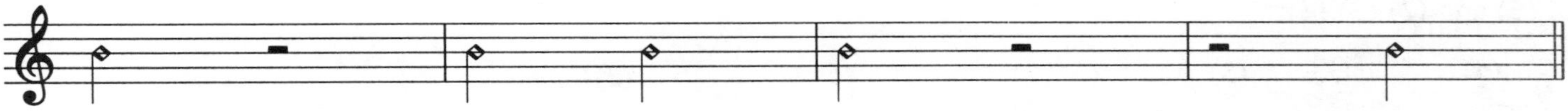

Now try using the following rhythmic interpretation of the above omission pattern over the II - V blues example.

Different string combinations and voicing sizes which are discussed in the following **Conclusion** chapter will only enhance these rhythmic concepts.

In most comping situations it is common to *attack* all four notes at the same time. The following exercises will explore attacking different string combinations at different times. This produces some interesting sounds as well as isolating different voice-leading situations between various string sets. It will enhance awareness of individual guide-lines as well as two and three note voicings. These different combinations also produce many unique and beneficial ways of *physically* preparing chord changes.

Any one of the following combinations could be used to alternate between *two* different string sets. Additional combinations are possible. Strings will again be notated as **bold** numbers in parenthesis.

1) Alternating between one voice and three voices;

| | | | |
|---|---|---|---|
| **(2)** and **(3)** | **(3)** and **(2)** | **(4)** and **(2)** | **(5)** and **(2)** |
| **(4)** | **(4)** | **(3)** | **(3)** |
| **(5)** | **(5)** | **(5)** | **(4)** |

2) Alternating between different two-note voicings;

| | | |
|---|---|---|
| **(2)** and **(4)** | **(2)** and **(3)** | **(2)** and **(3)** |
| **(3)** **(5)** | **(4)** **(5)** | **(5)** **(4)** |

3) Alternating between four-note voicings and one voice;

| | | | |
|---|---|---|---|
| **(2)** and **(2)** | **(2)** and **(3)** | **(2)** and **(4)** | **(2)** and **(5)** |
| **(3)** | **(3)** | **(3)** | **(3)** |
| **(4)** | **(4)** | **(4)** | **(4)** |
| **(5)** | **(5)** | **(5)** | **(5)** |

After establishing a two-bar rhythm pattern, chose one of the above combinations and alternate its string sets on every other attack of the rhythm pattern. The following rhythm pattern will use the above alternating string combination of **(5)** and **(2) (3) (4)**;

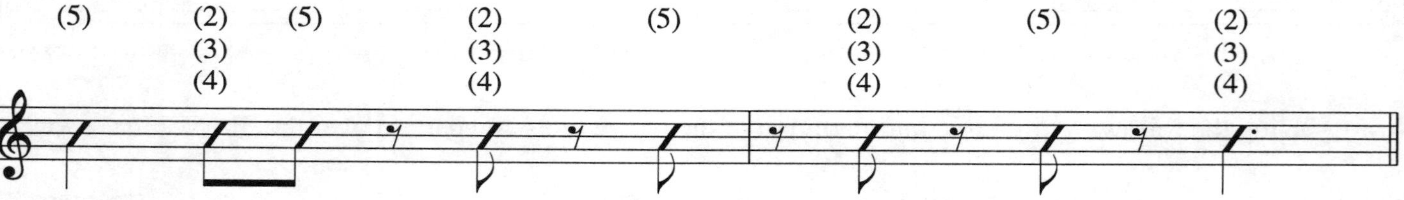


Now apply the above rhythm pattern–string combination to any of the previous examples or songs in this text. Some of the combinations might be easier with fingers in place of, (or with), a single pick.

The following chord progression will be used to demonstrate some of these concepts;

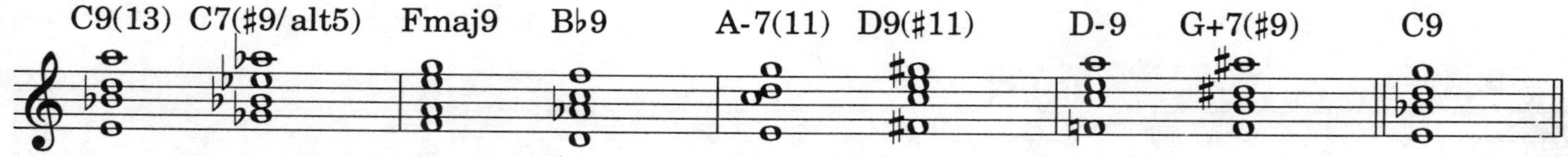


Addition of the above rhythm pattern–string combination to this progression;

"Legato" version;

Also try mixing two or more of the combinations as well as reversing some of the given ones. The following example will use the **(2)** and **(3)(4)(5)** combination on the first two bars while reversing the combination {**(3)(4)(5)** and **(2)**} on the last two bars;

The following uses the **(2)(3)** and **(4)(5)** combination on the first two bars while using the reverse combination **(4)(5)** and **(2)(3)** on the last two bars;

# Chapter Thirty.
## Conclusion

As stated in the **Introduction**, the intent of this text was to establish a simple and direct approach or system to chord construction, voice-leading, enharmonic realization, and supportive theory that would enable students to exercise and expand their knowledge and begin a process for future discoveries. The initial introduction of drop 2 type voicings with tension additions is a simple formula for many complicated voicings. By limiting those voicings to the middle four strings, more information on voice-leading, enharmonic substitutions, fingering possibilities, and theory could be presented. The enharmonic realization process was established as a means to the eventual discovery of new voicings which could ultimately be perceived as groups of specific intervals with twelve potential roots. These concepts can also be applied to various string sets and voicing sizes. The following comments will suggest some approaches to the various string sets and voicing types on the guitar.

Continuation of four-note voicing research on the middle four strings should include a thorough examination of seventh-width voicings and applicable voicings containing an "octave-doubling." Equally important are the three-note voicings available to the middle four strings, as well as later examination of additional three-string combinations. Perhaps the *two* three-string combinations that contain the same width as the four-string voicings presented; **[(2)(3)(5)]** and **[(2)(4)(5)]**, would be a logical starting point since they voice-lead well when mixed with the four-note voicings used in this text. Certainly one advantage that many three-note structures have over four-note voicings is their physical ease in fingerings. This might be an important consideration when music containing many chords is played at a fast tempo. Often just those four-note structures that produce difficult fingerings can be substituted by three-note voicings. The following example will illustrate this.

1) Passage using four-note drop 2 type voicings;

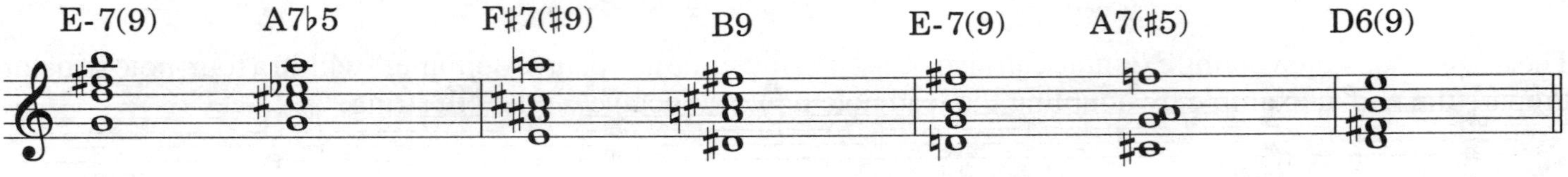


2) Above passage with some single voices removed to produce easier fingered three-note voicings;

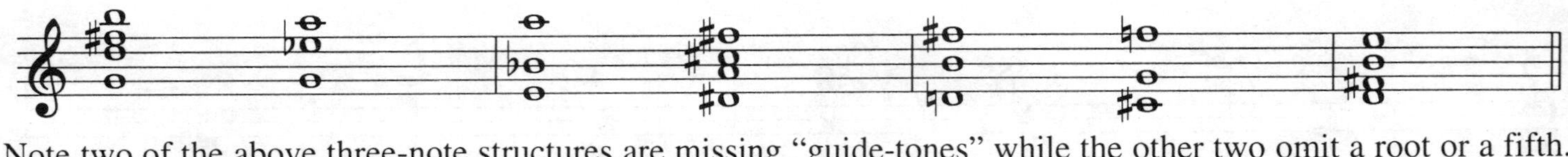

Note two of the above three-note structures are missing "guide-tones" while the other two omit a root or a fifth. Three-note voicings often produce "incomplete" structures, but as mentioned earlier in this text, certain tensions and predictable chord progressions can dictate the missing guide-tones. Also mentioned earlier, some of the best "sounding" voicings are in fact incomplete. Moreover, if two or more voicings are used on one chord, the guide-tones might be stated in one voicing while the other voicings remain incomplete.

The "ambiguous" nature of many three-note structures increases the amount of enharmonic chordal uses available to any one structure. The following will attempt to illustrate this;

| (Notes).............. | F | A | E | (minor modes) |
|---|---|---|---|---|
| Fmaj7................ | 1 | 3 | 7 | |
| G7(13/9)............ | ♭7 | 9 | 13 | (G dorian) |
| D♭7(♯9/♯5)......... | 3 | ♯5 | ♯9 | |
| A7(♭13)............. | ♭13 | 1 | 5 | (A aeolian) |
| B♭maj7(♯11)....... | 5 | 7 | ♯11 | |
| B-7♭5(11).......... | ♭5 | ♭7 | 11 | |
| Dm(add9)............ | ♭3 | 5 | 9 | |
| Esus4(♭9)........... | ♭9 | 4 | 1 | (E phrygian) |

An interesting exercise might be to take a nicely voice-lead four-note voicing example and remove various single strings to produce different three-note voicings. The following will serve as the four-note voicing example;

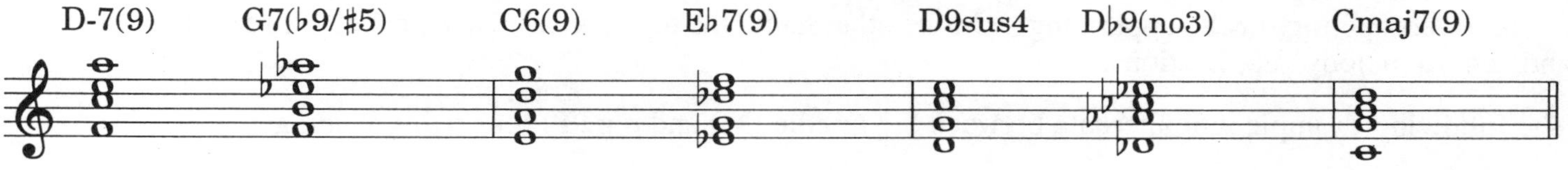


Using above example;

1) Play top three voices only.
2) Play bottom three voices only.
3) Play top two voices and bottom voice only.
4) Play bottom two voices and top voice only.
5) Alternating different three-note structures. As an example, alternate the following string sets on the above example; **[(2)(3)(5)]** and **[(2)(4)(5)]**;

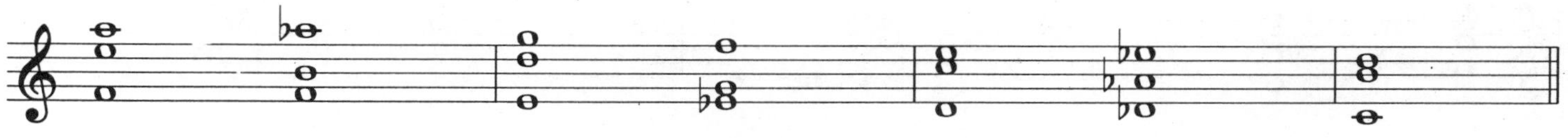

Additional three-string combinations using the *high* and *low* "E" strings, **(1)** and **(6)**, should also be examined, keeping in mind their limited use in a "comping" or band situation.

The above four-note voicing example can also be used to illustrate an "octave doubling" within a four-note structure. Prepare the above example by doubling the lead note down an octave on the 4th string;

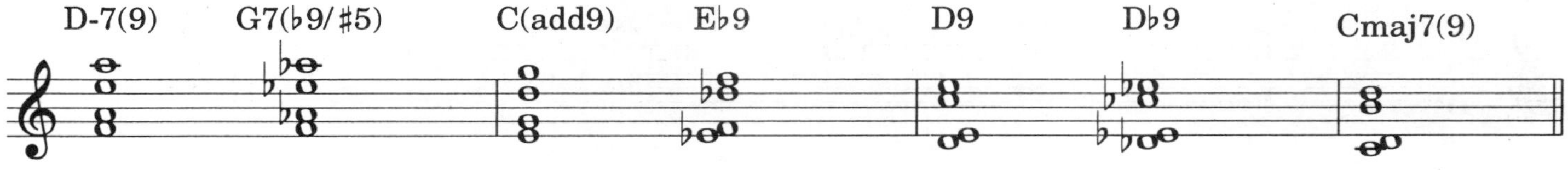


Now prepare the same example by doubling the bass note up an octave on the 3rd string;

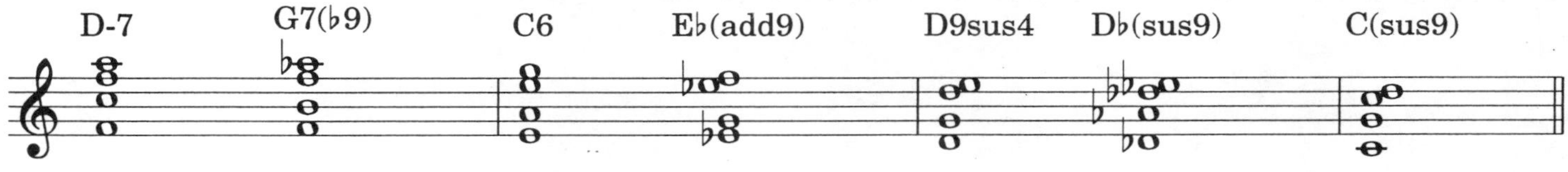


Physical consideration might dictate the use of *8vb* doubling on the first three chords and *8va* doubling on the last three chords with the E♭9 chord containing no doubling since it is difficult with either one;

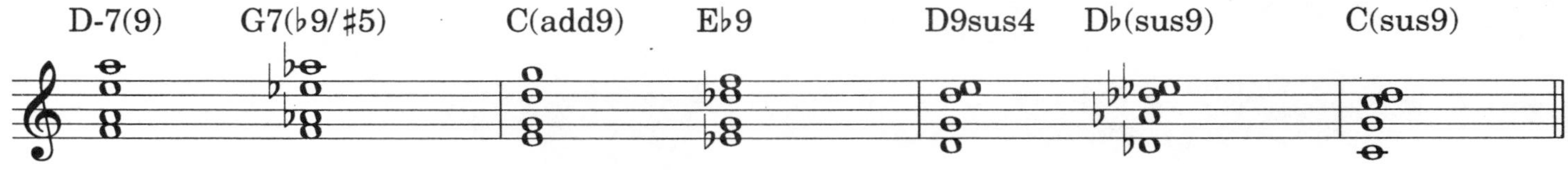


The next phase of harmonic study on the guitar should undertake the various string combinations available to this instrument. While three and four string combinations are the most common in a majority of comping situations, two and five string combinations are also worth examination. While five and six string voicings are probably most common to "solo" guitar, these structures might also be available over a "ballad" in a band situation.

Perhaps the first logical step in exploring different string combinations would be to transpose the voicings examined on the middle four strings to the top four strings. In fact, a majority of the drop 2 type voicings are physically more accessible on the top four strings while some of the non-drop 2 type voicings might prove more difficult. Keep in mind, the higher register of these voicings on the top four strings might at times produce conflicts with a melody or soloist competing for the upper range. On the other hand, the top four strings are excellent for "chord soloing" and "chord melody" applications.

The following example will alternate between the middle **(M)** and top **(T)** four string voicings;

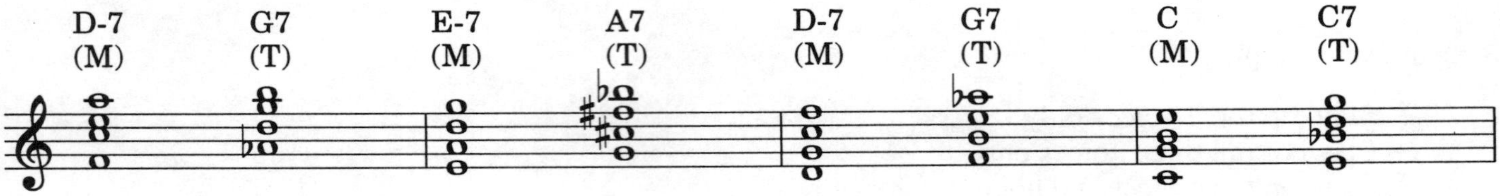


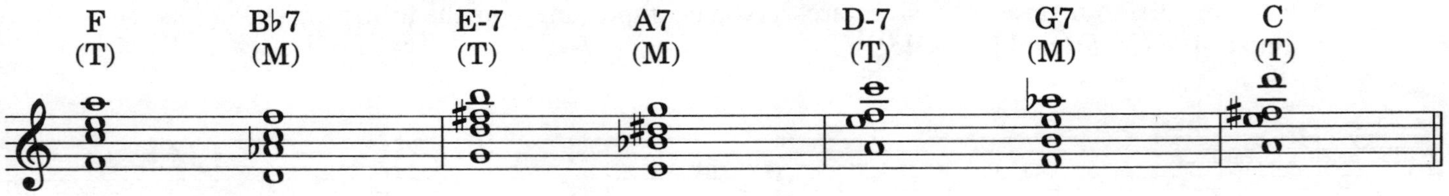


Note the physical advantages in alternating string sets as opposed to placing all voicings on the middle four strings. Also of interest is the melodic "pattern" over the entire exercise.

This last example will mix middle and top *four* string voicings with *three* note voicings. **(1)** will denote the top voice being placed on the 1st string while **(2)** denotes the 2nd string as the top voice;

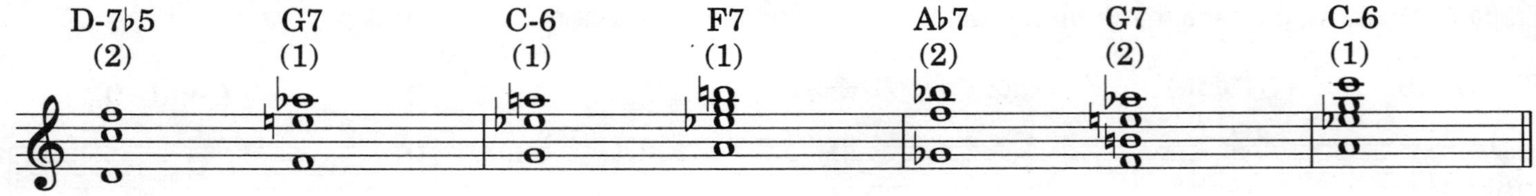


Note the physical "shapes" are the same on the last two voicings.

Colorful and sensitive comping is produced by the use of different string sets and various voicing sizes along with a variety of rhythms and space (rests). Have fun on your next comping trip!